www.wadsworth.com

wadsworth.com is the World Wide Web site for Wadsworth Publishing Company and is your direct source to dozens of online resources.

At *wadsworth.com* you can find out about supplements, demonstration software, and student resources. You can also send e-mail to many of our authors and preview new publications and exciting new technologies.

wadsworth.com
Changing the way the world learns®

From the Wadsworth Series in Mass Communication and Journalism

General Mass Communication

Shirley Biagi, *Media/Impact: An Introduction to Mass Media*, 4th Ed.

Shirley Biagi, *Media/Reader: Perspectives on Media Industries, Effects, and Issues*, 3rd Ed.

Louis Day, *Ethics in Media Communications: Cases and Controversies*, 3rd Ed.

Robert S. Fortner, *International Communications: History, Conflict, and Control of the Global Metropolis*

Kathleen Hall Jamieson and Karlyn Kohrs Campbell, *The Interplay of Influence*, 4th Ed.

Paul Lester, *Visual Communication*, 2nd Ed.

Cynthia Lont, *Women and Media: Content, Careers, and Criticism*

Joseph Straubhaar and Robert LaRose, *Media Now: Communications Media in the Information Age*, 2nd Ed.

Ray Surette, *Media, Crime, and Criminal Justice: Images and Realities*, 2nd Ed.

Edward Jay Whetmore, *Mediamerica, Mediaworld: Form, Content, and Consequence of Mass Communication*, Updated 5th Ed.

John D. Zelezny, *Communications Law: Liberties, Restraints, and the Modern Media*, 2nd Ed.

Journalism

Dorothy Bowles and Diane L. Borden, *Creative Editing for Print Media*, 3rd Ed.

Robert L. Hilliard, *Writing for Television, Radio & New Media*, 7th Ed.

Lauren Kessler and Duncan McDonald, *The Search: Information Gathering for the Mass Media*

Lauren Kessler and Duncan McDonald, *When Words Collide*, 5th Ed.

Alice M. Klement and Carolyn Burrows Matalene, *Telling Stories/Taking Risks: Journalism Writing at the Century's Edge*

Fred S. Parrish, *Photojournalism: An Introduction*

Carole Rich, *Writing and Reporting News: A Coaching Method*, 3rd Ed.

Carole Rich, *Workbook for Writing and Reporting News*, 3rd Ed.

Photojournalism and Photography

Fred S. Parrish, *Photojournalism: An Introduction*

Marvin Rosen and David DeVries, *Introduction to Photography*, 4th Ed.

Public Relations and Advertising

Jerry A. Hendrix, *Public Relations Cases*, 4th Ed.

Jerome A. Jewler and Bonnie L. Drewniany, *Creative Strategy in Advertising*, 6th Ed.

Eugene Marlow, *Electronic Public Relations*

Barbara Mueller, *International Advertising: Communicating Across Cultures*

Doug Newsom and Bob Carrell, *Public Relations Writing: Form and Style*, 5th Ed.

Doug Newsom, Judy VanSlyke Turk, and Dean Kruckeberg, *This Is PR: The Realities of Public Relations*, 7th Ed.

Juliann Sivulka, *Soap, Sex, and Cigarettes: A Cultural History of American Advertising*

Gail Baker Woods, *Advertising and Marketing to the New Majority: A Case Study Approach*

Research and Theory

Earl Babbie, *The Practice of Social Research*, 8th Ed.

Stanley Baran and Dennis Davis, *Mass Communication Theory: Foundations, Ferment, and Future*, 2nd Ed.

Sondra Rubenstein, *Surveying Public Opinion*

Rebecca B. Rubin, Alan M. Rubin, and Linda J. Piele, *Communication Research: Strategies and Sources*, 5th Ed.

Roger D. Wimmer and Joseph R. Dominick, *Mass Media Research: An Introduction*, 6th Ed.

THIS IS PR

THE REALITIES
OF PUBLIC RELATIONS

SEVENTH EDITION

Doug Newsom
Texas Christian University

Judy VanSlyke Turk
University of South Carolina

Dean Kruckeberg
University of Northern Iowa

Wadsworth
Thomson Learning™

Australia • Canada • Denmark • Japan • Mexico • New Zealand • Philippines
Puerto Rico • Singapore • South Africa • Spain • United Kingdom • United States

Mass Communication and Journalism
Editor: Karen Austin
Executive Editor: Deirdre Cavanaugh
Assistant Editor: Ryan E. Vesely
Editorial Assistant: Dory Schaeffer
Project Editor: Cathy Linberg
Print Buyer: Barbara Britton
Permissions Editor: Susan Walters

Production: Julie Kranhold / Ex Libris
Interior Design: Julie Kranhold
Copyeditor: Madeleine Clark
Cover Design: Delgado Design, Inc.
Cover Images: © PhotoDisc
Compositor: TBH Typecast, Inc.
Text and Cover Printer: R. R. Donnelley, Crawfordsville

For permission to use material from this text, contact us:
  web: www.thomsonrights.com
  fax: 1-800-730-2215
  phone: 1-800-730-2214

Wadsworth/Thomson Learning
10 Davis Drive
Belmont, CA 94002-3098
USA
www.wadsworth.com

International Headquarters
Thomson Learning
290 Harbor Drive, 2nd Floor
Stamford, CT 06902-7477
USA

UK/Europe/Middle East
Thomson Learning
Berkshire House
168-173 High Holborn
London WC1V 7AA
United Kingdom

Asia
Thomson Learning
60 Albert Street #15-01
Albert Complex
Singapore 189969

Canada
Nelson/Thomson Learning
1120 Birchmount Road
Scarborough, Ontario M1K 5G4
Canada

Library of Congress
Cataloging-in-Publication Data

Newsom, Doug.
    This is PR : the realities of public relations / Doug Newsom, Judy VanSlyke Turk, Dean Kruckeberg. — 7th ed.
        p.   cm.
    Includes bibliographical references and index.
    ISBN 0-534-55962-X
    1. Public relations.   I. Turk, Judy VanSlyke.   II. Kruckeberg, Dean.   III. Title.
    HM1221.N48   1999
    659.2—dc21   99-29237

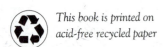

This book is printed on acid-free recycled paper

To Our Colleagues and Our Students,
Who Have Made Us
Better Teachers and Practitioners

DOUG NEWSOM, Professor of Journalism at Texas Christian University, is the senior coauthor of *This Is PR* and *Public Relations Writing,* 5th ed., with Bob Carrell. She is also the editor, with Bob Carrell, of *Silent Voices.* Dr. Newsom has been chair of the College of Fellows in the Public Relations Society of America, and has been president of the Association for Education in Journalism and Mass Communication, Southwest Education Council for Journalism and Mass Communication, Texas Public Relations Association, the North Texas Chapter of the Public Relations Society of America and the Greater Fort Worth Chapter of PRSA. She has also been chair of TCU's Faculty Senate. In 1982 she was named Educator of the Year by the Public Relations Society of America. In 1988, while a Fulbright lecturer in India, she gave public relations workshops and seminars throughout the country. In 1998–99 she was in Singapore on a Fulbright. She also has given workshops in South Africa (1992), Hungary (1995 and 1994), Bulgaria (1993), Poland (1995) and Vanuatu (1997), and has consulted in Romania and taught in London and Latvia.

JUDY VANSLYKE TURK, Dean and Professor at the College of Journalism and Mass Communications, University of South Carolina, was 1994–95 president of the Association for Education in Journalism and Mass Communication and was 1997 chair of the College of Fellows of the Public Relations Society of America. She was PRSA's Educator of the Year in 1992, and is a former co-chair of PRSA's Educational Affairs committee and Educators Academy. She currently serves PRSA as a member of the Task Force on the Future of Public Relations and the Commission on Public Relations Education. She is co-editor of a new scholarly journal, *Journalism Studies,* the first issue of which will be published by Routledge in 2000. Through grants from the United States Information Agency and the Soros Foundation, she has conducted workshops for public relations faculty and practitioners in Latvia, Estonia, Lithuania, Romania and Russia.

DEAN KRUCKEBERG, Professor and Coordinator of the public relations degree program in Communication Studies at the University of Northern Iowa, co-authored a book with Dr. Ken Starck called *Public Relations and Community: A Reconstructed Theory.* That book won the first PRIDE Award from the Public Relations Division of the National Communication Association. Dr. Kruckeberg was named the 1995 Educator of the Year by the Public Relations Society of America and is a member of PRSA's College of Fellows. He won the 1997 Pathfinder Award given by the Institute for Public Relations. He has served as the national faculty adviser to the

Public Relations Student Society of America, Midwest District Chair of PRSA and Chair of the Educators' Academy. He has been head of the Public Relations Division of the Association for Education in Journalism and Mass Communication and head of the PR Division of the National Communication Association. He is on PRSA's Educational Affairs Committee and co-chair of the National Commission on Public Relations Education. In 1994, he was a resident adviser for public relations education in the Department of Mass Communication, United Arab Emirates University, and part of the project team that developed its public relations degree program. In 1998 he taught in Latvia and Russia and presented workshops in Bulgaria.

BRIEF CONTENTS

Revising textbooks every three years brings authors to the reality of holding down two jobs—one for the university and one for the publisher. With limited "life" of an edition, on the surface it would seem that there's not much to change for each revision. However, as each edition is scheduled to be sent to the publisher, there's a last minute flurry—trying to squeeze in new developments and deciding what to remove in order to put in something new.

The real problem is that the field of public relations is changing and changing swiftly. Mapping the growth and development of public relations practice and education around the world is something we've been doing both academically and physically, and we all have rather ragged passports to prove it. You'll see more international emphasis in this edition than in the previous one, although, like earlier editions, the international aspects are integrated throughout the book. One reviewer suggested we write an international chapter, but trying to confine all that is going on globally and capture it in one chapter didn't seem to make sense—globalism is affecting everything about public relations from its definition to public understanding of what PR is and does.

We also focus on international aspects in the materials we've chosen for Info-Trac® College Edition, a new feature that Wadsworth is offering to amplify information about a particular area of interest (additional information is available on Info-Trac® that we wanted to incorporate into the text but didn't have room for). This on-line library offers a wealth of materials and is available 24 hours a day and updated daily. And it gives us a chance to keep adding to the book's knowledge base as we discover new articles or changes in the field.

The fact that InfoTrac College Edition can be offered shows the degree to which cyberspace has had an impact not only on the academy, but on everything we do—particularly this is true in pubic relations. The facility of getting information to publics certainly has improved dramatically with the Internet. Organizations have Web sites to communicate with any public who wants to log on, and Intranets that are secured for use only by special publics, each as members or employees. The digital world has changed the form and scope of all communications.

The positive aspects of this new world are as overwhelming to communicators as a truckload of candy is to a three-year-old. But there is a downside. The Internet has no editors, and anyone can put up a Web site. Organizations are having to combat rumors spread in chat sessions and deal with mock Web sites that imitate an organization and attack it, often viciously. Misinformation abounds. While crisis managers like to say each crisis offers an opportunity, some now could do with fewer opportunities. Managing public relations is a good bit more complex than before.

■ Perspectives

Our responsibility in *This Is PR, 7th Edition,* is to offer information that will be useful to the experienced practitioner as well as to the new student just learning about the field. We are objective in discussing communication theories and paradigms because we frankly don't believe there is a perfect fit for all situations. Our approach is comprehensive and provides a toolbox of useful information and examples to illustrate key points. There is a Glossary at the end of the text, which helps to clarify terms and is useful as a study aid.

Traditions for *This Is PR* include easy readability and gender-neutral language. In an effort to be sensitive in the use of language, we eliminated expressions peculiar to the USA because we've used this book all over the world and know that some of our readers—students, teachers and practitioners alike—live outside the USA.

As in previous editions, Part One sets forth some of the basic information about public relations practice, gives a brief summary of its development and indicates some trends that might predict the future.

This time Part Two begins with a chapter on publics because we don't think you can begin to think about public relations without that critical element. It then moves into a discussion of the two types of public relations research—one for planning and the other for monitoring and evaluating.

Part Three discusses theories that are the underpinnings of public relations practice, and then explores the ethical and legal environment for public relations practice.

Part Four takes you into the strategies and tactics used in public relations practice. Here you'll find chapters on management, communication channels, tactics, campaigns, cases and crises. The tactics, campaigns, cases and crises are just illustrations to round out your understanding of the total picture of public relations practice. There are books devoted to these topics, so perhaps this exposure will invite you to learn more.

As with earlier editions, we are also providing an *Instructor's Manual.* This useful instructor's manual comes replete with detailed chapter outlines, objectives and testing questions in a variety of formats.

■ Contributors and Critics

A word of advice to those who have never written a book: Don't try to do it without lots of friends. We are indebted to many for contributing ideas, examples and suggestions for changes. Especially good advice comes from students who are trying to learn from the text and teachers who are trying to teach from it. Those are informal reviewers. But, we also want to thank our formal reviewers for this seventh edition: William Briggs, San Jose State University; O. Patricia Cambridge, Ohio University; Melissa Motschall, Eastern Michigan University; John E. Guiniven, University of South Carolina; Bill Dean, Texas Tech University; Ann Marie Major, Pennsylvania State University; and Cynthia E. Clark, Boston University. And those for the sixth edition were Pam Creedon, Ohio State University; Timothy Coombs, Illinois State

University; Kathy Fitzpatrick, Southern Methodist University; and Gayle Pohl, University of Northern Iowa.

In the process of completing this book, we got a new editor, Karen Austin, and the Wadsworth Communication team got a new executive editor, Deirdre Cavanaugh. Fortunately for us, former editorial assistant Matthew Lamm, a wonderfully responsive helper, was a familiar voice on the phone; and assistant editor Ryan Vesely also provided continuity. We want to express our gratitude, too, for the production of the book to Julie Kranhold and thoughtful copyeditor Madeleine Clarke. And thanks finally to our research assistant Dalia Hamed.

DN, JVT, DK

CHAPTER 1

THE REALITIES
OF PUBLIC RELATIONS

Public relations practitioners should demonstrate a systematic approach leading to measurable results.

KIRSTEN BERTH AND GÖRAN SJÖBERG,
FROM *QUALITY IN PUBLIC RELATIONS*, ISSUED BY IPRA, CERP, ICO.

The public relations field, in all its variety, inventiveness, flamboyance and solemn pretentiousness, can perhaps best be approached, at the outset, by an examination of a representative sampling of its hardiest practitioners.

IRWIN ROSS, *THE IMAGE MERCHANTS*

Things start as promotions and when it goes beyond expectations and well beyond reason and into the realm of semi-belief, you might term it "hype."

HOWARD RUBENSTEIN, NEW YORK CITY PROMOTER QUOTED IN *USA TODAY* (AUGUST 31, 1993)

The mail box was full—the electronic mail box, that is, when the public relations practitioner found the correct connection for her laptop and plugged it into the wall socket in Caracas, Venezuela. A case study that was due at a London journal was getting some finishing touches by a colleague in Frankfurt, Germany. The entire project was in the e-mail bag to be read and dispatched electronically to the journal. An anticipated crisis brewing in Belgium needed attention, according to the on-site staff person who wanted her to call so they could discuss the strategy.

The other messages involved meetings in Caracas, relays via the home office from other worldwide clients, and a personal message from home. Prioritizing the responses was the first choice she had to make, and the major decision every public relations practitioner must make, because there is literally something to do every minute—no "down" time and very little personal "space."

Diversity of tasks and high pressure are part of the public relations environment. Furthermore, for individuals who are comfortable only in one culture, a career in public relations is less and less a realistic option—if, indeed, it ever was. And, while some people like to do only one thing at a time, that never has been the case in public relations. It is even less so now that businesses are reducing staffs and having much of their work, including public relations jobs, performed outside.

As the scenario illustrates, technology has changed the way we communicate. It's no longer necessary to be "on site" to handle an assignment. Business cards carry phone and fax numbers and e-mail addresses, as well as physical location addresses. The practice of public relations has emerged in recent years as a global phenomenon. The consistency of the practice, despite differences in the social, economic and political climates in various parts of the world, can be traced to the growing body of knowledge about and the general acceptance of what public relations is. The creator of public relations' international code of ethics, Lucien Matrat, offers these thoughts:

> Public relations, in the sense that we use the term, forms part of the strategy of management. Its function is twofold: to respond to the expectations of those whose behaviour, judgements and opinions can influence the operation and development of an enterprise, and in turn to motivate them. . . . .
>
> Establishing public relations policies means, first and foremost, harmonizing the interests of an enterprise with the interests of those on whom its growth depends.
>
> The next step is putting these policies into practice. This means developing a communication policy which can establish and maintain a relationship of mutual confidence with a firm's multiple publics.[1] [Emphasis ours.]

WHAT IS PUBLIC RELATIONS?

The public relations practitioner serves as an intermediary between the organization that he or she represents and all of that organization's publics.

Consequently, the PR practitioner has responsibilities both to the institution and to its various publics. He or she distributes information that enables the institution's publics to understand its policies.

Public relations involves research into all audiences: receiving information from them, advising management of their attitudes and responses, helping to set policies that demonstrate responsible attention to them and constantly evaluating the effectiveness of all PR programs. This inclusive role embraces all activities connected with ascertaining and influencing the opinions of a group of people. But that is just the communications aspect. As a management function, *public relations involves responsibility and responsiveness in policy and information to the best interests of the organization and its publics.*

The complexity of PR's role prompted the Public Relations Society of America (PRSA) to define fourteen activities generally associated with public relations: (1) publicity, (2) communication, (3) public affairs, (4) issues management, (5) government relations, (6) financial public relations, (7) community relations, (8) industry relations, (9) minority relations, (10) advertising, (11) press agentry, (12) promotion, (13) media relations, (14) propaganda. PRSA's definitions of these activities are listed in the Glossary.

Another organization produced a consensus definition of PR much earlier than PRSA did. The First World Assembly of Public Relations Associations, held in Mexico City in August 1978, defined the practice of public relations as "the art and social science of analyzing trends, predicting their consequences, counseling organizational leaders, and implementing planned programs of action which will serve both the organization and the public interest."

Yet another definition of public relations as "reputation management" has gained currency. The British Institute of Public Relations (IPR) offers this:

> Public relations is about reputation—the result of what you do, what you say and what others say about you. Public Relations Practice is the discipline which looks after reputation with the aim of earning

understanding and support, and influencing opinion and behaviour. *

As a practical matter, good public relations involves confronting a problem openly and honestly and then solving it. In the long run, the best PR is evidence of an active social conscience.

ORGANIZATIONAL ROLE & FUNCTION: 10 BASIC PRINCIPLES

As the definitions suggest, the result must be the real behavior of the organization and perceptions of that behavior by its publics. Therefore, among the various titles now being used for the role of the public relations function are communications management (or sometimes communications standards management), reputation management and relationship management. In delineating these, Fraser Likely, Canadian Public Relations Society, Inc., says all are managerial roles.[2]

We can describe the function and role of public relations practice by stating ten basic principles:

1. Public relations deals with reality, not false fronts. Conscientiously planned programs that put the public interest in the forefront are the basis of sound public relations policy. (*Translation:* PR deals with facts, not fiction.)

2. Public relations is a service-oriented profession in which public interest, not personal reward, should be the primary consideration. (PR is a public, not personal, service.)

3. Since the public relations practitioner must go to the public to seek support for programs and policies, public interest is the central criterion by which he or she should select these programs and policies. (PR practitioners must have the guts to say no to a client or to refuse a deceptive program.)

4. Because the public relations practitioner reaches many publics through mass media, which are the public channels of communication, the integrity of these channels must be preserved. (PR practitioners should never lie to the news media, either outright or by implication.)

5. Because PR practitioners are in the middle between an organization and its publics, they must be effective communicators—conveying information back and forth until understanding is reached. (The PR practitioner probably was the original ombudsman/woman.)

6. To expedite two-way communication and to be responsible communicators, public relations practitioners must use scientific public opinion research extensively. (PR cannot afford to be a guessing game.)

7. To understand what their publics are saying and to reach them effectively, public relations practitioners must employ the social sciences—psychology, sociology, social psychology, public opinion, communications study and semantics. (Intuition is not enough.)

8. Because a lot of people do PR research, the PR person must adapt the work of other, related disciplines, including learning theory and other psychology theories, sociology, political science, economics and history. (The PR field requires multidisciplinary applications.)

9. Public relations practitioners are obligated to explain problems to the public before these problems become crises. (PR practitioners should alert and advise, so people won't be taken by surprise.)

10. A public relations practitioner should be measured by only one standard: ethical performance. (A PR practitioner is only as good as the reputation he or she deserves.)

PR AND RELATED ACTIVITIES

Public relations involves many activities. People's participation in the activities of public relations and their subsequent assertion that, therefore, they are "in public relations" often cause confusion

---

PR News, October 10, 1994, p. 3.

in others' understanding of what public relations is. The *activities* of PR practice include: press agentry, promotion, publicity, public affairs, research (primary and secondary), graphics, advertising, marketing and merchandising support. But public relations is something greater than just this collection of activities.

Changes in the environment for public relations can shift the emphasis from one activity to another over time. Recently, advances in technology—such as significant differences in the way the news media operate—have driven many of these shifts. Another result of these advances has been increased globalization, affecting both internal and external communication and significantly altering the way crises are handled. All crises now get global attention which creates considerable urgency for appropriate organizational responses that are destined to be weighed in the world court of public opinion.

■ Press Agentry

Because PR's origins are associated with press agentry, many people think that press agentry and public relations are the same. But press agentry involves planning activities or staging events— sometimes just stunts—that will *attract attention* to a person, institution, idea or product. There is certainly nothing wrong with attracting crowds and giving people something to see or talk about, provided that no deception is involved. Today's press agents are polished pros who steer clear of fraud and puffery, unless it is done strictly in fun and is clearly recognizable as such.

■ Promotion

A hazy line separates yesterday's press agentry from today's promotion. Although promotion incorporates special events that could be called press agentry, it goes beyond that into *opinion making*. Promotion attempts to garner support and endorsement for a person, product, institution or idea. Promotional campaigns depend for their effectiveness on the efficient use of various PR tools, and in

many cases more is not better (see Chapter 4 on publics and public opinion). Examples of promotion are the various fund-raising drives conducted by churches, charities, health-care groups and conservation interests. Among the most successful promoters in the country are the American Red Cross, American Cancer Society and United Way. Promotion, fund raising and all the attendant drum beating constitute one variety of PR activities that may be incorporated into an overall public relations program. What makes promotion activities worthwhile is the merit of the cause. The legitimacy of the cause is also important from a purely pragmatic viewpoint: It won't receive media coverage if it isn't legitimate news and if it can't maintain public support.

■ Publicity

Because publicity is used to call attention to the special events or the activities surrounding a promotion, there is confusion about this term. *Public relations* is often used as a synonym for *publicity*, but the two activities are not the same. Publicity is strictly a communications function, whereas PR involves a management function as well. Essentially, publicity means *placing information in a news medium*—either in a mass medium (such as television, newspapers or the Internet) or in a specialized medium (such as corporate, association, trade or industry magazines, newsletters, brochures, including quarterly corporate reports or CD-ROMs).

Publicists are writers. Use of the term *public relations* by institutions to describe publicity jobs is unfortunate. Publicists perform a vital function— disseminating information—but they generally do not help set policy. Only PR counselors, usually at the executive level, are in a position to effect substantive management changes.

Publicity isn't always good news. In a crisis, for example, it's often important for the organization to tell its story before the news media develop it on their own. In these situations, the publicist is an inside reporter for internal and external media.

Publicity is *not* public relations. It is a tool used by public relations practitioners. Some writers do choose careers as information writers, but they are *publicists*, not public relations practitioners.

Public Affairs

Many public relations people use the term *public affairs* to describe their work, but this is misleading. Public affairs is actually a highly specialized kind of public relations that involves *community relations* and *governmental relations*—that is, dealing with officials within the community and working with legislative groups and various pressure groups such as consumers. It is a critical part of a public relations program, but it is not the whole program. For example, eighteen months before the Dallas/Fort Worth Airport was to open, two PR firms were hired—one to handle public affairs, and the other to handle media relations. There were good reasons for having two firms. The public affairs issues involved were complex, not only because the airport was paid for by cities in two different counties, but also because the airport was located astride two counties and within the municipal boundaries of four suburban cities. The media relations were complex, too, since they involved arranging special events, advertising and publicity connected with the opening; producing informational materials about the airport; and conducting media relations that were international in scope.

In agencies of the federal government, including the military, the term *public affairs* is commonly used to designate a broader responsibility than *public information*, which consists merely of publicity—handing out information. Thus a public information officer is a publicist, whereas a public affairs person in government often has policy-making responsibilities. Because a rather short-sighted law precludes government use of people identified as public relations personnel (see Example 1.1), military public affairs officers often have responsibility for all facets of internal and external public relations.

The unfortunate effects of this law could be countered at the very highest level of government, since the President of the United States appoints

EXAMPLE 1.1
Why the U.S. Government Uses the Term "Public Affairs"

An October 22, 1913, act of Congress often is interpreted as precluding governmental use of public relations talent. The prohibitive words were attached to the last paragraph of an Interstate Commerce Commission statute: "Appropriated funds may not be used to pay a publicity expert unless specifically appropriated for that purpose." The amendment to the bill was introduced by Representative Frederick H. Gillett and thus is referred to in public relations literature as the Gillett Amendment. Most public relations activity of that period was publicity, and the intent of the amendment was to identify and control publicity. Legislators were concerned that the government would become involved in propaganda directed at U.S. citizens. Most responsible PR practitioners would like to see this amendment repealed, since government currently carries out PR functions anyway, but masks them. As a result, taxpayers cannot get any information about how much money is spent on PR.

the country's most visible PR person, the presidential press secretary. It might make sense to rename the job "public relations counselor" and then employ an accredited public relations practitioner in that post. That person could name a publicity chief for news announcements. A public affairs department could then be set up to work with Congress, and a public affairs officer in the State Department could be appointed to handle relationships with other nations.

Research

The foundation of good public relations strategy is research—research on publics and public opinion, as well as on the situations and circumstances that have created the environment for public opinion. Public relations people do research to identify an organization's publics and to discover what they think. This research involves asking people questions and observing their behavior. Other observations include looking at the background behind a situation or problem to find out what issues or concerns are involved and how events have affected or been affected by public opinion. Public relations practitioners must think in broad terms about research and research methodologies; this entails recognizing the need for research and understanding how to apply research results.

PR people do both primary and secondary research. Primary research means generating new information. Secondary research means using data others have generated to arrive at some conclusions and recommendations. (One of those recommendations may be to do some primary research.) Technology has made research much easier because so much information is now accessible by computer.

Public relations students who think that their work on research-based writing will end with their last college term papers are in for a surprise. Research and the reports describing it look very much like term papers, only the "abstracts" are called "executive summaries."

■ Graphics

The way an organization's materials look has become especially important because a proliferation of media channels has increased the demands on a public's time and attention. All public relations audiences are "volunteer" readers and viewers who will reject any presentation that is unappealing or any message that is not "user friendly."

Public relations people have found computer wizardry with page design and computer graphics to be in great demand. Although some observers might classify these activities as part of "publicity," they often are not. The materials come prewritten, but they usually are in great need of editing and require format or design development. The graphics specialist's job is to enhance readability and attractiveness.

■ Advertising

Public relations differs from both advertising and propaganda. Matrat explains why:

> The strategy of advertising is to create desire, to motivate demand for a product.
>
> The strategy of propaganda is to generate conditioned reflexes which will replace reasoned actions. Public relations is the strategy of confidence, which alone gives credibility, to a message.[3] [Emphasis ours.]

Designing ads, preparing their written messages and buying time or space for their exposure are the tasks of advertising. Although advertising should complement a total PR program, it is a separate function. A public relations person who has no expertise in advertising should arrange to hire an agency to work under his or her supervision.

Advertising is needed for special events and for successful promotion. Although it is a major part of marketing, it has its own special needs for research and testing. Advertising, in the form of donated or paid-for time or space, is a PR tool often used to complement publicity, promotions and press agentry. (For the kinds of advertising most public relations practitioners tend to be closely involved in, see Chapter 11.)

■ Marketing

As in advertising, research and testing play a vital role in marketing, but the kind of testing used in advertising may be only a part of market research. Marketing specialists want to know two things: Is there a need or desire for a product or service? If so, among which audiences and in what form is it most likely to be well received? Marketing is directed toward consumers, although it also interacts with other publics such as the sales force, dealers, retailers and the advertising department. Market research is invaluable to the PR practitioner because it provides information about consumers—an important PR public.

In the 1980s the term *marketing/public relations* became popular as a way to describe public relations activities involved in marketing, but it caused further muddling of the component terms. In reality, the activities involved are not PR, but they do include promotion (usually sales promotion), press agentry (special events, special appearances) and publicity.

The 1985 definition of *marketing* adopted by the American Marketing Association (AMA) shows the relationship: "Marketing is the process of planning and executing the conception (product), pricing, promotion and distribution (place) of ideas, goods and services to create exchanges that satisfy individual and organizational objectives."[4] The AMA includes in that definition the activities (ideas and services) of nonprofit organizations, as well as products sold for profit.

Yet another development has created additional confusion. In the 1990s, the marketing/public relations function became "integrated marketing communication" (IMC) in many organizations. Marketing and advertising people began talking about "relationship building," which sounds a lot like public relations. Many public relations people reacted by calling IMC an "invasion" of "turf." Indeed, some seasoned PR people had been doing integrated communication at least since the 1940s and 1950s. Only in the 1950s did all of these functions become highly specialized—and thus disintegrated—in the first place (see Chapter 2). Some public relations people accepted the concept that all of the communication functions of an organization should be unified so that the organization would, in effect, "speak with one voice." However, the term they preferred was integrated communication (IC), eliminating the reference to "marketing." Subsequently, the IC and IMC terms began showing up in name changes for firms and in curriculum changes in some colleges and universities.[5]

Merchandising

In contrast to marketing, merchandising is concerned with the *packaging* of a product, an idea or perhaps even a president.[6] Its research asks what subtle emotions play a part in acceptance of the product, what shape of package is easiest to handle, what color is likely to attract more attention or what kind of display will make people react. The answers are important to salespeople and dealers and provide a valuable supplement to the marketing and advertising research in a campaign.

Technology has changed merchandising dramatically. Today it is tied more closely to marketing and other activities such as advertising and promotion. This change is seen in the diversity of messages delivered directly to potential customers by mail—print, cassette or compact disk (CD), as well as CD-ROM—and the direct response system of television shopping channels and ordering by fax or computer.

Merchandising experts are strong in graphics, color, tactile responses and emotional reactions to physical imagery. Their work is a frequent and vital part of the public relations milieu. However, it is not in itself public relations.

THE PR PRACTITIONER: PERSONAL TRAITS AND EDUCATION

Only a multitalented person can perform well the many activities encompassed by public relations. According to former PRSA president Pat Jackson, editor of *pr reporter*, the PR practitioner today needs to be a researcher, counselor, strategic planner, educator, communicator and cheerleader.[7] In this section, we look at the personal traits and educational background needed by a person choosing a career in public relations.

Personal Traits

PR practitioners have to master diverse skills. They must be creative in solving problems and well-adjusted enough to withstand the considerable stress involved in working between the institution and its various (and numerous) publics. Solving the problems encountered in public relations often requires teamwork and a tolerance for different views. As a public relations person, you must gather different views and help hammer them into a solution. At the same time, you must express confidence and hope that a solution can be found. In a crisis, people in an organization tend to look to the public relations person for answers. Confidence and hope depend on viewing and presenting problems with complete honesty and learning to live with some that seem (for the moment at least) insoluble, while diligently pursuing solutions. This leaves no room for viewing the job of public relations as being to provide a cover-up for problems or difficulties.

Edward L. Bernays listed eleven personal characteristics needed by the PR practitioner: (1) character and integrity, (2) a sense of judgment and logic, (3) the ability to think creatively and imaginatively, (4) truthfulness and discretion, (5) objectivity, (6) a deep interest in the solution of problems, (7) a broad cultural background, (8) intellectual curiosity, (9) effective powers of analysis and synthesis, (10) intuition, (11) training in the social sciences and in the mechanics of public relations.[8]

Most of these characteristics relate to the individual's effectiveness as a problem sensor and as a problem solver—critical roles for the PR person. In addition to these qualities, California practitioner Ronald E. Rhody has stressed that successful practitioners are those with "a strong sense of self confidence who aren't intimidated by pressure, who thrive on challenge, and who are comfortable in an environment of constant change and ambiguity."[9]

■ Education

As interest in public relations continues to grow, both in the USA and abroad, concern about what is being taught and who is teaching it increases. The late senior practitioner and author Sam Black, who wrote the International Public Relations Association's 1990s Gold Paper on public relations education, urged that there be more coordination

of educational standards.[10] He cited the conflict between proponents of skills-based study, to prepare technically competent people, and supporters of programs that prepare students for the upper-level skills of management counseling. Most educators agree that proficiency in both areas is necessary and that a liberal arts background is an essential starting point. Black suggested that most study beyond the level of basic skills should occur at the post-graduate level, but he was concerned about the lack of faculty.[11] He recommended that public relations curricula be built around the International Public Relations Association's "Wheel of Education" (see Example 1.2). "Unfortunately," Black observed, "there are times when public relations becomes a small spoke in the wheel of education for a related discipline."[12]

Because many practitioners come into public relations from other fields, and because public relations practice is constantly growing and changing, a practitioner's education can be divided into two parts: preliminary (pre-practice) education at either the undergraduate or the graduate level, and continuing education, which PRSA now requires of its more recently accredited members to maintain their accreditation.

Preliminary Education The exact contours of an ideal pre-entry education for the field of public relations are still a subject of debate among educators and practitioners, despite a great deal of research. The formal education of PR practitioners in U.S. colleges and universities has been developed through the cooperative efforts of professionals in PR education and in PR practice. The first nationally accepted standard for public relations education was developed in 1975[13] and was updated in 1981.[14] Because colleges and universities outside of the United States also began offering public relations courses, another model was developed to include all schools.[15]

In 1987, another study commission presented a report that called for mastery of specific skills, preparation in a second field and adoption of an approved curriculum for universities where PRSSA

EXAMPLE 1.2

The Wheel of Education for Public Relations

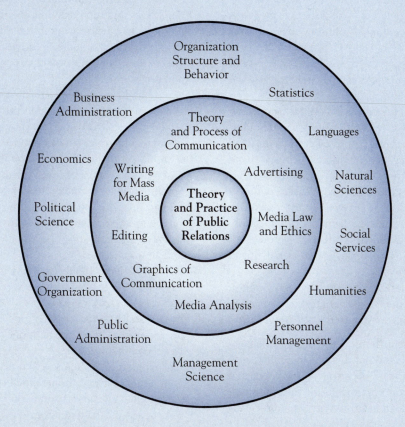

The educational curriculum for a student who wishes to enter the profession can be pictured as a series of three concentric circles. The smallest circle encloses subjects that specifically address public relations practice. The middle circle contains subjects in the general field of communication. The largest circle represents subjects taken in a general liberal arts and humanities course of study. All of the subjects named are essential elements in the background of a successful PR practitioner.

Source: Reprinted from "Public Relations Education—Recommendations and Standards" (September 1990), p. 2, with permission of the International Public Relations Association.

(Public Relations Student Society of America) chapters had a charter.[16] Four years before this commission's report appeared, another commission developed a model for earning a professional mas-

ter's degree in public relations,[17] and made recommendations for the doctoral program.

By 1997, so much had changed in public relations, especially with globalization and the new medium of the Internet, that the Public Relations Society of America appointed a new Commission on Public Relations Education with educator Dean Kruckeberg and practitioner John Paluszek as co-chairs. This commission will look at all levels of education, including continuing education for practitioners.[18]

Because educators have conflicting ideas about the academic level at which public relations should be offered, different institutions have taken varying approaches. Three areas of conflicting opinion were described by E. W. Brody as follows: (1) maintaining PR education at the undergraduate level versus transferring this function to the graduate level; (2) awarding a master's degree in PR after the traditional undergraduate education in PR versus awarding a master's degree in business administration after the same undergraduate education; (3) a stronger component of PR studies in the undergraduate education versus a traditional liberal arts program.[19]

Specific preferences about career preparation may vary, but experts agree that public relations practice demands expertise in the following:

- *Planning:* Ranges from counseling top management in problems other than PR to dealing with the details of the PR department's own organization and functioning; includes developing policy, procedures and actions and communicating these to other departments.
- *Managing:* Goes beyond managing the PR department itself to interpreting top management's directives to the entire organization, participating in association activities, coordinating all outside agencies and activities, accumulating information about the organization and preparing and allocating the corporate PR budget.
- *Advising:* Relates to researching the opinions, attitudes and expectations necessary to provide authoritative counsel, as well as educational and informational materials, to stockholders, lobbyists and others.
- *Analyzing:* Consists of examining trends and their consequences and preventing conflict and misunderstandings by promoting mutual respect and social responsibility.

- *Industry Relations:* Involves helping to attract and retain good employees and working with personnel to improve employer–employee relations; initiating communication systems with employees and suppliers; helping improve labor relations by participating in meetings and conferences with labor representatives; and working closely with labor negotiators in labor contracts and discussions.
- *Economic Relations:* Entails maintaining relations with competitors, dealers and distributors; encompasses advertising and promotion, which often require the practitioner to work closely with marketing and merchandising departments and to harmonize public and private interests.
- *Social Relations:* Includes being concerned with human relations—preservation of personal dignity, employee protection (security) and social welfare—incorporating recreational, medical and civic activities.
- *Political Activities:* Calls for being involved with the community's administrative, educational and religious groups, as well as with legislative bodies and international contacts; also implies an interest in the international affairs of the world community.
- *Communication:* Requires knowing how to communicate through mass media and specialized media via advertising and publicity and how to set up a system for a two-way flow of reliable information.
- *Educational Activities:* Covers working with all publics (educational institutions, employees, consumer groups and company representatives such as salespeople and dealers) arranging appearances and writing speeches for corporate executives and developing in-house educational activities such as employee training programs.

Continuing Education Offered and pursued sporadically at best, continuing education in PR consists largely of seminars given by educators and practitioners. In some of these seminars, continuing education credits can be earned while the practitioner prepares for an accreditation exam. Other seminars are developed by employers for their own employees. Growth in the field, especially in areas of specialization, forces many PR practitioners to perform demanding jobs using outdated skills.

Corporate and organizational management often faults continuing education programs for failing to teach public relations practitioners the business of the organization in which they work. This suggests that, as a means of learning a specialized area of public relations practice, workshops in communication may not be priorities for PR practitioners. Certainly a PR person benefits from learning the business of his or her organization—whatever it might be—in depth. For both the organizational staff person and the agency person, knowing the world of business is critical. This means understanding government and corporate regulations, as well as finances.

■ Career Job (Field) or Profession?

Some commentators argue that the very fact that anyone would question whether PR is a profession proves that public relations is *not* a profession. Another clue that it isn't might be inferred from the previous discussion about continuing education.

One criterion of a profession is that its practitioners have command over a *body of knowledge*. Although the Public Relations Society of America has developed a body of knowledge, it is for the USA only and has been criticized by the International Public Relations Association for its parochialism. Another criterion is general acceptance of a *standard educational curriculum*. While this exists to some degree in the USA, what is being taught in the USA isn't necessarily what is being taught elsewhere, where the availability of specialized education in public relations is growing at an explosive pace. Another criterion is *control over entry and exit* to the field, and public relations lacks any such control. One aspect of that control consists of requiring continuing education of all practitioners, to maintain standards of practice by ensuring that practitioners learn new developments and update skills. That is not a requirement for practicing public relations. In fact, there are no *requirements*.

THE JOB OF THE PR PRACTITIONER

While the basic duties of a public relations practitioner have not changed much over the past several decades, the demands on the practitioner and the way the practitioner carries out his or her duties have changed and will continue to change. There's more call for depth and diversity in knowledge for this field now that it is functioning at a global level. There's more accountability for public relations actions and greater damage if risk management and crisis communication are mishandled. There's less tolerance for "hype." Practitioners need more command of a greater array of communication technologies, and media relations now demands greater sensitivity to multiculturalism.

But some things have not changed. Former PRSA president Frank Wylie, now a Santa Cruz, California, consultant, notes that "every beginner is a 'go-fer,' and it's important that you not only go for something, but that you bring back something usable."[20] The retrieval emphasis implies reportorial skills, including knowledge of research techniques. Other skills Wylie stresses include thinking (first and foremost), writing of all types, speaking, being persuasive, understanding and appreciating media, knowing graphics and photography, respecting deadlines and developing an ability to deal with and solve multiple PR problems at one time.[21]

■ Three Basic Roles

The way a PR person applies his or her special skills depends on the role he or she plays in an organization. The three main roles are those of *staff member*, an *agency employee* and an *independent PR practitioner* who might from time to time function as a *PR counselor*. We will consider each of these roles separately.

Staff Members Staff public relations practitioners are employees of commercial or nonprofit organizations or of divisions of government such as local, state or federal agencies. They perform highly specialized tasks in their organization, but they get a paycheck just as other employees do, and they share the same corporate or institutional identity. Specific needs of the organization usually determine a staff member's job description.

Staff positions with small organizations often include responsibility for external relations. In the case of a small nonprofit organization, the PR person typically works either with volunteers who provide professional expertise of various kinds or with outside suppliers whose services may be bought on a limited basis or donated.

Staff positions with larger organizations can involve responsibility for all other communications functions that report to public relations, and in some instances for human resources (personnel) as well. Large organizations are likely to buy services such as research, audio-visuals (everything from employee training videos to video news releases and commercials) and perhaps even the annual report from outside suppliers. "Out-sourcing" of special public relation services is increasing as companies cut back on their total number of in-house employees.

Commercial and Nonprofit Organizations Public relations people in institutions—whether commercial or nonprofit—may have skilled jobs in a PR department, may be middle managers of some aspect of PR activity or may function as professional staff. Increased use of computer technology is likely to decrease the number of practitioners working at the lower-level jobs and increase the number working at the middle manager and professional levels; the rather small number of positions at the senior level of policy making is unlikely to be affected.[22]

Government Job descriptions for PR positions in government vary dramatically. Some people who are called "public information officers" are really publicists, while others with precisely the same title may have all the responsibilities of a corporate vice-president for PR.

Firm/Agency Employees Each agency or firm has its own internal structure, but generally the presi-

dent of the firm shares in handling accounts, as do the salespeople, who may also be account executives. A firm may employ a bookkeeper, a secretary, a publicity writer, an advertising or graphics specialist and an artist. In some instances the writer may prepare both publicity and advertising copy, and the artist may be responsible for illustrations and layout.

Large firms have copy editors, media specialists, several artists and a production facility. Most firms, even the largest ones, arrange contracts with printers, typesetters and photographers. More recently, desktop publishing has come to the aid of writers and artists by making their jobs more efficient and easier to coordinate. Computer software programs that include type and graphics make almost instantaneous page makeup possible in-house. These systems usually make the writer the production person as well, since the writer actually develops the final format of publication. The artist provides original designs and artwork.

Independent Practitioners/Counselors The *independent* public relations practitioner is usually hired to accomplish a specific task—one that is ordinarily (but not always) predetermined. Payment may take the form of a flat fee, a fee plus expenses or a base fee plus hourly charges and expenses. The less experienced the independent practitioner is, the more often he or she will have to work for a flat fee. Although some experienced independents prefer to bill for actual costs, they price a job based on the hours required to complete it multiplied by an hourly rate. They then increase these costs by a certain percentage to cover overhead and profit.

Independent public relations practitioners sometimes function as PR counselors. Indeed, some independent practitioners work almost exclusively as counselors.

A PR counselor is called in at an advisory level and works for a consultant's fee, which he or she sets, with hours and expenses added. The counselor studies and researches a situation, interviews the people involved, outlines recommendations and makes a formal presentation of these. The program is then implemented by other PR workers at the organization or at an agency. (See Chapter 10 for details of billings.) Counselors may work independently, or they may be associated with a firm as senior members. Some independent PR practitioners do various PR jobs, but most are strictly counselors.

Some counselors are sensitive about their role because people tend to view them as behind-the-scenes influence peddlers. Another misconception is that counselors are simply unemployed would-be senior staffers. Public confusion is understandable, however, because counselors are *advisers* who possess special areas of expertise, most of it gained in agency or corporate work. Their value resides in their experience; in the people they know and are able to call upon; and in their skill as researchers, analyzers, communicators and persuaders.

Some counselors develop reputations for helping institutions prepare for and handle crisis communication. Others are known for their ability to help institutions establish and maintain good government relations (at all levels, but primarily at the federal level). Still others are called on for their ability to help with internal problems, typically ones involving employee relations. Counselors, as senior practitioners, often develop staffs that include younger people who have particular strengths or specializations.

■ Specific Areas of PR Specialization

The breadth of PR services gives individuals a wide career choice. Many practitioners are experienced in more than one area.

Nonprofit Organizations Nonprofit organizations offer a practitioner several advantages and opportunities, although the compensation is often lower here than in other areas. The structure of these organizations (small production staff answerable to a volunteer board of directors) means that the nonprofit PR person generally has a great deal of freedom in designing a program. An attractive program that does not require a large bankroll probably will be accepted.

This kind of PR work usually entails a considerable amount of promotional activity and some-times also fundraising and foundation grant seeking. A particular plus, however, is the reception given to publicity materials by news media representatives, who usually make every effort to use information from nonprofit institutions as long as the preparation is professional. Even nonprofit advertising gets a break, with special rates (sometimes called "church rates"). The only drawback besides red ink is frequent dependence on volunteer support in many areas. Responsibility for training volunteers usually falls on the PR people, and they must recognize that volunteers' interest in and enthusiasm for the organization can be stimulated and sustained only by a viable program.

The number and variety of nonprofit organizations continue to expand rapidly, increasing the need for public relations practitioners in this area. Categories include museums, hospitals, social service and health-care groups plus professional organizations of all types.

Educational Institutions Educational institutions are usually nonprofit organizations as well, but they may be either public or private. The private institutions generally conform to the nonprofit organizational pattern. Although they have significant dealings with government, their work is quite unlike that of public institutions, which, being a part of government, are more open to the scrutiny of taxpayers and the whims of politicians. The type of PR practiced in state educational institutions is often suited to a person who enjoys dealing with the government.

PR people in all educational institutions are likely to be involved in development, which includes fundraising. The functions of PR and of development are separate, but the two groups must work closely together. In fact, the two functions are often lumped together under the umbrella term *institutional advancement* (a term used by CASE, the Council for Advancement and Support of Education).

The title "vice president for development" or "director of university relations" is commonly assigned to the individual who supervises both the PR and the fundraising functions. Sports information may be included under public relations or kept separate from it in an athletic department; in the latter case, the person responsible for it reports to the athletic director who in turn reports to the president. This arrangement can cause problems, however, because university sports are often involved in controversies that affect university relations.

Fundraising or Donor Relations Although many public relations people will tell you that they "don't do fundraising"—just as many others say that they "don't do advertising"—those who do it well are in great demand.

Fundraising is sometimes called donor relations. First and foremost, the fundraiser must identify sources of potential support through research. Then he or she must inform those sources of the value of the organization, so they will consider making a gift to it. In the case of individual donors, this usually means cultivating a relationship between that person and the organization over a period of time. If the source is a foundation, the informational task means writing a grant proposal that explains the value of the organization seeking the funds and identifies it closely with the mission of the foundation.

The third aspect of donor relations—the actual solicitation—takes many forms. It may involve an elaborate presentation book prepared just for that individual, or it may employ a videotape that can be used repeatedly in combination with personally directed appeals. It generally involves a series of letters requesting funds, and in broader appeals it may include brochures and telephone solicitations. Face-to-face meetings also are used for the personal appeal, and these can be one-on-one or one to a group of potential donors. In the case of large gifts, a strong tie is usually built between the institution (some element or some person in it) and the donor.

The next step is to provide some appropriate recognition for the donor that reflects the size of the gift and the nature of the appeal. (Nothing is more upsetting to a donor than getting an expensive "reward," since this signals that a good portion of the money raised is being spent on thank-yous instead of on the primary mission of the organization.)

Finally, the donor's relationship to the organization must be sustained in a way that is mutually satisfying. The fundraiser wants the donor to give again, especially if the organization has annual fundraising events (as public television stations, for example, do). Even if the gift was substantial and there is no reason to expect another, the fundraiser still wants the donor to have an ongoing relationship with the organization and to feel good about having given. Donors often attract other donors, but only when they feel good about their experience.

Research: Trend Analysis, Issues Management and Public Opinion Evaluation Some PR practitioners specialize in research that focuses on capturing information to help organizations plan better by anticipating currents of change. Some engage in analyzing trends to enable their organization to detect, adapt to and even take advantage of emerging changes. Issues management is centrally concerned with watching the horizons for change through many types of research. By determining in advance what developments are likely to become important to one or more of its publics, an organization can plan to meet the challenge, rather than being taken by surprise. Much of the research underlying trend analysis and issue anticipation consists of monitoring public opinion and evaluating the consequences of attitude changes to the organization and its publics.

In some situations public relations people may want to consult a futurist. Futurists are people whose occupation is forecasting future events, conditions or developments. By the mid-1970s, as many as one in five Fortune 500 companies had on the payroll a "futurist" whose role was to serve management as an early warning system.[23]

Detection of emerging issues and surveillance of social and economic trends continue to be important PR functions. These skills cast PR people in the role of social scientist. Information and intelligent analysis of issues and trends can help restore public confidence. The challenge facing PR practitioners is to provide leadership in developing creative, pragmatic communication programs that provide their publics with complete, candid, factual and understandable information. Further, PR workers must pioneer new skills to use in maintaining good relations with their publics.

All PR people, but especially those involved in research, must be good navigators of the information superhighway. Navigation means using the Internet to get where you need to go. This includes both gathering and disseminating information. Proficiency by PR practitioners is expected.

International PR for Organizations and Firms

The globalization of news media, the unification of the world's economy and the emergence of multinational companies have helped expand this area of public relations. *International PR* is not limited to businesses, however, because many nonprofit organizations and associations are international in scope. PR firms often have offices abroad to represent both domestic and foreign clients. Corporate PR people abroad function just as their counterparts do at home, working with community leaders, government officials and media. They provide a crucial link between the branch organization and the home office.

International PR requires extra sensitivity to public opinion because practitioners deal with people whose language, experience and frame of reference differ from their own. Areas of special concern are language (and knowledge of its nuances); customs affecting attitudes toward media, products/services and symbols that stem from customs; and laws. The last area is particularly significant, because incompatibilities between one country's laws and another's may make harmonious relationships impossible.

Financial PR or Investor Relations

This area includes such activities as preparing material for security analysts to study, developing an annual report that is acceptable to auditors and intelligible to stockholders and knowing when and to whom to issue a news release that could affect corporate stock values. It is a rather hazardous occupation because a wrong move can have such grave repercussions. On the other hand, it is exciting, remunerative and challenging.

Industry

Public relations for industry also requires a good feel for political PR–public affairs, because so much of industry is regulated by government. A person working for a company that handles government contracts must develop a high tolerance for bureaucratic delay. One PR staffer for a defense contractor has said that the average time required to get an "original" release—one with all new material—cleared for dissemination to the news media is twenty-three days. Since much of the emphasis in industrial public relations is on internal PR, and in particular on labor relations, a strong background in the social sciences and business helps.

Despite the trend toward deregulation in the utilities industry, PR practitioners still must work with both government and consumers. They must also know financial PR, because most utilities are publicly held. Finally, industry's PR practitioners may be involved in product promotion, which requires an understanding and appreciation of marketing and advertising activities.

General Business or Retail PR

This area is somewhat broader than the term *retail* implies. It involves working with government regulatory bodies, employees, the community, competitors and, generally, the full complement of publics both inside and outside the company. Consumers represent an increasingly significant external public because they talk to politicians and can arouse public opinion against a business. Product promotion—of a service or of goods—is another common aspect of general business. For that reason, the business setting is a likely place to find the *marketing/public relations* or IMC title.

Government

The four areas in this category all have the same focus, but their internal workings vary.

Federal, State or Local Government Employment Although the federal government is prohibited from labeling PR activities as such, it (like state and local governments) uses PR talent under a variety of titles: public information officer, public affairs officer or departmental assistant or aide.

Nongovernmental Organizations' Government Relations The term *public affairs* is also used by institutions to designate the working area of staff members who deal with government. Most institutions, whether commercial or nonprofit, have specialists who handle their relations with relevant departments of government on federal, state and local levels. In this context public affairs work consists of dealing with problems that come under the jurisdiction of elected or appointed public officials.

Political Public Relations Political PR involves working with candidates for office—and often continuing to work with them after their election—to handle problems, strategies and activities such as speech writing or publicity. Many PR practitioners will not support a cause or person they cannot conscientiously endorse. Others see PR advice as being like legal counsel and offer their services to anyone who is willing to pay for them.

For government, public affairs and politics, a strong background in government and history is useful. Political PR, like other areas of public relations, can be high-pressure, especially since the Freedom of Information Act has made government secrets more generally discoverable. In addition, recent restrictions on campaign financing mean that PR people must be even more judicious in collecting, reporting and spending money. State and federal laws must be obeyed to the letter.

Lobbying Many lobbyists are not public relations specialists at all (many are former government officials). But many public relations practitioners get involved in lobbying activities through their jobs with corporations or utilities. Some PR practitioners become professional lobbyists, at which point they generally represent a particular industry (such as oil and gas) or special interest (such as senior citizens or health-care organizations). Lobbyists work closely with the staffs of federal and/or state representatives and senators, who depend on them to explain the intricacies and implications of proposed legislation. Lobbyists draw on information furnished by their sponsors to try to persuade lawmakers to adopt a particular point of view.

Health Care Health maintenance organizations (HMOs), hospitals, other health-care agencies (such as nursing home corporations), pharmaceutical companies, medical clinics, health-science centers and nonprofit health agencies (for example, those combating heart disease, cancer and birth defects) all employ public relations personnel. The demand in this field is for PR practitioners who either know or have the educational background to learn about medical science, to translate that information accurately for the organization's publics. A heavy marketing component also exists in this area, which means that the PR person needs to have good advertising and public relations skills.

Sports Before sports became big business, the term *public relations* was sometimes used to describe a job that actually combined press agentry and publicity. Today, however, business enterprises in professional sports are of such size and scope that the PR title is legitimate. Professional teams have intricate relations with investors, their own players, competing teams and players, stadium owners, transportation and housing facilities (at home and on the road), community supporters, media (with regard both to publicity and to contractual obligations, as in live coverage) and other important publics. Most pro sports organizations employ full-time staff PR people, and they contract for special PR activities as well. Sports are also increasingly important to colleges and universities. Sports information officers in these institutions handle relations with media and fans.

Leisure Time The leisure-time market, which has been expanding since World War II, includes all recreation-related industries. It covers real-estate promotion for resort locations, public park development, resorts and hotels, travel agencies, airlines and other mass transportation systems, sports, hobbies and crafts and some educational, entertainment and cultural activities. The focus of PR activity in this market is promotions, and the only real hazard is the somewhat erratic international economy. Creative and inventive public relations generalists can function here quite comfortably.

THE FUNCTION OF PUBLIC RELATIONS IN BUSINESS AND SOCIETY

Traditionally, three functions have been ascribed to public relations. According to one point of view, public relations serves *to control publics,* by directing what people think or do in order to satisfy the needs or desires of an institution. According to a second point of view, PR's function is *to respond to publics*—reacting to developments, problems or the initiatives of others. According to a third point of view, the function of public relations is *to achieve mutually beneficial relationships among all the publics that an institution has,* by fostering harmonious interchanges among an institution's various publics (including such groups as employees, consumers, suppliers and producers).[24]

Stephen A. Greyser, a Harvard University business professor and consumer researcher, calls this third view of the function of PR, in which the consumer is seen as a partner of business, the *transactional model.* Greyser has developed two other models: the *manipulative model,* which looks upon the consumer as victim; and the *service model,* which sees the consumer as king. According to Greyser, the consumer still sees some distance between the current marketplace and the ideal service model.[25]

The three traditional views of PR are each discernible in the history of public relations (see Chapter 2). Greyser's manipulative model describes public relations during the era of communicating and initiating. His service model describes practices that predominated during the era of reacting and responding. His transactional model describes public relations during the era of planning and presenting.

The current era of professionalism has seen practitioners beginning to control PR's development, use and practice. This concept of the uniqueness of public relations is well expressed in the following words of the late Philip Lesly:

> Public relations people have the role of being always in the middle—pivoted between their clients/employers and their publics. . . . This role "in the middle" does not apply to any other group that deals with the climate of attitudes. Experts in other fields—journalists, sociologists, psychologists, politicians, etc.—are oriented in the direction of their specialties.[26]

James E. Grunig, who developed the "four models of PR practice" schema, defines public relations as "the management of communication between an organization and its publics."[27] Although many PR practitioners might argue that PR involves managing more than communication, few would fail to recognize the four models presented in Example 1.3.

Another way of talking about the different approaches to PR is from the standpoint of practitioner self-description. PR educator Lalit Acharya suggests that environment might explain the self-perceptions of a practitioner.[28] Self-described roles, largely the conceptual work of Glen M. Broom and George D. Smith,[29] include *expert prescriber,* an authoritarian and prescriptive model; *communication technician,* a supportive, skills-oriented model; *communication facilitator,* a liaison model; *problem-solving process facilitator,* a confrontational model; and *acceptant legitimizer,* a yes-person model. Acharya examined these descriptions in terms of "perceived environmental uncertainty" for the practitioner and concluded that a public relations practitioner (as an individual) may play a number of these roles, depending on the environment in which he or she functions in any given case.

Actually these self-described roles may be telescoped into only two: manager (who supervises technical staff and participates in planning and policy making as counsel to management) and

EXAMPLE 1.3

Grunig's Four Models of PR Practice

1. *Press Agentry/Publicity Model.* This model exemplifies the first historical stage of public relations, in which the aim is to "publicize the organization, its products, and its services in any way possible." Promotion of sports and theatrical events is typical. Product promotion in support of marketing objectives is also prevalent. These activities involve only one-way communication dedicated to "help the organization control the publics that affect it." The complete truth is not always told.

2. *Public Information Model.* This historically second stage of public relations seeks to "disseminate information to the public as truthfully and accurately as possible." It is used primarily by government agencies, nonprofits and associations. Practitioners in these organizations serve as "journalists in residence"; they try to represent both organizational and public interests.

3. *Two-Way Asymmetric Model.* This model is tilted in favor of the organization. It uses public relations to "persuade the public to agree with the organization's point-of-view." Feedback is used for manipulative purposes, i.e., "to determine what public attitudes are toward the organization and how they might be changed." Business firms in highly competitive markets use this model.

4. *Two-Way Symmetric Model.* Here the organization attempts to reach a "state-of-affairs" with its publics that is acceptable to all. The purpose of public relations is "to develop mutual understanding between the management of the organization and publics the organization affects." Instead of thinking of the organization as the source of communication and the publics as the receiver, both are conceived as groups engaged in a transaction.

Source: Reprinted with permission of *pr reporter*, Exeter, N.H.

technician (who performs the skills jobs that PR demands). A test of the conceptual research in which surveys were mailed to 136 PR practitioners in Washington state suggests that this is the case.[30] If the roles really are more diverse, as the earlier descriptive work suggests, the particular roles chosen may depend on the degree of encouragement or discouragement for individual initiative present in the public relations practitioner's own environment.

Acharya's work primarily describes practitioner behavior in terms of the external environment of public opinion, but internal environments (such as open or closed communication systems) also can affect practitioner behavior. In fact, some research indicates that PR practitioners who work in participative environments (where employees make job-related suggestions and generally take a more active role in determining their work environment) see themselves as less constrained than those who work in authoritarian environments (where employee input is strongly discouraged).[31] It may be that the self-described "technician" doesn't have the option of being a manager, because of authoritarian top management and a closed communication environment. Michael Ryan, who has investigated participative versus authoritative environments, observes:

> *Practitioners who work in authoritative environments might attempt to change those environments by educating management about the advantages—indeed, the necessity—of involving public relations persons in decision-making at the highest levels and of removing constraints on their freedom to act professionally.*[32]

While Ryan recognizes that the task of transforming an organization from authoritative to participative might not be included in a PR person's job description, he notes that accomplishing such a change might be among the most significant contributions a practitioner could make. In any case, Ryan suggests that "public relations persons would do well to seek out participative environments and to avoid authoritative environments."[33]

While most public relations practitioners accept the *idea* of there being distinct technician and manager roles due to the variety of activities that public relations incorporates, in reality public relations practitioners juggle the two roles simultaneously most of the time. The delineation might best be used to describe which role occupies *most* of the practitioner's time.

Typologies Aside

While these typologies are very useful, they often do not grasp the full range of factors affecting public relations practice. It makes a great deal of difference, for example, who is actually doing the PR. In many cases, public relations functions have been delegated to people from other fields: lawyers without any background in public relations or even communications; former media personnel who have been on the receiving end of public relations material but have no theoretical background; management-trained executives whose business school education did not include any courses in public relations; or marketing experts who have no knowledge of the overall communications components. If management doesn't know what the public relations function should be—and many do not—the function becomes what the person doing the job knows how to do best. (See Chapter 3 for a discussion of the effect this is having on public relations.) In other words, the *corporate communications environment,* the *education of the individuals* doing the job, the *type of organization* and the *culture* in which they function all significantly affect what actually happens under the name of public relations.

The Values of Public Relations

The lack of consistency in PR practice is also due to PR's rapid growth and the absence of any mechanism of control over both practice and practitioners. Public relations may still be observed *in practice* today that is typical of each of the eras Greyser and Grunig identify. The development of professionalism should give some consistency to PR practice and should strengthen the values of public relations, which include the following:

- Public relations represents and articulates the desire and interests of various publics to society's sometimes unresponsive institutions. While interpreting and speaking for publics, it also speaks to them for the institutions.
- Public relations helps establish smoother relationships between institutions and society by encouraging mutual adjustments to benefit society.
- Public relations offers ways to work out differences cooperatively so that coercion or arbitrary action does not become necessary.
- Public relations provides information for the communication system to help it keep people informed about various aspects of their lives.
- Public relations personnel can and frequently do help stimulate an institution's social conscience.
- Public relations functions in all aspects of life, since its principles reflect the basic human impulses of seeking acceptance, cooperation and/or affection from others. Public relations practice just formalizes that activity.[34]
- Public relations can help management formulate better objectives, advocate them and teach them.

Doing these things is part of the social responsibility of all institutions—public or private, profit-making or nonprofit.

PR as Counsel for Social Responsibility

Management must be responsible and responsive to its publics; otherwise, it will have to combat a hostile environment. Unfortunately, the pattern of action has often been just the opposite, according to social scientist Hazel Henderson, who identified the following "normal" pattern of business response to social issues: (1) Ignore the problem. (2) If publicity calls widespread attention to the problem, admit its existence but present business as a victim of circumstances it cannot alter. (3) When the public takes the problem to lawmakers, lobby, testify in legislative hearings and advertise to get opinion leaders to believe that the proposed solutions constitute government interference in the private economy. (4) After new regulations are final, announce that business can live with the new law.[35]

Not only does such behavior justify public pressure for government intervention as the only way to achieve needed changes—just what business does not want—but it also undermines a company's credibility. First, the behavior is reactive, as the late William A. Durbin, former chairman of Hill & Knowlton, pointed out. Second, it is defensive, suggesting that there is a fundamental conflict between public welfare and industry. Third, the posture business takes in explaining how it is a victim of circumstances evidences a preference for quantification (as in talking about "nonproductive dollars") when the public is focused on something qualitative like "clean air." Fourth, the pattern of response concentrates on the means and ignores the end—an end that business might actually support, like clean air."[36]

All large institutions, not only businesses, are challenged these days: governments, schools and colleges, professional sports, churches, health-care groups, fund-raising groups, even the news media. With the prevalence of such crises in public confidence, the role of the PR practitioner becomes critical.

Probably the biggest obstacles to "ideal" public relations, as media scholars David Clark and William Blankenburg observe, are economics and human nature:

> The plain fact is that managers are hired to make money for owners, and that a conscience can cost money. In the long run, it is money well spent, but many stockholders and managers fix their vision on the short run. Then, too, an abrupt change in corporate policy amounts to a public confession of past misbehavior—or so it seems to many executives. The natural temptation is to play up the good, and to let it go at that.[37]

As a result, in the 1970s a whole "new math" entered the corporate structure. Executives committed to being responsive and responsible attempted to explain social costs to chief financial officers, security analysts and stockholders. The *Wall Street Journal* called it "the Arithmetic of Quality":

> The social critics of business are making headway. Increasingly, corporations are being held to account not just for their profitability but also for what they do about an endless agenda of social problems. For business executives, it's a whole new ball game. Now they're struggling to come up with a new way to keep score.[38]

In the 1980s and into the 1990s, with downsizing and restructuring, the job became more difficult.

Many examples of the problems of accountability can be found. How can a profit-and-loss statement be made to reveal on the credit ledger the good a company does when its personnel advise minority businesspeople struggling to succeed in a ghetto? How can the installation of pollution control devices at a factory be calculated as a positive accomplishment, rather than as a drag on productivity? How can the expense of hiring school dropouts and putting them through company-financed training programs be manifested as a credit rather than as a debit? Conversely, how can the "bad" a company does (by polluting, using discriminatory hiring practices and the like) be measured and reflected as a negative factor in the company's performance?

Despite these problems, social responsibility is widely recognized today as an essential cost of doing business in the USA. A good indication of how seriously major companies now regard "social accounting" is the big jump onto the "green" bandwagon that occurred in the early 1990s. According to the *Wall Street Journal*, many companies have appointed environmental policy officers.[39] But some of these companies were merely being duplicitous—promoting some environmental efforts while continuing to pollute in another area.[40] Perhaps the reason for this is that some who espoused the environmental cause and wanted to devote more than "window dressing" to it found that the social accounting was quite costly, because it entailed top-to-bottom organizational reform. Still, a company does better to anticipate environmental accountability than to ignore it and eventually face a fine from the Environmental Protection Agency, as Disney Industries did in 1990. The pressure comes from consumers. PR firms with environmental specialists, such as GSD&M in Austin, Texas, find that explaining their clients' environmental activities (as opposed to telling people what they make, sell or do) consumes large amounts of time.[41]

Companies that claim to be doing good for society but aren't, and the public relations people who are their spokespersons, were soundly condemned in a 1997 book by John Stauber and Sheldon Rampton called, *Toxic Sludge Is Good for You: Lies, Damn Lies and the Public Relations Industry.* Many practitioners were outraged at being included in what the book called "today's multi-billion-dollar propaganda-for-hire industry." Nevertheless, the massive cover-ups by the tobacco industry revealed that same year should stand as a warning that deceit and misrepresentation have sometimes occurred on a massive scale in business and that PR people have been a part of it.

All of this criticism has meant that public relations has had to expand its role as (1) *a problem finder and problem solver or preventer* and (2) *an interpreter—a communication link.* Let's consider these two requirements individually.

PR as Problem Finder, Solver and Preventer PR people have to be problem finders and solvers and, preferably, problem preventers. Such work involves identifying issues and understanding what images are projected.

As long ago as 1965, former PR practitioner the late Philip Lesly outlined the six major problems he saw for business in the second half of this century.[42] These problems—which may also apply to large nonprofit institutions—are, Lesly said, "the most intangible, immeasurable, and unpredictable of all elements affecting a business":

1. The main problem in production is no longer how to increase the efficiency of factories and plants, but how to deal with the attitudes of people whose jobs will be changed or eliminated by the introduction of more efficient methods.

2. The principal problem of growth through innovation is not how to organize and administer development programs, but how to deal with the reactions of intended customers and dealers to the product.

3. The personnel problem is not how to project a firm's manpower needs and standards, but how to persuade the best people to work for the company—and then to stay and do their best work.

4. The financing problem is not how to plan for the company's funding, but how to deal with the attitudes of investors.

5. The problem in advertising is not how to analyze in minute detail the media, timing and costs, but how to reach the minds and hearts of the audience.

6. The problem of business acceptance is no longer how to demonstrate that an institution is operating in the public interest, but how to get people to understand that its cornucopia works better when it has a minimum of restraints.

Each problem Lesly isolated suggests a need for awareness of and sensitivity to what is going on in the public mind. To probe the public consciousness, PR people have turned to pollsters and futurists.

Years ago, no one foresaw the role that the public relations practitioner or consultant is now playing in relation to current social crises. No longer primarily a communicator, today's PR practitioner tries to prevent crises and, once they occur, tries to keep them from getting out of hand. Some of the tools used, such as personal contact and the media—mass and specialized—remain. However, the measure of performance is not how effectively the client's message gets across but whether a flareup that might injure a client's business can be avoided. One major obligation is to help clients conduct their business in a way that responds to the new demands made by concerned scientists, environmentalists, consumerists, minority leaders, employees and underprivileged segments of the community.

The most valuable type of public relations activity involves anticipating problems, planning to prevent problems, or at least to solve them while they are still small.

PR as Interpreter and Communication Link Perhaps, as suggested by Daniel H. Gray, a management consultant noted for his work on the social role of business, social accounting doesn't exist.[43] Indeed, the system needed may well be more concerned with communication than with accounting.

Communication audits—internal, external or both—have become common for institutions trying to track problem areas. Philip Lesly observed that institutions must function in a human climate, and thoughtful managers recognize that they don't have the expertise to deal with this element unaided. As human patterns become more complicated, they demand greater expertise and experience. Consequently, Lesly said, "Communications sense and skills, which have been vital and have always been scarce, are becoming more vital and scarcer still."[44]

This is where the PR practitioner comes in, of course. He or she must act as an interpreter or communication link between an organization and its publics. Lesly added,

> Public relations is a bridge to change. It is a means to adjust to new attitudes that have been caused by change. It is a means of stimulating attitudes in order to create change. It helps an organization see the whole of our society together, rather than from one intensified viewpoint. It provides judgment, creativity and skills in accommodating groups to each other, based on wide and diverse experience.[45]

In 1972, David Finn, cofounder of the PR firm of Ruder & Finn, wrote:

> Twenty years ago public relations had its eye on the social sciences, with the full expectation that new discoveries would soon be made which would elevate the art of mass communications into a responsible profession. Ten years ago some of us thought computer technology was going to do the trick and the phrase "opinion management" emerged as a possible successor to the long-abandoned "engineering of consent." As things turned out, it is not the technique of public relations which has changed so much as the subject matter with which we are concerned.[46]

Emphasizing PR's role as a communication link, Finn focused on four developments that he held to be true of the job: (1) resolving conflicts may require modifying many opinions, including those held by the public relations consultant and the client; (2) patterns of communication in the future may revolve increasingly around smaller groups; (3) the random benefits of public relations activities not directly tied to corporate interests will increase; (4) new methods of research now being developed will be especially relevant to situations where opinions change rapidly.[47]

His words were prophetic of the instant global communication system in which PR practitioners now work.

Public relations, one writer notes, does not "create the corporate image or reputation"; rather, "it interprets and advocates the policies, statements, and activities which qualify the corporation for its reputation."[48] In other words, PR cannot fabricate a corporate image; it must start with reality and seek to match the image to the truth.

Perceptions of Public Relations

For public relations to be an effective instrument in any situation, management must have a clear conception of the breadth of its role—such as in counseling, research and planning—beyond communication, and the PR practitioner must be prepared to assume any aspect of that role.

PR practitioners also must thoroughly know the organization and the environment in which it operates. In an article for *Harvard Business Review*, Robert S. Mason, then PR consultant and head of his own agency, cautioned management not to hire a new public relations director until the parameters of the job are clearly understood by all. If management only wants a communications technician, it should not hire a highly skilled public relations person who is qualified to participate in policy decisions. But since almost every policy decision has some public relations implications, Mason warned, management would do well to seek the more expensive, better-equipped public relations practitioner. As Mason noted, most PR directors have an independent orientation that adds a significant dimension to the decision-making

Calvin and Hobbes © Watterson. Reprinted with permission of Universal Press Syndicate. All rights reserved.

process. When the role is clearly defined, evaluation of PR performance is easier. Mason added, "Meaningful evaluation of PR's performance can only occur in an environment where PR itself is managed consciously as a rational function."[49]

One problem with PR evaluation, according to a professional newsletter, is the lack of agreement about how the function should be measured. It might be helpful to measure the PR function by determining how it contributes to an organization's financial health. At least seven contributions of PR to an organization's financial well-being are identifiable and measurable:[50]

- *Publicity and promotion* help pave the way for new ideas and products.
- *Internal motivation* can increase team effort and build morale.
- *Eliminating surprises* through interpretation of publics to the institution and vice versa may avoid disruptive controversies.
- *New opportunities* are identified by PR's outreach to all publics, as a result of which new markets, new products, new methods and new ideas may be discovered.
- *Protection of present position* can be handled by PR only when an institution is under siege, because then the public's perception of the institution's true values must be nurtured.

- *Overcoming executive isolation* enables management to know what is really going on.
- *Change agentry* helps persuade an institution's publics to overcome a natural resistance to necessary change.

For some time now, the role of public relations has been in flux. It has changed from being responsible for "making the cash register ring" to handling the "myriad social problems that beset the corporation," says Harold Burson, chairman of Burson-Marsteller.[51] There are three reasons for the change, Burson believes. The first is affluence: Energies once directed toward making a living are now diverted toward effecting social change. The second is technology, which has made bigness possible but has reduced the impact of the individual. The third is the transnational or multinational character of the large, modern corporation, which knows no boundaries. Burson's words (especially his third point) were even more true in the 1990s than when he spoke them originally in 1980.

Many people wrongly assume that public relations is preoccupied with image-making in the sense of creating a false front or cover-up. Unfortunately, this misperception of public relations is reinforced by periodic reports of just such behavior on the part of individuals identified as public relations specialists. For example, the term "spin

THE LITTLE WOMAN

"So you're in public relations. Is that where you get me to like something I wouldn't like at all if you didn't do what you do to make me like it?"

Reprinted with special permission of King Features Syndicate, Inc.

Times as saying, "You call in public relations operatives when the truth won't do. . . . That's why PR—the very letters evoke subtle maneuvers and manipulation of opinion—has become, in business and in politics, the substitute for genuine moral and ethical sense."[56] It's not uncommon for PR to be used as a pejorative term, and educating misinformed people about what PR really is and does poses a significant challenge.

OPPORTUNITIES AND CHALLENGES IN PUBLIC RELATIONS

Each year the Public Relations Society of America publishes statistics on career opportunities. In 1997, 40 percent of the openings for jobs at $35,000 and above were in corporations, 29 percent in PR firms and 22 percent in nonprofit organizations. Jobs with high-level titles included 5 percent for vice presidents, 21 percent for directors, 6 percent for account supervisors, 4 percent for senior account executives and 7 percent for account executives. The role of executive search firms for top-level positions had expanded. They handled 23 percent of these placements in corporations and firms, up from 16 percent in 1996.[57]

At the entry level, most of the public relations hiring comes through colleges and universities. Statistics compiled by the Association for Education in Journalism and Mass Communication show that the top salaries for students with bachelor's degrees in journalism and mass communication are commanded by public relations and advertising graduates. These figures, however, are only shown in comparison with graduates from news editorial and broadcast journalism programs, and do not take into account those entering public relations jobs from other fields, especially with master's degrees.

If other research findings of the 1990s hold true for you as a public relations practitioner, you'll change jobs with some frequency (every 3 to 5 years); devote a good bit of your time to such traditional tasks as media relations, special events and publicity; work in the corporate sector; and be paid on the basis of your gender (women in public

doctor," which suggests media manipulation through "doctored" (that is, deceptive) accounts or interpretations of events, was introduced in the late 1980s and gained currency in the 1990s.[52] In fact, a *New York Times* story about a media relations course being taught in business schools was headlined, "Media Manipulation 101."[53] At least most media relations instructors are teaching better answers than the following response received by a reporter investigating the troubled Los Angeles–based Security Pacific Bank: "[A] bank spokeswoman says that regulators aren't at the bank; she added that if they were, she wouldn't be permitted to say so."[54]

Students probably won't have to wait until they get a public relations job to discover the unfavorable perception of public relations some people have. In fact, in many departments of journalism and mass communication where public relations is taught, negative attitudes toward public relations as an area of study appear to be common.[55]

It doesn't help, either, when someone like Eugene Kennedy—Loyola University psychology professor and former priest—is quoted in the *New York*

relations earn generally less for the same work than men).

Whatever the PR job, some observations about career opportunities and challenges can be made uniformly. First, salaries are largely affected by gender, experience, education, age, job title and duties, as well as by the type, size and location of the organization. Generally speaking, though, the better educated the person is, the higher his or her average salary will be. This is true regardless of the person's college major, although age and gender are major factors.[58]

College-educated white women nationwide earn an average of $14,217 a year less than college-educated white men, and they earn only $794 a year more than white men who have never taken a college course. College-educated African-American and Hispanic women earn $2,558 less a year than white male high school graduates.[59]

According to a study by Catalyst, a New York research organization, these discrepancies persist at the management level. White female managers, they found, earn 59 cents for every dollar a white male manager earns; women of color get 57 cents; and men of color, 73 cents. Of all management jobs held by females, white women have 86 percent although they are only 77 percent of the female work force. African-American women make up 12.1 percent of the female work force, but hold only 6.6 percent of these management positions; Hispanic women make up 7 percent, but hold 5.2 percent of those positions; and Asian women represent

3.6 percent, but are only 2.5 percent of the female managers.[60]

Although more women are entering the field of public relations, as in other industries their pay and authority remain less than men's. Most women feel that their path to management is blocked, and women who are minorities feel that racism and sexism combine to keep them from the top. Many women have attempted to circumvent the problem by opening their own public relations firms.

A second general observation is that, since anyone can be designated as a public relations practitioner, two currently controversial areas in public relations are educational preparation and licensing for the practice.

A third point is that public relations practice, as interesting as it is, can be very stressful. A PRSA survey of practitioners in New York revealed that, while 82 percent of them consider PR a rewarding career, the stress level of their jobs has caused only 53 percent to say they definitely would still seek a PR career if they were starting over; another 27 percent said they weren't sure.[61]

PR practice has been listed as one of the top ten fields for stress. Psychologist Thomas Backer has identified eight reasons for this: (1) *negative leverage*, the result of the high visibility of mistakes PR professionals make, multiplies the stress impact; (2) *multiple bosses* (and publics) exist within the institution's structure (and there is the stress of a responsibility to all of the different publics as well); (3) *time pressures* are constant because almost all major tasks are on tight schedules; (4) *lack of understanding* of the PR role results in such disparaging labeling as "flacks"; (5) *intangible* results remain a problem, despite better gauges for measuring PR's effectiveness; (6) *lack of respect* for public relations work occurs because everyone thinks he or she can do it; (7) *values conflicts* often occur when the PR practitioner's personal values differ from those of his or her client or institution; (8) *multiple emergencies* are common in PR practice because crises tend to spark others.[62]

A fourth observation is that not all PR people appreciate that the information age has created a "global village." Several studies indicate that cross-cultural awareness penetrates the PR function only when the situation is forced by the activities of the institutions involved (multinational companies, high-tech companies, governments and nonprofit organizations with international ties). Clearly, educators and public relations practitioners in the field should be taking the initiative in creating such awareness among their publics.

POINTS TO REMEMBER

■ The practice of PR is now global, but some basic principles apply to it regardless of the culture and the geopolitical area where it is practiced.

■ Because a PR person has only credibility to offer, he or she is only as good as his or her deserved reputation. The organization's credibility is always at stake, too, which is why the British are offering "reputation management" as a definition of PR.

■ PR involves responsibility and responsiveness in policy and information to the best interests of the organization and its publics.

■ Disclosing an active social conscience is the best PR.

■ Whatever the title for the public relations function—communications, reputation management or relationships management—it is a *strategic* management function.

■ Public relations activities may include press agentry, promotion, publicity, public affairs, research, graphics, advertising, marketing and merchandising support.

■ The public relations function has an impact on the organization's policy. PR activities in and of themselves are not the public relations function. Use of the term *public relations* for activities such as publicity or integrated marketing communication is confusing and misrepresents the function. One exception is the term *public affairs* as used by government, which usually does represent the function of public relations.

- Public relations practitioners must be creative, well-adjusted, flexible and capable of mastering diverse skills, as well as having integrity and the courage of their convictions.

- More public relations practitioners in the field now have some educational background in public relations, but there is no uniformity of education for the field—especially since education for PR has sprung up throughout the world.

- Career preparation for public relations includes expertise in the following areas: planning, managing, advising, analyzing, industry relations, economic relations, social relations, political activities, communication and educational activities. The need for continuing education for practitioners continues to grow in importance.

- Public relations lacks the three major ingredients that qualify a field of activity as a profession: body of knowledge, standard educational curriculum and control over entry and exit.

- PR practitioner roles include being a staff member in a variety of institutional settings, being an agency or firm employee or being an independent PR practitioner.

- Specific areas of PR specialization include: nonprofit organizations, educational institutions, fundraising or donor relations, research, international, investor relations, industry, general business, government, health care, sports and leisure time.

- The three traditional interpretations of the function of public relations—controlling publics, responding to publics and achieving mutually beneficial relationships among all publics—correspond to the manipulative, service and transactional models of PR.

- Various typologies attempt to describe what public relations people do. However, who is doing the job, in what kind of communications environment, in what type of organization and in what culture all determine what is being done in the name of public relations.

- PR offers at least seven measurable values to society and the institutions it serves, most of them centering on PR's role in working out institutional and social relationships.

- Social responsibility, historically ignored by most institutions, increasingly is viewed as being an essential "cost" of doing business.

- PR people have to be interpreters, functioning as a communication link between an institution and all of its publics.

- Many people wrongly assume that public relations means image-making in the sense of creating a false front or cover-up.

- More women are entering the PR field, but for lower pay than men at the same level receive; women also have less access to the top.

- Four observations about PR: (1) the better the education, the better the jobs; (2) two currently controversial areas in PR practice are education and licensing; (3) PR jobs are highly stressful; (4) PR people must function effectively in a "global village."

NOTES

[1] Lucien Matrat, "The Strategy of Confidence," *International Public Relations Review*, 13(2) (1990), pp. 8–12. The quoted language is on p. 8.

[2] Fraser Likely, "The Knock and the Roles in Public Relations/Communications," *Journal of Corporate Public Relations* (1994–1995), pp. 7–13.

[3] Matrat, "Strategy of Confidence," p. 8.

[4] *pr reporter*, 28(36) (September 9, 1985), p. 1.

[5] Tom Duncan, Clarke Caywood, and Doug Newsom, "Preparing Advertising and Public Relations Students for the Communications Industry in the 21st Century," Report of the Task Force on Integrated Communications (December 1993).

[6] Joe McGinniss, *The Selling of the President, 1968* (New York: Trident Press, 1968).

[7] Pat Jackson, "The Practice of Public Relations, 1982," *pr reporter*, 25(1) (January 4, 1982), p. 3.

[8] Edward L. Bernays, *pr reporter*, 25(50) (December 20, 1982), pp. 1–2.

[9] Ronald E. Rhody, "The Game," Public Relations Honors Lecture at University of the Pacific, Stockton, California, March 30, 1995.

[10] Sam Black, "Public Relations Education—Recommendations and Standards," International Public Relations Association, Gold Paper no. 7 (September 1990), p. 5.

[11] Ibid., p. 6.

[12] Ibid., p. 8.

[13] Carroll Bateman and Scott Cutlip, "A Design for Public Relations Education," Report of the Commission on Public Relations Education (New York: Foundation for Public Relations Research and Education, 1975).

[14] Kenneth Owler Smith, "Report of the 1981 Commission on Public Relations Education," *Public Relations Review*, 8(2) (Summer 1982), pp. 61–70.

[15] IPRA Education and Research Committee with the IPRA International Commission on Public Relations Education, "A Model for Public Relations Education for Professional Practice," International Public Relations Association, Gold Paper no. 4 (January 1982).

[16] William P. Ehling and Betsy Ann Plank, "The Design for Undergraduate Public Relations Education," Report of the 1987 Commission on Public Relations Education (New York: Public Relations Society of America).

[17] Michael Hesse and Paul Alvarez, Report of the 1983 Commission on Graduate Education in Public Relations (New York: Public Relations Society of America). Also published in summary in *Public Relations Journal* (March 1984), pp. 22–24.

[18] Public Relations Society of America, Commission on Public Relations Education, Minutes of Inaugural Meeting, November 9, 1997, Nashville, Tennessee.

[19] E. W. Brody, "What Ought To Be Taught Students of Public Relations?" *Public Relations Quarterly*, 30(1) (Spring 1985), p. 8.

[20] Frank Wylie, "The New Professionals," Speech to the First National Student Conference, Public Relations Student Society of America, Dayton, Ohio (October 24, 1976); published by Chrysler Corporation, p. 6.

[21] Ibid., pp. 6–11.

[22] Daniel Goleman, "The Electronic Rorschach," *Psychology Today* (February 1983), p. 43.

[23] Liz Roman Gallese, "More Companies Use 'Futurists' to Discern What is Lying Ahead," *Wall Street Journal* (March 31, 1975), pp. 1, 10.

[24] Task Force on Stature and Role of Public Relations, "Report and Recommendations," Public Relations Society of America (November 1980).

[25] Stephen A. Greyser, "Changing Roles for Public Relations," *Public Relations Journal*, 37(1) (January 1981), p. 23.

[26] Philip Lesly, *Managing the Human Climate*, 54 (January–February 1979), p. 2.

[27] James E. Grunig, "What Kind of Public Relations Do You Practice? New Theory of Public Relations Presents Four Models," *pr reporter*, 27, *purview* (April 9, 1984), p. 1.

[28] Lalit Acharya, "Public Relations Environments," *Journalism Quarterly*, 62(3) (Autumn 1985), pp. 577–84.

[29] Glen M. Broom and George D. Smith, "Testing the Practitioner's Impact on Clients," *Public Relations Review* 5(47) (1979), pp. 47–59.

[30] Joey Reagan, Ronald Anderson, Janine Sumner and Scott Hill, "A Factor Analysis of Broom and Smith's Public Relations Roles Scale," *Journalism Quarterly*, 67(1) (Spring 1990), pp. 177–83.

[31] Michael Ryan, "Participative vs. Authoritative Environments," *Journalism Quarterly*, 64(4) (Winter 1987), pp. 853–57.

[32] Ibid., p. 855.

[33] Ibid., p. 856.

[34] Task Force on Stature and Role of Public Relations, "Report and Recommendations," PRSA (November 1980), p. 9. A 1991 task force did not change this assessment significantly except to focus on global public opinion as an increasingly significant factor and to acknowledge that international PR practice is growing in importance.

[35] Henderson is quoted by William A. Durbin, "Managing Issues Is Public Relations' Responsibility," in "tips and tactics," biweekly supplement of *pr reporter*, 16(9) (May 15, 1978), pp. 1, 2.

[36] Durbin, "Managing Issues," pp. 1, 2.

[37] David G. Clark and William B. Blankenburg, *You & Media* (San Francisco: Canfield Press, 1973), p. 175.

[38] Frederick Andrews, "Puzzled Businessmen Ponder New Methods of Measuring Success," *Wall Street Journal* (September 9, 1971), p. 1. Reprinted with permission of the *Wall Street Journal*, © Dow Jones & Company, Inc., 1971.

[39] Joann S. Lublin, "'Green' Executives Find Their Mission Isn't a Natural Part Of Corporate Culture," *Wall Street Journal* (March 5, 1991), pp. B1, B6.

[40] Ginny Carroll, "Green for Sale," *National Wildlife*, 29(2) (February–March 1991), pp. 24–28.

[41] Lublin, "'Green' Executives," p. B6. Charles T. Salmon in his preface to *Information Campaigns: Balancing Values in Social Change*, p. 9, says that there is a fundamental tension between social marketing and the social values influencing such activity.

[42] Philip Lesly, "Effective Management and the Human Factor," *Journal of Marketing*, 29 (April 1965), pp. 1–4. Reprinted by permission of the American Marketing Association.

[43] Andrews, "Puzzled Businessmen Ponder New Methods," p. 1.

[44] Philip Lesly, "Challenges of the Communications Explosion," *The Freeman* (October 1973), pp. 607–8.

[45] Ibid.

[46] David Finn, "Modifying Opinions in the New Human Climate," Ruder & Finn Papers no. 1, reprinted from *Public Relations Quarterly*, 17 (Fall 1972), pp. 12–15, 26.

[47] Ibid.

[48] John Cook, "Consolidating the Communications Function," *Public Relations Journal*, 29(8) (August 1973), pp. 6–8, 27–28.

[49] Robert S. Mason, "What's a PR Director for Anyway?" *Public Relations*, no. 21490, pp. 95–101; article reprinted from *Harvard Business Review*, no. 74510 (September–October 1974).

[50] "Eight Ways Public Relations Contributes to the Bottom Line," *pr reporter*, 26(1) (January 3, 1983), pp. 1–2. Used by permission.

[51] Harold Burson, "The 'Bottom Line' in Public Relations," *Burson-Marsteller Report*, 46 (November 1980), pp. 1–4; adapted from Burson's acceptance address when he was named Public Relations Professional of the Year.

[52] David Shaw, "'Spin Doctors' Provide New Twist," *Los Angeles Times* (August 26, 1989), sec. 1, p. 24.

[53] Claudia H. Deutsch, "Media Manipulation 101," *New York Times* (January 21, 1990), sec. 3, part 2, p. 29.

[54] Herb Greenberg, "Banking Blues," *San Francisco Chronicle* (January 14, 1991), p. C1.

[55] Peter Habermann, Lillian Lodge Kopenhaver and David L. Martinson, "Sequence Faculty Divided on PR Value, Status and News Orientation," *Journalism Quarterly*, 65(2) (Summer 1988), pp. 490–96.

[56] James Cox, "Bishops' Account Ignites PR Schism," *USA Today* (April 24, 1990), p. 28.

[57] *pr reporter*, 40(35) (September 1, 1997), p. 4.

[58] Current figures on job opportunities and salaries are available annually from PRSA.

[59] Business and Professional Women's Foundation, reported in *Intercom* (January 1998), p. 2.

[60] Leon E. Wynter, "Business & Race," *Wall Street Journal* (December 3, 1997), p. B1.

[61] "Public Relations Is Among the Most Stressful Occupations," *pr reporter*, 37(43) (October 31, 1994), p. 3.

[62] "Public Relations One of Top 10 Fields for Stress," *pr reporter*, 26(3) (January 24, 1983), p. 1.

Selected readings, activities and assignments appropriate to this chapter can be found in the *Instructor's Guide* or on InfoTrac if you are using the InfoTrac College Edition.

CHAPTER 2

PR'S ORIGINS

AND EVOLUTION

Public relations has always played a part in free societies and the democratic process, and it still does. I think we need to appreciate that heritage.

HAROLD BURSON, CHAIRMAN OF BURSON-MARSTELLER

Today's public relations worker has inherited a legacy of criticism.

FROM *THE MASS MEDIA AND MODERN SOCIETY*,
BY THEODORE PETERSON, JAY W. JENSEN AND WILLIAM L. RIVERS

New names for public relations abound, such as integrated communication. Old ones have become more prominent, such as corporate communication. Arguments exist that not all public relations tasks provide the practitioner with an appropriate claim to the umbrella title of "public relations." Public relations, by that view, should be reserved only for management jobs that involve strategic planning.

Given that the occupation continues to have difficulty defining itself, it should be no surprise that authorities disagree about where and when public relations started and how it got its name. Some historians credit Thomas Jefferson in 1807 with first combining the words "public" and "relations" into "public relations." Others say that the term was coined by lawyer Dorman Eaton in an address to the Yale graduating class of 1882.[1] Regardless, "public relations" was not used in its modern sense until 1897, when it appeared in the Association of American Railroads' *Yearbook of Railway Literature*.[2] The real success of the term can be credited to Edward L. Bernays, whom Irwin Ross calls "the first and doubtless the leading ideologue of public relations."[3]

Bernays was the first to call himself a "public relations counsel," which he did in 1921. Two years later he wrote the first book on the subject, *Crystallizing Public Opinion*,[4] and taught the first college course on PR at New York University. Thus it was around the turn of the twentieth century that PR came into being as a term, as an occupation and as an academic discipline.

Like his uncle, Sigmund Freud, Bernays devoted his career to the study of the human mind. His specialty was mass psychology—how the opinions of large numbers of people can be influenced effectively and honorably. When he arrived on the scene, public opinion was considered the province of philosophy. Sociology was in its infancy, and Walter Lippmann had just begun to define what Bernays called "the American tribal consciousness." Bernays' approach to psychology is exemplified in the advice he gave the Procter & Gamble Company several decades ago when it came to him with a problem: a boycott of its products by black people. Bernays advised Procter & Gamble to eliminate its racist advertising campaign, to hire blacks in white-collar jobs and to invite black people to open-house gatherings at the plant.

The Bernays style was often subtle. For example, he helped the Beech-Nut Packing Company sell bacon, not by promoting bacon itself, but by promoting what all America could respond to— a nutritious breakfast. In 1918, Bernays even changed the course of history by convincing Tomas Masaryk, the founder of Czechoslovakia, to delay announcement of that country's independence by a day in order to get better press coverage.

Bernays, who died in 1995 at the age of 103, adamantly believed that public relations is more than mere press agentry. He was not, however, above staging events. In 1924, he helped President Coolidge counteract his aloof image by staging a White House breakfast, to which Al Jolson and several other movie stars were invited. In 1929, he publicized the fiftieth anniversary of the electric light bulb by having Thomas Edison reenact its discovery in the presence of President Hoover.

On the other hand, Bernays turned down an appeal through an intermediary to provide PR as-

sistance to Adolf Hitler in 1933, just before Hitler came to power. A correspondent for the Hearst newspapers told Bernays, however, that—during an interview with Joseph Goebbels, Hitler's minister of propaganda, some years later—he saw Bernays' 1923 book, *Propaganda*, on the Nazi's desk.[5]

SEEKING THE PR "SOURCE SPRING"

For all his influence on the field of public relations, Bernays is not its "founder." In fact, some authorities say Bernays learned public relations while serving on George Creel's Committee on Public Information, which was dedicated to gaining popular support for the United States' war effort during World War I.

Public relations probably has no single "founder," but many public relations practitioners in the United States see Ivy Lee as the first practitioner of a modern-style public relations practice. Most of Lee's early efforts were strictly publicity, but later he and others working in this early era were called for some "media relations" assistance when a crisis occurred. More strategic planning and counsel developed in the Bernays' era.

Without a doubt, public relations developed faster in the United States than in other countries.[6] Historian Alan R. Raucher attributes this to the nation's social, political, cultural and economic climate, as well as to the power of its media to render all large public institutions vulnerable to public opinion.[7] Public relations practice also has become an important export service, as other nations have developed their own versions of the practice.

Public relations as a concept has no central, identifying founder, national origin or founding date because it focuses on efforts to influence—not only opinions but behavior. This very element has created the greatest criticism of public relations. Historians who view public relations as a significant positive influence regard it as a broker for public support of ideas, institutions and people. Others, however, contend that this entails the sacrifice of individual freedom, which is usurped by majority decision. Of course, the same tradeoff is central to the nature of democracy itself; but this does not dispose of the problem that public opinion can be misused (see Chapter 4).

■ PR Functions Throughout History

Since the effort *to persuade* underlies all public relations activity, we can say that the general endeavor of public relations is as old as civilization itself. For society to exist, people must achieve some minimum level of agreement, and this agreement is usually reached through interpersonal and group communication. But reaching agreement often requires more than the simple act of sharing information; it demands a strong element of persuasion on the part of all parties involved in the decision-making process. Today persuasion is still the driving force of public relations, and many of the tactics that modern PR people use to persuade have been used by the leaders of society for thousands of years.

Monuments and other art forms of the ancient world reflect early efforts at persuasion. Pyramids, statues, temples, tombs, paintings and early forms of writing announce the divinity of rulers, whose power derived from the religious convictions of the public. Ancient art and literature also celebrated the heroic deeds of leaders and rulers, who were considered gods or godlike. Speeches by the powerful or power-seeking used institutionalized rhetoric (artificial or inflated language) as a principal device for persuasion.

Looking at some of the early techniques and tools used in persuasion can help put today's PR activities in perspective. Certainly such an overview will reveal that, in the process of its development, PR has amalgamated various persuasive techniques that have proved their utility and effectiveness through the centuries (see Example 2.1).

As Theodore Lustig, professor and former Sun Chemical Corporation's communications manager, points out:

E X A M P L E   2 . 1
PR's Early Best Sellers

St. Paul wrote his *Epistles* to encourage membership growth and to boost the morale of the early Christian churches, which were spread about the Roman Empire. His PR campaign was a great success, and his slogans and words of encouragement are still quoted.

The Islamic prophet Muhammad would seclude himself briefly during certain periods of social conflict or crisis and emerge with *suras* (verses) attributed to divine authorship that offered arguments pointing toward a particular resolution of the controversy at hand. These and various more meditative *suras* became the text of the collection known as the *Koran*.

Dante Alighieri wrote his *Divine Comedy* in Italian rather than in Latin to reach a wider local audience. In the book, Dante, a political activist, eloquently put forth his moral, political and intellectual views.

William Shakespeare's historical plays contained poetry and ideas for the intellectuals and jokes and violence for the rest of the audience. But they also appealed to those in power by glorifying and reinterpreting the War of the Roses to justify the Tudor regime.

John Milton spent much of his career writing pamphlets for the Puritans. He also wrote for the Cromwell government. His greatest work, *Paradise Lost*, is a beautiful and influential statement of Puritan religious views.

The ancients had to make do with what they had. Two media, sculpture and coins, were particularly effective, and their use for political ends was refined between the fourth century B.C. and the establishment of the Byzantine Empire in the sixth century A.D., the beginning of the Dark Ages.[8]

Lustig cites as an example Philip II of Macedonia. By 338 B.C., Philip had subjugated all the city-states of the Hellenic peninsula under his dominion. Gold and ivory statues of Philip adorned temples along with those of the gods. Philip was thus a good role model for his son, Alexander the Great. In the thirteen years of Alexander's reign and conquests (336–323 B.C.), he managed to erect idealized images of himself across Africa, Asia Minor and India. According to Lustig, these image-making lessons were not lost on the first Roman emperor, Augustus.

All Roman emperors, from Augustus on, made use of the ultimate promotion campaign: they proclaimed themselves gods and required the people to worship them.[9] Augustus also had Virgil's *Aeneid* published, for propaganda purposes. This epic poem glorified the origin of the Roman people and, by implication, the house of Caesar.

PR Uses and Strategies Throughout History

Throughout history, PR has been used to promote wars, to lobby for political causes, to support political parties, to promote religion, to sell products, to raise money and to publicize events and people. Indeed, most of the uses modern society has found for public relations are not new, and modern PR practitioners have learned a lot by studying the strategies employed by earlier experts.

In 1095 Pope Urban II promoted war against the Muslim caliphate to the east. He sent word through his information network—cardinals, archbishops, bishops and parish priests—that to fight in this holy war was to serve God and to earn forgiveness of sins. It also gave Christians a once-in-a-lifetime chance to visit the holy shrines. The response was overwhelming, even though the Crusades were not an unqualified success.

In 1215 Stephen Langton, Archbishop of Canterbury, used promotion tactics to lobby for a political cause. He mobilized an influential group of barons to stand up for their rights against King John, and these men ultimately forced the king to agree to the terms of the Magna Carta—a document that has been used as a political banner ever since by people combatting political oppression

and control. In the fifteenth century, Niccolo Machiavelli, an Italian statesman and political philosopher, used his talents as a publicist to support a political party in power. His *The Prince* and *Discourses* are essentially treatises on how to govern people firmly and effectively. Machiavelli's political psychology seems quite modern. His work for Cesare Borgia relied heavily on opinion control and propaganda—techniques associated today with "issues management."

PR-related activities have been used to promote religion throughout the ages. In 1622 Pope Gregory XV established the *Congregatio de propaganda fide*, the Congregation for Propagating the Faith, to handle missionary activity. From that institution we have retained the word *propaganda*. In 1351 John Wycliffe called for reform of the Catholic Church and, in particular, for an English translation of the Bible to give the word of God more directly to more people. Wycliffe took his campaign to the people themselves, addressing them on the streets and in public places. Although it was forbidden, he and his followers also distributed books, tracts and broadsides.

Public relations scholars are aware, however, that a "battle/kings" approach to the history of famous people and remarkable events cannot totally explain the evolution of public relations; insights into societal developments are required for such understanding.

PR Tactics Throughout History

Various functions and uses of public relations have certainly existed throughout civilized history. The same cannot be said, however, for many of the *tactics* of twentieth-century PR, since these often depend on relatively recent inventions. For example, much of modern PR relies on electronic communication—telegraph, telephone, fax, telex, even satellites—and on electronic mass media—movies, radio and television. PR also has been radically affected by the rise of the computer, especially with the advent of the new media—the Internet and internal Intranets.

Of course, not all tactics of modern PR are of recent origin. PR still uses *rhetoric,* which is as old as human speech; *symbols,* which have been around as long as the human imagination; and *slogans,* which date back to people's first consciousness of themselves as groups.

Before the Industrial Revolution, the most significant period in the development of PR tactics was a 100-year period starting about 1450. During that time the Renaissance reached its height, the Reformation began and the European rediscovery of the New World occurred. These events gave people a new view of themselves, of one another and of their environment.

The period also marked the beginning of the age of mass media: around 1450 Johann Gutenberg invented printing from movable type, and the press was born. Few other inventions have had so profound an effect on human culture. Spinoffs of this discovery have been used by PR practitioners ever since, in books, advertising posters, handbills, publicity releases, party publications, newspapers and so on. Of course, these media existed before Gutenberg and his press, but never before could they be produced so efficiently to reach and persuade so many people at once.

THE BEGINNINGS OF PR IN THE UNITED STATES, 1600–1799

As Example 2.2 indicates, the United States has witnessed five periods or stages in the development of public relations.

During the early colonization of America, PR was used to sell a vital product, real estate. The Virginia Company in 1620 issued a broadside in England offering 50 acres of free land to anyone who brought a new settler to America before 1625. In 1643 PR was used in the colonies to raise money. Harvard College solicited funds by issuing a public relations brochure entitled *New England's First Fruits.*[10] Another college was the first to use a publicity release in the New World to publicize an event. King's College (now Columbia University)

sent an announcement of its 1758 commencement to various newspapers, where the item was printed as news.[11] Even sports sponsorship is not new. The first recorded intercollegiate competition was an 1852 rowing match between Harvard and Yale, sponsored by the Boston, Concord and Montreal railroads.

By the time of the American Revolution, substantial advances had been made in public relations uses and tactics. Although public relations as such did not exist in 1776, many of PR's functions, uses and tactics were already well developed by that time. The patriots who promoted the American Revolution overlooked no opportunity to use PR in their efforts to persuade—that is, to boost the war effort and to rally support for their new political plans. To this end they employed a wide variety of PR tools—newsletters, newspapers, heroes, slogans, symbols, rhetoric, organizations, press agentry and publicity—as well as rallies, parades, exhibitions, celebrations, poetry, songs, cartoons, fireworks, effigies and even crude lantern slides.

American patriots made the most of heroes (George Washington, Ethan Allen), legends (Yankee Doodle, the Spirit of '76), slogans ("Give me liberty or give me death!"), symbols (the Liberty Tree) and rhetoric (the speeches of John Adams and the writings of Thomas Jefferson, including the Declaration of Independence). They founded public-spirited organizations (the Sons of Liberty, the Committee of Correspondence). They grabbed every opportunity to interpret events in a light most favorable to their cause: a brawl on March 5, 1770, in which five unruly Bostonians were shot, was billed by the revolutionary press as the "Boston Massacre" and denounced as an atrocity to inflame passions against the British.

When there was no event to exploit, the patriots didn't hesitate to create one. On December 16, 1773, a group of them put on war paint and feathers, boarded a British ship and tossed its cargo of tea leaves overboard. The Boston Tea Party, whose main function was to attract attention, has been called an early example of American press agentry. Historian Richard Bissell states, "Of all the crazy hooligan stunts pulled off by the colonies against England, the Boston Tea Party was the wildest."[12]

EXAMPLE 2.2

Capsule History of PR in the United States

In the United States the development of PR has gone through five distinct stages:

1. **Preliminary period**—an era of development of the channels of communication and exercise of PR tactics (publicity, promotion and press agentry)

2. **Communicating/initiating**—a time primarily of publicists, press agents, promoters and propagandists

3. **Reacting/responding**—a period of writers hired to be spokespeople for special interests

4. **Planning/preventing**—a maturing of PR as it began to be incorporated into the management function

5. **Professionalism**—an effort by PR practitioners to control PR's development, use and practice on an international level

These stages of evolution are marked by particular periods in U.S. history, which fall into the following divisions:

1600–1799
Initial Colonization
American Revolution

1800–1899
Civil War
Western Expansion
Industrial Revolution

1900–1939
Progressive Era/Muckrakers
World War I
Roaring Twenties
Depression

1940–1979
World War II
Cold War of the 1950s
Consumer Movement

1980–Present
Global Communication

One of the best of the patriotic publicists was Samuel Adams, a man who had failed at every business venture he had previously tried. His specialty was what Bernays later labeled "crystallizing public opinion." Adams was one of the first to cry out against taxation without representation. He publicized the Boston Massacre, staged the Boston Tea Party and signed the Declaration of Independence. One historian offers the following assessment of Adams: "He was indignant, impassioned, incensed and outraged. He was the first American to get up in a public assembly and declare for absolute independence. As an agitator he makes Vladimir Ilich [Lenin] and Trotsky look like pikers."[13]

Adams understood that the press could be the emerging nation's most powerful weapon. When the American Revolution began, the colonies' thirty-seven newspapers served as a focal point for political appeals.[14] Many of these papers were owned and run by patriotic writers and editors such as Benjamin Franklin of the *Pennsylvania Gazette*[15] and Isaiah Thomas of the *Massachusetts Spy*—a man who often found it necessary to relocate his operations. A woman active in the cause was Hannah Bunce Watson, who took over publication of the *Connecticut Courant* at the death of her husband and contributed extensively to the revolutionists' propaganda war.[16]

The printing press was used for other forms of propaganda, too, such as books of political philosophy by Jean-Jacques Rousseau and inflammatory pamphlets by Thomas Paine. The works of both men were distributed widely to promote the spirit of rebellion.

Following independence, another massive effort at persuasion was necessary to push for reform of the short-lived Articles of Confederation. The men who drafted the Constitution conducted an intense PR campaign to sell the document to their colleagues and to the American people. Their propaganda took the form of eighty-five letters written to the newspapers. These letters, by Alexander Hamilton, James Madison and John Jay, became known as the *Federalist Papers,* and they did much to shape the political opinions of citizens of the young nation. The Bill of Rights, a propaganda piece supported by that spectacular campaigner Patrick Henry, guaranteed citizens numerous rights against the federal government, including freedom of the press. The resulting climate of free interchange encouraged the evolution of public relations into a full-fledged practice. If the Bill of Rights, especially with the provisions of the First Amendment, had not been adopted, public relations would never have become what it is today.

COMMUNICATING/ INITIATING: THE ERA OF PRESS AGENTRY AND PUBLICITY, 1800–1899

Although PR tactics were initially used in the United States for political purposes, as the nation developed and the nineteenth century progressed, all aspects of life fell under the influence of two PR tools: press agentry and publicity.

■ Government and Activists

In the 1830s, political sophistication got a boost from the PR innovations of Amos Kendall, the first man to function (although without the title) as a presidential press secretary—to Andrew Jackson. Kendall, an ex-newspaper reporter, held the official position of fourth auditor of the treasury,[17] but in fact he wrote speeches and pamphlets, prepared strategy, conducted polls, counseled the president on his public image, coordinated the efforts of the executive branch with other branches of government and with the public and constantly publicized Jackson in a favorable light.

PR techniques were also important in the heyday of the political machine. By the late 1850s, the Tammany Hall organization of New York was using interviews to gather information about the public mood. This marked the beginning of poll taking by special interest groups for strategic planning and publicity.[18]

Although public relations had always been employed in political campaigns in an effort to persuade, the 1888 Harrison–Cleveland presidential race showed a growing sophistication in its use. First, far greater use was made of the press—newspapers, pamphlets, fliers and the first official campaign press bureau—during that election year. The political campaign grew even more sophisticated during the 1896 race between Bryan and McKinley.[19] Both parties established campaign headquarters and flooded the nation with propaganda. Campaign trains and public opinion polls were also used extensively.[20]

Politicians were not the only ones to sell their ideas through PR. Agitators of many persuasions discovered that publicity could help change the nation's thinking. By relying mainly on appeals to public sentiment, groups such as the antivivisectionists, the American Peace Party and the Women's Christian Temperance Union met with varying degrees of success. Leaders of the women's suffrage movement publicized their cause at the 1876 Centennial celebration in Philadelphia; on July 4 Elizabeth Cady Stanton, Susan B. Anthony and Matilda Joslyn Gage staged a demonstration to dramatize that their rights as citizens had not yet been won.[21]

The most compelling protest movement of the nineteenth century was the abolitionist or anti-slavery movement, which consisted of many allied organizations. These organizations found that their cause was helped not only by news releases and press agentry stunts but also by getting public figures and newspaper editors to endorse their efforts and ideas. Forming an editorial alliance with a mass medium extended the reach of their message and gave it prestige and credibility.

Harriet Beecher Stowe used the partisan press to publicize the antislavery cause. Her best known work, *Uncle Tom's Cabin, or Life Among the Lowly*, was first published in serial form in an abolitionist journal. When the novel appeared as a book in 1852, some 300,000 copies were sold above the Mason–Dixon Line.

The fund drive, a very successful PR practice first used to raise money for military purposes, came into existence during the Civil War. During that war, the Treasury Department put Jay Cooke, a banker, in charge of selling war bonds to the public. Not only did the bonds finance the army, but the mass sales effort also roused public opinion in support of the Union cause.[22] Similar fundraising programs were later used to finance war efforts during World Wars I and II.

National Development

PR was also an important factor in the United States' westward development. The western frontier was sold like real estate by the forerunners of modern PR practitioners, who made the most of legends and heroes. As early as 1784, for example, John Filson promoted land deals by making a legendary figure out of Daniel Boone, an unschooled, wandering hunter and trapper.[23] Almost a century later, George Armstrong Custer was likewise made into a hero—partly to justify U.S. policy toward the Native American, partly to promote the settling of the West and partly to sell newspapers and dime novels.

In the 1840s, various publicists actively encouraged interest in the West. The Reverend Jason Lee and some Methodist missionaries promoted the Willamette Valley near Salem, Oregon, an area where Nathanial Wyeth had tried to establish colonies twice before. The missionaries were there to Christianize the Flathead Indians, and it wasn't until Lee's publicity that white settlers began to come. Lee wrote letters to religious publications and went on a speaking tour throughout the East

in 1838. The lower San Joaquin Valley was promoted by John Marsh, and Sacramento by John Sutter. Each man wrote articles for newspapers and magazines touting his preferred region for its healthfulness and playing up themes of patriotism and manifest destiny.

Perhaps the most effective publicist of westward expansion was *New York Tribune* publisher Horace Greeley, whose editorial "Go West, Young Man, and Grow Up with the Country" changed the lives of many people and the demographics of the entire nation.

But if the West was sold by PR techniques, it also was exploited by some of those same techniques. Press agent Matthew St. Clair Clarke brought Davy Crockett, the frontier hero, to the public's attention in the 1830s and used Crockett's glory to win political support away from Andrew Jackson. Two generations later, the adventures of Western personalities such as Buffalo Bill, Wyatt Earp, Calamity Jane and Wild Bill Hickock were blown out of all proportion (to the benefit of their promoters in the eastern press) to give people a glamorous picture of the American frontier. Even outlaws like Jesse James became adept at using the press for glory—and to mislead the authorities.

Entertainment and Culture

The role of PR in the growth of America's entertainment industry was substantial. In fact, the PR tactic of press agentry grew up with the entertainment business in the nineteenth century, a flamboyant era of road shows and circuses. P. T. Barnum was one of many circus showmen who employed press agentry (see Example 2.3).

Publicity stunts were even used occasionally to attract attention to books and their authors. For example, in 1809 the *New York Evening Post* ran a story about the mysterious disappearance of one Diedrich Knickerbocker from his residence in the Columbian Hotel. In followup stories, readers learned that Knickerbocker had left a manuscript, which the hotel's owner offered to sell to cover the cost of the unpaid bill. Later, the publishing house of Inskeep & Bradford announced in the same

EXAMPLE 2.3

Phineas Taylor Barnum (1810–1891)

The most famous and successful of nineteenth-century press agents was P. T. Barnum, who created, promoted and exploited the careers of many celebrities, including the midget General Tom Thumb, singer Jenny Lind and Chang and Eng, the original Siamese twins. Early in his career, in 1835, Barnum exhibited a black slave named Joice Heth, claiming that she had nursed George Washington 100 years before. Newspapers fell for the story, intrigued by its historical angle. Then, when public interest in Joice Heth began to die down, Barnum kept the story alive by writing letters to the editor under assumed names, debating her authenticity. Barnum didn't care what the papers said, as long as he got space. When Heth died, an autopsy revealed her age to be about 80. With the fraud exposed, Barnum claimed that he also had been duped.* Was this true? Why not? After all, "There's a sucker born every minute."

The great circus showman was himself often the center of public attention, for which he credited his own press agent, Richard F. "Tody" Hamilton.** However, the term *press agent* was first formally used by another circus. In 1868 the roster of John Robinson's Circus carried the name W. W. Duran with the title Press Agent.†

Barnum's circus museum in Bridgeport, Connecticut, celebrated its centennial in 1993.‡

*Edward L. Bernays, *Public Relations* (Norman: University of Oklahoma Press, 1952), pp. 38–39.

**Dexter W. Fellows and Andrew A. Freeman, *This Way to the Big Show* (New York: Viking Press, 1936), p. 193.

†Will Irwin, "The Press Agent: His Rise and Decline," *Colliers*, vol. 48, (Dec. 2, 1911) pp. 24–25.

‡Craig Wilson, "These Days Life Is but a Scheme," *USA Today* (August 31, 1993).

In the field of education, the value of PR was recognized even before the Revolution. In the nineteenth century, the trend continued. In 1899, Yale University established a PR and alumni office, showing that even the most established institutions were ready to enlist the budding profession to help them create favorable public opinion.[25] In 1900 Harvard University hired the Publicity Bureau—the nation's first PR firm, formed in Boston in 1900—but refused to pay the bureau's fees after about 1902. Nevertheless, the bureau continued to service the client for the resulting prestige.

■ Business and Industry

The development of industry during the 1800s brought about the most significant changes in the history of PR. The technological advances of the Industrial Revolution changed and modernized the tactics and techniques of PR. Steam power and inventions like the linotype made newspapers a truly democratic, nationwide mass medium.

Although the early industrialists used advertising to sell their wares and services to a growing market, they were not very interested in other functions of public relations. The prevailing attitude of the "robber barons" of the latter half of the century was summed up by William Henry Vanderbilt, head of the New York Central Railroad: "The public be damned."[26] J. P. Morgan, another railroad tycoon, echoed this sentiment when he said, "I don't owe the public anything." During the years between the Civil War and the turn of the century, industrial profit and power controlled and reshaped American life. Industrial magnates were answerable to no one and were immune to pressure from government, labor or public opinion.

An example of the corporate attitude at that time was the behavior of steel tycoon Andrew Carnegie during the Homestead Strike of 1892. When labor problems in his steel plant erupted into violence, Carnegie retired to his lodge in Scotland, 35 miles from the nearest railroad or telegraph. Carnegie wanted to be known as a cultured philanthropist, and he let the London press know that he remained aloof from the labor strug-

newspaper that they were publishing the manuscript, entitled *Knickerbocker's History of New York*. The whole story was a hoax, a publicity campaign conducted by the book's real author, Washington Irving.[24]

gle only to protect his company from his own generosity. But professionally, he had not amassed a fortune of $400 million by worrying about the working or living conditions of his poorly paid employees, and he was content to have his right-hand man, Henry Clay Frick, crush their strike and their union with the help of the state militia.[27]

In time, industry had to reckon with the monster it had created—a labor force unwilling to be further exploited by the likes of Carnegie, Morgan and oil magnate J. D. Rockefeller. As the twentieth century progressed, labor disputes came to be fought more and more with public relations, less and less with violence.

Nonetheless, even in the 1800s, a few large corporations recognized that in the long run they would have to woo the public's favor. In 1858 the Borden Company, a producer of dairy products, set a PR precedent by issuing a financial report to its stockholders.[28] In 1883 an even more important precedent was set by Theodore N. Vail, general manager of the American Bell Telephone Company. Vail wrote to the managers of local exchanges, urging them to reexamine the services they were offering and the prices they were charging.[29] His letter is significant because it shows concern for the consumer and an interest in improving relations between the telephone company and the public.

In 1877, Jay Gould opened a "literary bureau" for the Union Pacific Railroad, for the purpose of attracting immigrants to the West.[30] In about 1888, the Mutual Life Insurance Company hired an outside consultant, Charles J. Smith, to write press releases and articles to boost the company's image.[31] In 1889 the Westinghouse Corporation established, under the directorship of ex-newspaperman E. H. Heinrichs, what was essentially the first in-house publicity department in the USA.[32]

This was also the period when department stores first appeared in the United States. The originator of the concept, John Wanamaker, was also the best in the business at public relations. When his Philadelphia store opened in 1876, Wanamaker used publicity to generate interest in the new idea of a store that covered a full 2 acres. He gave visi-

tors copies of a self-printed 16-page "souvenir booklet" that explained the store's departments, hiring policies and dedication to customer service. Salespeople were instructed in how to capture quotes from visitors that could later be incorporated into news releases.[33] Wanamaker also founded the *Farm Journal*, which he published for years, and he began publishing *The Ladies Home Journal* to sell ladies' fashions.[34] Macy's, Bloomingdale's, Lord & Taylor and Marshall Field quickly caught on and began publishing their own magazines and souvenir books.[35]

■ Press Agents and Publicists

It has often been said that twentieth-century public relations primarily grew out of nineteenth-century press agentry. In some ways this is true. Certainly, many early PR practitioners got their start as press agents. Although few of these PR pioneers were as flamboyant as the great showman, P. T. Barnum, many were publicity writers whose main target had always been the press. The greatest of the publicity consultants was Ivy Ledbetter Lee (see Example 2.4).

Press Agentry Press agentry really began in about 1830, with the birth of the penny press. When newspaper prices dropped to a penny each, circulation and readership boomed, but so did the price of newspaper advertising. To reach the huge new audience without paying for the opportunity, promoters and publicity people developed a talent for "making news." The object was simply to break into print, often at the expense of truth or dignity. Press agents exploited freaks to publicize circuses, invented legends to promote politicians, told outrageous lies to gain attention and generally provided plenty of popular entertainment if not much real news.

The cardinal virtue of press agentry was its promptness. Indeed, it was often so prompt that its practitioners spent practically no time verifying the accuracy or news value of its content. But ultimately the effectiveness of a press release depended on its creator's imagination, and imagination remains a necessary talent for effective PR today.

EXAMPLE 2.4

Ivy Ledbetter Lee (1877–1934)

"THE FATHER OF PUBLIC RELATIONS"

After graduating from Princeton, Ivy Lee became a reporter in New York City but soon gave that up to become a political publicist. Then, in 1904, he and George F. Parker formed the nation's third publicity bureau. By 1906 he was the most inspiring success in the young field of PR and found himself representing George F. Baer and his associates (who were allied with the J. P. Morgan financial empire) in a public controversy over an anthracite coal strike. Lee tried a radical approach: Frankly announcing himself as a publicity consultant, he invited the press to ask questions, handed out news releases and presented his client as cooperative and communicative.*

Lee's "Declaration of Principles" issued in 1906 to city editors all over the country, won respect for public relations (and didn't hurt the Baer bunch either). That same year, Lee represented the Pennsylvania Railroad when an accident occurred on the main line. Instead of hushing up the incident, Lee invited the press to come, at company expense, to the scene of the accident, where he made every effort to supply reporters with facts and to help photographers. As a result, the Pennsylvania Railroad and the railroad industry got their first favorable press coverage in years.**

Lee's remarkable, straightforward style came from his frank admiration of industry and capitalism, and he made it his goal to get big business to communicate its story to the public. By the time he was 30, Lee had sired a profession, chiefly by introducing and promoting its first code of ethics.

Lee's career continued to be successful, if not so influenced by high ideals. He began working for the Rockefeller family in 1913, when he presented the "facts" about a coal strike in Colorado that resulted in an incident known as the Ludlow Massacre. Lee later admitted that the "facts" he handed out about the bloody affair were the facts as management saw them, and that he had not checked them for accuracy.†

Lee's many later clients included the American Russian Chamber of Commerce and the German Dye Trust, from whom he earned $25,000 a year and a sticky PR problem of his own—how to defend his work for a Nazi organization. He was also heavily criticized for his support of Stalin-era Soviet Russia and his encouragement of U.S.–Soviet ties.

Lee once wrote, "The relationship of a company to the people . . . involves far more than *saying*—it involves *doing*.‡ Nevertheless, it is perhaps an example of Ivy Lee's public relations talent that he is now remembered not so much for what he *did* at the height of his career as for what he *said* when he was still in his twenties.°

*Frank Luther Mott, *American Journalism* (New York: Macmillan, 1950), pp. 179–80.

**Irwin Ross, *The Image Merchants* (Garden City, N.Y: Doubleday, 1959), p. 31.

†Ibid.

‡Ibid., p. 32.

°For a defense of Lee's often-criticized international activities, see the letter to the editor of *PR Review*, 13(3) (Fall 1987), pp. 12–13, by James W. Lee, his son.

Publicity Many early publicists were no more careful with the facts than their press agent contemporaries; neither were many journalists of that day. Most publicists continually tried to "plant" stories in newspapers, hiding their source. In that respect, Ivy Lee represented a new kind of publicist (see Example 2.4). Perhaps the essential difference can be found in Lee's "Declaration of Principles" (1906), in which he defined the important ideals of public relations, his new profession: "Our plan is, frankly and openly . . . to supply the press and public of the United States prompt and accurate information concerning subjects which it is of value and interest to the public to know about."[36]

Lee's career spans the earlier era of communicating/initiating and the subsequent era of reacting/responding (1900–1939). At the dawn of the twentieth century PR's incubation period had drawn to a close. America was now a powerful, industrialized nation with sophisticated mass media and a well-informed public. The time was right for a mode of practice that would synthesize and coordinate the various talents—publicity, promotion, propaganda and press agentry—that had developed in tandem with the nation's growth.

REACTING/RESPONDING: THE TIME OF REPORTERS-IN-RESIDENCE, 1900–1939

Public relations developed significantly in the first four decades of the twentieth century, as publicists became spokespersons for organizations. As the age of unchecked industrial growth ended, industry faced new challenges to its established way of doing business. The new century began with a cry of protest from the "muckrakers"—investigative journalists who exposed scandals associated with power capitalism and government corruption. The term *muckraker* is a metaphor taken from John Bunyan's *Pilgrim's Progress*. It was first used in its modern sense by Theodore Roosevelt, who applied it pejoratively to journalists who attacked the New

York Police Department in 1897, while he was commissioner. Later as President, with a consumer protection platform and a trust-busting program, Roosevelt came to appreciate the muckrakers.[37]

The Turn of the Century

Perhaps the first of the muckrakers was Joseph Pulitzer, whose editorials supported labor in the Homestead strike of 1892. "The public be informed," his slogan for an earlier campaign in support of labor, parodied the contemptuous attitude of William H. Vanderbilt.[38] But the great age of muckraking journalism began in the twentieth century.[39]

Lincoln Steffens, staff writer for *McClure's* magazine, wrote articles and books exposing corruption in municipal politics. Frank Norris, who covered the Spanish–American War for *McClure's*, took on the railroads and the wheat traders in his novels *The Octopus* (1901) and *The Pit* (1903). Ida Tarbell's *History of the Standard Oil Company* (1904), which began as a series for *McClure's* in 1902 and consisted mainly of interviews with former Rockefeller employees, exposed the company's corruption and its unfair competition with smaller companies. In 1906, Upton Sinclair described the unsavory conditions that existed in the meatpacking industry in his novel *The Jungle*. These articles and books resulted in social legislation that remains the law of the land today.

Big business also was under fire from the government. President Theodore Roosevelt considered it the federal government's job to uphold the public interest in the battles that flared among management, labor and consumers. Using the Sherman Antitrust Act of 1890, he challenged big business—including U.S. Steel, Standard Oil and the Pennsylvania Railroad—to respond to popular displeasure.

An era of social consciousness was dawning. Proof that the former "public be damned" attitude was giving way came in 1899 with the founding of the first national consumer group, the National Consumers League (NCL), which was formed from state consumer leagues by Florence Kelley and Dr. John Graham Brooks.[40] The fledgling NCL supported the work of Harvey W. Wiley, a Department of Agriculture chemist who for more than twenty years gathered information to prove the need for a federal food and drug law. The first Pure Food and Drug Act was passed in 1906.

Industry *had* to respond. It could no longer afford simply to ignore the public and the press. Threatening to withhold advertising from uncomplimentary media did not have the desired effect. No longer could the railroads placate the press by giving free passes to reporters. No longer would the public buy statements like that of coal industrialist George F. Baer, who in 1902 told labor to put its trust in "the Christian men whom God in His infinite wisdom has given control of the property interests of the country."[41] When the coal industry came under fire again in 1906, the coal owners had learned their lesson. Instead of relying on puffery and rhetoric, they enlisted the talents of the young ex-newspaper reporter, Ivy Lee.

It is no coincidence that most of the first generation of public relations specialists came from newspapers. Newspaper advertising had long been the only way that many companies communicated with their markets. Newspapers also were the medium in which many companies were being attacked. And newspaper coverage had been the main goal of nineteenth-century press agents, whose legacy inspired the first publicity agencies of the twentieth century.

The first publicity firm, the Publicity Bureau, was formed in Boston in 1900.[42] The idea of publicity caught on quickly, and soon several such firms—composed largely of ex-newspaper people—had appeared, including the firm of William Wolf Smith in Washington, D.C., which specialized in publicity aimed at influencing legislators.[43] From a historical standpoint, however, the most important publicity bureau during this period was the one operated by George F. Parker and Ivy Lee. Although that company lasted only four years, it launched the career of Ivy Lee.

Before long, publicity became a standard and necessary tool for many businesses, individuals and organizations. Big businesses especially, such as communication companies, railroads and the automobile industry, found that publicity agencies and in-house publicity bureaus improved their relations with both the public and the government. In 1904 two major state universities—the University of Pennsylvania and the University of Wisconsin—set up publicity bureaus.[44]

By 1917, enough colleges had public relations and development officers for these individuals to form their own organization, the American Association of College News Bureaus. Later it was renamed the American College Publicity Association, and then the American College Public Relations Association; today it is known as CASE, the Council for the Advancement and Support of Education. CASE's roots in ACPRA make it the oldest public relations organization in the world.[45] (The first national association of public relations people was the Financial Advertising Association—later the Bank Marketing Association, formed in 1915 as a section of the Associated Advertising Clubs of the world.)[46]

Publicity also proved valuable for public service organizations. The Young Men's Christian Association (YMCA) employed a full-time publicist to call attention to its fund drive in 1905.[47] The National Tuberculosis Association started a publicity program in 1908, and the American Red Cross followed suit the same year.[48] The Marine Corps established a publicity bureau in 1907 in Chicago.[49] In 1909 the Trinity Episcopal Church in New York City hired Pendleton Dudley as a public relations counsel to help combat criticism of its ownership of slum tenements.[50] Three years later the Seventh Day Adventist Church established a formal publicity bureau to answer complaints about its opposition to Sunday closing laws.[51]

Publicity in support of a product was used by National Cash Register founders John and Frank Patterson, who employed newsletters, brochures and flyers in the world's first direct-mail campaign.

Many useful tactics and techniques were developed during this early period. One PR pioneer who contributed a number of new ideas was Samuel Insull, publicity expert for the Chicago

Edison Company.[52] Insull had a demonstration electric cottage constructed in 1902 to show how convenient the new technology was. In 1903 he communicated with the company's customers via bill stuffers and a house publication that was distributed to the community. In 1909 Insull became the first person to make PR-related movies.[53] (This was appropriate, since Thomas Edison himself was one of the first movie tycoons.)

Larger organizations, such as the Ford Motor Company, helped broaden business's interest in the public relations function. In 1908 Ford established a house publication, *Ford Times,* which is still printed today.[54] In 1912 the company began using public opinion surveys for market research.[55] And in 1914 Ford established the first corporate film department.[56]

The first formally designated press bureau in the federal government was founded in 1905 by the U.S. Forest Service.[57] The aggressiveness of its promotions is said to have been one of the elements leading to the 1913 federal ban on hiring public relations people (see Chapter 1).[58] However, Walter Lippmann's concern over the infiltration of German propaganda into American newspapers in the years immediately preceding World War I was another contributing factor, as was the growing resentment by newspaper reporters and editors of publicists.[59] Ivy Lee himself was attacked in muckraker Upton Sinclair's exposé of the newspaper business, *The Brass Check,* written in 1919.[60] Journalists particularly resented PR people's control over access to sources and their "prepackaged" news.[61] Advertisers, too, were unhappy with publicists for getting what they saw as "free advertising" in news columns.

Making the World Safe for Democracy

By the time the United States entered World War I in 1917, the war had been going on for several years (since 1914), and PR had proven itself an effective weapon of persuasion for Europeans. The British, in particular, directed a "hands across the sea" propaganda campaign at the United States

government and people, urging them to join the fight. They publicized the Allies' view of the *Lusitania* incident, for example, characterizing the Germans (whose submarine had sunk the ocean liner) as vicious "Huns." When President Wilson finally gave up his policy of peacemaking and neutrality, the United States entered the war with money, military might and a massive public relations effort. This PR effort was seen as essential to gain popular support in a country with many German immigrants and first generation German-Americans.

In selling the war as one destined "to make the world safe for democracy," the U.S. government solicited cooperation from many sources. The government convinced AT&T that the government needed control of the phone company for the war effort.[62] The press was persuaded to exercise self-censorship and to contribute free advertising space for the war effort.[63] Academics served too. College professors acted as a force of Four-Minute Men, meaning that they were prepared to speak for that length of time on propaganda topics relating to the war. The world, not just the classroom, was their forum.

The government also solicited cooperation directly from the public: Herbert Hoover's Food Administration persuaded American citizens to conserve food during this time of emergency. The greatest example of the government's salesmanship, however, was the Liberty Loan Drive, which financed the war.

The genius behind America's wartime public relations effort was George Creel, a former newspaper reporter whom President Wilson appointed as chairman of the newly formed Committee on Public Information. The success of the Liberty Loan Drive and the effectiveness of U.S. wartime propaganda at home and abroad were both attributable to the Creel Committee. (Creel's propaganda was not as heavy-handed as that of the British government. In particular, Creel toned down the assaults on the German character and emphasized loyalty more than fear as the basis for support.)

The committee also created a legacy for the PR profession. Many members of the committee who learned their craft in wartime went on to practice it in peacetime. Included among these were Edward L. Bernays[64] and Carl Byoir.[65] As assistant chairman of the Creel Committee, Byoir publicized the draft and was in charge of distributing the *Red White and Blue Textbooks*, which described the goals of the war. He went on to become one of America's most successful public relations practitioners.

The Advertising Boom and the Roaring Twenties

The early twentieth century was a period of tremendous growth in the advertising industry. In 1916 Stanley B. Resor bought the J. Walter Thompson Company, which had been founded in 1864 and was at the time the largest advertising agency in the world.[66] Resor focused the agency's work on fact finding and scientific research. He was co-founder of the American Association of Advertising Agencies in 1917 and also helped to found the Advertising Research Foundation, the Audit Bureau of Circulations and the National Outdoor Advertising Bureau.[67] Working with him was his wife, Helen Lansdowne Resor, who, as head of the copy department, worked to ensure that the ads were effective in their appeals to women.[68]

The 1920s were characterized by prosperity, power and pleasure. In spite of a national mood of isolationism, the United States' economic boom was heard around the world. Much of the boom was the sound of advertising, which continued its rapid expansion during this decade. In 1920, for example, the Illinois Central Railroad began what was to become the oldest continuous national advertising campaign in America.[69]

During this period, advertisers also discovered many new media. In 1921 an NBC radio station in New York broadcast the first paid commercial over the airwaves. Suddenly advertisers had a new medium to complement newspaper ads, billboards, streetcar signs and direct mailing. Advertisers in the 1920s also explored film, flashy trademarks and even skywriting. And advertising was itself adopted by health and public service organizations, by churches and by political parties and candidates. By 1929 advertising was a billion-dollar industry. Many sociologists attacked the economic wastefulness of the profession's mass media appeals, but none disputed the effectiveness of its sophisticated psychology.

Public relations in general also grew in scope and in stature during the 1920s. Books and courses were offered on the subject, and social scientists began to take notice. Among them was Walter Lippmann, a former adviser to President Wilson, who expressed concern over the implications of public opinion molding. In *Public Opinion* (1922), he wrote that the public no longer formed its own opinions, particularly about government policy; instead, people's opinions, like their knowledge, were fed to them by the media in the form of slogans and stereotypes.[70] He pointed out, however, that opinion molding is a two-way street. Society contains "innumerable large and small corporations and institutions, voluntary and semi-voluntary associations, national, provincial, urban and neighborhood groupings, which often as not make the decisions that the political body registers."[71]

Social scientists' interest in public opinion was shared by industry. Many companies, including AT&T, had learned from their experiences in World War I that social responsibility was good for public relations and hence good for business.[72] Thus the field of opinion research grew as companies developed tactics for finding out what their stockholders, their markets and the general community wanted. AT&T's cooperation with the government during the war had earned it the confidence of the government and of the pro-war public. When Arthur Page joined the company in 1927 as vice-president and in-house public relations expert, he stressed several opinions that have affected modern PR ever since: that business begins with the public's permission and survives because of its approval; that businesses should have public relations departments with real influence in top management; and that companies should find out what the public wants and make public commitments that will work as "hostages to performance." Page insisted that PR is built by performance, not by publicity[73] (see Example 2.5).

The New Deal

The mood of the 1930s differed drastically from that of the 1920s. Following the stock market crash of 1929, the U.S. economy plunged into a depression from which it did not fully recover for ten years. Public relations during this time faced many challenges, as industry was forced to defend itself against public distrust, a discontented labor force and strict regulation by the Roosevelt administration. The greatest challenge to PR, however, was the job of selling good cheer to a confused and frightened populace. The challenge was felt by government, and successive presidents responded by trying to convince the country that a return to prosperity was just around the corner and that the only thing to fear was fear itself. The challenge was also felt by industry, and in 1938 the National Association of Manufacturers and the U.S. Chamber of Commerce conducted a comprehensive campaign based on the slogan "What helps business helps you."[74]

PR continued to develop as a field of practice during the 1930s. The National Association of Accredited Publicity Directors was founded in 1936. The American Association of Industrial Editors, founded two years later, was an indirect descendant of earlier groups, including the Association of House Organ Editors, which had been formed in 1915. The American Council on Public Relations was founded in 1939 by Rex Harlow,[75] but it had no chapters. The National Association of Accredited Publicity Directors, which changed its name in 1944 to the National Association of Public Relations Counsel, had chapters and requirements for professional experience. This group merged with Harlow's ACPR in 1948.

Another significant development during the 1930s was the institution of the Gallup Poll, which gave a boost to the sophistication and credibility of opinion research.[76]

Many trends in the development of public relations during the 1930s are reflected in the history

---

EXAMPLE 2.5
PR at AT&T—A Long History

In 1938 Arthur Wilson Page, first vice-president for public relations of the American Telephone and Telegraphy Company, told an international management congress that "the task which business has, and which it has always had, is of fitting itself to the patterns of public desires." A familiar saying of the PR pioneer was that in a democratic society no business could exist without public permission nor long succeed without public approval. Page also helped to popularize opinion survey techniques. In doing so Page was following through on the philosophy of a predecessor who was very conscious of public opinion: Theodore Vail, AT&T president in the early 1900s, had sent a series of questions about service to Bell telephone exchange managers to inquire about how well Bell was serving its customers. He understood the power of public opinion, noting that it was based on information and belief. When public opinion was wrong, it was because of wrong information, and Vail said it was "not only the right, but the obligation of all individuals . . . who come before the public, to see the public have full and correct information." The long history of PR at AT&T makes even more amazing the public support of the 1982 consent decree that separated individual Bell companies from each other and from AT&T. Page's philosophy and views of public relations are kept alive today by members of the Arthur Page Society, a professional membership organization founded by Bell public relations practitioners.

Source: E. M. Block, "Arthur Page and the Uses of Knowledge," Inaugural Lecture, Arthur Page Lecture and Awards Program, College of Communication, University of Texas at Austin, April 22, 1982. Reprinted with permission of E. M. Block.

---

of General Motors. When Paul Garrett joined GM in 1931 as its one-man PR department, most people distrusted big business. GM's Board of Directors wanted Garrett to help the billion-dollar corporation look small to win public favor, but Garrett did not believe in this approach. Good PR, he felt, had to work from the inside out. Corporate policies in the public interest had to provide the basis for public acceptance.[77] Management had to earn the goodwill of the public by acting, not by selling a false image. Garrett insisted that it was in the company's best interest to "place the broad interest of the customer first in every decision of the operation of the business."[78]

Despite its adoption of Garrett's views, General Motors' problems were far from over. Events worked against GM in 1937 when the Congress of Industrial Organizations (CIO) got involved in a labor dispute that resulted in a forty-four-day sit-down strike.[79] At a time when public sentiment was strongly anti-union, the CIO won a major victory for labor by getting public opinion on its side and forcing the nation's third largest corporation to recognize the union. But although the corporation lost the battle with labor, under Garrett's leadership it continued to wage the war for good public relations. In 1938 Garrett said, "The challenge that faces us is to shake off our lethargy and through public relations make the American plan of industry stick."[80]

In 1939 *Fortune* magazine carried an article on Garrett, describing him as "carry[ing] out a long-range program of finding out what people like and doing more of it."[81] This was the first time an important magazine reported on a corporation's public relations, and the description itself showed how the function had evolved into one directly concerned with corporate policy.

The Increasing Influence of U.S. Presidents as Opinion-Makers

The management of news by U.S. presidents goes back to George Washington, who leaked his Farewell Address to a favored publisher who he knew would give it a good display. When Thomas Jefferson was in Washington's cabinet, he put a newspaper reporter on the federal payroll to establish a party newspaper that would represent Jefferson's point of view; later, when he became president, he relied heavily on his "party press" and limited other newspapers' access to him.

Abraham Lincoln sought out newspaper editors who he believed might convey his ideas sympathetically to the people and thus help win their support for his policies. The significance he placed on public opinion is apparent in his famous statement, "Public sentiment is everything. With public sentiment, nothing can fail; without it, nothing can succeed. Consequently, he who moulds public sentiment goes deeper than he who enacts statutes or pronounces decisions."

Theodore Roosevelt developed the "trial balloon" device, calling favorite reporters to the White House to get their reaction to his ideas before trying them out on the public. He was sensitive to media coverage and once waited to sign a Thanksgiving Proclamation until the Associated Press photographer arrived.[82]

However, Calvin Coolidge is credited with having arranged the first pure photo opportunity, some twenty years later, on the occasion of his 55th birthday. The taciturn president liked photo sessions because he didn't have to talk during them.[83]

Woodrow Wilson developed the first regular formal press conferences, although he later regretted the idea, for he was a reserved man and never won popularity with the press. He also complained that the press was interested in the personal and the trivial rather than in principles and policies— to which the press responded that presidents just want journalists to print what they tell them, not what the public wants to know.

Franklin Roosevelt's candor and geniality delighted reporters, but even he sometimes regretted holding press conferences; and once, in a pique, he said that he would like to award a Nazi Iron Cross to a news reporter whose stories he felt had earned it. Roosevelt staged a great many photo sessions so that photographers wouldn't take candid pictures that called attention to his paralysis.[84]

Roosevelt, more than any of his predecessors, used public relations tactics to sway public opinion; and the development of mass media technology during the 1930s enhanced his efforts (see

Example 2.6). In the decades following his death, he has drawn increased retrospective criticism for "managing news," as have more recent presidents and their spokespeople. There may be some justification for this criticism, since the executive branch can end most independent reportorial investigations into its affairs by claiming "executive privilege." No one expects to find out too much from the judiciary branch, because of restrictions on what can be discussed, in keeping with the American Bar Association's code of judicial conduct; but, in the legislative branch, what one party won't tell, the other will.

PLANNING/PREVENTING: THE GROWTH OF PR AS A MANAGEMENT FUNCTION, 1940–1979

With the advent of the 1940s, the nation's mood changed again. The country was soon at war, and, as in World War I, the most conspicuous public relations efforts either served the war effort directly or were obvious by-products of a wartime economy.

■ World War II

When the United states entered World War II, PR firms quickly seized the opportunity to enlist in the cause. Hill & Knowlton, for example, firmly established itself by representing war industry groups such as the Aviation Corporation of America, the American Shipbuilding Council and the Aeronautical Chamber of Commerce.[85] Overall, the PR effort during World War II was much more sophisticated, coordinated and integrated than the one during World War I.

Communications scholar Charles Steinberg believes that World War II caused public relations to develop into a "full-fledged profession."[86] In 1947 Boston University established the first full school of public relations, later renamed "public communications."[87] By 1949, more than 100 col-

EXAMPLE 2.6
PR Stands for President Roosevelt

Franklin Delano Roosevelt used every possible public relations device to sell the radical reforms of his New Deal to the American people. Advised by PR expert Louis McHenry Howe, FDR projected an image of self-confidence and happiness—just what the American public wanted to believe in. He talked to them on the radio. He smiled for the cameras. He was mentioned in popular songs. He even allowed himself to be one of the main characters in a Rodgers and Hart musical comedy (played by George M. Cohan, America's favorite Yankee Doodle Dandy). Of course, FDR's public image didn't succeed with everybody, and in some households *Roosevelt* is still a dirty word. But in general, the American people liked FDR, and they showed it by putting him in the White House four times.

Louis McHenry Howe also encouraged Eleanor Roosevelt to expand her public activities. She had joined the National Consumers League as an 18-year-old volunteer and was very interested in public issues. With Howe's help, she developed news conferences for women reporters only—"news hens," they came to be called. Nevertheless, they got exclusives from Eleanor, despite being excluded from most other news meetings because of their gender.

Source: L. L. Golden, *Only by Public Consent: American Corporations Search for Favorable Opinion.* Copyright © 1978 by L. L. Golden. Used by permission of Dutton, a division of Penguin Putnam, Inc.

leges and universities across the nation were offering courses in PR.

Two significant events in government affected the future of public relations. One was the appointment of former newscaster Elmer Davis as director of the Office of War Information (OWI)—the forerunner of the U.S. Information Agency (Service). Davis's program was even larger than George Creel's had been, but it was focused exclusively on the task of disseminating information worldwide. Unlike Creel, Davis was not an advisor to the president. At OWI evidence of government-planted disinformation began to appear.

The second event to affect PR practice was the creation of a War Advertising Council, which handled war-related public service announcements and created slogans like "Loose lips sink ships." The two organizations were tremendously successful in winning support for the United States at home and abroad, in helping to sell war bonds and in winning cooperation from the public, from industry and from labor.

The use of films for PR purposes expanded greatly during this period. In 1943, for example, Frank Capra made a documentary film for the U.S. Signal Corps to inspire patriotism and build morale.[88] The government was not alone in using film for PR, however; Hollywood also made countless movies glorifying American fighting forces. The persuasive power of film was not lost on industry officials. In 1948 filmmaker Robert Flaherty made the documentary "Louisiana Story"[89] for Standard Oil.

Individual companies adapted to the war in different ways, often with the help of PR. Because of wartime ink shortages, the American Tobacco Company had to change the color of the Lucky Strike package from green to white. Thanks to PR, the change caused the company only a moment's regret. It launched a new campaign promoting a new slogan: "Lucky Strike Green Has Gone to War." Lucky Strike smokers everywhere were proud of their new white package because it signified that their brand was doing its part for America.

For Standard Oil of New Jersey, the war created a public relations crisis. At hearings of Senator Harry Truman's Committee on National Defense, Assistant Attorney General Thurman Arnold charged Standard Oil with "acting against American intent."[90] The charge involved a deal that Standard Oil had made with a German company many years earlier. In response, the oil company's marketing director, Robert T. Haslan, mounted a public opinion campaign, sending letters to customers and stockholders and hiring Earl Newsom as outside PR counsel. Eventually, Standard Oil beat the charges and came out of it with public support.[91]

In 1945 the same public relations fervor that helped sell the war effort contributed to the postwar industrial recovery. In that year, Henry Ford II, the new president of Ford Motor Company, hired Earl Newsom as a PR consultant. Newsom helped Ford compose a letter to the United Automotive Workers (UAW) during a strike at General Motors, urging the union to be reasonable and fair. He also helped Ford with his speech to the Society of Automotive Engineers in January 1946 and with an important anti-labor address to the Commonwealth Club in San Francisco the following month. With Newsom's help, young Ford became a public figure—a respected and publicized spokesperson for responsible business management.[92]

Earl Newsom was one of the first of a new type of PR practitioner: the public relations counselor. He did not send out news releases or hold press conferences; he simply advised. But his advice was valued and effective. His career also demonstrated the power of PR counselors to affect the policies and behavior of their clients.

The Fabulous Fifties and the Military-Industrial Complex

During the 1950s, America again experienced a booming economy, this time based largely on rising production of consumer goods. The population was growing faster than ever, and more and more people were getting good educations and entering the white-collar workforce. Technology progressed on all fronts: television, satellites, atomic energy, the mainframe computer. Industry, in spite of "labor pains," continued to grow at home and abroad. Yet the mood of the nation reflected fear—of Communists, Russians, the atomic bomb, McCarthyism, technology, juvenile delinquency and mass conformity, to name a few. In 1955 Sloan Wilson examined society and described the American white-collar worker in his best-selling novel, *The Man in the Gray Flannel Suit*. The hero, Tom Rath, was an in-house PR person for a large broadcasting corporation.

Public relations grew with the economy. That Wilson's typical businessperson was a PR practitioner shows how well established the profession had become. In 1953 the International Chamber of Commerce set up a commission on public relations, and, in 1954, the Public Relations Society of America (PRSA) developed its first code of ethics.[93] A year later, the International Public Relations Association was founded. Its individual members currently represent more than 60 countries. Many public relations organizations in other countries also trace their founding to the period from 1955 to 1960.

By the end of the 1950s, a number of women had entered the field, including several who ranked among the nation's top PR people: Doris E. Fleischman Bernays, early PR pioneer; Denny Griswold, former editor and publisher of *Public Relations News*; Jane Stewart, then president of Group Attitudes Corporation; and Leone Baxter, former president of Whitaker and Baxter International in San Francisco.[94] In 1957, President Eisenhower appointed Anne Williams Wheaton his associate press secretary, drawing nationwide attention to PR as a potential career for women.[95]

The affluence of the 1950s encouraged businesses to find new uses for their money, and one job of public relations was to help them reinvest it in society—not only in tax-sheltering foundations, but also in health and community interest campaigns, public service drives and educational seminars. By encouraging corporate investment in society, PR gained greater respect and increased its own influence within corporations.

Television, which conquered America in the 1950s, had an enormous effect on the growth of public relations. This powerful medium's capacity for persuasion was evident from the start. Social scientists criticized television's pervasive control over public opinion, but it soon became clear that TV could create harmful as well as helpful PR. For example, Joseph McCarthy's credibility was weakened when his hectoring manner and his beard's five o'clock shadow were exposed to the scrutiny of viewers across the nation. The Revlon Company first enjoyed glorious PR from its sponsorship of the nation's most popular TV program, but when the "$64,000 Question" was exposed as a fraud, Revlon suffered acute embarrassment and a wave of public criticism for its failure to meet its social responsibility.

Honesty in public relations became a serious issue during the 1950s. In the bitter competition between truckers and the railroads to win the nation's long-haul freight business, both groups relied heavily on PR. The Eastern Railroad Presidents' Council hired Carl Byoir and Associates to represent it, and the Pennsylvania Motor Truck Association hired Allied Public Relations Associates. By 1953, the two parties also had hired lawyers, and the case was in court.

The truckers charged that the railroads (and their PR firm) were violating the Sherman Antitrust Act by trying to force the truckers out of business and by characterizing them as (in the words of federal judge Thomas J. Clary) "lawbreakers, road-hoggers, completely indifferent to the safety of others on the highway and moochers on the public through failure to pay their way."[96] Byoir and Associates created many "front" organizations with the single purpose of agitating against the trucking industry.

In response, Byoir's agency argued that the anti-trucking coalition did not violate antitrust laws but merely exercised fundamental rights of free speech. (Byoir himself died before the struggle was resolved.) A ruling from the U.S. Supreme Court in 1961 upheld Byoir's position and established the PR practitioner's right to represent a client's case in public even if the presentation is dishonest. Thus, the legal question was resolved, while the ethical one was raised to a new level of urgency.[97]

This and similar ethical problems led to PRSA's first code of ethics, a very brief statement promulgated in 1954. In 1959, PRSA adopted a Declaration of Principles and a more developed code of ethical behavior.[98] To avoid being accused of creating a paper tiger, PRSA established a grievance board in 1962 to conduct hearings whenever a PRSA member suspected another member of violating the code.[99] Two years later, PRSA approved a voluntary accreditation program open to all members of the society. This was simultaneously the first step in recognizing a level of professional accomplishment in public relations and the first step toward establishing and policing standards of behavior among practitioners.

■ Transition in the Turbulent Sixties and Seventies

The 1960s and early 1970s were years of great crisis and change in the United States. Public relations talent was called upon to cope with the drama and the trauma. Modern PR practitioners needed a broad knowledge of the social sciences, as well as communication and management skills. In addition, nonmarketing problems received new emphasis, more attention was given to the worldwide consumer movement, corporate–government relationships were scrutinized, PR people gained increasing responsibility within the corporate structure, a more demanding role emerged for PR in multinational companies and cries for help came from all sectors in dealing with dissident youth and minorities. Communication satellites, the awesome power of nuclear weaponry and the emergence of electronic information storage for data processing had made the globe smaller but had not diminished its problems.

One fundamental change in the United States actually began in the 1950s, signaled by the U.S. Supreme Court's landmark school desegregation decision of 1954, *Brown v. Board of Education of Topeka*, and involved a reassessment and legal reform of black and white race relations. During the 1950s in Montgomery, Alabama, Martin Luther King, Jr., began expressing his vision of what U.S. society could achieve if racism were ended. He used many public relations techniques to gain support for his cause, and he was skillful in working with the news media. His "I Have a Dream" speech and other eloquent sermons and addresses, as well as his adoption of nonviolent protest patterned on the approach developed by Mahatma Ghandi, helped launch a civil rights movement that produced many social changes, especially in the 1960s. King's assassination in April 1968 shocked the nation, and made his name a rallying cry for supporters of the continuing movement to achieve racial equality in the United States.

The nation seemed to divide on one point after another: civil rights, disarmament, the space program, the Vietnam war and the peace movement, conservation, farm labor, women's liberation, nuclear energy, the Watergate affair and on and on. In the debate over each of these issues, public relations was important to both sides. For example, PR professionals conducted seminars to train people within the power structure in how to respond directly to activists and how to answer them indirectly through news media and other public channels of communication. But the activists used PR just as effectively, capturing public attention with demonstrations, organizations and powerful rhetoric. Conservatives charged that the Chicago riots of 1968 smacked of press agentry. Radicals retorted that the same could be said of the Gulf of Tonkin incident, in which the North Vietnamese ostensibly attacked an American ship.

Dow Chemical Company faced a PR crisis when antiwar consumers boycotted its line of household products, including Saran Wrap, because Dow also manufactured the incendiary chemical napalm, used to great destructive effect in the Vietnam war. Industry was chagrined by such protests, since contributing to the war effort had always been good for public relations in the past. When no way could be found to popularize the Vietnam war, the United States signed a peace treaty ending the involvement of American troops—a decision that was announced (prematurely) during the last month of Richard Nixon's reelection campaign in 1972.

■ The Rise of Consumerism

In the United States, the consumer movement produced much of the criticism of institutions. Because of its increased visibility, many people assumed that the movement was new. It wasn't. The first national consumer group, the National Consumers League, had been founded from ninety state affiliates in 1899. Early issues it supported were minimum wage laws, improved working hours, occupational safety, abolition of sweatshops and child labor and improved working conditions for migrant farm workers. In supporting the 1906 Pure Food and Drug Act, the league formed food committees that set standards for food manufacture, inspected food manufacturing establishments and certified their safe working conditions by affixing a White Label, a logo similar to today's union label, to products.

Another organization that has been a longtime consumer advocate is the Consumers Union of the United States. It began as part of Consumer's Research, Inc., the first product-testing organization supported by consumers, and was established as a separate entity in 1936. Consumers Union is an independent, nonprofit organization that tests and evaluates such products as appliances, automobiles and packaged food. Since its founding, it has published the results of its tests in a monthly magazine, *Consumer Reports*, along with articles designed to help consumers spend their money more wisely and to make them aware of current consumer problems. The organization has always pressed for increased consumer protection by calling attention to what it believes are unsafe products. It has also concerned itself with weaknesses in consumer legislation and with the reluctance or failure of government regulatory agencies to act on behalf of consumers.

Sarah Newman, executive director of the National Consumers League from 1962 to 1975, has pointed out the major tactical differences between consumer-oriented organizations of earlier periods and those of the 1970s. For one thing, consumer advocates in the 1970s were more program-oriented. Consumer advocates during earlier periods did not resort to militancy. They also had to do much of the watchdog work themselves, because no regulatory agency was responsible for ensuring the safety of most consumer products. By the late 1970s, Newman's own group was involved in supporting such reforms as equal credit, no-fault insurance and uniform beef grading. The NCL also pushed for creation of an agency for consumer advocacy.

Until the late 1960s, the U.S. economy had run on the basis of increasing productivity. The supposition was that a ready market existed for all goods that could be conceived, produced, promoted and sold. Whatever it was, someone would buy it. This idea served as a cornerstone in the foundation of the American dream. But then a superabundance of goods resulted in a glutted marketplace and a surfeited public.

These surpluses led to more careful scrutiny of the consumer economy. At first only a few voices were raised, but the protesters found some dynamic allies, such as Ralph Nader. Their voices of dissent were eventually heard by some people sensitive to the sounds of the marketplace—people in public relations and advertising. Advertisers began finding flaws in the old edict of the business world: "If we can make it, you can sell it." As one disgusted advertising man exclaimed during this period: "I keep trying to tell those guys [his clients] that you can't fool the public." Although their clients may have been unaware of the changes that were occurring, many PR agencies certainly felt the mood of the marketplace; and in some of the largest and most prestigious, departments of consumerism or divisions of consumer studies began to appear.

Consumerism has been called "buyer's rights,"[100] "a cause or movement that advances the rights and interests of the consumer"[101] or a movement "seeking to increase the rights and powers of buyers in relation to sellers."[102] Whatever its title and definition, the essence of consumerism was clearly expressed by Margot Sherman, a retired senior vice-president of McCann Erickson (a New York agency), who had been in charge of setting up the agency's division of consumerism:

> On this business of consumerism, I suppose as a concept it was probably born in March 1962, when President Kennedy declared, "Every consumer has four basic rights—the right to be informed, the right to safety, the right to choose, and the right to be heard"!

Helping to craft those four rights was consumer advocate Helen Nelson, who produced a video documentary in 1995 chronicling the history of the movement, "Change Makers: The Struggle for Consumer Rights." Accompanying the video, which took her three years to write, is a teacher's guide of edited conversations with

35 consumer leaders interviewed for the video.[103] President Kennedy had identified consumers as the only important group in contemporary society that was not effectively organized. He then appointed ten private citizens to serve on a Consumer Advisory Council, including Nelson. Also he placed a consumer adviser, Esther Peterson, on his staff. Every U.S. president since Kennedy has followed his lead in having a staff consumer advisor.[104] Nelson advised two Presidents and Congress on consumer matters and was California's first Governor-appointed consumer advocate, from 1959–1966.[105]

The Sentiment Behind Consumerism The sentiment behind the consumer movement was best defined by Ralph Nader:

> Indeed the quality of life is deteriorating in so many ways that the traditional measurements of the "standard of living" according to personal income, housing, ownership of cars and appliances, etc., have come to sound increasingly phony.[106]

The sentiment was in fact a reaction to a "hostile environment." And the movement's character at any particular point in time, according to Edgar Chasteen, depended on the behavior of the "enemy," as defined by the movement.[107]

The enemy was business. In bewilderment, business looked on as a generation of consumers whose basic needs had been satisfied reacted adversely to old methods of persuasion. Evidently, the techniques that sold products also created expectations that could not be satisfied. A gap materialized between reality and the anticipation of rewards. In addition, consumer dissatisfaction was both the cause and the effect of another wave of investigative (or muckraking) journalism.[108]

To measure the intensity of consumer satisfaction/dissatisfaction, business used five common techniques: (1) statistics such as sales, profits and market share; (2) behavioral measures such as repeat purchases, acceptance of other products in the same line and favorable word-of-mouth publicity; (3) direct observation; (4) dissatisfaction indices such as recorded complaint data; (5) surveys and

interviews to unearth reticent respondents. The hazards of using these techniques and the difficulties involved in measuring consumer satisfaction and dissatisfaction are legion.[109]

A thorough look at the activist requires a look at the adversary as well. Ralph Nader has said that the principal concern of the consumer movement has always been the "involuntary subeconomy"—unwritten price-fixing for goods and services and inflationary agreements with labor and suppliers. These factors force up the costs of consumer goods and services, and the higher costs must be accepted because no other sources of the goods or services exist. Because there are no controls and no choices, the system is "involuntary"; because it underlies the economic structure, it constitutes a "subeconomy." Writing in 1973, Nader noted that the consumer movement had had limited success in improving regulatory action and encouraging private litigation. Its main achievement had been to create an awareness among consumers that they were being cheated and endangered. Nader conceded that the consumer movement had yet to devise an economic and policy-making framework to counterbalance or deplete the power of corporations to impose involuntary expenditures:[110]

> To some extent, consumerism as we know it was born of public frustration during a period of social turmoil, which saw unrest over civil rights issues and a divisive war in Southeast Asia. We entered a strobe-light existence, and with every blink of the flashing light, society had changed a little more before our very eyes! In short, the storm of the 1960s blew away many of the road signs that had helped us find our way comfortably along in the more predictable decades that came before.[111]

The Impact of Consumerism Most consumer activists of the 1960s and 1970s were members of what has been called the "silent generation." This generation was proportionally small because its members were Depression or post-Depression babies.[112] For it, quality of life was understood in terms of a standard of living.[113, 114] But not until confronted with the hostile accusations of the "anti-materialistic" younger generation of the 1960s did the silent generation recognize two salient questions: (1) At whose expense does a better living come? (2) What is the real value of all this? Robert Glessing has perceptively commented that "the unpreparedness of the silent generation was at least part of the cause of the student protest movements."[115]

But after taking a careful and critical look at its own lot, the silent generation began borrowing tactics from the youth revolt. Suddenly meat boycotts were being staged by matrons who were definitely over 40.[116] Although Rachel Carson's *Silent Spring* was published in 1962 and Ralph Nader's consumer statistics tips to Congress began appearing in 1960 (even before his 1965 publication *Unsafe at Any Speed*), the consumer movement did not become formidable until the early 1970s.[117] In 1972 and 1973, however, the Public Relations Society of America appointed a task force to examine the impact of consumerism on business.[118] By this time, class action suits were being filed; pressure was being brought to bear on regulatory agencies to enact stricter criteria and to enforce them; stockholders' meetings were losing their predictability because minor shareholders were appearing and demanding social accountability; employees were more likely to become litigants than loyalists.[119]

By 1967, President Lyndon Johnson had decided that consumer complaints were so politically significant that he appointed Betty Furness as his consumer advisory counsel.[120] By 1971, there were four national consumer organizations: the Consumer Federation of America, the Nader Organization and the two older associations, the National Consumers League and the Consumers Union.[121]

The consumer movement even reached that bastion of authoritarianism, the military. Complaints about the food in mess halls got a hearing, not a court-martial. Although the volunteer army may have influenced some of these changes, others clearly antedated it. For example, permissiveness in dress,[122] one of the first changes, was championed by the secretary of the Navy, Admiral Elmo R. Zumwalt, in 1970, three years before the end of the draft.[123]

Communication Problems and Public Opinion

The consumer movement clearly demonstrated some lack of communication between business and consumers, a deficiency that the following statement makes clear:

The consumerism movement not only mirrors the inability of the business sector to discern what factors of inherent consumer motivations promulgate (dis)satisfaction, but also reflects a growing concern for the "quality of life," which seems to be a popular cause, as well as a goal to collectively attain.[124]

In commenting on a 1977 Louis Harris survey, financial columnist Sylvia Porter asked how closely the views of senior business managers, consumer activists and government regulators matched the views of the general public. The answer was "not closely," with senior management "less in touch with public opinion than are any of the other groups." As Porter said:

Consumer activists would prefer to concentrate on electric utilities, the advertising industry, nuclear power plants and banks.

Business executives want reforms in hospitals, the medical profession, garages, home building and the legal profession.

Only one common perception is shared by every group surveyed: mistrust of the honesty and accuracy of advertising.[125]

The Harris survey had found that more than a third of all adults were bothered by poor-quality or dangerous products that failed to live up to advertising claims. They were distressed at the failure of companies to show legitimate concern for the consumer. They were bothered by poor after-sales service and repairs and by misleading packaging or labeling. More than half of the respondents thought they were receiving a worse bargain in the marketplace than they had been getting ten years earlier. Moreover, consumers expected things to get worse in three areas: product durability, product repair and the reliability of manufacturers' claims for products. Although the public expressed a desire for more information about subjects relevant to consumers, the poll found little public confidence in the accuracy and reliability of media news.

The Scope of the Problem The word *corporate*, as used in the consumer movement, should be interpreted in its broadest sense. Under fire, in addition to businesses, were all large institutions—hospitals, fund-raising public health associations, major-league sports teams, public and private educational institutions at all levels and religious groups. The biggest guns of all have been leveled at government administrators. The news media have suffered from adverse public opinion, too, as have newsmakers themselves, due to lawsuits, public attacks and threats of government intervention.

The harsh realities are clearly set forth by mass media scholars David Clark and William Blankenburg:

> The sturdiest obstacles to "ideal" public relations are economics and human nature. The plain fact is that managers are hired to make money for owners, and that a conscience can cost money. In the long run, it is money well spent, but many stockholders and managers fix their vision on the short run. Then, too, an abrupt change in corporate policy amounts to a public confession of past misbehavior—or so it seems to many executives. The natural temptation is to play up the good, and to let it go at that.[126]

The Impact of the Sixties and Seventies on Public Relations

The urgency of the problems that PR practitioners handled during the crises of the 1960s and 1970s and the expectations of those hiring PR talent gave the role new dimensions. But the new demands also created a crisis of confidence inside and outside public relations. In 1968 the Public Relations Student Society of America formed,[127] and, as public relations continued to gain status as an academic discipline, the field for the first time became dominated by people specially trained for the job.

In 1973 the U.S. Supreme Court handed down a decision that fundamentally changed the role of the PR practitioner. In the *Texas Gulf Sulphur* case (discussed further in Chapter 14), the Supreme Court upheld a 1968 decision of the U.S. Circuit Court of Appeals in New York requiring immediate disclosure of any information that may affect the market value of stock in publicly held corporations.[128] This ruling meant that PR had to concentrate more on dealing with public information and less on selecting what information to make public. The Supreme Court also ruled that PR practitioners involved in such cases were "insiders" and therefore were subject to the same trading restrictions as other members of the corporation whose knowledge of special circumstances prohibited them from buying or selling stock.[129] The insider trading scandals of the 1980s severely tested the SEC's ability to enforce insider trading rules.

The Growth of Public Skepticism Between 1966 and 1977, public confidence in corporate leadership dropped by 31 percentage points. While many executives besieged by negative public opinion bunkered down or toyed with the idea of resigning, one public relations officer decided to take the offensive. Mobil Oil's Herb Schmertz, a lawyer, began running Mobil's issue advertising in 1970. Following the oil shortages of the 1970s and the price acceleration they caused, Schmertz expanded Mobil's aggressive ad program and sought favorable opinion by convincing the corporation to sponsor public television's "Masterpiece Theater."

In some ways, Schmertz's combination of communication tactics rediscovered earlier mixes of advertising, publicity and promotion and prepared the way for the increased integration of communication tactics that occurred later in the 1970s and early 1980s. Schmertz emerged from the 1970s as a public relations personality. He engaged another PR person, William Novak, to memorialize Schmertz's version of the transformation and experience.[130] In 1988, Schmertz resigned from Mobil to start his own PR firm.

Pulling together as many communication devices as possible to influence public opinion was a response to deepening public disaffection and distrust, including the beginnings of widespread genuine mistrust of government. This development was not without foundation. Throughout the 1960s and 1970s valid grounds for public skepticism existed. Although the term *disinformation* didn't gain currency until the 1980s, the U.S. government was giving its citizens a good bit of it all along. One such campaign was engineered by former Assistant Secretary of Defense Paul Nitze. In 1975 intelligence-gathering activities of the CIA revealed that the Soviets' defense industry was *half* as efficient as had previously been supposed. It was therefore costing the Russians twice as much to build their weapons as U.S. analysts had previously thought. But in October 1975, Secretary of Defense James Schlesinger disclosed that "new intelligence" showed the Soviets were *spending* twice as much, implying that the Soviet military capacity was twice as great as had been estimated theretofore. News of the Soviet spending increase was reported in the mass media and thus was placed on the public agenda. With then CIA Director George Bush's help, Nitze put together a study group to reevaluate the CIA data; subsequently, the group "leaked" to the *New York Times* its conclusions that the CIA had been "dangerously complacent" in earlier evaluations of Soviet capacity and that the Soviets now had a first-strike capability. The leak was timed for one month before Jimmy Carter took office. So much for his vow to cut the defense budget.[131]

The Seventies in Summary The Middle East garnered a great deal of attention in the United States in the 1970s. The effects of the oil shortage created by policies of the coalition of oil-producing nations (OPEC—the Organization of Petroleum Exporting Countries) began to be felt as world demand for oil outstripped the supply from non-OPEC sources. In Iran the Ayatollah Khomeini and his fundamentalist Islamic followers overthrew the U.S.-backed shah. Soon thereafter, the American Embassy in Tehran was seized and its staff held hostage by "revolutionary guards" whose exact relationship to the new Iranian government was never satisfactorily clarified. Other acts of terrorism in the region suggested that the U.S. government was unable to defend its interests in that part of the world.

Problems in the Middle East added to a loss of confidence in the U.S. government at home. Another contributing factor was double-digit inflation, which eroded the economy and caused a serious decline in the standard of living. The nation's first military defeat, in Vietnam, drained people's feelings of nationalism, although the 1976 bicentennial helped revive these to some extent.

During the 1970s, the cultural monopoly of the traditional American family disappeared. More couples lived together outside marriage, and some were of the same sex. Married couples divorced at high rates, and, after the 1950s "baby boom," fewer children were born each year, especially to white couples.[132] The ethnic mix in America changed as the black and Hispanic populations, respectively, grew at twice and six times the rate of the white population. The Hispanic community was enlarged by numerous political and economic refugees from Latin America. Southeast Asian refugees, fleeing their homelands in the wake of communist victories there, added another ethnic piece to the American mosaic.

While consumerism and environmentalism both made great strides during the decade, the main social movement of the 1970s was the women's movement. Opponents succeeded in blocking modification of the Equal Rights Amendment to the Constitution, but the movement helped bring about some fundamental changes in society. Women began to view themselves as complete equals to men and demanded equal treatment in the workplace. Of the 3 million new people in the workforce, 2 million were women; almost half of all married women were employed, one-fourth of them with children under the age of six. Women's wages, though, were only 60 percent of men's. Women in legal careers doubled. Women getting medical degrees accounted for 22 percent of all those who sought such degrees in traditional medicine and 23 percent in veterinary medicine. The percentage of financial officers who were women rose from 18 percent to 30 percent in the decade, and women economists increased from 11 percent to 23 percent. Women in operations system research and analysis more than doubled, and women entered the public relations field in unprecedented numbers.

Presidential Power and Public Opinion in a Climate of Increasing Skepticism In the 1950s, President Dwight Eisenhower acknowledged the needs of television and radio news media and allowed them to record his press conferences. John Kennedy permitted live TV coverage of his meetings with the press.

Richard Nixon, who blamed TV for his 1960 defeat for the presidency, was determined to master his television technique and did. President Nixon's press secretary was not permitted much candor in his interactions with the media, however, and was not a professional public relations practitioner. In fact, Ronald Ziegler was experienced only in advertising. The only person with media experience, Herb Klein, was relegated to working with newspapers in the "hinterlands." The only person on Nixon's staff with PR background, William Safire, was strictly a speech writer.

Jimmy Carter hired Jody Powell as his press secretary when he first took office. However, when President Carter felt his work was not being understood correctly by the citizenry, he hired Gerald Rafshoon, the man who had managed his media campaign during his candidacies for governor of Georgia and president of the United States, to co-ordinate policy statements within the executive branch so that unity and cohesiveness of position were maintained. In response to media descriptions of his role as an "image maker," Rafshoon said he was coordinating, not creating.

PROFESSIONALISM: PR IN THE ERA OF GLOBAL COMMUNICATION: 1980–PRESENT

The 1960s were a time of tremendous social and economic upheaval. The 1970s were a decade of uncertainty. Most Americans worried about economic problems and shortages of natural resources, especially energy. Many people also lacked confidence in American institutions. These concerns continued into the 1980s, giving impetus to planning based on predictions of internal company development and external social, political and economic conditions.

The confrontations, challenges and turbulence of the 1960s and 1970s led to polarization in the 1980s. This polarization crossed every imaginable social and political boundary. The resulting struggles increased global as well as national tensions between fundamentalists and secularists. At the same time, the centrist position narrowed dramatically.

■ The Reagan Eighties

President Ronald Reagan's deputy press secretary, Pete Roussel, said he faithfully adhered to what he called the "Press Secretary's Prayer": "Oh, Lord, let me utter words sweet and gentle, for tomorrow, I may have to eat them."[133] Roussel was one of several public-opinion-sensitive specialists on Reagan's staff. Reagan came to be called "the Great Communicator." Recognizing that some people who didn't like what Reagan said nonetheless continued to like him, Colorado Congresswoman Pat Schroeder nicknamed him the "Teflon" president: nothing unpopular that his administration did seemed to stick to him personally. Reagan's administration also employed pollster Richard Beal, whose job was to look at public views on questions likely to arise as issues in the future.

In doing this, Reagan was following a trend that started with John F. Kennedy's use of polling, according to Sidney Blumenthal, author of *The Permanent Campaign*.[134] Blumenthal called Reagan "Communicator in Chief" and made this observation:

> *Reagan is governing America by a new doctrine—the permanent campaign. He is applying in the White House the most sophisticated team of pollsters, media masters and tacticians ever to work there. They have helped him to transcend entrenched institutions like the Congress and the Washington press corps to appeal directly to the people.*[135]

In addition to filling the administration's major public relations posts with experienced professionals, Reagan appointed PR pros to many positions not traditionally considered public relations jobs. Of the three top advisers to the president, two were lawyers and one, Michael Deaver, was a public relations professional. Deaver was indicted for influence peddling after he left the White House, and Bernard Kalb of the State Department left in protest when the government got involved in a disinformation campaign.

After press secretary Jim Brady was severely injured in the assassination attempt on Reagan, Larry Speakes became acting press secretary. Speakes sometimes felt that he wasn't sufficiently informed by other administration officials, and some news people agreed. However, Speakes said, not knowing is the lesser of the two sins of a press secretary; lying was a "cardinal sin" and unforgivable. Then, after he had left the administration—first to work for a large public relations firm, and then to direct public relations for a major brokerage firm—Speakes acknowledged he had "made up" quotes he attributed to President Reagan!

There is protection in not knowing because then you can't lie outright. However, if you don't know, you may commit a near-equivalent to lying—misleading. Not knowing everything, Speakes said, left him vulnerable in briefings because he ran the risk of saying something that might embarrass the president. About a fourth of the time, he was bound by strict guidelines concerning what he could say to the news media.[136]

The Reagan presidency was one of the most controlled in the history of the office. One indication of this was the number of orchestrated photo opportunities.[137] Additionally, during the Reagan administration, the U.S. Information Agency grew in power and influence. As the U.S. Information Service, it now has offices worldwide and controls an extensive television service called Worldnet, which broadcasts to 100 cities in 79 countries. Concern about Worldnet was expressed in 1987 by Florida Congressman Dan Mica, who observed that it had an "untapped and unlimited potential." The Congressman was concerned "that a particular

Administration could use Worldnet as its private propaganda vehicle."[138] Current USIA efforts are directed toward working with other government and nongovernmental groups abroad.

■ Integrated Communication Trend Begins

Beginning in the late 1970s and early 1980s, several large public relations firms were acquired by advertising agencies. In one transaction, J. Walter Thompson acquired Hill & Knowlton for $28 million. In another important merger, Dudley-Anderson-Yutzy, a PR firm, became a part of Ogilvy and Mather, an advertising firm, which was renamed the Ogilvy Group. Then, in 1989, the Ogilvy Group and J. Walter Thompson merged, through a hostile takeover, into the British-owned WPP Group. WPP grew even faster than its chief competitor at the time (also British) Saatchi & Saatchi PLC, now called Cordiant. In addition to owning then the world's largest PR firm, Hill & Knowlton, WPP got the largest custom market research company, Research International, and the largest direct-marketing company, Ogilvy Direct.[139]

Mergers also created giant communications operations with advertising and public relations capabilities. For instance, Young and Rubicam bought Burson-Marstelller and Marsteller, Inc., for about $20 million, and Benton and Bowles acquired Manning, Selvage and Lee for $2 million. The first big merger (1978) was of Carl Byoir & Associates (one of the oldest PR firms) with Foote, Cone & Belding.

Many advertising agencies moved into related fields: public relations, specialized advertising to and for select groups (doctors, for example), merchandising (including package design), direct marketing and/or sales promotion. Some agencies bought successful companies to put under a corporate umbrella. Others created their own divisions. Some integrated the various units into a superteam. Others operated the units separately and independently but found an advantage in presenting themselves as a "full-service" agency. The late PR counselor Philip Lesly expressed a fear that the trend could limit PR to a narrow communications role, subservient to marketing and stripped of its counseling role. Although some agencies used PR mostly for product/service support, others allowed PR free rein to pursue its full range of functions.

The intertwining function that these mergers produced was recognized by some colleges and universities, which combined the academic programs of advertising and PR, sometimes calling them integrated communications or integrated marketing communications.

 ## Global Impact on Public Relations Practice and Education in the 1980s and 1990s

The growth and evolution of public relations practice and of education for public relations internationally continued at an even faster pace during the 1980s and 1990s. Technology connected the world as never before, and this emphasized the need for and use of communication. Cultural awareness became increasingly important—not only in international communication, but also within nations—as political and economic disruptions the world over created a tide of refugees. Natural disasters added to the displacement of people from their homelands.

The formal combination of advertising and public relations tactics that began in the 1970s increased. The results were greater emphasis on "strategic planning" to coordinate the integrated communication elements and greater awareness of the need to integrate an organization's different "voices" to ensure consistency of message statements and to enhance credibility.[140] To put this phenomenal global growth of public relations into perspective, we must look at the social and political environment in which it occurred.

Historical Developments in the 1980s and 1990s

The interconnectedness and shared experience of our global society was demonstrated in international reactions to everything from natural events

such as the return of Halley's comet (1985–1986) to calamities like the Chernobyl nuclear power plant accident in the Ukraine (April 25, 1986) to the world stock market disaster of Black Monday (October 19, 1987), which was precipitated by a drop of 508 points in the Dow Jones industrial average. Individual investors fled the marketplace and complained bitterly about the havoc wreaked by the speculators. In 1989 the "Big Board" in the United States initiated a major public information campaign aimed at the 47 million Americans who owned stocks or shares in mutual funds. By 1991 there was some evidence that individual investors had returned to the stock market.

Discoveries of a supernova and of a superconducting substance, as well as breakthroughs in genetic coding research, revitalized American confidence in our ability to understand and shape the world. But the proliferation of the deadly virally-induced condition AIDS (Acquired Immune Deficiency Syndrome) was humbling and defied explanation and control. Both in the United States and abroad, advertising and public relations programs were undertaken to educate the public about AIDS and to impede its progress into a pandemic.

Faith in U.S. institutions was severely shaken in 1986 by a series of events. The first of these was the January 28 explosion of the Challenger space shuttle, which temporarily ended manned space explorations by the United States. NASA's return in 1989 was with the launches of the Magellan and Galileo space probes and with the brilliant success of Voyager 2's flyby of Neptune at the conclusion of its 12-year journey. Then there followed the first-ever pictures of the surface of Venus. Despite these successes, however, NASA was forced by the national budget crunch to economize, sometimes to the detriment of its projects. Nothing typifies the agency's mixture of triumph and fallibility better than the launch of the Hubble telescope in 1990. A simple mathematical error produced a flawed lens shape, which for a time prevented the remarkable telescope from transmitting the exquisite views of the heavens it had been expected to provide. Subsequent delicate (and expensive) maneuvers in space brought the telescope to its full operational capacity.

Falling oil prices in 1986 caused such economic chaos in the Sunbelt states that more banks failed that year than ever before in the nation's history. The drop in oil prices hurt not only the banks themselves and U.S. oil-producing states, but also Latin American countries that had used their petroleum assets as collateral for loans from U.S. banks that they suddenly had no means of repaying.

Worldwide television audiences witnessed the exposure of an unelected subgovernment in the United States during the Iran–Contra hearings, which investigated unauthorized sales of overpriced arms to Iran, supposedly in exchange for American hostages held in Lebanon, with some of the profits from the sales going to the Nicaraguan Contras. President Ronald Reagan claimed to have been unaware of these activities, and Marine Lieutenant Colonel Oliver North of the National Security Council enjoyed a brief career as a national hero before being indicted and sentenced in 1989. (His convictions were overturned later when an appeals court decided that the evidence proving his guilt had not been sufficiently insulated from testimony North gave to Congress under a grant of immunity from prosecution. North pronounced himself "totally exonerated" by this ruling and ran [unsuccessfully] for the Senate in 1994.) Before the dust from the Iran–Contra debacle had settled, a new (but lesser) scandal involving Pentagon defense contracts further eroded public confidence in government.

Television audiences also watched the downfall of TV evangelists Jim and Tammy Bakker and Jimmy Swaggart and the collapse of the Bakkers' organization, an event that indirectly led to Jerry Falwell's resignation as head of Moral Majority, the leading fundamentalist organization in the United States.

In the face of falling U.S. prestige, Soviet Prime Minister Mikhail Gorbachev introduced a new climate of *glasnost* (openness) in the USSR. He sent young, effective communicators to represent his nation in preliminary peace talks and agreed to many U.S. positioning statements, much to the dismay of U.S. diplomats. In 1987, he came to the United States and showed that he, too, knew how to handle a media event. But, by 1991, Gorbachev was in serious trouble at home, trying to keep the USSR glued together as one state after another voted for independence. By year's end the Soviet Union was defunct, and Gorbachev was head of a Russian "think tank."

The United States hosted another important world leader in 1987, Pope John Paul II, who found his followers in a restive mood as he refused to modify his conservative views on the issues of marriage for priests and nuns, abortion, birth control and homosexuality. The world of public relations got directly involved in that issue because the United States Catholic Conference (USCC) asked Hill & Knowlton to represent it in a public anti-abortion campaign. Robert L. Dilenschneider, then president and CEO of Hill & Knowlton, agreed to take the account, but he didn't anticipate that USCC would announce that fact before he had a chance to tell employees about it. Many of his staffers were quite upset, and some even quit. Dilenschneider later conceded that the internal handling of the affair was not ideal, but he defended his decision to accept the account as a first amendment issue—a rather problematic line of argument because it implies that, much like lawyers, PR practitioners have a societal duty to provide their services to anyone who wants (and can pay for) professional help in framing and disseminating ideas, regardless of how repugnant those ideas may be. Taken to an extreme, this reasoning would find an obligation to provide PR services to hate groups, on the theory that the First Amendment guarantees them, not merely the right to free speech, but the right to effective speech. In the fall of 1991, Dilenschneider resigned, citing loss of control to the parent company, WPP Group PLC.

Hill & Knowlton also had the account of the Citizens for a Free Kuwait, which it obtained shortly after U.S. troops started their campaign to recapture that country on January 16, 1991. The Desert Storm war, perhaps because of its brevity, success and multinational force, restored a strong feeling of patriotism to citizens of the United States. However, the war's aftermath, especially the Kurdish refugee situation, reminded the international community of the lingering horrors of war. The war also left a substantial number of Kuwaiti oil fields on fire (the last of these fires was put out some six months later) and an oil-drenched, ecologically damaged Persian Gulf. Cynicism replaced patriotism in some quarters after the war, as people became more aware that the "reality" of the coverage they had been exposed to more nearly resembled managed news. The backlash among media personnel against PR control of war information was strong.

The stock market collapse of Black Monday in 1987 represented a frightening but graphic example of imagery and public opinion. The lingering weakness of the market was attributable in part to global discomfort at the U.S. debt, which had reached the trillions of dollars, and at the deadlock between the Reagan administration and Congress over how to deal with it. The friction in philosophies between the executive and legislative branches was apparent in the Iran–Contra hearings, the budget negotiations, and most dramatically in the Senate's refusal to confirm strict constructionist Robert Bork to the Supreme Court. Opposition to his nomination revived the activism of civil rights and feminist constituencies. Four years later, the nomination of Clarence Thomas to replace Thurgood Marshall on the Supreme Court opened a rift within the black community when law professor Anita Hill's allegations of sexual harassment by Thomas created a national furor over the nature and prevalence of this previously ignored type of crime. Although many people found Hill's testimony at the resulting hearing both plausible and compelling, the U.S. Senate's ninety-eight men and two women narrowly voted to confirm Thomas's appointment to the court.

The most dramatic historical development of the late 1980s was the downfall of communist regimes in Eastern Europe. In the spring of 1989, with neighboring borders relaxed, East Germans began leaving the state in droves. Then in November, the East German government resigned en masse, and on November 10 the Berlin wall began

to come down. Pieces of the wall sold as souvenirs in U.S. department stores at prices from $15 to $25. By 1990, the U.S. Information Agency had opened the first "American University Bookstore" in East Berlin. The two Germanies were united in October of 1990. Another notable development in November of 1989 was Hungary's withdrawal from the Warsaw Pact; and later in the same month Hungarians voted in their first free election in forty-two years. In Czechoslovakia, voters elected prominent dissident playwright Vaclav Havel president in 1989. But within four years, the national government gave in, reluctantly but peacefully, to the secession of Slovakia from the union with the subsequently renamed Czech Republic in 1993. The Solidarity trade-union leader Lech Walesa was chosen premier of Poland in August 1989. By 1990, the Voice of America had opened its first Polish office, in Warsaw. Meanwhile, in Bulgaria, seeing the tide of change in 1989, Communist party leader Todor Zhivkov resigned.

The most dramatic climax may have been in Romania. In December 1989, after his communist government had collapsed, Nicolae Ceausescu was captured, tried in secret and, along with his wife, executed by a firing squad on Christmas Day. Mass graves of suspected government opponents were exhumed, and U.S. families began to adopt orphaned and abandoned Romanian children. This turned out to be a problem by 1991 when it became clear that many private adoption homes in Romania were placing children who had been relinquished (either abandoned or sold) by poor families. The U.S. State Department responded by refusing for a time to grant adopting parents visas for the children.

In the Western Hemisphere, Fidel Castro began issuing visas that permitted some people to leave Cuba legally for the first time.

With restraints loosening in much of the communist world, the Western world was shocked to watch on television as Chinese students participating in a pro-democracy movement were attacked by armed troops and tanks near Beijing's Tiananmen Square. Especially apprehensive were the Chinese citizens of Hong Kong, since that island city would revert to China in 1997. Many of the students who weren't captured in the subsequent crackdown escaped with the help of an underground movement operating out of Hong Kong.

Two unique elements in the tragic event point out the globalization of today's world. First, the students in revolt were receiving fax messages from Chinese students and sympathizers abroad; second, the authorities later used television footage to identify the students and track them down. Some received severe prison sentences. This led some U.S. citizens to push for revoking China's "most favored nation" trading status, but President Bush opposed this measure and committed the administration to a policy of keeping the market open. The subsequent Democratic administration of Bill Clinton did not reverse the Bush policy on China.

The mostly nonviolent revolutions of Eastern Europe were followed in 1991 by the disintegration of the Soviet Union into its constituent republics (loosely allied as the Confederation of Independent States). Czechoslovakia split to become two independent nations. A destructive secessionist movement occurred in Yugoslavia, where forty-five years of cooperative existence between neighboring states gave way to older enmities and a bitter civil war.

The world's turbulence and turmoil opened markets and new opportunities for public relations practitioners who could cope with the demands of global communications. The new Russian commonwealth presented a particularly challenging opportunity. In response to the new European Union market formed by the Maastricht Treaty, the United States, on President Bush's initiative, opened expanded trade with Canada and Mexico, as a part of a "united continent" concept. The North American Free Trade Agreement (NAFTA) was ratified in 1994.

A year later, the U.S. Congress approved a General Agreement on Tariffs and Trade (GATT), which further opened up international trade and had significant domestic economic consequences as well. The GATT agreement vote in the U.S. Congress came after voter anger in the 1994 elections had ousted many politicians and put both houses of Congress into Republican hands for the first time in forty years. The level of public hostility

and distrust toward government (including President Clinton) was at a 1960s level. However, the GATT agreement, like some other legislation of the period, showed some new political alignments being forged in an effort to find out what citizens wanted. In Latin America, the new Southern Cone Common Market (Mercosur) began to attract other nations.

At a time when social and political systems were being abandoned in other countries, the USA began to question its entitlement programs such as social security and welfare. The national health policy that President Clinton came into office vowing to establish was disassembled by partisan political disputes and interest-group wrangling. At the same time, new concerns, such as for people with disabilities came to the forefront in legislation protecting the rights of the disabled, to accommodations in the workplace and in educational institutions.

Technological advances have made the environment for people with disabilities potentially more friendly, with all sorts of electronic devices to compensate for physical losses. However, as many of these systems came into the consumer market, their origin—the space industry—was threatened as never before. Changes in the political environment had an impact, as did costs and some spectacular failures such as the Mars Observer in 1992, the loss of some key satellites in 1993, a cut in the size of the space station and the aforementioned problems with the Hubble space telescope.

Advances in technology dominated the early 1990s, especially with regard to computers. Even hotels and airplanes had to accommodate computer users. The key phrase "Information Superhighway" created all sorts of opportunities and problems. Facsimile messages went all over the world and became almost as commonplace as telephones in some countries. Voicemail message systems meant 24-hour answering, even at home. Telephones went on board airplanes for in-air use, and countries without reliable permanent phone systems found hand-held cell phones in great demand. Many addresses on business cards and letterheads included both phone and fax numbers and, in addition to a physical location, an "e-mail" address, a location on the information superhighway. International travelers used money cards in electronic machines for access to their accounts and moved money across national boundaries with ease.

Friendships also moved across national boundaries. As computer network "correspondents" plugged in internationally, whole new publics and media, in a public relations sense, developed. Teenagers could communicate with people their age all over the world, and the elderly found a whole new group of friends worldwide at the touch of their keyboards. In addition to these new publics, new media developed. Some "publications" became available only electronically, and traditional "library" information became available in CD-ROM format. "Desktop publishing" not only meant publishing at home by an individual who wanted to create a newsletter, but meant having the capacity to send that information electronically around the world.

The problems technology brought involved disputes over copyrights, something ignored by certain countries, and laws involving pornography, libel and slander. Computer networks had developed some protocols or procedures to which users generally adhered. These protocols worked fairly well when there were few users, but they fell into an abyss when many users came on line.

Conflicts as well as opportunities are a part of the new technology revolution or evolution. The impact of these changes on the practice of public relations has been profound.

■ PR Developments in the 1980s and 1990s

During the 1980s, PR newswire services responded to the new technology by using satellite transmissions. "Clipping" services functioned electronically too. In addition to the greater dispersion and collection of information, computer technology brought the microcomputer to the public relations office and, with it, an array of microcomputer techniques. Desktop publishing improved the look of in-house publications and made possible sophisticated graphics for reports, speeches and ads.

The World Wide Web has created a whole new medium for public relations, presenting new opportunities and problems. From home pages and chat rooms to e-mail ListServs, all sorts of institutions and individuals have a presence on the Web. Within organizations, the e-mail system has also deeply affected employee relations, since it has become a powerful means of internal communication.

The Web has significantly changed media relations as well. A good Web page gives basic information about the organization and access to additional information and includes text, pictures and graphics. News releases are often posted on organizations' Web pages, and media can seek sources from a number of different sites.

The media's use of their own Web pages to release stories that may be speculative has created new difficulties for public relations people. Individuals can also use the Web to circulate rumors that often have serious consequences. With their lack of editors, chat rooms and independent Web pages can pose problems even more troublesome than stories released by major media organizations. And while the Web has become a preferred fact-finding tool because of its easy access, the verifiability of Web information remains a problem.

Improvements in computers also added to the explosion of the PR research industry. Its dependence is such that a major concern of the 1990s was to bring computers into compliance with "Year 2000" standards. Most of the older programs could not cope with any date after 1999.

Changes in the economy throughout the world created a situation where many companies began to cut their numbers of employees and to depend on suppliers for services previously provided within the institution. This "out-sourcing," as it is called, also affected public relations. Many public relations practitioners began to work for themselves because they were let go by organizations that had employed them; as independent contractors, they established their own clientele, servicing many customers, often including their previous employers. The electronic technology that had allowed their employers to reduce the number of in-house employees also made it possible for them to work from their homes and service clients all over the world.

The global aspect of public relations was underscored by the demand abroad for public relations expertise both in the field and in the classroom. Developing nations with a growing middle class began to expand public relations activities, and newly democratized nations found a need to talk to citizens who had new liberty to make political and economic decisions. As a result, the International Public Relations Association began to develop a global body of knowledge designed to be more comprehensive than the PRSA body of knowledge.

An effort to make public relations a profession through control over entry and exit was launched by Edward L. Bernays who filed bills in the House and Senate of the Commonwealth of Massachusetts in 1992 that would have licensed public relations practice. That effort failed.

Bernays' licensing proposal called for an examination that would require mastery of a body of knowledge and adherence to a recognized code of ethics. With the globalization of public relations, educational standards for public relations and the body of knowledge on which these would be based are more diverse than ever before. The code of ethics is a bit of a problem, too; although the IPRA code has broad international acceptance, it lacks the specificity of the PRSA code. A new code developed by the International Association of Business Communicators (IABC) attempts to deal with contemporary international issues.

Public relations practitioners in the United States now compete with practitioners throughout the world and will continue to do so. Lack of international experience is a problem for some public relations practitioners who might never have imagined they would need it. More and more companies and nonprofit organizations are involved in international activities.

For example, buyouts of U.S. companies by companies headquartered in foreign nations has put a new and complicated burden of responsibilities on PR practitioners in the United States. The buyout of Standard Oil by BP (British Petroleum) has been cited as a "textbook example of the complications that arise in such a transaction."[141] In 1986, when BP was still only a partial owner, Sohio (Standard Oil of Ohio) dropped its name because management felt that its activities were too international to justify using the name of a single state. During the February 1986 name change, the company was restructured and twenty subsidiary companies were sold, requiring an extensive investor and media relations campaign.

Another full-blown information campaign was developed for the May 1987 merger, but it had to be put aside after the British government announced in July 1987 that it was privatizing its one-third share ownership of BP. During that time, under both U.S. and British securities regulations, BP America was forbidden to engage in internal or external communications activity until the share issue was no longer in the registration process—and this process lasted from the end of July until December.

To make matters worse, the British government's BP share offering occurred on Black Monday. To prevent company shares from being bought from a stockbroker at less than the government's asking price, the government promised to support a floor price to reduce risks to brokers who had agreed in advance to buy the full issue.

Finally, in January 1988, BP America began to tell its story with a three-page ad that ran during the first week of the year in most major U.S. dailies. The ad pointed out that BP America "is the 12th largest company in America . . . but you probably never heard of it." The ads were part of a comprehensive campaign that included an intensive media relations emphasis for the business and financial press.[142] Later that year, BP America was able to extend its presence by purchasing Amoco, the former Standard Oil of Indiana.

Another trend in public relations was the continued stream of women into the field, as documented and examined in "The Velvet Ghetto."[143] While male PR practitioners moved into CEO slots, women did not. Most women in public relations held lower-status positions and earned considerably less than men in similar positions. Most women at the top reached it by heading their own agencies, although there were exceptions such as Jean Way Schoonover, former vice-chairman of Ogilvy Public Relations Group. Alma Triner was vice-president of corporate communication for Arthur D. Little, Inc., until she and several others went into business handling the promotion of entrepreneurial ventures.

President Clinton had a woman media spokesperson in DeeDee Myers, until she resigned late in 1994. He appointed his wife, Hillary Rodham Clinton, to be the point person on the health plan. These women, like some of Clinton's other female appointees, attracted a great deal of criticism. One Clinton appointee who handled her role well was Janet Reno, U.S. Attorney General, who found herself center stage after the raid on the Branch Davidians in Waco, Texas, resulted in a holocaust. Another appointee didn't fare so well. Health Secretary Joycelyn Elders was asked to resign in December 1994 because she was "too outspoken."

In part the unpopularity of these women was attributable to the backlash that some pundits say also was reflected in the Republican success in the Congressional elections of 1994. According to surveys, white males voting Republican do not support women's rights, and women voting Republican are not likely to see any reason to support women because of gender.[144]

1975 was declared International Women's Year, and the world conference in Mexico City that year proclaimed 1976–1985 the United Nation's Decade for Women: Equality, Development and Peace. The New Decade of Women was to have begun in 1986, concluding in 1995. Actually, the progress is not encouraging.

Internationally, the female spokesperson who gained highest visibility in the early 1990s was the very articulate Hanan Ashrawi. As spokeswoman for the Palestinian delegation to the U.S.-initiated Middle East peace talks from the time they began in early 1991, she commanded world attention and praise for her ability to present the Palestinian case effectively in the court of public opinion.

Another highly visible international appointment occurred in the United States. In 1989 the Episcopal Church (Anglican Communion) elected as its first woman bishop a former public relations practitioner, Barbara Harris. The African-American activist broke a 2,000-year-old barrier for women in Anglican communion.

Another trend of the 1990s was the growth of ethnic public relations organizations. The consolidation of people of like background in these organizations almost certainly highlights the failure of inclusiveness and diversity in the longer-established public relations organizations. However, it may help ethnic practitioners to eventually get a better foothold in other firms since they will be more identifiable to those companies and institutions that want to diversify and are looking for talent.

It's difficult to study the careers of women and minorities in the field because public relations careers are not high profile. The role of the public relations practitioner in fact often requires avoiding the spotlight. The result is that public relations history has produced only a few identifiable personalities, even though the histories of all institutions, profit and nonprofit, have embedded in them the influence and work of men and women from all sorts of ethnic backgrounds and nationalities.

Media coverage of public relations in the 1980s and 1990s was extensive and often hostile—usually because of the perceived manipulation of public attitudes by sophisticated PR campaigns. An unpublished PRSA survey showed that most CEOs evaluate the quality of their public relations as being only fair. The principle weaknesses they cite are their internal and external public relations advisers' inability to grasp management's needs fully, to understand the institution's goals and to chart a way to meet these goals.

In 1998, the Association of Public Relations Firms was established with Jack D. Bergen as its first president. This is the first trade association to represent the professional, ethical and financial interests of the US PR industry.

Although the term public relations is widely used now, it is generally applied erroneously. Public recognition of the term without full knowledge of what it means leads more people on the fringes of the field to call themselves public relations practitioners.

A close examination of how media use the term *public relations* nevertheless shows that, overall, positive references outweigh negative; most of the focus is on agencies, publicity and support to marketing. Probably because of that, the most attention to public relations by news media occurs in New York, Los Angeles and Washington, D.C. The government's use of public relations is not always seen positively—as, for example, in the negative reactions to the government's handling of information about the Gulf War. Writers for the mass media still refer to "putting public relations spins" on news and using "PR gimmicks."

Nevertheless, the use of public relations talent worldwide is increasing daily, and education for public relations continues to grow steadily in the USA and elsewhere. More universities throughout the world have begun adding public relations courses to their programs, and professional public relations organizations are providing continuing education for public relations.

POINTS TO REMEMBER

■ While public relations practice as we identify it today has only existed since the beginning of the twentieth century, it has grown from ancient sources.

■ The particular political, economic and social climate in the United States allowed public relations to establish itself here first, so the practice is now firmly identified with this country.

■ Historians who view the practice of public relations positively see it as a broker for public support of ideas, institutions and people, but critics say this is done at the expense of individual autonomy.

■ In the United States, the development of public relations has gone through five distinct stages, each related to the type of public relations predominantly practiced during that period.

■ The government's effort to get support for World War I through the "Creel Committee" resulted in on-the-job training of many of the founders of the first public relations firms.

■ The economic crash of the 1930s stirred industry's concern for social responsibility as a way to regain public esteem and confidence.

■ The PR effort during World War II was much better focused than was the one in World War I, but it also injected an element of disinformation; unlike Creel, Davis was not a presidential adviser.

■ The postwar period saw PR counseling come into prominence and begin to develop toward professional status.

■ The fractionalization of the nation in the 1960s and 1970s underscored the need for public relations people who were good social scientists and good social counselors.

■ The consumer movement was the origin of current environmentalism, which has general public support, although hype by institutions has created some skepticism about its positive value to the public.

■ Business lost consumer loyalty during the postwar period, and employee loyalty became almost nonexistent.

■ The stage of the 1980s and 1990s saw technology transform the world into a global neighborhood; this stage created an international demand for public relations talent, especially in developing and newly democratized nations.

■ This need is being met by continuing education for practitioners by professional associations and by public relations courses added to university curricula.

■ The high visibility of public relations, due to its stature and the increasing pervasiveness of news media, has resulted in increasing criticism.

■ Many users of public relations talent don't think PR people understand their organization's real needs and goals and how to help meet these.

■ Cutbacks in employees, partly as a result of technology, have resulted in the out-sourcing of many services including public relations.

■ Many public relations practitioners who have left institutions have gone into business for themselves, keeping their former employers as clients and adding clients throughout the world, which they easily can service through technology.

NOTES

[1] According to a report by Professor Eric Goldman of Princeton University, referred to by Edward L. Bernays in the International Public Relations Association (IPRA) *Review* (September 1977), p. 4 of reprint. However, according to Sanat Lahiri of Calcutta, IPRA president, in *pr reporter* (December 17, 1979), the phrase "public relations" was used much earlier by Thomas Jefferson, and this reference appears in the first edition of Scott Cutlip and Allen Center, *Effective Public Relations* (Englewood Cliffs, N.J.: Prentice-Hall, 1952), p. 40.

[2] Ibid.

[3] Irwin Ross, *The Image Merchants* (Garden City, N.Y.: Doubleday, 1959), p. 51.

[4] Edward L. Bernays, *Public Relations* (Norman: University of Oklahoma Press, 1952), p. 84.

[5] Based on Irwin Ross, *The Image Merchants* (Garden City, N.Y.: Doubleday, 1959), pp. 51–64.

[6] J. A. R. Pimlott, *Public Relations and American Democracy* (Princeton, N.J.: Princeton University Press, 1951), pp. 235–41.

[7] Alan R. Raucher, "Public Relations in Business: A Business of Public Relations," *Public Relations Review*, 16(3) (Fall 1990), p. 19.

[8] Theodore Lustig, "Great Caesar's Ghost," *Public Relations Journal* (March 1986), pp. 17–20.

[9] Theodore H. White, *Caesar at the Rubicon* (New York: Atheneum, 1968), p. 9.

[10] Marcus Lee Hansen, *The Atlantic Migration, 1607–1860* (New York: Harper & Row, 1961), p. 30. Also see E. I. McCormac, *White Servitude in Maryland, 1634–1820* (Baltimore: Johns Hopkins University, 1904), pp. 11–14.

[11] Scott M. Cutlip and Allen H. Center, *Effective Public Relations*, 4th ed. (Englewood Cliffs, N.J.: Prentice-Hall, 1971), p. 49.

[12] Richard Bissell, *New Light on 1776 and All That* (Boston: Little, Brown, 1975), p. 26.

[13] Ibid., p. 32.

[14] Frank Luther Mott, *American Journalism* (New York: Macmillan, 1950), pp. 26–28.

[15] Ibid., p. 33.

[16] Susan Henry, "Work, Widowhood and War: Hannah Bunce Watson, Connecticut Printer," Connecticut Historical Society Bulletin 48 (Winter 1983), pp. 24–39.

[17] Frank Luther Mott, *American Journalism* (New York: Macmillan, 1950), pp. 179–80.

[18] Jerome Mushkat, *Tammany: The Evolution of a Political Machine* (Syracuse, N.Y.: Syracuse University Press, 1971), pp. 373–74. "Public opinions" are noted, not "polls" specifically, in this reference. See also Gustavas Myers, *The History of Tammany Hall* (New York: Gustavas Myers, 1901).

[19] Stanley L. Jones, *The Presidential Election of 1896* (Madison: University of Wisconsin Press, 1964), pp. 276–96.

[20] Ibid., p. 295.

[21] Deborah J. Warner, "The Women's Pavilion," in Robert C. Post, ed., *1876: A Centennial Exhibition* (Washington, D.C.: Smithsonian Institution, 1976).

[22] Vernon L. Parrington, *Main Currents in American Thought* (New York: Harcourt Brace, 1938) pp. 31–43, especially p. 40.

[23] Cutlip and Center, *Effective Public Relations*, 4th ed., p. 49. See also John Walton, *John Filson of Kentucky* (Lexington: University of Kentucky Press, 1956). Also in Cutlip, Center and Broom 7th ed. (1994), p. 107.

[24] Bernays, *Public Relations*, pp. 36–39.

[25] Cutlip and Center, *Effective Public Relations*, 4th ed., p. 83.

[26] The rest of the remark, made in 1882 in his private railroad car while being interviewed by reporters, was "I don't take any stock in this silly nonsense about working for anybody's good but our own because we're not. When we make a move we do it because it is in our interest to do so." Roger Butterfield, *American Past* (New York: Simon & Schuster, 1947), p. 476.

[27] Richard Bissell, *The Monongahela* (New York: Rinehart, 1952), pp. 184–91.

[28] John Brooks, "From Dance Cards to the Ivy League Look," *The New Yorker* (May 18, 1957), p. 74.

[29] Vail also sought third-party credibility by subsidizing the writing of favorable editorials and by giving newspaper editors free long-distance service. For more on this aspect of Vail, see Marvin N. Olasky, "The Development of Corporate Public Relations 1850–1930." Journalism Monographs 102, April 1987

(Columbia, S.C.: Association for Education in Journalism and Mass Communication, 1987).

[30] William R. Faith, "The American Public Relations Experience: 400 Years from Roanoke to Reagan" (New York: Institute of Public Relations Research and Education, unpublished manuscript).

[31] Scott M. Cutlip and Allen H. Center, *Effective Public Relations*, 5th ed. (Englewood Cliffs, N.J.: Prentice-Hall, 1978), p. 73. Also in Cutlip, Center and Broom 7th ed. (1994), p. 98.

[32] Forrest McDonald, *Insull* (Chicago: University of Chicago Press, 1962), pp. 44–45.

[33] Ronald A. Fullerton, "Art of Public Relations: U.S. Department Stores, 1876–1923," *Public Relations Review*, 16(3) (Fall 1990), p. 69.

[34] Ibid., p. 71.

[35] Ibid., p. 72.

[36] Sherman Morse, "An Awakening on Wall Street," *American Magazine*, 62 (September 1906), p. 460.

[37] Faith, "The American Public Relations Experience."

[38] W. A. Swanberg, *Pulitzer* (New York: Scribner's, 1967), pp. 73–122.

[39] Cornelius C. Regier, *The Era of Muckrakers* (Chapel Hill: University of North Carolina Press, 1932).

[40] Douglas Ann Johnson Newsom, "Creating Concepts of Reality: Media Reflections of the Consumer Movement" (Austin: University of Texas, unpublished Ph.D. dissertation, 1978).

[41] Ross, *Image Merchants*, pp. 29–30.

[42] Cutlip and Center, *Effective Public Relations*, 4th ed., p. 72. In 7th ed., p. 101. See also Scott M. Cutlip, "The Nation's First Public Relations Firm," *Journalism Quarterly* 43 (Summer 1966), pp. 269–80.

[43] William Kittle, "The Making of Public Opinion," *Arena*, 41 (1909), pp. 433–50.

[44] Cutlip and Center, *Effective Public Relations*, 4th ed., p. 83. In 7th ed., pp. 107–08.

[45] Personal letter from Paul Ridings, PR practitioner and son of J. Willard Ridings, founder of the Department of Journalism at Texas Christian University and ACPRA president 1941–1942. When Paul joined in 1940, they were the association's first father–son team. Paul Ridings, Jr., is also a public relations professional.

[46] Cutlip and Center, *Effective Public Relations*, 4th ed., p. 91. Also in 7th ed., pp. 115–16.

[47] Scott M. Cutlip, *Fund Raising in the United States: Its Role in America's Philanthropy* (New Brunswick, N.J.: Rutgers University Press, 1965).

[48] Ibid.

[49] Ibid.

[50] Ibid. (letter from Pendleton Dudley to Major Earl F. Storer).

[51] Howard Weeks, "The Development of Public Relations as an Organized Activity in a Protestant Denomination" (Washington, D.C.: American University, unpublished master's thesis, 1963).

[52] McDonald, *Insull*, p. 3.

[53] David L. Lewis, "Pioneering the Film Business: *Public Relations Journal* (June 6, 1971), pp. 14–18.

[54] Cutlip and Center, *Effective Public Relations*, 4th ed., p. 82.

[55] Ibid.

[56] Lewis, "Pioneering the Film Business," pp. 14–18.

[57] Stephen Ponder, "Progressive Drive to Shape Public Opinion, 1898–1913," *Public Relations Review*, 16(3) (Fall 1990), p. 95.

[58] Ibid.

[59] Alan R. Raucher, "Public Relations in Business: A Business of Public Relations," *Public Relations Review*, 16(3) (Fall 1990), p. 21.

[60] Ibid.

[61] Ibid.

[62] L. L. Golden, *Only by Public Consent: American Corporations Search for Favorable Opinion* (New York: Hawthorn Books, 1968), pp. 37–39.

[63] George Creel, *How We Advertised America: The First Telling of the Amazing Story of the Committees on Public Information That Carried the Gospel of Americanism to Every Corner of the Globe* (New York: Harper & Row, 1920), especially pp. 18–19.

[64] Bernays volunteered to help on the Foreign Press Bureau and had to have his loyalty investigated by military intelligence, since he was Austrian-born.

[65] *Who Was Who in America*, vol. 3 (Chicago: Marquis–Who's Who, Inc., 1960), p. 129.

[66] Peggy J. Kreshel, "The 'Culture' of J. Walter Thompson, 1915–1925," *Public Relations Review*, 16(3) (Fall 1990), p. 81.

[67] Ibid., p. 86.

[68] Ibid., pp. 87, 88.

[69] Cutlip and Center, *Effective Public Relations*, 4th ed., p. 90.

[70] Bernays, *Public Relations*, p. 84.

[71] Walter Lippmann, in Clinton Rossiter and James Lare, ed., *The Essential Lippmann* (New York: Vintage Books, 1963), p. 96.

72 Golden, *Only by Public Consent*, pp. 37–39.

73 Cutlip and Center, *Effective Public Relations*, 4th ed., p. 91. See also George Griswold, Jr., "How AT&T Public Relations Policies Developed," *Public Relations Quarterly*, 12 (Fall 1967), pp. 7–16.

74 Golden, *Only by Public Consent*, p. 386.

75 Cutlip and Center, *Effective Public Relations*, 4th ed., pp. 674, 675.

76 Philip Meyer, *Precision Journalism* (Bloomington: Indiana University Press, 1973), pp. 144–45; see also George H. Gallup and Saul Forbes Rae, *The Pulse of Democracy* (New York: Simon & Schuster, 1940), pp. 41–56.

77 Bernays, *Public Relations*, p. 112.

78 Ross, *Image Merchants*, p. 25.

79 Golden, *Only by Public Consent*, p. 386.

80 Ross, *Image Merchants*, p. 27.

81 Bernays, *Public Relations*, p. 112.

82 George Juergens, *News From the White House: The Presidential Press Relationship in the Progressive Era* (Chicago: University of Chicago Press, 1981), p. 29.

83 Rodger Streitmatter, "The Rise and Triumph of the White House Photo Opportunity," *Journalism Quarterly*, 65(4) (Winter 1988), pp. 981–86.

84 Ibid.

85 Ross, *Image Merchants*, p. 102.

86 Charles S. Steinberg, *The Creation of Consent* (New York: Hastings House, 1975), p. 27.

87 Bernays, *Public Relations*, p. 145.

88 Richard Meran Barsam, *The Nonfiction Film* (New York: E. P. Dutton, 1973), p. 129.

89 Ibid., pp. 151–56.

90 Golden, *Only by Public Consent*, pp. 163–72.

91 Ross, *Image Merchants*, p. 93.

92 Ibid., pp. 87–88.

93 Cutlip and Center, *Effective Public Relations*, 4th ed., p. 673. See also comments in Golden, *Only by Public Consent*, pp. 347–50, and the Public Relations Society of America.

94 Richard W. Darrow et al., *Public Relations Handbook* (Chicago: Dartnell Corporation, 1967), pp. 55–56.

95 *Facts on File*, vol. 17, "National Affairs" (New York: Facts on File, 1957), p. 116.

96 "The Railroad–Truckers Brawl," *Fortune* (June 1953), pp. 137–39, 198–204.

97 PRSA *Register*. See also Golden, *Only by Public Consent*, pp. 347–50.

98 Ibid. (PRSA).

99 Ibid.

100 Stephen A. Greyser and Steven L. Diamond, "Business Is Adapting to Consumerism," *Harvard Business Review* (September–October 1974), p. 38.

101 Public Relations Society of America, "Frustration Shock," slide presentation script, 1974, p. 2. [Hereafter cited as PRSA, 1974.]

102 Greyser and Diamond, "Business Is Adapting," p. 38.

103 Rebecca Smith, "Before Nader, there was Helen Nelson," *Dallas Morning News* (Sept. 24, 1995), p. 7F.

104 PRSA, 1974, p. 7.

105 Smith, "Before Nader," p. 7F.

106 Ralph Nader, "A Citizen's Guide to the American Economy," in Robert R. Evans, ed., *Social Movements* (Chicago: Rand McNally College Publishing, 1973), p. 217.

107 Edgar Chasteen, "Public Accommodations," in Robert R. Evans, ed., *Social Movements* (Chicago: Rand McNally College Publishing, 1973), p. 379.

108 PRSA, 1974, pp. 3–4.

109 D. J. Aulik and L. J. Saleson, "Client Satisfaction: Conceptualization, Measurement, and Model Development—A Perspective," paper presented at School of Business, University of Wisconsin at Madison, May 12, 1975.

110 Nader, "A Citizen's Guide," p. 220.

111 PRSA, 1974, p. 3.

112 According to the 1970 U.S. Census, this age group accounted for 11 percent of the population.

113 Louise Cook, "Consumer Voices Being Heard," *Fort Worth Evening Star-Telegram* (May 18, 1976), p. 7A.

114 Anthony M. Orum, ed., *The seeds of Politics: Youth and Politics in America* (Englewood Cliffs, N.J.: Prentice-Hall, 1972), p. 3.

115 Robert Glessing, *The Underground Press in America* (Bloomington: Indiana University Press, 1970), p. 51.

116 *1966 Facts On File*, p. 526.

117 Bo Burlingham, "Popular Politics," *Economic Working Papers* (Summer 1974), pp. 5–14. See also Cook, "Consumer Voices," op. cit.; Richard Flacks, "The Liberated Generation," in Orum, ed., *The Seeds of Politics*, pp. 267–68; Orum, *The Seeds of Politics* p. 3.

118 PRSA, 1974, p. 1.

[119] Ibid., p. 3.

[120] 1967 *Facts on File*, p. 85.

[121] 1971 *Facts on File*, p. 801.

[122] 1970 *Facts on File*, p. 834.

[123] 1973 *Facts on File*, p. 84.

[124] Aulik and Saleson,"Client Satisfaction," p. 2.

[125] Sylvia Porter, "'Fair Deal' Wanted, Anybody Listening?" *Dallas Morning News,* May 18, 1977, p. 5C.

[126] David G. Clark and William B. Blankenburg, *You and Media* (San Francisco: Canfield Press, 1973), p. 175.

[127] 1970 *Facts on File*, p. 830.

[128] *Facts on File*, vol. 29, "U.S. Developments" (New York: Facts on File, 1969), pp. 266–67; see also vol. 28, p. 625.

[129] Ibid.

[130] Alexander Cockburn and Andrew Cockburn, "Flacks: They Clarify, They Edify, They Stupify—They're PR Specialists and They Get Paid to Change Your Mind," *Playboy* (January 1987), pp. 195–96.

[131] Ibid., p. 196.

[132] Andrew Hacker, "Survey of the 70s," *Britannica Book of the Year, 1980*, pp. 129–37.

[133] Dave Montgomery, "A Texan Meets the Press (and Says a Little Prayer)," *Fort Worth Star Telegram* (April 10, 1983), p. 29A.

[134] Sidney Blumenthal, "Brave New World: Marketing the President," Dallas Morning News (September 20, 1981), p. G1.

[135] Ibid.

[136] Maureen Santini, "Presidential Spokesman Speaks on Life under Fire," *Fort Worth Star Telegram* (February 22, 1983), pp. 1, 2.

[137] Streitmatter, "Rise and Triumph of White House Photo Opportunity," p. 985.

[138] Howard Greene, "USIA's TV Network Could Be 'Most Powerful' Propaganda Instrument in History of World," *TV Guide*, 1987, news release, pp. 27–29.

[139] Randall Rothenberg, "Brits Buy Up the Ad Business," *New York Times Magazine* (July 2, 1989), p. 14.

[140] Tom Duncan, Clarke Caywood, and Doug Newsom, "Preparing Advertising and Public Relations Students for the Communications Industry in the 21st Century." Report of the Task Force on Integrated Communications (December 1993), Appendix C.

[141] PR Strategies Staff, "Foreign Buy-outs of U.S. Companies Set up New PR Challenge," *PR Strategies*, 1(1) (February 1–15, 1988), p. 4.

[142] Ibid.

[143] Carolyn Cline, Hank Smith, Nancy Johnson, Elizabeth Lance Toth, Judy VanSlyke Turk, and Lynne Masel Walters, "The Velvet Ghetto" (San Francisco: IABC Foundation, summary report, 1986).

[144] Richard Morin, "And How Did the Voters Judge the Media," *Washington Post National Weekly Edition* (December 5–11, 1994), p. 37; Dennis Farney, "Elite Theory, Have Liberals Ignored 'Have-Less' Whites at their Own Peril," *Wall Street Journal* (December 14, 1994), p. 1.

Selected readings, activities and assignments appropriate to this chapter can be found in the *Instructor's Guide* or on InfoTrac if you are using the InfoTrac College Edition.

CHAPTER 3

PR TRENDS

*Public relations has now reached its Rubicon . . . Because public relations, as a vocation, is saddled with disagreement as to its identity and confusion regarding its direction, it cannot step boldly into the new century without first re-evaluating **what it is** and **where it is going.***

EDWARD L. BERNAYS (1992)

[T]he field is searching for the balance between (a) communications products manufacturing and (b) strategic counsel & training of all members of organizations for their responsibility—since relationship-building is everyone's job.

PR REPORTER 41(1) (JANUARY 5, 1998), P. 1.

We will need to understand the overall, to broaden our view of the world we live in and of the institutions that employ us. To provide strategic advice, we must understand and identify with the business we're in—not only the public relations part, but the business itself, the business of our client and of our employer.

HAROLD BURSON, CHAIRMAN OF BURSON-MARSTELLER

The future of public relations depends to a large degree on success in defining what PR is and does, and how to measure its contribution to the bottom line. Some practitioners contend that people simply don't "understand" public relations, including the CEOs who hire PR talent.

When "spin doctors" work under the name of public relations, the whole PR profession becomes associated with their deceptions. Casual references to public relations in the news media often reinforce the notion of public relations as duplicitous and untrustworthy. A *Wall Street Journal* story about AT&T's justification for job cuts said, "He (Harold W. Burlingame, AT&T Human Resources) denies AT&T is engaging in a public relations spin."[1]

In a story about the increasing significance of investor relations, the field was written about as something entirely different from public relations rather than a subset of PR practice. The Associated Press writer said:

As companies report their latest quarterly earnings this month, the gift of gab is just not cutting it anymore.

Companies used to let public relations people tell their stories to Wall Street. But as investors become more sophisticated, companies are finding they need employees who can deal with them on an equal footing: investor relations professionals.

Put another way, blarney may be good—but financial training is better.[2] Even cartoonists get into the act (see the *Apartment 3G* cartoon).

The situation was serious enough in 1997 that the lead story in the first issue of *PR News* focused on the fact that most public relations leaders felt their own field needed a better image. "What we need is a PR campaign for PR—we need to do some image control," *PR News* was told by Delena Roth of Lord, Sullivan & Yoder PR in Columbus, Ohio.[3]

Part of the difficulty, as *pr reporter* sees it, is that the field has been undergoing two critical changes:

1. Finding its way beyond print-oriented mass communication practices that overcommunication, new technology and changing personal interests & values have made obsolete & ineffective —toward relationship-building activities that can motivate stakeholder behavior.

2. Sorting out the role, size, personnel makeup, assignment mode & services package of pr firms, while simultaneously reengineering the role, size, budget and accountability of internal pr dep'ts.[4]

In summary, what *pr reporter* was finding is the tension mentioned in Chapter 1 between public relations activities, or, as *pr reporter* called it, "communications products manufacturing," and genuine public relations which deals with strategic issues and affects organizational policies, or as *pr reporter* defined it, "strategic counsel & training of all members of organizations for their communications responsibility."[5]

Confusion within PR about what PR should be and do is part of the problem, but not all of it. John Budd has called for more doing and less whining about being misunderstood. "The hard truth," according to Budd, is that "we've been looking for solutions in the wrong place, the wrong way and on the wrong premise. It is not CEOs who need tutoring (about PR's value). We need to educate

APT. 3-G/ by Alex Kotzky

ourselves about CEOs. Do we really know them? We're selling; they're not buying. Why?"[6]

Budd explains the role of a public relations counsel:

> My premise is that the relationship between a CEO and his top pr officer has to be unlike any other relationship the chief may have with other executives—because to be truly effective you have to be his alter ego. You write his speeches, defend his reputation, protect his credibility. All of this is very personal. You and he have to be so close that you can finish each other's sentences and actually talk in a shorthand that comes only from total compatibility.[7]

As these comments indicate, some of the difficulties PR is having are self-induced, and some are the result of changes within the environment. We can see how dramatic these changes are, though, when efforts arise to rename PR itself. British practitioners now use the term "reputation management," while Burson-Marsteller, the world's largest public relations firm, prefers "perception management." Add to this mix "integrated communication" which unites all of the communications of an organization so that it speaks with one voice. Still others talk of "brand management," which comes from the integrated marketing communications concept.

THE GLOBAL ENVIRONMENT FOR PRACTICING PR

Technology has turned long-established business practices upside down. The ability to direct communication almost anywhere from almost anywhere has emphasized dramatically what is communicated. The global demand for public relations risks the possibility that, despite cataclysmic change, public relations practitioners will continue to do what they have been doing without rethinking the process and the consequences. In the USA where public relations is well-established, senior counsel John Budd says that PR needs to be *reinvented*, not just *reengineered*.[8] Add to that the late Edward L. Bernays' suggestion that PR is at its Rubicon,[9] a time of real decision making, and the future of public relations appears anything but clear.

Budd's comment is premised on the idea that too many PR people have become satisfied with the status quo, failing to voice "divine dissatisfaction" and always anticipating management's problems with all and any of its publics. Twenty-year corporate PR practitioner Dale Basye says it's worse than that. Most corporate PR departments in the USA now are run by "figureheads"—unqualified vice-presidents who don't understand the public relations functions, he says, and so are likely to accept cutbacks in their staffs and budgets, even to the point of putting the reputation and bottom line of the company at risk.[10] Consequences for the future seem dependent on restructuring and refining.

Restructuring PR Roles

While it is true that the corporate downsizing and subsequent out-sourcing discussed in Chapters 1 and 2 have affected public relations dramatically, Budd says that public relations in the future will emphasize two major functions: (1) editorial, and (2) public policy and programming.[11]

The editorial function Budd lists is like the PR communication or technician role described in Chapter 1. This function, Budd says, will "attend to the high priority, high profile, high leverage communication needs of the organization. These positions will be staffed by fast writing, highly skilled, facile, expository and news writers and researchers. They'll focus on principal corporate communication objectives. Local divisional or special departmental communication functions will be the responsibility—and budgetary obligation—of the subsidiaries, units and major product line departments. All special, one-time needs (e.g., video production) will be out-sourced."[12] This is what is called PR activities in Chapter 1.

The public policy and programming function that Budd describes is similar to the PR management role described in Chapter 1. Budd calls this "the heart, soul and nerve center of the operation. It is comprised of the principal officer—vice president public policy—and experts in two disciplines critical to sound public policy from a public relations perspective—social science (either sociology or anthropology) and opinion research. They identify major issues and make recommendations on public policy strategic actions."[13]

Bernays saw the management function as the core of the problem facing public relations now and into the future. Public relations, Bernays said, currently lacks an identity because the term means many things to many people.[14] To save the term *public relations counsel* from "meaninglessness," Bernays said public relations must become a genuine profession. And to Bernays that meant defining what one does and how one does it and maintaining control over entry into and exit from the field, through licensing.

As he noted, "Public relations should not become a catch basin for failed lawyers, unemployed businessmen [sic] and inactive stockbrokers hoping for some additional income. The risks to the public and the value of the vocation are too great. I am afraid that without some seriously considered fundamental changes, it will suffer a continued erosion of public faith and structural obtuseness."[15]

The problem with downsizing and out-sourcing is that many corporate vice-presidents (seldom called public policy vice-presidents) whose background is strictly in the business field of their employers, whether that be chemistry or engineering, are given administrative oversight over public relations, increasingly called "corporate communication." The reason given by many chief executive officers for putting someone other than a public relations practitioner in charge is that public relations people, while they are experts in communication (technicians), have not really bothered to learn the field they are working in (the real business of the organization).

The reality of the situation is that many people working in public relations today, not just in the USA, but throughout the world, are women. As one Indian public relations professional, Prema Sagar of Genesis PR, said, "Public relations is a field which is still looked down upon. The simplest example of this is that there are very few men doing this job." This quotation is from India, a nation where the practice of public relations and the education for the field are growing explosively.[16]

All over the world, it remains rare to find women in the management role of public relations. In companies in the USA, varying reasons are given for not putting a woman in charge of corporate communications. Women talk of the "glass ceiling" phenomenon that prevents them from breaking through to top management ranks. In multinational companies, the reason often given for not putting a woman in charge is that the culture in the host country may not accept a woman. Usually that isn't the case. As long as the woman is from another culture: she isn't necessarily expected to conform to norms in the host country's culture. This, many women say, helps those in the host culture bring about changes in the way women are viewed.

The fact of out-sourcing has meant that many more women are joining the ranks of technicians and suppliers of public relations talent—the editorial role that Budd talks about. The reason is that much of this work can be done at home. Women with children can work around demands on them to fulfill their domestic roles and still meet the needs of their clients. It does mean needing to get "instant" childcare assistance sometimes, but most women have found that this is a very manageable situation. Of course, not all out-sourcers are women—or technicians. Many are men who work in a counseling as well as a technician function.

The problem of not being taken seriously as counselors and managers remains an issue for women, though. Their increasing visibility in the field is viewed with alarm by some PR practitioners and with enthusiasm by others. one enthusiast is Tom Peters, co-author of *In Search of Excellence*. He sees women as likely to make better managers for the future business world because business "must become: less hierarchical, more flexible and more fluid."[17] The increasing economic and social power of women is one major ongoing trend in North America, according to Patricia Aburdene, principal in Megatrends Ltd. in Washington, D.C., and co-author with John Naisbitt of the best-seller, *Megatrends*. She also thinks public relations will take a leadership role in the future.[18]

On the other hand, many public relations practitioners fear that the presence of increasing numbers of women in the field is already causing corporate "layering" that lowers the status of the PR function on the corporate ladder. Others believe that, in a global society where women have lower status than men, delegating the PR function to women will denigrate the profession. Few critics are brave enough to voice these concerns loudly, but their murmurings can be heard.

According to Carolyn Cline, one of the co-authors of "The Velvet Ghetto," research suggests that "the major problem facing public relations' move into top management today may be not only the large percentage of women in the field, but the dominance of the profession by the intuitive."[19] An intuitive worker "seeks the furthest reaches of the possible and the imaginative, and is comparatively uninterested in the sensory reports of things as they are." This conflicts with the methodology of a sensate worker, who "prefers an established way of doing things, relying upon skills already learned, working steadily, and focusing on now." The sensate type of worker accounts for 70 to 75 percent of the American population, Cline says.[20]

For whatever reason—psychological predisposition or gender—women in public relations constitute an unpopular majority and face discrimination in wages and jobs. Of course, this situation might well change if Peters's view of what qualities are needed in management prevails.

Also subject to widespread discrimination are public relations practitioners of color, although their value has increased as businesses have begun to recognize the value of the ethnic market. Just as women have set up their own organizations to improve their prospects for success in the field, so have public relations practitioners of color. They also have their own professional organizations, although a few are members of the predominately white professional organizations as well. The discrimination that forces minorities to set up their own firms and organize their own professional associations may change if Aburdene is correct in seeing cultural diversity in the workplace as a megatrend of the 1990s. Due to a shortage of experienced practitioners in the labor market in the USA, she says, managers in the future will be hiring new workers from among women, minorities and immigrants.[21] Although Aburdene is talking about the workplace in general, her analysis could certainly apply to public relations. In the future, the more astute public relations firms and staffs will rely on cultural diversity among their own practitioners to maintain their sensitivity to issues and audiences on a broad scale. They will not hire a practitioner from a specific ethnic group just to reach that constituency. Aburdene says that managers will need to possess "superb cross-cultural skills" just to achieve successful superintendence of the diversified American workforce.[22]

Issues of ethnicity and other cultural problems are not restricted to the practice of public relations in the USA. Abroad, serious divisions of social class exist that are difficult to bridge even in a professional setting. Furthermore, in some countries, even where people of color are in the majority, discrimination about the degree of color persists.[23]

Managing employees in public relations, as well as in other fields, will be more complicated because, as tomorrow's practitioners focus on becoming more professional in what they do, their ties to any specific organization or institution will weaken. Public relations employees whose positions were eliminated in the mergers and consolidations of the 1980s found that what they needed was not demonstrated loyalty to an employer but "portable professionalism."

The growing trend on the part of public relations people to see themselves as PR people first and only secondarily as employees of a particular organization has some advantages for the field as a whole. Ronald Rhody says that, whereas employees see themselves as a unitary part of their organization, a professional should have a different perspective. While employed by a particular organization, the PR person must demonstrate something short of blind loyalty, because a professional "sees himself or herself as hired to bring expert professional skills or talents to bear on the problems and opportunities at hand."[24]

In some ways, PR practitioners may be reflecting a national trend in the United States—an increase in individualism at the expense of communalism or a sense of belonging. This extends beyond the workplace to encompass various other social, economic and political institutions. But while the increasing commitment to self-interest is readily apparent in the United States, it is not a part of all cultures. In fact, many cultures pride themselves on their sense of community and on their readiness to put the common good above personal benefit.

Understanding different perspectives is especially important to public relations practitioners who work globally and are responsible for employee communications. "Many communicators are not equipped intellectually, educationally and culturally to cope with globalization," says Taki Andriadis, president of Intercultural Public Affairs in Wilmington, Delaware.[25]

Inability to cope with the international scene may be costing U.S. public relations organizations their former preeminence in the world. Although public relations isn't unique to the USA, it did develop most rapidly in the USA, and for many years public relations expertise has been a major service export. But the recent change has been dramatic. Writing in 1990, Jean Farinelli of Creamer Dickson Basford in New York commented, "A decade ago, the world's five top PR firms were American owned. Today, only one is."[26]

Furthermore, Farinelli said:

> [A] study of 400 U.S. and U.K. CEOs found the British are more active users of PR than are Americans. Over half formally integrate PR into corporate planning systems, compared with a third of American companies. PR managers in 50 percent of the British companies report directly to the board compared to a third (generous estimate) in U.S. companies.[27]

She went on to say that "superb work is coming out of Europe," and she observed that the PR industry in Europe and Japan had grown to 15 to 20 percent

of the size of the PR industry in the USA, whereas only ten years ago it was considerably smaller.[28]

This trend suggests that the practice of public relations may be losing its association with the USA, and that it may eventually be defined in terms quite different from those we now use, as the emphasis shifts toward strategies and away from tactics. The two components that Harold Burson identifies in the public relations process are strategy and execution;[29] as he sees it, PR's greatest contribution is strategy:

> Our true value, our unique and vital contribution to our clients and employers is the knowledgeable advice we bring to the decision-making process. . . .
> [T]here's growing importance in the strategic component, in providing input that produces the most effective decision—first about what to do, then about what to say and how.[30]

The execution of the strategy, Burson notes, usually involves communication, which will continue to be important (and increasingly challenging) as the channels of communication—the available media—proliferate.

◼ Some Organizational Changes

Whether you call them "management and editorial" (Budd's words) or "strategy and execution" (Burson's) or "strategy and tactics," everyone seems to agree that these different terms describe fundamentally different categories of work in public relations. In most small public relations departments and firms, a practitioner cannot tell you precisely how much time he or she spends doing which. In larger operations, though, the way the two units work together affects the structure of public relations within companies and as stand-alone agencies or firms. A characteristic of both models is flexibility.

The number of acquisitions and mergers during the 1990s affected all types of companies, including those involved in advertising and public relations. For companies engaged in business other than communications, two ways of organizing the public relations function emerged:

1. the in-house corporate model, if the company is national or international in its scope, usually with charges to the business units within the company calling on it for services (a mix of strategy and tactics);

2. a small core of specialists with outside contracting for regional or smaller companies (primarily strategist with tactics services bought).

For communications firm/agencies, three models emerged:

1. the account director (strategist) for international communications groups who can call on resources from the firm/agency worldwide for the client as well as those of independent contractors when necessary;

2. the account director in each separate firm within the larger group who negotiates resources with other group units or goes outside for resources to independent contractors;

3. the account director who is only a strategist and either uses the client's own resources or contracts outside for all tactical help.

There are two significant outcomes of this reorganization: a more critical role for the strategist, and an increase in the accountability demanded from the strategist by the client or company.

Growth of the PR Role   The public relations function has expanded its role so that more types of public relations activities are now included as responsibilities of an organization's public relations practitioner. These include issues management, public affairs, community relations, shareholder/stakeholder relations, corporate contributions/fundraising (nonprofit), all types of organizational advertising and employee communication. The increased workload has not translated into bigger public relations departments, but it has meant that many organizations that never previously had a public relations person now do.

In the larger organizations, where the public relations function is well established, economic conditions have caused staff reductions. Typically, the workload from these reductions has been farmed out to public relations specialists rather than to larger firms. Many PR firms struggling to meet the demands of the expanded PR function have extended themselves to offer a full range of services to clients, and many firms associated with advertising agencies have taken on entire public relations campaigns. The tendency is for firms/agencies to handle campaigns but not routine public relations projects. The routine work—such as producing employee publications, newsletters and annual reports and developing and maintaining Web sites—has gone to specialists. Because of the complexity of global communication in some organizations, specialty media firms are often used to disseminate their news releases and to monitor their use.

Increased Organizational Demands for Accountability   Both within the organization and outside it, most public relations practitioners are experiencing pressure for greater accountability, in association with management's increased tendency to set PR goals and to demand evidence of their accomplishment. The evidence deemed acceptable is mainly physical, such as increased market share, successful media placement, funds raised or employee involvement in events. Few organizations use research about opinions and attitudes to measure changes in awareness, understanding and acceptance of the organization and what it is doing. In an occupation whose primary role is to serve as counselor and strategist, at least one major area of effort and achievement remains concealed because employers fail to perform the necessary opinion research.

Technology's Impact on Strategy and Tactics

Fax messaging, e-mail, satellite "meetings" and jet travel permit practitioners to manage, quickly and directly, situations that used to take at least a day or two to reach physically or to make sense of. The convenience that technology brings to ordinary day-to-day business matters is extraordinary. But there are problems, too.

"In-your-face" contact can result in culture clashes and personality friction that didn't occur as much when there were time lags and intermediaries. For some public relations practitioners, technology brings isolation. Since most of what practitioners need in order to do their job is now accessible electronically, practitioners can feel chained to their desks. Because contacts are global, there's an element of timelessness as practitioners work across time zones. It's possible to work around the clock, and sometimes practitioners have to.

Technology is changing relationships even within organizations. Employee computer networks make it possible to "know" someone online that employees may never meet face-to-face. Messages travel instantaneously on electronic bulletin boards; but this means that, if the wrong message gets out, it goes to more people faster and with greater impact. For some reason, computer messages seem harsher anyway, and electronic communiqués are often hastily conceived because the speed of the technology encourages it. Technology can be efficient, but it can be damaging, too.

It's possible to do all public relations research electronically—even survey research. It's possible to send all messages electronically. A practitioner can present a speech somewhere by videocassette, which is a bit more reliable than a satellite "send." It's even possible to get material changed from one language to another electronically. However, that particular technological option is only for those who enjoy living dangerously, since public relations requires interpretation rather than just translation.

Technology can also enable practitioners to learn about other countries and gain a world view. People in different parts of the world approach problem solving and communication differently. Media ownership and control differ dramatically across cultures and these differences affect what words and illustrations can be used in messages. Culturally based misunderstandings will occur, but misunderstandings occur even within cultures, and even within families.

Trends

The major trends affecting public relations in the 1990s are anticipated to continue into the new millennium. These include changes in who will be doing public relations and with what kind of background, how the Internet will affect public relations practice, the increased diversity of PR publics, a heightened need for good internal public relations, increased government use of PR, and growing environmental concerns.

Increased Struggles over Turf The demand for results and the spread of public relations activities has created new turf battles, since many individuals whose competence lies in other areas feel qualified to handle PR. Encroachment from marketing appears on the consumer relations side, from finance and financial accounting firms on the investor relations side, from human resources on the employee relations side, from political scientists on the public affairs side, and from management consulting firms and lawyers in the counseling/strategy area. As a result of the litigation journalism trend, there has been invasion from lawyers into the area of media relations, which previously was being contested for by former television news producers. Other PR practitioners complain that crisis management is often handled by outsiders trained in emergency and disaster response or by risk management specialists.

Organizations continue to take people who are specialists in the area where the organizational mission is concentrated and make them public relations directors—often because the PR people do not learn the nuances of the organization's business as well as they should.

Sometimes, turf battles may be solved by having the "encroachers" make formal use of public relations talent. Their increased appreciation of public relations as a result of this experience might discourage them from persisting in their "anyone can do PR" attitude. For example, the two most threatening encroachers—law and marketing/advertising—now use public relations firms.

Lawyers use public relations firms to improve their competitive edge and image.[31] The law firm of Winston & Strawn in Chicago is believed to have been the first to hire a public relations specialist, Loren A. Wittner, as a salaried partner.[32] Wittner, formerly an executive vice-president at Edelman Public Relations Worldwide, had practiced law before joining Edelman and currently works with the law firm's outside public relations firm.[33]

Having an in-house public relations person is not new to ad agencies, but having a public relations specialist on staff to help improve the position of the agency itself is new. Increasing competition in an era marked by recession has caused agencies to employ someone to look after their own interests, not just those of their clients.[34]

Internet   How PR will use the Internet remains to be seen. There's no question that the Internet can be effective for promotion, monitoring of publics, research, improving relationships with special publics like employees and for instant responses in a crisis. On the other hand, public relations people also recognize that the Internet can be an extraordinarily effective weapon for antagonists. There are no editors, so rumors can be generated easily on the Internet and gain not only momentum but also credibility. Organizations and individuals who are often the target of special interest groups are keenly aware that activists have discovered the Internet as a significant tool. Denise Jones, who gives workshops for environmentalist groups, says it is "the most powerful activist tool ever reckoned with."[35] Speaking for Greenpeace USA, Jay Townsend said, "We've always been frustrated at the limitations of trying to communicate complex campaign issues through commercial radio, tv and newspapers. . . . Through our Web page, people around the world can read about an issue or project that may not have been reported by their local newspapers. It's the ultimate freedom of the press."[36]

Traditional news media organizations appear to agree with Townsend on this point. Most major media have launched Web sites, and are likely to release information there before using it on the air or in their newspapers. This is often done simply as promotion for pieces in their traditional outlets. Some media, however, have used their Web pages to release information which they felt might be subject to legal restraining orders. Perhaps the greatest use of the Web at a single time occurred on September 11, 1998, with the release of independent counsel Kenneth Starr's report of President Clinton's relationship with a White House intern.

Generally, public relations people have to do a lot of monitoring of the Internet to keep abreast of what issues regarding their organization may be out there. The Web sites of antagonists, news media and competitors should be tracked, not to mention the chat room "conversations" on issues which may affect their organization, its personnel or products and services.

Increased Diversity of PR Publics   The publics addressed by public relations are more diverse than ever before, and the stereotypes that once permitted mass communication in each haven't worked for some years. More people are living with unrelated people in a family unit, and more people are choosing to live alone. There are many single fathers in the United States today—and even more single mothers. The age-bracket populations are becoming more evenly divided, so that youth no longer dominates. While economic and political changes abroad have enlarged the middle class internationally, in the USA many formerly middle-class people (especially single mothers) have joined the ranks of the poor.

Since married couples make up a smaller share of "families" than previously in the USA, significant differences in family and household income exist. The two-income family is looking at itself as an economic unit. The person with the best job offer is likely to cause a move of the household, or even a distance marriage with the partners together only on weekends. Some couples are separated by thousands of miles and keep up with each other by e-mail and phone. When there are children, they are likely to stay with the parent who has the most flexibility in being able to care for them, or even more pragmatically, where schooling and after-school care is most affordable and desirable.

The look of most countries is changing, and the USA is at the forefront of diversity in its population. There are more Asians in the USA now than ever before in its history, because many immigration restrictions have been lifted. Also, immigration from Latin-American nations is increasing so rapidly that Spanish is heard as frequently as English in some border states.

Organizations that are not sensitive to the complexity that diversity brings to a population have a crisis waiting to happen. The organization that owns Denny's restaurants, Advantica (then Flagstar), faced such a crisis in the 1990s. An incident with a group of African-American students in San Jose, California, accelerated into a seven-year siege of discrimination suits from minority customers in Denny's restaurants all over the USA. Karen Randall, director of public relations for Advantica, notes that today Denny's is a new company with zero tolerance for discrimination and a strong track record in embracing diversity. The restaurants have been cited in news media such as *Fortune* for this "cultural overhaul," and received the NAACP's Fair Share Corporate Award for minority business development in 1997.[37]

Heightened Need for Good Internal PR

You might expect that organizations' internal relations would be smoother than their relations with external publics, but that is not the case. The level of employee satisfaction has been low for nearly a decade. One cause of employee alienation is management changes. The dilution of affirmative action laws in the USA has also contributed to some workers' unhappiness on the job. However, several Supreme Court decisions on the subject of discriminatory firing have offset this effect somewhat.

A major factor in low employee morale is the failure of management to communicate with employees. The critical phrase here is "communicate with," as opposed to "talk to." Anecdotal information indicates that top management has no idea what the people lower in the organization think, want or need.

The problem with some CEOs, to paraphrase philosopher R. D. Lang, is "not that they're in the dark—but that they're in the dark that they're in the dark." This observation introduced an article by Steve Rivkin titled "Mutiny in the Cafeteria," published in PRSA's, *The Strategist*.[38] The article simulated a pep talk by a CEO, how he assumed his employees responded to it, and the real conversa-

tion that occurred after he left. The situation was imagined, but the reality isn't. As countless employee opinion surveys of the 1990s revealed, employees are "disgruntled, disenchanted, disaffected and highly skeptical." The result, Rivkin concludes, is the risk of a "steady decline in employee morale and productivity."[39] That, and a bad interaction with the organization's other publics. This can hurt the organization's reputation, since employees are any organization's PR front line.

Growing Government Use of PR

All governments are making increasing use of public relations, especially as many of the previously centralized Eastern European governments undertake a democratization process. Developing nations (some of which are democracies) frequently have a critical need for public relations. According to Saudi Arabian professor Abdulrahman H. Al-Enad, a considerable gap may exist between the expectations of citizens and the actual benefits that a government still engaged in building infrastructure can deliver. He sees a pressing need to develop a realistic understanding between the citizens and the government.[40] The role of public relations has often been poorly understood by the USA government, too, although any democracy depends on the consent of its citizens. Harold Burson states it succinctly: "Call it what you will, but there it is: advancing information in the public forum, for the purpose of contributing to public opinion. That is public relations. It's implicit to the democratic process."[41]

Another thing implicit to the democratic process is the opportunity for feedback. But, because this remains a problem in the USA, special interest groups have grown to fill the void. Finding ways to respond to government actions is even harder in developing nations that traditionally have a more hierarchical communication system. If governments and their citizens can find ways to communicate better, the result should be an improved level of political and economic stability. Public relations can help develop such relationships in democratizing and developing nations, but PR practitioners must be well trained in understanding different cultures and in communicating among them.

Increased Environmental Concerns Concern for the "environment" within an organization is critical, but many organizations see a marketing advantage in devoting at least public attention to the global environment, as well. However, the global environment is not an easy subject for organizations to handle, because it pits publics against each other in sometimes dire conflict, creating a no-win situation for the organization.

One of the more memorable international tugs of war between corporate interests and environmentalists occurred in the spring and summer of 1995 when Shell Oil, part of the Royal Dutch/Shell Group, announced its decision to sink its Brent Spar oil platform in the North Atlantic. Greenpeace activists launched a major assault on the issue, putting people on the tubular-shaped platform, and television showed Shell water cannons aimed at the activists clinging precariously to their perch. Even British Prime Minister John Major got into the act when he said publicly that he had approved the decision to sink the platform.

Shell defended its decision as environmentally the best choice. The problem was that it had initially gotten bids from local contractors to determine the cost of hauling in the Brent Spar and taking it apart on land rather than sinking it. Learning that they were not to get the contracts after all, the contractors alerted Greenpeace, which launched a massive and spectacular campaign to prevent the sinking. Protests came from all over Europe, including from some European Union leaders. Shell was correct. It was environmentally better to sink the platform, and Greenpeace later publicly admitted that some of its statements about oil being on the Brent Spar were wrong and apologized, somewhat, to Shell.

Nevertheless, it wasn't until January of 1998 that Shell and the environmentalists came to an agreement about what to do with the controversial Brent Spar. Shell would spend $42 million to salvage the platform, more than twice what it intended to pay to dump it at sea.[42] The platform was

to be sliced into sections, cleaned and filled with solid materials to be support for pillars in a pier extension in Mekjarvik, Norway. The town is near Norway's southwestern port of Stavanger where the Brent Spar had been relocated since the disagreement with Greenpeace. Although this plan was agreeable to both parties, it may not resolve Shell's public relations problem. The deputy executive director of Greenpeace in the United Kingdom, Chris Rose, predicted that the Norwegian pier would forever be associated with the Brent Spar and Shell's public relations blunders.[43]

Shell might have learned something from the ordeal of Johns-Manville, which was forced into bankruptcy by personal injury claims in 1982. Even the company name was abandoned partly to avoid its association with asbestos (although it was reclaimed in 1998). In 1990, then Manville CEO Tom Stephens told the World Economic Forum that the company was compelled to share its experience.

Among the things company management had learned, Stephens said, were (1) to listen to society very carefully, rather than relying on the law, because the company would be held accountable in the *future* for what it did; (2) to reflect on what is ethical, rather than what is expedient; (3) to control its own destiny rather than waiting for government to step in; (4) to be aware of the power of persistence and of how dedicated employees can help an organization through its problems; (5) to seize the environmental initiative. Our policies, he said, must be real, not rhetoric.[44]

▰▰▰ ■ FUTURE FOCUS

In the field of public relations, the focus of future challenges will be on credibility, accountability and responsibility.

Credibility From time to time, pollsters publish the results of surveys that ask people in the USA which occupations they respect. Implicit in the word *respect* is confidence and trust. As a group, politicians don't enjoy it, and neither do business leaders. There is no point in even asking about the public relations field per se as long as the term *public relations* is used pejoratively. "That's just a public relations explanation" means "That's just something said to make the speaker look good, and it is only slightly related to the truth." In that sense, public relations is considered by many to be a tool used by the untrustworthy to deceive the unwitting. Thus, neither public relations nor those who use it are trusted, and the very service that is supposed to help an organization win credibility is itself suspect. Marketing doesn't fare any better, since it is seen as just trying to sell or "pawn off" on the credulous some product, service or idea. The unstated but assumed view is that the product, service or idea is probably worthless.

Why worry about credibility for the future? There are two reasons: first, credibility is difficult to win and easy to lose; second, we live in a global village where credibility is not just a domestic issue.

Credibility is based on the realities of behavior as well as on favorable perceptions of that behavior. Public relations professionals face immense challenges in trying to maintain credibility for institutions that have myriad publics in a range of cultural, economic and political settings.

Will public relations practitioners be up to the task? In the 1960s, when institutions turned to their "public relations" people to solve problems, more often than not they found communication specialists—not social scientists who could tell them what to expect and what to do about the problems. A substantial number of public relations practitioners dropped out of the field during that time. What will happen now that the audience is the world? PR practitioners will have to understand media, political and economic systems throughout the world, but even that is not enough. To be effective, they will also have to understand the business of their own institutions, just as well as specialists in the field do, in order to explain the nuances and anticipate the potential impacts of policies to global publics.

Just as important, the public relations practitioner must ensure that the organization communicates with one voice, so that internal and external messages are unified and credible. This means establishing strong liaisons within every facet of the organization's activities.

Accountability   The second important challenge is accountability, which consists of providing substantive verification for the contributions of public relations and establishing a baseline for all publics against which public relations actions can be measured. This means that the contribution of public relations actions must be quantitatively measurable. When public relations people report to operations officers in terms that these officers understand, they win respect for their PR expertise and gain tangible arguments for their budgets. If public relations is ever replaced by marketing, it might be because marketing people are experts at measuring. They have to measure markets, and they have to measure results, so they become experts at offering quantifiable justifications for what they do.

In the past, public relations people claimed results and offered publicity instead of proof, while claiming that public relations was more than publicity and promotion. The future will belong to PR people who can hold their own in doing research, buying research and analyzing the resulting data. In many cases public relations people will be engaged in measuring changes in behavior.

Discovering what PR adds to the bottom line in a tangible way is the substance of a project, "Return on Communications," launched by the Swedish Public Relations Association. The project lists the five segments of business influenced by public relations: 1) markets, customers and suppliers; 2) investors and financial categories; 3) employees; 4) community; 5) leadership, strategies and visions. These are to serve as "main accounts" in a new type of balance sheet that looks at how public relations contributes to the non-material assets of an organization, such as awareness, confidence, preference, relationships and loyalties among designated groups of people who can affect profits (or resources in a nonprofit). Tools used in developing the evaluation include: a structure that focuses on four major groups—markets, investors, employees and community; a checklist that serves as a benchmark for monitoring an organization's strengths and weaknesses; a range of performance measures to assess non-material assets; and value links that tie the performance measures to factors that determine company profits.[45] The preface to the report, written by the CEO of the Stockholm Stock Exchange, claims that such evaluations would help to predict how companies might perform in the future. Traditional accounting, he notes, is based on past performance and isn't always a good platform for prognoses.[46]

Responsibility   One difficulty with responsibility is measurability, but another difficulty relates to the question of who is practicing public relations and with what credentials, how much expertise and how much current experience.

Top management expresses some exasperation in trying to identify acceptable public relations talent. It's not like locating a CPA or an attorney—both of whom come with formal credentials. (This is why Edward L. Bernays argued in favor of licensing PR practitioners.) Most people don't have any idea what IABC's ABC means or what APR represents, and certainly they have no knowledge at all of the PRSA code of ethics. The professional transgressions that this code forbids are precisely the things most people imagine that public relations people do routinely (see Chapter 8). They are even less likely to have heard of the standards set by the International Institute for Quality in Public Relations. (See Chapter 1.) In the future, some way will have to be found for public relations talent to be recognized by the public, and something other than self-declaration will have to be offered to justify functioning at certain levels of expertise.

PR people are also going to have to demonstrate real knowledge and mastery of the industry or field they represent, whether it be chemicals, banking, agriculture, music or fine arts. A CEO can't send a public relations person who doesn't know the field in depth to serve as a spokesperson to knowledgeable employees, to suppliers or to the trade press. You can't speak for the field without understanding it thoroughly and without knowing all the nuances of the written and spoken words that are used to describe it. A PR person who fails to master the field in which he or she works is limited to performing in the role of technician.

Another area of responsibility involves management. Whether it operates in a small office or in a large institution, management must make important decisions regarding budgets, personnel and other routine business activities. Learning on the job can be costly, since most PR people are hired for important jobs because of their track records.

Public relations practitioners of the future will not only have to be good, they will also have to be capable of guiding the best talent they can find—male or female. Finding the best talent also means making a special effort to attract minorities.

Four critical issues remain problems in public relations: the lack of a codified body of knowledge in public relations, one that incorporates work done in other countries as well as the USA; the lack of generalized educational standards for working and for teaching in public relations; the measurement of a person's career experience and education to control entry to the field (who gets hired with what credentials); and how one can be kept from practicing public relations if certain standards of practice are not upheld (control over exit from the field).

▮ Problems

Every field of endeavor has problems, but the difficulties that public relations faces are especially visible because of the nature of the work: counseling management executives whose decisions may subsequently be criticized as poor "public relations" moves (whether or not the action taken was what the PR person advised); interacting with globally connected media, so that PR mistakes are magnified; issuing printed materials that can later come back to haunt the organization because of factual or judgmental errors. The larger public relations grows internationally, and the more sophisticated its audiences become, the more likely PR is to be a target of criticism.

Research   Perhaps the most serious uncorrected problem in public relations practice is the failure of PR practitioners to use research. Millions of dollars may be spent on messages that haven't been pretested. Followup research is too often oriented toward exposures to messages, rather than toward the messages' impact. And PR planning frequently operates on the basis of routine rather than on the basis of serious study of publics and policies.

Area-specific Problems   Other problems are specific to certain areas of public relations practice—employee relations, investor relations, media relations and organizational counsel.

Employee relations involves two major problems: (1) how to maintain a strong PR front line (which employees represent) when many employees are in jobs, not careers, and when those who are in careers are primarily interested in their area of expertise and not in the organization that employs them; (2) how to get volunteer readers/listeners/viewers to review employee communications when employees have many other demands on their time and a great deal of competition for their attention.

Investor relations has at least four major problems: (1) how to make investors understand long-term benefits that may not report out well on quarterly statements; (2) how to involve individual investors who are buying shares indirectly (that is, through accounts or funds); (3) how to encourage employee investments; (4) how to capture and sustain analysts' attention.

Media relations includes at least two areas of concern: (1) how to develop continuity of coverage (that is, how to get media to follow an organization over time so that a deeper understanding of the organization is developed); (2) how to use specialized media more successfully to communicate to priority publics, given that no "mass medium" is truly "mass" in its ability to reach publics.

Organizational counsel (the highest level of PR practice in an organization) encompasses two areas that raise special problems: social responsibility and competition.

Social responsibility itself contains two major areas of concern: (1) how to communicate the good a company is doing, in order to create a climate of goodwill and trust in a generally cynical society; (2) how to coordinate all communications (employee, marketing, product/service publicity and so on) so that areas of conflict don't destroy credibility.

In the area of competition, two problems arise: (1) how to issue challenges without engaging in negative attacks (which tend to make already distrustful audiences even more so); (2) how to communicate advantages without hyperbole.

One fundamental problem in the field of public relations involves the connection between public relations practice and education for PR. Many practitioners feel that too many students are being prepared for public relations careers in the first place, and that many of these are taking courses in mass communication theory rather than learning relevant skills—although many PR practitioners also say that they would just as soon train a liberal arts graduate who had no skills. Since all schools accredited by the Accrediting Council on Education in Journalism and Mass Communications must offer liberal arts degrees, the presumption that a liberal arts problem exists constitutes something of a mystery. Actually, most university degrees require only about 30 hours in the major, whatever it happens to be; so out of 120 total hours, typically consisting of forty courses of 3 hours each, only ten classes (one-fourth of the total) are in the major—any major! Therefore, that particular complaint from the field defies easy explanation. The future of education in public relations, however, raises a number of broader issues.

PR IN THE CLASSROOM

The future of public relations education has to be considered on two levels: that provided for full- or part-time college or university students, and that provided for continuing education. Educators should be taking the lead in both, but they aren't. This lack of leadership may stem in part from the limited supply of public relations educators in academic institutions who are available to teach the burgeoning crowds in PR. In any case, higher education has not shown itself able to focus attention on continuing education.

Instead of coming to the educators' rescue with needed resources, most practitioners have focused on setting up their own training facilities. One reason for this is that many people teaching public relations in colleges and universities were pressed into service without having much experience in the field, and many practitioners had little confidence in what was happening in the classroom. Certainly they weren't looking at PR education as the "cutting edge," where practitioners could go to learn how to do their jobs better. The decision not to invest in continuing education at universities—even at universities where public relations programs existed—remains widespread today, and it does not bode well for the future of the field.

Growing demand for PR courses at academic institutions has increased the need for public relations educators with advanced degrees. In response, many academics with public relations interests began doing quantitative research in the field, but this made them seem even more remote to practitioners in the field who did not do any research and did not even pretend to understand it—even when they were buying it from commercial research organizations. This state of affairs has changed somewhat as more researchers holding doctorate degrees have been hired to work in the research departments of public relations firms. However, during the period when demand for public relations education was exploding in the USA the gap between education and practice grew, and the courses and workshops that practitioners set up outside the universities for people they were hiring primarily addressed "nuts and bolts" concerns. So much for continuing education at the university level in the USA.

Abroad, as education for PR grows rapidly, the focus has been on institutions of higher learning and on professional organizations.

If public relations is going to achieve professional status, it will have to switch to the mode adopted by law and medicine, where faculties teaching the field are expected to be at the forefront of the field's practice. In that mode, the field's intellectual resources lie in higher education, not in the practice.

Such a statement suggests that graduate schools for public relations should be centers for research and knowledge; and some are. But controversy continues, in the academic community and in the practice, over whether public relations should even be taught at the undergraduate level. Nevertheless, most PR jobs go to students who have learned public relations in undergraduate programs. In the future, universities will have to fulfill their responsibilities at both undergraduate and graduate levels and will have to live with the continuing debate over what courses they should offer.

Despite years of effort by curriculum committees and commissions made up of educators and practitioners, experts still disagree over what should be taught and who should teach it. Many academics, stung by criticism that they didn't know the field, have gotten experience on the side. Many practitioners who wanted to teach have gone back to school to learn how to do scholarly research.

A by-product of the push to require public relations professors to hold doctoral degrees is that they often learn about public relations secondhand without having gained professional experience. Consequently, rather than actually teaching public relations, they are more likely to be teaching *about* public relations. In some academic environments, this means taking the critical-cultural approach. That tendency is particularly evident in institutions which already use that approach to look at the mass media. Public relations, in that context, is seen as a related discipline.

This is not to say that we shouldn't have theorists taking a critical approach to public relations. That is needed in any discipline. But before one conducts research from that perspective, it is important to have some fundamental knowledge of how public relations is practiced. Globalization of public relations practice has exacerbated the problem. Most public relations practitioners don't have doctorates. Public relations is new to the curriculum in most universities abroad, so most people teaching have no significant experience.

A 1997 Gold Paper issued by IPRA, *The Evolution of Public Relations Education and the Influence of Globalisation*, reported the results of a survey conducted in eight countries—Australia, Brazil, Japan, Singapore, South Africa, Switzerland, the United Kingdom and the USA. Surveys were sent to chief executive officers and chief operating officers, public relations managers and consultants. The major finding was a need for continuing education. The question is, where will that come from and who will be teaching the courses. After reviewing recommendations and standards for mid-level and senior level practitioners, the Gold Paper held that public relations should be viewed, and taught, as an applied social science and a management discipline. But even if we agree that this discipline—and its attendant theory—will be taught in the universities, how to find an academic "home" for public relations is not obvious.[47]

The question of where the public relations sequences should be housed has been an ongoing problem in the USA. Most PR courses were originally developed in programs of journalism and mass communication, and the Department of Education's designated accrediting body for public relations is the Accrediting Council on Education in Journalism and Mass Communications (ACE-JMC), which accredits journalism-based programs, usually. However, news editorial faculty often have negative attitudes toward public relations courses, the students who take them and their own colleagues who teach them.[48] This creates academic friction and hinders advancement of the field's status, since news editorial faculty still tend to be the heads of journalism and mass communication units.

While some journalism and mass communication units would like to get rid of their public relations sections, speech communication units have generally welcomed them. Few speech communication units qualify for accreditation, however. Many authorities advocate teaching public relations in business units, but the business schools

scarcely recognize public relations as a field and certainly not as a management function—although some see it as allied (but probably subordinated) to marketing. Naturally, this low esteem doesn't sit well with public relations educators and practitioners.

Ultimately, the squabbling has unfortunate consequences for public relations education and practice. As one of this book's authors said,

> *Public relations educators, like those who actually practice public relations, haven't even been able to agree upon a definition of what it is they do and how they're supposed to do it, much less achieve the parameters of professionalism that should guide their endeavors. Is it any wonder, then, that public relations education—and, indeed the entire public relations practice—faces a lack of credibility and fails to earn support, encouragement and understanding?*[49]

POINTS TO REMEMBER

■ PR's future depends to a large degree on the success of a search for what PR is and does and how to measure its contribution to the bottom line.

■ The reputation of PR has been damaged by "spin doctors" and disparaged by the news media.

■ Confusion between public relations activities and public relations as a management function continues to obscure understandings.

■ Adding to the confusion are various names now being given to public relations practice such as reputation management, perception management, brand management and integrated communication.

■ The future of public relations is anything but clear. Bernays said that public relations must become a genuine profession, which means defining what one does and how one does it, as well as licensing to ensure control over entry into and exit from the field.

■ All over the world, women are still rare in public relations *management* positions.

■ Out-sourcing has meant that many more women are joining the ranks of "technicians" and "suppliers" of public relations talent—what Budd calls the "editorial" role.

■ Public relations practitioners of color are subject to widespread discrimination, although businesses have begun to recognize the value of the ethnic market.

■ Discrimination may decrease if cultural diversity in the workplace becomes a megatrend throughout the 1990s. Managers will need cross-cultural skills to superintend the diversified American workforce.

■ Inability to cope with internationalism may be costing public relations organizations in the USA their former preeminence in the world.

■ The practice of public relations may be declining in the USA, and the field may eventually be defined in terms quite different from those we now use, as the emphasis shifts toward strategies and away from tactics.

■ More types of activities are now included as responsibilities of an organization's public relations practitioners.

■ The number of acquisitions and mergers in the 1990s had an impact on the public relations function in companies and in communication agencies and firms.

■ Different structures for the public relations function emerged in companies outside and inside the communication industry. The most significant outcomes of the reorganization were the increased importance of the strategist and the greater accountability demanded by the client/company for measurable results.

■ The tendency is for firms/agencies to handle campaigns but not routine public relations projects.

■ Most public relations practitioners are experiencing pressure for greater accountability.

■ Few organizations use research about opinions and attitudes to measure changes in awareness, understanding and acceptance of the organization and what it is doing.

■ Technology's impact on strategies and tactics has introduced an element of timelessness as communication goes across time zones, and the direct contact that technology has created often results in culture clashes if the PR practitioner is unaware of others' sense of time and approaches to problem-solving.

■ Knowledge of different languages is increasingly important, as is an understanding of other countries' laws and media.

■ Organizations tend to take people who are specialists in the area where the organizational mission is concentrated and make them public relations directors—often because PR people do not learn the organization's business as well as they should.

■ The publics addressed by public relations are more diverse than ever before, and assumptions about the effectiveness of mass communication haven't been true for several years.

■ Internal PR is needed; a major factor in low employee morale is failure of management to communicate effectively with workers.

■ Increasing use of public relations is being made by all governments, especially those engaged in a democratization process.

■ Concern for the environment is increasing. It is international in scope, and the issues are diverse, numerous and complex. Managements will have to anticipate future problems as well as worrying about the current ones.

■ The focus of future challenges in public relations will be on credibility, accountability and responsibility.

■ Perhaps the most serious uncorrected problem in public relations practice is the failure of PR practitioners to use research.

■ The future of public relations education has to be considered on two levels: that provided to full- or part-time college or university students, and that provided to practitioners for continuing education. Educators should be taking the lead in both.

NOTES

[1] John J. Keller, "AT&T Tries to Put New Spin on Big Job Cuts," *Wall Street Journal* (March 18, 1996), pp. B1, B6.

[2] *Associated Press*, "Investor Relations Role Gets Serious," *Dallas Morning News* (February 1, 1998), p. H5.

[3] Tom Moore, "Issues 1997: PR Execs Hope to Boost Their Industry's Image," *Phillips PR News*, 53(1), pp. 1, 7.

[4] "Prediction: '98 Will See Profession Decide Its Future," *pr reporter* 41(1)(Jan. 5, 1998), p. 1.

[5] Ibid.

[6] John Budd, "Physician, Heal Thyself.—Luke 4:23," *plain talk*, a supplement to *pr reporter*, 8 (December 2, 1996), p. 1.

[7] Ibid.

[8] "PR Needs to be Re-Invented, Not Just Reengineered: Budd," *pr reporter*, 37(39) (October 3, 1994), pp. 1–2.

[9] Edward L. Bernays, speech at the annual convention of the Association for Education in Journalism and Mass Communication, Quebec, Canada, August 6, 1992.

[10] "Evidence PR Is Losing Its Value," *pr reporter*, 37(39) (October 3, 1994), p. 2.

[11] "PR Needs to Be Re-Invented, Not Just Reengineered: Budd," *pr reporter*, p. 2.

[12] Ibid.

[13] Ibid.

[14] Bernays speech, p. 4.

[15] Ibid.

[16] Punam Thakur, "Trends, in Their Own Image, Professional or Otherwise, the Business Public Relations Is Picking Up," *Sundays* (May 8–14, 1994). See also Doug Newsom, "Gender Issues in Public Relations Practice," Hugh M. Culbertson and Ni Chen, eds., *International Public Relations: A Comparative Analysis* (Hillsdale, N.J.: Lawrence Erlbaum Associates, 1995).

[17] Tom Peters, "The Best New Managers Will Listen, Motivate, Support," *Working Woman* (September 1990), p. 142.

[18] Patricia Aburdene, speech to the 1990 National Convention of the Public Relations Society of America, New York, November 1990.

[19] Carolyn G. Cline, Michael H. McBride, Kate Peirce, "A Functional Gender-Aschematic Approach to the Feminization of Public Relations: A Review of the Literature and the Possibilities." Paper presented to the Committee on the Status of Women at the annual convention of the Association for Education in Journalism and Mass Communication, Minneapolis, Minn., August 1990.

[20] Ibid.

[21] Patricia Aburdene, "How to Think Like a CEO for the 1990s," *Working Woman* (September 1990), p. 137.

[22] Ibid. See also Leon E. Winter, "Theater Program Tackles Issues of Diversity," in "Business and Race," *Wall Street Journal* (April 18, 1991), p. B1.

[23] Newsom, "Gender Issues in Public Relations Practice," pp. 107–17.

[24] Ronald E. Rhody, "The Matter of Survival," speech at the Public Relations Society of American Management Seminar, Palm Springs, California, June 26, 1990. Reprint #3124 by Bank of America, Box 37000, San Francisco, Calif. 94137.

[25] *Public Relations News*, 46(24) (June 18, 1990), Special Report, Part II.

[26] Jean Farinelli, "You'd Better Learn to 'Speak International,'" in *tips & tactics*, supplement to *pr reporter*, 28(9) (June 25, 1990), p. 1.

[27] Ibid.

[28] Ibid.

[29] Harold Burson, "Beyond 'PR': Redefining the Role of Public Relations," speech for the Institute for Public Relations Research and Education, New York City, October 2, 1990, p. 16.

[30] Ibid.

[31] Ellen Joan Pollock, "Lawyers Are Cautiously Embracing PR Firms," *Wall Street Journal* (March 14, 1990), p. B1, B2.

[32] Amy Dockser Marcus and Stephen Wermiel, "Public-Relations Executive Joins Big Law Firm as Salaried Partner," *Wall Street Journal* (February 27, 1990), p. B8.

[33] Ibid.

[34] Thomas R. King, "Agencies Use PR Firms to Attract Clients," *Wall Street Journal* (March 28, 1990), p. B6.

[35] "Internet Activism," *purview*, a supplement to *pr reporter*, 426 (September 1, 1997), p. 1.

[36] Ibid.

[37] Karen Randall, "Anatomy of A Nightmare: Denny's Discovers Diversity," *Public Relations Strategist*, 3(4), pp. 14–19.

[38] Steve Rivkin, "Mutiny in the Cafeteria," *Public Relations Strategist*, 3(4), pp. 20–23.

[39] Ibid.

[40] Abdulrahman H. Al-Enad, "Public Relations' Roles in Developing Countries," *Public Relations Quarterly*, 35 (Spring 1990), pp. 24–26.

[41] Harold Burson, "Beyond PR."

[42] Associated Press, London, "Shell Makes Move To End Dispute Over Oil Platform," *Wall Street Journal* (January 30, 1998), p. B6A.

[43] Ibid.

[44] "Nothing Like the Asbestos Nightmare Must Ever Happen Again, We at Manville Are Compelled to Share What We Have Learned From That Experience—Mainly About Anticipating Issues," *pr reporter* 33(26) (June 25, 1990), p. 1.

[45] "Blockbuster Swedish Project: Getting Relationships & Other Non-financial Indicators Included in Accounting," *pr reporter* (March 10, 1997) 40 (10), pp. 1–4.

[46] Ibid.

[47] International Public Relations Association, "The Evolution of Public Relations Education and the Influence of Globalisation: Survey of Eight Countries," Gold Paper No. 12, (November 1997), published by IPRA, UK.

[48] Peter Habermann, Lillian Lodge Kopenhaver and David L. Martinson, "Sequence Faculty Divided on PR Value, Status and News orientation," *Journalism Quarterly*, 65(2), pp. 490–96.

[49] Donald K. Wright and Judy VanSlyke Turk, "Public Relations Education: The Unpleasant Realities: Questions and Challenges for a New Decade." Report published by the Institute for Public Relations Research and Education, 1990.

Selected readings, activities and assignments appropriate to this chapter can be found in the *Instructor's Guide* or on InfoTrac if you are using the InfoTrac College Edition.

CHAPTER 4

PUBLICS AND
PUBLIC OPINION

As I see it, PR is defined in terms of public opinion and behavior. Public opinion is a powerful lever that can motivate an audience to a desired behavior.

HAROLD BURSON, FOUNDER OF BURSON-MARSTELLER

We can now distinguish ourselves based on our ability to deliver our highest value information directly and immediately—and in direct response to the perceived needs of stakeholders.

JEFFREY HALLETT, CHAIR OF THE PRESENT/FUTURES GROUP IN FALLS CHURCH, VA
AND FOUNDER OF NEW MEDIA PUBLISHING INC.

People work and play in the digital world. They inhabit virtual communities, where they socialize, find employment, share information. . . . This collection of fierce individualists is also a powerful community-building entity.

JON KATZ, NOVELIST, MEDIA CRITIC AND AUTHOR OF *VIRTUOUS REALITY*

Public relations or communications? Just as what to call the person handling a public relations job is undergoing some changes, so is the subject of that public relations activity. You'll find many references to *stakeholders*, rather than *publics*. The idea comes from the term stockholders—people who have bought into a publicly held company and thus have a vested interest. However, there are many others with vested interests in an organization, such as employees who may or may not actually own stock. Thus the term "stakeholders" has evolved to capture that broader concept.

Stakeholders can be employees, suppliers, customers, government, investors, a local community or even many local communities where an organization operates, special interest groups affected by the organization and others. The concept is a good one because stakeholders have expectations of an organization and the organization owes them some level of accountability. However, for the purpose of this discussion, the more traditional term publics will be used because of its close tie to the other concept in this chapter, public opinion.

IDENTIFYING AND DESCRIBING PUBLICS

In any public relations situation, whether it is at the management level or the communications/tactical level, you can't even start without first identifying your publics.

Every discipline seems to develop its own terminology; sometimes, the same term is used in different ways by people in different disciplines and professions. In this book, one exceedingly important term is *public*, which has a very specific meaning in public relations. It is essential that a practitioner grasp the distinction between a "public" and an "audience."

The term *public* has traditionally meant any group (or possibly, individual) that has some involvement with an organization. Publics thus include the organization's neighbors, customers, employees, competitors and government regulators. Publics and organizations have consequences for each other: what a public does has some impact on the organization, and vice versa. You might imagine that "public" and "audience" are synonymous. But in important ways they are not.

From a public relations perspective, the term *audience* suggests a group of people who are recipients of something—a message or a performance. An audience is thus inherently passive. But this conflicts with the goal of most public relations programs, which is to stimulate strong audience participation. To help resolve the semantic conflict, the term public evolved to distinguish between passive audiences and active ones.

In public relations, the term *public* ("active audience") encompasses *any group of people who are tied together, however loosely, by some common bond of interest or concern and who have consequences for an organization.* The best way to understand this concept is to think of various publics that you, as an individual, might be part of (see Example 4.1).

First, you belong to a group of consumers that, no doubt, has been well-defined by marketing people. You may, for instance, be in the eighteen- to twenty-one-year-old "college" market. This market receives a great deal of attention because—although you may not believe it—it is responsible for a vast outlay of cash. Second, you may have an organizational identity. For instance, if you belong to a social or civic organization—the Rotary, Lions, PTA, League of Women Voters, a fraternity, political action group, professional society or athletic team or club—you are a member of a public. You also belong to other publics because of your race, religion, ethnic group or national origin. You probably would not want to be thought of as a member of "the general public," and you're not. No one is. *No such public exists.* Instead, you are a member of many definable, describable publics. It is the job of public relations practitioners to identify these publics as they relate to the practitioners' organizations.

In traditional public relations literature, publics are divided into two categories: external and internal. *External publics* exist outside an institution. They are not directly or officially a part of the organization, but they do have a relationship with it. Certain external publics, such as government regulatory agencies, have a substantial impact on the organization.

Internal publics share the institutional identity. They include management, employees and many types of supporters (investors, for example). Occasionally, the term *internal publics* is used in public relations practice to refer exclusively to employees—that is, workers. This usage is unfortunate, however, because it results in employees being considered as unrelated to management instead of as part of the same team. Such thinking has a ghettoizing effect that creates serious communication problems. In a strong union situation, the separation is real and a team concept is not as likely. Still, the adversarial relationship can be healthy as long as communication between the two groups is maintained.

Realistically, the categories *internal* and *external* are too broad to be very useful in identifying

EXAMPLE 4.1
One Person's Publics

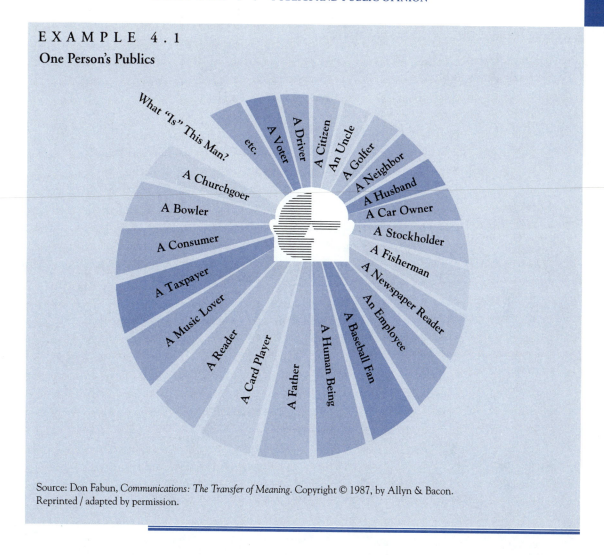

Source: Don Fabun, *Communications: The Transfer of Meaning.* Copyright © 1987, by Allyn & Bacon. Reprinted / adapted by permission.

publics. A more definitive typology has been developed by Jerry A. Hendrix, who identifies the following major publics: media, members/employees, community, government, investor, consumer, international and special (see Example 4.2). Every organization needs to thoughtfully compile a comprehensive list of its publics.

Any particular public, regardless of its broad category, may become the focal point for a public relations effort. When that occurs, the public singled out for attention is called a "target public" or a "priority public."

Not everyone approves of the connotations of the term "target" in the context of an important public. The "dean" of communication researchers, Wilbur Schramm, was one authority who early on disparaged it.

For nearly thirty years after World War I, the favorite concept of the mass media audience was what advertisers and propagandists often chose to call the "target audience." . . . A propagandist could shoot the magic bullet of communication into a viewer or a listener, who would stand still and wait to be hit! . . .

EXAMPLE 4.2
Discovering Major Publics

Publics for any organization fall into these categories developed by Jerry Hendrix.

MEDIA PUBLICS

Mass media
  Local
    Print publications
      Newspapers
      Magazines
    TV stations
    Radio stations
  National
    Print publications
    Broadcast networks
    Wire services
Specialized media
  Local
    Trade, industry, and association publications
    Organizational house and membership
      publications
    Ethnic publications
    Publications of special groups
    Specialized broadcast programs and
      stations
  National
    General business publications
    National trade, industry, and association
      publications
    National organizational house and membership
      publications
    National ethnic publications
    Publications of national special groups
    National specialized broadcast programs and
      networks

EMPLOYEE PUBLICS

Management
  Upper-level administrators
  Mid-level administrators
  Lower-level administrators
Nonmanagement (staff)
  Specialists
  Clerical personnel
  Secretarial personnel

Uniformed personnel
  Equipment operators
  Drivers
  Security personnel
  Other uniformed personnel
Union representatives
Other nonmanagement personnel

MEMBER PUBLICS

Organization employees
  Headquarters management
  Headquarters nonmanagement (staff)
  Other headquarters personnel
Organization officers
  Elected officers
  Appointed officers
  Legislative groups
  Boards, committees
Organization members
  Regular members
  Members in special categories—sustaining,
    emeritus, student members
  Honorary members or groups
Prospective organization members
State or local chapters
  Organization employees
  Organization officers
  Organization members
  Prospective organization members
Related or other allied organizations

COMMUNITY PUBLICS

Community media
  Mass
  Specialized
Community leaders
  Public officials
  Educators
  Religious leaders
  Professionals
  Executives

Bankers
Union leaders
Ethnic leaders
Neighborhood leaders
Community organizations
    Civic
    Service
    Social
    Business
    Cultural
    Religious
    Youth
    Political
    Special interest groups
    Other

GOVERNMENT PUBLICS

Federal
    Legislative branch
        Representatives, staff, committee personnel
        Senators, staff, committee personnel
    Executive branch
        President
        White House staff, advisers, committees
        Cabinet officers, departments, agencies, commissions
State
    Legislative branch
        Representatives, delegates, staff, committee personnel
        Senators, staff, committee personnel
    Executive branch
        Governor
        Governor's staff, advisers, committees
        Cabinet officers, departments, agencies, commissions
    County
        County executive
        Other county officials, commissions, departments
    City
        Mayor or city manager
        City council
        Other city officials, commissions, departments

INVESTOR PUBLICS

Shareowners and potential shareowners
Security analysts and investment counselors
Financial press
    Major wire services: Dow Jones & Co., Reuters Economic Service, AP, UPI
    Major business magazines: *Business Week, Fortune,* and the like—mass circulation and specialized
    Major newspapers: *New York Times, Wall Street Journal*
    Statistical services: Standard and Poor's Corp., Moody's Investor Service, and the like
    Private wire services: PR News Wire, Business Wire
Securities and Exchange Commission (SEC), for publicly owned companies

CONSUMER PUBLICS

Company employees
Customers
    Professionals
    Middle class
    Working class
    Minorities
    Other
Activist consumer groups
Consumer publications
Community media, mass and specialized
Community leaders and organizations

INTERNATIONAL PUBLICS

Host country media
    Mass
    Specialized
Host country leaders
    Public officials
    Educators
    Social leaders
    Cultural leaders
    Religious leaders
    Political leaders
    Professionals
    Executives

(continued)

EXAMPLE 4.2 (continued)

Host country organizations
  Business
  Service
  Social
  Cultural
  Religious
  Political
  Special interests
  Other

SPECIAL PUBLICS

Media consumed by this public
  Mass
  Specialized
Leaders of this public
  Public officials

Professional leaders
Ethnic leaders
Neighborhood leaders
Organizations composing this public
  Civil
  Political
  Service
  Business
  Cultural
  Religious
  Youth
  Other

Source: Reprinted with permission from Jerry A. Hendrix, *Public Relations Cases*, 4th ed., pp. 16–19 (Belmont, Calif.: Wadsworth, 1998). Copyright © 1992 Wadsworth Inc.

By the late 1950s the bullet theory was, so to speak, shot full of holes. Mass communication was not like a shooting gallery. There was nothing necessarily irresistible about mass communication or mass propaganda. Many influences entered into the effect of the mass media. The audience was not a passive target; rather, it was extraordinarily active.[1]

Certainly most PR practitioners would agree that a target public tends not to be passive and may exhibit unpredictable behavior. Still, the idea behind the term is valid—as a silhouette or a statistical profile, and not as a life-size, full-color portrait. Although *priority public* might be more accurate, the term *target public* continues to be used today to signify some definable audience for whom advertising and information are specifically prepared. The "mass audience" is indeed a myth, and using the scattershot approach to reach target publics is both foolish and uneconomical.

■ Identifying Priority Publics

To see how a public becomes a *priority public*, consider the example of health-care programs and

President Clinton's efforts to create a national health-care system. When any national health-care program is proposed, the opinion of the American Medical Association—as a public—is critical; therefore, pro-health-care-reform PR forces must be concerned with AMA members as a priority public. Priority publics are generally chosen for economic or political reasons. You don't try to reach everyone—only the members of a priority public you have *chosen* to receive a specially designed message.

Sometimes priority publics are determined by large-scale changes in socioeconomic or sociopolitical environments. For example, Otto Lerbinger identified several relationships that American corporations had to reassess to compete more successfully in the global marketplace: competitors (more cooperation), suppliers (more long-term relationships), capital (money), employees (partnership) and government (cooperative).[2]

As a public relations practitioner, you must carefully study your comprehensive list of publics and identify each priority public that is especially pertinent to your particular project. You must also

EXAMPLE 4.3
Prioritizing Publics

Prioritizing publics may be done in several ways. One informal method is called the PVI index: P, the organization's Potential to influence a public, plus V, the organization's Vulnerability to that public (which may change over time and in different situations), equals I, the Impact of that public on the organization. The higher the I value, the greater the impact. Here is a tabular form for "computing" a PVI index.

	P	+	V	=	I
Audience or Public	*Potential for Organization to Influence (Scale 1–10)*		*Vulnerability of Organization to Being Affected (Scale 1–10)*		*Importance of Audience to Organization*
————	————		————		————
————	————		————		————
————	————		————		————

designate publics not on your initial list that might be affected in the future. One way to isolate these peripheral publics (which are not normally a part of your contact list) is to determine how you would get names, addresses and phone numbers if you needed to contact *each* member of that public directly.

The PVI (Public Vulnerability Importance) index has been developed to help organizations identify target or priority publics. The potential *P* of a public plus the vulnerability *V* of the organization to action from that public equals the importance *I* of that public to the organization and to its public relations program (see Example 4.3).

Another measuring tool for PR publics, called PR Quotient, has been devised by Richard W. Muller. PR Quotient uses a list of forty questions with weighted responses to evaluate the importance of various publics.

The key to identifying and rank-ordering (that is, prioritizing) target publics accurately is *research* —finding out who these publics really are and what they actually think. The danger of not doing research and only *assuming* what a priority public

thinks or knows is quite serious. Alert public relations practitioners consider not only the collective or majority opinion of each public, but also the opinions of dissenters.

To develop sensitivity to the attitudes of various priority publics, a PR person must develop empathy for each one, much as an actor studies a role and then becomes the character. The PR person must ask, "If I were this public, with this background, these situations, this set of concepts, how would I react to the set of circumstances being introduced by the institution I represent?" Developing such empathy for a public—trying to imagine how that public will react—not only helps in planning for a specific situation, but also helps in media selection.

Each institution has its own particular *primary* publics, all or many of whom are *priority* publics— although the terms are not necessarily synonymous. A business, for example, has internal primary publics (stockholders, employees, dealers and sales representatives) and external primary publics (customers, government regulatory agencies, suppliers, competitors, the financial community—security analysts and investors in addition to their own stockholders—and the local community). At any time, depending on the issue or situation, one or more of these primary publics can become a target (that is, a priority) public.

■ Describing Priority Publics

Priority publics can be described in any of three ways: nominatively, demographically or psychographically. The nominative form of description consists merely of giving the public a name, such as "stockholders." The demographic approach involves looking at the public's statistical characteristics such as age, gender, income, education and so on. The psychographic method examines the public's defining emotional and behavioral characteristics. These psychographics often show how one primary public resembles another in interests, attitudes, beliefs or behavior.

Such descriptions are becoming more and more important as the diversity of publics increases. Telling evidence of that appeared in the *Wall Street Journal* in a story about jury selection.[3] In the USA one is supposed to be judged by "peers," which has meant that lawyers selecting a jury have used demographics. However, some realize that demographic profiles corresponding to their client's may not yield as favorable an opinion as expected, in spite of the attitudes attributed to certain groups. One assumption, for example, has been that women are less likely to vote for a death sentence than a man. But this cannot be relied upon. According to research by the American Bar Association, demographics account for no more than 15 percent of the variation in jury-verdict preferences. Then why are demographics so commonly used? Because they're easy. Marketers frequently make the same mistake. Assumptions about demographics are risky.

More sophisticated approaches examine core personality traits such as values and look at attitudes as well as lifestyles. An example is the psychographic casting done by SRI international which uses a system called VALS 2 to profile consumers in the USA.[4] The conceptual framework of the system is based on self-orientation and a definition of resources. The self-orientation concept says that people are motivated to choose what they buy based on principle, status or action. Their resources include not only material means but also education and intelligence, health and energy, self confidence and willingness to buy.

The VALS 2 system designates eight categories of consumers. *Actualizers* are successful people with high self-esteem who are open to change and whose lives are characterized by richness and diversity. *Fulfilleds* and *believers* are principles-oriented. They differ from each other in that while fulfilleds are practical consumers, looking for durability and quality, believers, having more modest income and educational levels, are more likely to favor established brands. *Achievers* and *strivers* are status-oriented. While image is important to achievers, they value structure and predictability over risk and stick to purchases they know will demonstrate their success to their peers. Strivers, on the other hand, are limited by resources but want to be stylish and often are impulsive. *Experiencers* and *makers* are action-oriented and want to demonstrate their impact. Experiencers are usually young, disdainful of conformity and authority and are likely to spend money on entertainment and clothes. Makers, conversely, are more traditional and conservative and not impressed with anything that doesn't have a functional purpose. *Strugglers* are so constricted by income and education that they are usually focused on meeting their most urgent needs. They constitute a limited market but tend to be loyal to certain brands.

Media cross referencing was used in a Roper Starch Worldwide global study that surveyed the views of 1.5 billion people. Roper interviewed 35,000 people aged 13 to 65 in 35 nations on all continents using one-hour, 1,000-answer questions in face-to-face interviews. The questions were based on what Roper called 58 "guiding principles" for their lives. (See Example 4.4.) From these 58, the top ten global values were: 1) Protecting family; 2) Honesty; 3) Respecting ancestors; 4) Au-

EXAMPLE 4.4
Global Values

THE SIX VALUE SEGMENTS

Altruists: slightly older, slightly more women than men

Strivers: more male, median age

Fun-seekers: more men than women, younger

Creatives: evenly split between men and women

Devouts: older, more women than men; anchored in religion, faith, tradition

Intimates: slightly more women than men, younger, focused on personal relationships

Generally, we move between groups as we age. In our teens, we're generally Fun-seekers. In our 20s, more are Creatives and Strivers. In our 30s and 40s we become more concerned with personal relationships and move into the Intimates group. In our 40s and 50s we move into the Altruist or Devout groups.

- Examples: Asia has a high number of Strivers; developed Asia, a large number of Fun-seekers; whereas developing Asia has more Devouts.

A CLOSER LOOK AT VALUES SEGMENTS

Devouts:

- Primary values: respect for ancestors, also protecting the family, honesty, faith and duty. Neither faith nor duty are among global top 10
- Lowest weekly TV viewership and listenership of radio
- Lowest media involvement, excepting religious media
- High concentration of Devouts in Middle East, Africa, Indonesia, Saudi Arabia, India and China

Altruists:

- Protecting family, honesty and justice are among their primary values; justice not in global top 10
- Average overall media involvement
- High concentration in Latin America, Russia, Kazakhstan, Turkey, Spain, Argentina, Mexico and Japan

Intimates:

- Primary values: family, honesty, stable personal relationships, friendship and self esteem
- Higher than average media involvement and they are most interested in media that can be shared with others, i.e., music, television
- High concentration in Judeo-Christian-based societies like Western Europe, Eastern Europe, the USA and the UK (4 in 10 Britons are Intimates)

Strivers:

- Top values are family, material security, health and fitness, wealth, respecting ancestors
- Next to the devout group, are the lowest users of media. They're too busy working for leisure time and social pursuit
- Print media is important to them
- Highest concentrations in Asia/Pacific, Hong Kong, Korea, China, Malaysia, Thailand

Creatives:

- Most important values are honesty, freedom, authenticity, self esteem and learning
- Personal improvement is important to this group
- This is the group most engaged in media, especially print media, personal computers
- Highest concentrations in Latin America, Western Europe, USA, Chile, Australia, Columbia

Fun-seekers:

- Key values are enjoying life, having fun, friendship, freedom, protecting the family
- Heaviest users of video and recorded music, average overall media usage
- Highest concentrations of this group are in the developed world, i.e. those with the economic ability to be fun seekers—Malaysia, Thailand, Japan, Germany, Italy

MEDIA USE:

- Across cultures and values segments, consumers say they watch between $2\frac{1}{2}$ and 3 hours of TV every day

(continued)

EXAMPLE 4.4 (continued)

- All groups describe the kind of shows they like as "interesting"
- Intimates average 2½ hours of radio every day
- Creatives are most interested in new media and books and are the most technologically advanced
- Newspapers are not an efficient way to reach Fun-seekers or Intimates, but Devouts and Creatives love newspapers

CONCERNS:

- The #1 concern in the USA and worldwide is crime and lawlessness
- For Creatives, greatest concerns are environment and quality of education
- For Devouts, the greatest concern is government corruption

SOME CHARACTERISTICS:

- *Sports and leisure:* while soccer is still #1 sport in the world, basketball is quickly catching up—and

is more gender balanced. Michael Jordan is the most recognizable person globally
- *Music:* "MTV generation" is real. "Music transcends cultural, national and even personal values of people worldwide." It's a universal language
- *Technology:* people in the USA, France and other places as diverse as Kazakhstan and Paraguay use new media (computers, WWW, etc)

3 INTRINSIC FACTORS DRIVE GLOBAL MARKETS

To understand people in a personal way, PR pros must take into account:
- personal values
- lifestage (where you are in your life, age-wise and lifestyle-wise)
- nationality

Source: Reprinted with permission from *pr reporter*.

---

thenticity; 5) Self esteem; 6) Friendships; 7) Freedom; 8) Health and fitness; 9) Stable personal relationships; 10) Material security. These values are used to describe six psychographic categories, including important variations in patterns of media use.[5] The way these are interpreted by public relations practitioners may be dramatically affected by the increased use of the newest medium, the Internet, although this is not significant in terms of "mass" use yet. (See Example 4.5.)

Psychographic researchers realize the difficulty of predicting behaviors from attitudes, but attitudes remain easier to measure than behavior (without invading privacy). Some research indicates that behaviors can best be predicted from attitudes under the following specific circumstances: (1) when multi-item, detailed and highly relative instruments are used; (2) when a common understanding of the attitude questionnaire is shared among respondents and between researcher and respondent; (3) when the behavioral measure is familiar to the respondent; (4) when the attitudinal and behavioral objects are defined so as to achieve common interpretations; (5) when the attitudinal response and behavioral response are defined similarly; (6) when belief intentions (probability that a person will perform a particular act) and normative pressures (group norms tending to induce conformity) are taken into account.[6]

To improve educated guessing before a final decision is made, demographic and psychographic information should be cross-referenced with other statistics. Numerous firms correlate such data with the outreach potential of various forms of the media. The study by Roper Starch Worldwide described above, for example, was one that effectively used media cross-referencing.

■ Media Research, Media Use

Audience research is used by media to help sell advertising time and space and by media buyers to de-

EXAMPLE 4.5
Public Opinion (USA) Toward Organizations/Institutions

Current public opinion of organizations/institutions:

Organization/Institution	Very Favorable	Mostly Favorable	Mostly Unfavorable	Very Unfavorable
Business	11%	55%	23%	5%
Media	7	43	34	14
Military	22	56	13	5
Federal government	4	34	41	18
State government	10	56	22	7
Local government	12	56	18	7

Rating ethical and moral practices:

Occupational Group	Excellent	Good	Only Fair	Poor
Federal government officials	2%	29%	47%	21%
State/local government officials	3	40	44	11
Leaders of business	2	31	47	16
Journalists	4	29	41	25
People like you	16	53	27	3

Media use:

How Often Do You:	Regularly	Sometimes	Hardly Ever	Never
Watch news on TV	72%	20%	6%	2%
Read newspapers	62	24	10	4
Listen to news on radio	50	26	15	9
Listen to talk radio that discusses current events, public issues and politics	18	28	25	29
Go online to get info on current events, public issues or politics	11	13	14	62

Source: Reprinted with permission from *pr reporter*.

termine how to maximize their budgets to reach their publics most effectively. Some media specialty firms offer combined databases that they sell to media buyers. Research information firms often supply this data at a lower cost than subscribing to all of these databases, some of which might be used only occasionally; certainly this is easier than trying to maintain a usable library of information in-house. Media relations people also use media specialty firms, some of which also offer placement of both advertising and publicity. An important

service that specialty firms can provide is interpretation of information from the database.

A confounding new problem for media use researchers is how to interpret "audiences" on the Internet. Although Web pages abound on the World Wide Web and "hits" can be counted, it is difficult to determine who is doing the hitting. Web pages are set up by organizations to put out information, publicity and advertising, and to engage publics, especially priority publics, in responding. Exactly who is accessing Web page information and responding is becoming increasingly significant to know in a global society comprised of fragmented publics.

One aspect of this fragmentation is the growing number of people, especially the USA, who feel inundated with information from all kinds of media. Specialized media invade their privacy by phone calls and unsolicited, unwelcomed mail. Of course, part of this comes from the ability to electronically track all kinds of personal information about people from just their daily living: credit card use, telephone calls, plane and hotel reservations, banking services and the like. The result of all of this data is the growth of services that sell information about individuals, some of which is sold on the Web. Buyers of this personal data can be anyone, but usually it is someone trying to sell something. The effect on marketing and market research has been great enough that the Direct Marketing Association now requires its members to publicly disclose how they gather and use data.[7]

Many people have responded by effectively "tuning out" all of these media, mass and specialized. This backlash against the information society has forced those trying to reach them with messages to develop new methods, especially more personal approaches such as meetings, conferences and other participatory activities. Also increasing is the use of intranets within organizations and listservs on the Internet to reach special publics. Participation is the key that media users hope will facilitate messages getting through.[8]

That sort of participation on the Internet, though, serves to underline the fragmentation of publics, inasmuch as it works through the building of definable constituencies. For example, one of the appeals of the Internet to teenagers is its anonymity, a quality which is also appealing to fringe groups afraid to speak openly on controversial issues. For the elderly, who were written off early as not likely users of the Internet, it has become a way to socialize and keep up with family, but it also has resulted in a large number of people who can focus on issues that concern them, such as medicare and medicaid.[9]

The benefits of these groups on the Web has been significant for public relations people who can use Web sites and chat rooms as a part of their issues identification and monitoring. The down side of the Internet for public relations people is that constituencies can attack the organization directly by setting up rogue Web sites, for example, which mimic the real site but contain negative information.[10] In other cases, the constituencies coalesce in much the same ways as any fragmented, disenchanted public. They are outside the bounds of traditional institutional spheres of influence and can affect an organization's operations and well-being.[11] Included in these constituencies are some important conventional publics, such as employees or customers of a particular ethnic group or women who have had some relationship with the organization, or those who may become concerned about an issue and use the Internet as a platform to attract others to their concerns.

Important Publics: Employees, Women & Minorities

Employees are always an important public because they are any organization's public relations "front line." Employees are seen as knowledgeable about the organization with the special insight of an insider's experience and information, so they are credible to other publics. Also, employees often have direct contact with other publics, such as customers or suppliers. Women and minorities may be a part of an employee public, but additionally, from a broader perspective, they constitute significant publics who can damage an institution's reputation. Insensitivity to women and minorities in all types of relationships has cost profit and nonprofit groups both money and status.

Employees The workplace has become much more demanding as organizations, profit and nonprofit, have cut back on the numbers of employees but increased the amount of work to about 47 hours a week, and for less pay. Employees are also insecure about their jobs.

In comparing 1977 with 1997 the Families and Work Institute found that businesses are discovering the cost of ignoring conflicts between work and employees' off-duty obligations. Child care is just one of those because twenty-six percent of the workforce also cares for an elderly parent or relative.[12] To fit in all the demands on their time, employees are seeking more flexibility. Some organizations faced with the costs of high employee turnover have examined more flexible work hours at all levels. Companies who have gone through significant downsizing and realized how costly it has been in terms of lost expertise are trying to make employees feel more secure by rewarding longevity. However, what seems to cause most employees to respond with loyalty is being made to feel valued.[13] The key to feeling valued for most employees is not salary and benefits as much as it is the quality of their work life—space and improved communication from management, which helps build stronger relationships. PR people can make important contributions in this area.

Women Although women are a majority of the world's population, many are in economic, social and political environments where they are a minority in terms of power. They are nearly half of the workforce, but fewer than 10 percent are in positions of authority.

Because most women are working in male-dominated environments with little authority, many experience sexual harassment. Only a fraction of those complain about it, but in the USA some of those cases have resulted in class action lawsuits with high profile trials. The damage is not just monetary. A company that gets a reputation for abusing women as employees or customers may fail to get both. This is an issue that needs to be addressed in any organization before it creates a problem. The same is true for treatment of minorities.

Minorities Minorities can be ethnic or religious groups, and they can be physically present in a nation or represented by a constituency abroad—one now connected to its counterparts any place in the world by the Internet. This is an important consideration in issues identification and monitoring. Although an issue can cause diverse groups of any religion or ethnicity to coalesce, it's important to remember that these groups often have no real homogeneity.

Hispanics, for example, now constitute the largest minority in the USA. The greatest number are of Mexican origin, but there are important groups from other places, such as Cuba and Puerto Rico. These groups should not be casually lumped together—not by politicians, advertisers or public relations people. Spanish is common, but not at all uniformly spoken. Their cultures and histories are very different. Moreover, the gulf between recent immigrants and those with many generations in the USA can often be even more significant than differences of national origin.

The sheer numbers have attracted the attention of businesses since the average income for an Hispanic household in 1996 was $31,582, compared with $43,133 for all USA households. As the financial industry, for example, has become aware of this large, relatively untapped market, firms such as NationsBank and discount broker Charles Schwab have begun advertising their bilingual services.

The problem is finding the right Spanish, for one thing, but there also needs to be some confidence that the translated message fits the culture. The California Milk Processor Board, for example, discovered that their "Got milk?" campaign couldn't be literally translated because the result meant something like "Are you lactating?" Worse than that, the notion of running out of milk in the household was not funny because it implied that the provider had failed to meet family responsibilities. A California-based Hispanic ad agency was hired to develop a campaign just for that state. Rather than focusing on deprivation, the campaign by Anita Santiago Advertising, Los Angeles, instead showed milk as an important ingredient in recipes handed down from grandmother to mother to daughter in traditional Mexican families.[14] While this was not an issue that angered anyone, the research showed that simply translating the original campaign would not only have been confusing, it also could have been very embarrassing.

Not being sensitive to the differences created by the diversity of cultures exposed to messages is part of what makes the role of issues identification and monitoring so important.

ISSUES: IDENTIFICATION, MONITORING, EVALUATION, MANAGEMENT

Identifying issues that are likely to create problems for a company or nonprofit organization is the first step in the process of monitoring not only the issue but the socio-economic and political climate for any event or development that could have an impact on any of the organization's publics. Not everything that appears on the PR-radar can be dealt with, but each must be evaluated for its potential to create some serious problem or to offer an opportunity. Monitoring helps management foresee when opinion is likely to build around incidents or trends.

Anticipating problems makes it easier to deal with them before a major difficulty arises and a crisis ensues. Not all problems result in crises. Some issues can be managed, at least from the perspective of the organization's response. In many cases, the emergence of an issue creates an opportunity, and even a crisis may in the long run be turned into a beneficial experience.

Handling issues demands an integrated approach to communication. The issue, the public, and the situation in which an issue develops all require that an evaluation consider strategies which use any communication tools available. This is where the artificial barriers in an organization, especially among its communication units, can be extraordinarily detrimental. The organization needs to speak with one voice and that voice must be clear and unambiguous.

Issues

The handling of issues once they have been identified is not a linear action that concludes when a favorable solution is achieved. Instead, as consultant John Bitter suggests, it is a cyclical process with five steps: (1) sensing the problem (research); (2) defining the problem (through judgment and priority setting); (3) deriving solutions (through policy and strategy selection); (4) implementing

them; (5) evaluating outcomes (see Example 4.6). The process can recur as each portion of a solution is worked through. The feedback causes adjustments in the plans, which in turn cause the next step of the solution to return to step one each time.[15]

Philip Lesly cautioned that emphasizing "issues" can lead to a siege mentality. He called the entire procedure *monitoring,* and pointed out that the process lends itself to discovery of both issues and *opportunities.* The term *issues monitoring* suggests the need to be flexible and responsive to developing situations and trends.

Lesly developed a comprehensive checklist for issues and opportunities (see Example 4.7).[16] Many organizations have issue-tracking systems, and some use a computer software program that performs a content analysis of daily news from various wire services.

Issues Evaluation and Management

In many instances, the appropriate strategy to use depends on the life-cycle stage of the issue, according to John F. Mahon of the Boston University School of Management.[17] He suggests three strategies: (1) containment, for an emerging issue; (2) shaping, for one that has media attention and therefore is on the public agenda; (3) coping, for issues that face legislative, regulatory or interest group action. When an issue is emerging, Mahon recommends dealing directly with it or with those who are promoting it, to defuse the situation. The most aggressive stance an organization can take is to shape or define the issue in its own terms. Shaping strategies include total resistance, bargaining, capitulation, termination and cessation of activity. If the issue has reached the coping stage, Mahon says, the organization has no choice but to change its behavior substantially.

Accepting the cyclical nature of issues, many theorists argue for the revised catalytic model (See the theory for this in Chapter 7.) In this model, the issue is guided through its life cycle toward a resolution that is in the organization's favor. This takes

EXAMPLE 4.6

The Issues Management Process

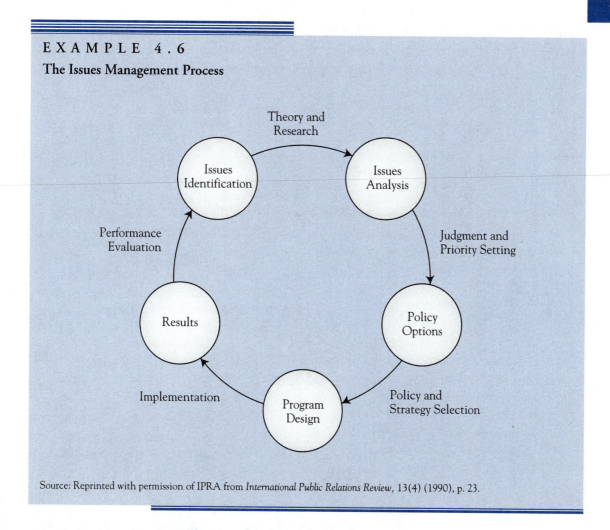

Source: Reprinted with permission of IPRA from *International Public Relations Review*, 13(4) (1990), p. 23.

into consideration an intense examination of the publics involved in the issue and their potential receptiveness to information about the issue, how that message can be presented and how the organization can frame the issue and set the agenda for public discussion to gain a favorable resolution.

Handling issues management internally is sometimes difficult, because it is likely to cross many lines of authority and require several levels of technical expertise. A process has to be in place to allow for efficient and effective response. One such process, developed by Dow Chemical, is shown in Example 4.8. In any event, enough publics must be

convinced that the issue is of *legitimate concern* to them to motivate them to take or support action in response to it.

Polling helps determine this, as do advisory boards, but the organization most closely associated with the issue must evaluate legitimacy and the implications of action in terms of each of its key publics before setting policy.

One of the hardest parts of handling issues is convincing management that an issue needs to be addressed. Richard Long suggests a four-step process: (1) state the issue or problem in the most specific terms possible, and describe the various effects

EXAMPLE 4.7

Lesly's Checklist for Issues and Opportunities

In the model developed by Philip Lesly, issues and opportunities are evaluated by following procedures outlined in Part II of his chart. Priority publics can then be established by selecting the appropriate ones from Part III. Appropriate activities should be subjected to the usual pretests, to make sure that the right message is communicated through the most appropriate medium, as Part IV of the chart suggests. Some of this is contingent on time elements, as Part V indicates, and on budget, as in Part VI. Built into each of the activities in Part IV should be some method of monitoring for ongoing effectiveness, as well as a system to accommodate final evaluation, as Part VII recommends.

Managing the Human Climate: Guidelines on Public Relations and Public Affairs

I. Structure
   1. Public Issues and Opportunities Task Force
      - Corporate planning
      - Operations
      - Finance
      - Marketing
      - Production
      - Law
      - Government relations
      - Public relations
      - Human resources
      - Outside counsel

II. Preparation for Each Issue or Opportunity
   1. Research what is known about the issue or opportunity
      1.1 Analyze causes
         - Technical factors

- Supplier fault
- Company's procedures
- External problems (blockages, weather, etc.)
- Snag in employee communication
- Snag in communication with customers
- Snag in communication with stockholders
- Snag in communication with government agencies
- Snag in communication with legislators
- Snag in relations with external organizations (environmentalists, minorities, etc.)

1.2 Study facts, reports, experts within company

it can have on the organization; (2) identify adversaries and friends; (3) develop a strategy that includes deciding whether to take the initiative; (4) determine whether to involve coalitions.[18]

ISSUES AND THE ROLE OF THE PR PRACTITIONER

More than any other executive (except the chief executive), the PR practitioner must know what is going on inside and outside the organization and how the organization's activities and functions interrelate and relate to those of others. He or she also is expected to bring awareness and objectivity to the job and to inject unvarnished, usable facts into the decision-making process.

The PR person learns about what is happening outside the organization by being exposed to pressures generated by various groups seeking support. The role of the practitioner here is sensitive and complex.

Sometimes the PR practitioner must play devil's advocate, raising all the salient arguments

1.3 Review outside sources
- Government
- Other industry
- Associations
- Libraries
- Suppliers
- Publications

1.4 Analyze the present climate
- In government
- Competitors
- Other industry
- Critics' groups
- In media
- In journals

1.5 Conduct opinion surveys
- Among groups affected by issue
- Activists
- Employees
- Stockholders

1.6 Determine what others are doing on this issue (avoid duplication, coordinate, counteract)

2. Establish company's position on the issue
  2.1 Write policy as guide for all in company
  2.2 Distribute on need-to-know basis

III. Publics to Be Dealt With
  1. Employees
    1.1 All

  1.2 Select groups
    - Executives
    - Operating staff
    - Subsidiaries' staff
    - Local plant and office level

  2. Government
    2.1 Federal elected officials
    2.2 Federal appointed officials
    2.3 State elected officials
    2.4 State appointed officials
    2.5 Local elected officials
    2.6 Local appointed officials

  3. Financial community
  4. Stockholders
  5. Customers and prospective customers
  6. Unions
  7. Suppliers
  8. Plant and office communities
  9. Academia
  10. Other opinion leaders—churches, civic groups
  11. News media
    11.1 Press
    11.2 TV and radio
  12. Other media
    12.1 Books and reference works
    12.2 Business publications
    12.3 Trade publications
    12.4 Alternative press

(continued)

against a proposed course of action and explaining which decisions will have an adverse effect on certain groups. Sometimes actions must be taken that will offend a major public, and management should be warned in advance and offered some way of successfully explaining to the public why the action is necessary.

Years ago, no one foresaw the role public relations now plays in relation to current issues and social crises. No longer primarily a communicator, the PR practitioner must act as an intervenor and relationship builder who tries to prevent a poten-

tial problem from getting out of hand. Indeed, the most valuable public relations activity consists of formulating and convincing management to take steps designed to prevent problems or at least to solve them while they are small.

Some of the tools the PR practitioner uses, such as personal contact and mass media, remain the same. The proper measure of performance is not how effectively the client's message gets across, however, but whether a flareup that can stop a client's business can be avoided. The public relations practitioner has an obligation to help

EXAMPLE 4.7 *(continued)*

IV. Activities
1. Prepare authoritative document on the issue or opportunity that can be the key source for all concerned with it
   - Distribute to affected government officials and personnel, colleges, journals, public media, other industry members, associations
2. Designate company representatives on this issue or opportunity, and establish lines of authority for communicating on it
3. Prepare executives for questioning by media, testifying to committees, conducting meetings
4. Prepare testimony before Congress, government agencies, etc.
5. Prepare fact cards on the issue and company sources (with home phone numbers) for distribution to media
6. Set up emergency plan
   - Line of authority
   - Facilities for the media on the site
7. Statements ready as responses to charges or questions
8. Press conference
9. Press releases
10. Fact sheets and photos for the media
11. Videotape

- Record events
- Provide proof of developments and deter media distortion
- Prepare news footage for TV
12. Literature
13. Employee bulletins or letters
14. Employee publications
15. Advertising
16. Scripts for radio broadcast
17. Customer information—letters and literature
18. Letters to stockholders
19. Bulletin boards
20. Community meetings
21. Speeches
    - Key executives
    - Others at local levels
V. Set Timetable (with built-in flexibility)
VI. Establish Budget
VII. Review and Evaluation
1. Conduct survey as a measure against analysis of problem or opportunity at the start
2. Analyze cost of manpower utilization in terms of alleviation of the problem or progress in fulfilling opportunity

Source: Philip Lesly, "Checklist on Issues and Opportunities," *Managing the Human Climate* 68 (May–June 1981). Reprinted with permission of *pr reporter*.

employers or clients conduct their business in a way that responds to the new demands made by concerned scientists, environmentalists, consumerists, minority leaders, underprivileged segments of the community and employees.

Internal and External Publics

Management's perception of priority publics—both internal and external—is not always accurate, as the following story demonstrates.

The owner of a specialty store with a reputation for expensive, high-quality merchandise was asked by other local retail merchants to join them in a downtown promotional campaign. The owner was skeptical. "We have the carriage trade," she said, "and a great deal of out-of-town, even international business. Frankly, I can't see that it would be worth our time." But then someone who had noticed that the specialty store was highest both in dollar volume and in individual receipts asked the owner where the store's volume of business was

EXAMPLE 4.8

Format for Issue Analysis

ISSUE ANALYSIS WORKSHEET

This worksheet is intended as a guide in developing constructive company programs for dealing with emerging and/or current issues. Completion of the worksheet might logically lead to the following steps:

1. An Issue Overview Statement or executive summary which describes the scope, intensity and direction of an issue; no more than two typewritten pages.
2. A Public Affairs Strategy Proposal which spells out a particular course of action for management review and support.
3. A Company Position Paper which defines, in a paragraph or two, the company's response and/or policy on the issue; this should be particularly useful in handling media queries.

ISSUE ANALYSIS

Issue: _____

Management responsibility for the issue:

Who is in *overall* charge? _____   Research: _____

Public Affairs: _____   Government Affairs: _____

Commercial: _____   U.S. Area Management: _____

Manufacturing/Division: _____   Corporate Management: _____

Legal: _____

Who is responsible for handling media calls on this issue?

1. Primary _____   2. Backup _____

Describe the level and intensity of media interest to date. Who are the key reporters and their organizations? Are any "themes" emerging from the news coverage?

What is the potential impact of this issue on the company's operations and/or its reputation?

Describe any state or federal *legislative* implications:

What, if any, are the state or federal *regulatory* implications?

What are the key *legal* implications, e.g., litigation filed or trial dates pending?

What do we know about the public opinion on this issue? Does the evidence suggest that public opinion is (or can be) susceptible to change?

What are the geographic considerations of this issue?

(continued)

EXAMPLE 4.8 *(continued)*

On a scale of 1–10 (10 being the worst), what is our vulnerability to:

____ Bad publicity	____ Congressional testimony	____ Community unrest/fear
____ Significant lawsuits	____ Plant shut-down	____ Security concerns
____ Customer backlash	____ Regulatory action	____ Product recall/ban
____ Employee morale problems	____ Drop in stock price	____ Terrorist activity
____ New legislation	____ Network television coverage	

STRATEGIC CONSIDERATIONS

What are the toughest questions we will be asked by key parties in this controversy? What are our answers?

What might [Name of Company] say and/or do to defuse or minimize this issue? How might it be turned into a plus?

Are there opportunities for a coalition approach to the issue? Who are our likely allies, and how can they help us?

Are there opportunities for compromise or joint study of the problem? If this issue has not yet flared, what steps might be taken to begin or accelerate dialogue with our adversaries?

What specific actions must be taken (and by whom) to improve our understanding of this issue?

Source: This format was developed by The Dow Chemical Company and is reprinted here with permission.

centered. Might the customers responsible for all those receipts be young professionals, many of whom worked downtown? They were the kind of people who could afford only a couple of high-priced outfits but were willing to make the investment to get the style and quality the specialty store offered. And might these people, since they were climbing the career ladder, tend to buy smaller-priced gifts simply to get the store's label? Intrigued, the owner did some research. She found to her amazement that, although she did have the carriage trade, which made substantial purchases, her daily volume came from downtown career workers. She participated in the downtown promo-tion and became as excited as any businessperson with a new market discovery.

Knowing who your target publics are implies knowing what to say to them and how to say it (see Exercise 4.9). You need to know how your messages are likely to affect the various publics you depend on for goodwill. A university administrator once forgot this when, during a talk to prospective students and their parents, he thoughtlessly said, "To maintain high standards of teaching, we try to have as few teaching assistants as possible." His remark, dutifully reported in the university's student newspaper, aroused a predictably hostile reaction from graduate students who served as teaching

EXAMPLE 4.9

Internal and External Publics and Media

PR people prioritize publics by knowing the characteristics of members of the various publics, which they discover through advance research.

Internal

Publics

Management (top and middle)

Staff and employees (union and nonunion employee organizations)

Stockholders

Directors

External

Publics

Direct (marketing communications)	*Indirect (institutional communications)*
Customers	Potential customers
Sales representatives	Potential investors (stockholders)
Traders and distributors	Financial community
Suppliers	Special community of institution
Competitors	Government (local, state, federal)
	Community (environmental)

Media

Personal (person to person/person to group)

Audiovisual (specialized media: films, slides, videotape, closed circuit TV, computer networks, i.e., intranets)

Publications (specialized media: books, magazines, newspapers, newsletters)

Direct mail

Exhibits (including posters, bulletin board materials and personalized items such as pins and awards)

Critics (individuals and institutions)

E-mail

FAX (facsimile)

CD-ROMs

Web page

Media

Personal (person to person/person to group)

Audiovisual (films, slides, videotape, mass media, specialized media available to external audiences such as slide presentations, etc.)

Publications (mass and specialized, including controlled and uncontrolled publicity, as well as institutional and commercial advertising)

Direct mail (personalized, institutional and sales promotion)

Exhibits (mass and specialized, including product packaging, graphics and point-of-sale promotions)

CD-Roms

Broadcast FAX

Listserv (e-mail)

Internet (such as one on the World Wide Web)

Source: Adapted from Doug Newsom and Bob Carrell, *Public Relations Writing*, 5th ed. (Belmont, Calif.: Wadsworth, 1998), p. 12.

assistants. The president did not set out to offend the TAs, of course; it was just a thoughtless remark, but one he might not have made had he been particularly conscious of the composition of his audience.

Awareness of publics and their responses requires heightened sensitivity, constant alertness and a lot of guessing, unless you have and regularly update a statistical profile of these publics. A trend in public relations away from the artistic to the scientific is noticeable. More and more clients ask practitioners to back up their advice with scientific evidence. As Wayne Danielson summarizes:

> The point is simply this: Interest in science and in asking the scientific question is part of the spirit of our times. Professional communicators cannot avoid these questions. They encounter them all the time. They frequently ask them themselves. And they cannot indefinitely avoid giving a scientific as opposed to an artistic answer.
>
> This is basically what communication research is all about. It is an attempt to give scientific answers to scientific questions about communication.[19]

Being aware of publics and their opinions depends on having ready access to information that helps give an accurate picture of where they stand on issues facing an organization. Institutions accumulate a wealth of information in their daily operations. Unless some thought is given to how that information might be used, though, it is useless.

Research for sound public relations planning can be built into a record-keeping system, provided that retrieval is also carefully considered. Information about PR audiences is critical. (See Chapter 5 Research for Backgrounding and Planning.)

The president of one research company uses a method he calls cross-tabulation of data to develop profiles of his clients' PR publics. He takes a company's own fact-finding operation and extracts from it a general picture of its publics. He combines this with more generally available research in the field, such as published public opinion studies, to get a broad picture. Then he develops a set of questions to use in interviewing small segments of these publics. The *quantitative* information furnishes the base from which he can go after specific *qualitative* information—a technique he laughingly calls "coloring by numbers." There may be a broad outline and a number suggesting what color to use, but until colors—the qualitative research—are applied, the picture is not complete. (See Chapter 6 on Research Methods.)

Internal Publics and Perceptions of the Organization   One important aspect of an organization's internal publics is their perception of the organization: its image in their eyes. A word needs to be said about "image" in connection with public relations. Most PR practitioners would gladly ban use of the word *image* because it's so often misused and misunderstood and because they don't like being depicted as "image makers." Nonetheless, *image* does describe the perception of an organization or individual, and this perception is based largely on what the organization or individual does and says. Of course, the organization seldom is perceived in exactly the same way by all of its publics at any given time, but we will return to this aspect of the subject a bit later.

A major contributor to virtually every public's perception of an organization is the organization's employees. To complicate matters, employees are themselves an organizational public that has its own perceptions of the organization. The role of employees is a significant concern in most PR efforts.

The lack of homogeneity in any public poses problems for the public relations practitioner trying to evaluate it. This is especially true of employees, since they exist on many different levels: salespeople, clerks and receptionists, technicians, professionals, administrators. Moreover, within each group, some people see themselves as embarked on a career while others see their work only as a job. Beyond that, subgroups exist in all of the main categories; professionals, for instance, may include engineers, researchers and lawyers.

The way these people work together and the way the administration works with them create a corporate or organizational culture, which strongly

Reprinted with permission of Punch Ltd.

affects how employees behave in relationships to each other and to outsiders. This in turn affects how the organization is perceived. Furthermore, with increased diversity in the workforce and with increasing international ownership and operational linkages, such differences among employees can be profound.

Collective perceptions about an organization by its publics, based on what it says and does, constitute its image. "Every organization has an image. The only question is whether it has the image it wants to have—in fact as well as in fantasy,"—according to Harry Levinson, a clinical psychologist. Levinson explains:

[Psychoanalyst Sigmund] Freud points out that individuals in any cohesive organization identify with the ego ideal [ideal stereotype] of their leader. As an organization expands and matures, this ego tends to become the collective aspirations of its people. Diffuse as this may sound, it is real. Industrial psychologists have long known that people, if they have any choice in the matter, will not work for an organization when they disapprove of its image, its self-image, and its ego ideal.[20]

In other words, employee attitudes often accurately reflect an organization's image of itself. Employees who are indifferent to the organization's ideal of itself may stay on the payroll, but they will do nothing beyond the minimum demanded.

For employees to react in any way to an organizational ideal, that ideal must be defined, communicated and understood. Many institutions have never tried to define theirs accurately, and the result is often a fragmented reaction to the institution, its policies and its products. In other instances, the ideal is too vague or is just rhetoric. When an oil company says it believes understanding and goodwill must be earned through the application of sound and ethical principles in the conduct of every phase of its business, but then embarks on a path of conduct that raises ethical questions, one might suspect that the company is only engaging in rhetoric.

The real difficulty is not in stating an ideal, but in living up to it. When an organization fails to act consistently with its projected ideal, employees, customers and the community are disillusioned. But while customers may simply take their dollars elsewhere, employees express their disillusionment in other ways, particularly if economic circumstances do not permit them to quit. If they stay, they often have feelings of depression, apathy, alienation and outright anger. These feelings are compounded if a company advertises that people are its most important asset, but its own employees have a different experience. They will, of course, see their leaders as hypocrites and will react with open or covert hostility.

Negative feelings may also result when employees cannot contribute toward attaining an ideal. For example, a company's pride in the steel panels it makes may be shared by all employees except those in the paint department, who know that the paints they apply will wear off quickly because the company has not invested in the necessary process for baking on the enamels. The resulting cynicism causes high turnover in that department and may undermine morale elsewhere in the company.

Clinical psychologist Harry Levinson has compared an organization to a human being:

> If you want to understand a person, you examine him. You may do so systematically, as a physician does, or you may get to know much about him over a long period of time, as a friend does. First, you try to learn who and what he is. Second, you try to learn how he behaves under various circumstances. Third, you want to know what he believes and how he sees the world, how he presents himself to the world and why he does so that way. If there is a wide gap between the image he projects and the person he really is, emotional conflicts are inevitable.[21]

The measures Levinson recommends for determining an organization's image are as follows (see Example 4.10):

- *What it does*, as evidenced in its products and services and in the way it regards its employees ("economic units to be purchased and directed" or "capable, mature people").

- *What it says*, through communication with employees ("exhortation and persuasion" or "mutual definition of common problems") and with its customers ("someone to be conned by promising more than can be delivered" or "to be duped by clever packaging").
- *What people believe it to be.*

Although the best way to find out what various publics think is by conducting scientific research, you can also ask a few information questions: (1) If the institution has an image, does it live up to it? Or does it say one thing and do another? (2) If the organization has an image, can employees live up to it? Or do conflicting demands, low pay or other factors render this impossible? (3) When an image change is necessary, have the employees been helped to make the change through participative management? (4) If the company has no recognizable image, does this result in confusion, limited identification and disparate values?

Internal publics are likely to be particularly sensitive to how an institution is presented to an external public because, as a part of that institution, their ego is involved. All sorts of communication from the organization to other publics must reflect most employees' experiences as closely as possible, especially the institutional presentations such as Web pages and advertising. Furthermore, all internal publics are seen as authorities on the organization, which is the reason they need to have access to as much information as possible.

Realizing that each member of an internal public is a potentially significant public relations asset could make most public relations directors' jobs easier. The best way to promote the use of internal publics as PR's front line is to make employees feel involved. PR researcher James Grunig says that a person involved in a situation seeks information, and that a person motivated to communicate about a situation is also motivated to develop a solution for it. For example, a city having difficulty with old gas meters that record higher levels of consumption than actually exist needs to inform those on the front line—the meter readers. They will be in contact with customers, and if they understand the problem and what the company is do-

EXAMPLE 4.10
Institutional Image

PROBLEM PROFILE

1. What an institution's employees think it is. ○
   What employees want it to be. ⬭

2. What an institution's management thinks it is. △
   What management wants it to be. ▽

3. What an institution's external publics think it is. ☐
   What external publics want it to be. ⬭

Difficulties occur when the two profiles overlap and the lines are not harmonious. For example, in problem profile 3, the public wants the institution to be ⬭ (buses to all major shopping districts on the hour, six days a week, for 50 cents fare), but it is ☐ (buses to three major shopping districts, 10 a.m. to 6 p.m., five days a week, for 75 cents fare plus area add-on tolls). The result is ⬓, a poor fit.

LEVINSON'S IMAGE THEORY ILLUSTRATED

	Problem Profile	Positive Profile
What an institution does.	○	○
What it says.	☐	○
What people believe it to be.	△	○
How these fit.	⧈	◎

Levinson says that an institution is a mix of what it does and what people believe it to be. If these fit, the image is consonant.

ing to solve the problem, they are more likely to communicate. If the company goes farther and provides them with information to give customers, the typical communication constraint—that it's someone else's job—is removed. If the company generally keeps its front-line meter readers, receptionists and so on informed, the effectiveness of the PR front line will be much improved.

Internal surveys to find out what employees think of their organization are now as common as external ones. Evidence suggests that labor strife can be reduced by *regular* employee attitude surveys. Such surveys often influence organizational decisions on personnel policies, work practices, communication, productivity, compensation, organizational structure and physical plant improvements (see Example 4.11).

The organizational behavior of employees who produce the corporate or organizational culture contributes significantly to the organization's image. Joseph F. Coates has described the concept of corporate culture as recognizing that every stable human organization has consistent patterns of behavior reflecting implicit and explicit beliefs and values. Coates says that the cultural characteristics of an organization are usually expressed in positive terms by employees, who often fail to see how outsiders may perceive the same company behavior or policy in negative terms—for example, as "paternalistic," "moralistic" or "intrusive into personal matters," rather than as "offering counseling" or "genuinely concerned."

Coates identifies two widely held beliefs regarding the corporate culture. One is that the culture comes from the top down. The other is that it determines or strongly influences a corporation's willingness to embrace change, promote innovation, tolerate dissent, encourage criticism, experiment and allow for other qualities that characterize a competitive firm. Organizations with especially strong corporate cultures *may* enjoy a more cohesive image, but they tend to be less flexible and don't adapt well to change. Furthermore, the influence of the corporate culture is also shaped by its environment (location), its business (for example, TV or manufacturing) and the primary societal

EXAMPLE 4.11
Production-Line Problem

Should you always take workers' complaints at face value? Think twice before you do! Maybe communications problems are the real cause of the trouble.

St. Louis public relations consultant Alfred Fleishman, in his [1973] book *Troubled Talk*, tells of a client who was having "all kinds of problems" at one of his plants. In this plant, two identical production lines existed side by side.

Employees on the first line complained about their physical working conditions. It was "too cold in the winter, too hot in the summer." There "wasn't enough light. The machines were too close together." Employees complained about high accident rates and other matters. Absenteeism was high.

But researchers noted that employees on the second production line had few complaints, low absenteeism and a low accident rate. So instead of making the physical changes in the factory called for by the first group, the investigators dug deeper. And here's what they found.

In answer to the question "How does your boss criticize you, in public or in private?" more than 75 percent of the first group said the boss always criticized them in public. This compared with about 10 percent in the second group. Other questions revealed similar differences between the two groups. The answers convinced Mr. Fleishman that neither new lights nor new air conditioning and heating systems would solve the problem.

Instead, the supervisor of the first production line was taken off his job and sent back for more training. The supervisor of the second group replaced him. Months later, a follow-up study showed that the first group's complaints had dropped sharply, along with absenteeism and accidents. Nothing physical had changed; only the boss.

Source: Alfred Fleishman and William D. Meyer, *Troubled Talk* (San Francisco: International Society for General Semantics, 1973); printed in "persuasion," 21, edited by Chester Burger, May 27, 1974, supplement of *pr reporter*, Exeter, N.H. Used by permission.

---

culture of its employees (for example, American or Japanese).

Typically, PR practitioners are not asked to convince employees that they should accept the corporate culture. People usually go to work in a place where they are comfortable. The more common problem public relations must deal with is *changing* a corporate culture when new leadership arrives.

Such PR efforts are particularly important in an era of downsizing that demands what communication consultant Jayme Rolls calls "transformation communications"—relationship communication that helps employees attach to a new reality. Rolls notes that a lack of congruence between organizational rhetoric and action results in employee withdrawal, anxiety or anger. If communication is authoritarian, employees know any organizational change for supposed improvement is only lip ser-

vice. Rolls says that communication should help employees keep in touch with themselves and with the outside world.[22]

Coates recommends that employees be "brought along" with a change in corporate culture through discussions and requests for their input, although he concedes that the job is not easy. Philip Lesly expressed more pessimism. He said it is akin to "turning over an elephant with a shoe horn."[23] People are more likely to change their jobs than to change their values.

External Publics and Perceptions of the Organization External publics are not the exclusive property of any institution. Any external public may become a target for public relations activities. For example, high-school students and recent graduates who might become college freshmen are target publics for university recruiting. Other prospective candidates for college are students in community colleges and working people who might want to return to school or enter for the first time.

Looking at the different subsets of people who constitute an organization's external publics helps PR practitioners avoid the fallacy of considering external publics as a "mass public." There is no such thing as a "mass audience or public." External publics usually consist of larger segments of people than do internal publics, but never should external publics be thought of as an undifferentiated "mass."[24]

External publics may be a supportive constituency—like the residents of cities that have a professional sports team—or they may be adversarial—as antinuclear advocates are to electric utilities that use nuclear energy. Both types must be considered in public relations planning and communication strategies. External publics also have a great deal to do with an institution's image. When external publics and internal publics share similar perceptions of what the institution is and what it should be, the institution's image is likely to be sound because it is consistent.

The perception of an organization's image may vary from public to public, and it may change over time, owing to significant economic, technological and demographic changes in the business environment.

Organizations should always monitor perceptions of their identity but must reexamine their identity under the following circumstances:

- When public perceptions of a company do not reflect reality. Vestiges of past management mistakes, poor earnings, environmental problems, and the like may still be having a negative impact.
- When external forces such as a new competitor, a breakthrough product, deregulation, or an existing competitor's new identity require identification countermeasures.
- When competitors are slow to form clearly defined and effectively projected corporate and/or product presentation. In this sense, identity is opportunistic and can become a competitive advantage in itself.[25]

In looking at relationships with external audiences, you should keep in mind the differences between attitudes, opinions and beliefs. Although some people use the terms *attitudes*, *opinions* and *beliefs* interchangeably, social scientists generally define each of them differently. **Attitudes** are tendencies or orientations toward something or someone—a state of mind, a manner, a disposition, a position. **Opinions** are expressions of estimates or judgments—generally something not as strongly held as a conviction, but articulating a sentiment or point of view. **Beliefs** are convictions firmly fixed in the bedrock of one's value system, embodying one's sense of truth.

Priority Publics and Planning Tailoring public relations programs to fit various priority publics requires careful and specific identification of the publics and their characteristics (through both formal and informal research methods), translation of this information into a sensitive understanding of each public's needs, and knowledge of how to communicate with each (see Example 4.12). To develop a program that is both real and realistic—not merely a facade of imagery that produces disillusionment and alienation when its insincerity is detected—you must have respect for and empathy with the target publics.

A public is a priority not only when it is centrally affected by a PR recommendation, but also when it is the group most influential in determining whether an idea, policy, event, decision or product recommendation will be accepted. Once identified as a priority public, the group must be studied for its other relationships. Insensitivity to the composition of publics, their interrelationships, their relationships with members of other publics (as well as to your organization), their ideals and their attitudes may lead an organization to waste much time, effort and money on public relations programs that bore or offend the intended recipients or have a negative effect on unintended recipients.

The importance to successful planning of knowing a particular priority public becomes clear when you consider the variety and disparity of different publics. A PR practitioner must have the

EXAMPLE 4.12

Tips on Influencing Publics: Advice from a Psychologist

This article, by S. Plous, Ph.D., University of Illinois, is excerpted with permission from Animals' Agenda, *the voice of the animal rights movement. The article is intended to stimulate more effective activism by critiquing tactics often used by activists. The author bases his insights on lessons from the nuclear freeze movement and psychological research on attitudes and behavior. The advice given is a succinct text for any practitioner to instill behavioral change.*

1. If the goal is attitude change, do not use graphic images unless they're accompanied by specific actions people can execute.

Both the nuclear freeze campaign and the animal rights movement began by relying heavily on graphic images of death and destruction. Although these images are essential to a complete understanding of the issue, they run the risk of pushing people away rather than drawing them in. *Disturbing presentations rarely lead to sustained attitude change, and they are worst when people feel unable to prevent a negative outcome.* In fact, studies show this can actually reduce intentions to act.

2. Go to the public instead of asking the public to come to you.

Most people are well intentioned but will never become directly involved. By recognizing the limits of public interest and improvement, activists can develop realistic strategies that capitalize on public goodwill without demanding more than people are willing to give.

3. Don't assume that attitude change is necessary for behavior change.

A large body of psychological research casts doubt on the proposition that the best way to change behavior is to begin with attitudes. Attitudinal change often follows change in behavior, rather than the other way around. Yet even when attitudinal change precedes behavioral change, sustained changes in behavior are rare. Any event organizer frustrated by the discrepancy between interest and actual attendance can attest to this.

Informing smokers of the link between cigarettes and cancer is easier than persuading them to quit. Informing people how a leghold trap works is easier than persuading them to support a ban on trapping.

Assuming attitude change would lead to legislative change, the nuclear freeze movement devoted most of its resources toward education and persuasion. The result was little legislation and no nuclear freeze. Of course, changing attitudes can be a worthy goal in its own right, and there is nothing wrong with allocating resources to this end—*as long as it's viewed as an end in itself.*

4. If behavior change is your goal, use moral arguments as adjuncts rather than main arguments.

---

acumen of a political scientist and the instincts of a politician to work effectively with, for example, the countless government agencies that directly regulate or indirectly affect an institution. A thorough knowledge of all levels of government and of the political system itself is essential, as is maintaining open lines of communication with elected representatives and administrators. Better to receive a

warning from a friend and have some time to cope with the emerging problem than to read about it in the newspaper and then have to improvise.

The news media are often overlooked as a target public by PR practitioners in their planning. Those who regard the press as "the enemy" generally find this attitude reflected in news coverage of their organization. In contrast, a corporation that

Moral views are difficult to change. It is much easier to gain support for a nuclear freeze by stressing practical advantages of arms control than by emphasizing the immorality of the arms race. Similarly, it's much easier to convert most people to a meatless diet by discussing the health benefits of vegetarianism than by discussing whether the Bible gives people dominion over animals.

Even though the activists may be moved by moral arguments, they should not assume these arguments will affect others the same way. Moral arguments are useful adjuncts, but in most cases, they are not sufficient to change how people behave.

5. Embrace the mainstream.

It's absolutely critical that activists embrace people from all walks of life. Otherwise, [a] movement runs the risk of being discounted as radical or faddish. One problem the nuclear freeze movement encountered in building a broad constituency was that many sympathizers didn't support a nuclear freeze per se.

The animal rights movement suffers from a similarly restrictive title: many people who care about animals do not believe in animal rights. Some are uncomfortable with the arguments, or view such arguments as irrelevant to animals' welfare. It would be a tragedy to lose the support of these people based on a restrictive definition of the movement.

6. Do not offend the people you seek to change.

Research on persuasion shows that influence is usually strongest when people like the persuader and see him/her as similar to themselves. Unfortunately, animal rights activists often alienate the very people they seek to change. For example, rather than courting the cooperation of veterinarians, a recent cover article in *Animals' Agenda* characterizes the views of vets as "standard fodder," "schizoid," "pusillanimous," etc. Readers are told that "vets and animal rights advocates make unlikely bedfellows," even though it mentions prominent counter-examples.

This is not to say that the American Veterinary Medical Association has championed the cause of animal welfare—far from it. The point is more circumscribed: by using derogatory language, activists make it unlikely that others will respond positively. Inflammatory language is rarely persuasive—particularly to those who are derogated—and it's unbecoming of a movement based on compassion.

No matter how much some practices deserve criticism, activists will be more effective if they are able to understand and empathize with people whose views differ from their own. As Zen master Thich Nhat Hanh wrote in connection with the nuclear freeze movement, "The peace movement can write very good protest letters, but they are not yet able to write a love letter. We need to learn to write a letter to Congress or the President of the U.S. that they will want to read, not just throw away. The way you speak, the kind of understanding, the kind of language you use should not turn people off."

Source: Reprinted with permission from "tips & tactics," supplement of *pr reporter*, Exeter, N.H. 30(1), January 15, 1990.

had always cooperated with the news media continued to do so when its plant was wracked by explosions. The explosions received front-page coverage, but only for one day—and the coverage was generally sympathetic to the business. Media reports described what the company was doing to help the victims and how it was attempting to discover the cause. Clearly, the PR practitioner can benefit from keeping in close contact with both mass and specialized media such as trade, industry and association publications.

An important but seldom mentioned public is the competition. The competition is an important public to know, communicate and work with. Institutions that maintain fair and honest dealings with their competitors usually establish this relationship through trade or association organizations. It is harder to insult someone you know personally. In addition, mutual respect within an industry or profession helps prevent open hostilities that could damage everyone.

PERCEPTIONS AND PUBLIC OPINION

An American Airlines pilot training manual contained copy that proved embarrassing when it was made public in 1997 during a pre-trial hearing in a lawsuit over the crash of one of the airline's planes in Cali, Columbia, in 1995. The manual said that Latin American passengers are frequently unruly and intoxicated. Some Latin American passengers may even call in a false bomb threat to delay a plane if they are running late. On the other hand, it was also claimed that Latin Americans generally don't expect to depart on time. To make matters worse, the *Latin America Pilot Reference Guide* contained instructions for flying into Latin American airports which fell below USA safety standards.

For an airline that is the leading carrier in the Latin American market, this was an unfortunate disclosure. The airline's senior vice president for Latin America and the Caribbean, Peter Dolara, himself a Latino, said he was offended by the manual, which he noted got its bad information from Eastern Airlines when American acquired Eastern's Latin American routes in 1989! A spokesperson for the airline expressed regret over the generalizations and promised that they would rewrite the guidebook to delete any inaccuracies and misrepresentations.

That was seen as superficial action by some members of the offended communities who fly on the airline to Latin America and the Caribbean. "When we caught them, they supposedly apologized. How many other stereotypical beliefs do they have in place that haven't been revealed?" asked Rosa Martha Zarate, co-manager of Quetzal Travel in San Bernardino, California.[26]

Perception is the reality for publics. A warning about image and reality was sounded by Frederick

D. Watkins. The age of public relations has created confusion between image and substance, he said, and PR practitioners may be tempted to settle for the role of image maker. But, he advised, public relations people should do more than serve as mouthpieces: "They can help us develop an outward-looking managerial philosophy that will be translated into actions proving our concern for the public interest."[27]

Public relations can help develop the proper management philosophy by listening and responding effectively—or as Watkins put it, in one of those dog-chasing-its-tail definitions of PR, "by working to interpret the needs of the public to the industry . . . and reflecting back to the public the actions taken in response to those needs."[28] When listening and responding effectively go together, the conscience of management takes on a new perspective. In an institution whose policies are inconsistent and whose management lacks integrity, no public relations effort can be effective.

American Airlines' problem with its pilot training manual came to light in a pre-trial hearing for a lawsuit brought against it. Often before and during a trial, the case is taken by the lawyers to the court of public opinion. This has been called, variously, *litigation journalism* (since the media are used) or *litigation public relations* (since the lawyers are acting as spokespersons for their clients and talking to news media in a media relations role).

What this means for those involved in the conflict is a battle for the minds and hearts—because the appeals are often emotional—of a variety of publics. (For more on litigation journalism/public relations see PR and the Law, Chapter 9.) All media are used in these battles, and the Internet is becoming increasingly important. Attempts to influence public opinion are made in formal settings such as news release postings in established Web sites, in special Web sites often with links to media Web sites and informally in chat rooms. Keeping information available and monitoring the media are essential in these cases that are tried in the court of public opinion.

This is not only true for particular cases; issues can be tried in the court of public opinion too. As noted in *pr reporter*, "When unfair, greedy or anti-social actions or policies become sufficiently wide-spread to cause outrage, the public turns its wrath onto *institutions*. This contrasts with attacks on specific organizations, which is perpetual and more immediate." One example of "institutional on-slaught" cited by *pr reporter* is the cost of higher education.[29] (See Example 4.13.)

Perception and Personality

In these battles for public opinion, organizations attempting to disseminate public issue or public policy messages might be interested in a study finding that the meaning of political advertising rests not only in the content of the message, but also in the minds of its receivers. In other words, both the message and the perception of the message count.[30]

The role played by personality in the perception of messages has long been understood by attorneys trying cases before juries. In cases involving a great deal of property, some attorneys have asked prospective jurors questions from the Minnesota Multiphasic Personality Inventory, a psychological assessment test updated in 1989 to remove some of its racial and gender bias. Prospective jurors' responses to some questions from the MMPI often indicate how they might vote on the central issues of the case to be tried. PR practitioners now recognize and take into account the importance of personality, especially when dealing with message construction and direction.

Getting a Handle on Public Opinion

Public relations practitioners function in a climate of public opinion that often conditions their own perceptions and responses. Climates of public opinion can be as broad as that of the international community with regard to a nation's presumed leadership in an arms race or as narrow as that of security analysts when a company's bonds are rerated downward.

Public opinion is what most people in a particular public think; in other words, it is a collective opinion of, for instance, what voters or teenagers or senior citizens or politicians think about a specific issue.

Bernard Hennessy says, "Public opinion is the complex of preferences expressed by a significant number of persons on an issue of general importance."[31] Hennessy, who does not distinguish between opinion and attitude, says that public opinion has five basic elements. First, public opinion must be focused on an issue, which Hennessy defines as "a contemporary situation with a likelihood of disagreement." Second, the public must consist of "a recognizable group of persons concerned with the issue." A third element in the definition, the phrase "complex of preferences," Hennessy says, "means more than mere direction and intensity; it means all the imagined or measured individual opinions held by the relevant public on all the proposals about the issue over which that public has come into existence." The fourth factor, the expression of opinion, may involve any form of expression—printed or spoken words, symbols (such as a clenched fist or stiff-arm salute) or even the gasp of a crowd. The fifth factor is the number of persons involved. The number of people in a public can be large or small, as long as the impact of their opinion has a measurable effect. The effect may be as much determined by the intensity of opinion and the organization of effort as by the size of the public. Hennessy's definition of public opinion does not deal with what could be called latent public opinion. He would reserve that term for "describing a situation in which a considerable number of individuals hold attitudes or general predispositions that may eventually crystallize into opinions around a given issue." In any case, public opinion has to be expressed in order to be measured.[32]

Public opinion expresses beliefs based not necessarily on facts but on perceptions or evaluations of events, persons, institutions or products. In the United States, many people assume that "public opinion is always right." Perhaps this view should be expected in a democracy, in which elected officials must be concerned with public opinion. Long before the pollsters were on the scene, nineteenth-century essayist Charles Dudley Warner said,

EXAMPLE 4.13
Trial of an Issue in the Court of Public Opinion

CAUSES OF THE PROBLEM

1. **Tuition increases**, in most cases annual hikes, above the inflation rate. Top colleges cost in the $20,000 range per year total. With all costs considered, that's about $100,000 for an undergraduate education. Even state universities keep raising rates, and some are quite high.

2. **Faculty intransigence**—as critics term it. Tenure protects them from the pressures of most jobs . . . often researching subjects that seem irrelevant . . . free to express views that upset various constituencies etc. Current example: Faculty union push for spousal benefits for homosexual or unmarried households. That businesses as different as Levi Strauss and Coors offer them doesn't quiet critics.

3. **Administrative overload**, which enrages tax-reduction groups and divides campuses when faculty gripe about too many managers or support staff.

4. **Graduate anger** when degrees don't guarantee the jobs they want. Curricula and professors' teaching abilities get blamed, rightly or wrongly. Flip side is **employer anger** when graduates seem unprepared or are not targeted to the job categories where the need is at the moment.

5. **The cushy campus life**—summers off, course load means teaching 3 or less courses per semester, time is measured in terms of school years or semesters, lots of athletic and cultural amenities (all subsidized) et al.

WHY THIS HAS THE MAKINGS OF AN ATTACK BY THE PUBLIC

1. Healthcare, public schools and government each had **virulent internal cleavages**: doctors vs. administrators, providers vs. third party payers, teachers vs. school boards, civil servants vs. downsizing political appointees. The fractiousness of cases like Harvard's clerical workers strike, Tennessee's budget cuts by a governor who's ex officio chairman of the board of trustees, faculty union battles for raises and rule changes, increase in student crime (or reporting of it) especially rape and athletes' misdoings—these evidence a house divided.

2. **Linkage to current emotional issues.** To cite a few: a) Gay and lesbian faculty members, b) supposed dumbing down of courses (e.g. attack on Georgetown for eliminating a Shakespeare re-

---

"Public opinion is stronger than the legislature, and nearly as strong as the Ten Commandments."

Obviously, public opinion can be misused or manipulated—as Adolf Hitler's master propagandist Joseph Goebbels, demonstrated. And it can be based on a lack of accurate information—as in the period before World War II when many Americans applauded Mussolini's efforts at "straightening out the Italians" (tourist translation: getting the trains to run on time), while many Italians were beginning to live in fear of the black-shirted fascist militia.

Public opinion also is notably unstable. That is why the "bottom line" for political strategists is election day itself, when the actual votes are tallied, not public opinion poll results from earlier in the campaign. Public opinion's reliability as a measurement resembles that of body temperature. For accuracy, doctors say, "The patient's temperature was 101 degrees at 7 A.M.," not "the patient's temperature is 101 degrees" (unless the thermometer has just been read). PR people would be a lot safer in their judgments if they would take the same precautions. Exposure to new information or events can quickly change public opinion, rendering recent polling research obsolete.

"Majority opinion is a curious and elusive thing," columnist Charles Frankel points out:

People's opinions on a public issue depend very much on how the issue is posed to them, and on the circumstances in which they are asked to express them-

quirement), c) political correctness rules, d) minorities demanding to live together and sitting together rather than mixing (which fueled attack on affirmative action).

Add these elements to the "factual" case outlined on the previous page and the classic formula for a Big Issue is in place.

PR'S ROLE IN FENDING IT OFF

1. **Environmental scanning** would quickly alert administration to the impending crisis. Doesn't help higher education today because few PR departments are doing it, too many administrators think PR = news bureau.
2. **Issue anticipation teams** can take the issues identified from scanning and fill in the particulars—so execs can remove or resolve the issues before they explode. PR is the lead player in establishing and guiding such teams.
3. **Explaining what $100,000 buys as an investment** over a lifetime. Yes, it's a lot of money, but amortized over 40–50 years of a career it brings huge returns in earnings and job satisfaction. Consider that med school grads' *debts* at graduation run $60–100,000.

4. **Making the undeniable case** that economic development and technical survival are an essential societal and personal investment. There can be no successful city or state today without a great university, as the economic developments pros tell it.

HOW HIGHER ED DUCKED BEFORE—AND MAY AGAIN

Alumni/ae of universities are the elite, the opinion leaders. Called into action in previous crises, they quelled the storm. Will or can they do it again, when the loudest critics are from their own ranks?

Competition is also changing. Once-underrated community and tech colleges have improved mightily. Vast numbers of students begin—even end—their education there. True, many go on to a university and become its alums—but they seem to have far less of the rah-rah spirit. Community and technical schools also compete to fill the training and night school void, taking dollars away from universities. But, is this creating a 2-tier system based on students' wealth—fueling the issue? Or is the collective clout of 3200 colleges and universities beyond the reach of public opinion?

Source: Reprinted with permission of *pr reporter*, Exeter, N.H.

selves. *A minority today may well be a majority tomorrow, depending on what transpires between today and tomorrow.*[33]

Frankel also discusses the nature of majority opinion on a particular issue:

[It] may not in fact express opinion on that specific issue. It may express a general party loyalty; it may express the individual's sense that he should go along with a coalition of interests with which he is broadly sympathetic even if he disagrees with the particular policy at issue; it may reflect simply his judgment that he does not know enough to have a reliable opinion on the specific question he has been asked, and his decision, therefore, to accept the opinion of people in authority.[34]

To keep pace with constantly changing public opinion, you must accept a few basic precepts. Not everyone is going to be on your side at any one time. The best you can hope for is a majority consensus. To achieve this, you need to retain the partisans you have, win at least provisional support from the undecided or uncommitted bloc and neutralize or win over the opposition.

Winning over the opposition is the most difficult part. Most of us read and listen for reinforcement of our own ideas. We do not like to hear ideas that conflict with our own, and we make every effort to reject them. For example, we may simply tune out and fail to hear or remember what we have been exposed to. We may discredit the source, without objectively determining the legitimacy of its evidence or argument. We may reduce the conflicting argument to a crude caricature whose fallacious elements we have no difficulty pointing out. We may distort meanings so that what we hear or read conforms to what we believe. No doubt you have seen letters to the editor of a magazine from two different people, each complimenting the publication for an editorial they interpreted in opposite ways; the readers simply read into the editorial what they wanted the publication to say. For a comprehensive list of the most important factors to consider in attempting to change public opinion, see Hadley Cantril's "laws" in Example 4.14.

Public Opinion as a Moving Target

The importance of the private, individual "opinion" (attitudes and beliefs) that underlies public opinion was described as follows by Daniel Katz:

> The study of opinion formation and attitude change is basic to an understanding of the public opinion process even though it should not be equated with this process. The public opinion process is one phase of the influencing of collective decisions, and its investigation involves knowledge of channels of communication, of the power structures of a society, of the character of mass media, of the relation between elites, factions, and masses, of the role of formal and informal leaders, of the institutionalized access to officials. But the raw material out of which public opinion develops is to be found in the attitudes of individuals, whether they be followers or leaders and whether these attitudes be at the general level of tendencies to conform to legitimate authority or majority opinion or at the specific level of favoring or opposing the particular aspects of the issue under consideration. The nature of the organization of attitudes within the personality and the processes which account for attitude change are thus critical areas for the understanding of the collective product known as public opinion.[35]

The capriciousness of public opinion is due to its fragile base in perceptions. Celebrities know (or soon learn) how fickle public opinion is. Influenc-

ing it requires constant effort directed toward viable—that is, credible and supportable—positioning of the organization (or person) vis-à-vis the competition. Positioning can sell a product, as Bernays proved when a promotional campaign he developed made smoking in public socially acceptable for young women—a feat he later felt less proud of. Positioning can also sell a person, as many elected officials can testify.

Ideas can be sold, too. During World War II, a massive PR effort by government and industry convinced the American public that the international situation made it appropriate for large numbers of single and married women to enter the paid labor force.[36] That effort put women in jobs never before imagined as "women's work," but it also returned them to hearth and home when those jobs were needed by returning veterans. In moving from one major model of American womanhood to another—each based on American myth—the tide of public opinion was manipulated each time to suit the government's perceived needs.

Measuring Public Opinion

Because public opinion changes so often and can be influenced so easily, measuring it is big business. Most public relations people make use of published public opinion surveys, and many buy public opinion research. Published surveys, for instance, are available by subscription to the Roper Center for Public Opinion Research. Issues of its *The Public Perspective* are also available online in Nexis (file PUBPER). It often includes polls, such as those taken by Louis Harris, George Gallup or news organizations, which sample the nation's moods and pass on the information through public outlets. Other public opinion research is offered by a variety of groups for a fee. Some studies—many done by academics or research institutions—are available without charge, or at minimal cost.

Public relations practitioners will often perform similar research themselves, although this is usually proprietary—owned by the organization paying for it, and unavailable to other firms or clients. Even when no original research is done,

EXAMPLE 4.14
Hadley Cantril's "Laws" of Public Opinion

1. Opinion is highly sensitive to important events.

2. Events of unusual magnitude are likely to swing public opinion temporarily from one extreme to another. Opinion does not become stabilized until the implications of events are seen with some perspective.

3. Opinion is generally determined more by events than by words—unless those words are themselves interpreted as an "event."

4. Verbal statements and outlines of courses of action have maximum importance when opinion is unstructured, when people are suggestible and seek some interpretation from a reliable source.

5. By and large, public opinion does not anticipate emergencies—it only reacts to them.

6. Psychologically, opinion is basically determined by self-interest. Events, words, or any other stimuli affect opinion only insofar as their relationship to self-interest is apparent.

7. Opinion does not remain aroused for any long period of time unless people feel their self-interest is acutely involved or unless opinion—aroused by words—is sustained by events.

8. Once self-interest is involved, opinion is not easily changed.

9. When self-interest is involved, public opinion in a democracy is likely to be ahead of official policy.

10. When an opinion is held by a slight majority or when opinion is not solidly structured, an accomplished fact tends to shift opinion in the direction of acceptance.

11. At critical times, people become more sensitive to the adequacy of their leadership—if they have confidence in it, they are willing to assign more than usual responsibility to it; if they lack confidence in it, they are less tolerant than usual.

12. People are less reluctant to have critical decisions made by their leaders if they feel that somehow they, the people, are taking some part in the decision.

13. People have more opinions and are able to form opinions more easily with respect to goals than with respect to methods necessary to reach those goals.

14. Public opinion, like individual opinion, is colored by desire. And when opinion is based chiefly on desire rather than on information, it is likely to show especially sharp shifts with events.

15. The important psychological dimensions of opinion are direction, intensity, breadth, and depth.

Source: Selections from Hadley Cantril, "Some Laws of Public Opinion," in *Gauging Public Opinion*. Copyright © 1944, renewed 1972, by Hadley Cantril. Reprinted by permission of Princeton University Press.

however, familiarity with research methodology is essential to be able to successfully apply the many published surveys to a particular company, market or client.

Walter K. Lindenmann, of Ketchum, says that the most sophisticated public relations practitioners measure outcomes—that is, changes in opinion, attitude and behavior. The practitioner relies on such techniques as before-and-after polls; experimental research designs; observation, participation and role-playing; perceptual mapping; psychographic analysis; factor and cluster analysis; and multi-faceted communication audits.[37]

Although attitude research must be used promptly because opinion is so unstable, old data should not be discarded. Information from old polls can be used later in developing simulated tests that will yield some probable responses. For instance, when John F. Kennedy was running for president in 1960, his campaign strategists used cards from the

Roper Public Opinion Research Center in Wil-
liamstown, Massachusetts (depository for the old
cards of the Gallup and Roper polls), to design a
program simulating how people around the United
States would react to various critical questions and
issues, based on how they had reacted in the past.
In fact, the simulation came closer to predicting
the November election outcome than did the public opinion polls taken in August. The reason,
Philip Meyer explains, is that the simulation, designed by Ithiel de Sola Pool,

> . . . was acting out how the voters would react to
> a [campaign] strategy that had not been fully imple-
> mented. After it was implemented and the voters be-
> gan to react, the polls began to reflect the results and
> came into closer correlation with both the simulation
> and the final outcome.[38]

Most political research organizations are identified with one party or the other. Yet, the private
pollsters say, politics and partisanship do not prevent them from doing honest research. They use
the same measurements as the public pollsters, and
they report objectively to their clients. Indeed,
they cannot afford to do inadequate research.

The reliability of polls has from time to time
been questioned. Nevertheless, both Gallup and
Harris claim that polls are generally accurate.
Gallup says that, since 1948, his organization has,
on the average, been off the actual balloting in important elections by a little less than one percentage point.

The problem with public understanding of any
poll, but particularly political polls, was stated succinctly by authors and researchers Charles Roll and
Albert Cantril:

> There is nothing immutable about the results of a
> poll. The way polls are treated by the press and politi-
> cians, one might be led to think otherwise. However,
> what a poll provides is a picture of the public's view at
> only one point in time and on only the questions that
> were asked. Yet, inferences of sweeping proportion
> are frequently drawn from a poll, leading to funda-
> mental misunderstandings of what the state of public
> opinion really is.[39]

Politicians are not alone in polling public
opinion. Business and nonprofit associations and
institutions also measure the climate in which they
operate. The accuracy of such surveys is often, as
one reporter noted, "a matter of interpretation."
This Associated Press reporter offered as an example two reports about small business in the United
States—one optimistic and the other showing conditions deteriorating. The pessimistic report was
from the National Federation of Independent Business, which had an eight-year track record of surveying the climate for small business in the United
States. The report represented its own summary of
the current survey. The optimistic report was a
public relations firm's interpretation of a survey
done for Dun & Bradstreet. The survey researcher
told the AP reporter that the total number of responses was 444, not "nearly 500" as the PR firm's
news release had said. The release had also stated
that "more than half the respondents felt that inflation would decrease"; in fact, however, the survey results actually recorded 33 percent saying it
would increase, 32.7 percent saying it would decrease and 23 percent saying it would remain the
same. The erroneous "more than half" assertion
had come from a breakdown of companies with
revenues of more than $1 million. Indeed, 52 per-
cent of these did expect a decrease, but of the 444
respondents, only 100 were companies with revenues of more than $1 million.[40]

Another difficulty with both interpretation
and process is reported by anthropologist–market
researcher Steve Barnett, who notes that most
opinion polls are adequate for assessing public feeling on superficial questions but says that people
often behave differently from how they say they
will on important questions.[41] He cites research his
firm did for a group of electric utilities. Their fuel-
use projections, which were based in part on poll-
takers' reports of customer interviews, were falling
short of reality. To find out why, Barnett put TV
cameras in the room where the thermostat was
kept in 150 homes. He discovered that the discrepancy was due to "guerrilla warfare" over the thermostat between the person who paid the bill and
everyone else. The constant adjusting changed the

level of heat use, and the actual amount of heat used differed substantially from the poll-based projections.

Something else may be going on as well. The very act of communicating an opinion has consequences on public opinion. For example, a male candidate for governor in one USA state appeared to be leading until the final hours of the election, but his opponent, a woman, won without a runoff. What was going on with the pre-election polling? Two factors may have come into play. First, early polls had asked how the respondent was going to vote and what he or she thought others would do. While many women said they intended to vote for the woman candidate, they doubted that other women would. Misperception of others' opinions is a common phenomenon. People often see themselves as holding different opinions from their friends' or neighbors'.[42]

The second element that skewed the early projections involved social relationships theory.[43] Not only were women talking with other women about the election, they were getting more ideas from these discussions than from the mass media. People often won't talk about how they feel or are going to vote if they think their friends, family, neighbors and others close to them will disagree. Many women were not saying openly (in mixed company) that they intended to vote for the woman candidate because they didn't want to argue with male family members, office colleagues or bosses.

Some might say that another contributing factor is embodied in the Noelle-Neumann "spiral of silence" theory.[44] This theory, which assumes a "powerful effects model" for media, states that media can suppress public expression of opinions opposed to those presented in the media, creating a "spiral of silence" that grows until the media's picture of reality becomes reality itself. This might have been a factor in the miscall of the Salvadoran elections in 1990. In any case, one way to compensate for this factor in polling may be to look at alternative media, according to a study by Hernando González.[45] He looked at the 1986 revolution in the Philippines that brought Corazon Aquino to

power and found that the alternative media "broadened the context in which key events could be interpreted and influenced those segments of the audience that provided new leadership." In other words, the alternative media gave voice to opposition and helped form a media base for expressing dissident points of view.

PUBLIC OPINION RESEARCH AND PUBLIC RELATIONS

The difference between public opinion researchers and PR people was stated many years ago by Fred Palmer, a partner in the PR firm of Earl Newsom and Company: "The public opinion researchers' function is to know, measure, analyze, and weigh public opinion. The practitioners' function is to help people deal constructively with the force of public opinion."[46]

The study of public opinion ties public relations research to both behavioral psychology and economics. Opinion research reflects seasonal and other types of trends in attitudes that raise questions about behavior patterns, and these in turn often require researchers to look at the economic picture to determine whether the roots of the problem might be there. Anyone who questions this sort of correlation might find some adequate, if unscientific, support in simple observation. Read the frontpage headlines of the newspaper, and check the Dow Jones averages. Any security analyst or stockbroker will tell you that a correlation exists between news on the AP and UPI wires and subsequent information on the Dow Jones ticker.

The study of public opinion is particularly important to public relations people for another reason. Information and opinion are fundamentally different. Appreciating that difference means recognizing how understanding and knowledge differ. Hadley Cantril, public opinion authority and pollster, observed that public understanding is "knowledge that is functional, that has been built up from experience, that has been tested by action."[47] Public knowledge, on the other hand, is more in the nature of intellectual data that do not play a role in concrete perception. Cantril suggested that public opinion surveys should watch for occasions when "knowledge" is used for "understanding" and should inquire into the reasons for its being linked to purpose and brought to bear on decision making.

Many public relations projects now involve behavior modification. One of these is the American Heart Association's efforts to get young people to take care of their hearts in a lifelong program. Here, as in any attempt to modify behavior, public relations people are dealing with perception versus reality. Therefore, what Cantril said about perception is particularly important.

There is still no continuing system of measurement for the "climate of public opinion." Specific tests measure public opinion on a particular issue at a given time, but no continuing study of a public's state of mind exists to reveal, for example, how much they are willing to sacrifice in craftsmanship in return for less expensive, mass-produced products. Who knows what the real religious temper of the nation is, what spiritual values are held and by whom, and why and when these values change? Such attitudes can have political consequences, as the Italians demonstrated in 1974, when they finally voted to provide a legal process for divorce in that Catholic country.

How much freedom are people in the United States willing to relinquish in return for security? This question was raised repeatedly in 1994 political campaigns throughout the United States, in discussions on topics ranging from gun ownership to teen-age curfews. It is a question politicians and businesspeople alike would benefit from knowing. The Opinion Research Corporation makes such probes, and *Collectivist Ideology in America* is its most comprehensive study to date. One of the few long-term series of public opinion polls in the United States is the Link Audit, by the Psychological Corporation, which tests attitudes toward eight large U.S. companies. This kind of continuing research has considerable application potential.

In recent years, the advertising industry has shown an awakened responsiveness to public opinion. As advertising commentator Herbert D. Maneloveg noted in *Saturday Review* back in 1970, the brightest marketing people move to the client's side rather than to the agency's, and the brighter clients seek help from people more in tune with the times—people oriented to new needs and lifestyles. The ad agencies have been forced to meet the mood of consumerism, which demands that ads tell what the public wants to know about a producer or service, rather than what the company wants to tell.

■ Dealing with Public Opinion

Many publics share knowledge or work together on various issues. Hence, organizations sometimes find, to their dismay, coalitions of unlikely political partners involved in a boycott or other hostile action against them. Computerized information banks, electronic mail, facsimile (FAX), video-teleconferencing and special-interest organizations create loosely affiliated publics with strong emotional ties to particular issues. Because of crossover of communication among these loosely connected publics, it pays to make sure that a message designed to respond to one public doesn't offend another.[48] Many subsets of very tightly woven communities are tied together by common experiences (children of alcoholics, COAs) or situations (disabilities or illnesses) or interests (animal rights). These webs of relationships are interlocking even for a single individual.

Even though different publics often share some common interests and values, it is increasingly dangerous to assume that people share common sets of values. Thus, an organization trying to determine a socially responsible course of action must simultaneously try to respond to special interest groups interested in changing broader public opinion. An example is a revision of a high-school history textbook that discusses Abigail Adams' role in the American Revolution at greater length than that of her husband. The book's author, Henry F. Groff, says the changes resulted from his having raised two daughters and from scholarship that has illuminated the historical role of women (women's studies and the women's movement).[49]

The PR manager often feels caught in the force field of special interest groups. But allegiance to a mission statement can keep PR efforts from being scattershot and can work, instead, to strengthen the organization's image and the public's perception of its organizational values.

Public opinion results from relationships formed between individual organization representatives and those with whom they come into contact.

Melvin L. Sharpe delineated the following set of principles to help organizations maintain favorable public opinion:

1. That the economic and social stability of an organization of any type depends on the attitudes and opinions of the publics within its total operational environment.

2. That all have the right to voice opinions in relation to decisions that will directly affect them and, therefore, have the right to accurate information about pending decisions relating to them or their welfare.

3. That an organization's management of communications is essential to ensure accurate and adequate feedback from both internal and external publics, in order to ensure the organization's adjustment and adaptation to the changes necessary for longevity.

4. That, although technology may be responsible for the fractionalization of today's society, technology can be used to reach out to these various publics.[50]

POINTS TO REMEMBER

■ The term *public* ("active audience") encompasses any group of people tied together, however loosely, by some common bond of interest or concern and who have consequences on an organization. No "general public" exists. *External publics* exist outside an institution; *internal publics* share the institutional identity. An *audience* is a group of people who are recipients of something—a message or a performance.

■ A "mass audience" is a myth, and the scattershot approach is both foolish and uneconomical.

■ *Publics* can be described in three ways: nominatively, demographically and psychographically.

■ Priority publics are those most important to an organization in terms of their potential impact on the organization.

■ Certain priority publics are stable, such as employees who are always important, but others may change as issues or situations develop.

■ Psychographics are increasingly important for describing diverse publics. One system for analysis of USA consumers is VALS 2 (Values, Attitudes and Lifestyles) which puts consumers into eight categories. An international study by Roper Starch Worldwide uses six psychographic categories, and identifies a list of "top ten global values."

■ Increasingly, people are not using traditional media, which furthers the fragmentation of publics.

■ The "tuning out" of traditional media, mass and specialized, is partly the result of saturation, including messages which people perceive as violations of their privacy.

■ Organizations are trying to reach some fragmented communities by using intranets and listservs to benefit from interactive participation.

■ The newest medium, the Internet, is drawing more use because it is participatory, offers anonymity and affords the development of "communities."

■ Many of the communities develop into constituencies that can be on-line critics of organizations, even to the extent of setting up rogue Web sites and otherwise using the Web to legitimize their criticism.

■ Employees are always an important public because they often have direct contact with a number of other publics. With their insiders' experience and information, they are perceived as knowledgeable and credible. Keeping employees informed and loyal is crucial for maintaining this PR "frontline."

■ Women in the workplace and women customers can create serious problems with an institution's reputation if they are victims of harrassment or discrimination and make that case publicly.

■ Minorities can be ethnic or religious, and it should not be assumed that they represent any sort of homogeneity. Failure to recognize that they can be in the nation or represented by a constituency abroad is also a serious mistake.

■ Sensitivity to the culture of a minority is as important as being aware of and using its language effectively.

■ Identifying issues that are likely to create problems for a company or nonprofit organization is the first step in the process of monitoring not only issues but also the socio-economic and political climate for events and developments that could affect any of the organization's publics.

■ Handling issues demands an integrated approach to communication. The issue, the public, and the situation in which an issue develops all require that an evaluation consider strategies which use any and all available communication tools.

■ Issues are cyclical in nature. Understanding that cycle helps to determine at what stage it is important to act.

■ The catalytic model aims to seize the opportunity to frame the issue, and to guide it through its life cycle toward resolution in the organization's favor.

■ One of the most difficult parts of handling issues is convincing management to address an issue in a timely way.

■ More than any other executive, other than the president or chief executive officer (CEO), the staff public relations practitioner needs to know what is going on both inside and outside the organization and how the organization's actions and plans will relate to its publics.

■ The job of the PR person is to bring awareness and objectivity to the job and to inject unvarnished, usable facts into the decision-making process. This is not always a popular position, but it is essential for the PR person's role in strategic planning.

■ The type of information on internal and external publics and the media used to reach them must be as verifiable as possible, which means research that employs a mix of scientific measurements.

■ *Image* describes the perception of an organization or individual. It is the collective perceptions of an organization by all of its publics, based on what it says and does, which constitute its "image."

■ The way employees and management work together creates a corporate or institutional culture that strongly affects how employees behave in relationships to each other and to outsiders. This, in turn, affects how the organization is perceived.

■ The corporate culture impacts the image that external publics have of an organization. Mergers and acquisitions can, consequently, create some confusion about the new entity.

■ An external public may be a supportive or adversarial constituency. Thus, the perception of the organization varies from public to public and may change over time due to significant changes in relationships or in the environment.

■ *Attitudes* are tendencies or orientations toward something or someone—a state of mind, a manner, a disposition or a position. *Opinions* are expressions of estimates or judgments—generally something not as strongly held as a conviction but articulating a sentiment or point of view. *Beliefs* are convictions firmly fixed in the bedrock of one's value system, embodying one's sense of truth.

■ *Public opinion* is a collective opinion—that is, what most people in a particular public think.

■ Public opinion expresses beliefs based not necessarily on facts but on perceptions or evaluations of events, persons, institutions or products.

■ Tailoring public relations programs to fit various priority publics requires careful and specific identification of the publics, an understanding of their needs and knowledge of how best to communicate with them.

■ A public is a priority not just because the organization says so, but because the public is influential in the success or failure of an idea, policy, event, decision or product.

■ Attempting to influence publics means being sensitive about their reaction to imagery, going to them instead of expecting them to come to you, not assuming attitude change is necessary for behavior change and using moral arguments only as adjuncts not main points, embracing the attitudinal public mainstream and not offending the people you want to change.

■ Insensitivity or unawareness of the interconnectedness of publics is a formula for failure.

■ Knowledge is power. That is why fact-finding is so important, and why understanding how organizations and institutions work is critical.

■ Often overlooked in research about publics are the news media and competitors, two publics that have the potential to do the most harm.

■ Not everyone is going to be on your side at any one time. The best you can hope for is a majority consensus.

■ There is still no continuing system of measurement for the "climate of public opinion." Specific tests measure public opinion on a particular issue at a given time, but no continuing study of a public's state of mind exists.

■ Internal communications can become public communications, so these should always be prepared with a consideration for the sensitivities of all publics, not just those for whom they are written.

■ Perception is the reality for publics, so when image and experience conflict, opinion of the institution takes a nosedive.

■ Public relations people who think they can only be image-makers or spokespersons for whatever management wants to say are borrowing trouble and abdicating their role as institutional strategists.

■ Legal cases often are tried in the court of public opinion, resulting in what is often called litigation journalism or litigation public relations.

■ Issues, such as the cost of higher education, can also be tried in the court of public opinion.

■ In battles for public opinion, personality plays a role in how messages are interpreted by individual members of publics.

■ Public opinion is what most people in a particular public think—a collective opinion. Groups of those publics can be seen as having an opinion about an organization or institution. In order to be measured, however, public opinion has to be expressed.

■ Public opinion is unstable and is only as good as the information involved in its formation.

■ Pollster Hadley Cantril developed some concepts about public opinion that have stood the test of time and of theoretical assessment.

■ Public relations practitioners measure outcomes, changes in opinion, attitude and behavior to determine the effectiveness of persuasive efforts.

■ One of the ways to measure opinion is by using polls. But in order to interpret results correctly it is important for public relations people to understand the mechanics of polling as well as communication theories that affect gathering information.

■ Some information about public opinion is available in public sources, and other information can be bought; but research done by firms for clients or done by companies for their own use is proprietary and not available.

■ Public opinion researchers know, measure, analyze and weigh public opinion; but the PR practitioners' job is to help their organizations and clients deal with the *impact* of public opinion.

■ Information and opinion are different. Appreciating that difference means recognizing how understanding and knowledge differ, and being careful about which are used in decision making.

■ Different publics may share some common interests and values, but it can't be assumed that there is enough homogeneity in a public to make assumptions about how fully values are shared.

■ Organizations depend on the opinions of their publics, so they need to be sure that these publics get accurate information and can communicate with the organization, especially about decisions that may impact them.

NOTES

1 Wilbur Schramm, *Men, Messages, and Media: A Look at Human Communication* (New York: Harper & Row, 1973), pp. 243–45.

2 Otto Lerbinger, ed., "Relationships Are Refined and Strengthened by Modern Corporations," *purview*, 275 (January 22, 1990). From George Lodge and Richard Walton, "The American Corporation and Its New Relationships," *California Management Review*, 31 (Spring 1989), pp. 10–24.

3 Andrea Gerlin, "Jury Pickers May Rely Too Much on Demographics," *Wall Street Journal* (December 16, 1994), pp. B1, 8.

4 SRI International, VALS Program, 333 Ravenswood Ave., Menlo Park, California 94025.

5 Tom Miller, Roper Starch Worldwide, reported in "New Psychographic Study Covers 1.5 B People Worldwide," *pr reporter*, 40(49) (December 17, 1997), pp. 1–3.

6 Alexis S. Tan, *Mass Communication Theories and Research*, 2d ed. (New York: John Wiley, 1985), pp. 217–18.

7 For insight on the consequences of this see David Buckingham, "News Media, Political Socialization and Popular Citizenship: Towards a New Agenda," *Critical Studies in Mass Communication* 14 (1997), pp. 344–366.

8 See special Technology section of *Wall Street Journal*, "The Corporate Connection" (November 18, 1996) and special Internet section of *Wall Street Journal* (December 8, 1997).

9 Scott McCartney, "Society's Subcultures Meet by Modem" and Jared Sandberg, "Fringe Groups Can Say Almost Anything And Not Worry About Getting Punched," Marketplace, *Wall Street Journal* (December 8, 1994), pp. B1, 4, 5, 10.

10 Don Middleberg, "How To Avoid A Cybercrisis," *Public Relations Tactics*, PRSA, 3(11) (November, 1996), pp. 1, 15.

11 Richard R. Mau and Lloyd B. Dennis, "Companies Ignore Shadow Constituencies at Their Peril" *Public Relation Journal*, 50(5) (May 1994), pp. 10–11.

12 Harriet Johnson Brackey, "Survey: Workplace Is More Demanding," *Florida Herald* (February 7, 1998), pp. 1C, 3C.

13 Sue Shellenbarger, "Employers Are Finding It Doesn't Cost Much To Make A Staff Happy," *Wall Street Journal* (November 19, 1997), p. B1.

14 Leon E. Wynter, "Group Finds Right Recipe for Milk Ads in Spanish," *Wall Street Journal* (March 6, 1996), p. B1.

15 John Bitter, "A Basic Training Document: Following a Problem Solving Cycle Steadies the Course in a Crisis," *pr reporter*, "tips and tactics" (January 24, 1983), pp. 1–2.

16 Philip Lesly, "Checklist on Issues and Opportunities," *Managing the Human Climate*, 68 (May–June 1981).

17 Otto Lerbinger, ed., "Issues Management Strategies Suitable for Different Lifecycle," *purview*, 277 (March 26, 1990). From John F. Mahon, "Corporate Political Strategy," *Business in the Contemporary World*, 2 (Autumn 1989), pp. 50–62. For a comprehensive look at issues management and its implications, see Robert L. Heath, "Corporate Issues Management: Theoretical Underpinnings and Research Foundations," in Larissa A. and James E. Grunig, eds., *Public Relations Research Annual*, vol. 2 (Hillsdale, N.J.: Lawrence Erlbaum Associates, 1990), pp. 29–65. For a good discussion of the application of theory to the process, see Gabriel M. Vasquez *Journal of Public Relations Research* 6(4) (1994).

18 Richard K. Long, "Understanding Issue Dynamics," in Darden Chambliss, ed. *Public Affairs in the New Era* (New York: PRSA, 1986), pp. 22–24.

19 Wayne A. Danielson, speech to Sigma Delta Chi, University of Texas at Austin, October 26, 1967.

20 Harry Levinson, "How to Undermine an Organization," *Public Relations Journal*, 22(10) (October 1966), pp. 82–84.

21 Ibid., p. 84.

22 Jayme Rolls, "Employee Communication Has a Change of Heart," *HR Magazine*, 38(10) (October 1993), pp. 132–34.

23 Philip Lesly, "Turning Over an Elephant with a Shoehorn," *Managing the Human Climate*, 90 (January–February 1985). For the ethnoecology approach to corporate culture, see James L. Everett, "Organizational Culture and Ethnoecology in Public Relations Theory and Practice," in Larissa A. and James E. Grunig, eds., *Public Relations Research Annual*, vol. 2 (Hillsdale, N J.: Lawrence Erlbaum Associates, 1990), pp. 235–51.

24 Melvin L. DeFleur and Sandra Ball-Rokeach, *Theories of Mass Communication*, 5th ed. (New York: Longman, 1989), p. 159. "Mass society refers to the relationship that exists between individuals and the social order around them. In mass society . . . individuals are presumed to be in a situation of psychological isolation from others, impersonality is said to prevail in their interaction with others, and they are said to be relatively free from demands of binding social obligations."

25 Stephen M. Downey, "Corporate Identity's Role in Economic Recovery," *PRSA Newsletter*, 11(4, 5) (April–May 1983), p. 1.

26 Keith L. Alexander, "American Airlines Apologizes for Manual," *USA TODAY* (August 21, 1997), p. 2B.

27 Frederick D. Watkins, "Top Insurance Men Meet to Discuss Industry's Public Relations," *pr reporter*, 17(5) (February 4, 1974), p. 2.

28 Ibid.

29 *pr reporter*, 40(32) (August 18, 1997) pp. 1, 2.

30 Deirdre D. Johnston, "Image and Issue Political Information: Message Content or Interpretation?" *Journalism Quarterly*, 66(2) (Spring 1989), pp. 379–82.

[31] Bernard Hennessy, *Public Opinion*, 4th ed. (Monterey, Calif.: Brooks/Cole, 1981), p. 4. Social scientist Ithiel de Sola Pool also said: "An opinion is a proposition, while an attitude is a proclivity to be pro or anti something." For his discussion of public opinion, see "Public Opinion," *Handbook of Communication* (Chicago: Rand McNally, 1973), pp. 779–835.

[32] Hennessy, *Public Opinion*, pp. 4–8.

[33] Charles Frankel, "The Silenced Majority," *Saturday Review* (December 13, 1969), p. 22.

[34] Ibid.

[35] Daniel Katz, "The Functional Approach to the Study of Attitudes," *Public Opinion Quarterly*, 29 (1960), p. 163.

[36] Maureen Honey, *Creating Rosie the Riveter: Class, Gender and Propaganda During World War II* (Amherst: University of Massachusetts Press, 1984), p. 212.

[37] Walter K. Lindenmann, "An 'Effectiveness Yardstick' to Measure Public Relations Success," *Public Relations Quarterly*, 38(1) (Spring 1993), pp. 7–9.

[38] Philip Meyer, *Precision Journalism* (Bloomington: Indiana University Press, 1973), p. 184.

[39] Charles W. Roll, Jr., and Albert H. Cantril, *Polls: Their Use and Misuse in Politics* (New York: Basic Books, 1972), p. 117.

[40] John Cuniff, "Accuracy of Surveys a Matter of Interpretation," *Fort Worth Star-Telegram* (November 20, 1981), p. 5C.

[41] Frederick C. Klein, "Researcher Proves Consumers Using Anthropological Skills," *Wall Street Journal* (July 7, 1983), p. 21.

[42] Carroll J. Glynn, "The Communication of Public Opinion," *Journalism Quarterly*, 64(4) (Winter 1987), pp. 688–97. See also Charles T. Salmon and Hayg Oshagan, "Community Size, Perceptions of Majority Opinion, and Opinion Expression," in *Public Relations Research Annual*, vol. 2, pp. 157–71.

[43] Melvin DeFleur and Sandra Ball-Rokeach, *Theories of Mass Communication* (New York: Longman, 1989), p. 192.

[44] Elizabeth Noelle-Neumann, "Turbulences in the Climate of Opinion: Methodological Applications of the Spiral of Silence Theory," *Public Opinion Quarterly*, 40 (1977), pp. 143–58, and *The Spiral of Silence—Public Opinion Our Social Skin* (Chicago: University of Chicago Press, 1984).

[45] Hernando González, "Mass Media and the Spiral of Silence: The Philippines from Marcos to Aquino," *Journal of Communication*, 38(4) (Autumn 1988), pp. 33–34.

[46] Fred L. Palmer, "Opinion Research as an Aid to Public Relations Practice," address at International Conference in Public Opinion Research, Eagles Mere, Pennsylvania, September 13, 1948.

[47] Hadley Cantril, *Understanding Man's Social Behavior* (Princeton, N.J.: Office of Public Opinion Research, 1947), p. 31.

[48] Jolie Solomon and Carol Hymowitz, "Team Strategy: P&O Makes Changes in the Way It Develops and Sells Its Product," *Wall Street Journal* (August 11, 1987), p. 12.

[49] Bob Davis, "Scholastic Work, Many Forces Shape Making and Marketing of a War Schoolbook," *Wall Street Journal* (January 3, 1985), p. 1.

[50] Chester Burger, "30 Years After Sputnik—The Revolution in Communications," speech to Public Relations Society of America Detroit Chapter, Detroit, Michigan, February 3, 1987.

Selected readings, activities and assignments appropriate to this chapter can be found in the *Instructor's Guide* or on InfoTrac if you are using the InfoTrac College Edition.

RESEARCH FOR BACKGROUND AND PLANNING

Research is the one important source of ideas for public relations practice.
EDWARD J. ROBINSON, MANAGEMENT TRAINING AND DEVELOPMENT AUTHORITY

We can't manage what we don't measure.
DAVID R. DROBIS, CHAIRMAN, CEO, KETCHUM PUBLIC RELATIONS WORLDWIDE

You have a new public relations job, and you are anxious to get started on your responsibilities. Before you can function effectively, you must find out what you are supposed to do, for whom and why. You must ask a lot of questions, and you must look for materials to read—perhaps at the library. Once on the job, you begin discovering helpful information that you can put into your computer or file away where you can find it.

You are doing research. Furthermore, you are using the same general methods that every researcher uses: reading available material and questioning people. These two categories of research methods are *secondary* (reading or consulting available materials that someone else has already compiled—that is, searching "the literature") and *primary* (collecting raw data that no one else has yet compiled). This chapter deals with secondary research; primary research is discussed in Chapter 6.

In public relations, the need for systematic research is critical and continuous. Keeping well-organized records as you go along will save you from a lot of frantic scurrying when you have to locate specific information. Maybe you've already learned this lesson to the extent of keeping a list of your information sources' phone numbers handy, and updating it regularly.

You have to do formative research initially to gather facts. Then you have to monitor your progress to see whether what you have planned is going all right or whether changes need to be made. Finally, you must evaluate what was accomplished, in order to determine how you need to plan for the future. There's no simple all-purpose formula to follow, because research in public relations is a never-ending process. Example 5.1 indicates the high value organizations place on up-to-the-minute information.

Public relations research concentrates on finding the answers to these questions: Who are our publics? What is our action/message? What channels of communication reach our publics? What is the reaction to our efforts? What should we do to keep in touch? With every public relations activity, we should consider: How is this activity going to be understood by everyone whom we are trying to inform or persuade? What are they going to say or do as a result of our efforts? What is their feeling about us and about what we are doing and saying? Research is used for exploration, description, explanation and prediction.

Research in public relations supports audience, media and trend analysis; message testing; and issue monitoring, forecasting and evaluating. It often provides essential data for effectively presenting information. This chapter discusses the importance of keeping records and other data, of finding and using existing reports and information and of using research in planning, monitoring and evaluating PR programs.

THE BASICS: RECORD KEEPING AND RETRIEVING

Getting started with a new public relations job or a new client means doing a lot of preliminary research and setting up a system for accumulating and accessing information. Some large organizations have information systems officers and librarians. Information systems officers manage the current flow of information generated by the organization. Librarians maintain past records and archives such as files and documents. You will find that both are invaluable as you gather the information you need.

EXAMPLE 5.1
Information Gatherers in Washington, D.C.

There's a high value in being the first to get important facts in the decision-making atmosphere of Washington, D.C., so public relations and accounting firms often hire fact-finders, at salaries as high as $50,000 a year, to sit outside committee meetings until they break up and then grab quick briefings from participants. These information gatherers often make getting to know congressional and committee staff people a part of their job, so they have steady sources of strategic information. In discussing this new "paper chaser" role, the *Wall Street Journal* gave the example of a tax analyst for Hill & Knowlton who stationed himself at 7:15 A.M. outside the room where the House Ways and Means Committee was to meet. This committee writes the nation's tax laws, and the H&K researcher needed to be there to talk to people as soon as the meeting adjourned or even as people came and went. The *Journal* noted that, by the time the Ways and Means Committee convened (which was several hours after the H&K researcher took his post outside the room), he had 100 or more people behind him, all doing what he was doing—trying to get critical bits of information for their employers. Sometimes the researchers are on all-night "stake-outs" as meetings go on until early morning. They are prepared to pass the word to their employers even if it's 3 A.M. The information is often critical to decision making, and a client's strategy may depend on a few key facts. The *Journal* said that two rules govern the behavior of these new-style researchers: be accurate and transmit what you get as soon as possible.

Source: *Wall Street Journal* (August 3, 1990), p. B3A.

■ Keeping Records

The kinds of records you will need to accumulate fall into several categories: information about the organization itself (when it was begun, its mission statement, what it makes or does, its history); information about personnel (biographies of current and past leaders); and information about ongoing organizational activities. You will need file copies of all of the organization's formal communication—magazines, newsletters, annual reports, advertising, films and videotapes. These may be on file in the organization's library, but you will also need to have all of the current information readily accessible in your office.

Retrieving Information

Systematic record keeping—fact collecting—can be an interesting and "fun" part of your job, because you are being paid to learn. It also can supply critically needed information (such as a record telling you what you did last year when the same problem cropped up), help you plan (by telling you what you need to put onto your calendar) and help you flesh out stories or identify a news peg. Maintaining a file on all major activities, as well as a general how-to file, facilitates planning and reduces strain on the nerves—provided that you can find what you filed.

Recorded information must be kept in a logical, well-organized and easily retrievable form. It is not valuable unless you can quickly find it. For example, suppose that you have been touting the high nutritional value of your company's canned peaches, and a competitor releases a "market study" showing that its frozen peaches have more nutritional value because much nutrition in yours is destroyed in canning. A newspaper food editor calls you for a comment. If it takes you too long to find the nutritional information you need, the competition may win the headlines that day, and you may have to settle for a less prominent display of your "second-day" story.

RESEARCH SOURCES

There are two broad categories of research sources: scholarly and commercial. Academic institutions and faculty do scholarly research, sometimes with funding from the government, from foundations or

from professional associations. Government research in the USA and in many other nations is free and available in print or off the World Wide Web. Commercial research is done by research firms, advertising and public relations firms/agencies and other marketing-related companies. Much of it is also available in publications such as annual reports and at Web sites.

Research results that are funded by academic institutions or by professional associations or societies are usually published in scholarly or professional journals and made public. The results of much commercial research are proprietary and generally are not made available to others. Scholars, however, may be given limited access to the results. Normally research findings are withheld unless the commercial organization sees some benefit in releasing them.

Finding and Using Existing Reports

Research results of all kinds are available. Databases from general and specialized sources can be accessed either on a subscription basis, through purchased searches conducted by reference librarians or on the Internet. Familiar databases include CompuServe, The Source, Dow Jones News Retrieval and Nexis/Lexis. MARS serves the field of marketing, advertising and public relations.

PR people often need to use general communication databases, as well as specialized ones, for their organization and clients. Many of these are available at Web sites. The Ragan's Interactive Public Relations Newsletter is one guide to sources in cyberspace that are useful to PR people.

Most useful in communicating with publics is communication research that shows profiles of audiences and provides credibility ratings for various communication tactics and tools. Research to answer such questions has usually already been done. You simply need to know where to find it. You must also know enough about research techniques and methodologies to interpret the results correctly and then apply them. If, for instance, you are interested in advertising for the youth market, you would be interested in a published study by

Professor Stephen Unwin, who concluded that "differences in opinion of the advertisements and the products advertised were predictive of response difference between cultures but not between generations and sexes."[1] However, you would also note that this study was published in 1973—over 25 years ago—and you would want to seek out any related newer studies. Social science research also provides a wealth of information. Although such research often is not directly applicable to a particular public relations problem, the PR practitioner can learn how to extract what can be used most effectively.[2]

Because of its easy access, the principal source for research findings used today is the Internet. One good reference for the new cyberspace researcher is *The Internet Handbook for Writers, Researchers and Journalists* by Mary McGuire, Linda Stilborne, Melinda McAdams and Laurel Hyatt (1997, Trifolium Books, Inc. 238 Davenport Rd. Suite 28, Toronto, Ontario, Canada M5R 1J6). This handbook's organization makes it easy to help you both find information on the Web and create information for the Web.

If you are relatively comfortable with the Internet, a useful site is the ALL-IN-ONE SEARCH PAGE which has a collection of search software with brief descriptions of each and is updated about every 48 hours. The collection is organized into groups: The World Wide Web, General Internet, Desk Reference, Publications/Literature and Other Interesting Searches/Services. Each entry gives you a brief description and search strategy.

Web sites offer an abundance of useful information literally at your fingertips. For example, the State Department lists travel warnings to various places in the world. Other sites give you information on world time, international events, advisories about foreign countries—with political/cultural information, places to avoid, and so on. The Securities and Exchange Commission has a database of publicly traded companies where you can access 10-K and 10-Q reports filed on-line. *Forbes* Magazine offers daily updates of the Dow Jones and other stock market indices, as well as copies of its current and past publications.

These Web sites have information that is well-documented. However, practitioners should be cautious about the validity of information on the Internet. This is especially the case with personal Web sites, ListServs and newsgroups, although sites maintained by recognized organizations are generally more reliable.

ListServs and newsgroups are subscribed to and you have to initiate the request. One source of information about available ListServs is the Liszt web site at http://www.liszt.com where you can get background information on them. One for PR is PRFORUM. Information in ListServs is more like what you'd get from conversations because that's what participants do—send messages back and forth. More structured sources are newsgroups, where you can find quite a few journalistic organizations. Access to information about subscribing to newsgroups is available through CompuServe. CompuServe also is one way to subscribe to the oldest PR discussion group, one founded in 1984, the PR & Marketing Forum.

Useful compilations of research information that describe emerging trends are available in books and government periodicals as well as quasi-government entities such as the United Nations. Membership in an organization such as the Newspaper Advertising Bureau, Inc., can provide ready access to additional useful research data.

Periodicals are yet another source of useful information. The public relations newsletter, *pr reporter*, shares studies that its subscribers and readers grant it permission to use. The newsletter often directs readers who want additional information to contact the agency that conducted the survey.

The results of national surveys are usually obtainable from several sources. Some national surveys have individual applications. Thus, if you obtain permission to use the same questionnaire and methodology as the national survey, you can compare your publics with the nation at large.

Research organizations also are sources of information. Research institutions such as Opinion Research Corporation, which was founded in 1938, offer comprehensive reports compiled from various clients' projects. These reports are not inexpensive (each costs several hundred dollars), but they probably are considerably cheaper than any comparable research project you might do yourself.

Good survey research is costly. Small organizations, therefore, depend heavily on careful analysis and application of the results of surveys taken by others that have been published or made available within the industry. Such surveys are commonly performed by professional associations and then made available to their members. Social problems and issues with significance to government or to social agencies are studied and published by public polling agencies. Recent examples include studies that have focused on projecting the numbers of future AIDS (Acquired Immune Deficiency Syndrome) victims and the cost of their treatment.

Mastery of a unique body of knowledge is one of the marks of a true profession. In 1988, a task force appointed by the Public Relations Society of America developed an outline of subject matter essential to the professional practice of public relations. This *Body of Knowledge* is a comprehensive bibliography within which each entry is annotated (summarized). The International Public Relations Foundation, founded by the International Public Relations Association but which is now a separate body, has published a book, *Global Sources*, which is an international bibliography of public relations that cites articles and books published in English since 1990.[3]

From the U.S. Government Printing office, you can order a catalog of booklets published from government-funded research. You can also get research information, especially demographic information and economic statistics, from state and local governments. The U.S. Census Bureau is *the* source for demographic information, and many community libraries have much of this information on file. In addition, some university libraries are government document repositories that can provide a wealth of information to PR practitioners.

Fortunately much research is available in electronic data banks. A good bit is even accessible to personal computer users, due to the development of the CD-ROM (for compact disk–read only memory) technology and on the World Wide Web.

Some even offer sound. If you don't have the capacity to access such information with your own computer, you can pay a research librarian to perform the search for you. If you are fishing in unfamiliar waters, a research librarian can be very helpful with descriptions—the key words you use to tap into data banks—and with the choice of data banks themselves. Once you find information, you need to be sufficiently knowledgeable about research methodology to interpret its meaning in relation to a particular client or organization.

What to Look for in Research Data   Much of the information that public relations practitioners seek involves public opinion—the reported views, values and attitudes of designated groups of people. Since public opinion is composed of the collective individual views expressed about a product, service or organization by segments of a community, both demographics and psychographics must be used to put public opinion into its proper context. The public relations practitioner needs to be sure that the research data contain sound demographic and psychographic information.

Demographics identifies the size of a population and its capacity to expand or decline. It also provides information about a population's gender, level of education, occupation, income and related "hard" factual data. **Psychographics** reveals the personality traits of an audience. Its value lies in its ability to show likenesses in audiences of great demographic variation. Thus, psychographics can reveal what an eighty-year-old engineer and a twenty-five-year-old stockbroker have in common. Perhaps they both prefer classical music to popular music, or they both like to grow roses. Psychographics also tells us about lifestyles.

Public relations practitioners are interested in the geo-demographic information contained in the research data, as well. Geo-demographics—also known as "cluster demographics," "indirect psychographics," "zip clustering" and "geo-marketing"—identifies geographic areas that are populated by consumers who share demographic and psychographic characteristics. The demographic and psychographic profile of an area is matched against the penetration of a product or service into that same area. Sound geo-demographic information causes universities to recruit new students in areas where large numbers of their alumni live, and it persuades the U.S. Armed Services to recruit in neighborhoods where they have gotten qualified applicants in the past.[4]

Applying Research Information You'll find yourself relying heavily on survey data for guidance. But you should ask two questions before you use survey research. First, is it valid? That is, does it measure what you initially assumed and want it to measure? Second, what does it mean to you or your client? That is, does it measure something central and important to your employer or client? If the answer to the first question is "no" or "probably not," there is no point in using the information. The answer to the second question can serve as a warning signal to the alert public relations practitioner that a problem is brewing. If the answer is "Some of this research does not really apply to our situation," then you must take care to use only the portion of the research that *is* relevant and to do some primary research of your own to get at your problem directly. For instance, a church or denominational office might react to a Gallup religion survey by checking its own statistics on attendance. If attendance is sliding, the prudent move would be to design a survey to answer questions directly relevant to that church or denomination.

Surveys and polls can be extremely useful as long as they are interpreted correctly. The key to successful interpretation is a realistic and objective viewpoint. To help people interpret and apply poll data correctly, the National Council on Public Polls (NCPP) has issued some standards for releasing poll data. NCPP considers it essential that the following information be specifically incorporated in published or broadcast reports on polls: (1) who sponsored the poll; (2) dates of interviewing; (3) method of obtaining the interviews (in-person, telephone or mail); (4) wording of the questions; (5) population that was surveyed; (6) size of the sample; (7) size and description of the subsample, if results are based on less than the total sample.[5]

One of the biggest stumbling blocks to overall acceptance of market research is implicit in the question, "Who is going to test-market the test-marketers?" The Advertising Research Foundation undertook to find out just how objectively market research firms were operating and how valid their findings were. The foundation asked research firms to allow it to audit their research techniques. Its findings were then made available to foundation member firms, and participating research companies received the "Registered for the ARF Open Audit Plan" seal.[6]

USING RESEARCH FOR PLANNING

Research is critical at every step of public relations work, from planning and goal setting to identifying and prioritizing publics to evaluating results for purposes of future planning and action.

The May 1994 *Public Relations Journal* identifies six ways to use research: (1) to formulate strategy; (2) to gauge success; (3) to test messages; (4) to size up competition; (5) to get publicity; (6) to sway opinion. Depending on how such categories are broken down, there undoubtedly are other public relations–related uses.[7]

Research information is particularly useful at the initiation stage of a public relations effort. A public relations practitioner interested in putting together a program to bring an organization's goals and objectives to a public's attention begins by examining all available research information indicating how various publics view the organization (or similar organizations). Any other information about the organization's publics also deserves close study.

When a public relations practitioner reaches the point of planning messages for various publics, audience research becomes critically important. If sufficient information about how a target group is likely to respond to a particular type of message is not readily at hand, the practitioner must make every effort to locate it. This may involve asking specific departments, such as sales or product re-search, for available information. However, the practitioner must be cooperative toward and con-siderate of the work schedules and time commit-ments of those approached for help.

Sometimes information about how a particular audience will respond to a particular type of mes-sage simply cannot be located. Original research must then be performed (see Chapter 6).

Vast quantities of material are available for public relations planning. PR consultant Steve Lee once astounded a British client by presenting a 2-inch thick book of information for public relations planning—all from available research sources.

The main stages of the planning phase of research are issue forecasting, learning about pub-lics, planning media use and considering possible outcomes.

■ Issue Forecasting

Issue forecasting is the research part of issues man-agement and environmental scanning. In issue forecasting, an organization uses collected informa-tion to determine how it and its publics might re-act to a future event, trend or controversy.

Kerry Tucker and Bill Trumpfheller cite a five-step plan to establish an issues-management system:

1. Anticipate issues and establish priorities by ask-ing these questions: What changes do we project in economics, social trends, government and politics, technology and the competition?

2. Analyze issues once priorities are set by devel-oping a formal situational analysis or issue brief.

3. Recommend an organizational position on issues.

4. Identify publics/opinion leaders who can help advance your position. (Formal research can vali-date assumptions about groups with a stake in the issue and can help identify opinion leaders who are likely to be allied with your position.)

5. Identify desired behavior of publics/opinion leaders.[8]

■ Learning About Publics

After you have accumulated all the facts you need about a given issue or situation, you must begin ex-ploring the publics involved. Reexamine their pro-files to see how each might be affected by the situation. This is a critical area, and it is important not to overlook any public. In this manner you will often discover areas that present conflicts of in-terest between divergent publics. For example, a college PR administrator frequently encounters conflicts of interest among the college's varied pub-lics—trustees, administrators, alumni, faculty, staff, parents and students. Each public might react quite differently to the same issue or situation.

The two main tasks involved in exploring pub-lics consist of prioritizing them by issues and inter-preting their behavior.

Prioritizing Publics by Issues   In each planning situation, you have to decide which are the major publics and which the minor ones of your organiza-tion. For example, some nonprofit organizations that depend on fundraising are very sensitive to news media coverage, as are all government agen-cies. But a privately held company that manufac-tures equipment for a specific industry may not have to rank news media very high on its list of publics. On the other hand, on *specific* issues, you may have to revise your general ordering of publics. If that privately held company were charged with polluting a major source of drinking water, news media might suddenly rank very high on its list of publics.

"It's not exactly deciding whom you can afford to offend," one practitioner said. "It is more decid-ing which one has to be appealed to most effec-tively and figuring out how to do that while offending the others the least." To do this at all, you must be aware of what these publics know and what they think they know. Only research will tell you how many real facts a public has, what myths it holds and what rumors it has embraced. Some re-search professes to have discovered how a public is *likely* to think and what it might do. This claim is worth examining, but cautiously.

Research also helps you examine the dynamics of your publics—how they act collectively. This is something more and more institutions are investigating through employee surveys.

Surveys are one way to measure a public's dynamics on issues and problems, but some managements use a more direct approach with employees and consumers. Managers—even CEOs—sit down with a few employees at a time at different sites to listen to them air complaints and suggestions. For example, officers, accompanied by some directors, of some companies go to different locations to present employee awards and to hear about problems. Most CEOs now get e-mail from employees, meet one-on-one with them and with units to hear what they have to say.

Some companies have adopted a Japanese technique called "quality circles," in which groups of employees meet regularly with managers to review problems. Listening to the people who are doing the work and interacting with consumers and suppliers may be good for morale, even if nothing is done to change the existing setup. On the other hand, if employees or consumers don't see some tangible evidence of the upward flow of communication, they may lose interest or use the meetings strictly for personal or political benefit. The dynamics of a public often provide clues to possible approaches for effective communication.

Interpreting the Behavior of Publics James Grunig, public relations professor at the University of Maryland, says likenesses between and among publics may depend entirely on specific situations. Any examination of publics, Grunig says, should consider first a grouping by the nature of that public's communication behavior and then a grouping by the similarity of that public's situational perception and behavior—that is, how people look at certain situations and how they behave in them. For example, an ordinarily outgoing and talkative person may be silent and reserved in particular situations. Thus, Grunig says, we must take into consideration that people *control* their behavior. Grouping publics in the two ways that Grunig recommends may help us predict the attitudes people

will assume in certain specific situations, as well as offering us a way to understand what is going on in those situations.

Grunig tells us to expect different communication behaviors from information seekers than from information processors.[9] (See persuasion and communication theories in Example 7.6.) An information seeker is interested enough in the problem or situation to want to know more about it. An information processor is aware of the communication and may be touched by the message but does not actively seek the information.

For example, suppose that the professor in your class announces that Friday is the last day to add and drop classes. If you are interested in adding or dropping a class, you will try to find out more information about how to do it on or before Friday. You are therefore an information seeker. However, if you have no intention of adding or dropping a class, then you do not need the information. Hence, you will process it but not seek additional data. Subsequently, if your roommate says, "My schedule is all messed up; I wonder when the deadline is for changing," you might say, "Well, it's Friday, but that's all I know."

The roommate has demonstrated *problem recognition*—one of the communication states that Grunig explains. Problem recognition increases the probability that a person will communicate and seek information about a situation. Communication is reduced, though, if the person thinks that limitations restrict his or her behavior. Grunig calls this behavior *constraint recognition*. These two concepts combine to produce four types of perceived situations: problem-facing behavior (high problem recognition, low constraint recognition); constrained behavior (high problem recognition, high constraint recognition); routine behavior (low problem recognition, low constraint recognition); and fatalistic behavior (low problem recognition, high constraint recognition).

Now add another variable, the *referent criterion*. A referent criterion is a guide or rule by which a person measures a new situation in terms of an old experience. A person who is confronted with a new situation employs an old criterion to handle it.

If the old criterion doesn't work this time, the person develops a new criterion to guide his or her behavior (including communication behavior) in the new setting. Grunig has found that, when a person is motivated to communicate about a situation, he or she is also motivated to develop a solution for the situation—an attitude. Therefore, why a person communicates or does not communicate in a situation can be explained by these three variables: problem recognition, constraint perception and referent criterion.[10]

A fourth variable that helps determine whether a person will be an information seeker or an information processor is *perceived level of involvement*. A person seeks information if involved in a situation but only processes it if not involved. Grunig's four variables now produce sixteen types of communication behavior (four combinations of problem recognition and constraint recognition, subdivided by the presence or absence of a referent criterion and again by the level of involvement). Recent studies have shown less effect from referent criterion than the other variables. The examination presents probabilities that can be used to decide whether either information seeking or information processing by a particular public is likely to be worth the investment involved in preparing information (such as brochures, videotapes and Web pages) for that group.

Consider, for example, a new admissions policy that would affect students transferring from two-year colleges. Many of these students may not even be thinking about going on to a four-year institution, while others might entertain the idea if they thought they had a chance to be admitted. Information about a nonrestrictive policy would have to be communicated to the latter group to show them how to qualify for admission—how to overcome obstacles. They constitute a very cost-effective public, since they are actively interested in finding out what to do and what is going on. However, money is wasted on students who are not very interested in a college education, who think getting admitted is impossible and who really want to obtain a vocational rather than an academic education.

Planning Media Use

Research indicating what media different publics use is widely available from professional, trade and academic journals. Occasionally, research reports from polls appear in the popular press, as well. As a PR practitioner, you want to know how people use media, which media they use and who the users are. When you want to know about a specific medium, you can consult reference publications such as *Standard Rate and Data* and the Audit Bureau of Circulation reports, as well as industry guides such as *Editor & Publisher*. In addition, a medium will provide its own research data to help sell time or space or to provide editorial guidance.

Considering Possible Outcomes

Any time you consider a public relations plan, you should closely examine everything that can go right and everything that can go wrong. Even just discussing these possibilities can often prevent a poor plan from progressing beyond the talking stage. Few practitioners are willing to share "wild ideas" that were scrapped in the planning stages, but often people with public relations awareness wonder whether certain actually adopted plans were ever put to the "possibilities test."

A university discovered that it would have to increase dormitory room rents. Except for the administration and the school's business office, however, no one knew of the plan—until housing contracts were sent to students who planned to return the following year. The shock and resentment at the last-minute notification caused many students to cancel their contracts and to move off campus, while other students felt lingering bitterness toward the institution. You have to wonder why no one asked, "What will be the reaction when these contracts are received?"

Examining the possibilities of any plan often reveals that unexplored areas exist. You must then decide whether additional research is needed. Is the missing information likely to be critical enough to justify the cost? Usually the answer is yes. This is particularly true when you are developing a campaign.

Moreover, even though existing research in each area—the situation, the publics and the media—may have been applied, pretesting is essential. Secondary research—materials and information from other sources—is certainly important, but each situation is unique and may merit its own testing before you launch an entire campaign. For this reason "case studies" must be viewed cautiously. Similar campaigns by other organizations may have involved many different variables that made the outcome of their campaign potentially far different from what you may find.

If you receive in the mail one bar of soap of a brand you have never seen before, the accompanying information will probably reveal that you are in a "test market." Sometimes different ads will appear in one split run of a magazine as a test. Or a person may interview you and show you several different ads to get your reaction to each. All such pretests are worth the investment if they prevent an expensive error, indicate an unanticipated response or suggest a different approach.

USING RESEARCH FOR MONITORING

It is important to arrange for feedback after a plan has been set in operation. Careful planning may have preceded a public relations program, but that does not ensure success. A campaign should be monitored as it is being carried out, and evaluative research should be performed at the campaign's conclusion to determine its degree of success or failure.

In developing goals, you must use an "operational" procedure that will allow you to measure later on whether you have achieved these goals. To accomplish this, you have to build monitoring into your plans. Monitoring can reveal problem areas before they become crises. Monitoring a PR operation involves performing a specific check on results, as opposed to engaging in general monitoring of the climate of public opinion, which goes on in issues management. Monitoring is also different from the final evaluation, which allows you to determine whether your completed program has achieved all your specific goals.

Monitoring can be as simple as reading a community newspaper to determine whether and where a news release was published. On the other hand, it may be as difficult as finding out whether a public's behavior is being changed. The benefits of monitoring are illustrated by the example of a resort area's hurried decision to buy radio time after discovering that a magazine story counted on to increase Labor Day crowds would, in fact, hit the newsstands the day after the holiday instead of two weeks before.

The importance of keeping up with events was not lost on one politician's campaign manager. He had hired youngsters one Friday morning to set up stake signs in supporters' yards. The following Monday he could find no signs in place. He arrived at the office ready to yell at a bunch of kids; but instead he had to answer a call from city officials, who informed him that his signs had been removed because all 500 had been placed in the easement area just behind the curb. That was city property, and political signs could not be displayed there. How had the city officials known about this infraction? The candidate's opponent had been "monitoring," of course. Monitoring media use of your news releases is another important part of your work. You need tangible evidence that the message is getting out. For publicity monitoring, you can use services that will clip and tape stories in the media that have mentioned your organization. Some services, such as Media Link which is international in scope, also will perform extensive analyses of the media coverage. If you are monitoring advertising, you also generally get reports with the bill when you buy time or space in a medium. However, you need to have someone visually check to confirm that billboards and posters went up on time.

USING RESEARCH
FOR FINAL EVALUATION

The public relations function doesn't end with the achievement of particular goals or objectives. But certainly you want to look at each goal to see whether and by how much it was achieved. This is the purpose of the final evaluation. After-the-fact measurements of goals provide an objective estimate of achievement and indicate where problems may persist.

Most major agencies have elaborate evaluation systems in place. Ketchum's Effectiveness Yardstick measures everything from a client's news clippings to behavioral shifts, and Burson-Marsteller uses a proprietary method to measure subtle perception shifts.[11]

You should check the effects of your public relations effort on each public, if possible. If that is too costly, at the very least you should look at its effects on your most important publics. You also need to see how the accomplishment of certain goals has modified or changed your overall objective. Here, measurements could suggest a shift in emphasis.

It is therefore wise to adopt the following procedures:

1. Compile the goal results, and interpret their significance to the specific objective set, to the organization's overall objectives and to its mission.

2. Evaluate the impact of actions taken on your publics to see what their attitudes are now toward the organization (and its products, services, management and so on).

3. Determine how the organization's overall objective and mission have been affected.

4. Measure the program's impact in three areas: (a) *Financial responsibility*—going beyond market share to the publics' perception of how an organization gets and spends its money; (b) *Ethics*—the perception by publics of an organization's standards of behavior, a moral judgment of the consequences of what it says and does; (c) *Social responsibility*—publics' perception of whether an organization is a good citizen; for example, whether it contributes to the social, political and economic health of global society.

Research can yield specific information about publics that may prove useful. For example, one survey produced evidence that two-thirds of the public (68 percent) said that knowing more about a company generally makes them think more favorably about it;[12] and almost nine out of ten (87 percent) said that, if given a choice of similar products or services, they would choose the one from the company with the best reputation. Both points held up across socioeconomic lines for all major segments of the public.[13]

Ongoing research efforts can assess information about both the public and the message. In one such project, the American Heart Association tested the impact of its annual Food Festival on grocery shoppers to see if awareness of heart-healthy foods had increased. The survey for the first Food Festival was measured against a prefestival baseline survey, and the survey for succeeding Food Festivals was measured against previous ones and against the baseline. Conducted by the Home Testing Institute, the survey collected information from shoppers who were asked about the types of food consumed in their households and about their attitudes toward food consumption. The overall findings were positive from a health standpoint, which also reflected well on the credibility of the American Heart Association.[14]

■ The Cyclical Effect

Using research helps the public relations practitioner anticipate problems, evaluate ongoing programs, pretest the effectiveness of certain tools, profile a public and its attitudes, accumulate information about effective uses of media and evaluate completed programs and campaigns.

What results is a cycle of research activity (see Example 5.2) that can be described as follows:

1. Research is begun either as routine record keeping or specifically to gather facts for planning purposes.

E X A M P L E   5 . 2

The Continuing Cycle of Research

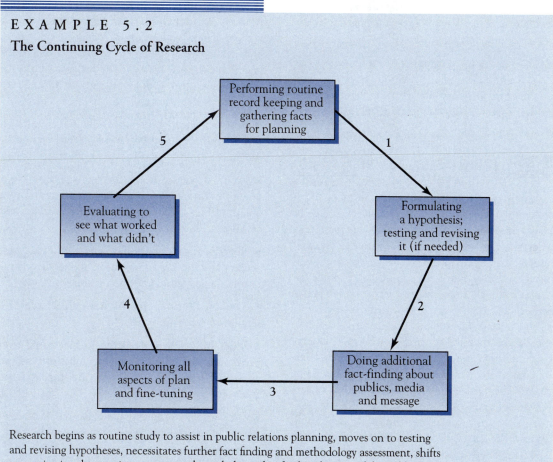

Research begins as routine study to assist in public relations planning, moves on to testing and revising hypotheses, necessitates further fact finding and methodology assessment, shifts to monitoring the ongoing program and concludes with a final evaluation of the public relations plan, which provides information to help in planning for the future, thus completing (and restarting) the cycle.

2. After the PR objective is determined, facts gathered from research are used to formulate a hypothesis, test the hypothesis and make revisions if the hypothesis is disproved.

3. Once the PR objective has been developed, additional fact finding may be necessary to determine what needs to be known about the situations, publics or media to be used. Here we consider how best to present the PR objective to a particular public. We must evaluate the image the public holds and determine whether to keep or modify the present identity. We must also devise methods of reaching the audience and decide what type of message is likely to be most effective—publicity, speech, meeting, display, Web page or advertising. In addition, we need to consider the best timing for activities and messages.

4. To ensure that the plan is working properly, we monitor.

5. Afterward, an evaluation should be conducted to see what went according to plan, what deviated and why. This evaluation can help clarify a public's profile or suggest greater use of a particular medium, and it may be used as resource information in developing future plans.

Thus, a continuing program of research needs to be developed for each public relations situation. The greater the continuity of any research project, the greater its potential validity and reliability.

TYPES OF RESEARCH

Research can be either informal or formal. Both are useful, and both have limitations. You have to know when informal methods are adequate and when more formal methods are required. Formal research can be divided into two categories: qualitative and quantitative. Qualitative research includes historical and legal research, some types of field studies and the like. It is descriptive and informative but not measurable. Quantitative research can be experimental research done in the laboratory or survey research done in the field. Field studies can be observational and thus qualitative, but most field studies in public relations consist of survey research. Quantitative research allows mathematical analysis because it produces measurable results. There is a place for all types of research. The choice depends on the purpose of the research and on the degree of accuracy the client requires (and will pay for).

Increasingly, the public relations practitioner must learn electronic forms of information retrieval—for instance, Internet navigation tools and software systems that allow worldwide search and retrieval of research data for the public relations practitioner astute enough to use them.

How to do your own research is discussed in Chapter 6, which also provides guidelines for evaluating research that you buy from a supplier.

POINTS TO REMEMBER

■ The two basic categories of research methods are *secondary* and *primary*.

■ Research in public relations is a never-ending process that includes formative research to gather facts, research to monitor programs and campaigns and evaluative research to determine your campaign's success and how you need to plan for the future. There's no simple all-purpose formula to follow in doing research.

■ Research in public relations includes audience, media and trend analysis; message testing; and issue monitoring, forecasting and evaluating.

■ Information systems officers manage the current flow of information generated by an organization; organizations' librarians maintain past records and archives such as files and documents.

■ Records the public relations practitioner must accumulate include information about the organization, its personnel and its ongoing activities.

■ Two broad categories of research sources are scholarly and commercial.

■ Much research is available in electronic data banks, and some is accessible to users of personal computers through CD-ROM and through the Internet.

■ *Demographics* provides "hard" factual data about a population: its gender, level of education, occupation and so on.

■ *Psychographics* reveals the personality traits of a public.

■ *Geo-demographics* identifies geographic areas that are populated by consumers who share demographic and psychographic characteristics.

■ The key to successful interpretation of surveys and polls is a realistic and objective viewpoint.

■ The main stages of the planning phase of research are issue forecasting, learning about publics, planning media use and considering possible outcomes.

■ A five-step plan to establish an issues-management system includes: (1) anticipate issues and establish priorities; (2) analyze issues by developing a formal situational analysis or issue brief; (3) recommend an organizational position on issues; (4) identify publics/opinion leaders who can advance your position; (5) identify desired behaviors of publics/opinion leaders.

■ In each planning situation, decide which are the major publics and which are the minor ones.

■ Expect different communication behaviors from information seekers than from information processors.

■ After-the-fact measurements of goals provide an estimate of objective achievement and indicate where problems may persist.

■ After the PR objective is determined, facts gathered from research are used to formulate a hypothesis, test the hypothesis and make revisions if the hypothesis is disproved.

■ Formal research can be divided into two categories: qualitative and quantitative.

■ Qualitative research is descriptive and informative, but it is not measurable.

■ Quantitative research can be experimental research done in the laboratory or survey research done in the field. Quantitative research permits statistical analysis because it produces measurable results.

■ There is a place for all types of research. The choice depends on the purpose of the research and the degree of accuracy the client requires and can afford.

NOTES

[1] Stephen J. F. Unwin, "How Culture, Age and Sex Affect Advertising Response," *Journalism Quarterly* (Winter, 1973), p. 743.

[2] For an excellent description of research sources, see Jacques Barzun, *Modern Researcher*, 6th ed. (Orlando, Fla: Harcourt Brace Jovanovich, 1998).

[3] Danny Moss and Andrew Newman, *Global Sources* (Basingstoke, UK: Hampshire House Publications, 1996).

[4] "Geo-Demographics—Aid in Marketing and Recruiting," *pr reporter's purview* 168 (January 14, 1985), p. 2; see also Ronald L. Vaught, "Demographic Data Banks: A New Management Resource," *Business Horizons*, 27 (November–December 1982), pp. 38–42.

[5] Statement issued in 1978 by the National Council on Public Polls, 1990 M Street, N.W., Washington, D.C. 20036: President Albert H. Cantril, Vice President Burns W. Roper, Secretary-Treasurer Frederick P. Currier and trustees Archibald M. Crossley, Mervin Field, George Gallup, Louis Harris and Richard M. Scammon.

[6] *Advertising and Sales Promotion* (February 1972), p. 38.

[7] Anonymous, "Six Ways to Use Research," *Public Relations Journal*, 50(5) (May 1994), pp. 26–27.

[8] Kerry Tucker and Bill Trumpfheller, "Building an Issues Management System," *Public Relations Journal*, 49(11) (November 1993), pp. 36–37.

[9] James E. Grunig, "An Assessment of Economic Education Programs for Journalism Students." Paper presented to the Public Relations Division, Association for Education in Journalism annual convention, Houston, Texas, August 5, 1979.

[10] Grunig has since stopped using the referent criterion variable because he has found that the other variables yield the same predictions.

[11] Gary Levin, "Role of Research Rises in Public Relations," *Advertising Age* (May 16, 1994), p. 28.

[12] Harry O'Neill, "A Good Company Image Can Mean Higher Sales," *ORC Issue Watch*, news release.

[13] Ibid.

[14] American Heart Association, 1986 Food Festival Public Awareness Survey.

Selected readings, activities and assignments appropriate to this chapter can be found in the *Instructor's Guide* or on InfoTrac if you are using the InfoTrac College Edition.

CHAPTER 6

RESEARCH PROCESSES, PROCEDURES AND TECHNIQUES

Demonstrating accountability through research is not only necessary to get behind the mahogany doors, but to avoid being outplaced. . . . To reaffirm the central strategic role of public relations/corporate communications, we need to be vigorous and persistent in systematically capturing and analyzing information from key stakeholders and in keeping the organization informed and focused on the stakeholders' needs. We need to be the organizational radar, taking soundings and providing early warnings to help the senior management team steer clear of public relations problems and charting the course to building a desired corporate reputation.

ANDERS GRONSTEDT, PUBLIC RELATIONS COUNSELOR

Good research and management's openness to communication, working in tandem, generate a favorable climate for public relations.

PETER FINN, RESEARCH & FORECASTS, INC., NEW YORK

Any superimposing of preconceived ideas which forces patterns upon people's reports loses the richness, the uniqueness, the flavor or the authenticity of what they are trying to say about themselves. What is needed is information which transmits reliably, in people's own terms, what they are feeling.

HADLEY CANTRIL, SOCIAL PSYCHOLOGIST

In addition to providing public relations with a new medium, the World Wide Web has given it a new research tool. That's a mixed blessing. The Web is easier to use than a traditional library because it is literally at your finger tips. You can count on the general reliability of data available at sites like the CIA's World Factbook http://www.odci.gov/cia/publications/nsolo/wfb-all.htm, or the General Social Survey http://www.icpsr.umich.edu/GSS. However, even the USA's National

Election Survey and the Census—two other frequently used sources—have problems that are fairly typical of all survey research. Issues may arise from how the question was worded, when it was asked and of whom.

Of course the Web is full of all sorts of other facts that didn't come from survey research, facts offered by organizations, institutions and individuals about themselves. Reliability may sometimes be a problem not because of outright deceit, but simply failure to update the site. Then there are sources where information is offered without any effort to check on its accuracy. Unfortunately, this is occasionally the case for some of the media sites because the media have a tendency to use their Web sites for speculative stories that may or may not make it into print or airtime.

So, the Web as a research tool may be quick and easy, but may not be all that accurate. On the other hand, all secondary research—information already gathered and available—always needs to be carefully considered and compared with other available data, including primary research you gather yourself. An important key to doing and using research well is to employ a number of research tools. Look at secondary data first. Then in using primary data, compare informal and formal research information and always consider a mix of qualitative and quantitative information.

If you are already thinking that you know why many public relations practitioners don't use research, then stop a moment and consider this. Informal research is really what the previous chapter is all about. We collect facts all of the time, personally and professionally. The difference in what we call informal research is building these miscellaneous bits of knowledge into a useful database. This chapter tells you how to give structure to information and how to use some special informal research techniques to fill in your knowledge gaps.

Formal research falls into two categories: qualitative and quantitative. It's easy to remember which one is which if you remember that quantitative comes from quantity, as in counting. The qualitative, from quality, gives an added dimension that doesn't reduce to numbers. The two complement

each other. That is why most public relations practitioners employ both.

The next question you may be asking is why you need to know this if you don't intend to do any research. You may never actually do any formal research yourself, but you will need it.[1] That means you'll have to get it from a source. You'll need to know enough to know how reliable that research is. If you are buying it, you'll also need to know whether or not it is worth what you are being charged.

INFORMAL RESEARCH

Informal research is research conducted without generally agreed-upon rules and procedures that would enable someone else to replicate the same study. The results of such research can be used only for description and not for prediction (see Example 6.1).

Among the categories of techniques frequently used in informal research are unobtrusive measures, journalistic research, opinion and communication audits and publicity analysis. Intuition and experience also play significant roles, and ethical considerations must be given full weight in all research endeavors.

Unobtrusive Measures

Informal research makes extensive use of unobtrusive measures to gather information. Such measures permit researchers to study someone or something without interfering with or interrupting what's going on. Field experiments are often designed to incorporate these techniques. Unobtrusive measures give a researcher a general notion of what has occurred, but no real proof. If, for example, you use several different sources to issue color-coded tickets to an event, you can count how many people used each color of ticket, but you cannot tell from where they got them. A classic example of the flawed use of unobtrusive research measures comes from a

EXAMPLE 6.1
Informal Research: Pluses and Minuses of Various Techniques

Technique	Pluses	Minuses
Unobtrusive measures	1. No "intrusion" that affect publics 2. Physical evidence 3. Can be less costly, more convenient	1. Investigator error 2. Recorder error 3. Fixed data 4. Some physical evidence is not appropriate to psychological or sociological study.
Audits	1. Make it possible to locate "problems in the making" 2. Can detect breaks in the communication chain 3. Help develop images that are held by different publics	1. Special sensitivity to "guinea pig" effect—awareness of measure 2. Sensitivity to confidentiality 3. People with less formal schooling may give socially acceptable responses at variance with real views 4. Response to visible clues from interviewer
Publicity analysis	1. Shows evidence of efforts 2. Suggests other opportunities	1. Same as unobtrusive measures 2. Incomplete documentation 3. Difficult to put into context 4. Not a measure of audience impact

survey conducted by a museum. Museum administrators assumed that a display's popularity could be judged by the amount of wear on the carpet in front of it. Unfortunately, they failed to take into account the fact that some displays lay along routes that the public often took to get to restrooms and water fountains.[2]

Journalistic Research

When it comes to gathering data, journalists and public relations researchers have a lot in common. For one thing, both rely heavily on unobtrusive measures. Philip Meyer, author of *Precision Journalism*, observed that "the role of the fire-engine researcher may come naturally and readily to journalists. The ground rules are no different from those on which we've always operated: find the facts, tell what they mean, and do it without wasting time."[3] Like other researchers, the journalist is trained to get information from two principal sources: secondary (public records, media files, libraries) and primary (mainly interviews). Practicing sound interviewing techniques is essential. The journalist learns to phrase questions neutrally, to avoid asking "leading" questions or putting words into the mouth of the respondent. A good journalist also learns how to organize questions in a logical sequence, offering the easiest one first. The rapport a journalist becomes skillful at developing with interview subjects contributes significantly to eliciting answers from people who are under no obligation to give them. A journalist also learns how to pin down an evasive respondent to get at something only suggested or implied by earlier answers.

The journalist also learns that listening and observing are extremely important to both the reporter and the public relations researcher. A few journalists can recall entire conversations, although most rely on audio and video recorders. These methods, as well as the records journalists use and their observations constitute unobtrusive measures.[4]

The tools of reporting are the tools of any other form of primary research. Furthermore, the general researcher, like the journalist, must try to make sense out of all the information he or she has collected. Both must also be sensitive to trends, contradictions and conflicts and must be able to communicate their findings efficiently and effectively—usually under deadline pressure.

Opinion and Communication Audits

Informal research also makes wide use of opinion audits and communication audits. The typical procedure for either type of audit is identical (see Example 6.2). Opinion audits may be social, economic or political. Some opinion audits use survey research, but many concentrate on observational data such as economic indicators, trends that note what is happening but do not explain why and experiential reporting (people recounting individual experiences).

Communication audits attempt to evaluate various publics' responses to an organization's communication efforts (see Example 6.3). Opinion audits and communication audits can both be done with publics inside or outside an organization. Moreover, either can be used prior to a change (such as at the beginning of a campaign) to establish a benchmark or baseline against which subsequent results can be measured.

Publicity Analysis

Publicity analysis is another often-used tool of informal research. Clippings from print media and transcripts from broadcast publicity can be analyzed to determine the quantity and quality of coverage. Analysis is usually broken down by audience, medium, message and frequency. The prestige of the publication or broadcast source is often taken into consideration as well, to weight the value of the publicity to intended audiences.

Risks and Responsibilities

The validity of sources used in informal research is always a serious issue. For example, in looking at audiences that media claim to reach, figures should always be suspect. In the USA where print media are examined by the Audit Bureau of Circulations, some confidence can be placed in the numbers, but many international publications only estimate circulation whether paid or controlled by distribution. Even in the USA, magazine publishers routinely overestimate. The consequences affect researchers, media buyers and, of course, the advertisers, although for the advertisers the magazines usually offer cash refunds or offer extra space called "make-goods."[5] Broadcast numbers, even audited ones, are also suspect, as the information in the formal research section shows.

The consequences of taking any source for granted can be serious. For example, when Ross Perot was trying to defeat the North American Free Trade Agreement (NAFTA), he said the agreement would put 5.9 million U.S.A. jobs at risk. That figure came originally from a brochure produced by a start-up investment fund, Ameri-Mex, that wanted to raise $50 million to buy some small companies that paid workers between $7 and $10 an hour and locate them in Mexico. Using Ameri-Mex's figures but adding some large high-tech companies and even some defense industries that couldn't move for security reasons, analyst Pat Choate published a study showing a higher number.[6]

When using secondary information, always cross-check information with at least three sources before accepting its validity. Your responsibility in using and disseminating information from informal research is especially critical because other researchers are less likely to check the results. There's

EXAMPLE 6.2

Typical Audit Procedure

This audit procedure applies to either opinion audits or communication audits. It uses both formal and informal research techniques.

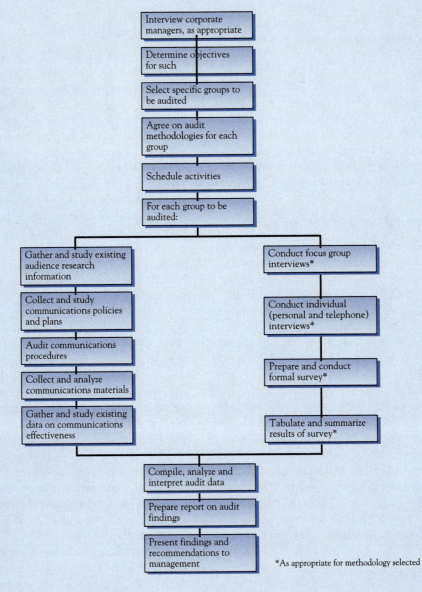

Source: Reprinted with permission of Jim Haynes.

EXAMPLE 6.3

Communication Audit

A communication audit for an organization involves searching for differences in opinion about the organization among various publics to improve the "fit" so that publics develop the same ideas about what the organization is, does and should be.

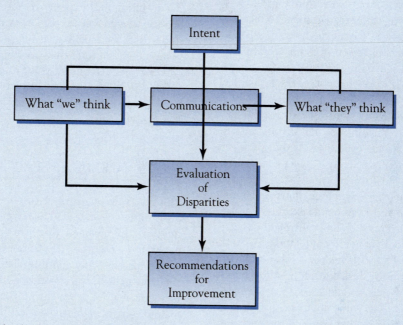

Source: Reprinted with permission of Jim Haynes.

not the process of replication that formal research offers.

Upholding ethical standards in gathering information is important too. You must be sure respondents understand how the study is being conducted, what the purpose is, and how the results will be used. You should protect respondents by guaranteeing them anonymity.

Anonymity is especially critical in the audit process, which is usually done with employees. It's important too in processes that use employee suggestions either put in boxes or sent by e-mail. Another process for gathering ideas to identify problems or to solve them is a Crawford Slip-Writing Method. The CSM asks participants (cus-

tomers, employees, volunteers or any other public) to write a response to a focused question in 5 to 10 minutes. The process can use as many as 3 questions resulting in a 30-minute session. The involvement of the public in the process gives special insights to management and creates participation on the part of the public, but it also raises expectations. Beyond that, sorting the slips is a concentrated, analytical and evaluative process that can be time consuming. However, Crawford's research shows 4–6 percent of the ideas generated are immediately usable.[7] The importance in this process lies in keeping confidences. More ideas are generated when anonymity is promised and must, therefore, be kept.

The Role of Intuition and Experience

Much informal research is "soft," that is, based on available information and/or intuition. A good example of this is a piece developed by John W. Felton when he was vice president of corporate communications for McCormick & Company, Inc. (he is now president of the Institute for Public Relations). In trying to get management to recognize the impact of generational experience in attitudes, he developed a comparison of trends from the 50s through the 90s including styles of dress, basic beliefs, meaning of work, thoughts of the future, feelings about employment, use of time, use of money, individual vs. collective sense of responsibility and education. Felton's point was that if you are trying to talk to people, you need to know that their generational experience is likely to affect the way they hear and respond to what you say. His effort affected all employee communications and public presentations by other corporate executives.[8]

An informal research tool called PVI discussed in Chapter 4 looks at publics in relationship to the organization. PVI's developer, consultant Jim Haynes, takes into consideration how much control over the Public or audience an organization has compared to the Vulnerability of the organization to any action by that public in order to estimate potential Impact. This is not guesswork, as many factors have to be known, but it is informal.

The mix of informal and formal within both qualitative and quantitative research is critical. One of the largest national organizations interested in affecting public policy says it compiles membership information from letters, phone calls, e-mail, use of products, activities and services. It also tracks and analyzes social, economic and demographic trends, reviews research done and reported by news media and research organizations, and examines financial trends and studies, some of which it initiates. Additionally, it conducts focus group interviews on special topics and surveys a random sample of its 30-million plus membership several times a year. The mix is essential for putting information into the proper perspective.[9]

Much informal research is conducted to confirm or deny the validity of concepts that are ultimately based on intuition or experience: someone simply feels that something is true or that something is happening. Research typically cannot *prove* that the intuition or experience is valid or invalid, however; it usually only *indicates* that it is. But intuition and experience are very important, because they may lead to a larger and more formal study that does yield scientific evidence. While some people assert that formal research only proves what everyone already knows, the results of formal studies sometimes reveal that "common knowledge" is in error—indeed, little more than shared myth.

FORMAL RESEARCH

The two types of formal research—qualitative and quantitative—can be conducted either in the laboratory or in the field (see Example 6.4). While qualitative research describes, quantitative research measures (by counting). Both types follow the same general steps, and in both the researcher is responsible for representing the study honestly, maintaining confidentiality and interpreting data objectively. The responsibility is great because many people are suspicious of research.

Steps in Formal Research

The formal research process usually consists of the following steps:

1. State the problem.

2. Select a manageable (and measurable) portion of the problem.

3. Establish definitions to be used in the measurement.

4. Conduct a search in published literature for studies similar in subject or research approach.

5. Develop a hypothesis.[10]

E X A M P L E   6 . 4

Formal Research: Pluses and Minuses of Various Techniques

QUALITATIVE

Technique	Pluses	Minuses
Historiography, case studies, diaries	1. Give insight into situations 2. Suggest further research to examine the "whys" that the research indicates 3. Provide detail that can put other research into perspective	1. Difficult to generalize from 2. Often lack rigor of scientific method 3. Time-consuming and require boiling down a lot of data that are sometimes selectively presented.
In-depth interviews	1. Allow interviewers to follow up on new line of questioning 2. Permit respondent to describe in detail so that more information is available 3. Permit questions to be broader, more comprehensive	1. Difficult to transcribe and code for content analysis 2. Interviewer sometimes "leads the witness," or otherwise influences response 3. Responses often include basically meaningless information
Focus groups	1. Some are quick and less expensive than other research methods 2. Flexible in design and format 3. Elicit more in-depth information and often point out "whys" of behavior, as well as showing intensity of attitudes held	1. Often used as conclusive evidence when they are merely tools to be used with other research 2. Sometimes not handled well by moderator, so not all participants express opinions 3. Sometimes not representative of population
Panels	1. Same as for focus groups 2. May be chosen to represent a population	1. Same as for focus groups 2. Same people used over time "learn" some of the reasons for difficulties and cease to be representative

QUANTITATIVE

Technique	Pluses	Minuses
Content analysis	1. Shows what appeared, how often, where and in what context 2. Allows comparison with other data, especially about publics 3. Useful in tracking trends and in monitoring change	1. Expensive and time consuming 2. Provides no information about impact of messages and audiences 3. Some information may not be in the media

(continued)

EXAMPLE 6.4 *(continued)*

QUANTITATIVE *(continued)*

Technique	Pluses	Minuses
Survey research	1. Flexible	1. Respondents may not tell the truth, because they don't remember accurately or because they want to appear different from how they really act
	2. Varied—administered by mail, telephone, computer, personal or group interview	2. Inflexibility of instrument doesn't allow for in-depth expression and intensity of true feelings
	3. Capitalizes on enjoyment of expressing opinion	3. Wrong questions may be asked of wrong people

6. Design experiments.[11] This step includes defining the universe or population you want to study and then choosing a sampling method and a sample.

7. Obtain the data.

8. Analyze the data.

9. Interpret the data to make inferences and generalizations.

10. Communicate the results.

A somewhat different formulation of these research steps is given in Example 6.5.

Stating the problem with precision certainly aids in the second step: deciding which part of the problem most requires study or which part lends itself to testing that may cast light into other dark corners. Because they ignore this step, many inexperienced practitioners design unwieldy research projects that attempt to examine too much at once.

A realistic researcher usually designs simple projects that keep the significance of the research in proper perspective. This involves, in each case, isolating a testable portion of the problem and knowing specifically what information is needed. You must take care to spell out what you want to know. Don't set a goal like "Find out how to establish effective communications with employees"

when you really want to know whether they would like to have an employee publication. If the latter is the question, find out what kind of publication they want, how often it should be published and what subjects it should cover.

By establishing definitions, you also set parameters for your research. If you want to find out what people think about the Center for Battered Women, first decide what you mean by "people"—social workers? battered women? everyone in the city or county? residents of the neighborhood in which it is located? The purpose of your study is the determining factor in establishing these definitions.

Conducting a literature search simply means seeing if someone has already done some work for you. Has someone conducted research that you can apply or use as a model? To answer this question, you must consult relevant research journals in the social sciences, communication and business. Buried deep in one or more of these may be precisely the information you need to obtain a unique insight into your research project.

■ Qualitative Research

Many people are more comfortable with qualitative research than with quantitative, because they are suspicious of statistics and feel that numbers

EXAMPLE 6.5

The Research Process

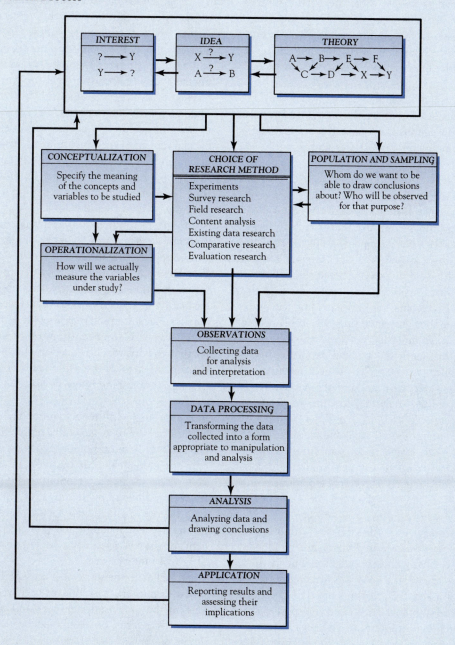

Source: Reprinted with permission from Earl Babbie, *The Practice of Social Research,* 7th ed., Wadsworth, 1995, p. 101.

neglect the human side of the story. Undeniably, statistics can be used to obscure, distort or exaggerate. Consider, for example, the debates about how many homeless people there are in the United States and how many people may go hungry here (not necessarily the same people). The percentages might be comparatively small, but whatever they are, the human suffering involved is indeed intolerable.

Although much formal research could be classified as qualitative, three distinctive techniques are generally employed in qualitative work: historiography (including case studies and diaries), in-depth interviews and focus groups.

Historiography, Case Studies, Diaries People who write biographies or historical narratives about actual happenings must first collect facts from informed sources—both secondary sources (books, articles, journals and so on) and primary sources (people who were involved in some way). The researchers then organize these facts to provide the necessary background for understanding the problem or issue they are examining. When PR people produce background papers or position papers, they rely on this methodology and reporting technique—called *historiography*—which reconstructs the past in a systematic and orderly manner. It involves recording, analyzing, coordinating and explaining past events.

Case studies use all available factual data to examine issues, events and organizations systematically. Diaries are used in field studies and consist of detailed reports of personal experiences and actions.

In-depth Interviews As is the case with informal audits, most in-depth interviews are conducted with a specifically chosen audience. But in these formal interviews, the questions are pretested and are usually asked of all respondents. The questions are designed to produce open-ended responses that the researcher must interpret. The respondents selected are encouraged to talk freely and fully. This technique is used extensively in motivational research—the study of the emotional or subcon-

scious reasons that lie behind decision making. However, motivational research requires highly trained interviewers and skilled analysis.

Open-ended questions are often used with in-depth interviewing because they give the interviewer an opportunity to follow up equivocal answers with more probing questions. For example, while trying to ferret out employer bias toward hiring members of minority groups, some in-depth interviewers asked general questions at first and then zoomed in with questions like this: "If you had two applicants absolutely equal in terms of educational background and experience, and one was a woman or a member of a minority race, or both, which would you hire?" The employer's answer could then be interpreted directly, based on a particular response.

Some researchers also feel that open-ended questions reduce error in reply, since the interviewee can respond in his or her own words rather than having to fit his or her answer into a category set up by the researcher. Errors are often made in evaluating such questions, however, because interviewers may interpret responses in light of their own opinions. Consequently, most researchers prefer that the answers be coded in the office rather than in the field by the interviewer. This reduces the impact of the interviewer's bias.

Focus Groups In the focus group technique, the interviewees chosen generally represent one specific public, because homogeneous groups usually converse more freely. Alternatively, however, focus groups may include representatives from each of a number of different publics. In a university setting, such publics might include faculty, staff, administrators, students, alumni and perhaps parents, regents or trustees. Generally, a focus group consists of 12 to 15 interviewees.

The key to the session's success is the moderator, who must be a skillful interviewer, adept at keeping the conversation moving and tactful when acting as referee or devil's advocate. Research groups often videotape these sessions, too, and they often use a live monitor so that viewers—the researchers or the client—can slip notes to the moderator during breaks in the session and get additional questions on the agenda. The focus interview is often used as a prelude to developing a questionnaire.

Misuse of this technique appears when reported results are used to make judgments without benefit of more specific research. Focus groups should only be used as a *preliminary* or *guidance* technique.

Focus groups are not the same as panels, although the two research techniques share some advantages and disadvantages. Panels (groups of people queried on several occasions) are sometimes used for discussions in issue development, but they are not generally considered appropriate for formal research. Focus groups are.

Five steps are followed in focus group research, some of which are identical to the steps involved in overall research methodology:[12]

1. Define the problem to be examined.

2. Choose the part of the problem to be looked at by the participants.

3. Decide how many focus groups are needed, and choose the participants. (Because group selection methods are likely to create nonrepresentative groups, more than one group is necessary in almost every situation.)

4. Work out all the details of the session, including notification of the participants, selection of the moderator, physical arrangement of the interview area and compensation of the participants.

5. Prepare all materials that the group will need, including a list of basic questions to serve as a guide for the moderator.

■ Quantitative Research

The difference between qualitative research (which is based primarily on description) and quantitative research (which is based primarily on measurement) is that quantitative research offers a higher degree of predictability. It is easier to generalize from results of this research in order to make predictions about the larger population from which

the participants were drawn. Quantitative measures include content analysis and survey research based on descriptive and inferential statistics. (Descriptive statistics describe data by intelligible category; inferential statistics help the user draw conclusions, often about a population, from the sample studied.)

Content Analysis Transcripts of panel discussions or interactions, in-depth interviews and focus group interviews are often subjected to content analysis, as are broadcast media transcripts and newspaper and magazine clippings. Content analysis allows for the systematic coding and classification of written material that relates to the public relations practitioner's organization or client. Content analysis tells what has been published or broadcast and the context in which it was presented. This provides helpful clues to the kinds of information various publics are being exposed to (although not necessarily what they consume and believe).

As a data-gathering technique, content analysis can also be used to assess what is being said about the goals set by the organization and about its specialized areas of interest, such as proposed legislation. The main difficulty with the technique consists in setting up a model that will give an unbiased analysis.

The classic definition of content analysis was provided by Bernard Berelson, who called it a research technique for the "objective, systematic, and quantitative description of the manifest content of communication."[13] The content analysis research procedure developed by H. D. Lasswell is one of the earliest quantitative measures of communication and follows Berelson's definition. It is *objective* because categories used in the analysis are both precise and normative, with no evaluative terms (good–bad) used. It is *systematic* because selection proceeds by a formal, unbiased system that does not permit subjective collection of data. It is *quantitative* because the results are usually expressed in some numerical way—in percentages, ratios, frequency distributions, correlation coefficients or the like. It is *manifest* because it is a direct measure: no effort is made to figure out the intent of the person using the words; only the fact that the words were used is registered. Some content analysis research designs are more complicated, because they apply symbol or phrase coding to allow for mention of the "context" of the words used.

Content analysis uses variables related to the medium: typography, makeup and layout for print; and camera angles, editing, shot selection, pace and scene locations for broadcast. PR content analysis usually is concerned with the time or space given to an organization and its spokespersons. In broadcasting, the concern is with whether the spokesperson does the talking, the announcer describes the situation or the two work in combination.

Hypotheses can be tested with content analysis, and comparisons can be made with normal or real situations by designing a representation of the "normal" or "real world." Sometimes the comparison shows how a group is represented, in contrast to their real role in society. An example might start with a television drama that depicts a two-working-parent family with two children. This might then be compared to the current reality, which is often a family headed by a single parent who works.

Of course, content analysis is limited to recorded communication. Unless you are studying communication processes per se, validity problems are likely. However, the tangibility of the materials studied makes reliability likely.[14]

Some research steps in content analysis are different from those in the basic research process. Once you format the research questions, construct a hypothesis, identify the population and select a sample, you must go on to define a unit of analysis, construct the categories to be analyzed and write descriptions of the categories. After you establish a way to choose material for the various categories uniformly, you must train coders and make sure that they categorize the items the same way. You can test that ability by applying a coder reliability formula that measures whether the definitions are consistently applied. After the collected data are categorized, you analyze them, draw conclusions and then try to develop some statements indicating a situation or circumstance that supports your hypothesis.

Survey Research   Survey research attempts to measure the practices and preferences of a specified public by tabulating responses to a standardized series of questions. Such research has become an essential basis for assessing a public's actions and opinions. Two types of statistics are used in survey research: descriptive and inferential. Descriptive statistics consists of talking about data in manageable ways. Inferential statistics lets you use what you found in the sample to draw conclusions about a population.

Basics of Quantitative Research

A PR practitioner must master at least the basics of quantitative research. These basics include a practical understanding of sampling, probability and how to pose research questions.

Sampling   Since a public normally contains a large number of people, it's usually possible to question only a representative sample of this population to determine what the public as a whole thinks. The sample need not be large. Large samples cost too much, and they do not improve the investigation's accuracy much, once a certain sample size is reached. At very small sample sizes, predictability increases rather dramatically with each additional member of the sample; but once the sample reaches a certain size, error becomes a factor. (*Sample error* is the degree of discrepancy between the representativeness of the sample and the larger population.) Thus, a sample of 1,000 is not likely to be much better than a sample of 500, although a sample of 100 is considerably more reliable than one of 50. That explains why, in a country of more than 260 million people, reliable national estimates are made based on samples of only 1,500 to 3,000. Researchers do this work within a margin of allowable error. The size of the sample depends on how much error can be tolerated in the results—that is, how close a call you need to make.

Sampling is more than a matter of convenience. A "universe" is everyone you would want to be included in a study, and you're not likely to reach everyone unless that universe is small. One attempted study of a large universe is the USA's census which in 1990 missed about 4 million people but was upheld by the Supreme Court.

Probability Sampling is based on probability. The researcher is gambling on how probable it is that a sample accurately represents a population. But the gamble is not wild. The people selected for a sample can be chosen *randomly,* and a random sample is usually free of bias or substantial error with regard to such things as the income of those chosen. The use of a mechanical method for random selection eliminates any bias that the researcher might have or any peculiar homogeneity that might exist within a group or segment of a group selected for study. (*Bias* is the tendency of an estimate to deviate from the true value.) In a random sample, each member of a population has an equal chance of being selected. For example, students in a mass communication class were used as subjects for a survey on media use. To select a random sample from the class, the researcher gave every *other* student seated in the classroom a survey to complete. Since seating was a matter of the students' choice, and not simply assigned, every student had an equal chance of being selected for the sample. This is random selection.

But while this group of students constitutes a random sample of the population of students in the room, it does not constitute a sample of people living in that area or of students attending that college or even of students taking classes in mass communication at that college. The population from which the sample was drawn was one particular classroom of students, and that remains the population to which information discovered in the sample survey can legitimately be extrapolated.

In dealing with any large number of events that occur by chance, we can make predictions (or educated guesses) based on the relative frequency of occurrence of certain events among all events that are observed. This involves applying rules of probability. To return to the example of the student survey, because every other student in the classroom was chosen, half of the students (one out of every two) completed the questionnaire. Thus, each student had a 1:2 (or .5) chance of being se-

lected, and this is the probability that any given student would be chosen.

Two types of errors can occur in research that uses probability sampling: sampling errors and nonsampling errors. Sampling errors are the chance difference between an unrepresentative sample and the larger population from which it was drawn. They can occur if a sample is too small for the audience or population being sampled or if the selection is not random enough. *Nonsampling errors* are simply mistakes made by the research team in gathering, recording or calculating data. Nonsampling errors are reduced when fewer data have to be recorded and calculated—another argument for using a small sample size.

As researcher W. Edward Deming observed long ago, a survey's usefulness and reliability "may actually be enhanced by cutting down on the size of sample and using the money so saved to reduce the nonsampling errors,"[15] such as by tracing wrong and missing information. (*Reliability* is the extent to which a test always yields the same results. *Validity* is how well the evidence explains what is occurring—whether the empirical measures are really measuring the desired situation or concept. Thus, questions of reliability ask, "Is the measurement accurate?" while questions of validity ask, "Does this measure what it says it measures?") These savings, Deming pointed out, might free up more time and money for constructing the questionnaire, hiring better interviewers, providing better training and supervision in the field and making more callbacks to people not previously at home.

Not all samples are chosen randomly. In fact, three major types of nonprobability or nonrandom sampling exist: accidental, purposive and quota. A reporter who stands outside the campus cafeteria and asks people leaving what they think of the food is getting an *accidental* sample; it is accidental because those who come out at that time may not be representative of everyone who eats there. (Suppose you catch all the members of the football team, and they all liked the ground round?) A *purposive* sample is conducted by a reporter who interviews teachers and students in the food and nutrition department about the quality of food in the college cafeteria. (They have been chosen because of their particular expertise or background, and they can be expected to have different ideas about food from their counterparts in, say, engineering.) A *quota* sample is used by a reporter who tries to match the school's population in miniature: the proper proportion of freshmen, transfer students, sophomores, juniors, seniors, staff, faculty. The sample in this case would be improved if the reporter already knew what percentage of these different groups ate regularly in the cafeteria. Each group could then be represented in the sample in the same proportion as its presence in the entire population of students who ate in the cafeteria.

Stratified sampling is similar to quota sampling in that both re-create the population in microcosm and both have population representation. However, the selection process is different. In *stratified sample measurement*, selection is *random* but the overall population has been divided into categories or strata. Selection is therefore a matter of probability. In quota sampling, the interviewer selects participants nonrandomly.

Posing Research Questions Most quantitative research attempts to answer, "what if" or "I wonder if" questions or speculations. Research questions are often asked about matters that haven't been looked into often or in depth. Such *exploratory* research looks for indications, not causes. It attempts to get preliminary data so that research questions can be refined for future study and so that hypotheses can be proposed. You might wonder, for example, what conditions (if any) could change the results of your exploratory research, or how other elements of the research questions are related. In doing this, you are attempting to make a prediction (hypothesis) that states your assumption of what is or could be. The reverse of that assumption—what is not or could not be—is called a *null hypothesis*. It expresses the assumption there is no relationship.

Prediction comes after preliminary or exploratory research and before hypothesis testing. At the exploratory stage, you are saying, "I wonder." At the prediction stage, you are saying, "I think." When you start to test an idea or a hypothesis in quantitative research, your particular re-

search project will dictate whether you should use parametric or nonparametric statistics. You will use parametric statistics for interval and ratio data—data about populations, means and variances. You will use nonparametric statistics for nominal and ordinal data. The numbers contained in interval data reflect the existence of meaningful, consistent-sized increments between numerical values of each variable. Ratio data are similar to interval data but in addition possess a true zero reference point. Nominal data are organized into exhaustive and mutually exclusive categories for each variable. Ordinal data are arranged by rank order of the underlying measurements.

Hypothesis testing is always done within some theoretical framework. Most public relations people use communication or persuasion theories. There are five commonly accepted bases for communication theories and two general bases for persuasion theories (see Chapter 7).

The five-step procedure for testing a hypothesis is quite simple:

1. State your hypothesis—what you think is true of the population or universe (generally a PR public) in general. Make sure that the variable you want to measure in your population can be quantified or counted.

2. State the opposite of your hypothesis—the null hypothesis. This is simply a statement of what would be the case if your hypothesis were not true.

3. Determine the probability that you would see the same differences in the population or universe that you see in your sample, if the opposite of what you believe turned out to be true. This is the null hypothesis's probability of being true, based on your sample's results.

4. If that probability is slight—less than .05, say—then you can reject the null hypothesis, with (in this case) at least 95 percent confidence that what you thought was true is true.

5. If the sample probability that the null hypothesis is true is significantly larger—even though it is much less than .5 (that is, 50/50)—you should not reject the null hypothesis, since you can't be sufficiently confident that your original hypothesis is true.

Hypothesis testing uses descriptive and inferential statistics.

AUDIENCE INFORMATION

Most sampling relies on a small subgroup of the audience that the researcher uses to represent the larger group. The subgroup is chosen with the demographics of the larger audience in mind. Some of the research most valuable to people interested in persuasion goes beyond telling who an audience is to describing who the audience thinks it is—or better still, who it wants to be. Information about *who* makes up an audience—age, sex, level of education, geographic location, occupation and such—is called the *demographics*[16] of that audience. But demographics alone isn't enough. A group of individuals, even a large one, may fall into one category in which all demographic data match, and yet the individuals in the group may not think at all alike. A key to how people are likely to respond often lies in their value systems. The study of what goes on inside audience members' heads is termed audience *psychographics.*[17]

A demographer is a social scientist who keeps an ongoing record of the size and characteristics of human populations and how they change—their births, deaths, longevity, migrations and so on. Demographic statistics are important because of the dollars-and-cents consequences of these changes. Demographic information is important to planners trying to develop educational systems to meet future needs, to utilities managers furnishing equipment and services to changing populations and to many others.

Psychographics is a specialty of psychologists employed by polling and attitudinal research firms to help determine what is going on in the minds of people who are members of a particular demographic group. Advertisers have been interested in psychographics for a long time because of the science's relevance to a marketing strategy called "positioning."[18] For example, many commercial products are chemically identical and have equal qualities; how they are presented makes all the difference in competitive marketing.

The most familiar processes for data gathering by samples are cross-section surveys and survey panels. The most frequently used instrument is the questionnaire, which has many formats.

Cross-section Surveys

Three types of samples are widely used in cross-section surveys: probability samples, quota samples and area samples.

In a *probability sample*, people are chosen at random—ordinarily by using a random number table or a mechanical formula such as every nth name on a list together with a random start, a method called "systematic sampling" or "interval sampling."

In a *quota sample*, a population is analyzed by its known characteristics, such as age, sex, residence, occupation and income level. A sample selection is made by choosing a quota of people with desired characteristics in the same proportion as these characteristics exist in the whole population.

In an *area sample*, geographical areas, such as cities or units of cities, are used; an area sample can be designed by using city directories as sources for housing units. Using a *cluster plan* in an area sample may reduce the time and money spent on travel, although it also reduces the randomness somewhat. (In a cluster plan, areas are selected and sample small block clusters from each area are drawn. A random sample may then be drawn from each cluster.)

Survey Panels

Businesses and institutions often use survey panels, such as consumer panels, in their research. One unusual consumer panel employed by a toy company consists of panelists five years old and under. Once a panel is selected, the members are interviewed several times over the duration of the panel. The toy manufacturers get around verbal communication problems by watching their consumer panel. Some research firms videotape panel sessions so that the client can see the results without inhibiting the panelists by being there. (Using one-way glass in the viewing area doesn't fool many panelists.) Videotaping aids in analyzing the sessions too, because it permits body language as well as words to be evaluated.

Survey panelists are usually selected on a cross-sectional basis and generally by quota, which is effective for controlled experiments. Seldom, if ever, are panelists chosen randomly. One disadvantage of panels is that, over time, they tend to become less representative. For example, newspaper editors have found that citizens chosen for small panels of readers from the community tend to become less critical as they learn more about the problems of getting out a daily paper.

Not all survey panels actually meet. Some may participate through teleconferencing. Some may respond only to mailed inquiries of various types, including diaries and questionnaires. Sometimes a panel represents people with vested interests, presumably participating with the inducements of improved goods or services. But members of some panels are rewarded with gifts.

■ Questionnaires

The most familiar survey data-gathering device is the questionnaire. A questionnaire is often administered in face-to-face personal interviews, with the interviewer asking the questions and noting the interviewee's responses on a form.

One important benefit of face-to-face contact is the ability to better understand the questions. Research has shown that even listeners whose hearing is not impaired understand better if they have visual cues. Interestingly, one use of this research has been the development of computerized talking heads with synthesized speech, which enable questions to be asked more precisely and to offer visual cues that aid understanding.[19]

In the future, technology may replace the face-to-face interview. E-mail is being used, especially for employee or membership surveys, and these al-

low for instant responses. Of course questionnaires can be printed and sent by direct mail, handed out at a meeting or left in a facility such as a hotel room or restaurant and they can be printed in any medium, either mass or specialized such as an organization's publication.

When physical contact is not feasible, the next choice has usually been the telephone, although a number of problems may shift polls to another medium. One of the major problems is that fewer questions can be included, because the interview may be interfering with the interviewee's activities. Asking too many questions shortens responses and upsets respondents' tempers. Moreover, only homes with listed telephones can be reached by telephone book-based samples, and up to 30 percent of the telephones in any area may have unlisted numbers. Thus a telephone survey sample is less likely to represent the entire market accurately. One solution to this problem is to obtain from the telephone company a list of local exchanges (the first three numbers in a seven-digit telephone number) and the number of telephones served by each. A computer can then be programmed to draw four digit numbers at random to add to the prefix. This method is reliable enough to be used by national research companies. However, such random dialing includes business telephones and phones of others who might not be eligible respondents. Furthermore, many exchanges and area codes are changing in the USA, making it difficult to keep phone lists updated, even computer-generated ones.

The caller, often a machine, is likely to get another machine, the respondent's answering machine. Many people use their machines not only to capture calls they want but also to screen out calls they don't want. Caller ID and blocking devices that can come with it also prevent unsolicited calls from reaching respondents.

Even if a person answers, the interviewer (actual or automated) may get an immediate hang up. The reason is that marketers have used a survey technique in an effort to make sales over the phone. While many people say they wouldn't mind answering legitimate public opinion surveys, often the caller is not given a chance. Refusal rates are as high as 58 percent in the USA,[20] and when an answering machine is used, that may be filtering out the higher income level respondents so results are seriously skewed.[21]

Computers are used more widely today to administer questionnaires electronically. They are used for polling, in market research to determine product demand and even in personnel interviews. Techniques for using computers vary. In some cases, a person may be seated in front of a screen and asked to type simple responses or to punch numbers on a telephone in answer to questions asked by a mechanical voice. Some researchers say that people hang up more often when they are reached by a computer; however, others say that many people prefer to give private information to a computer, because the machine is nonjudgmental.

Media organizations often put polls on their Web pages, as do other organizations, profit and nonprofit, including various government agencies. The problem with these polls is that respondents are not likely to be very representative of any public except the one that regularly keys into that Web page. Nevertheless, the results are often touted as though these surveys were as representative as administered ones. Television stations, even networks, have questions that they ask viewers to respond to by calling in. In most cases this constitutes a promotional use of the survey rather than a genuine effort to discover public opinion.

Often questionnaires are sent by direct mail. When this is done, the researcher can increase the proportion of responses by enclosing a self-addressed, postage-paid envelope. Such questionnaires can be longer than those used in telephone or personal interviews, but a long, formidable-looking questionnaire will draw few responses.

One important element in the rate of return is the respondent's interest in the subject. For general questionnaires sent to a large sample, you can only expect a 5 to 20 percent return. But when the rate of returns is this small, the respondents usually do not represent the population well. In contrast, a 30 to 80 percent response to a carefully designed questionnaire is likely if respondents have a vested

interest in or some special knowledge of the subject. Members of a professional organization, for example, are more inclined to answer a long, detailed questionnaire that asks about their professional interests. Appeals for cooperation based on the significance of the study, the personal appreciation the researcher would feel or any other altruistic motive on the respondent's part were ineffective. But evidence is mixed on the efficacy of explaining the role and importance of the respondent in the survey.[22]

Increases in postage rates have forced researchers to examine content and systems very carefully to stay within budgets. Some research agencies use Western Union Mailgrams or other electronic mail systems for both speed and drama. The implied urgency of the communication system commands attention.

Women in Communications, Inc., reported a 75 percent return on a salary questionnaire sent to all its members without a return envelope. Texas Instruments Corporation tried a special gimmick. It got almost a 60 percent response from shareholders to a questionnaire printed on the back of dividend checks.

When people don't have a vested interest, offering them money to cooperate is the best way to elicit a response. For years, researchers have provided monetary incentives to encourage people to respond to questionnaires. For affluent respondents, a gift in their name to a charity may work.

In a study collating findings from surveys conducted in the social sciences since 1935, Arnold S. Linsky concluded that researchers may need to change their overall strategy to ensure a high return on mail questionnaires. He found the following devices (listed in descending order of effectiveness) worked best:

1. Send one or more followups, such as postcards or additional letters, as reminders. More intensive followups, such as phone calls or letters sent by special delivery or registered mail, work best.

2. Contact the respondent in some way before the questionnaire is sent. Again, the most effective method of doing this is by phone.

3. Send mail by some type of special handling, such as special delivery, and use a hand-stamped return envelope rather than a postage permit envelope.

4. Send a reward with the mailing. Promises to send something on receipt of the questionnaire are less effective.

5. Make sure that the sponsor of the survey and the name of the person signing the cover letter are both impressive to the audience you are trying to reach.

Linsky's study did not show that guaranteeing the anonymity of respondents constituted a decided asset.[23] Personalizing the questionnaires seems to be somewhat effective, but it also confounds the anonymity issue, so the situation and the issues involved in the research might be the deciding points to consider here.

How to Prepare a Questionnaire   The best way to encourage a good level of response to a survey is to write a good questionnaire (which is usually called the "instrument" by social scientists). The questionnaire should be clear, simple, and interesting (see Example 6.6). You must decide whether the questions should require specific answers or be open-ended to elicit free response. (The latter type is much more difficult to tabulate and usually demands time-consuming content analysis to codify responses.)

Some formats dictate the type of questions. In all cases, though, you must try to elicit all pertinent information easily, quickly and in analyzable form. It takes skill to break a general question down into its logical parts. Questions should be definite and separate, not overlapping, and they should invite answers. Be especially careful of your phrasing because personal queries often meet with some resentment.

Because the source of a questionnaire may bias the answer, it is sometimes important to hire an outside agency to administer the instrument. An interviewer conducting a door-to-door survey for an aluminum foil company received a long list of the many ways one woman used aluminum foil in

her kitchen, but when the interviewer talked to the woman's next-door neighbor, who was also her daughter, he was told, "Don't bother going over there. My mother lives there and she doesn't cook a thing. She eats every meal with us." Obviously, the mother just had not wanted to disappoint the interviewer.

It is important to group questions in a logical sequence so that the arrangement encourages response. If a respondent is to fill out a questionnaire unaided, the instructions must clearly specify whether responses are to be checked, underlined or crossed out (see Example 6.7). Many survey results have been skewed because respondents put x's by choices they thought they were deleting. Every question must be accounted for, but there should also be an allowance for "Other," "Does not know," "Does not wish to answer" or "Omitted."

Another source of skewed results is artificial polarization of opinion in which response options are framed as narrowly and starkly as possible. Otherwise, the interviewees tend to adopt a non-committal position, not because that reflected their true views but because they thought that by giving such an answer they could evade the responsibility of defending their real opinion.

One way to ensure developing a good questionnaire is to pretest it by asking a few people to complete it before you adopt it for the research project. Pretesting may tell you which questions are ambiguous or cause resentment. Examples 6.8 and 6.9 show an advertisement created by the American Heart Association and a survey questionnaire conducted by National Family Opinion, Inc., to pretest this ad's impact and effectiveness before running it.

Some questionnaires that require a specific response provide no gauge for measuring the *intensity* of the response. However, researchers can use semantic differential scales or summated ratings to get at intensity.

The point about pretesting questionnaires cannot be made too strongly. Words change meaning in different contexts, for one thing. For example, the word "family" has many meanings. A biological family means parents and their children, but the term "simple family" can include formally adopted

EXAMPLE 6.6

Tips for Framing Questions

There are . . . some general questions you should always ask yourself when drafting a survey. Some of these questions, and examples of those that may not be obvious to most people, include:

1. Are the words understandable?

2. Do they contain abbreviations or unconventional phrases/jargon?

3. Are the questions technically accurate?

4. Are there appropriate time references?

5. Are they too vague?

6. Are they biased? Bias can occur at least four ways:

   a. *Bias from behavioral expectation*

   QUESTION: More people have attended pro football games than any other sport. Have you ever seen a pro football game?
     1. Yes
     2. No

   REVISION: Have you ever attended a pro football game?
     1. Yes
     2. No

   b. *Bias from leading information*

   QUESTION: If the election were being today, whom would you vote for: Bill Clinton, the incumbent; Bob Dole, the Republican challenger; or Ross Perot, the independent?
   REVISION: If the presidential election were being held today, whom would you vote for: Bill Clinton, Bob Dole, or Ross Perot?

   c. *Bias due to unequal comparison*

   QUESTION: Who do you feel is most responsible for the high oil prices?
     1. Service station owners
     2. People drilling for oil
     3. Executives of the oil companies
   REVISION: Who do you feel is most responsible for the high oil prices?
     1. Service station owners who pump it

     2. Refiners who process it
     3. Businessmen who operate the oil companies

   d. *Bias due to unbalanced categories*

   QUESTION: Currently our country spends about $40 billion a year on social services. Do you feel this amount should:
     1. Be increased
     2. Stay the same
     3. Be decreased a little
     4. Be decreased somewhat
     5. Be decreased a great deal

   REVISION: Currently our country spends about $40 billion a year on social services. Do you feel this amount should:
     1. Be increased significantly
     2. Be increased a little
     3. Stay the same
     4. Be decreased a little
     5. Be decreased significantly

7. Are questions offensive? If so, there are at least three ways to overcome offensive questions:

   a. *Using a series*

   QUESTION: Have you ever had an abortion?
   REVISION: As you know, there is a great deal of controversy about abortion in this community. Some folks think it's a serious problem, others do not. Do you consider abortion to be a serious, moderate, slight or no problem at all in your community?
     1. Serious
     2. Moderate
     3. Slight
     4. Not at all

During the past few years do you think the number of abortions has increased, stayed the same, or decreased in the community?
     1. Increased
     2. Stayed about the same
     3. Decreased

(continued)

EXAMPLE 6.6 *(continued)*

Please try to recall the time when you were a teenager. Do you recall personally knowing anyone who had an abortion?

1. No
2. Yes

How about yourself? Did you ever consider having an abortion?

1. No
2. Yes

If yes, did you actually have one?

1. No
2. Yes

b. *Using general categories to overcome offensive questions*

QUESTION: How much money did you earn in 1994?

_____ dollars

REVISION: Which category below best describes your income during 1998?

1. Less than $20,000
2. $20,000 to $29,999
3. $30,000 to $39,999
4. $40,000 to $49,999
5. $50,000 or more

c. *Using narrative material to overcome offensive questions*

QUESTION: "Big business is the root of society's problems." Do you:

1. Agree
2. Disagree

REVISION: Next, let's talk about your feelings about the relationship between big business and society. Here are various popular opinions, both negative and positive. With each statement, check whether you are in agreement or disagreement.

"Big business is the foundation of our society's problems."

1. Agree
2. Disagree

"Big business is the root of society's problems."

1. Agree
2. Disagree

(Other statements could follow.)

8. Do they require too much effort to answer?

QUESTION: What percentage of your time each month is spent on meetings? _____

REVISION: How many hours do you spend a month in meetings? _____

How many hours do you spend on the job each month? _____

Source: Adapted from "The Communication Audit—Your Road Map to Success," *Journal of Organizational Communication*, 10(2) (February 1981), p. 16. Reprinted with permission of John R. Wirtz and revised to reflect contemporary choices.

---

children. Other references to this unit are nuclear family, natural family, immediate family, primary family or restricted family. Parallel research terms exist in other cultures: elementary family (British) or Kleinefamilie (German). Beyond that, all people belong to their birth/adoptive family and to the new family they create if they marry.[24] Family, then can mean extended family, including grandparents and/or aunts, uncles, cousins.

Also, in some cultures, polygamy is practiced. What then is family? A questionnaire going to

those countries would need to clarify a form to include these multiple family units. In some cultures, if a head of household dies the entire family goes to the next ranking male who has his own "family." The status of each unit within the "family" must be clarified. What a scientific researcher would understand as a definition of "family" might make little sense to a person familiar with customs, but not science.

When surveys have to be translated, testing of the translation process is critical for the translation

E X A M P L E   6 . 7

Sample Opinion Survey

The first portion of this survey is designed to elicit responses to nostalgia questions.
The bottom half is attitudinal and value-oriented.

GOOD OLD DAYS

THE "GOOD OLD DAYS", WHILE SUBJECT TO SOME DEGREE OF "SELECTIVE MEMORY", ARE FILLED WITH FOND THOUGHTS OF EVENTFUL TIMES IN OUR LIVES WHEN WE WERE GROWING UP AND/OR ENGAGED IN ACTIVITIES THAT WERE VERY IMPORTANT TO US. MANY TIMES, THE AUTOMOBILE PLAYS A SIGNIFICANT PART IN THOSE MEMORIES.

FIRST

PLEASE TAKE A MENTAL TRIP DOWN "MEMORY LANE" THROUGH SOME OF THE PERIODS AND POSSIBLE MILESTONES IN YOUR LIFE THAT WE'VE SELECTED BELOW, AND TELL US THOSE SITUATIONS IN WHICH A PARTICULAR CAR STANDS OUT IN YOUR MIND.

CHECK (✔) THOSE PERIODS/EVENTS WHICH BRING TO MIND A SPECIFIC CAR YOU OWNED OR PARTICULARLY LIKED AT THAT TIME.

1. WHEN YOU WERE "JUST A KID", AND THINKING ABOUT BEING ABLE TO DRIVE
2. WHEN YOU GOT YOUR DRIVER'S LICENSE AND HAD ACCESS TO A CAR AT LEAST PART OF THE TIME
3. WHEN YOU FIRST ACQUIRED A CAR TO CALL YOUR OWN
4. WHEN YOU WENT OUT ON YOUR FIRST DATE IN A CAR
5. WHEN YOU BOUGHT YOUR FIRST NEW CAR
6. WHEN YOU GRADUATED AND WENT TO WORK FULL TIME (if applicable)
7. WHEN YOU WERE ENGAGED TO BE MARRIED
8. WHEN YOU RETURNED HOME FROM MILITARY SERVICE (if applicable)
9. WHEN YOU STARTED "DOING WELL" IN YOUR JOB OR PROFESSION (if applicable)
10. WHEN YOU REACHED THAT POINT WHEN YOUR LIFE STYLE COULD ACCOMMODATE THE KIND OF CAR YOU REALLY WANTED

ANY OTHERS YOU CAN THINK OF? _____

SECOND

NOW, PLEASE SELECT 4 OF THE MOST SIGNIFICANT PERIODS/EVENTS FROM THE LIST ABOVE IN TERMS OF YOUR MEMORIES OF AUTOMOBILES .... AND TELL US MORE ABOUT THEM.

MOST SIGNIFICANT 4 OR 5 PERIODS/EVENTS (Write in ID Number From the List Above)	OUTSTANDING CAR IN YOUR MIND (Write in Make and Car Line)	OWN IT	DID YOU... HAVE ACCESS TO USE IT (CHECK ONE)	JUST ADMIRE IT	U.S. CAR	WAS IT A ... IMPORTED CAR (CHECK ONE)
		1	2	3	1	2

THIRD

THINKING NOW OF THE PRESENT TIME, WHAT CAR (MAKE AND CAR LINE) WOULD BE YOUR "MOST WANTED" CAR, IF PRICE WERE NO OBJECT?

MOST WANTED CURRENT CAR _____ (MAKE) _____ (CAR LINE) DO YOU: OWN IT [ ]1 ADMIRE IT [ ]2 IS IT: A U.S. CAR [ ]1 OR AN IMPORT [ ]2

RELATIVE TO YOUR INDIVIDUAL TASTES AND PREFERENCES FOR DIFFERENT KINDS OF CARS THROUGHOUT YOUR LIFETIME, PLEASE TELL US YOUR AGREEMENT OR DISAGREEMENT WITH THE FOLLOWING STATEMENTS.

(5 = STRONGLY AGREE ...... 1 = STRONGLY DISAGREE)

. WHILE MY "NEEDS" MAY HAVE CHANGED THROUGHOUT MY LIFE, I STILL HAVE THE SAME "TASTES": I PREFER "PLAIN VANILLA"...OR A "SPORTY FLAIR"...OR A "TOUCH OF LUXURY", ETC.   5 4 3 2 1

. PEOPLE GROWING UP TODAY HAVE DIFFERENT VALUES FROM THOSE OF YESTERDAY....I THINK WE WILL SEE A DIFFERENT PATTERN OF CAR PREFERENCES (by size...type...U.S. vs. Import, etc.) IN THE FUTURE THAN IN THE PAST.   5 4 3 2 1

. YOUNG PEOPLE'S ATTITUDES GO IN CYCLES. THE RADICALS OF THE 60'S HAVE BECOME QUITE CONSERVATIVE IN THE 80'S. THERE'S NO REASON TO THINK THEY WON'T LIKE THE SAME KINDS OF MATERIAL THINGS SUCH AS THE TYPES OF CARS THAT OLDER PEOPLE LIKE TODAY.   5 4 3 2 1

. YOUNG PEOPLE TEND TO FAVOR SMALL ECONOMY OR SPORTY CARS BUT AS THEY GROW OLDER, THEY USUALLY CHANGE TO SOMETHING BIGGER AND MORE COMFORTABLE.   5 4 3 2 1

. MAYBE WE'LL NEVER GET BACK TO THE ULTRA BIG LUXURY CARS OF THE PAST, BUT THERE ALWAYS WILL BE A DEMAND FOR RELATIVELY LARGE, LUXURY CARS AS WELL AS ECONOMY CARS, SPORTY CARS, ETC.   5 4 3 2 1

. IMPORTS HAVE BEEN GOOD FOR ECONOMY ...AND SPORTS-CARS, BUT FOR FAMILY NEEDS, U.S. CARS TRADITIONALLY HAVE BEEN BETTER.   5 4 3 2 1

. WHEN I BOUGHT MY FIRST CARS, IMPORTS FIT MY BUDGET, AND WHEN I PROGRESSED IN MY "ABILITY TO PAY", I JUST NATURALLY STAYED WITH THE IMPORTS.   5 4 3 2 1

. IMPORTED CARS MAY BE REALLY NICE CARS, BUT I HAVE A STRONG BUY-AMERICAN ATTITUDE.   5 4 3 2 1

. MANY YOUNG PEOPLE DRIVING IMPORTS TODAY WILL SWITCH TO U.S. CARS AS THEIR NEEDS AND TASTES CHANGE WITH AGE.   5 4 3 2 1

. I DON'T THINK MOST PEOPLE ARE LOYAL TO EITHER IMPORTS OR U.S. CARS PER SE, BUT THEY BUY ACCORDING TO THEIR PARTICULAR NEEDS AT THE TIME.   5 4 3 2 1

. ONCE A PERSON OWNS EITHER AN IMPORT OR A U.S. CAR AND HAS GOOD LUCK, HE IS LIKELY TO "STAY LOYAL" TO THE SAME KIND OF CAR NEXT TIME.   5 4 3 2 1

. FOR SOME PURPOSES, U.S. CARS OFFER THE BEST CHOICE, WHILE FOR OTHERS, AN IMPORT IS MUCH BETTER, SO MANY FAMILIES OWN ONE OF EACH.   5 4 3 2 1

E X A M P L E   6 . 8

Advertisement Published by the American Heart Association

This advertisement was one of seventeen created by the American Heart Association and pretested by National Family Opinion, Inc. (see Example 6.9). Respondents rated the photograph as gripping, the message as strong and the entire ad as eye catching.

This kind of family reunion happens all too often these days. Because too many people don't realize that heart disease, stroke and related disorders will be responsible for almost half of all deaths this year. And that affects a lot of families. Don't wait until it's too late. Don't smoke. Eat a low-fat, low-cholesterol diet. And keep your blood pressure under control. Urge your family members to do the same. And make sure your next family reunion is an especially lively one.

Source: Reproduced with permission. "This is no way to attend a family reunion," PSA, 1987.
Copyright American Heart Association.

of the question and the translation of the responses. The researcher may be asking questions in the language that was not the one intended, and thus the responses when retranslated may not be a good fit.

Even within countries speaking the same language, terms can be confusing, such as elevator (USA) and lift (UK). The names of mealtimes can be different in different parts of the world and even different parts of the country, such as "dinner." Be-

longing to different generations can make a difference too. A health questionnaire that went to teenagers and asked about "snacks" got confused responses, but a similar one that went to people on a weight-loss program also got mixed responses because they were eating small "meals" six to eight times a day.

Noting the problems this can create, one researcher conducted a study of seven questions drawn from national health surveys and using

EXAMPLE 6.9

Survey Questionnaire Conducted by National Family Opinion, Inc., for the American Heart Association

This survey questionnaire was used to pretest seventeen candidate advertisements for the American Heart Association on a sample audience. Responses were used to help identify the most effective and positively received advertisement (see Example 6.8).

1. Have you smoked any cigarettes in the last week?
   - 1 ☐ Yes
   - 2 ☐ No

2. Are you presently trying to reduce fat or cholesterol in your diet?
   - 1 ☐ Yes
   - 2 ☐ No

3. Has your doctor ever told you that you have high blood pressure?
   - 1 ☐ Yes
   - 2 ☐ No
   - 3 ☐ Never been tested for high blood pressure

4. I have personally experienced the difficulties of heart problems because I, someone in my family, or someone close to me has had to deal with them.
   - 1 ☐ Yes
   - 2 ☐ No

5. Have you made a donation to the American Heart Association in the last year?
   - 1 ☐ Yes
   - 2 ☐ No

6. Please indicate your age and sex
   - Age: _____ years   Sex: 1 ☐ Male
   - 2 ☐ Female

7. Please tell me how much you agree or disagree with each of the following statements. (✔ one box for each statement)

	Completely Agree	Somewhat Agree	Neither Agree Nor Disagree	Somewhat Disagree	Completely Disagree
The ad was eye catching	1 ☐	2 ☐	3 ☐	4 ☐	5 ☐
The ad showed me nothing that would make me change my habits	1 ☐	2 ☐	3 ☐	4 ☐	5 ☐
The ad was clear and easy to understand	1 ☐	2 ☐	3 ☐	4 ☐	5 ☐
The ad was very informative	1 ☐	2 ☐	3 ☐	4 ☐	5 ☐
The ad was alarming	1 ☐	2 ☐	3 ☐	4 ☐	5 ☐
I would be more likely to donate money to the American Heart Association because of this ad	1 ☐	2 ☐	3 ☐	4 ☐	5 ☐
The ad really does not apply to me	1 ☐	2 ☐	3 ☐	4 ☐	5 ☐

(continued)

EXAMPLE 6.9 (continued)

8. What would you say is the main idea that the ad is trying to communicate? (Please be as specific as possible) _____

_____

9. What, if anything, do you particulary like about this ad? (Please be as specific as possible) _____

_____

10. What, if anything, do you particularly dislike about this ad? (Please be as specific as possible) _____

_____

Source: Reprinted by permission of National Family Opinion, Inc., and the American Heart Association.

special pretest procedures found that when the questions were revised to clarify the definition of key terms, significantly different estimates resulted.[25] The Roper Center publishes compilations of different surveys on the same issue and compares the different phrasing of questions and the different responses these elicit.

These problems are compounded when gathering information in other countries. Survey research may need to be handled differently for both cultural reasons and because of differences in infrastructure (see Example 6.10). There are also many governments that do not permit collection of opinion data of any kind. The most sensitive, of course, is political polling. Even some governments that permit opinion polls on social, economic and political issues restrict or limit their publication. If an election is in the near future, many governments, including western democracies, put restrictions on the publication of opinion data. The World Association for Public Opinion Research considers the situation so serious that it has created the Foundation for Information which battles the efforts by governments worldwide to restrict the gathering and dissemination of public opinion.[26]

■ Questionnaire Formats

The way respondents are asked to answer surveys also affects the type of answers. Some question-

naires mix different types for responses. Evaluative formats you might consider are: semantic differential, summated ratings, scale analysis and respondent-generated questionnaire.

Semantic Differential Scales A semantic differential questionnaire accounts for intensity by measuring variations in the connotative meanings of objects and words.[27] In this procedure, the respondent rates the object (person or concept) being judged within a framework of two adjectival opposites with seven steps between them. In rating a person, for instance, adjectival opposites might be active–passive or strong–weak. A political pollster may use a semantic differential scale in asking respondents to select qualities, positive or negative, they attribute to persons or issues.

The application of semantic differential scales to marketing was advanced by William Mindak, who views it as a useful tool in rating images of brands, products and companies.[28] As many as nineteen rating scales will reduce to five factors, and a varimax factor analysis can be used for measurement.[29] Weighting of responses is based on the value of the attribute (such as colorful–colorless, measured as positive or negative) to the factor (appearance).

Complex questionnaires and tests have been designed, using the semantic differential technique, to measure changes in attitudes, personality,

EXAMPLE 6.10

Survey Methods of Different Nations

Survey research is handled differently in other countries than it is in the United States, for both cultural and logistical reasons. In some countries, asking personal opinions is considered invasive. Moreover, many countries lack the infrastructure for polling by telephone, for instance. And many countries don't have devices useful to researchers such as city directories that are cross-listed with names followed by addresses and with addresses followed by names, sequential phone numbers followed by names and addresses. The following outline shows the result of a survey of some countries by Louis Harris and Associates researcher Humphrey Taylor to compare systems for information gathering.

I. Normal Methodology for Public Opinion Surveys

1. **Normal Sample Sizes**
   Vary from 500 (one firm in the U.K. and one in Italy) to 3,600 (one organization in Japan) with substantial variations within countries.

2. **Basic Methods**
   Uniform
   All or mostly in-person probability: Australia, South Africa.
   All or mostly in-person quota: U.K., Mexico.
   All or mostly telephone: US, Canada, Germany, Denmark.
   Mixed
   Japan (in-person probability, telephone, mail and self-completion).
   Brazil (in-person probability, in-person quota).
   Portugal (telephone, in-person quota).
   France (telephone and in-person quota).
   Italy (telephone and in-person probability).

3. **Timing**
   Number of days in field: varies from 1 to 14 (several firms said "usually only one day"). Whether usually includes weekends: Yes (almost everywhere, except for one German firm).

II. Weighting

Germany: Past voting, geography, sex, age.
UK: Geography, sex, age, socio-economic class, housing, working/not working[1], past voting[1], number of eligibles in household.[1]
Australia: Geography, sex, age.
Denmark: Past voting, geography, sex, age, socio-economic class, education, working/not working, housing.
USA: Sex, age, race, education, number of telephone lines[1], number of eligibles in household[1], how often at home[1].
South Africa: Geography, sex, age, race.
France: Past voting, geography[1], sex[1], age[1], socio-economic class[1], working/not working[1].
Brazil: No weighting.
Mexico: Sex, age, socio-economic class, working/not working.
Canada: Sex, age, race (language)[1] (one Canadian poll: no weighting).
Portugal: Past voting, geography, sex, age, working/not working.
Japan: No weighting.
Italy: No weighting of telephone surveys; weighting of in-person survey by geography, sex and age.

III. Telephone Surveys

1. **Sampling Methodology**
   Random digit dialing (RDD): USA, Canada.
   Directories: Denmark, Portugal, Germany, Italy.
   Other (including "database quota"): France.
   Mixed (RDD and directories and "database"): UK, Australia.
   Mixed (voter registers and directories): Japan.

(continued)

EXAMPLE 6.10 *(continued)*

2. Clustering
   Unclustered: Australia, UK, Portugal, Denmark, Italy.
   Mixed (some clustered, some unclustered): US, Canada, Japan, France, Germany.

3. Telephone Surveys—Selection of Individual
   Random selection grid: Germany[2], USA[2], Portugal[2], Denmark, Canada[2].
   "Youngest male" method: Australia[2], USA[2], Canada[2].
   Quota: UK[2], Portugal[2], France, Australia[2], Italy.
   Birthday method: UK[2], Canada[2], Germany[2].
   List of named individuals: Japan.

4. Telephone Surveys—Number of Call-backs (re-calls)
   Varies from zero (0) to 6 or more.

IV. In-Person Surveys

1. Clustering In-person Surveys
   Number of clusters varies from 50 to 400.

2. In-person Quota Samples: Quota Controls
   Mexico: Sex, age, socio-economic class, working/not working.
   UK: Sex, age, socio-economic class, working/not working.
   Brazil: Sex, age, education, working/not working, industry.
   Portugal: Sex, age, working/not working.
   France: Sex, age, profession.

3. In-Person Probability Samples—Basic Methodology
   Germany: Area probability, random walks.
   Australia: Area probability.
   South Africa: Area probability and household listings.
   Japan: Voting register, residents/household (inhabitants) listings.

V. Election Forecasts (Last National Elections)

1. Methodology
   Telephone: Denmark, Germany[3], Australia, USA, Canada, Portugal[3], Japan[3].

In-person quota: UK, Portugal[3], France, Mexico.
In-person probability: Japan[3], Brazil, South Africa.

2. Use of Turnout Questions to Determine Likelihood of Voting
   Not normally used in countries with mandatory voting. Otherwise generally used, except for two firms in Canada.

3. Timing
   Number of days in field: from 1 to 8.
   How long before election fieldwork ended: from 1 to 8 days (except where laws forbid publication of late surveys, where it ends sooner).

4. How undecided (Including Not Sures/Don't Knows) Voters Allocated
   In proportion to decided voters: Denmark, UK[1], USA[1], Australia[1], Canada, Portugal[1], Japan, Germany[1]
   Based on replies to other questions: Australia[1], Mexico, USA[1].
   Based on experience of previous elections: Australia[1], Portugal, Germany[1].
   Other methods: UK[1], Brazil.
   Note: In USA, France, South Africa, Canada and Japan some firms do not allocate undecided voters at all.

5. Use of Follow-Up Question to "Squeeze" Undecided Voters: Generally used except for most firms in Japan, one firm in France and one firm in Brazil.

[1] Some firms only.
[2] Different firms use different methods or some firms use different methods.
[3] More than one method used in country.

Source: Reprinted with permission of the Roper Center from *The Public Perspective*, February/March, 1995.

knowledge and behavior against a background of such variables as education, income, religion, social status, gender, occupation and race. One writer has listed the following measurement dimensions and examples of semantic differential adjectives for each:

- *General evaluative dimension:* pleasant–unpleasant, valuable–worthless, important–unimportant, interesting–boring
- *Ethical dimension:* fair–unfair, truthful–untruthful, accurate–inaccurate, biased–unbiased, responsible–irresponsible
- *Stylistic dimension:* exciting–dull, fresh–stale, easy–difficult, neat–messy, colorful–colorless
- *Potency dimension:* bold–timid, powerful–weak, loud–soft
- *Evaluative dimension:* accurate–inaccurate, good–bad, responsible–irresponsible, wise–foolish, acceptable–unacceptable
- *Excitement dimension:* colorful–colorless, interesting–uninteresting, exciting–unexciting, hot–cold
- *Activity dimension:* active–passive, agitated–calm, bold–timid[30]

Summated Ratings Summated ratings are similar to semantic differential scales. Here, however, the responses to a series of statements are selected from among the options, "strongly approve, approve, undecided, disapprove or strongly disapprove." A weight of from 1 to 5 is assigned to each option, so that the high score consistently represents one of the two extremes—for example, 5 for "strongly approve" and 1 for "strongly disapprove." After testing, the weights are totaled and each individual is given a single numerical score. Those who score high and those who score low are selected for further study. Then each question on the questionnaire is evaluated by determining whether the high scorers respond to the particular item with a higher score than do those who are low scorers. Internal consistency in the questions ensures that no correlation of answers appears between these extreme groups. If correlation is found on some questions, these are deleted from the scoring, so that only the items reflecting consistent divergence of opinion are used as a scale.

Scale Analysis In its simplest form, scale analysis involves dichotomous questions—such questions as "Is your grade point average 4.0 (yes or no)?" and "Is it 3.5 (yes or no)?" Questions of this type often appear on questionnaires about salary and position in relation to years of experience in professional fields. Other questions may be posed along lines of increasing or decreasing agreement or disagreement. These may be presented in a multiple-choice format.

Respondent-generated Questionnaire: The DELPHI Process Developed by a Rand Corporation research group, the DELPHI process is a method of polling an audience in order to reach a consensus. An organization's management might use this method to improve relations with employees. The process involves six steps. First, a questionnaire is designed to allow open-ended responses. Second, the sample is chosen on the basis of cost and acceptable level of sampling error. Third, the questionnaire is sent to respondents in the sample as individuals—not handed out by a supervisor or given to the respondents in a general assembly. Fourth, the responses received are organized into a single composite list. Corrections in spelling and grammar are made as a common courtesy, but no value judgments are made, such as discarding an idea because it is too costly or has been tried before. Fifth, each respondent is given a copy of the composite list of responses, together with a rating scale, such as high to low from 5 to 1, and asked to order the responses. Tabulations of this second series of responses—that is, a ranking of items on the list—can be made on a computer. When a number of issues from the list are rated in the highest category, they are grouped according to some relationship of ideas. Once categories of ideas have been developed, the items can be rank-ordered within the categories, according to what the responses were. Sixth, a copy of the ordered list is sent back to each respondent along with his or her individual responses. Of course, this cannot be done if the responses are anonymous; however, if the respondents' anonymity is important, you can provide an automatic copy that they tear off and keep to compare with the overall results.

One result of the DELPHI process is that employees can see if their opinions are shared by the majority of their peers. If the results of the polling are to be reported to management for some action, those in the minority may want to present a minority report also. This opportunity to participate in issue description and prioritization has given employees a greater sense of contributing to the organization's overall planning, and it certainly aids in communication.

A new approach to polling was taken in Britain on May 8, 1994 when the first "deliberative opinion poll" was broadcast over Channel 4. The deliberative poll, as defined by political scientist James Fishkin, is different from a survey of what people are thinking in that it "attempts to model what the public would think, if it had a better opportunity to consider the questions."[31] Fiskin explains, "The deliberative poll has a recommending force: these are the conclusions the people would reach if they were better informed and had the same opportunities for intensive face-to-face discussions as the members of the sample did."

The sample, in the British situation, were 869 citizens randomly selected from the electorate by an independent research institute based in London. The sample was representative of the nation in age, class, geography, gender, education and other significant attributes. All 869 were invited to the Granada Television studios in Manchester, England April 15–17. The 302 who accepted and completed the weekend were considered representative of the entire country. Since they knew they would be on national television, Fiskin says, they probably became less representative from the moment they got the invitation in that they began to learn more about issues and to discuss them with neighbors and friends. Fiskin later held a National Issues Convention in Austin, Texas to which 600 scientifically-selected Americans were invited to discuss issues and question the presidential candidates in 1995.[32]

This type of deliberative polling has supporters and detractors within the polling community, but it is something to consider in that most surveys elicit response from a mix of people who may or may not be informed about the issues.

Public opinion polling methods differ throughout the world, and researcher Humphrey Taylor says that "Survey methods which are standard practice in some countries would be regarded as gross malpractice in others." When working across borders it's important to know which criteria are being used.[33]

Do-It-Yourself Versus Supplier Types of Research

In do-it-yourself research, the following points are important:

1. The types of surveys you can best handle yourself are those dealing with (a) the audience (the listeners, viewers or readers of your messages); (b) the market in which you operate (the consumers and users of your products or services); (c) public opinion (what people think about issues, conditions, governments, their lives).

2. Confine your survey to your precinct, city, metropolitan area or county. Difficulties arise when a beginning researcher attempts to cover more extensive territory.

3. Collect information by telephone or face-to-face interviews or observation. Mail surveys have some value, although their applicability is limited in view of the costs involved.

4. Question interviewees directly, but avoid asking them for information about others in the family. Use a standardized questionnaire. Self-administered and leave-behind forms are generally not recommended.

5. Primarily use closed-ended or structured-type questions, eliciting explicit replies. Although open-ended questions are sometimes necessary, they are more difficult to handle, both during the interview and during tabulation.

6. Make interviews relatively short—from 1 or 2 minutes up to a maximum of 15 minutes. Professionals can successfully handle interviews lasting an hour or more, but such questioning requires wide experience, and the analysis can be ponderous.

7. Gather the information through sampling—a cross-section of relatively few people—rather than through a complete enumeration of the population.

8. An adequate sample can be as small as 100; it is seldom more than 1,000.

The following situations usually call for hiring an outside professional research supplier:

1. Advertising effectiveness can now be measured in new and intriguing ways, but these usually require more technical know-how than the average businessperson or beginning researcher has. Many problems arise in attempting to measure not only advertising effect on sales but exposure to advertising—commercials, print, outdoor and others. It may seem perfectly natural to ask, "What led you to buy that?" or "What type of advertising helps you most?" but such simple approaches usually yield misleading results because respondents are likely to give superficial responses and may not understand what really motivated them.

2. *Motivation research* has become a popular term, but it is widely misused. Properly it refers to research that describes *why* people act as they do. Using it usually requires training in psychology or at least knowledge of techniques developed by behavioral scientists. You can ask people their reasons for many things, but don't expect to probe their subconscious for basic motives if you are equipped only with everyday research tools. In-depth interviewing is one of the techniques of motivation and attitude research. An in-depth interview that probes intensively behind expressed opinions and reactions demands research skills most public relations practitioners do not possess.

3. Conditional questions are dangerous. Asking a respondent what he or she would do if certain changes were made or if other conditions existed seldom produces realistic results. Perhaps

you cannot completely avoid questions like "If the 6 o'clock evening newscast were changed to 7 P.M., would you listen to it more, or less, or about the same?" But such questions give you, at best, a general indication—not a precise estimate.

4. Identifying use of products by volume is difficult. Consumers can readily tell you whether they use a product or not, but it is quite another thing to find out how much they use.

5. Loaded surveys mislead. Some advertising researchers have attempted to "document" what they don't actually have by using "research." Going through the motions of a loaded survey does not produce facts. And even if you proceed in good faith, your eagerness to make a good showing may cause you to bias a survey unconsciously.

6. Trend measurements are not taboo, but for one result to be comparable to a later one, the comparability of each survey in a series must be maintained on several levels—as to method, timing and manner of being conducted.

7. Panels, requiring that the same people be reinterviewed at intervals or that they do something between intervals, are best left to specialists.

8. Store audits also call for specialists. Although simple in concept, they demand more control than a nonspecialist can exercise.

9. Consumer tests—taste tests, advertising copy tests, package tests and the like—are highly specialized and should be used cautiously, if at all.

10. Internet site activity is measured for users' reaction to editorial material, for marketing information drawn from who is using the site and to determine advertising potential from the number of "hits" on the site. Most companies are trying to do all three themselves, but there are more sophisticated measurements available from professionals.[34]

11. Ratings—the measurements that tell how many people are listening to a given radio or television station at a given time—are not recommended as part of electronic media do-it-yourself research. There is much more to station research than ratings. Demand for ratings research by radio and television has, indeed, been high, but for many reasons they should be left to specialists.

Broadcast Research

Audience Measurement   Some questions and methods are peculiar to broadcast research and some of this research is of value to public relations practitioners. One question often asked is, "How big is my audience?" The three main methods used in broadcast research are diaries, interviews and mechanical audience recorders.

Although it might seem to be a simple task, accurate measurement of audience size is highly technical. One need only read the congressional hearings on ratings to become aware of the intricacies and pitfalls. The National Association of Broadcasters is active in the effort to police ratings through the Broadcast Rating Council, which audits the operations of the major rating services. To be effective and useful, ratings must be comparable from market to market; so they must be tallied by organizations that operate nationally. Ratings are available from such services as American Research Bureau, Hooper, Mediastat, Nielsen and Pulse. Only if you intend to use audience estimates *internally* and can't afford to retain a professional firm should you try to conduct ratings research yourself. The simplest and least expensive method is usually the telephone coincidental—calling a sample of homes during the time segment you wish to measure.

Evaluating the impact or effect of media on publics can be done in several ways, but among the ones most commonly used by broadcasters is the control group study or experiment in which two groups are selected to be matching samples. One is then exposed to the program, while the other is not. The differences in the two groups' views subsequently are determined through panel studies or surveys, and thus the impact of the program is measured. The survey method is generally used here when a program has been activated in one geographical area and not in another. The panel method may use the already selected advisory group. However, the problem with this test involves matching the two sample populations. Another measurement technique consists of studying similar groups over a long period of time. The measures may involve observable changes over the time span, as well as measurable differences in individual and group reactions. The in-depth interview is a valuable tool for determining reactions to various aspects of a program.[35]

The Diary   When used to measure a program's audience, the diary method requires that some member of a household keep a written log of the household's program listening or viewing. The same information can be obtained by attaching a recorder to the TV or radio to measure the frequency of viewing and channel selection, although the automatic device does not tell when the TV or radio is playing in an empty room.

The Interview   Broadcast researchers use several different types of personal and telephone interviews.

The *personal coincidental* method consists of personal interviews made during a given time period or during a specific program. Respondents are simply asked what program they are listening to or watching at that moment.

The *personal roster recall* consists of showing respondents a list of programs and stations and asking them to indicate which they watched or listened to within the given time span (usually the day before or the week before).

The *unaided personal recall* seeks the same type of information, but respondents are asked to identify what they listened to on the radio or watched on TV during the survey time span without referring to a list. Thus respondents must remember the names of programs and stations through independent recall.

The *telephone coincidental*, a survey method that local stations or area research bureaus can use effectively, is identical to the personal coincidental method, except that it is conducted over the telephone. Along the same lines, the *telephone aided recall* is like the personal roster recall, and the *telephone unaided recall* is essentially the same as the personal unaided recall.

Broadcasting researchers also use *combinations* of these tests: the combined telephone coincidental and telephone recall, the combined telephone coincidental and personal roster recall or the combined telephone coincidental and diary.

Mechanical Audience Recorders The two main types of mechanical audience recorders for broadcast audiences are people meters and program analyzers. People meters are devices that can be held in the viewer's hand or can rest on top of the TV set. People using these devices can record who is watching as well as what is being watched. The A. C. Nielsen Company has replaced its diary system of 2,400 participants with people meters, and the results have been rather dramatic. The meters indicate that network TV audiences are far smaller than had been suggested by the diary system, and this led to a drop in advertising on TV and an effort by the networks to find a new measuring system. Recently, broadcast networks have decided to do their own research because they find fault with the Nielson process.

Another device for obtaining viewer information is the program analyzer. It is now used exclusively by panels; but as cable television becomes more widespread, its use may be extended to general audiences. To analyze a program, the viewer or listener presses a button or switch that records his or her reaction to a specific part of the program. There are two buttons—Like and Dislike—and the viewer's reactions are recorded on tape and then matched with the program to see which parts of the show elicited which response. Cable systems equipped with such response buttons have been used to register instant ratings, but only on an experimental basis.

■ Measuring Web Audiences

Another form of automatic measurement much like broadcast measures is what is being used to find out who is "surfing" what on the Net. In 1998 two competing research firms merged. Media Metrix, Inc., with a sample of 30,000, used something like the diary system where the selected users mailed in

floppy disks each month to tell what sites they visited. However, when Independent Counsel Kenneth Starr's report on his investigation of President Clinton was released, rival RelevantKnowledge, Inc. broke into the news because of its more immediate system of tracking. RelevantKnowledge's 10,000 sample users downloaded software into their computer systems which then beam all the data about the Websites they have visited back to the research company. This system enabled the company to give instant reports of the "hits" to the Internet site with Starr's report. The merged company now uses both technologies and is called Media Metrix Inc.[36]

APPLIED RESEARCH: MIXING QUALITATIVE AND QUANTITATIVE MEASURES IN INTERNAL AND EXTERNAL SETTINGS

Research conducted within an organization is often done informally. When formal, it usually mixes qualitative and quantitative techniques: conferences with employees involved in a particular problem, studies of the organization's records, reviews of employee suggestions and surveys of employee opinions. Some internal research also may take into account external opinion: ideas of opinion leaders that affect the organization's management; incoming mail; reports from field agents or sales personnel; press clippings and monitoring reports on electronic media; opinion polls, elections and legislative voting patterns or similar reflections of public opinion that may be shared by internal audiences; and the work of advisory committees or panels of people experienced in a particular field. The trouble with internal research is that it is seldom representative and almost always lacks objectivity.

External research is almost always formal. It may involve public opinion—that is, the opinions of large groups of the public (such as a nation) which are usually described demographically—and it always involves monitoring specific target audiences outside the organization that are of particular significance to it. Both qualitative and quantitative methods are used.

Monitoring publics and their environments suggests an old southwestern ranching phrase, "riding the fences." The original phrase refers to checking all the boundaries of a property periodically to make sure that the fences are up and in good repair. In public relations, it means checking the parameters of the institution to see what areas need mending or rebuilding because something either has changed or is likely to change.

When you ride the PR fences, you identify issues both inside and outside the organization, analyzing the opinion of publics in both places and monitoring the climate of public opinion in both places. You may also be trying to build or rebuild relationships with various publics. And you may be evaluating the effectiveness of your work by measuring conditions before and after to see what the results are.

More and more companies conduct employee surveys to check on the quality of their products, the effectiveness of their advertising and the extent of employee involvement in the local community. Organizations in the USA that use total quality management (TQM) concepts find employee feedback to management is critical.[37]

Many nonprofit organizations recognize their members as an internal public and try to find out what these people are interested in. Many national organizations with local chapters have become keenly aware of the grassroots perception of many members that the national office doesn't benefit them directly. Some organizations conduct formal, scientific surveys to keep in touch with their membership and its concerns. Others, like the Public Relations Society of America (through its *Public Relations Tactics*), may use informal readership surveys. One nonprofit organization, the Dallas Museum of Art, has conducted a number of formal audience surveys and has assembled visitor profiles over the years. It has also employed unobtrusive measures, such as tracking membership attendance at previews.[38]

Some organizations use outside research firms that provide not only linear data, but use artificial intelligence and fuzzy logic techniques to link variables so that relationships between variables that might not otherwise be linked are discovered. The links sometimes identify problems in the making and in other cases help sort out priorities. An example would be how menu prices being changed in ink or pencil makes customers question food quality.

RESEARCH AND PROBLEM SOLVING

Three types of people don't want to hear about an institution's problems: the ones responsible for them, because the problems make them look bad; the ones whose egos are involved, because the problems are a threat to their expertise; and the helpless, who are usually employees or suppliers, because they can't do anything about the problems and are likely to become victims of any institutional shakeup. When people don't want to hear about a problem, they may either ignore the information that points to it or deny that the information is accurate.

In either case, the messenger who draws attention to the problem—for example, a public relations practitioner armed with information obtained through research—is always at considerable risk. People who feel threatened are likely to lash out at the most convenient and visible target. To avoid getting involved in battles that can't be won, you must be a diligent fact-finder and an expert communicator. You must also be sensitive to the natural resistance to certain messages that exists within each public, and you must compensate for the resistance. Finally, you must anticipate that some resistance will be put up in response to any action that you or your organization takes to solve problems. Consequently, in addition to riding the fences, and identifying needed action, you have to be prepared to supervise the action, monitor its likelihood of success and report objectively on the results.

A PR person must above all maintain objectivity in "riding the PR fences." You have to be the one to say, "That looks shaky, and a good strong wind is going to blow it down. It's going to cost plenty to fix it, but it has to be fixed now and fixed right." Or, you might have to say, "There's the hole where the livestock are getting out. We have to repair it now, even if we don't get anything else done." Finding the holes and the potential breakdowns is your job.

An organization's reaction to its problems is determined in part by its structure and its corporate culture, which also influence how it communicates about its problems. Organizations maintain either closed or open systems of communication. For example, banks have traditionally maintained closed systems, saying little publicly when they have faced problems. Deregulation of the industry, however, has forced them to adopt much more open systems. The first banks to find themselves on a list of troubled institutions in danger of closing experienced a rude shock. The industry had operated for years within the secure confines of confidential practice. Banks rarely spoke publicly about themselves, justifying their silence on grounds of protecting the privacy of their clients. But suddenly they had to communicate with their publics.

Hospitals, too, have traditionally operated as closed systems. But while many closed systems still exist, the marketplace has obviously become more competitive in recent years. Major corporate restructuring, brought about as the result of a takeover or a parent spinoff, has also changed how organizations communicate.

Corporate restructuring continues at a rate that alarms some observers. Various spokespersons have observed that this restructuring is not particularly good for either business or its customers, although it usually benefits stockholders in the short term. Restructuring almost always disassembles the corporate culture. This is important because communication first occurs internally, within the framework of an institution's culture.

External communication—even deliberate external communication, such as marketing—follows from and reflects internal communication. A person who functions objectively within the institution—for example, by communicating honestly with employees—is sometimes perceived as not being a team player and not adhering to the corporate point of view. Objective communication to external audiences may be seen as even more threatening. But objective communicators are valuable assets to an institution. They are alert to problems and potential problems because they have been riding the fences with their eyes and ears open, basing their recommendations and actions on objective research. The idea of doing systematic research isn't always supported by management, often because the results can be threatening, but there is no substitute for such information in times of need.[39]

■ Research for Problem Identification

A good way to begin identifying problems is to ask an organization's insiders about them. Employees know an institution better than anyone else. They may only know parts of it expertly, but they also interact with people in other sections of it, and they talk among themselves. Listening to voices of dissent within an institution often provides good clues as to where fences need mending. Unfortunately, this is a little-used technique, perhaps because it strikes management as being subversive. Public relations practitioners, of course, recognize that employees are the front line for public relations because they *are* the institutional image. They have a strong sense of what an institution really is, what its problems consist of and what its customers think about it. They also represent the institution to its publics. In their neighborhoods and among their friends, they are the authority on the institution. Finding out what employees know or think they know about an institution is a critical monitoring operation.

Employees respond to an external environment, as the public relations practitioner well knows. Anticipating reactions of various publics under certain circumstances is part of the job of the PR person as a social scientist within management. Unfortunately, this role often calls for the PR person to become a devil's advocate, posing hard questions about proposed actions. This can be risky, and it explains why a communication audit is a good research technique for riding the fences. Such an audit combines internal and external research with some quantitative and qualitative evidence.

The right time to do a communication audit is not after you have already detected a problem, but regularly as a part of normal monitoring. A communication audit is especially needed before major changes are anticipated, to give you a benchmark or baseline against which to measure internal and external attitudes in the future. The audit begins with an account of what is—a look at policies, procedures, materials and any available data on communication effectiveness. Publics are then studied to identify what is perceived versus what is; research tools used for this purpose include focus group interviews, individual interviews and perhaps a formal survey. The result provides a comparison of policies and procedures with the image they cast.

Audits can be useful problem predictors. Sometimes you know fences are going to need mending, but you don't know exactly where, when and how much. One predictable problem involves policy changes. Philip Lesly has called public relations practitioners "the bridge for change," and a PR colleague observed, "That's right. It means you get walked on." Anticipating problems and dealing with them while they are small are two major public relations contributions to management. Policy changes (indeed, changes in general) usually mean problems. The role of the public relations practitioner is to help smooth the way for changes by eliminating surprises and building interest and anticipation. The PR person also may have to assume the role of negotiator to help effect a change.

Another type of problem is a *crisis*—anything from an internal breakdown, where someone has embezzled funds or leaked corporate secrets, to a primarily external controversy, where the institution is accused of creating a public hazard. Your institution will inevitably have a crisis of one sort or another. Anticipating the crisis will make it easier to cope with (see Chapter 15).

■ Research for Problem Analysis

Dissecting a problem sounds simple when you work step-by-step through the procedures. Yet what is initially identified as the problem rarely turns out to be the problem. It's usually an effect or result of the underlying problem. The only way to get to the root of the situation is to describe in clear declarative sentences what has happened or is happening. Then you have to do some research—formal or informal (and probably both)—to see if you can get at the true cause or causes.

Once you have identified the problem, you should be able to express it in one simple sentence. The next step is to state what you want the outcome to be, again in one simple sentence. Even if the situation is as complex as an attempted takeover, you should express the desirable outcome in a simple statement.

If the desired outcome cannot be stated, you should set down some possible outcomes as goals, together with the consequences, pro and con, of each. This step involves selecting strategies and the tactics to implement them, as well as research techniques for measuring progress toward your goals. The research can be unobtrusive (such as monitoring phone calls or mail) or formal (such as a survey). Once your action strategies are set, you must identify the publics and the appeals likely to affect them. Finally, you must choose the media most likely to reach those publics.

Now the easy part begins. You have to orchestrate the organization's efforts so that it carries out the strategies and tactics needed to meet the goals, on a timetable and within a reasonable budget.

Constraints on time or resources may force you to modify your goals, but creative thinking usually will enable you to overcome these constraints. On the other hand, even when resources are unlimited, you have to set some priorities. This entails deciding what you need to achieve first for a strategy to work. Once you have decided that, you can begin work on a more mechanical timetable that tells you what has to happen first.

For example, if you determine that you have to get neighborhood agreement on the rezoning of some property before the architect's plans for a proposed development are completed, you need to make sure that these meetings are going on while you are working with the architect. You must allow enough lead time to avoid any risk that the finished plans will be "leaked" before the neighbors agree to the zoning change. If this is not done properly, the whole deal could be torpedoed. Once you have made this determination, the mechanics become clear. The staff first has to get in touch with neighborhood group leaders to set up meetings and to prepare information for presentation at those meetings, before work begins on a brochure that will feature the architect's plans and schematics.

In problem situations, your concern is to influence public opinion in a positive way. Case histories show that successful plans to influence opinion share five problem-solving characteristics: assessment of the needs, goals and capabilities of target publics; systematic campaign planning and production; continuous evaluation; complementary roles of mass media and interpersonal communication; and selection of appropriate media for target audiences. All of these depend on sound research.

In some problem situations, you may be attempting to change behavior rather than opinions. Four problem-solving characteristics are associated with successful behavior change: education; enforcement (legal measures to force behavior change); engineering (constructing preventives or barriers); and entitlement or peer support. The communication requirements in behavior change are problem awareness, problem acceptance (belief that it is a real problem) and a feeling that something can be done about it.

Research for Program Development and Implementation

When you develop a program to address a problem, you focus on three major components: the publics involved (prioritized and described in terms of demographics and psychographics); the message statements to each of these publics (slanted for special appeal to each public—but essentially the same, so that the institution speaks with one corporate voice—and phrased as a simple statement); and the media to reach each public (primary and secondary, evaluated for their usefulness in delivering the message in an appropriate, economical and timely manner).

You should plan the program in parts and set achievement goals for each part. Research tech-

niques are built in, so you can measure how well the plan is working. Any plan has to be flexible enough to allow for changes as you work through it. The purpose of measuring (monitoring) your achievement as you go along is to fine-tune the plan by eliminating what is not working. This kind of midcourse correction research may also reveal at some point that you must go in an entirely different direction. If this happens, you must be prepared to make the necessary changes in course.

The danger in measuring results as you go along, however, is that you might draw erroneous conclusions, especially regarding cause and effect. For instance, you might conclude that, because customers said in a survey that they liked your product, they can be expected to buy it. In the social sciences, you deal with people who respond differently under different circumstances. As a result, cause and effect are difficult to determine without extensive replication. In this kind of research, you also run the risk of throwing out information that seems irrelevant but may later turn out to be meaningful. On the other hand, you can become confused and led astray by information that you think is useful but is fundamentally unrelated to the problem.

Deciding which research data are relevant and which are irrelevant is critical to objective thinking. Ego involvement always presents a major problem in any effort to think objectively. The problem is lessened if plans are made by a group rather than by an individual. Information about progress can then be shared with all members of the group. At some point, however, someone has to make critical decisions. It may be the public relations person, or it may be someone else in the management group, acting after receiving an appropriate recommendation from the public relations person.

In any case, the best way to proceed is to make your recommendation as objectively as possible, based on your research findings, anticipating as you do so the positive and negative effects it may have on various publics. These potential effects should not be guessed at. They should be anticipated, based on past responses in similar situations and on what research has shown is likely to happen.

POINTS TO REMEMBER

■ Informal research is conducted without generally agreed-upon rules and procedures that would enable someone else to replicate the same study. The results of informal research can be used only for description, not prediction.

■ Unobtrusive measures permit researchers to study someone or something without interfering with or interrupting what's going on.

■ Informal research makes wide use of opinion audits and communication audits. Both can be done with publics either inside or outside an organization.

■ Clippings from print media and transcripts from electronic publicity can be analyzed to determine the quantity and quality of coverage.

■ Informal research carries some particular risks and responsibilities. There is risk in using information from secondary sources that may not be valid and are difficult to verify, so cross-checking sources is critical. The main responsibility involved in gathering information from people informally is to protect their anonymity.

■ Much informal research is conducted to confirm or to deny the validity of concepts based on intuition or experience.

■ The two fundamental types of formal research are qualitative and quantitative.

■ Secondary sources include books, articles and journals. Primary sources are people who are involved in some way with what is being studied.

■ Case studies use available factual data to examine issues, events and organizations systematically; diaries provide detailed reports of personal experiences and actions.

■ One practical difference between qualitative research (based primarily on description) and quantitative research (based primarily on measurement) is that quantitative research offers higher predictability.

■ Survey research attempts to measure the practices and preferences of a specified public by tabulating responses by members of that public to a standardized series of questions.

■ Sampling is based on probability. Most sampling relies on a small subgroup of the target audience, which the researcher uses to represent the larger group. A random sample is usually free of bias or substantial error. Bias is the tendency of an estimate to deviate from the true value.

■ Three major types of nonprobability or nonrandom sampling are accidental, purposive and quota.

■ In a probability sample, people are chosen at random; in a quota sample, a population is analyzed by its known characteristics; in an area sample, geographical areas are studied.

■ The best way to encourage a good response in a survey is to write a good questionnaire. Pretest this "instrument" by asking several people to complete it before you use it on the actual sample to gather research data. Pretesting helps you avoid ambiguous questions and questions causing resentment among respondents.

■ Questionnaires that go to people in other countries often must be translated as well as the responses. Pretesting helps to ensure that the translations convey the appropriate meaning.

■ Cultural barriers, the lack of a comparable infrastructure in some countries and outright legal restrictions against opinion gathering and reporting can make accumulating data difficult.

■ The way questionnaires are structured also affects responses. Some evaluative formats you may want to consider are semantic differential, summated ratings and scale analysis.

■ The six-step DELPHI process is a method of polling an audience to reach a consensus; it begins with a questionnaire designed to allow open-ended responses.

■ Three main methods used in broadcast research are diaries, interviews and mechanical audience recorders. The two main types of mechanical audience recorders are people meters and program analyzers.

■ Internal research often is done informally. When formal measures are used, it is often a mix of qualitative and quantitative measures. A frequent problem with internal research is that it is seldom truly representative and often lacks objectivity.

■ External research is almost always formal and generally employs both qualitative and quantitative measures. It is used to monitor publics and identify issues that need consideration. Most formal research is done by outside providers.

■ Although most formal quantitative research is linear only, some research firms can provide unexpected linkages among variables by using artificial intelligence and fuzzy logic.

■ Response to research findings is not always positive because at least three types of people don't want to know about problems: those responsible for them, those whose egos are involved because they will look bad and those who are helpless to do anything about them.

■ It's important for the public relations person to maintain objectivity in ordering or doing research, and certainly in evaluating and reporting on it.

■ An organization's corporate culture has a great deal to do with its receptiveness to research that identifies problems. The more open the communication climate within the organization, the more receptive it is to objective reporting of research.

■ The idea of doing research systematically is not always supported by management because the results can be threatening. But in a crisis the information is critical.

■ Research among insiders is one of the best ways to identify an organization's problems. As an organization's PR front line, employees have a great deal of knowledge that needs to be tapped.

■ In examining research for problem identification or potential problem identification, the public relations person often has to play the role of devil's advocate. This is not always a popular stance for management which can misinterpret it as not being a team player.

■ Audits are useful problem predictors.

■ Problem analysis is difficult because what often appears to be the problem is only a symptom.

■ Defining a problem means being able to express it in one simple, declarative sentence. From that point, the desirable outcome(s) can be stated, goals developed and a timetable established for achieving them. Recognition of constraints in meeting goals is an important factor in achieving success. Be realistic.

NOTES

[1] Each year Dr. Walt Lindenmann updates a *Guide to Public Relations Research*. The reference manual for practitioners is available for a fee from the Research and Measurement Department, Ketchum, 292 Madison Ave., New York City, NY 10017.

[2] Eugene J. Webb, Donald T. Campbell, Richard D. Schwartz and Lee Sechrest, *Unobtrusive Measures: Nonreactive Research in the Social Sciences* (Chicago: Rand McNally, 1966).

[3] Philip Meyer, *Precision Journalism* (Bloomington: Indiana University Press, 1973), p. 15.

[4] Eugene J. Webb, Donald T. Campbell, Richard D. Schwartz and Lee Sechrest, *Unobtrusive Measures*, p. 3.

[5] Patrick M. Reilly and Ernest Beck, "Publishers Often Pad Circulation Figures," *Wall Street Journal* (September 30, 1997), p. B8.

[6] "Perot Got Numbers on Jobs At Risk From A Brochure," *Wall Street Journal* (September 15, 1993), p. A16.

[7] William Sledzik, "Research Tool from the 20s Opens Idea Process for the 90s," *tips & tactics*, supplement of *pr reporter*, 33(10) (June 19, 1995), pp. 1–2.

[8] John W. Felton, President, The Institute for Public Relations, The University of Florida, Box 118400, Gainesville, FL 32611–8400.

[9] Constance Swank, *Modern Maturity* (March–April 1998), p. 81. Swank is the director of research for the American Association of Retired Persons (AARP).

[10] In exploratory or descriptive research (which is often done in public relations), you develop, instead of a hypothesis, a simple statement of what you want to find out. You must do this as specifically as possible.

[11] In designing an experiment, you must pretest it even if it is exploratory. You will be dealing with respondents' interpretations of your questions, so you need to discover any misconceptions that might skew results.

[12] Roger D. Wimmer and Joseph R. Dominick, *Mass Media Research* (Belmont, Calif.: Wadsworth, 1983). See especially "The

Methodology of Focus Groups," pp. 99–100. The book also has a moderator's guide in the Appendix.

[13] Bernard Berelson, "Content Analysis in Communication Research," in Bernard Berelson and Morris Janowitz, eds., *Reader in Public Opinion and Communication*, 2d ed. (Glencoe, Ill.: Free Press, 1953), p. 263.

[14] Earl Babbie, *The Practice of Social Research*, 8th ed. (Belmont, Calif.: Wadsworth, 1998), pp. 318–19.

[15] W. Edward Deming, *Sample Design in Business Research* (New York: John Wiley, 1960), p. 61.

[16] Demography is the science of vital statistics. An important factor in this science is the tolerable margin of error. Thus, demography asks, how wrong can you be—5 percent? 10 percent? 20 percent?

[17] Psychographs are charts outlining the relative strength of fundamental personality traits in an individual.

[18] PR clients, like products, can be "positioned," whether they are individuals or institutions. Images are important to positioning, and this means finding an emotional appeal that will segment the market.

[19] Max Glaskin, "Did You See What I Said?" *Times of London* (June 30, 1995), p. 31.

[20] Richard Morin, "Leave A Message At The Beep, Unless You're A Pollster," *Washington Post National Weekly Edition* (August 2–8, 1993), p. 37.

[21] Carolyn Barta, "Public's Refusal Rate May Skew Results of Phone Surveys," *Dallas Morning News* (March 15, 1997), pp. J1, 10.

[22] Arnold S. Linsky, "Stimulating Responses to Mailed Questionnaires: A Review," *Public Opinion Quarterly*, 39(1) (Spring 1975), pp. 82–101.

[23] Ibid.

[24] One useful guide for terms is the *Dictionary of Social Sciences*.

[25] Floyd Jackson Fowler, Jr., "How Unclear Terms Affect Survey Data," *Public Opinion Quarterly* 56:218–231 (1992), pp. 218–231.

[26] Richard Morin, "Not So Free to Gather Public Opinion," *Washington Post National Weekly Edition* (January 19, 1998), p. 34.

[27] Some researchers disagree, saying semantic differential measures *degree* of response but not *intensity*. But others argue that degree itself reflects intensity.

[28] William A. Mindak, "Fitting the Semantic Differential to the Marketing Problem," *Journal of Marketing*, 25 (April 1961), pp. 28–33.

[29] Varimax gives a clearer separation of factors. Most students use computer programs to handle reserve data, but for an explanation of the mathematics see Jae-On Kim and Charles W. Mueller, *Factor Analysis Statistical Methods and Practical Issues* (Beverly Hills, Calif.: Sage, 1978).

[30] Hugh M. Culbertson, "Words vs. Pictures: A Comparison as to Perceived Impact and Connotative Meaning," *Journalism Quarterly* (Summer 1974), pp. 226–37.

[31] James S. Fishkin, "Britain Experiments with the Deliberative Poll," *Public Perspective* (July/August, 1994), p. 27.

[32] Wayne Slater, Sam Attlesey, Nancy Kruh, "Interview: James Fiskin," *The Dallas Morning News* (December 10, 1995), p. J1, 10.

[33] Humphrey Taylor, "Horses for Courses: How Different Countries Measure Public Opinion in Very Different Ways," *Public Perspective* (February/March, 1995), pp. 3–7. For this article see INFOTRAC.

[34] Merrill Goozner, "Advertisers Gauge Internet Site Potential by Measuring Usage, Studying Users," Tarrant Business section, *Fort Worth Star-Telegram* (December 30, 1996), p.6, originally printed in the *Chicago Tribune*. A single measurement tool is being sought to measure on-line advertising, and that might have broader applications.

[35] Adapted from *A Broadcast Research Primer* (Washington, D.C.: National Association of Broadcasters, 1973), pp. 10–12.

[36] Rebecca Quick, "Rivals to Merge to Measure Web Audiences," *Wall Street Journal* (October 13, 1998), p. B8.

[37] Susan L. Fry, "Establishing a Total Quality Structure," *Public Relations Journal*, 48(4) (April 1992), p. 4.

[38] Robert Milbank, Jr., "DMA Visitor Profile," *Dallas Museum of Art Bulletin* (Summer 1986). See also John C. Pollock and Michael Winkleman, "Salary Survey," *Public Relations Journal* (June 1987), pp. 15–17.

[39] Jennie M. Piekos and Edna F. Einsidel, "Roles and Program Evaluation Techniques Among Canadian Public Relations Practitioners," in Grunig and Grunig, eds., *Public Relations Research Annual*, vol. 2, p. 107. Also see Hugh M. Culbertson and Dennis W. Jeffers, "The Social, Political and Economic Contexts: Keys to Front-End Research," *Public Relations Quarterly* (Fall 1991), pp. 43, 48.

Selected readings, activities and assignments appropriate to this chapter can be found in the *Instructor's Guide* or on InfoTrac if you are using the InfoTrac College Edition.

CHAPTER 7

PERSUASION AND COMMUNICATION THEORIES

Public relations embraces what I call the engineering of consent based on Thomas Jefferson's principle that, in a democratic society, everything depends on the consent of the public.

EDWARD L. BERNAYS, AUTHOR OF FIRST PR TEXT

Thank God, communication isn't a disease, because we know so little about it.

BILL MARSTELLER, FORMER CHAIRMAN AND
CHIEF EXECUTIVE OFFICER, MARSTELLER, INC.

A s you learned in Chapter 4, public opinion is the collective opinion of groups of people. You can count on two things about public opinion: first, it will change; second, those who hold an opinion were somehow persuaded to think as they do. Although people do sometimes respond collectively, as when they applaud or join in a boycott of a product or store, they always initiate their responses individually. These individual responses indicate attitudes that reflect feelings or convictions. Each person individually decides to clap or not to clap, to buy or not to buy and to patronize or not to patronize. Consequently, we must look at individual reactions first. Then we try to figure out how these reactions of individuals affect the reactions of other individuals to produce a collective response.

It is important to keep in mind that responses are always individual before they are collective. Many faulty mass communication theories have been based on the mistaken idea that there is only a mass response. Looking at publics collectively can create a number of difficulties for public relations practitioners, as can looking at what publics say without explaining what they *do*.

EXAMPLE 7.1
Two Theoretical Models Underpinning Public Relations Practice

Communication Model

Sender encoding message → Medium → Audience → Decoding → Response

Feedback

Behavioral Model

Awareness → Latent readiness → Triggering event → Behavior

According to *pr reporter*, the behavioral model "basically shifts the objective, and with it the focus of thinking, strategizing and planning, away from the traditional model's emphasis on creating or retaining awareness."* Step 1, **awareness**, may involve creating awareness, changing levels of awareness or maintaining awareness, but in every case relevance to the individual is the key to getting attention. In this step, the diffusion process of communication—the two-step flow—contributes either positively or negatively to the next step. In other words, information goes *from* mass media *to* opinion leaders and is then passed along to individuals who have some contact with the opinion leader. Step 2, **latent readiness**, precedes action and involves referencing existing experiences, information, attitudes, values and beliefs and every other resource. The mental computer of each member

of the target public is checking and matching, confirming or rejecting. In step 3, the **triggering event**, some circumstance arises, accidentally or intentionally, that causes action. Step 4, **behavior**, is that action. The initial action may only be preliminary to the final action—the ultimate, desired behavior. This is a modification of the six-step persuasion model (see Example 7.2, where the behavioral response to each phase of the symmetrical process model of persuasion is represented as a boxed event).

* "Behavioral Model Replacing Communications Model as Basic Theoretical Underpinning of PR Practice," *pr reporter*, 33(30) (July 30, 1990), pp. 2–3.

Source: Reprinted with permission of *pr reporter*, Exeter, N.H., 33(30) (July 30, 1990), p. 1.

SOME MODELS TO CONSIDER

The attitudes and opinions of publics greatly interest the PR practitioner, but even more important is what these publics are *doing*. This point is reflected in the replacement of the communication model

by the behavioral model as the theoretical underpinning of public relations (see Example 7.1)[1]

Edward L. Bernays held this view all along, which is why he insisted that public relations must be viewed as a social science. To be useful and appropriate for public relations practitioners, a com-

EXAMPLE 7.2

Symmetrical Process Model

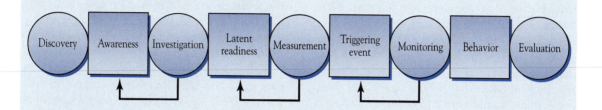

The symmetrical behavioral model involves five steps (represented as circles in the above schematic diagram): first, **gauging** existing levels of awareness and discovering conditions under which publics are likely to respond positively to an effort to create, enhance or increase awareness of some desired behavioral goal; second, **investigating** responses to the attempt to create, raise or sustain awareness, to determine any problems with the desired behavior goal that may already be apparent and should cause goal modification (or even abandonment) with respect to one or more publics; third, **measuring** latent readiness to act, so that the action's direction can be anticipated, depending on certain conditions; fourth, **monitoring** responses to the triggering event, to anticipate the level of resulting behavior, and interceding with action or communication or both if the behavior seems likely to be undesirable; fifth, **evaluating** behavior to determine why that particular action was taken, whether it is likely to be sustained and (if it is desired) what is needed to sustain it. Each of these five stages builds in the opportunity for publics to communicate their desires, needs and concerns so that goals can be adjusted or at least a mutual understanding can be negotiated.

Source: Reprinted with permission of *pr reporter*, Exeter, N.H., 33(30) (July 30, 1990).

munication model must encompass publicity, publications, advertising and special events that attract attention. All of these practices serve either to create or to maintain levels of awareness, and all emphasize messages designed to affect attitudes and opinions; but as *pr reporter* notes, "Every dieter facing the dessert tray understands the difference between attitude and behavior."[2] The behavioral model also suggests that communication in public relations should focus less on "mass" appeal and more on direct, personal impact on members of a defined public. Still, the behavioral model suggested here does not allow for the type of reciprocal action envisioned in the symmetrical model for public relations. The behavioral model is clearly asymmetrical, although it could be modi- fied to accommodate symmetrical behavior (see Example 7.2).

PERSUASION AND CHANGE

When someone holds a strong opposing opinion, you are probably wasting your time trying to win that person over to your view. Usually, all you can hope to do is to limit whatever effects the person may have on others who are undecided or uncommitted. In particular, you should not waste time on recent converts to the opposition, since new converts to anything react with more emotion than reason and are almost impossible to reach with factual materials, much less with a persuasive argument. You should concentrate your efforts, then, on preserving what favorable opinion exists and on winning over undecided individuals to your point of view.

There are three basic ways to get people to do what you want: power, patronage and persuasion. Power involves the use of authority and the implied or overt threat of compulsion. One obvious source of power is the legal system, which has laws that demand compliance. Other sources of power may be more subtle, but they are equally binding. For example, employees may not be legally bound to follow a supervisor's suggestions, but if they don't they may soon be looking for other jobs. Because groups can exert substantial pressure internally, peer groups are also a strong source of power. (If you don't believe that, consider how often you hear, "But I must have one. Everyone else has.") Public relations practitioners use power, for example, in helping promote blood donation drives, where they rely on the tactic of asking employers to get commitments from their employees. The request is for a good purpose—an honest cause, certainly—but it still involves the use of power.

Forms of patronage used as a means of changing people's behavior may be as crude as bribery, or they may be quite delicate, particularly if a favorable opinion is sought or if there is an implied threat of denial. Patronage may involve paying a celebrity money to make advertising endorsements or public appearances on behalf of a campaign, or it may involve making a substantial contribution to a civic improvement project in a key neighborhood or area.[3]

Persuasion involves using communication to win people over. Whatever the goal of the persuasion, there are essentially six steps in the persuasion process—not that each act of persuasion necessarily follows these sequentially.[4] The first step is *presenting*. A person must be in a position to receive a persuasive message—that is, both physically accessible and mentally receptive. You can present something and have the presentation ignored, however, so the second step in the persuasion process is *attending*, which means that the receiver must pay attention to the persuasive message. Beyond attending to the message, the receiver has to understand it. Therefore, the third step is *comprehending*. To satisfy this step, the message must be presented in symbols the receiver can understand. The fourth step is *yielding*, in which the receiver accepts the message and agrees with the point of view it expresses. The next (fifth) step is *retaining* the transmitted information, which explains why repetition is so fundamental to the persuasion process. People have to be reminded of the message, even after they have accepted it. The sixth and final step is *acting*. The persuader must be able to observe the results of persuasion in the receiver's behavior.

Some strategies that will get receivers to one point in the process will not carry them all the way through to the final step.[5] So persuasion strategy has to be planned and monitored to ascertain whether it is having the desired effect at each stage, and if it is not, why not. Parallels between the persuasion model and the behavior model are easy to see. The behavior model's awareness stage incorporates the persuasion model's presenting and attending. The latent awareness stage corresponds to comprehending, yielding and retaining. The triggering event essentially offers a demonstration of the receiver's retention, resulting in some sort of behavior. If this behavior matches the desired action, the persuasion process has succeeded.

Despite the protestations of some practitioners to the contrary, public relations frequently employs the techniques of persuasion to articulate a point of view that differs from that of members of a public. Examples include public relations or advertising campaigns, which are generally highly visible because of the attendant publicity. In persuasion, the critical factor in opinion change usually is information or the lack thereof and how this information is presented or withheld. Information is power, as social scientist Herbert I. Schiller points out, and information resides in controllable sources—among the upper echelons of government, business and education. It tends to be made available to the public, Schiller says, through public relations people who have the power to control its flow. Their access to information and their selective use of it combine the tools of power and persuasion. Schiller rails persuasively against such "mind managers," but his arguments fail to take into account the social responsibility exercised by these institutions or their representatives, plus the social responsibility assumed by news and advertising personnel in the media.[6]

Public relations persuasive strategies are planned around three elements: media, message and source.

Media Orientation

PR people use no black magic in their efforts to win over public opinion. First and foremost, public relations involves deciding what to tell, whom to tell it to, how to tell it and through what media to communicate. The choice of medium is critical. It must be a believable source, able to reach the priority public and technologically capable of carrying the message. Television, for example, has high credibility and mass penetration. Safety officials who want to alert residents about an impending hurricane invariably take to the airwaves. But something complicated like a change in Social Security benefits cannot be communicated as well through this medium. All television can do is alert people to the change and tell them were to find the information: a print medium is better at explaining details.

People also turn to different media for different types of gratification and rewards. Many different measures have been used in examining *media use* and *gratification* motives, but three seem especially well-suited: environmental surveillance, environmental diversion and environmental interaction.[7] According to these measures, people use media to see what's going on that might interest them or for sheer entertainment or to prepare for anticipated conversations or interactions with others.

How people use media for gratification may change as they change, as their circumstances change and as their relationships with others change. A young woman might become an avid reader of the sports pages while she is dating a sports enthusiast. A young man might begin to subscribe to computer magazines if he becomes in-

terested in a young woman who is a computer science major. In either case, the individual's interest in the specialized medium may not outlast his or her enthusiasm for the human relationship being pursued at the moment.

Message Orientation

In selecting a persuasive strategy, you must also evaluate the message itself. We do not always act as rational beings, relying on calculated judgments. We know that too much coffee is not good for us, but we may drink six cups a day anyway because we like it. Yet we may proceed cautiously in deciding about buying a car. Thus, to be effective, persuasive appeals must combine the rational and the emotional.

Think about an effective speaker you have heard recently. No doubt he or she illustrated the facts in the talk with examples—anecdotes that entertained you and helped you recall the major points. Compare that with a talk in which you took notes furiously to get down the flurry of facts. How much of the latter presentation do you remember? Unless you were compelled to take notes and to review them later, you probably don't recall a single significant fact. When given a choice, as you are in most instances involving public relations material, you probably would not choose the straight facts over the fact-story.

The complexity of the individual in the audience or public has been addressed by William McGuire (see Example 7.3). McGuire's chart indicates that, to be persuasive, a message has to present something of value to the target public. It must also be compatible with that public's motives. If your public has to make some adjustments to accept a new or different idea, you must provide a clear statement of that adjustment and the rationale for making it. In a free society where communication is open, the person being persuaded chooses which messages to attend to. If your message challenges your public's sense of security or self-image, you must provide an ego defense; otherwise, members of the public will repel the argument, instinctively defending their egos. If you are suggesting acceptance

EXAMPLE 7.3

Motivational Theories Behind Communication/Persuasion Research

INITIATION OF ACTION / Need		Stability		Growth	
TERMINATION OF ACTION / State	PROVO-CATION / RELATIONSHIP	Active	Reactive	Active	Reactive
COGNITIVE	Internal	1. Consistency	2. Categorization	5. Autonomy	6. Problem-solver
	External	3. Noetic	4. Inductional	7. Stimulation	8. Teleological
AFFECTIVE	Internal	9. Tension-reduction	10. Ego-defensive	13 Assertion	14. Identification
	External	11. Expressive	12. Repetition	15. Empathy	16. Contagion

To use McGuire's chart, look first at what caused a response—a seeking (need) or a reaction to some stimulus (provocation). Then observe the likely effect in a stable (status quo) environment in two categories—an active response and a reactive response. Then check the growth category in both the active and reactive columns. Trace these back to the cognitive (intellectual) response and the affective (emotional) response. Consult the internal versus the external to get some idea of demonstrable effects.

Source: William McGuire, "Theoretical Foundations of Campaigns," in Ronald E. Rice and William J. Paisley, eds., *Public Communication Campaigns* (Beverly Hills: Sage, 1981), p. 55.

---

of something that has been rejected before as socially taboo, you must offer a value that can be adopted to replace it or rationalize it. For instance, although it may be difficult to get white Americans to adopt American-born children of other races, they may adopt *foreign* children of other races—as they did in the 1975 Vietnam "babylift"—because of an emotional appeal to guilt or conscience. Some of this can be explained by the theory of *cognitive dissonance*. When something we are persuaded to do collides with what we think we should do, we resolve the conflict by justifying our action, rationalizing our behavior and modifying our opinion.[8]

News media often are credited with the ability to bring about change in a free society; but according to agenda-setting theory studies, the most they can do is give importance or significance to a message or to an issue by giving it news coverage. Sometimes the news media are so out of touch with the "average" citizen that real public opinion on an issue grows independently, despite its being totally ignored by the news media.

Research suggests that media coverage can be crucial throughout the life of an issue, although perhaps less so when publics are split on their support. Thus, public agenda-setters might want to keep up bursts of coverage to maintain popularity of a position on an issue. Also, agenda setters can influence issue priorities by increasing media coverage of those issues that are international or otherwise unobtrusive, i.e., those issues that people cannot experience directly.[9]

Source Orientation

The source of information has such a big effect on persuasion that producers of commercial advertising go to great lengths to decide what qualities the person or persons featured in the commercial should have. Organizations take the same care, especially in times of crisis, to select the best spokesperson for the effect that is sought. President Clinton, anticipating the release of Kenneth Starr's Grand Jury report, went directly to the people, confessing to an "inappropriate relationship" with White House intern Monica Lewinsky. Also, carefully selected and well-rehearsed Clinton spokespeople tried to counteract, or at least soften, the impact of the release of the videotapes of President Clinton's testimony to the Grand Jury.

People tend to believe sources that are like them, like they want to be or like they perceive themselves to be. People also seek authority in sources, most of the time. But they can be emotionally swayed into accepting someone else's advice. For example, the U.S. Surgeon General's initial appeal to people in the 1980s to use condoms to avoid possible contagion from the AIDS virus had only a marginal effect. Planned Parenthood could have told him that the appeal would have little impact. Planned Parenthood has been trying for years to prevent unwanted pregnancies, but it often has to compete with someone emotionally close to the decision maker and with the decision maker's own emotions. Part of the acceptance of authority is credibility, much of which is based on trust. People almost always trust someone close to them more than they do any authority figure. Some analysts contend that the influence of traditional authority is generally in decline—both because of cultural changes among baby boomers and "Generation X," and because electronic communi-

cation and globalization have tended to erode institutional hierarchies.[10]

Useful guidance on the effects of media, source and message on receivers of persuasion is available in secondary research (see Example 7.4). Some research has suggested that source credentials may not matter as much as a message's plausibility and message quality, at least when the reader is not highly involved in the topic. In this view, questions of source expertise and bias tend to have less influence on people's beliefs than the quality of the message itself.[11]

PERSUADERS AND THEIR APPEALS

We have all practiced persuading others to do our bidding since we discovered as babies that crying brought us a bottle. As adults, we persuade people to come with us to see a film they don't want to see, or to take us to pick up our car at the shop or to come for us when the car breaks down. Although these may be considered deeds of friendship, they actually are negotiations. We used something in the bargaining process, stated or unstated. If you doubt that, think of the times you have heard, "I'd have to call in some chits [favors granted and not yet returned] to get that done," or "I don't have any leverage with her. You're in a better position to ask." You might even say in response, "I'll ask. She owes me one."

Personal Persuaders

Organizations and authorities, family members and what sociologists call "significant others"—people you care about—exercise leverage over you. Organizations that you belong to ask for money regularly, and you usually give. They ask you to obey certain codes of conduct and to be present for certain events, and you comply. You may belong to the organization for social, religious or political reasons or for economic reasons (as with the organization that employs you). In the workplace,

EXAMPLE 7.4

What Research Tells Us About Sources, Messages, Media and Receivers of Persuasion

SOURCES

1. Self-persuasion (internalization) seems to be the most permanent source of persuasion, followed by identification and compliance.

2. High-credibility sources, when recalled, produce more opinion change.

3. Credibility of source does not affect message recall.

4. Information from low-credibility sources does not increase over time.

5. Powerful, attractive, biased sources can be more effective than unbiased sources in reinforcing opinions.

6. Biased sources are less likely to be believed if they are also perceived to be experts.

7. Expertise adds more to persuasive impact than trustworthiness, and we are more likely to be influenced by experts than by peers.

8. Attractive sources are more effective than unattractive ones, but source credibility has more impact.

9. Unattractive sources are more effective when they advocate unexpected positions.

10. Retention of a message is higher if the message was not expected from that source.

11. Sources offering rewards are more effective than sources that threaten.

12. Mild threats may be internalized and may lead to compliance, while strong threats stimulate defiance.

13. A source that threatens one of several punishments for noncompliance may be as persuasive as one that promises rewards.

14. Source credibility may not matter if the messages themselves present reasonable arguments.

MESSAGES

1. Messages with explicit conclusions are more effective than messages that allow the recipient to draw her or his own conclusions.

2. Good news presented first increases acceptance of a message, even if the message also contains bad news.

3. Information at the beginning and end of a message is recalled better than information in the middle.

4. Telling both sides in a message (telling the other side and refuting it) is advisable if the recipient is educated, is likely to hear the other side anyway, is familiar with the issue or is opposed to the side being advocated.

5. High-fear appeals can be more effective than low-fear ones when receivers have low chronic anxiety or don't see themselves as vulnerable and when the recommendations are specific, clear and easy to follow.

6. Generally there's no difference in the persuasive impact of emotional versus rational appeals.

7. Increased comprehension of a message increases agreement.

8. Learning increases with message repetition, but repetition can eventually cause an increase in counterargumentation and a decrease in favorable thoughts.

9. Repeated exposure to a message can increase agreement, but too much can lead to boredom and reduce agreement. A period of nonexposure can overcome effects of overexposure.

10. Generally, comparative and noncomparative ads are equally effective, but comparative ads are more effective on television than in print or on radio. Comparative ads are most effective when used with new or novelty products, when market share is small or when the desired public doesn't have established preferences.

(continued)

BOTH SOURCE AND MESSAGE

1. If there's little supporting evidence for a message, source credibility is more important.

2. Communicators are evaluated more favorably to the extent that their messages have the following qualities: listenability or readability, human interest, vocabulary diversity and realism.

MEDIA

1. Live or videotaped messages are most effective in changing attitudes, followed by oral (audiotaped) messages. Written messages are least effective.

2. Television involves its audience more than does radio, which is more involving than print.

3. Written messages—especially complex ones—are more easily learned and remembered than either videotaped or audiotaped messages.

4. When the message is simple, videotapes are more effective than written presentations.

5. Trustworthy sources are more effective in changing attitudes when they use television rather than print or radio media, both of which may give untrustworthy sources an advantage.

RECEIVERS

1. A message that contradicts an existing opinion may not suffer peremptory rejection if it appears to reward the receiver.

2. Perception is often subjective. Even when information is not adequate, receivers tend to use what is there (or what they perceive is there) to serve an immediate need or purpose.

3. Accurate and favorable perceptions of a message can be facilitated by establishing early bonding with the target public, by using familiar objects and categories and by using message cues that the public can easily recognize.

4. There is no evidence of selective retention of information based on the receivers' attitudes and behaviors.

5. Publics tend to disregard supportive messages that are easy to refute and nonsupportive messages that are difficult to refute.

6. Most mental and personality traits of receivers have diametrically opposed effects on message reception and yielding. Intelligence, for instance, facilitates reception but inhibits yielding.

7. Adjusting messages to minimize differences between the source and extreme receivers facilitates greater acceptance.

Source: From Alexis S. Tan, *Mass Communication Theories and Research*, pp. 141–43, 164–65, 176–77, 204–5. Copyright © 1985 by Allyn & Bacon. Adapted by permission.

certain people are in positions of authority—those who have special responsibilities. When you work for someone or when you are a conscientious member of an organization, you generally comply with the requests of those in authority. You also generally do what close friends and members of your family ask you to do. Recognition of authority in families is long-lived when it grows into respect or when someone has the leverage of purchase (that is, inheritance). Often personal persuaders can get you to do things contrary to your own desires, best interests or values. Their persuasive control is potent.

■ Impersonal Persuaders

Less potent and influential are the impersonal persuaders. These are found in the mass media in the forms of editorials and advertisements. They are found in the content of various types of entertainment and among persons who perform. They are found as well in educational and governmental institutions and in the commercial institutions that we depend on for goods and services. In some countries, all of these may be government-operated or -controlled. These impersonal institutions may persuade you through your fear of the punishments that they have available for noncompliance or because of the personal persuasiveness of their representatives. A specific teacher in a school or a specific sales clerk in a favorite store moves the relationship beyond the impersonal and into the personal.

Some of these impersonal persuaders qualify as opinion makers because they influence significant numbers of people. Some are opinion makers because of their public status (as in the case of celebrities and other newsmakers), and others because they manage the news. Some of the most visible opinion makers are both public figures and news managers.

■ Opinion Makers and News Managers

A news manager may be someone who creates an event that becomes news when it is made to happen, usually on a carefully detailed and prearranged schedule. The event may be Mickey Mouse's visit to a children's hospital or the bombing of American embassies in Kenya and Tanzania. It may continue over an extended period of time, as did the 1979–1980 hostage crisis at the American Embassy in Tehran, Iran. A news manager may also be someone who focuses media attention on an event that might otherwise be overlooked. In addition, a news manager may attempt to control information, as President Clinton tried to do in the Kenneth Starr Grand Jury. This is not new, however. As media critic William L. Rivers noted, "Nothing is quite so absurd as thinking of news control by government as a modern phenomenon. . . . Information policy has been at the very center of governing the United States from the beginning."[12]

■ Public Relations and Opinion Molding

What is true of news management by government is true of any group in business, science, education or elsewhere that possesses specialized information:

Those in command of information control its dissemination. The public's only defense lies in being aware that someone is always trying to influence its opinion. A sophisticated person will ask, "What am I being asked to think? What am I being asked to do? By whom? Why?"

In a democracy, these questions often are raised by members of some opposition, resulting in a struggle for favorable public opinion. That struggle confounds some other nations whose form of government makes it possible to ignore public opinion. But the freedom to compete for public opinion is inherent in our concept of democracy. PR practitioners become involved in such struggles because each side in a controversy employs them as professional advisers or spokespersons. Practitioners usually represent the side corresponding to their own beliefs, although some ethical practitioners will, like lawyers, serve any client with loyalty whether or not they personally subscribe to the client's position. What differentiates the professional practitioner from the unprofessional news manager—who unfortunately is often mistaken for the PR person—is strict adherence to a code of ethics that upholds a strong sense of overall social responsibility. Professional public relations practitioners never lie to the news media, although in the interests of a client they may sometimes have to say to the press, "I know, but I cannot tell you." The success of those who control certain areas of information in affecting public opinion is only as strong as their credibility. Credibility is thus among the most important assets a public relations practitioner possesses.

■ Propaganda and Persuasion Appeals

People who want to sway opinions use a variety of persuasion appeals—not all of them honest. The following list identifies some propaganda devices commonly used to mislead publics:

1. *Name calling:* The characterization can be positive or negative. Someone can be called "wise and conscientious" or "a liar and a cheat" (or the matter can even be left open to interpretation, as with "He's a character!").

2. *Glittering generalities:* Many nebulous words can be used here—for example, "enthusiastic crowds" or "throngs of greeters."

3. *Transfer:* This occurs when a movie star or other celebrity campaigns for a politician or product with the result that some of the famous person's aura is transferred to the less well-known person or product.

4. *Testimonial:* This is an actual endorsement, as opposed to a transfer device. A common advertising technique, it involves having professional athletes and other celebrities encourage consumers to buy a product by saying that they use it.

5. *Plain folks:* A favorite of politicians, this device involves using homey language or appeals to down-to-earth concerns to convince a public that, despite their high office or aspirations thereto, the politicians are still "one of us."

6. *Bandwagon:* This compelling device is used to sway undecided people to go with the majority, however slight the majority might be. The bandwagon device is considered so powerful that networks avoid telecasting projected results of election returns in the East until polls close in the West. Some research evidence indicates, however, that such coverage has no impact on people who have not yet voted.

7. *Card stacking:* Telling "one side of the story" involves selecting facts that represent one point of view, while obscuring other facts. The result is distortion and misrepresentation.

8. *Emotional stereotypes:* These evoke all kinds of images, and are so designed: "good American," "housewife," "foreigner" and so on.

9. *Illicit silence:* This device is a subtle form of propaganda, like innuendo, suggestion and insinuation. It involves withholding information that would correct a false impression.

10. *Subversive rhetoric:* An offshoot of card stacking is the device of discrediting a person's motivation in order to discredit the idea, which may be good and useful. For example, someone may discredit the mayor's plan to build a bridge on grounds

that the mayor owns property on the other side of the river. In the meantime, viewed objectively, the bridge-building plan may still be a good one for opening up commerce, traffic or tourism.

Obvious forms of these propaganda devices are easily recognizable, but history offers numerous examples of skillful users wielding them with great subtlety and effectiveness. Anyone who communicates may employ propaganda devices—spoken, written, pictorial or whatever. Such devices also may take the form of synthetic events. The 1960s were filled with "demonstrations"—all of them propaganda devices. And among the most skillful of that era's news managers were the youths. Reared on television and other media, they knew how to use propaganda devices and media effectively.

Although it encompasses some techniques that are used to mislead, the word *propaganda* should not be thought of as totally negative. Indeed, when one of the authors was working professionally for a large organization, a European colleague always introduced him as a member of the organization's ministry of propaganda, meaning no insult. Certainly, there is nothing inherent in the nature of propaganda that prevents it from being used to change attitudes and behavior in a constructive way. Propagandists differ from educators in that educators try to teach people how to think, but propagandists try to teach people what to think.[13] Propaganda also has been used to appeal to basic human emotions in order to effect opinion changes in the public interest (see Chapter 9).

Social legislation, income tax, Medicare, civil rights laws and other public policy initiatives all reflect changes in public opinion that were sensed and acted upon by politicians. Generally, such public opinion is an emotional response to information or events. Social psychologist Hadley Cantril developed some "laws" purportedly governing this emotional response (see Example 4.14). Although critics say that no law can account for something with as many variables as public opinion, Cantril's laws do suggest five basic ideas that seem common to all studies of opinion expression: (1) events are most likely to affect opinion; (2) demands for action are a usual response; (3) self-interest must figure heavily if people are to become involved; (4) leadership is sought, and not always objectively and critically; (5) reliability is difficult to assess.

Another five elements have been isolated by psychology professor Robert Cialdini, who identifies these as being elements of self-persuasion, the strongest and most effective type of persuasion. All are tied to the social persuasion strategy discussed earlier. Cialdini explains the elements as follows:

1. *Consistency:* After committing themselves to a position, even in some trivial way, people are more likely to perform behaviors consistent with that position. When people decide to comply with a request, they check to see if they have already done something that is consistent with the request. For example, in one American Cancer Society charity drive it was found that homeowners who had previously gone on record as supporting the Cancer Society (by accepting and wearing a small lapel pin for a day) were nearly twice as likely as others to give a monetary donation a week later when the charity drive began. However, not all small, initial commitments are equally good at producing consistent future behavior. They are most effective in this regard when the commitments are active, public and not coerced.

2. *Reciprocity:* One question people ask themselves before agreeing to another's request is, "Do I owe this person something?" If the answer is yes, they are more apt to comply, often when they would otherwise have declined and even when what they agree to do is more significant than what they received earlier. For this reason, charities mail unsolicited token gifts.

3. *Social validation:* People are more influenced to perform an action or hold a belief when they see that others are doing so. An important piece of evidence people inspect in deciding what is appropriate conduct for themselves in a situation is how others are acting. For this reason, advertisers love to include the words "fastest growing" or "largest selling" in their product descriptions. They don't have to say directly that the product is good; they only need say that others think so, which seems to be proof enough.

4. *Authority:* People are more willing to follow the suggestions of someone they consider a legitimate authority in terms of knowledge and trustworthiness. Demonstrating knowledge can usually be accomplished by showing evidence of superior experience, training, skill or information. Establishing trustworthiness is trickier. One device, in pitching a story to an editor, is to back off from this week's story but promise real newsworthiness with the following week's item—for example, "I know this item isn't exactly what you want, but wait until you see what we have for you next week!"

5. *Scarcity:* People try to seize items and opportunities that are scarce or dwindling in availability. This accounts for the success of the "deadline," "limited number" and "can't-come-back-later" sales tactics. Research indicates that people want a scarce item more than ever when they are in competition with others for it, or when they believe they have an exclusive.[14]

Earl Newsom's four principles of persuasion build on the concept of personal identification with an idea or problem, and suggest actions that people will take in response to a personal appeal:

1. *Identification:* People will relate to an idea, opinion or point of view only if they can see it as having some direct effect on their own hopes, fears, desires or aspirations.

2. *Suggestion of action:* People will endorse ideas only if the ideas are accompanied by a proposed action from the sponsor of the idea or if the recipients themselves propose it—especially a *convenient* action.

3. *Familiarity and trust:* People are unwilling to accept ideas from sources they don't trust, whether the sources are people or institutions. Thus a goal of PR is to ensure that an institution deserves and obtains such confidence, that it increases the trust of many people and that it keeps the trust of those it counts as friends.

4. *Clarity:* The meaning of an idea in an event, situation or message has to be clear in order to be persuasive.[15]

Successful advertising copywriters certainly know the importance of the last two principles—namely, that the people doing the buying have to trust those doing the selling, and that those doing the selling must communicate clearly to have any effect at all.

The element of trust needs to be emphasized in any study of opinion change. All of us are more likely to assume attitudes and accept ideas uncritically from persons we love and trust. Observers predicted all kinds of voting patterns for eighteen-year-olds in the USA before they were given the right to vote. What actually happened? Most youths voted like their parents—probably because they loved and trusted them. However, even if they did not love and trust their parents, they did receive information from them over a long period of time. One communication theory—called the "sleeper effect"—suggests that the source of a persuasive message, even if it is a distrusted source, is apt to be forgotten after a long period of time, leaving a residue of information accepted as fact.

Identification and suggestion of action are also important. As for identification, most of us feel an association with others—by education, religion, occupation, social or economic status or other category. What our identification groups say and do suggest courses of action for us. These associations have potential power because, when events so demand, opinion can be mobilized along lines of self-interest. According to Philip Lesly, such mobilization can be activated by highly visible leaders. Lesly said that at least three separate groups are discernible in the "leader" category:

1. *Vocal activists* who devote themselves to high-profile advocacy of cause.

2. *Opinion leaders*, both mass-media and individual thought leaders throughout society.

3. *Power leaders*—legislators, government officials, judges and regulators who have the power to take actions that affect organizations and society.

Increasingly, the focal group in persuasion is the power leaders. They have the ability to make things happen. Vocal activists, influential individuals and groups, the media and the general public provide input to the power leaders, but they have little power themselves. The input that reaches the power leaders is much greater from vocal activists and from opinion leaders than from the public and from most private organizations.[16]

Opinion mobilization by a leader creates a pressure group. Even if we are not directly involved in a particular controversy, we are still likely, because of our personal loyalties, to side with the pressure group that claims to represent us. For example, during the 1970s strife in Ireland, international problems resulted when Americans of Irish descent became involved in gunrunning.

■ Persuasion Strategies

Persuaders use one or more of five specific strategies to enlist compliance: stimulus-response, cognitive, motivational, social appeal and personality appeal.

The *stimulus-response* (S-R) strategy, borrowed from behavioral research, presupposes that audiences can be conditioned to respond automatically to certain stimuli, such as answering the phone when it rings. But sometimes S-R doesn't work as planned. For example, capricious association may occur, in which the stimulus elicits a different response from the one desired because the mind makes a different (and unexpected) connection. Another problem arises from the need for repetition before learning can occur. If not enough repetition takes place, the response can differ markedly from the one anticipated. A third problem is that the exposure necessary for repetition is usually expensive and is not always cost-effective, because the association may be forgotten. Nonetheless, long-term payoffs from embedded recall do result when S-R works.

Anticipating an S-R response of some kind can affect the type of message sent, according to *Glimpse*, a now discontinued newsletter of the

International Society for General Semantics. The newsletter noted that this anticipation can lead to another propaganda technique:

> Once told that an event or action signals a particular response, we may assume uncritically that earlier learning has established such a connection, as the word signal suggests. Unaware how we do so, we may come to believe that a particular event or action serves as a signal because someone labels it a "signal."
>
> Thus our reasoning and conclusions may be shaped by this propaganda ploy.[17]

The newsletter offers some example of this ploy from columns and letters in the *New York Times*, including this one: "It would send the wrong signal to the Russians if [former Defense Secretary Caspar] Weinberger is not included in the Geneva delegation [to a summit]," a Pentagon official said. "It would make it look like we're too eager for a deal."[18]

The *cognitive* strategy reasons that learning factual information in the context of a message can persuade if the information is retained. However, this strategy works only with individuals who have no stake in the outcome or who have no negative preconceptions about what they are being persuaded to do. Additionally, because it is cognitive, suitable alternatives have to be proposed, and the persuasion has to be presented in a context, as part of a bigger picture. For example, the purpose of exercise is not just to lose weight; it may also make you feel and think better.

The *motivational* strategy involves creating a need or stimulating a desire or want. It relies on a learned behavior, and not everyone that you want to reach can be motivated. To succeed, this strategy must offer a real or at least a perceived reward.

The *social appeal* strategy concentrates on calling attention to social conditions. Many appeals to alleviate conditions for the poor and needy use this strategy, as do appeals designed to correct behavior (like those sponsored by Mothers Against Drunk Driving). Often the appeals are tied to job-related norms.

The *personality appeal* strategy is designed for people who are outer-directed rather than inner-directed. It is based on tolerance (as opposed to intolerance) levels. Some nonsmoking and smoking appeals are personality-based, as is the appeal that promotes self-employment: "Own your own business; be your own boss."

Effectiveness of Persuasion

In making persuasive appeals to various human motives, you must consider two possibilities: that cognitive dissonance could occur, and that truth may be personal.

A theory of cognitive dissonance by sociologist Leon Festinger describes what people do when they act inconsistently with their own beliefs—as a result of pressures from power, patronage or persuasion.[19]

According to Stanford University psychology professor Philip Zimbardo, subtlety is sometimes the best persuader. He believes that more attitude change can sometimes be produced by *less* social persuasion. If people think themselves free to make decisions that run counter to their values, they sometimes need only a gentle push to take the plunge. Some smokers, for example, abandon their habit when subtly persuaded that smoking impairs the health of others, such as expectant mothers and small children. No one had to pressure them to abandon the habit; they simply became aware of the health hazard through media reports. They view themselves as having made a free choice and remain unaware that they were coaxed into changing by gentle social persuasion.

To see that truth is personal and value-oriented, we need only look at the religions of the world. All disciplines claim that their religion represents *the truth*, yet there are obviously many conflicts in doctrine among different sects and denominations. Certain objective truths are generally accepted—such as that "football is a contact sport"—but many less definitive "personal truths" exist as well, and these are often circumstantial, such as the different definitions of "sex" that arose in the Clinton-Lewinsky scandal.

Is manipulation of public opinion only a matter of communication skills and knowledge? Not always. PR practitioner Earl Newsom pointed out an example of a major failure in a six-month "skilled persuasion" effort in an Ohio city. The campaign distributed 59,000 pieces of literature aimed at getting people to view the United Nations in positive terms. But it failed miserably because, during the campaign, the United Nations itself was particularly ineffective. It is not true, Newsom said, "that if you have enough money to pay for printing, advertising, and 'propaganda,' you can change people's minds."[20] It is also possible to overcampaign, arousing suspicion and backlash when people notice that a lot of money is being spent on the media.

Such overcampaigning may have been part of the problem with the U.S. government's unsuccessful (1971–1978), $5 billion war on cancer. A cure for cancer is not yet in sight, and public support for the battle lags. Some government officials feel that too simplistic an approach to the disease was taken originally, stimulating false hope. Others believe that the source of disillusionment and confusion was the government's decision to ban various products that cause cancer in animals[21] but have not been tested adequately on humans. Ultimately, the public's increasing refusal to join the "war on cancer" may be attributable to disillusionment over the false promise implicit in its initiation. Some legislators talked of having the battle won by the 1976 bicentennial. But "actions speak louder than words"—which was also the real lesson of the United Nations effort.

Overcampaigning probably also occurred in the effort to control smoking. Smokers clearly understood that their addiction caused cancer, but after a certain point the campaign against smoking began to falter. Then coalitions of antismokers began to obtain results that the original campaign could not produce. These groups brought about restrictions on smoking in public places by pressuring airline management, government officials and private business owners. Today, it is difficult to find an indoor public place where people are permitted to smoke.

Persuasion occurs face to face and through mass media. But while interpersonal persuasion can result in cognitive changes, mass media tend to focus their efforts on channeling attitudes and existing behavior changes in a particular direction.[22]

COMMUNICATION CONCEPTS AND THEORIES

Many theories about communication are borrowed from the social sciences. A theory, according to sociologist George Homans, is something that enables researchers to derive a wide variety of findings under a number of different conditions from "a few higher order propositions."[23]

Another definition states that a theory is "an abstract, symbolic representation of what is conceived to be reality . . . a set of abstract statements or rules designed to 'fit' some portion of the real world."[24] This definition appears with two sets of rules for using "a theory (a set of symbolic statements)." One set, called the *correspondence rules*, states that some of the symbols (called "conceptual independent variables") must relate with others (called "conceptual dependent variables") and to what occurs (behavior of an object or person in a situation). The other set of rules, called *functional relationships*, describes how to manipulate the symbols of the theoretical concepts to derive testable hypotheses.

In communications, the propositions resulting from various theories are constantly undergoing examination, testing and revision. They will continue to do so as we get more deeply into relatively new media, such a VCRs and expanded cable TV choices.

The propositions that have survived testing so far suggest certain principles that may provide a useful framework, both practical and theoretical, for the day-to-day operations of public relations.

When you do research, your hypothesis testing always proceeds within some theoretical framework—usually a communication or persuasion theory. There are four commonly accepted frameworks for communication theories and two general persuasion models.

The four general communication theories are as follows:

1. *Structural functionalism* (Plato's *Republic*, Durkheim, Merton, Parsons): This theory holds that the organization or structure of society provides its stability. As a result, the forms of media and mass communication depend on their society and contribute to social equilibrium.

2. *Evolutionary perspective* (Darwin, Spencer): This theory holds that social change follows a set of natural laws and that mass communication systems have grown and developed with technology and with decision makers' needs for communication.

3. *Social conflict* (Hegel, Marx, Engels): This theory holds that social struggles occur between groups with competing needs and goals. The mass media are competitive and active in a number of areas of conflict, such as being a watchdog over government.

4. *Symbolic interactionism* (Charles Horton Cooley—environment over genes—and George Herbert Mead—language symbols in collective and individual life): This theory holds that the media present constructs of reality that offer information from limited sources, resulting in individual and collective creations of reality.

These general theories are social paradigms (sets of assumptions or systems of beliefs). Some competing psychological theories are usually discussed as a single framework, chiefly because in the study of mass communication the first four theories provide a good launching pad for discussions of collective action or effects. Nevertheless, we have to turn to a psychological paradigm for the effect of communication on the individual. Several approaches can be isolated within the psychological framework. One is the neurobiological approach, which concerns itself with the effects of communication on the nerves and the brain. Another is the comparative approach, which focuses on the effect of communication on humans versus its effect on other living creatures. A third focus is the behavioral approach, which derives from stimulus-response psychology and is closely related to the

neurobiological and the comparative. A fourth is the psychoanalytic approach, which studies unconscious reactions. A related fifth orientation is the cognitive approach, which examines what people do to and with sensory input. This is the most commonly used approach in studies of the effects of mass communication.

The two general persuasion models are as follows:

1. *Sociocultural paradigm:* This model attempts to account for sociocultural variables that enable a particular individual to interpret or present reality as in the mass media.

2. *Psychodynamic model:* This model, based on the cognitive paradigm, studies how an effective message makes a person do something (deliver an overt response) that the communicator desired as an effect. One of the most valuable theories drawn from this model is Ball-Rokeach's Theory of Value Change. People who are given a value test and who are then compared with others like them or whom they want to be like will change specific values to accommodate the others' values.

If you keep these various paradigms in mind as you develop a hypothesis, you will maintain a consistent theoretical framework. Developing a sound hypothesis has three benefits: it gives focus to the research; it eliminates trial and error research; and it allows you to quantify (measure) variables. Words that you can't quantify don't belong in a hypothesis.[25]

How We Communicate

Much public relations theory about communication rests on Carl Hovland's idea that to change attitudes you must change opinions, and that attempting to do this requires communication. For communication to be effective, the object of the communication effort must pay attention to the communication, understand it, accept it and remember it. Once such communication reaches the level of acceptance, the question of credibility enters in. Earl Newsom made the following comment about credibility:

It does seem to be true that the attitudes of people are formed by what they see us do and say—not by our insistent attempts to tell all about ourselves and persuade them that we deserve their confidence. It does seem to work out in practice that before we can move people to have confidence in us we must appear to them to be solving the problems they want to see solved—to be headed where the people are headed.[26]

The second part of the Hovland approach is raised in the question posed by H. D. Lasswell: "Who said what to whom with what effect?"[27] The "Who" here is the source of the communication. If the source is a PR practitioner, that person speaks for an entire institution whose credibility depends on the public's perception of its power, competence, trustworthiness, goodwill, idealism and dynamism, as well as on the similarity between the source and the public's self-perception. (A source can be either a person or a medium of communication, as in the expression "the *New York Times* said today.") The medium used for a communication conveys information, either factual or emotional, intended to cause an opinion change in the public.

The final part of Lasswell's question is critical for public relations people: "to whom with what effect?" That is, who was the public, and what effect did the communication have on it? We will examine these questions in the following subsections. But keep in mind that trying to change attitudes is complicated; it involves convincing a person to relinquish one way of looking at the world (or part of the world) in exchange for another. What publics do with a message defines its effect.

Reception Test for Media Although media research departments can show tables of statistics that theoretically profile their audiences, you should still ask some probing questions. For example, are the selected "receivers" chosen from a physical or from an intellectual base? A university (for instance) may define all those to whom it mails its alumni magazine as "readers," yet a substantial number are probably "nonreceivers" (they throw the publication away without ever lifting the cover) and another segment may be "lookers"

(they thumb through the magazine but never read anything except photo captions). The real readers are those who read at least one article per publication in the time period sampled. The same applies to news releases. To quote former Ohio State University PR professor Walter Siefert:

> *Dissemination [of news releases] does not equal Publication, and Publication does not equal Absorption and Action! Which means, in simpler words: All who receive it won't publish it, and all who read or hear it won't understand or act on it.*[28]

Credibility Test for Media Another relevant question concerns a medium's credibility. How much do surveys couched in terms of numbers reached tell you about reception? If you send out a news release to the media, not all media will publish it, and many people who ultimately do read or hear it will not pay any real attention to it. For instance, a presentation designed by the Magazine Publishers Association to show the impact of magazine advertising claimed that certain ads reached women in the twenty-five to thirty-five age bracket who, it was asserted, do most of the buying. The presentation offered supporting data to show such women's response to and recall of specific advertising messages, but it did not state the *proportion* of readers recalling these messages. And just as some people read editorial content and ignore advertising, others do just the opposite.

Thus, in talking about public reception of media, we first have to talk in broad terms of publicity and advertising. Many studies are available on the subject of receptivity of advertising, because of its ties to marketing. Publicity is more difficult to measure because the use (much less the reception) of publicity materials released to the mass media is almost impossible to evaluate. Publicity is assumed to have a higher degree of credibility than advertising because it appears as a nonbiased "news" source— one often referred to as *third-party credibility*.

Studies bear out these generalities. Ethnic and religious publications have a higher credibility with their readers than other media do with theirs. Industry, trade, association and professional print media also rank high with their selected audiences. Suburban and small-town weekly publications (generally newspapers) rate next highest in credibility. Specialized magazines also rate high—again, perhaps, because their readers have a concentrated interest in the subject matter. Recent studies tested readers' *affinity* for a publication—an emotional reaction, rather than an intellectual one. The strength of that affinity is a measure of how high the credibility of the publication is with its reader.[29]

Among mass (as opposed to specialized) media, television dominates. Possible reasons for this are the widespread belief that "seeing is believing" and TV's capacity to disengage the critical senses. Daily newspapers have more credibility than their critics often are willing to concede and a higher persuasive impact than their publishers and editors may be willing to admit. Radio stations, owing to their specialized appeal and the emotional impact of the medium, significantly affect their own loyal audiences, but these are comparatively small. At the bottom of the credibility ratings come company publications, which get mixed reviews for credibility, perhaps because they are so diverse in quality. In an era when everything else about the government seems suspect, government publications consistently get rather high credibility ratings—particularly those that include unbiased consumer-oriented studies.

Although the narrowness of their appeal makes the specialized media and the smaller mass media (suburban papers, radio) easier to evaluate, the mass media present a complex study. Studies among young people show television news rated higher in credibility than newspaper news. A college sample gave newscasts a 3-to-1 lead over newspapers.[30] A high-school sample rated TV as the preferred news source because viewers could see the news happening. Radio and newspapers almost tied for second place with this high-school audience, but newspapers were cited as more believable; news magazines rated last.[31]

An understanding of the agenda-setting role of research is also valuable to the public relations practitioner. The term *agenda setting* refers to the variable degrees of attention the mass media give to certain ideas, issues or themes, lending them more or less significance. A symbiotic relationship (mutually beneficial coexistence) seems to exist between message source and medium, in that mass media may pick up ideas that seem likely to represent broad appeals and then popularize them. The media agenda may also suggest to leaders some exploitable public concerns, although some evidence suggests that the power of agenda setting is diminished when the issue is abstract (federal budget deficit) rather than concrete (drug abuse).[32] There is no clear-cut "cause and effect" in agenda setting, but the impact of the mass media in calling attention to an idea, regardless of its source, is considerable.

How to Choose the Right Message

Communication theory states that, after you estimate a medium's reception and credibility, you must plan a message that is appropriate for it. If you are using billboards, you must do more than simply conclude that someone driving at 55 miles per hour cannot possibly read twenty words of copy and still be a safe driver. You also have to consider the purpose of the message, as well as its form, its color and its language.

The Purpose of a Message   The purpose of a message depends on the objective of the communication. What do you wish to accomplish? The goal should be something measurable, such as increasing the enrollment of a university, and not something nebulous, such as improving the image of the institution. PR pioneer Edward L. Bernays was adamant about refusing to use the word *image* in a public relations context. Bernays said the word suggests that PR deals with shadows and illusions when in reality it deals with changing attitudes and actions to meet social objectives.[33]

The reality of the PR practitioner's job is reduced to basics—experience, not imagery—by

EXAMPLE 7.5

Maslow's Hierarchy of Human Needs

Physical Needs	Safety Needs	Love Needs	Self-Esteem Needs	Self-Actualization Needs

Food
Sleep
Health
Body needs
Exercise
Rest
Sex
	Safety
	Security
	Protection
	Comfort
	Peace
	Order
		Acceptance
		Belonging
		Group
		  membership
		Love,
		  Affection
			Recognition
			Prestige
			Confidence
			Leadership
			Success
			Knowledge
				Self-fulfillment
				Creative
				  challenge
				Reality
				Intellectual
				  curiosity

Secretarial	Organizational Maintenance	Services	Programs	Advocacy

Organizations ⟶

Source: "Hierarchy of Needs" from *Motivation and Personality* by Abraham H. Maslow. Copyright 1954 by Harper & Row, Publishers, Inc. Copyright © 1970 by Abraham H. Maslow.

former Southwestern Bell Telephone area public relations director Jim Pattillo. Pattillo is blunt and very specific: "All the image building goes down the drain for the telephone industry the very first time the customer starts having a hard time with his telephone service or with company representatives."[34]

Some problems of institutional credibility cited by PR practitioner Philip Lesly can be attributed directly to peddling images instead of dealing with realities.[35] Some data indicate that deceptive persuaders are more likely to use rationale or explanation than truthful persuaders, who tend to employ positive and negative attributes of a situation.

Once the purpose of the message has been clearly defined, the motivation and inspiration decisions are easier. Psychologist Abraham H. Maslow has devised a hierarchy of human motives (see Example 7.5).[36] Although no longer held as reliable as

it once was, it suggests ways a message may appeal to the appropriate need within this hierarchy:

- *Physical needs*—for food, drink, sex, rest and such—are the most fundamental motivations.

- *Safety* is the need for protection against violence, economic hazards and unpredictable reality.

- *Love* is more than a need for affection. It encompasses the need to belong to a group and the longing for a friendly social environment. The strength of this motivational need pulls young people, particularly teenagers, together into a seemingly impenetrable peer group.

- *Self-esteem* includes the needs for achievement and for recognition of that achievement by others. It also involves the face-saving compromises we often engage in to rescue our self-regard, such as settling for a fancier title instead of a salary increase.

■ *Self-actualization* is the need to develop individuality and to make constructive use of one's abilities. This extends to creativity and aesthetic appreciation. One subtle aspect of this motive is the need to know and to understand.

Some principles go along with these needs. One is *homeostasis*. People constantly make an effort to maintain their own status quo. Another is the principle of *deprivation*. Related to physiological needs, it never wanes in intensity. If people are deprived of a physiological goal (for instance, food), they will continue to seek it. (One compulsive chocolate eater explained that a childhood allergy had deprived her of the pleasure of eating chocolates when very young!) When deprivation involves social goals, however, it often retains its effectiveness as a motivation only up to a point. Beyond that point, it loses intensity and people may abandon a goal; for instance, they may resign themselves to a certain social class or status. The principle of *satiation* weakens physiological drives and can weaken social motives, but it seems to have no effect on emotions—good news for lovers, perhaps. The principle of *goal evaluation* is based on tension, as in a straining to achieve something—to earn a karate black belt, to be a master at bridge. Goals that are not socially acceptable, however, either must be abandoned or must find support from another principle. This occurs also when certain goals prove impossible to achieve. For example, if you can't be an "A" student, perhaps you can be a "solid B" student. One other principle works in these basic motives, the *barrier* principle. A barrier placed between people and the fulfillment of their goals will enhance the appeal of the goal unless the barrier proves too great, in which case they will probably change their goals.

Our goals are tied closely to what we want to be. An advertising creative director, for example, may steadfastly maintain that everyone is a snob of one kind or another—for example, if well-educated, probably an intellectual snob. The promoter of a national magazine keyed to intellectuals (*Harper's*) adopted that very thesis in a mailing piece sent in a "plain brown envelope" that carried this question in the lower left corner: "Should you be punished for being born with a high IQ?" The envelope probably was opened by most recipients. What we value is often a key to our personality.

The Texture of a Message   Once you know which needs and values you want to appeal to, you understand the purpose of your message and which persuasive appeal is likely to work; then you can choose the texture of the message for its persuasive effect. The medium dictates to some extent the range of textures. Television has the widest range—color design, movement and sound. A close competitor is the computer which has all of these, plus interactive control. But pictures and sound on computers are still not as good as what TV offers—especially High Density (HD-TV) television. In print, the size, shape and feel of an object—as people trained in graphics know—may determine whether a brochure is picked up (much less read), whether a package is taken off a supermarket shelf, and whether an ad catches people's attention.

Motivational studies involving texture need to be interpreted by public relations practitioners as well as by marketing people in approaching particular problems. Regarding color, for instance, most businesspeople will not respond to a questionnaire printed on hot pink, will make little response to one on blue, but will give many answers to a questionnaire printed on green, beige or white. Several people complained at the 1994 National Conference of the Public Relations Society of America that the gray display type in the program was difficult to read in the available indoor light.

Most of us psychologically favor certain colors. This is likely to manifest itself in our choice of colors for clothes, cars and furniture. The public relations person needs to know which colors will appeal to a particular audience and how well those colors reproduce in the medium chosen for communicating with that audience. One despairing art director, after having to change colors for a campaign owing to problems in reproducing them in different media, said with some resignation, "I'm ready to go back to the basics: red, white and blue."

Nonverbal symbols are also part of a message's texture. Be particularly careful to avoid those that suggest bias, such as a woman standing beside a man seated at a desk or an ethnic or racial minority in a subservient posture in relation to a majority figure. Nonverbal cues say things that words do not, and today's diverse and culturally sensitive audiences will be quick to notice them. Be sure that the symbolism your message projects matches your intentions. Well-chosen nonverbal cues can greatly enhance the message communicated by the accompanying words. Carelessly chosen cues can completely destroy an intended message and alienate an audience.

The Language of a Message Problems in communication are often caused by semantics. The words you use must mean the same thing to the receiver that they do to you. It doesn't matter whether the words you use to say something are the ones that *you* think sound the best or most authoritative; rather, you must focus on what words have the most forceful and desirable impact on the viewer or listener.

Only people can bestow meanings on words, says communications specialist Don Fabun, adding, "When we act as if we believed that a word symbol is the event that was originally experienced, we ignore all the steps that have made it something else."[37]

The English author Samuel Johnson once made a bet with his companion James Boswell that he could go into the fish market and reduce a Billingsgate stall tender to tears without saying a word she could understand. Here is what took place:

Johnson began by indicating with his nose that her fish had passed the stage in which a man's olfactories could endure their flavor. The Billingsgate woman made a verbal assault, common enough in vulgar parlance, that impugned the classification in natural history of Johnson's mother. The doctor responded with, "You're an article, ma'am." "No more an article than yourself, you bloody misbegotten villain." "You are a noun, woman," "You . . . you," stammered the

woman, choking with rage at a list of articles she could not understand. "You are a pronoun," said Dr. Johnson. The woman shook her fist in speechless rage. "You are a verb . . . an adverb . . . an adjective . . . a conjunction . . . a preposition . . . an interjection!" the doctor continued, applying the harmless epithets at proper intervals. The nine parts of speech completely staggered the old woman and she dumped herself down on the floor, crying with anguish at being thus blackguarded in a set of terms unknown to her and which, not understanding, she could not answer.[38]

Jargon and obfuscation abound in government, education and elsewhere. Sometimes even attempts to clarify go wrong. A classic example occurred in 1972, when Pennsylvania's education secretary reportedly exhorted his underlings in a memo to write English instead of bureaucratese. Ironically, he wrote the memo in the sort of language he was out to eliminate: "A determination has been made that the communications effectiveness of department personnel suffers from low prioritization of clarity and correspondingly high thresholds of verbosity and circuitous phraseology."[39]

Important factors in language choice include clarity, emotional impact and context. A message's consistency with other messages from the same source and its level of repetition are also significant.

Clarity Obscurity in language has reached ridiculous proportions in American usage, as today's technical society embraces a whole vocabulary of words that would not have been understood even a decade ago. And since PR practitioners are not around to explain what their messages mean, the language they use had better be self-explanatory. You must choose your words with a feeling for the associations the receivers will make, based on their individual frames of reference; the images the words will conjure up for them, based usually on stereotypes they hold; and the simple fitness of the word itself. As an instance of clarity, John F. Kennedy's inaugural address ("Ask not what your country can do for you . . .") was written almost entirely in single-syllable words and was comprehensible, as well as elegant and eloquent, to almost all

Reprinted with permission of Copley News Service and Mike Thompson.

who heard it. Readability can be tested. Computer software can be used to check the clarity and reading level of your writing.[40]

Emotional Impact This element of language has nothing to do with clarity; it depends on emotional association. Emotional impact is, of course, a significant weapon in all propaganda battles. In World War II, Axis Sally and Tokyo Rose, two sultry radio personalities and propagandists, tried to entice American defections; however, two incomparable commanders of the English language, Winston Churchill and Franklin D. Roosevelt, urged their countrymen on with eloquent propaganda, raising the morale and resolve of those on the front lines as well as those at home.

The emotional impact of icons—emotionally arousing images, events or verbal metaphors—is an important mechanism for affecting public opinion. While this is not a revelation, as anyone who has seen Leni Riefenstahl's film for Hitler, *Triumph of the Will*, can attest, there are some new studies of emotional campaigning. Robert Blood, strategic communications analyst in the United Kingdom, says "Icons infect people's beliefs and they replicate by communication—they are the viruses of persuasion." His studies indicate that three factors influence the rate at which an icon spreads through the public consciousness: emotiveness, resonance and benignity. Emotiveness is the icon's measure of emotional arousal; resonance, its degree of agreement with existing beliefs and anxieties; benignity, its lack of a direct effect on the individual exposed to it. The actual cost of a new environmental policy, for example, may be quite benign for an individual since often the government and/or businesses are most directly affected. This factor can be separated from whether the policy has any emotive or resonant qualities. Blood's analysis helps explain how public opinion is affected by pressure groups and the news media.[41]

Context The context of messages—their verbal settings—is also important. As one writer advises:

> There is no easy way of choosing words. They must not be so general in meaning as to include thoughts not intended, nor so narrow as to eliminate thoughts that are intended. Let the meaning select the word.
>
> A word is ambiguous when the reader is unable to choose decisively between alternative meanings, either of which would seem to fit the context.
>
> A great deal of unclear writing results from the use of too many broad, general words, those having so many possible meanings that the precise thought is not clear. The more general the words are, the fainter is the picture; the more special they are, the brighter.[42]

Repetition and Consistency Because people both seek and avoid messages, it is important to consider the significance of *repetition* and *consistency* in public relations messages. Repetition increases the opportunity for exposure. Consistency helps increase credibility. Communication scholars who have conducted experiments on cognitive discrepancies and communication call the act of seeking "information search" and the act of avoiding a message "information preference."

Making sure that a message gets through to an intended receiver is the first goal, and repetition increases your chances of accomplishing this. Making sure that the message is believed is the next goal, and consistency helps here. But both of these techniques are based on a time element, and communications scholars have made some disquieting discoveries in this area. First, they found that, when pressed for time, people often make decisions based on less information than they would normally require (an especially significant fact in political PR). Second, writers must decide whether their target public needs information piece by piece (which is all right if members of the public already have made their decisions) or whether they need an evaluative structure or frame of reference to permit making comparisons between alternatives.[43]

Receiving and Accepting Messages

Evidence suggests that people who have grown up with lots of television (which means most readers of this book) learn to tune out messages they do not wish to receive. Everyone does this to some degree—otherwise we would all be drowning in noise. But the high degree of unconscious selectivity exercised by members of the electronic generation poses particular challenges to the PR person trying to reach them.

Great stock was once put in the two-step flow theory, which holds that ideas flow from opinion makers down to the public at large.[44] The theory suggests that opinion leaders attending to mass or specialized media are early adopters of new ideas. Their adoption influences others, starting with people who are like themselves—those in the same occupations or social/economic class. In the past several decades, however, politicians have successfully conducted public opinion studies to see what people are interested in and concerned with and then have enunciated those feelings as ideas or policies. Presidential programs reflecting this upward flow are John Kennedy's War on Poverty, Lyndon B. Johnson's Great Society and Jimmy Carter's New Foundations, as well as Bill Clinton's tax revision efforts.

Sources of a Message How publics perceive the source of a message is a significant factor in whether they accept the message. One effective source is people. We are in almost constant conversation with people, and the information we get in this way has a higher credibility than any other—depending on the attitude we hold toward the speaker. Is it someone we like? respect? consider smart? Is it someone who resembles us or who accepts and likes us?

The credibility of "people" sources fluctuates. Recent polls show clergy, educators and physicians at the top of the credibility list, winning back the position they had relinquished for a while to celebrity sports or television figures. We tend to seek out as sources not only people but media that reflect our opinions and attitudes. For this reason, many PR veterans recommend not trying to persuade vehement opponents to change their minds, but instead trying to neutralize them so they will do minimal harm.

Everyone seems to recognize that a sender must encode messages—that is, translate information into something personally meaningful to an intended receiver. However, we tend to forget the static and interference created by competing messages, credibility disturbances and the interference of selectivity on the part of the receiver. If the receiver does accept the message, it must be decoded, after which a response to the message may be encoded.

Considering the environment of distortion that exists in our family, social, educational, religious and ethnic life, it is a wonder any communication gets through to us at all. And of course, many messages do not get through. In other instances, our intended messages are contraindicated by our "body English" or other symbols.[45] Indeed, symbols are important, whether in advertising or in art, whether as trademarks or as company logos, in conveying the meaning we intend.

In utilizing symbols, we often resort to stereotyping, a mental shorthand that can be useful in processing information. The word *chair* makes you think of a certain type of chair because you have *all* chairs filed under that mental image. Often this is adequate for communication and for understanding a situation. However, the context may make you seek a particular symbol. Thus your mental image may go from your basic chair to a desk chair in a classroom setting.

But stereotypes—the pictures in our heads—are personal and may misrepresent reality. As a result, communication, imprecise at best, takes on an even greater risk when using stereotypes.[46] If you were dealing with a clearly defined target public

and you had a well-grounded knowledge of which stereotypes you could use effectively and appropriately with this audience, you might proceed with some confidence. But there are some monumental examples of the hazards of stereotyping.

For example, look at various situations where ways of representing women resulted in boycotts, demonstrations and even loss of elections. The stereotyping of females in advertising, television programming and news columns and by public speakers (especially politicians) has lessened in the face of activity by women's groups, but it is still in evidence. The main criticism of using stereotypes to represent roles people perform or to view groups of people is that, for many, the image becomes the reality. During the civil rights movement in the United States, for example, objections by blacks to racial stereotyping were based on concerns that people who had limited contact with blacks accepted the representation as the reality.

Effects of Stimuli Public interpretation of different message stimuli is constantly being measured. Advertisers are not the only ones to take advantage of the capability to add scent to print. McCormick Foods scents its annual report. Many greeting cards offer scent, sound and optical effects.

■ Responses to a Message

Information processing is critical in evaluating the impact (or potential impact) of communication. Carl Hovland established the idea of changing attitudes in order to change opinions, and this became known as the Yale approach to persuasion. He pointed out that effective communication involved attention, comprehension, acceptance and retention. Using Lasswell's model of who said what to whom with what effect, Hovland identified source, message, audience and audience reaction as the elements of the processing cycle. The source had to evidence power, competence, trustworthiness, goodwill, idealism, similarity (to audience) and dynamism. The credibility (trust, goodwill, idealism, similarity) and authority (power, compe-

Peanuts reprinted with permission of United Feature Syndicate, Inc.

tence, dynamism) of the source are the major conceptual factors in the Yale model.

William McGuire saw a flaw in the Yale information-processing theories. Hovland and his associates, McGuire felt, had ignored the relationship between comprehension and acceptance. Instead of emphasizing the *source*, McGuire focused on the *receiver*. His modifications clarified the relationship between comprehension and acceptance, indicating their separate effects on a persuasive message's impact. Personality traits of message recipients, he said, affected comprehension, acceptance of messages and persuasion in general. McGuire reduced the steps of the Yale model to two—receiving message content and yielding to what is comprehended—arguing that, to make a change of attitude or opinion possible, a person has to receive a message effectively and then yield to its point.

McGuire, like Hovland and associates, assumed that new cognitive information was learned from the content of the messages. That supposition was challenged by Anthony Greenwald, who said that people did not learn message content, but rather created their own covert messages idiosyncratically in response to the original message. However, Greenwald's cognitive response approach tells more about "the *covariation* between self-generated messages and their effects than it does about *why* covert conditions generate cognitive realignments and behavior changes."[47]

Other theories of social and cognitive behavior also help explain message effects. Social psychologist Kurt Lewin observed that people process information and "compute" attitudes to make logical combinations.[48] *Group dynamics* are important in this process because individuals try to adjust their opinions and perceptions in response to group norms and pressures toward uniformity. Motivation, said Lewin, is socially based, which means that the group has the power to reward for compliance or to punish for deviation.

Leon Festinger's *theory of cognitive dissonance* states that people strive to reduce discrepancies that exist within their own cognitive system. Experiences may be consonant (compatible with values), dissonant (conflicting with values) or irrelevant. The greater the ratio of dissonance to consonance, the more deeply the dissonance is felt. Of course, for cognitive conflict to occur, the opposites have to be important to the person. *Cognitive overlap* occurs when more than one choice is available; the choice closest to compatibility creates the least dissonance. J. W. Brehm and A. R. Cohen suggested that the dissonance would be greater if a person committed him- or herself to a course of action while recognizing that another path was possible, whereas Eliot Aronson said that becoming aware of dissonance was a consequence of violating expectations or rules, especially regarding one's self-concept. Hence, for example, honest persons are presumably more bothered by lying than thieves are.

Explaining people's efforts to make sense of others' behavior is called *attribution theory*. According to Fritz Heider, two types of causes are used to explain behavior: situational (external) causes and dispositional (internal) causes. The type we choose depends on some suppositions. If people often do unusual things in different situations for reasons we can't discern, we may attribute their behavior to an internal or dispositional cause. The problem with such assumptions is that analysts tend to oversimplify and overestimate people's consistency in behavior and tend to see an internal reason when the external situation might have had more bearing. Clearly people do take behavior cues from their environment, and they also have some reason to explain their behavior. The question is which comes first: the reason or the behavior?

Social learning theory holds that continuous reciprocal interaction and continuous feedback occur between a person's internal cognition and the situation. What we learn through experience, observation, listening or reading and establishing symbolic relationships teaches us to expect different consequences in different situations for the same behavior. In addition, according to the theory, reinforcements are different for various people, depending on such factors as value systems. Another element of social learning theory states that, in order for learning to occur, a person must remember and expect something to occur again. Extinction is one way to change behavior. Extinction may occur when the anticipated result of an action is withheld (for example, when a parent does not respond with attention to a child's tantrum as the child expects). Rules, instructions or communications can also be used to change behaviors.

The public relations practitioner thus has a choice of several theories to apply in planning message strategy to reach a goal. The option selected may be to encourage people to belong (Lewin). It may be to avoid a message that conflicts with values or—if people are already in a state of cognitive dissonance—to help them reconcile the value conflict through rationalization (Festinger). Self-persuasion, remember, is the most successful form of persuasion. The strategy might also be to provide environmental cues (Heider) that are likely to appeal to a target group (such as using an impressive setting—for example, a black tie event—to mark the opening of a new building). Or it may be an ongoing educational program to develop expectations (as in the case of antismoking campaigns that aim at making smokers feel uncomfortable whenever they light up in a public place).

Some researchers feel that a model devised by Martin Fishbein is useful in predicting group attitudes. The Fishbein model can be used to identify and categorize consumers according to criteria that are significant to the consumers themselves, and for this reason it may have practical implications for marketing specialists in particular.[49]

Fishbein himself has contended that his model can measure both a person's emotional evaluation of a concept or object and his or her beliefs about that object. He has asserted further than it can be used to demonstrate that a person's belief may change independently of attitude, with the result that two people may differ in belief but have similar attitudes.[50] For example, after having read USA Special Prosecutor Kenneth Starr's report and having viewed the Grand Jury videotape, some people might have opposed impeaching President Clinton because they believed the president had not perjured himself and because they considered his relationship with White House intern Monica Lewinsky to be the private business of those directly affected. Others, however, might also have opposed impeachment but for a different reason: they felt such proceedings would be unduly harmful to the country.[51]

Some researchers say that opinions and facts both represent answers to questions, making it impossible to draw a sharp line between them. A fuzzy line may separate opinions and attitudes as well, although opinions can be verbalized, while attitudes often cannot (they may be subconscious).

The opinions, attitudes and actions of people are all affected by family, friends, informal work groups and formal groups such as clubs and organizations. Group influence and pressure become particularly apparent during controversy, according to research evidence. When issues are clear, group pressure influences at most only a third of the people, with two-thirds standing firm. If even a small countervailing voice comes in, the third shrinks away. Only when ambiguity and confusion reign can you count on a bandwagon effect, which means that factors other than the propaganda device itself determine media effectiveness.[52]

Getting people to believe something is easier than preventing them from accepting something you don't want them to believe. One popular idea is that early exposure to some opposing arguments will inoculate hearers against future belief in the opponents. Other evidence suggests, though, that any preliminary message may weaken the impact of a persuasive opposing attack that might follow. Some evidence also suggests that trying to elicit a critical viewpoint in a public can either inhibit or enhance the effect of a message that is to come. If you try to turn people against a message or against the messenger, your efforts could have the opposite effect of inoculating them against further negative criticisms. The effect could be to make them more vulnerable to future persuasive appeals by opponents. But reception and acceptance of a later persuasive appeal are determined by both the target of criticism and the nature of the critical act. Therefore, the situation could be manipulated to have some bearing on the outcome.

The purpose of a persuasive communication is often concealed, becoming apparent only after careful examination. Comparing the obvious content with its intent may be done in examining such organized propaganda campaigns as those launched internally by a government or directed by one government against another, as in psychological warfare. Psychological warfare is as old as war itself. Although it has become sophisticated, its goals remain basically the same: first, to convert subjects from one allegiance to another; second, to divide the opposition into defeatable groups; third, to consolidate existing support; fourth, to counteract or refute another propaganda theme.[53]

Certain kinds of persuasive language can diminish people's critical thinking skills, although such language doesn't completely eliminate the ability to think critically. Rather, persuasive language triggers mental processes that are related to memories, imagery and emotion more so than to analytical thought. Jacobs warned that, if a captivating speaker persuades people that a particular action will ultimately lead to a desired end, and if many other factors related to the emotional stability of people also come into play, some horrific results can occur.[54] Examples include cult members'

deaths during the April 19, 1993, standoff at David Koresh's compound in Waco, Texas, and the 1997 mass suicide of Marshall Herff Applewhite's Heaven's Gate cult in Rancho Santa Fe, California.

Regarding retention of information, researcher Carl Hovland finds that, during an initial period, people forget verbal material rapidly; this forgetfulness gradually decreases until little further loss is noticeable. (Sometimes, in fact, the amount remembered over a period of time actually increases.) He also has found that people retain meaningful material better than obscure material, but that overusing even good material in order to emphasize it can have a boomerang effect. Moreover, the more completely people learn material initially, the longer they will remember it. Hovland also found that repeating a message up to three or four times usually increases the degree of people's attention, but that too frequent repetition without reward is likely to lead to inattention, boredom and disregard of the communication.[55]

Communications researcher Steuart Henderson Britt developed a whole set of learning principles that apply to consumer behavior:

1. Unpleasant appeals can be learned as readily as pleasant ones.

2. Appeals made over a period of time are more effective.

3. Unique messages are better remembered.

4. It is easier to recognize an appeal than to recall it.

5. Knowledge of results increases learning of a message.

6. Repetition is more effective when related to belongingness and satisfaction.

7. Messages are easier to learn when they do not interfere with earlier habits.

8. Learning a new pattern of behavior can interfere with remembering something else.[56]

One thing is certain about communication: You can never tell whether you have achieved understanding of your message unless you provide the recipient with a way to respond. Measuring

EXAMPLE 7.6
Grunig's Theory of Message Receptiveness
Conditional Probabilities for Information Processing and Information Seeking

Audience potential is important to cost-effective communication. This diagram of Grunig's theory of message receptiveness in communication behavior attempts to illustrate that importance.

Publics:	Active	Active	Active	Active	Active reinforcing	Latent	Aware
Behaviors:	Problem facing	Problem facing	Constrained	Constrained	Routine	Routine	Problem facing
Variables:	Problem recognition	Problem recognition	Constraint recognition	Constraint recognition			Problem recognition
	Referent criterion		Referent criterion		Referent criterion		Referent criterion
	High involvement	High involvement	High involvement	High involvement	High involvement	High involvement	Low involvement
Information seeking:	High	High	High	Moderate	High	Low	High
Information processing:	High	High	High	Low	High	Low	High
Cost-effectiveness scale, 1–10 (10 best)	5	4	7	6	3	8	10

understanding—rather than just message reception—was the task undertaken by two researchers, M. Beth Heffner and Kenneth Jackson.[57] They used pictures and verbal descriptions of the pictures to see whether the verbal descriptions resulted in the same mental impressions on readers as the pictures. Results showed that understanding seems to occur independently of the messages received verbally (which can occur without their being understood). Conversely, understanding can occur when messages are altered. The researchers also found that having a cognitive frame of reference helped students determine meaning. If students had the same basis for organizing information, it increased their comprehension of the messages' meaning. Some verbal descriptions were more reliable than the picture themselves. Another thing noticed was that symbols can be mis-

understood. This has happened occasionally when American advertising has been "exported" without due research into the culture or mores of another country.

The complexities of operations in an international community are heightened by the sophisticated technology of instantaneous satellite communications and the Internet. While the satellite picture or e-mail message might be technically clear, the message can be easily misunderstood. This increases the communicators' responsibility to ensure the fidelity of message reception through conscientious research, attention to research findings and cultural sensitivity.

Because information processing is such a critical factor in communication, models that predict behavior successfully are important in planning a communication campaign. Grunig's model (see Ex-

Aware	Latent/ Aware	Latent/ Aware	Inactive/ Latent	Inactive/ Latent	Latent	Latent	Inactive	Inactive
Problem facing	Constrained	Constrained	Routine	Routine	Fatalistic	Fatalistic	Fatalistic	Fatilistic
Problem recognition	Constraint recognition	Constraint recognition						
	Referent criterion		Referent criterion		Referent criterion	Referent criterion	Referent criterion	Referent criterion
Low involvement	Low involvement	Low involvement	Low involvement	Low involvement	High involvement	High involvement	Low involvement	Low involvement
Moderate	Low	Low	Low	Low	Moderate	Low	Low	Low
High	High	High	High	Low	Low	Low	Low	Low
9	2	1						

ample 7.6) attempts to illustrate the importance of audience potential to cost-effective communication. Of the four independent variables Grunig identifies, three explain when a person will communicate: problem recognition, constraint recognition and the presence of a referent criterion. The fourth variable is the controlling variable, which explains when and how a person will communicate; the level of involvement here will result in either information processing (low level) or information seeking (high level of involvement). Beyond that, recognition of a problem and awareness of some constraints yield four types of perceived situations: problem facing, constrained behavior, routine behavior or fatalistic behavior.[58] The result anticipates that, in a communication effort, four of the sixteen possibilities will be so low in cost-effectiveness as to be scarcely worth any invest-

ment: those that combine low-level (information-processing) routine behavior and fatalistic behavior. Twelve will be fairly high in cost-effectiveness. Among these, the active publics constitute a *second* target audience because an active public needs organizing communication and the active reinforcing effort needs maintenance communication. The primary publics to win are the latent, aware and latent/aware publics.

Recent research supports two aspects of Grunig's model. The research shows that individuals are more likely to seek and process information if they anticipate that it will help them solve a problem and if they are personally involved in trying to solve the problem. The research also supports the prediction that people who are constrained (and therefore would not be free to implement a solution if they had one) are less likely to seek or process information, although this relationship was largely explained by other independent variables. Contrary to the Grunig model, an individual's knowing a solution to the problem (or a "referent criterion" in Grunig's terminology) was negatively related to information seeking and processing.

Much of a public's response to persuasive information in a situation that requires a behavioral change has to do with where it lies in the diffusion cycle. The diffusion cycle has six phases:

Phase I: Awareness (also called *presenting*, as in presenting information)—The public learns about an idea or practice but lacks detail.

Phase II: Information (also called *attending*, as in getting someone's attention)—The public gets facts, develops interest, sees possibilities.

Phase III: Evaluation (also called *comprehending*, an understanding of the appeal)—The public tries it mentally, weighs alternatives.

Phase IV: Trial (also called *yielding*)—The information achieves social acceptability, experimentation.

Phase V: Adoption (also treated as one aspect of *retaining*)—The public adopts the information for full-scale use.

Phase VI: Reinforcement (also treated as the other aspect of *retaining*)—The public displays continued, unswerving commitment.[59]

Other studies show that when there's a conceptual match between attitudes and behavior, there is a stronger relationship between the two.[60]

Discussions about how people's behavior can be affected through persuasion make many of us uncomfortable, even though most of us have been doing it all our lives. You learned as an infant what kind of behavior gained attention. As you got older, you learned the right words and the best timing to use in asking for money from a parent.

Behavioral psychologist B. F. Skinner made the following observation about the positive aspects of affecting what people do:

I am concerned with the possible relevance of a behavioral analysis to the problems of the world today.

We are threatened by the unrestrained growth of the population, the exhaustion of resources, the pollution of the environment, and the specter of a nuclear holocaust. We have the physical and biological technology needed to solve most of those problems, but we do not seem to be able to put it to use. That is a problem in human behavior, and it is one to which an experimental analysis may offer a solution. Structuralism in the behavioral sciences has always been weak on the side of motivation. It does not explain why knowledge is acquired or put to use; hence it has little to tell us about the conditions under which the human species will make the changes needed for its survival. If there is a solution to that problem, I believe that it will be found in the kind of understanding to which an experimental analysis of human behavior points.[61]

Not only did Skinner point to a critical flaw in the effort to use today's theoretical knowledge to predict what people will actually do, he also alluded to another difficulty. Today's problems are global, but today's theories are culture-bound. Most research has been done in Western societies; and even within them, little attention has been paid to nonwhite minorities—who, of course, are the majority in much of the world and who (according to some predictions) will become the majority in the United States during the next century. Much remains to be discovered.

POINTS TO REMEMBER

■ When someone holds a strong opposing opinion, you are probably wasting your time trying to win that person over to your view. Usually, all you can hope to do is to limit whatever effects the person may have on persons who are undecided or uncommitted.

■ There are three basic ways to get people to do what you want: power, patronage and persuasion.

■ Public relations involves persuasion as well as accommodation. At the least, public relations involves articulating a point of view that may differ from that of members of a public.

■ People use media to see what's going on that might interest them or to be entertained or to prepare for anticipated conversations or interactions with others.

■ To be persuasive, a message has to present something of value to the target public.

■ Sources of messages are significant contributors to persuasion.

■ Studies of agenda-setting theory suggest that the most the news media can do is give importance or significance to a message or an issue by giving it news coverage. Icons are an important mechanism for public opinion formation.

■ People tend to believe sources that are like them, like they want to be or like they perceive themselves to be.

■ Impersonal persuaders are found in the mass media in the forms of editorials and advertisements.

■ We are more likely to assume attitudes and accept ideas uncritically from persons we love and trust.

■ The *stimulus-response* strategy presupposes that audiences can be conditioned to respond automatically to certain stimuli; the *cognitive* strategy reasons that learning factual information in the context of a message can persuade if the information is retained; the *motivation* strategy involves creating a need or stimulating a desire or want; the *social appeal* strategy concentrates on calling attention to social conditions; and the *personality appeal* strategy is designed for people who are outer-directed rather than inner-directed.

■ A *theory* enables researchers to derive a wide variety of findings under a number of different conditions from a few higher-order propositions.

■ Much public relations theory rests on the idea that, to change attitudes, you must change opinions and that attempting to do this requires communication.

■ Leon Festinger's theory of *cognitive dissonance* states that people strive to reduce discrepancies that exist within their own cognitive system. The greater the ratio of dissonance to consonance, the more deeply the dissonance is felt.

■ Explaining people's efforts to make sense of others' behavior is called *attribution theory. Social learning theory* holds that continuous reciprocal interaction and continuous feedback occur between a person's internal cognition and the situation.

■ You can never tell whether you have achieved understanding of your message unless you provide the recipient with a way to respond.

NOTES

[1] "Behavioral Model Replacing Communications Model as Basic Theoretical Underpinning of PR Practice," *pr reporter,* 33(30) (July 30, 1990), p. 1.

[2] Ibid., p. 2.

[3] Somewhat different motivational patterns are given by Daniel Katz and Robert Kahn in *The Social Psychology of Organizations* (New York: John Wiley, 1966), p. 341. Given as "motivational patterns for producing various types of required behaviors" are the following: (1) legal compliance; (2) the use of rewards or instrumental satisfactions—either individual rewards or "system" rewards such as earned memberships or seniority, earned approval of leaders or affiliations with peers that win social approval; (3) internal patterns of self-determination and self-expression; (4) internal values and self-concept.

[4] William J. McGuire, "Persuasion, Resistance, and Attitude Change," in Ithiel de Sola Pool et al., ed., *Handbook of Communication* (Chicago: Rand McNally, 1973), p. 221.

[5] Ibid., p. 223.

[6] Herbert I. Schiller, *The Mind Managers* (Boston: Beacon Press, 1973), pp. 134–35.

[7] Gregg A. Payne, Jessica J. H. Severn and David M. Dozier, "Uses and Gratification Motives as Indicators of Magazine Readership," *Journalism Quarterly,* 65(4) (Winter 1988), p. 909.

[8] Leon Festinger, "The Theory of Cognitive Dissonance," in Wilbur Schramm, ed., *The Science of Human Communications* (New York: Basic Books, 1963), pp. 17–27. See also Festinger's *A Theory of Cognitive Dissonance* (Stanford, Calif.: Stanford University Press, 1982); and Philip B. Zimbardo, Ebbe B. Ebbesen and Christina Maslach, *Influencing Attitudes and Changing Behavior: An Introduction to Theory and Applications of Social Control and Personal Power,* 2d ed. (Reading, Mass.: Addison-Wesley, 1977).

[9] Jian-Hua Zhu, James A. Watt, Leslie B. Snyder, Jingtao Yan and Yansong Jiang, "Public Issue Priority Formation: Media

Agenda-Setting and Social Interaction," *Journal of Communication*, 43(1) (Winter 1993), pp. 8–29. See also Samuel Coad Dyer, "Descriptive Modeling for Public Relations Environmental Scanning: A Practitioner's Perspective," *Journal of Public Relations Research*, 8(3) (1996), pp. 137–150. Dyer operationalizes an agenda-setting model for research in public relations issue monitoring.

[10] Jay A. Conger, "The Necessary Art of Persuasion," *Harvard Business Review*, (May–June 1998), pp. 84–95.

[11] Michael D. Slater and Donna Rouner, "How Message Evaluation and Source Attributes May Influence Credibility Assessment and Belief Change," *Journalism & Mass Communication Quarterly* 73(4) (Winter 1996), pp. 974–991.

[12] William L. Rivers, *The Opinionmakers* (Boston: Beacon Press, 1965), p. 1.

[13] Zimbardo et al., *Influencing Attitudes*, p. 156.

[14] Robert B. Cialdini, Joyce E. Vincent, Stephen K. Lewis, José Catalan, Diane Wheeler and Betty Lee Darby, "Reciprocal Concessions Procedure for Inducing Compliance: The Door in the Face Technique," *Journal of Personality and Social Psychology*, 31 (1975), pp. 206–15.

[15] From Earl Newsom's published speeches: "Elements of a Good Public Relations Program," presented to public relations conference of Standard Oil (New Jersey) and affiliated companies, December 3, 1946; "A Look at the Record," presented to Annual Public Relations Conference of Standard Oil (New Jersey), December 16, 1947; "Our job," presented to Reynolds Metal's executives, March 21, 1957.

[16] Philip Lesly, "Guidelines on Public Relations and Public Affairs," in *Managing the Human Climate*, no. 24, adapted from *The People Factor: Managing the Human Climate* (Homewood, Ill.: Dow Jones-Irwin, 1974).

[17] "Another Propaganda Technique," *Glimpse*, 39 (March 1987), p. 2.

[18] *Glimpse* (October 14, 1985).

[19] Leon Festinger, "The Theory of Cognitive Dissonance," in Wilbur Schramm, ed., *The Science of Human Communications* (New York: Basic Books, 1963), pp. 17–27. See also Festinger's *A Theory of Cognitive Dissonance*, and Philip Zimbardo et al., *Influencing Attitudes*.

[20] Earl Newsom, "Elements of a Good Public Relations Program."

[21] Rich Jaroslovsky, "Elusive Quest, Cancer Research Drive, Begun with Fanfare, Hits Disillusionment," *Wall Street Journal* (October 24, 1978), p. 1; and "Elusive Quest, War on Cancer Is Hurt by Animal Test Fight, Moves to Ban Products," *Wall Street Journal* (October 26, 1978), p. 1.

[22] Mary John Smith, *Persuasion and Human Action* (Belmont, Calif.; Wadsworth, 1982), pp. 320–22.

[23] George C. Homans, "Contemporary Theory in Sociology," in Robert E. L. Faris, ed., *Handbook of Modern Sociology* (Chicago, Ill.: Rand McNally, 1964), pp. 951–52. Also, Wilbur Schramm's definition of *theory* is helpful: "a set of related statements, at a high level of abstraction, from which propositions can be generated and tested by scientific methods the results of which help explain human behavior." This definition appears in "The Challenge to Communications Research," in Ralph O. Nafziger and David M. White, eds., *Introduction to Mass Communication Research* (Baton Rouge: Louisiana State University Press, 1972), p. 10.

[24] Zimbardo et al., *Influencing Attitudes*, p. 53.

[25] Melvin L. DeFleur and Sandra Ball-Rokeach, 5th ed. (New York: Longman, 1989), pp. 29–43.

[26] Earl Newsom, "A Look at the Record."

[27] H. D. Lasswell, "The Structure and Function of Communication in Society," in Lyman Bryson, ed., *Communication of Ideas* (New York: Harper & Row, 1948), pp. 37–51.

[28] Walter Siefert, personal communication.

[29] "Seventy-six Percent Trust What They Read in News Publications According to Simmons' Affinity Study Pilot Test," *PR Newswire* (Oct. 8, 1997).

[30] Raymond S. H. Lee, "Credibility of Newspapers and TV News," *Journalism Quarterly*, 55(2) (Summer 1978), pp. 282–87.

[31] Paul A. Atkins and Harry Elwood, "TV News Is First Choice in Survey of High Schools," *Journalism Quarterly*, 55(3) (Autumn 1978), pp. 596–99. Also, the Roper poll study for the Television Information Office showed TV having better than a 2-to-1 advantage over newspapers for credibility (*Trends in Attitudes Toward Television and Other Media* [New York: Roper Organization, 1983]).

[32] Aileen Yagade and David M. Dozier, "The Media Agenda-Setting Effect of Concrete Versus Abstract Issues," *Journalism Quarterly*, 67(1) (Spring 1990), p. 3. For a good summary of agenda-setting theory and an insight into the role of persuasion, see Ellen Williamson Kanervo and David W. Kanervo, "How Town Administrators' View Relates to Agenda Building in Community Press," *Journalism Quarterly*, 66(2) (Summer 1989), pp. 308–15.

[33] Edward L. Bernays, "Down with Image, Up with Reality," *Public Relations Quarterly*, 22(1) (Spring 1977), p. 12.

[34] Jim Pattillo in a speech for a public relations workshop in New York City, January 1977; taken from a copy of his address printed by American Telephone and Telegraph (1977), p. 8.

[35] Philip Lesly, "Another View of the Communications Gap," *Managing the Human Climate*, newsletter published by the Philip Lesly Company, Chicago, Ill., (44) (May–June 1977). For the information on truthful and deceptive persuaders, see James W. Neuliep and Manfran Mattson, "The Use of Decep-

tion as a Compliance-Gaining Strategy," *Human Communication Research*, 16(3) (Spring 1990), pp. 409–21.

[36] Abraham Maslow, *Motivation and Personality* (New York: Harper & Row, 1954). See also Maslow's *Toward a Psychology of Being* (New York: Van Nostrand Reinhold, 1962).

[37] Don Fabun, *Communications: The Transfer of Meaning* (Encino, Calif: Kaiser Aluminum and Chemical Corp., distributed by Glencoe Press, 1969), p. 19. Copyrighted 1968 by Kaiser Aluminum and Chemical Corp., and reissued in 1987 by Macmillan Publishing Company.

[38] Herbert R. Mayes, "Trade Winds," *Saturday Review* (October 19, 1968), p. 12.

[39] Reported in *El Dorado* (Kansas) *Times*, July 13, 1972.

[40] For further information about readability indexes, see (1) Robert Gunning, *The Technique of Clear Writing*, rev. ed. (New York: McGraw-Hill, 1968); (2) Rudolph Flesch, *How to Test Readability* (New York: Harper & Row, 1951); *The Art of Plain Talk* (New York: Harper & Row, 1946), p. 197; and "A New Readability Yardstick," *Journal of Applied Psychology*, 32 (June 1948), p. 221; (3) Edgar Dale and Jeanne Chall, "A Formula for Predicting Readability," *Educational Research Bulletin*, 27, Ohio State University (January–February 1948); (4) Wilson L. Taylor, "Cloze Procedure: A New Tool for Measuring Readability," *Journalism Quarterly*, 30 (Fall 1953), pp. 415–33; and "Recent Developments in the Use of 'Cloze Procedure,'" *Journalism Quarterly*, 33 (Winter 1956), pp. 42–48. You might also want to read Irving E. Fang, "The Easy Listening Formula," *Journal of Broadcasting*, 11 (Winter 1966–1967), pp. 63–68; B. Aubrey Fisher, *Perspectives in Human Communication* (New York: Macmillan, 1978); Rudolph F. Flesch, "Estimating the Comprehension Difficulty of Magazine Articles," *Journal of General Psychology*, 28 (1943), pp. 63–80, and "Measuring the Level of Abstraction," *Journal of Applied Psychology*, 34 (1950), pp. 384–90; Davis Foulger, "A Simplified Flesch Formula," *Journalism Quarterly*, 55(1) (Spring 1978), pp. 167, 202.

[41] Robert Blood, "Icons and the Influence of Public Opinion," *Journal of Communication Management* 2(1) (1997), pp. 83–91.

[42] "The Discipline of Language," newsletter, Royal Bank of Canada.

[43] Steven H. Chaffee, Keith K. Stamm, Jose L. Guerrero and Leonard P. Tipton, "Experiments on Cognitive Discrepancies," *Journalism Quarterly Monograph* (December 1969). Illustrations are as follows: (1) Deadline pressures affected the selection of wire copy by wire editors; when under such constraints their biases affected the selection of material whereas on other occasions, with no time pressures, they were impartial. (2) In an election campaign there are one-sided exposures early and late that attempt to persuade voters of the opposition to cross over; these should be timed to coincide with the period when they are likely to listen to arguments that run counter to their loyalties—certainly not at the last minute, however, such as an election eve telethon.

[44] For the evolution of the two-step flow theory, see Elihu Katz and Paul Lazarsfeld, *Personal Influence: The Part Played by People in The Flow of Mass Communications* (New York: Free Press of Glencoe, 1955), pp. 15–42; Katz, "The Two-Step Flow of Communication: An Up-to-Date Report on a Hypothesis," *Public Opinion Quarterly* 21 (Spring 1957), pp. 61–78; Paul Lazarsfeld and Herbert Menzell, "Mass Media and Personal Influence," in Wilbur Schramm, ed., *Science of Human Communication* (New York: Basic Books, 1963); Johan Arndt, "A Test of the Two-Step Flow in Diffusion of a New Product," *Journalism Quarterly*, 45 (Autumn 1968), pp. 457–65; Melvin L. DeFleur and Sandra Ball-Rokeach, *Theories of Mass Communication*, 5th ed. (New York: Longman, 1989), pp. 192–95, 318.

[45] "Albert Mehrabian, *Silent Messages*, 2d ed. (Belmont, Calif.: Wadsworth, 1981).

[46] Walter Lippmann, "Stereotypes," in Morris Janowitz and Paul M. Hirsch, eds., *Reader in Public Opinion and Mass Communication* (New York: Free Press, 1981), pp. 29–37.

[47] Alexis S. Tan, *Mass Communication Theories and Research*, 2d ed. (New York: John Wiley, 1985), pp. 124–25.

[48] Kurt Lewin, "Studies in Group Decision," in Dorwin Cartwright and A. F. Zander, eds., *Group Dynamics* (Evanston, Ill.: Row Peterson, 1953); and *Group Dynamics, Research and Theory*, 3d ed. (New York: Harper & Row, 1968).

[49] Jose L. Guerrero and G. David Hughes, "An Empirical Test of the Fishbein Model," *Journalism Quarterly*, 49 (Winter 1971), pp. 684–91.

[50] Martin Fishbein, "Investigation of Relationship Between Belief About an Object and Attitude Toward That Object," *Human Relations*, 16 (1963), pp. 233–39.

[51] While the illustration used here, for simplicity, involves individuals, the validity of the Fishbein model as a predictive tool for *individual* attitudes is disputed by Guerrero and Hughes, op. cit., who see its best application as being to *group* attitudes—certainly a significant observation for PR.

[52] Solomon E. Asch, "Effects of Group Pressure upon the Modification and Distortion of Judgment," in H. Guetzkow, ed., *Groups, Leadership and Men* (Pittsburgh, Pa.: Carnegie Press,1951), pp. 177–90; R. S. Crutchfield, "Conformity and Character," *American Psychologist*, 10 (1955), pp. 191–98. See also Asch and Crutchfield, quoted in Rex Harlow, *Social Science in Public Relations* (New York: Harper & Row, 1957), pp. 64–69.

[53] Michael Burgoon, Marshall Cohen, Michael D. Miller and Charles Montgomery, "An Empirical Test of a Model of Resistance to Persuasion," *Human Communication Research*, 5(1) (Fall 1978), pp. 27–39.

[54] Don Trent Jacobs, "The Red Flags of Persuasion," *et cetera*, 52(4) (Winter 1995–96), pp. 375–392.

[55] Carl I. Hovland, Irving L. Janis and Harold H. Kelley, *Communication and Persuasion: Psychological Studies of Opinion Change* (New Haven, Conn.: Yale University Press, 1953), p. 270.

[56] Steuart Henderson Britt, "Are So Called Successful Advertising Campaigns Really Successful?" *Journal of Advertising Research*, 335 (June 1969), pp. 3–9. Also in Britt's *Consumer Behavior in Theory and Action* (New York: John Wiley, 1970), pp. 46–48.

[57] M. Beth Heffner and Kenneth M. Jackson, "Criterion States for Communication: Two Views of Understanding," paper presented to Theory and Methodology Division, Association for Education in Journalism convention, Carbondale, Illinois, August 1972.

[58] James E. Grunig, "Communication Behaviors and Attitudes of Environmental Publics: Two Studies," *Journalism Monograph* 81 (March 1983).

[59] *pr reporter* (January 6, 1986), p. 2.

[60] Min-Sun Kim, "Attitude-Behavior Relations: Meta-Analysis of Attitudinal Relevance and Topic," *Journal of Communication* 43(1) (Winter 1993), pp. 101–42.

[61] B. F. Skinner, "Origins of a Behaviorist," *Psychology Today* (September 1983), p. 31.

Selected readings, activities and assignments appropriate to this chapter can be found in the *Instructor's Guide* or on InfoTrac if you are using the InfoTrac College Edition.

CHAPTER 8

PR ETHICS AND
RESPONSIBILITIES

Never, never do anything or say anything that you are unwilling to see in print.
LEE JAFFE, FIRST FEMALE PUBLIC RELATIONS GOLD ANVIL WINNER, 1965

Nothing is more indivisible in a company than its reputation and the climate in which it does business. These are the concerns of the company's public relations, which must be unified as the antenna, the conscience, and the voice of the whole corporation.
PHILIP LESLY, AUTHOR AND PR COUNSELOR

The "morality" or "ethical" nature—the correctness or rightness—of any action . . . is to be judged in terms of the degree to which it includes and integrates the purposes, and provides for the potential development of those purposes, of all other people concerned in the action or possibly affected by it.

HADLEY CANTRIL

A public relations professor approached a colleague in philosophy to ask about offering a communications ethics course crosslisted with philosophy, offering the philosophy professor some codes of ethics from journalism as well as public relations. The philosophy professor shook his head incredulously. "I didn't know you folks had any ethics."

Outside the university, others question the attempt to teach ethics in college courses. One argument is that it's too late by the time people reach college age. Another is that ethical behavior is culture-bound. Certainly culture is a factor in what is considered ethical behavior.

Ethics are founded on moral principles that are themselves grounded in effects. This holds true whether you subscribe to the idea that a moral judgment must fulfill only *formal* conditions that are universal and prescriptive or whether you think it must also meet a *material* condition for the welfare of society as a whole. In either case, "ethical behavior recognizes and rests within a shared interest," according to Ivan Hill, writing for the Ethics Resource Center.[1]

Judgments about an organization's standing are made in three areas: ethics, social responsibility and financial responsibility. An organization's sense of commitment toward its publics (which often have conflicting interests) has to be articulated and demonstrated. When Arthur W. Page was hired by AT&T in 1927 as the first corporate vice-president of public relations ever in the United States, he advocated this philosophy: "Be sure our deeds match our words"—and vice versa.[2]

Ethics and responsibilities are public relations concerns on two levels. We have to consider the behavior of the individual practitioner and that of the institution she or he represents. Public relations has been called the "conscience" of management, which underscores PR's role in reminding an organization of its social responsibility to all of its publics.

Actually, most research supports the idea that top management sets the ethical tone for an organization. Management, after all, chooses both inside public relations staff and the outside firm or agency that may be employed to complement or supply public relations work. If those public relations people see themselves as simply functionary "order takers" for management, and that management is unethical, then there's little hope for financial and social responsibility. Highly visible ethical lapses by organizations with PR staff or contracted firms have received a great deal of public attention in books, magazine articles and television shows. Such attention has not done much to improve the reputation of public relations people who are supposed to be advising management of ways to gain and maintain their own good reputations.

The challenge for internal and external public relations people is to guide those who hire them to responsible actions that are founded on integrity. To maintain standards of practice for public relations that don't allow representation of unethical behavior means having the courage to stand up for ethical codes as well as having a strong set of personal values. It also means having

the courage of one's convictions and refusing to do what is unethical.

A sound approach to ethical conflicts in society is to teach ethics across the board—to all disciplines and to engage the community as well as the campus in discussions of ethical issues. One university with an endowed chair in ethics is attempting just that. Dr. William F. May, Cary M. Maguire Center for Ethics and Public Responsibility at Southern Methodist University, takes on the issues that affect all fields, from businesses to physicians to artists and everything in between. Dr. May says ethics poses the question of "What ought to be."[3]

In recent years, observers have expressed some concern about the sense of moral values preprofessionals—students—are bringing to their studies. The author of *The Moral Dimension*, Amitai Etzioni, wrote of his efforts to teach ethics to Harvard University MBA students, "I clearly had not found a way to help classes full of MBAs see that there is more to life than money, power, fame and self-interest."[4]

The reaction of Etzioni's students is not surprising. The casual way university students respond to plagiarism and other forms of cheating has caused concern on the part of professors and administrators. The University of Maryland began offering its students discounts at local shops if they promise not to cheat. The Student Honors Council offered discount cards to students who would sign pledges against cheating.[5] Many of those students may be doing just what they did in high school. A 1993 poll of 2,000 super achievers in *Who's Who Among American High School Students* revealed that 78 percent of them admitted cheating. Of those, 67 percent said they copied the homework of another student and 40 percent said they cheated on a quiz.[6]

Perhaps they learned it at home. Student applications for financial aid often are based on false answers about need, and many of these are completed by students' parents who submit phony tax returns. Perhaps the worst part is that if they are caught—and not many are—all that happens is that the student loses the aid. The financial fraud goes unpunished.[7]

Concerns about the morality (or lack thereof) demonstrated by public school children have generated some pressure on their teachers to teach moral values in the classroom—a task teachers generally resist.[8] California, New York, New Jersey and New Hampshire ask their teachers to teach separate classes in morality and to include moral values in other classes, such as history, social studies and language arts. Efforts are not always successful, although relevant teaching materials are available. Many teachers worry that such lessons will merely stir up controversy in ethnically and economically diverse classrooms. They are probably correct. In practice, principles of ethics are susceptible to many interpretations, cultural and otherwise, and students already make questionable decisions in response to the moral choices that face them.

Although extremely complex, the study of ethics falls into two broad categories: comparative ethics, which is the purview of social scientists; and normative ethics, generally the domain of philosophers and theologians. Comparative ethics, sometimes called *descriptive ethics,* is a study of how different cultures observe ethical standards. Both diversity and similarity are of interest to social scientists. However, the social scientist looks for evidence that can be verified, and in a study of ethics such questions as whether ethical behaviors are a part of human nature spill over into other areas, such as theology and philosophy.

According to PR educator Hugh Culbertson, the philosopher and author Sissela Bok takes a near-absolute position that decisions are either morally right or wrong.[9] But there is another basis for decision making—the technique often referred to as *situational ethics,* which sees ethical standards not as constant but as varying or flexible in application to specific occasions or situations. Culbertson's observations of students suggest that they lean more toward situational ethics. Bok, too, recognizes that lies can sometimes serve a good purpose, says Culbertson. (One example is protecting Jewish house guests from discovery by Nazi storm troopers by lying about their presence. A more ordinary example might be telling a friend who asks your opinion that you think her new and expensive outfit is becoming when you think it isn't.) But, Bok asserts, in choosing between lying and truth telling, the presumption is always against lying, for the following reasons:

1. Dishonesty leads to lack of trust and cynicism—such as when a reporter later discovers that a PR person has told half-truths resulting in an inaccurate story.

2. Lying is an exercise in coercion, forcing someone to act differently from the way he or she would have behaved if given the truth.

3. Lying is resented by those deceived, even if the deceived are liars themselves.

4. Dishonesty is likely to be discovered, and no climate for credibility can be reestablished.

5. Decisions about when to lie are often made without calculating either alternatives or consequences.

6. A lie often demands another lie to cover it up, and then others to maintain the prevarications.[10]

Dishonesty is seldom ambiguous, but some public relations actions are.

COMPLEXITIES IN ETHICAL DECISION-MAKING

Part of the problem for public relations people trying to behave in an ethical way is that they are hired to be advocates, whether they are employees of an organization or employees of a firm hired to represent an organization. Public relations people have a role to play as educators or informers, telling what an organization is and does, but also as persuaders, convincing publics to support that organization.

One reason the two-way symmetrical model for public relations, discussed in Chapter 1, is seen as desirable is that it allows for input from all affected publics and for negotiations about policy decisions. The reality, however, is that negotiation with all of an organization's publics is simply not practical. Nothing would get done! In practice, though, what can occur is that an organization should try to act in such a way that even when its actions negatively affect one or more its publics (such as through the closing of an unprofitable facility), those who are affected will understand and accept the decision, even if they don't like it. Furthermore, publics can change the organization as much as the organization's public relations efforts can change the beliefs, attitudes, opinions and even behaviors of publics.

Two theoretical paradigms may help in understanding the ethical conundrums public relations practitioners face. Danish educator Susanne Holmström has posed two major sociological theories in juxtaposition, those of Jürgen Habermas and Niklas Luhmann. Both theories deal with the relation of the individual and the social structure.[11] Habermas's position is that an on-going dialogue in the public sphere is necessary to reach consensus so that the actions of an organization gain legitimacy. He sees two spheres in society: a lifeworld, which has a cultural and social basis, and a system, which has an economic and administrative basis. In today's world these two have become uncoupled, hence the need to communicate to gain legitimacy for the actions and policies of organizations.

While Habermas's approach is critical in attempting to set forward some normative theories, Luhmann's systems approach does not make any judgments about what is good or bad but looks at how society functions. Modern systems theory denies the integration that Habermas talks about. To Luhmann, everything, even cultural elements such as art, is a system with boundaries that must be maintained for society to continue to function. A system evaluates things from its own logic, and that creates a view of the world. The systems do and must interact, and that interaction involves negotiation. But in Luhmann's theory, there can never be a collective concept of what is socially responsible.

Both paradigms, Holmström says, have their "blind spots," but together they represent fundamentally different interpretations of the concepts of conflict and social responsibility. Because of their opposing perspectives, these are especially useful in examining criticism of public relations practice. She notes that public relations practice is commonly seen as managing social responsibility while avoiding or solving conflicts between an organization's behavior and public perceptions of what is right or socially responsible.

The paradigm from theories of Habermas, Holmström says, "make it possible to disclose the ideal perception which seems to prevail in the self-understanding of public relations practice while, at the same time, setting out normative ideas for the practice." Holmström calls this the *ethical, communicative or normative paradigm of public relations*. Key to understanding this paradigm, which she calls the *inter-subjective*, is the self-understanding of public relations practice while at the same time setting out normative ideals for the practice. The public relations practitioner using this paradigm acts as an individual through communicative action. The ideal is to re-establish connections between an organization and its social and cultural environment (lifeworld).

On the other hand, Luhmann's theories position public relations practice within social systems that define the actions of the public relations practitioner. In Luhmann's paradigm, Holmström says, "Public relations is a matter of functional issues in a cognitive perspective." She calls this the functional, reflective or cognitive paradigm of public relations with the key element being establishing public trust in the context-regulated society, that being a social order where social systems are in constant negotiation to maintain interaction. In this paradigm, social responsibility will never be an agreed upon "norm," but depends on communication to resolve conflicts and disagreements.

What does this mean to the public relations practitioner? Holmström says both paradigms put public relations practice in the "conflict zones between the different rationalities of societies." But, the nature of the conflict is different in the two paradigms. With the Habermas theory, the public relations practitioner is acting as a individual in the common interest. In the Luhmann paradigm, the practitioner acts as the system's representative in the special interest. You'll see the tug between these two theories in the many discussions of the role of public relations.

Ethics and Values

Certainly someone who is ethical would tell the truth, right? One problem is inherent in the use of this word to mean factually accurate, in which case one can be factually accurate and still deceive. The other problem is that for something to be a fact, it has to be something about which most people agree. There still is a Flat Earth Society, even after photos from space testify to the earth's roundness. Most people accept the photos and other evidence that the earth is a sphere. This is a verifiable truth. Some "truths" are actually people's perceptions of events, data and pictures. Our own bias or view of the world affects how we see things and react to information. Then, too, our beliefs and personal values influence how we define "truth." (If you don't want to accept that, just think for a moment about why we have so many different religions in the world. Which one is the "truth"?)

Two ethical issues illustrate this difficulty, one involving gun control and the other the tobacco industry. The National Rifle Association has a lobbying and research arm called the Institute for Legislative Action. An Institute research coordinator, Paul H. Blackman, began using a pseudonym, Theodore Fiddleman, during the 1970s when he began writing letters to various publications supporting the NRA's agenda. When his identity was unveiled in 1995, he said he only did it because it was easier to get letters published if he didn't let people know he worked for the NRA. Also, he said he could write the letters without taking the time to get NRA approval. Although he said his superiors were unaware of his deception, others in the NRA have said the practice of employees using fictitious names in letters is widely known.[12] Blackman was identified when a letter to the *Journal of the American Medical Association* caused the editors to check. Blackman said at the time that

Fiddleman was staying with him, and the JAMA editor spoke to someone who said he was Fiddleman. The editor asked for a resume, which never was sent, and checked on a university association Fiddleman claimed, which wasn't true. During this time, other publications, from *The New York Times* to *Roll Call*, the Capitol Hill newspaper, printed his letters and essays without identifying him as an employee of the NRA. What about this? Just doing his job, or lying?

The tobacco industry has been in the news almost daily during the 1990s. Its first promoter was John W. Hill, founder of Hill and Knowlton. Hill started the Tobacco Industry Research Committee in 1953 to combat the notion that smoking was injurious to one's health. He even ended his long career (1927–1962) battling the health community and denying that tobacco caused addiction and death. In a case study by Scott Cutlip, the educator doesn't fault Hill for representing the tobacco industry in the court of public opinion, but he does fault Hill for misrepresenting facts about tobacco. Cutlip wrote, "Public relations counselors too often define 'the public interest' in their client's or corporation's self-interest, which after all is their self-interest too. Is the legality of a product all that matters to a corporation or to a counselor?" he asked.[13]

As a practical matter, Arthur W. Page offered six management principles:

1. Tell the truth. Let the public know what's happening and provide an accurate picture of the company's character, ideals and practices.

2. Prove it with action. Public perception of an organization is determined 90 percent by doing and 10 percent by talking.

3. Listen to the customer. To serve the public well, you need to understand what it needs and wants. Keep top decisionmakers and other employees informed of public reaction to company products, policies and practices.

4. Manage for tomorrow. Anticipate public reaction and eliminate practices that create difficulties. Create goodwill.

5. Conduct public relations as if the whole company depended on it. It does. Corporate relations is a management function. No corporate strategy should be implemented without considering its external and internal public relations impact. The PR practitioner is a policy maker, not just a publicist.

6. Remain calm, patient and good-humored. Lay the groundwork for public relations miracles with consistent, calm and reasoned attention to information and contacts. When a crisis comes, you will be prepared and know exactly what to do to defuse it.

These principles underscored the Page philosophy: "Real success, both for big business and the public, lies in large enterprise conducting itself in the public interest and in such a way that the public will give it sufficient freedom to serve effectively."[14]

An organization's standing depends on its actions, and an organization's *good* standing depends on its acting in an ethical manner. An organization also is judged on how ethical its publics *perceive* it to be. For example, if your organization's board of directors adopts an antitakeover device—a poison pill—and your news release says that the pill is not to prevent takeovers, whom are you kidding? If your organization is a bank that is reported to be failing, and you deny that you are looking for help to avoid failing, how do you think you look to the people who are considering helping you? Depositors fearful of losing their money will withdraw funds immediately because you obviously can't be trusted.

Once again, beliefs are important to the public perception of an organization. When you measure a public's view of your ethics, you are asking if it thinks you deserve to exist. Don't be surprised if your organization is seen as undeserving.

Ethics are often defined as just "doing what's right." But, in different cultures, "right" may be "wrong." The fact that ethics are culture-bound creates some difficulties for global public relations practice. The view of an organization's ethics is likely to be based not so much on a definition of morality as on an understanding of the consequences of what the organization says and does,

which are seen as either moral or immoral by its publics. Beliefs about social responsibility strongly influence whether and to what extent publics see the organization as being a good citizen, either locally or globally.

PUBLIC CONSENT

PR pioneers Arthur W. Page and Edward Bernays both emphasized that organizations in democratic societies exist with the consent of their publics. In that light, it is appropriate to look at the issue of responsibility in detail.

Social responsibility, another term for good citizenship, means producing sound products or reliable services that don't threaten the environment and contributing positively to the social, political and economic health of society. It also means compensating employees fairly and treating them justly, regardless of the cultural environment in which you operate. Clearly translated, this means no poorly paid "slave" labor and no discriminatory or "sweat shop" practices. It means never offering overpriced or potentially dangerous junk in the guise of a high-quality product. It means refusing to misuse this small planet and its creatures. It means restoring and protecting anything your organization might damage or threaten during normal business operations.

Financial responsibility generally refers to an organization's fiscal soundness, as indicated by such measures as market or audience share; but it also includes how the organization interacts with investors and investment advisers. Public relations has its own financial responsibility: to detail its own contribution to the bottom line (an organization's profit margin).

These traditional measures of responsibility are important, of course, but just as significant are the perceptions people have about how a for-profit or nonprofit organization gets and spends its money. These facets of financial responsibility are too often overlooked in attempts to measure public images. Yet beliefs about an organization in these areas are strongly tied to confidence, trust and loyalty. For example, should we try to measure loyalty? If our organization becomes embroiled in a takeover fight, investors' loyalty may be absolutely critical. How many of our large individual stockholders will retain their holdings in the face of escalating offers?

As public relations people, we hope that our organization's image will influence our stockholders to retain their confidence in the organization's leadership. And the same goes for "stakeholders." Suppose that you represent a nonprofit organization—a museum, say—and you are trying to recruit volunteers to serve in it at a time when it is receiving heavy public criticism. You must rely on the long-standing goodwill of the public toward the museum and on the ability of current volunteers to reinforce this in the community. The goodwill must be a strong resource, however, because you'll need it to bolster current volunteers' morale. The key point here is that traditional measures of financial responsibility most often are *not* adequate.

In all three areas—ethics, social responsibility and financial responsibility—publics are likely to believe that public relations people may, on occasion, be trying to influence them. The fact that PR does work to change people's views causes the individual practitioner's ethics to be closely entwined with the organization's social responsibility. The frequent tension inherent in the role is clearly articulated by educator Marvin Olasky. He says that free-market competition forced PR practitioners (as voices for corporate America) to seek government regulation as a means of eliminating competition while they spoke publicly of supporting free enterprise. But the very pursuit of "social responsibility," Olasky says, has fostered the popular notion that there are no "private" areas of business—that is, no areas that are off-limits to public scrutiny. In attempting to say *something* while at the same time protecting an organization's business, the PR person often deceives, according to Olasky. Olasky also asserts that, the closer business moves toward government, the more likely it is to try to affect the political process.[15]

While corporate PR poses serious hazards for the practitioner, political PR can be even worse.

Political PR people often find themselves caught in the middle of conflicts resulting from use of news media by public officials and vice versa.

Social/Financial Responsibility and Values

Just as with ethics, efforts to be socially and financially responsible are closely tied to values, which are anything but universal. However, the choices can and should be defensible. Patagonia founder Yvon Chouinard claims that "everything we do for the right reason ends up making us more money. That's the message I've got to get across to corporate America." Chouinard tithes 10 percent of pretax profits or one percent of sales to environmental groups. In 1996, Patagonia gave more than $1.1 million to 200 groups. Not everyone likes the choices. Some employees have protested and have threatened to go to work somewhere else. Chouinard responds that they may find an employer who doesn't support any nonprofit organizations at all. Some customers have sent back clothing or have asked to have their names taken off the mailing list. Each protester gets a personal letter asking him or her to consider all of the recipients on the list, not just the one objected to. Internally, Chouinard looks for employees who have families, and half of his staff are women. For new mothers, Patagonia has lactation consultants, a nursing room and an on-site nursery next to the cafeteria, separated by a plate glass window.[16] For responsibility to be credible, there must be significant real evidence of commitment.

Even with such commitment, however, conflicts can still arise over how that responsibility is interpreted. The shirt maker, Phillips-Van Heusen Corp., has a code of conduct that says employees will be treated fairly with regard to wages, benefits and working conditions; that the legal and moral rights of employees will never be violated; that children will never be employed by the company directly or indirectly, and that the company is committed to monitoring its facilities and those with whom they do business. CEO Bruce Klatsky's role as a human rights advocate is well known. He is on the board of an advocacy group, Human Rights Watch, and serves on a White House committee to eliminate sweatshops. He also lectures about an executive's responsibility to protect human rights in all of its operations, including those abroad.

Nevertheless, his company has been accused of violating human rights. One accusation focuses on a Guatemalan plant. PVH and some of its contractors are said to pay below poverty wages, to intimidate union organizers and to buy from suppliers who use underage workers. At issue is a question all or most global employers face: can they really protect human rights and keep labor costs low? Confronted with evidence of the credibility of his accusers, Klatsky says that a lack of direct dialogue with associates is part of the problem. He also noted that, "if I knew about Guatemala what I know now, I wouldn't have put the plant there. I don't have a pure, clean easy answer to the morality of producing products in such countries." But even if he didn't have a plant there, another response is probably even more telling: "We aren't bad people. Are we perfect? Absolutely not. Are there going to be some mistakes made? Absolutely."[17] The problem is that it is the slips that create a credibility gap, which is why social and financial responsibility are so difficult to establish and maintain.

RESPONSIBILITY TO WHOM?

There will always be some people in the business world who are convinced that all they need is a lawyer to keep them out of jail and a PR practitioner to keep bad news out of the paper.

Actually, public relations must create constant awareness by management of the institution's responsibility to all its publics. Most professional PR practitioners recognize that they and their organizations have ethical responsibilities to at least ten different publics:

1. *Clients:* Being responsible to a client means not only being judicious with his or her money, but also (sometimes) saying no, because the customer is *not* always right. When a client is wrong, it is important to say so—to tell truths substantiated by facts discovered through honest research.

2. *News media:* These deserve honest and valid use of their channels; that is, you should not involve them in compromising situations, such as by lying or feeding them misleading or incomplete information. PR practitioners are accused by news media more often for sins of omission than of commission. A responsible PR person may not be expected to call news media attention to bad news but should be expected, when asked, to respond with a straightforward and complete presentation of the facts when the news media are pursuing an unfavorable story. Exceptions might occur in legal cases where specific or complete disclosure is required by law (for example, SEC regulations) or is prudent (where events are matters of public record or otherwise legally accessible).

3. *Government agencies:* The PR person should be a source and resource for substantive information needed and required by the government.

4. *Educational institutions:* There should be a good two-way system for sharing research, ideas and resources and for offering learning opportunities for students. Both sides can enhance their riches through close, professional cooperation.

5. *Consumers of your client's products and services:* An increasingly skeptical and demanding customer public can be exasperating, especially to those watching the profit-and-loss sheet, but sincerity and quality go a long way here. Consumers have a right to expect goodwill and integrity in products and services.

6. *Stockholders and analysts:* Many PR practitioners owe their jobs to investors in their business and to those who counsel such investments, since such investors provide the economic framework and the overall climate of confidence in an organization. Both investors and investment counselors need adequate information to make good decisions, and this calls for lucid interpretations of financial status, reliable annual reports and full explanations of company developments.

7. *Community:* Because the local community often provides critical elements such as utilities, tax breaks, cooperative zoning plans and chamber of commerce promotion, a community has a right to expect environmental protection, a fair tax return, employment of local people and corporate contributions of funds and executive time to community projects.

8. *Competitors:* Other businesses have a right to expect from PR-advised firms a fair competitive environment that stays within the limits of the law and does not violate individual rights or privacy. The obligations of PR practitioners are set forth in the codes of ethics or standards for behavior promulgated by various professional PR organizations. (The Public Relations Society of America's Code of Professional Standards for the Practice of Public Relations, with Interpretations, the IABC code and the IPRA code are included in the *Instructor's Guide* for this text.)

9. *Critics:* Public relations practice is likely to generate criticism from all of the preceding publics, but its very existence as an organizational role and function is criticized from at least two philosophical points of view. One set of critics complains that public relations practitioners impede rather than facilitate corporate social responsibility by rationalizing corporate actions and manipulating public opinion. For these reasons, they add, corporations do not bear the full measure of hostility they deserve from their various publics for ignoring quality-of-life factors that economic indicators may not reflect. These critics may not be fundamentally opposed to the capitalistic system, only to what they consider its abuses. They think the institutions of our society should voluntarily provide improvements in quality of life as well as economic well-being. They see public relations people as a cushion between management and the public's demand for social responsibility.

Another philosophical set of critics might be categorized as human rights defenders. This group tends to speak out against public relations practitioners who represent unpopular clients—for example, leaders of countries that are reputed to be repressive.

10. *Public relations practitioners:* Other practitioners in the field itself expect practitioners to uphold standards of behavior that will win respect for the practice of public relations. This impulse provides the basis of the PRSA, IPRA and IABC codes and lies at the root of the discussions of licensing.

Public relations codes of ethical behavior or standards of practice have been called self-serving, but they do provide guidelines and, in some cases, an argument against pressures in the workplace.

Hadley Cantril succinctly identified the basis for appraising ethical public relations conduct:

> The "morality" or "ethical" nature—the correctness or rightness—of any action . . . is to be judged in terms of the degree to which it includes and integrates the purposes, and provides for the potential development of those purposes for all other people concerned in the action or possibly affected by it.[18]

RESPONSIBILITY IN PRACTICE

Some areas of public relations practice considered legitimate by most practitioners nonetheless cause public concern and arouse criticism. Among the most obvious of these are how to conduct research (and how to use the resulting information), how to handle internal battles you lose with management and what to do about international activities when these involve working with foreign governments that operate according to codes of ethics that might conflict with your own.

Research and Persuasion

Research is critical in all areas of public relations. (Chapters 5 and 6 of this book were devoted to the subject.) Finding out all that you can about the demographics and psychographics of your publics enables you to reach and communicate with them effectively. However, the uses of PR research and the purposes of persuasion must be examined by the practitioner to minimize opportunities for abuse.

The first ethical problem to resolve is how to collect the data. Whether you do the research yourself—in-house, so to speak—or buy research services, you have to maintain certain standards toward the subjects used in the research. Earl Babbie, a well-established social science researcher, identifies the following practices that must be safeguarded in a research study: (1) ensuring the voluntary participation of all subjects, including employees when the research is of internal publics; (2) preventing harm to the subjects, either psychologically (through participation itself or as a result of facing issues they would prefer to avoid) or through analysis and reporting (when self identification could cause damage to self-image); (3) protecting participants through anonymity and/or confidentiality, the latter occurring when the researcher identifies the participant but does not reveal the information; (4) avoiding deceiving participants, something not always possible but highly desirable; (5) reporting and analyzing results fairly and accurately so that others are not misled by the findings. Incidentally, when you buy research, you should know that members of the American Association for Public Opinion Research are pledged to uphold a code of professional ethics and practices.[19]

The second ethical problem in research involves the actual accumulation and storage of information. Probably no PR practitioner can match any level of government in its accumulation of data on an individual. Most people are in ten to thirty local and state files as individuals. In addition, the U.S. government classifies individual citizens according to more than 8,000 separate record systems. Many government records are supposed to be off limits to commercial researchers. Nevertheless, one company, Metromail Corp., a subsidiary of R. R. Donnelley & Sons, was able to obtain California voter-registration rolls. Another acquired driver's license information and photos from the South Carolina Department of Motor Vehicles in 1999 and was sued by the state for misusing the information. In addition to using the voter rolls, Metromail callers claimed they were from the Survey Research Bureau in Lincoln, Nebraska, asking questions about ice cream. But the survey was bogus. What they were after was the ages of people in the household because that information is marketable.[20] Such accumulated data offers an opportunity for compilations that can profile individuals and families.

Concern over possible misuse of this kind of data was partly why legislators passed the Freedom of Information Act and a consumer credit bill which allow people to see just what information government and business had compiled on them. Nevertheless, both public and private institutions continue to gather substantial data, owing to the many different types of public registration (auto and boat licenses, building permits and so on) and mailing lists that are maintained.

Among the users of such purchased lists has been the Internal Revenue Service, to examine data drawn from surveys in which people have revealed their level of income. The IRS can use these lists to look for tax evaders. Social scientists (and marketing researchers) are afraid such use will discourage participation in surveys.[21]

But market research in and of itself is a cause for some concern. Purchases are monitored, and even cable subscribers' use of electronic data banks is watched. Another important issue involves how you represent yourself in gathering facts. Some market survey techniques call for researchers to represent themselves as "clients" for a company's service, which is tantamount to lying to get information. One responsible market researcher who was asked to use this approach declined, saying, "I can get better data honestly." This researcher was alluding to the fact that research data are frequently misrepresented to a client.

A third problem has to do with how research information is used.

A campaign against disposable diapers had been launched, and more than a dozen state legislatures were considering bans, taxes and warnings on disposable diapers, which supposedly do not deteriorate in land fills. The campaign was engineered by a PR firm that had gotten a cloth diaper account in an era of disposables. But public opinion took another shift after publication of results of an Arthur D. Little study commissioned and paid for by Procter & Gamble Co., then the nation's largest manufacturer of disposable diapers. The study showed disposable diapers were no worse for the environment than the reusable cloth kind. Enter the battle of researchers for public opinion. This tactical research has dominated debates about issues as well as products, issues such as abortion, gun control, family leave, school choice, the speed limit, and so on.[22]

In public relations you become a consenting agent of attitude change. What sorts of questions should you ask yourself before you get involved in a persuasive effort?

First, you need to consider what you are trying to change. If behavior change is your objective, is it something people must be aware they are changing (as in stop-smoking campaigns waged by several of the national health agencies), or is it something people will change without being aware of it (such as automatically turning out lights without thinking consciously of energy conservation)? Second, you must ask whether the attitude change is one that will benefit the involved publics. Do you believe in what you are doing? Ultimately, you will have to live with the consequences of your professional work. Then you need to look at how specific the desired change is. Does it involve a particular attitude (such as how the public feels about the hospital you are working for) or a general set of attitudes (how the public feels about health care in the United States, in general)? You need to examine how long the change will have to last and how many people are involved in it.

Some measure of the effect of your effort must be built into the program, since the effect might not be what you anticipated. In addition, you may have to consider here how your role will be perceived and whether your public constitutes a captive audience. Is it an audience with whom you will be having other dealings? Do you have misgivings about being identified as a persuader on this particular issue? What is at stake for you in the ef-

fort: personally? professionally? You may find that some roles put you in conflict with other roles you perform. As a volunteer public relations person for the American Cancer Society, for example, you could find yourself at odds with your professional duties of effectively representing a tobacco company client.

■ Internal Battles and Defeat

Public relations people generally try to persuade management to act in socially responsible ways toward all publics. Occasionally, though, the interests of two or more publics conflict, or the profit interests of the company conflict with the interests of one or more of its publics. Management decisions are not always in line with what the PR person recommends. What happens then? The PR person can first try to reach a compromise (if one is possible). If that doesn't work, he or she must review the situation to decide just how serious the conflict is.

Public relations practitioners are constrained in their efforts to influence management by at least four factors: (1) lack of access to management; (2) restraints on information collection; (3) roadblocks to dissemination of timely, accurate information; (4) a narrow definition of the role of public relations.[23] Of these factors, the first two pose the most serious problems. Researcher Michael Ryan concludes that practitioners need to find environments suitable to them. The most innovative practitioners should seek the most constraint-free environment; those who prefer routine tasks may be able to function well in an environment where management imposes considerable constraints on employees' behavior.[24]

Senior executives are sometimes accused of talking about ethics but failing to follow through. A 1998 Walker Information study of USA employees said only 45 percent of CEOs and other executives live out ethical values in their day-to-day behavior. While 81 percent of senior managers said ethics is used in daily decision-making, 43 percent of employees said it is routinely overlooked, and 30 percent of the employees responding to this survey said their company ignores ethics at least some of the time and knowingly breaks the law. Workers who had a high opinion of their company's ethics were more committed, and said a company's ethical integrity directly influences their decision to work there.[25]

Employees must assume responsibility too. Some practitioners label themselves "team players" and carry out each management's decision as though it were their own. Others may carry out decisions imposed from above, but not as effectively as they would have worked on their own—a subtle form of sabotage that raises an ethical question in itself. The alternative is to move on to another place where the ethical climate is more compatible.

One practitioner asserts that leaving is difficult to do. "Your ethics may be as good as your credit rating. No one with a big mortgage and lots of bills takes too many risks for a 'cause'." But this is not always a valid rule. Doing something you feel is wrong is often worse for you personally and professionally than having to go job hunting. Moreover, if the action taken violates the PRSA or IABC code, you have to leave. If you don't, you risk being reported for the code violation by another practitioner. Fortunately, crises of confidence rarely occur because most people gravitate toward managements with goals compatible with their own.[26]

Foreign Governments and Locations

Working within, with or for foreign governments poses some complex ethical questions because of different cultural patterns. One CEO from a multinational corporation said, in confidence and with some degree of exasperation:

> I wish each nation's government would make paying bribes explicitly illegal. We pay bribes abroad—all kinds—to do business. Those crooks just soak us—all the way from border guards to get materials moved among the countries to the heads of state. We have to pass the costs on to our customers. I hate it. It makes me sick. But there is simply no other way to get things done abroad.

Anyone who has lived in such an environment can appreciate his comment, even without agreeing that bribery is necessary.[27]

In response to the surfacing of "questionable payments" by corporations doing business abroad, legislation was passed in the United States making bribery illegal. But where do you draw the line between bribes or kickbacks and such traditionally acceptable practices as tips, gratuities and gifts? When do these become conditions for doing business? Even in foreign countries where bribes and kickbacks are illegal, such practices may exist in custom, which is difficult to work around.

In Egypt, as in the USA, regulations bar payment of commissions on contracts. But despite regulations in both nations, Lockheed Corp., just prior to its merger with Martin Marietta in 1995, pleaded guilty to having paid an Egyptian lawmaker $1 million for helping the company sell C-130 aircraft there.[28] Following the documentation of 100 cases between April 1994 and May 1995 in which USA firms lost contracts valued at $45 billion to foreign companies that pay bribery, an editorial in the *Wall Street Journal* commented that it doubted that a global anti-bribery law is workable. Corruption, it noted, is just "the usual slime found on the still waters of any system."[29]

Some companies, like multinational Ingersoll-Rand, have tried to protect themselves by establishing a committee of outside directors charged with investigating all business practices. From an outside director's point of view, the role of adviser is probably preferable to that of police inspector. However, all companies—multinationals, in particular—are trying codes of conduct, outside directors and anything else they can think of to undergird corporate morality. Multinationals have a social responsibility to all of their publics, not just to the nation in which they were originally chartered.

Furthermore, public relations firms in the USA are being purchased or merged with agencies based in other countries, which creates the potential for differing cultural beliefs.[30] Ethical conflicts in these areas can arise over the status of women and children, hiring practices (especially where sex, class or caste are factors), job descriptions (especially ones that might violate some religious observances), conditions for promotion, the treatment of animals and contracts or agreements with suppliers or the government, just to name a few.

Working directly for foreign governments poses even more ethical questions. Some questions have been raised about U.S. political strategists, pollsters and political PR campaign managers who handle candidates in other countries—even when the elections are free and open. Although attorneys represent clients with public and professional impunity (in fact, their services are supposed to be available to all), public relations firms share the image of their clients. Not only the firm, but also the individual handling the PR account, may find it difficult to defend working for a country that has a reputation for being repressive.

Many countries with records of human rights violations have turned to U.S. public relations firms for help. And the desire to look good in world public opinion is not the only reason for doing so. U.S. aid payments are bigger to nations with better reputations in this area. Tourism may increase as well. Some companies accept only foreign clients with reputations as responsible world citizens; but as one said in discussing the Iranian takeover of 1979, such a judgment gets more and more difficult to make.

Burson-Marsteller chairman Harold Burson made no apology for his firm's agreeing to take on Argentina as a client before the 1983 installation of a civilian regime in that country. The firm told the government it had an image as a dictatorial regime and warned it to halt any campaign that denied civil liberties or human rights. The agency's counsel can play a beneficial role in such situations—if the client heeds the advice it is paying for. If advice is not heeded, practitioners representing that nation in the USA as a foreign agent are sure to be criticized, as Burson has been.

Foreign governments rely increasingly on U.S. (and British) public relations firms for both government contracts and media relations. A recent example is Kuwait's use of a major U.S. public relations firm to interpret the Persian Gulf War to U.S. citizens and government officials. Some media people say that the PR firms aren't effective and that the embassies of the countries could do the same job. Others consider the embassies less skilled at media relations. Apparently the only effective PR people are those whom media people accept as credible sources. When their own media contacts haven't worked, foreign countries have often turned to advocacy advertising.

The ethical practices of the world's media are yet another issue because they factor in the media relations aspect of public relations and have an impact on opinions. In a study of Europe's media systems, three functions seem to be held in common: accountability to the public, accountability to sources and referents, and protection of professional integrity. But, three other functions illustrate the tensions within most media in the USA, Europe or anywhere else: accountability to the employer; accountability to the state, and the protection of the status and unity of the profession.[31] The role of media ethics is significant not only because of editorial content, but also because of the advertising.

RESPONSIBILITY IN ADVERTISING AND SPONSORSHIPS

The soap-opera actress Martha Byrne really wanted to be a star in the music industry, and in 1997 she got a backer that offered a superstar boost to her singing career. Her backer gave her a top studio, producer and back-up musicians for recording a CD, then heavily promoted a 10-city tour as the CDs were released to the stores. So, what's the problem? The CDs were not available at record stores, but they came with the purchase of two packs of Virginia Slims everywhere the cigarettes were sold. The CDs were advertised in newspapers, magazines and by direct mail. Philip Morris saw a threat to conventional advertising so it developed a new tactic to get its Virginia Slims brand to young women. A major strategy is its own recording label, Women Thing Music, drawn from the Virginia Slims' slogan, "It's A Woman Thing."[32]

The company also figured in another controversial advertising effort—this time a traditional advertising campaign—but the message was anything but traditional. Miller Brewing's Molson Ice beer, owned by Philip Morris, had based its advertising on the product's higher alcohol content printed on the label. It's against federal law to promote a beer's alcoholic "kick" in advertising, though, so the Bureau of Alcohol, Tobacco and Firearms began an investigation. Miller denied its ads were unlawful, saying that the label was approved and that it's legal to show them in ads. Miller also admitted that its representatives may post the alcoholic content of its ice beers in public places, but said these are also in compliance with federal law.[33] What is legal, though, is less of an issue than what is ethical. "Kids drink to get drunk," according to George Hacker, director of the alcohol policies project for the Center for Science in the Public Interest. "That's more of what they want in a beer." Miller's Lite Ice brand uses the slogan, "More of What You Want: Less of What You Don't Want. New Rules."[34]

That advertising message is direct, but what about subliminal advertising? Subliminal advertising comes up for discussion from time to time, often in a classroom setting. Books have been written on the subject. However, most social scientists discount the effectiveness of such advertising, and mass media gatekeepers (advertising directors in particular) deny that such ads, if submitted, would be published. Nevertheless, subliminal suggestion is possible. You can buy tapes that supposedly help you learn while you sleep, relax or are otherwise occupied. The eye can physically detect and relay to the subconscious symbols (words and art) that the conscious mind doesn't react to at the time. But it is unlikely that subliminal advertising is created on any significant scale, much less that it abounds.

Responsibility in advertising also extends to the agencies involved in developing the campaigns and in buying time and space. The commission the agencies get for that service is often misunderstood. Consider this scenario:

An advertising executive, the vice-president of a locally owned agency in another metropolitan area, called one evening to put off a dinner conference for another hour. She is her agency's time buyer and had stayed at her desk all day trying to work out the best broadcast buys for a client. Experienced in all media, she is particularly suited for the latitude her agency's owner and president has given her: "Change the schedules any way you want. What we are after are the best media buys for our customers." She is liked and respected by the media salespeople, who know she will give them a polite hearing and examine their contract suggestions carefully and considerately. She is trusted by the agency's clients, who know there is no competition within the agency to place the ads in a particular medium in order to increase personal commissions. They also know the bills they get have been carefully checked and the time purchases monitored. For that service agencies used to get a 15 percent commission. That has been replaced for the most part with discounting deals. If a client buys time or space directly from the media, the time or space is sold according to the rate for which the client qualifies—local, national, nonprofit or whatever. The media then prepare the ads or commercials and charge the client for the time or space and (usually) for any production costs. If the client wants to preserve some kind of uniformity in advertising and engages an advertising agency, the advertising that the agency prepares goes to the media ready for instant use. The agency's media discount theoretically covers the convenience of its having prepared material (instead of leaving the task to the media) and of its having brought the media some business.

The harshest critics of advertising say stimulating people to buy what they do not need or to buy something instead of spending or saving prudently is also unethical. These kinds of choices, though, seem to be a permanent feature of the free marketplace.

■ Protecting the Client

Just as a client's name should be respected, so should its rights to a trademark, logo or trade name. Protecting these forms of property can be difficult. For one thing, only the name of the specific design may be protected; there is no law against stealing ideas. This may explain the similarities often found in symbols, names and even in advertising ideas.

The only recompense for a copied idea is the realization that imitation is the sincerest form of flattery. If your trademark or logo is copied, you may be able to sue for damages, but only if the *precise* design is used. In general, it does not make any difference legally that the public might fail to distinguish between your design and the thinly disguised copied one. For instance, the symbol of the famous Texas Boys Choir, a silhouetted choirboy in bow tie holding an open music book, was appropriated by a civic girls' chorus. In the altered design, the choir boy's ears were covered with shoulder-length hair and the pants legs were filled in to resemble a skirt. A copyright authority stated that the changes were sufficient to prevent a suit. The alternative was simply for the Boys Choir to stop using the symbol it had created, which it did for several years until the other group's use of it declined.

If you are watchful, you can find numerous examples of close copies, especially with logos or creative advertising concepts and designs. Packaging similarities are found in crayons (green and yellow box with old-fashioned lettering), in bleaches (white plastic container with predominately blue label) and corn chips (red and yellow packaging)—all prompted by imitation of very successful brand-name products.

Trade names are also legally entitled to protection, but this often becomes virtually impossible to enforce when they fall into generic use, such as "Kleenex," "Band-Aid" and now (almost) "Xerox."

■ Protecting the Consumer

Efforts to protect the consumer cover a wide range of areas, but we will focus on three: products, politics and promotions.

Products A PR person should warn a client when his or her product is being erroneously confused with another (thus violating consumer confidence) or when the product itself is creating a consumer problem.

Criticized for using the cartoon character Joe Camel to sell cigarettes, RJR Nabisco launched an educational campaign advising children not to try the product until they were old enough to make a "mature" decision about smoking. The company refused to stop using its popular character (which has high recognition and appeal among youngsters) in advertisements until legally compelled to do so.

Constrained at home, USA tobacco companies are moving abroad to increase sales where restrictions are considerably fewer. The question this effort raises is how responsible is this? In addition to the health risks, other countries complain about the well-financed campaigns that compete with their own national products and actually are more pervasive in their exposure than their companies can afford to be.

Cultural issues can arise at home, though, as a hair care product discovered. Shark Products, a white-owned company, makes the popular African Pride hair-care line. It was well accepted by the African-American community until it sued a black-owned company that was marketing similar products called African Natural. Although over three quarters of Shark Products employees are black, resentment grew against its use of black symbols. "People who come into our community using our symbols, then try to restrain us for using them, should not be allowed to sell in our community," said the Rev. Al Sharpton of New York. Sharpton wanted to pressure national chains to drop African Pride, and the Rev. Jesse Jackson's Rainbow Coalition got African Pride pulled from 350 Southeastern stores owned by Big B Drugs of Birmingham, Alabama.[35] Cultural sensitivities have been an issue with a number of products directed toward different ethnic groups, and often what begins as a national issue in the USA travels abroad, due to international media coverage.

The impact of media content, editorial and advertising, cannot be underestimated. For example, corporate advertising when a company is in litigation can cause legal problems, as discussed in

Chapter 9 under litigation journalism, but it also can raise ethical issues. For example when Dow Chemical was going on trial in New Orleans over silicon breast implants, Dow began running ads on TV and radio playing up its corporate citizenship. One spot was placed by a nonprofit organization. A little girl is shown with a life-saving silicone shunt in her brain, and her mother says, "Silicone is not the problem. The personal-injury lawyers and their greed is the problem." A New Orleans attorney for the breast-implant plaintiffs accused Dow of trying to influence the jury, but the state judge refused to take any action against the company.[36]

Companies are getting more and more aggressive about protecting their advertising. For example, before its actions gained a lot of publicity, Chrysler had been demanding to know the editorial content of publications in which its ads would be run prior to publication. As an example, *Esquire* editor in chief Edward Kosner pulled a short story about a gay man who writes college term papers in exchange for sex after his publisher warned him that Chrysler would pull four pages of badly needed ads. Chrysler's ad agency had sent 100 other magazines a letter January 30, 1996, saying, "Each and every issue that carries Chrysler advertising requires a written summary outlining major theme/articles appearing in upcoming issues. These summaries are to be forwarded to PentaCom, the agency, prior to closing in order to give Chrysler ample time to review and reschedule if desired."[37] The threat was acknowledged by many media as being fairly typical of big advertisers. The ensuing publicity for Chrysler, though, caused it to back away to some extent since it was seen as a censor of editorial content.

Most publications adhere to standards of ethical behavior which would disallow yielding to such a threat from advertisers. And these standards may also cover their ability to reject advertising that they see as offensive or objectionable. Standards of ethical behavior in advertising are set forth in the advertising profession's own code and in an elaborate two-tiered mechanism to deal with truth and accuracy in national advertising—although, of course, there is nothing to prevent those who do

not subscribe to it from plying their trade. But even if advertisers ignore their own code, the media may provide the restraint—at least in matters of taste.

Politics   Although the Internet has yet to yield to any meaningful or far-reaching legal restraints, legal and ethical issues can be controlled on Intranets, those internal computer systems within organizations. Academic institutions have come into the forefront of these issues with their efforts to control content, and they have been challenged over issues of free speech. University bulletin boards have drawn most of the focus. Some Canadian colleges have blocked discussions of sex. A California community college journalism professor was suspended for running a computer bulletin board on which male students wrote messages that allegedly harassed a female.[38] As more courses are taught on-line with virtual classrooms and chat rooms set up specifically for the class, this issue is likely to grow in importance. What are the ethical issues here? What about harassment, hate speech, and such? The Internet culture is fiercely protective of freedom of expression, but Intranets are another issue.

The digital age has created another monster of sorts in new televised political ads. Some standard techniques accepted in commercial ads such as speeded up or slowed down motion or sound can be devastating in political advertising. Candidates' voices can be speeded up or slowed down, made higher or lower. Presidential candidate Steve Forbes found that Bob Dole's camp had a political ad before the New Hampshire primary that showed him in grainy black and white footage speaking in slow motion with every movement exaggerated. The advertisers' defense is that these technologies are available to the other side too. In any case, they say, the public is not misled by these images.[39] Perhaps not, but what about the impact of the images themselves? Is this ethical?

What about ads like the one many campus newspapers got that said the Holocaust didn't happen? The ad, called "The Holocaust Controversy: The Case for Open Debate," came from Bradley Smith, co-director of the California-based Committee for Open Debate on the Holocaust. Some universities ran the ad, citing freedom of speech. Others refused the ad because it looked like editorial copy, and others because it was "hateful."[40]

An historic judgment call of that sort was made by a Dallas newspaper. Late in the afternoon of November 21, 1963, a full-page ad, headlined "Welcome Mr. Kennedy," was given to the *Dallas Morning News*. It read, in part:

> Mr. Kennedy, *despite contentions on the part of your administration, the State Department, the Mayor of Dallas, the Dallas Chamber of Commerce, and members of your party, we free thinking and American thinking citizens of Dallas still have, through a Constitution largely ignored by you, the right to address our grievances to you, to disagree with you and to criticize you.*

This was followed by a dozen questions regarding government policy, each addressed to the President with a boldface "Why?" The ad was signed by "American Fact Finding Committee, an unaffiliated and nonpartisan group of citizens."[41] In the case of all political advertising, payment with copy is required. A check for more than $1,000 was presented, and the ad was accepted.

The advertiser had another $1,000-plus check for the city's other daily newspaper. By the time the advertiser reached the fifth-floor offices of the *Dallas Times Herald*, some ten blocks away, most of the advertising staff for that afternoon paper had already left for home, since they usually checked in at 7 or 8 A.M. A young salesperson read the copy and refused the check, saying, in effect, "We don't accept advertising like that at this newspaper." Although newspapers have the prerogative as private institutions to accept or reject advertising, the timing of the ad was unfortunate for the *News*. It appeared in the newspaper the morning of November 22, the day President John Kennedy was assassinated.

Broadcast stations have less flexibility in rejecting political advertising because of the *equal-time provision*. This provision appeared in the 1934 Broadcast Act through the incorporation of language from the 1927 Radio Act stating that, if a li-

censee permits any person who is a legally qualified candidate for any public office to use a broadcasting station, the licensee has to give equal opportunity to all other such candidates. Furthermore, the licensee (broadcast station) has no power of censorship over the material broadcast. This stipulation was regarded somewhat ruefully by Atlanta, Georgia, broadcasters who in 1974 had taken the advertising of one political candidate and then, under FCC regulations, had to accept the spots of his opponent, Democratic candidate J. B. Stoner. Stoner's taped messages said: "I am the only candidate for the U.S. Senate for white people. The main reason why niggers want integration is that niggers want our white women. I am for law and order. You can't have law and order and niggers." The messages, broadcast over radio station WPLO and WSB-TV, evoked a deluge of protesting phone calls, but the spots ran for a week anyway.

The equal-time provision was amended in 1959 by the *fairness doctrine,* which stated that legally qualified candidates can appear on bona fide newscasts, news interviews, news documentaries or on-the-spot coverage of news events without the licensee's having to provide equal time to opposing candidates. But another clause proved more difficult to interpret: because stations are supposed to operate in the public interest, they must afford reasonable opportunity for the discussion of conflicting views on issues of public importance. The fairness doctrine had been interpreted to include advertising as well as program content and was the basis on which two networks, ABC and CBS, refused Mobil's explanatory advertising on the energy crisis.

The FCC discontinued the fairness doctrine in 1987. Print media supported the broadcasters in their effort to get rid of the requirement. Congress then tried to enact the fairness doctrine as law, but the bill was vetoed by President Reagan.

The problem for public relations people involved in politics is that people tend to see all campaigns as "public relations" efforts, regardless of who actually runs them. The campaign for a risky candidate usually involves strict control of exposure, limited access to media and voters, no discussion of issues or philosophy of governance, and as much television commercial time as available money allows. The unfortunate consequence of the last feature is that only candidates who have money or the ability to raise it can even compete. This narrows the field.

During an election campaign period—which now lasts at least a year, and sometimes extends to eighteen months, the "public relations" tactics employed by various candidates arouse a great deal of resentment toward public relations practice in general. In fact, however, many political election campaigns are not handled by mainstream PR practitioners who adhere to the highest standards of professional practice. There may be several reasons for this. First, if the PR practitioner is a member of PRSA, he or she must comply with specific standards governing the practice of political public relations. These standards state, among other things, the following:

> It is the responsibility of PRSA members practicing political public relations . . . to be conversant with the various statutes, local, state, and federal, governing such activities and to adhere to them strictly. This includes, but is not limited to, the various local, state and federal laws, court decisions, and official interpretations governing lobbying, political contributions, disclosure, elections, libel, slander and the like. In carrying out this responsibility, members shall seek appropriate counseling whenever necessary. It also is the responsibility of members to abide by PRSA's Code of Professional Standards.[42]

The PRSA code itself requires, among other things, conducting business in the public interest, dealing fairly with the public, adhering to standards of accuracy and truth and not knowingly disseminating false and misleading information or corrupting the integrity of the channels of communication.

There's more. PRSA members must represent their clients or employers:

> . . . in good faith, and while partisan advocacy on behalf of a candidate or public issue may be expected, members shall act in accord with the public interest and adhere to truth and accuracy and to generally accepted standards of good taste.[43]

Furthermore, members are forbidden to:

> issue descriptive material or any advertising or publicity information or participate in the preparation or use thereof that is not signed by responsible persons or is false, misleading, or unlabeled as to its source, and are obligated to use care to avoid dissemination of any such material.[44]

Beyond that, PRSA members cannot use campaign posts to garner commissions from suppliers or media without their client's consent. Nor are they allowed to use their post as a step toward government employment. PRSA members are to "avoid practices that might tend to corrupt the processes of government," and they "shall not make undisclosed gifts of cash or other valuable considerations that are designed to influence specific decisions of voters, legislators, or public officials on public matters."

Other restrictions are included in the code as well, one of which deserves specific mention here: "Members shall not, through use of information known to be false or misleading, conveyed directly or through a third party, intentionally injure the public reputation of an opposing interest." It's hard to play in the election ball game following those rules. Yet many did, or tried to.

Unfortunately, everything that goes on in a political race is called "public relations." Public relations counselors now find themselves wondering how to deal with the problem of negative campaigning itself, the popular perception that public relations people are responsible for it and the notion that these are "legitimate" public relations practices. Another worthwhile item to put on the agenda might be an effort to make individuals who hold the nation's top public relations jobs (such as "press secretaries") accountable to a code of professional practice. The code does cover deceptive practices regarding the media.

Promotions Most promotions are part of a larger campaign, and in some cases may be so controversial that they incite an opposing campaign. That's what occurred with the launching in 1996 of *Our Stolen Future*, a book about the environmental threat of common synthetic chemicals. Written by zoologists Theo Colborn and John Peterson Myers, and journalist Diane Dumanoski, the book describes a decade of investigations that uncovered horror stories about the effect of chemicals on plants and animals, including humans. They reported, for instance, the effect that some widely-used chemicals might be having on hormonal systems.

With a forward by Vice President Gore, *Our Stolen Future* was loftily promoted as "the next *Silent Spring*," referring to the book by Rachel Carson that became a cornerstone of the environmental movement. They were not the first authors to raise these issues, but the prominence of *Our Stolen Future* was taken so seriously that a counter-campaign was launched by chemical industry groups determined to discredit it.[45] What are the ethics in a situation like this? What role do values play?

Another controversy has developed over drug makers' addressing promotional advertising directly to consumers. Formerly, drug companies advertised only in medical journals. But people are demanding more control over their health-care options and are choosing generic drugs, often from a mail-order catalog, to avoid higher costs. Because of consumer changes, drug companies are going directly to the marketplace. Some consumer activists, who might have been expected to support such a direct approach, are actually against it. They believe that the more extensive public campaign will cause drug prices to rise. Some activists who oppose direct sales of drugs to the consumer point to practices that they consider misleading, such as promotion of calcium to women as a preventative for osteoporosis.[46]

Some promotions are deceptive because they are personalized. An advertising tearsheet arrives with what appears to be a handwritten Post-It attached that says something like the one that came to one of the authors: "Douglas, Try this it works! Y" The signature could have been a "T." In any case, it was attached to an ad about making speeches. As it turns out, the "signature" must have been a "J" because James Durham, director of business development for the law firm Mintz, Levin, Cohn, Ferris & Glovsky, sent his second e-mail in two years to members of the firm explaining that he is not the "J" on the Post-It note that had people calling him from all over the country asking

him if they really should buy the book. Presumably it was a book about law or some legal issue. In any case, the Better Business Bureau of Washington, D.C., has issued a cease and desist order to the Georgetown Publishing House responsible for this promotion, but to no avail.[47]

Another deceptive promotion practice is to blur advertising and editorial photographic formats, something increasingly common in magazines where product advertising seems to enjoy making a mystery of what is being offered for sale. These single documentary-like photos or photo essays in some cases simply show the photos and the advertiser's logo, often in a very subtle presentation. Preliminary research shows these to be more memorable, a key factor in advertising. But is this ethical?[48]

The challenge for public relations practitioners involved in promotions is to test their own value system for what they are advocating. A critical issue is beyond that: is it responsible?

RESPONSIBILITY IN PUBLICITY

The ethical question of when and how to acknowledge the PR source of news is extremely important. Critics question the ethics of having news appear in the mass media precisely in the form submitted by a PR person. They feel that PR-originated news should carry some identifying label to alert the reader or viewer. Many PR and media people regard this as impractical and (for different reasons) undesirable. They argue that it is the job of newspeople to know the source of the information they use and to employ discrimination and good editorial judgment about what to disseminate and whether to include attribution.

PR as a Source

The relationship between PR people and newspeople is rarely the kind of contest in which the PR practitioner plots to sneak misleading or nonnewsworthy material into print, and the reporter tries to "get" the PR practitioner's client. Publicity is supposed to *facilitate* the news-gathering process. PR people expect news people to regard news releases critically, and to use or not use the news release at their own discretion. The release can be rewritten, incorporated with other materials, or not used at the time and used at a later date, sometimes in an unflattering way that is not so helpful. That is part of the risk in being a source.

The same is true of video news releases, although some have accused public relations people of deceiving the public. Video news releases go to news directors who can decide, the same as any other newsperson, what, if any should be used. The television station can, and often does, identify the footage they use as supplied by a company or organization. But the practice is seen as deceptive because many people may not realize that public relations people are the source for some of the information.[49]

Sometimes complaints are legitimate. For example, a content analysis of tobacco industry information in two children's publications, *Weekly Reader* and *Scholastic News,* showed that the industry's viewpoint predominated in the *Weekly Reader* as did coverage.[50] It is reasonable to question why the industry tried to place stories in either children's publication. And what was the responsibility of the editors in presenting news that involves a health risk for children?

There are other abuses in the publishing world. For instance, the U.S. government sometimes arranges to have opinion-making "policy" books printed by a commercial publisher (for example, Ralph P. Slater's *The Sword and the Plow* [New York: Praeger, 1965]) so that the reader not only has no idea of the actual source of the book but also pays for it three times: (1) through the subsidy given by the government to the freelance writer to research and write the book; (2) through the subsidy given to the commercial press to print the book; (3) through the retail cost of the book. Meanwhile, readers are also paying for a national printing service, the U.S. Government Printing Office, which can produce books relatively inexpensively.[51]

During any election year, look for books about candidates who are already officeholders, and watch out for any heavily promoted books that seem to support a principal plank in a party platform, especially when that party is currently in power.

One deceptive publicity practice that has invaded the magazine field (coming perhaps from small newspapers) involves specialized magazines, and is relatively transparent. A company that buys an elaborate ad—always four-color, usually double-truck (two pages side by side), and sometimes with a foldout—is almost always featured in an article with several pictures in the same issue. Sometimes the article carries no byline. When it does, the professional identity of the writers is seldom disclosed. In all likelihood, the writers are publicists for the advertisers. In one case, an aviation magazine that carried a prominent four-color advertisement for an airplane manufacturer's new model also published an illustrated four-page article on the plane and gave it the cover.

Some magazines that compete with commercial publications for readership and advertising are actually public relations tools themselves. Among these are American Express's publications *Travel and Leisure* and *Departures,* another is Ford's (one of the oldest). *Smithsonian* is actually a government publication because the Smithsonian Institution, which publishes it, is a government entity.

Although professional communicators express concern over the lack of a clear division between news and advertising copy, the public seldom seems to give it a thought. Study after study has indicated attention to *content,* with little understanding of the difference between commercial content and editorial content. Or perhaps this just shows an advanced level of calloused disbelief.

Interconnections among advertising, marketing and public relations are impossible to sever. It is best to accept that at the outset. Just as people don't separate the content in publications, they don't discriminate between the separate "voices" of an organization's advertising and its publicity.

World Wide Web pages further blur the lines between advertising and publicity. Many organizations use their Web page to post news releases, illustrate information with graphics such as financial charts, show pictures, engage Web surfers with games, offer opportunities for questions to be asked, and give information about new products, services or promotions. Of course, there's no deception in that since anyone logging on to the organization's page will know the source of the information. Problems begin when others use the information there too, such as newspeople. Whether or not they credit the source is their responsibility.

■ Art/Photos

The digital world offers opportunities in terms of photos and art but these opportunities can pose ethical issues. It's not that pictures haven't been manipulated before. Certainly they have, but now it's easier to do and more difficult to detect. Some organizations have published standards for altering imagery, but others will do anything that's effective. People in fashion may improve a model's physical characteristics; political ads have used morphing (showing a candidate turn into someone else), and news media have altered images to emphasize a point or get a laugh.[52]

News organizations have different standards, just like other organizations, for what they will and won't change, and if *National Geographic* will move the pyramids closer together for a good cover, then what can you expect? Photo fiction is likely to continue, and that expectation has led the photography profession to suggest some way to keep its credibility by telling people when an image has been manipulated.[53] The trouble is, not everyone will. The amount of photo manipulation connected to the O.J. Simpson trial is a good indication that it won't—everything from the bruises on Nicole Brown Simpson's face to the unflattering *Time* magazine cover of O. J. Simpson. Using photo illustrations or digitally enhanced images of any kind calls for the viewer to interpret the symbolic intent instead of accepting it as reality.[54] That may not always occur. When it doesn't, the viewer is deceived.

■ Money Matters

What happens when you, as a publicity writer, have a story accepted by a publication? Are you entitled to compensation for the story or pictures? No! Publicity is free; magazine editors know it and won't offer payment. Many will give you a byline, and some will identify you as a guest author in that issue. But make sure your identification carries your relationship to the piece you are writing.

What if a magazine staff writer writes a story suggested by a PR firm and allows his or her expenses to be paid by the firm? What if the writer accepts a fee as well as expenses from the firm? The ethical problem here is not only that the magazine staffer is "on the take" but also that the PR people are inducing the misconduct. It is permissible for a public relations practitioner to suggest a story to a publication, and if the idea is accepted and a writer assigned, the practitioner may make arrangements for accommodations and may see that all expenses involved in getting information for the story are covered. Almost all publications permit such arrangements on expenses, but many want to pay for transportation and accommodations themselves. Some are flexible about the accommodations.

Increasing criticism has been voiced about junkets—all-expenses-paid excursions for movie reviewers to the location of a filming, for travel editors to the opening of a new resort hotel or amusement park, for fashion editors to the site where a new line (cosmetics, shoes, sportswear, anything) is being introduced, or for real estate editors to the opening of a new luxury development in a remote area. Critics charge that such junkets amount to the purchasing of editorial talent. Many PR practitioners see nothing wrong with them, however, particularly since there is no control over what the wined and dined reporters write. And most practitioners use a careful screening process to separate the professionals from the freeloaders. Sometimes a strict publication will allow its reporter to go but will insist on paying for the transportation and accommodations. Others permit these to be paid for if the reporter acknowledges the fact in his or her copy. Still others permit reporters to accept trip packages because they believe the gratuities will not affect how the reporters handle the story.

Some observers feel that this debate should be extended to the situation where the information source (sometimes a public relations person and sometimes not) pays the expenses of a freelance travel writer.[55] News media tend to ignore this situation and treat the article as a submission by a freelancer who used her or his own resources to get the story. At least three major newspapers (*New York Times, Chicago Tribune* and *Boston Globe*) will not take any subsidized travel stories and insist on documentation. On the other hand, Barry Anderson, former president of the Society of American Travel Writers, says he doesn't think freelancers can survive without some travel assistance, and the PRSA Code of Professional Standards permits practitioners to provide free trips for media representatives, including travel writers, if the purpose is to allow coverage of a story with legitimate news interest, if the trip is made available to all writers, and if no preferential treatment or guarantees are expected or implied. Some public relations people compare this to the free access to events provided to sportswriters and theater and music critics, although some news media insist on paying for these as well.

Broadcasters appear to have more flexibility, especially in situations where it's clear to the viewer that the resort area featured in the travelogue obviously cooperated in the production. Features of this type are usually broadcast on special channels or in quasi-commercial programming. But how do these TV magazine format features differ from newspaper travel sections?

The Society of Business Writers was the first to respond to this problem. It adopted a code of ethics that specifically outlaws junkets and "freebies." A member may not accept any special treatment or any gift of more than token value; all out-of-town travel must be paid for by the writer's employer. Other professional journalism organizations followed suit, as did individual newspaper corporations. Most publications had already prohibited outright gifts to their editorial staff members, either directly or through people in their own advertising

departments. Some specialized publications, though, such as *Car and Driver,* only ended staff freebies in 1991.

Newspapers always seem to watch this practice especially closely. Some will not allow their reporters to accept any gifts whatsoever; others are aware that their reporters often receive small gifts from PR sources but only worry when many stories appear from a single source or when a gift seems large enough to be potentially compromising. One relevant consideration is a ruling by an administrative law judge for the National Labor Relations Board in a case involving the Madison (Wisconsin) *Capital Times* that gifts to newspeople were part of a news employee's wages and could not be prohibited by the newspaper. Editorial publisher Miles McMillan appealed the decision to the full NLRB, which upheld the newspaper's right to establish a code of ethics preventing freebies. One fashion editor often receives free cosmetics, gimmicks and gadgets of all descriptions—but at the risk of the givers. She reports on such gifts and doesn't hesitate to point out bad features. Her editor doesn't worry about news sources compromising *her* integrity.

There is another side to this, though. Public officials are also on PR gift lists. Many companies have certain public officials they want remembered and tell their PR person to "buy something." Many city, county and state governments have strict regulations about what public officials may accept, but just as many don't. Common prudence suggests that all gifts should be "token" rather than substantial. One executive who shops the catalogs every year for gifts to suggest to his clients offers this rule of thumb: "When I choose something, I always think, how would I feel if I suddenly saw this on the 6 P.M. news? That curbs my buying sprees considerably."

Another kind of remuneration—one that inflates the ego as well as the pocketbook—is the awarding of prizes, and this affects both press and public officials. Does a reporter embark on a series about arthritis to enlighten the newspaper's readers or to increase the writer's chances for tangible recognition from the Arthritis Foundation? Does a local television station do a documentary on possible fire hazards during the summer to warn its viewers or to receive recognition from the Firefighters' Association? Does a network choose its documentary for overriding public interest or a chance to win an Emmy or Peabody? Does an ambitious lawyer offer to head the local symphony drive for the arts out of love of music or because his eye is on a civic club's annual outstanding citizen award? Commercial as well as nonprofit institutions engage in these incentive programs, but these seem to meet with greater editorial acceptance than junkets, even though many awards are cash prizes.

A more blatant type of remuneration is the moonlighting that some reporters and photographers do at part-time publicity jobs. Although most media executives do not condone the practice, few actively try to stop it. As one newspaper's photo chief said, "Are you kidding? All my good people would quit. They can't live on what this paper pays them." Nevertheless, there are all sorts of ethical ramifications. For instance, does a feature photo taken by a photographer working part-time for a public relations department get published in the community newspaper because of her favored status as a full-time news photographer for that publication?

Favor can also be shown by PR people in the gifts their organization makes to nonprofits. Public relations people often control more than their own departmental budgets. Generally the corporation's investments in the community—gifts to civic, social, even national organizations—are within the control of the PR department. This is especially true of national organizations to whom the company gives its support. These relationships are scrutinized by special-interest groups that monitor such gifts to ensure that minorities and other disadvantaged groups are not excluded. Their reviews can also put an institution in a bad position if its funds go to groups that do exclude minorities or that practice discrimination or that have labor policies that could be criticized as unfair.

Public relations practitioners are accustomed to providing for the media, but usually on a tempo-

rary basis. The situation is different for public affairs officers in government. In 1978 attention became focused on the facilities provided for news media in public places (government centers), such as courthouses and state capitols. In many of these places free parking spaces, a paging system and a complete writing facility with desks, typewriters, telephones and even attendants were provided. The taxpayer was picking up the tab, of course. Much of the furor over such perquisites ("perks") originated in the Washington, D.C., news media's criticism and exposure of congressional perks. Suddenly government perks for reporters came under scrutiny everywhere, much to the consternation of some government people hired to handle the news media. When the reporters moved out, the working relationships of these staffs with the news media became a lot more complicated. However, news agencies could preserve their integrity by paying rent for the facilities and furnishings.

Some state governments, whose constitutions required them to provide the media with free space and prevented reimbursement, found themselves in a bind. However, few people working in the public relations role for government saw the facilities issue as a threat to the free press system, and several pointed to an observation made by some newspeople themselves—that lack of facilities really inhibited news coverage. The bigger organizations could afford to foot the bill, but some of the smaller media, whose reporters tend to look carefully at what their constituents' representatives are doing, were forced to abandon coverage and use the more general wire-service copy.

The Puppet Show

When governments offer space to newspeople, the relationship between the two groups is direct, at least. But less obvious connections exist between many organizations and special interests in our society. For example, the false front organization is an old public relations gimmick that hurts PR credibility and violates the PRSA code of ethics. When a product or a person needs a forum, a club (which appears to be a collection of people with a common interest) is created. Best recognized is a fan club for a star. But such clubs seldom begin spontaneously.

"60 Minutes" co-editor Morley Safer was sharply critical of Hill & Knowlton in his comments at the first Harland W. Warner seminar on ethics in Public Relations in May 1994. Safer criticized the PR agency for its activities on behalf of Citizens for a Free Kuwait, particularly for failing to identify a witness who appeared before a congressional committee as the daughter of Kuwait's U.S. ambassador and for denying that it represented the Kuwaiti government when nearly all the funding for Citizens for a Free Kuwait came from that government.[56]

As part of its representation of the "Citizens for a Free Kuwait," Hill & Knowlton presented to the Congressional Human Rights Caucus a Kuwaiti girl (later identified as the daughter of the country's ambassador to the USA) who told a story of Iraqi soldiers taking infants out of incubators and leaving them on the hospital floor to die. For months subsequently, however, no direct evidence such as eyewitnesses to these atrocities could be found. After the war, H&K was accused of creating the story for its client. Finally, a year and a half after the incidents alleged, Kuwaiti officials presented news media with a nurse who claimed to have witnessed the atrocities; no explanation was offered for the delay by the nurse in coming forward.

In another alleged breach of ethics, H&K was accused of representing the Bank of Credit and Commerce International (BCCI) as a respectable, legitimate institution. Even if H&K was deceived by its clients, it remained responsible for learning the truth before spreading the information. The BCCI case has resulted in legal action against the PR firm.

PACs: Political Action Committees

Political action committees (PACs) are clearly identifiable legal organizations registered and incorporated in states to raise money for politicians whom they favor. The corporate political war chests they command are sizable. For example, a

law firm's PAC fund contributions may exceed $100,000, and one state's professional organization for CPAs has a political fund of more than $200,000. PACs are also developed by unions and by activist groups ranging from anti-abortionists to homosexuals. Most states require that PACs maintain public records of their names, affiliations and assets and the names of those who make donations to them above a given amount. However, in some cases the information is not easy to get. Public relations ethical questions arise over how the money is raised (through pressure put on employees, for example), how the money is spent (on political candidates who may not behave in the best interests of society), how much information is made public about the institution's PAC and whom it supports. Although big business and big labor dominate PAC activity, many professional and trade associations are also involved. These institutions defend their right to bankroll the candidates they feel will support them most staunchly when in office. Critics of PACs insist that they invite abuse of the electoral process.

News Media and Political PR

Politicians and the news media are natural adversaries. The cause for conflict, as William Blankenburg identifies it, is that "undefinable thing called news that mixes two combustibles, timely disclosure and objective truth, one of which is chaotic and the other coercive."[57] Caught in the middle of the conflict is the political PR person. Although government officials are public servants and should respond to the public (represented by news media), the Pentagon's distrust of such responsiveness has gone to the extent of administering lie detector tests even to top-level officials to make sure that no "unauthorized information" goes to a reporter. Often the problem with unauthorized information is that its release would make certain individuals in positions of authority look bad. The PR person is always suspect and therefore occupies a high-tension spot. The tension is heightened by the way public officials use the news media and vice versa.

In international PR practice, media play by different rules. In the People's Republic of China, for example, newspaper space is limited, since most papers may print only four pages. A PR person seeking publicity must therefore go to the China News and Culture Promotion Committee and buy the services of its members in order to get into either print or broadcast news. Advertising is another problem, since space is so limited that an advertiser may have to wait weeks or months for an opening. Cash up front and freebies are the standard cost of getting media time and space.[58]

Leaks compromise the integrity of news channels. In countries where the integrity of news channels is taken seriously, that integrity can be jeopardized when a spokesperson takes his or her role too literally and issues quotes from conversations that never took place. Although "creating quotes" is routine in public relations, it is done only when statements are prepared prior to an event and approved by the person to whom they are ascribed. Later, when a newsmaking event occurs—when, for example, a speech is given—the person frequently uses the prepared remarks, making them his or her own by conveying the information they contain in his or her own words.

■ The Public's Right to Know

The media's right to know is related to the public's right to information. The Freedom of Information Act has given individuals access to certain types of information, and the media derive their right to that information from the public's right. The act, however, protects certain kinds of information from public exposure. Information that the government believes is important to national security remains confidential, as does information that pertains to ongoing criminal investigations. Of course, the act has nothing to do with financial and commercial information generated by private sources. Other state and local regulations, such as the open-meeting and public record laws, also protect certain kinds of information. Governmental bodies still have the right to discuss such things as collective bargaining and certain personnel matters in executive session.

Although some information remains hidden from the media, some critics believe that the media are now privy to too much information. Other critics maintain that the media do not treat privileged information with sufficient discretion or respect.

Many problems that the news media encounter are attributable to the fact that we as a public do not agree on what we want to know. We do not agree because our basis for deciding what we want to know is a value system; since we have different value systems, complete agreement appears to be impossible. Nevertheless, the law says we have a right to know everything that does not invade an individual's privacy—and the privacy of public figures in some instances—and everything that does not defame a person or a group.

The limits on these two crucial freedoms—to be informed and to be left alone—have been set, but they continue to evolve in court cases, because these rights come with obligations. The news media are not the only ones who fail to uphold their obligations to tell the public what they need to know in order to make rational decisions. In the past, the commercial sector has often withheld health and safety information from consumers and employees. Additional examples continue to come to light.

In surveys of journalists and face-to-face presentations where both journalists and PR people participate, some guidelines have evolved. First and foremost, be sure anyone speaking to the news media on behalf of the organization has media training so that news media protocols such as "for background only" are understood. Secondly, be sure spokespersons are available when news media call. If not, the news media will "go with what they have," which may not include your side of the story at all. The problem is that most people outside the news media don't understand the urgency of deadlines, which are even more immediate now that stories can go out electronically before being presented formally in the medium. Third, be sure that reporters have an opportunity to ask questions and that the spokesperson keeps in mind that, however biting the question, the response must not be hostile. Fourth, although "no comment" can be an invitation for disaster, in fact reporters do understand when a spokesperson says that nothing can be said about a case that is in litigation, or simply that spokespeople don't have all of the information now but will get it. Of course reporters understand that trade secrets and competitive information are not disclosable under ordinary circumstances. If information needs to be withheld to meet government restrictions or to protect the privacy of an individual, that situation must be explained or it's not likely to be believed by reporters. Not responding to protect the reputation of the organization is certainly not acceptable to reporters, and not responding isn't the best way to accomplish that anyway. (See Chapter 15 on crises.)

Promotions and Public Opinion

Although many organizations climbed on the environmental bandwagon in the 1990s, not all of the tie-ins have been successful. For example, Procter & Gamble advertised its Pampers and Luvs brand diapers in an Earth Day magazine to be sold at Hardee's restaurants. The purpose, P&G said, was to educate consumers about new technology for composting the diapers. Critics responded that the ad was misleading because the technology for the composting was not widely available.[59]

Some organizations have been criticized for promoting environmental sensitivity while continuing to pollute with other products or operations. The irony of some corporate efforts was pointed out by *National Wildlife* magazine, which noted that the nation's eight largest petrochemical manufacturers had contributed $2 million each in seed money for plastic recycling centers that now produce polystyrene pellets used in beach park benches from which visitors can watch "waves of tar balls washing up."[60]

One company that decided its environmental efforts should be more than hype is McDonald's Corporation. The company is working with the Environmental Defense Fund on its waste-reduction effort. The effort goes beyond McDonald's announced abandonment of the plastic box for take-outs. The joint task force of the advocacy group and the company has arrived at forty-two initiatives to help McDonald's reduce by 80 percent the 238 pounds of waste each of its 11,000 restaurants generates daily.[61]

When an organization does something that appears to benefit the public, but actually benefits the organization more, the rationale needs to be clearly stated or the action is seen as self-serving and thus suspect. Genentech got itself into just such a situation when one of the biotech industry's largest and most profitable companies began funding a nonprofit group, Human Growth Foundation, that identifies short schoolchildren who may have only a cosmetic need for a high-priced Genentech growth drug. The charity trains gym teachers to measure students and keep charts. Parents of children who fall into the lowest 5 percent get a letter urging them to see their physicians or the charity if they are concerned about their child's height or weight. Neither the letters nor the charity identify Genentech as their major funding source. Most schools don't know either. The second largest funder for the charity is Eli Lilly, which has 30 percent of that market. Members of both companies have been on the charity's board and advisory committee. What has aroused public attention to this is that the disorder is not always easy to define and some see a risk in giving the drug to children who may not turn out to be truly disadvantaged by their size.[62] This is definitely a situation with two sides to it, but an organization getting involved in such a project needs to be prepared for any criticism its support may draw.

INDIVIDUAL RESPONSIBILITIES

Ethical performance amounts to doing what's right to preserve your integrity, in accordance with your value system. But values are culture-bound, which is why difficulties often arise across cultures. In the USA, honesty is valued, but it isn't rewarded very well. In short, as any "whistle-blower" can tell you, there's not much reward for ethical behavior. (-*Whistle-blowers* are individuals who call public attention to problems within their own industry, business or organization. As a result of their revelations, they often lose their jobs and have trouble finding other employment. Women and minorities who file anti-discrimination lawsuits often encounter the same difficulties, even when they win.)

Two Columbia business school professors investigated the material value of ethics training by surveying 25 years of alumni experience.[63] They discovered that, of the 1,070 alumni from the classes of 1953–1987 who responded, 40 percent said they had been implicitly or explicitly rewarded for taking some action they considered to be ethically *troubling* (emphasis ours), and 31 percent of those who had refused to take some ethically troubling action said that they had been directly or indirectly penalized for their choice.

Two writers for the *Harvard Business Review*, seeking to test the hypothesis that "honesty pays," found the opposite to be true. Their study led them to conclude that "power can be an effective substitute for trust." According to these researchers, "Trustworthy behavior does provide protection against the loss of power and against invisible sniping. But these protections are intangible, and their dollars-and-cents value does not make a compelling case for trustworthiness." Then why be trustworthy? The authors say, "Only our individual wills, our determination to do what is right, whether or not it is profitable, save us from choosing between chaos and stagnation."[64]

There may be faint comfort in that. These writers' research suggests that conscientious public relations practitioners must attempt to function ethically and responsibly in settings where a different culture may support different values, in a larger society in the USA that lauds ethical behavior but seldom rewards it, and in situations where others are using entirely different standards reflecting divergent underlying values. In fact, the student views discussed earlier in the chapter may signal that values in American society are changing. You might want to test your own business ethics in Example 8.1.

There may be a difference between ethical decisions and what Joseph L. Badaracco, Jr. calls a "defining moment." Ethical decisions, he says, are between right and wrong, while defining moments present choices between two ideals in which we deeply believe, and have no truly "correct" answer. However, the way these decisions are made over a period of time define one's character. The question "Who am I?" can be a corporate one, "Who are We?" The answer is in the values of the organization, which is why most organizations faced with a difficult decision go to their mission statement for guidance.[65]

What many public relations professionals do is turn to their code of ethics or standards of behavior. The problem with most of these is that they are seen as self-serving. The problem for public relations professionals is that they must uphold not only their own code, but the codes of news media. These codes are a form of self-policing, so they are not infallible. But what efforts to be responsible in all relationships do is establish a level of trust.

■ Reciprocal Trust

An area of major importance in PR involves keeping confidences with the media and with other publics. For example, a reporter on the trail of a story deserves the exclusive he or she is ingenious enough to identify and develop. A PR practitioner should not pull the rug out by offering a general release before the reporter has had an opportunity to use the material. Also, a news medium has the right to expect a practitioner to be entirely aboveboard in offering information. Feature ideas, suggestions and pictures should be offered on an "exclusive use" basis. Certainly magazine editors expect stories and pictures submitted to be exclusives. A magazine editor who finds the same or a similar story in another magazine will never trust you again.

A story issued in printed form "for general release" notifies an editor that other news media have the story. However, a story marked "Special to the Banner" should be just that. No other news medium in that circulation area should receive the story. (If you do send it to other newspapers, you should let the editor know.) The quickest way to destroy your welcome in the newsroom is to plant the same story all over the place. Even if the same story is given to the morning and evening editions of the same newspaper, you are in trouble. Each deserves different stories with different approaches.

EXAMPLE 8.1

Business Ethics: What Are Your Personal Standards?

Hard work, fairness and honesty were the values we grew up with, but do they exist today? Influence peddling in Washington, insider-trading scandals and fraud among TV ministers are common headline themes. Are there similarly unsavory developments in the average office, store or hospital? This confidential questionnaire was used by Working Woman *magazine to measure how its readers would make the tough choices business people make on a daily basis.*

OFFICE DILEMMAS: WHAT IF . . .

1. *One of your associates obtains a confidential report from a competitor. It contains information crucial to your sales effort. You . . .*

Return it to your associate, saying it is unethical to take such information ☐

Read it and use it ☐

2. *Some of the doctors you work with prescribe an expensive brand of medication even though cheaper ones are available. You suspect it is because the manufacturer regularly treats them to expensive entertainment. You . . .*

Blow the whistle to the local standards board ☐

Say nothing ☐

3. *One of the purchasing agents you sell to makes very sexist comments to you. He buys more of your product than other companies do and gives you a good price. You . . .*

Stop selling to the sexist purchasing agent ☐

Sell to the sexist purchasing agent ☐

4. *You have to pick up your child from school early even though you have an important meeting at work. This has happened four times in the last month. You . . .*

Make up an excuse ☐

Tell your boss the truth ☐

5. *The doctors in your unit routinely overcharge for their services. The government makes them resubmit many bills, but some get through. You . . .*

Do nothing ☐

Report them ☐

6. *You've been working late and on weekends. Recently you had lunch with an old friend and picked up the tab. When the bill comes you . . .*

Put it on your next expense account ☐

Write a personal check ☐

7. *Your boss confides that your company will relocate to another state. Fellow employees ask you to confirm or deny rumors. You . . .*

Tell them the truth in confidence, even though the company may suffer and you could be fired ☐

Keep quiet until the official announcement ☐

8. *One of your employees is a heavy drinker. You have never seen her drunk at work, but it could be a problem. You . . .*

Fire her rather than risk insurance problems ☐

Tell her to stop drinking or else risk dismissal ☐

CODES OF ETHICS

1. *Do you feel business ethics have become worse, improved or stayed the same over the last ten years?*

Become worse ☐

Improved ☐

Stayed the same ☐

2. *In your opinion, do the huge sums of money on Wall Street corrupt people?*

Yes, money corrupts ☐

No, the people were originally corrupt ☐

3. *Which of the following kinds of ethical violations have you observed where you work? (Check as many as apply)*

Lying to employees ☐
Expense-account abuses ☐
Violating confidentiality ☐
Bribery ☐
Sexual harassment ☐
Lying to make a sale ☐
Taking credit for others' work ☐
Favoritism/Nepotism ☐
Discrimination ☐

4. *How do you react when you see unethical behavior at work?*

Report it to superiors ☐
Report it anonymously ☐
Confront the person but don't report it ☐
Do nothing ☐
Never happens ☐

5. *How often are the ethics of business decisions discussed where you work? Are they informal or formal discussions?*

	Informal	Formal
Very often	☐	☐
Sometimes	☐	☐
When a problem arises	☐	☐
Seldom/Never	☐	☐

6. *Is there a written code of ethics where you work?*

Yes ☐
No ☐
Don't know ☐

7. *If there is no written code of ethics, do you think one would be useful?*

Yes, it would be useful ☐
No, it would not be useful ☐
No, it is not necessary ☐

8. *Please indicate where you learned to make ethical decisions on the job. (Check as many as apply.) Which one was most influential?*

	Where Learned	Most Influential
Family	☐	☐
Religion	☐	☐
College (general)	☐	☐
College business class	☐	☐
Friends	☐	☐
Business colleagues	☐	☐
Books, magazines or newspapers	☐	☐
Special course on ethics	☐	☐
Boss	☐	☐
Nowhere in particular	☐	☐

9. *Have you ever worked for a company or institution that got into trouble over ethical violations?*

Yes ☐
No ☐
Don't know ☐

YOUR VALUES

Here are some statements people sometimes make about business. Please circle the number that indicates how strongly you agree or disagree with each statement.

a. *The question of right or wrong depends on the particular business situation.*

Strongly agree		Neither		Strongly disagree
1	2	3	4	5

b. *Sometimes it is necessary to break the rules to get ahead.*

1	2	3	4	5

c. *Most successful people occasionally have to compromise their principles.*

1	2	3	4	5

(continued)

EXAMPLE 8.1 (continued)

d. If business cannot operate ethically, it should be regulated by government.

1   2   3   4   5

e. Most women are more ethical than most men.

1   2   3   4   5

f. Most business people basically are honest.

1   2   3   4   5

g. The bottom line is the only standard for judging a business.

1   2   3   4   5

h. There are absolute ethical standards that every business should adhere to.

1   2   3   4   5

INDUSTRY STANDARDS

1. Here is a list of various occupational groups. Which ones do you feel have the greatest incidence of unethical behavior? (Check up to three.)

Banking ☐   Manufacturing ☐
Finance ☐   Media ☐
Government ☐   Medicine ☐
Law ☐   Sales ☐

2. Suppose you are job hunting. Would you work for any of the following?

	Yes	No	Maybe
An energy company with a history of environmental accidents	☐	☐	☐
A manufacturer with a bad worker-safety record	☐	☐	☐
A financial company indicted for insider trading	☐	☐	☐
A law firm that defends known racketeers	☐	☐	☐
A cigarette manufacturer	☐	☐	☐

3. One of your employees has purchased a top secret report from a competitor's company without your knowledge. What do you do when you find out? (Check as many as apply.)

Fire the employee ☐
Reprimand the employee ☐
Reward the employee ☐
Do nothing
Send back the report ☐
Keep the report ☐

4. You have a close friend in a competing company. You occasionally trade information about company products and plans. This is . . .

A major ethical violation ☐
A minor ethical violation ☐
Not a problem ☐

SEX AND THE WORKPLACE

Here are some situations involving sexual behavior. Please indicate which ones you are aware of in your workplace. Also tell us whether they are major or minor violations or if they have nothing to do with business ethics.

	Aware of	Major	Minor	No Problem
Flirting to make a sale	☐	☐	☐	☐
Having sex with clients to make a sale	☐	☐	☐	☐
Doing business with clients who are sexist	☐	☐	☐	☐
Having sex with co-workers on company time	☐	☐	☐	☐
Becoming sexually intimate with the boss	☐	☐	☐	☐

THE PROBLEM WITH PERKS

1. *Please indicate whether you consider each of the following a serious problem, a minor problem or not an ethical problem at work.*

	Serious	Minor	No Problem
Taking office supplies home	☐	☐	☐
Copying computer software for personal use	☐	☐	☐
Making personal calls on a company phone	☐	☐	☐
Calling in sick when you need a mental-health day	☐	☐	☐
Sharing company discounts with a friend	☐	☐	☐
Padding expense accounts	☐	☐	☐

2. *At what level does entertainment or a gift become a bribe?*

$25 to $49	☐
$50 to $99	☐
$100 to $499	☐
$500+	☐
None; any gift that achieves its purpose is acceptable	☐

WHAT IS ETHICAL?

Please indicate how you feel about each of the following situations. (Circle the appropriate number.)

a. *Your boss secretly treats her best clients to cocaine.*

Illegal	Unethical	Neutral	Acceptable Practice	Good Idea
1	2	3	4	5

b. *An account exec refuses to attend an important client's party because she feels uncomfortable about the amount of drinking.*

1	2	3	4	5

c. *An administrative assistant routinely makes up excuses for her boss when he takes long lunches with his secretary.*

1	2	3	4	5

d. *A public relations officer makes the financial picture of her company appear rosier by withholding critical information.*

1	2	3	4	5

e. *A real-estate agent is showing a house. She doesn't point out that the basement floods.*

1	2	3	4	5

f. *A manager has accumulated many sick days. She takes a few days off and calls in sick.*

1	2	3	4	5

g. *A procurement officer recommends her brother-in-law's company for one of her projects without revealing the connection to her boss.*

1	2	3	4	5

h. *A book publisher gives his college-age niece a highly sought-after unpaid summer internship.*

1	2	3	4	5

i. *An executive learns his company is about to be sold, which is bound to send its stock price soaring. He leaks the information to two of his biggest clients as well as to several of his friends.*

1	2	3	4	5

j. *After a year of poor sales, a sales representative convinces her boss to let her give expensive gifts to prospective clients. The tactic works, and sales increase.*

1	2	3	4	5

k. *Company policy forbids employees to discuss their salaries But two people trade information to negotiate better with their boss.*

1	2	3	4	5

l. *A job applicant finds out the morning before her job interview that she is pregnant. She decides not to say anything rather than jeopardize her chances.*

1	2	3	4	5

(continued)

EXAMPLE 8.1 *(continued)*

SUCCESS AND SATISFACTION

1. *Altogether, how many years have you worked full-time?* _____

2. *Overall, how successful have you been over the course of your career?*

Consistently successful ☐

Mostly successful ☐

Some ups and some downs ☐

Mostly unsuccessful ☐

Consistently unsuccessful ☐

3. *Please circle the number that indicates how satisfied you are by your job.*

Very unsatisfied				Very satisfied
1	2	3	4	5

4. *How successful are you at your current job?*

Very unsuccessful				Very successful
1	2	3	4	5

5. *Overall, how satisfied are you with your life?*

Very unsatisfied				Very satisfied
1	2	3	4	5

6. *Have you ever taken an ethical stance that has affected your career? If so, was the effect positive or negative?*

Yes–positive ☐

Yes–negative ☐

No ☐

7. *Have you ever been accused of making a bad ethical decision at work?*

Yes, I was fired ☐

Yes, I was given a hard time ☐

No, never happened ☐

8. *What kinds of ethical decisions in your job make you most uncomfortable?*

_____

_____

_____

INFORMATION, PLEASE

1. *How old are you?* _____

2. *Your sex?*   Female ☐   Male ☐

3. *What is your marital status?*

Single ☐

Single, living with partner ☐

Separated, divorced, widowed ☐

Married or remarried ☐

Your age at first marriage: _____

4. *What is the highest level of education you have completed?* _____

5. *Are you employed . . .*

Full-time? ☐

Part-time? ☐

Not currently employed ☐

6. *What is your occupation?* _____

7. *What is your title?* _____

8. *Do you work for yourself or someone else?*

Self-employed ☐

Partnership ☐

Work for others ☐

9. *What is your total annual income? If you are married or living with someone, what is your partner's total annual income?*

	Mine	Partner's
Less than $9,999	☐	☐
$10,000 to $19,999	☐	☐
$20,000 to $29,999	☐	☐
$30,000 to $44,999	☐	☐
$45,000 to $59,999	☐	☐
$60,000 to $74,999	☐	☐
$75,000 to $99,999	☐	☐
$100,000 to $149,999	☐	☐
$150,000 or more	☐	☐

10. *What is your zip code?* _____

Source: Reprinted with permission from *Working Woman* magazine. Copyright © 1990 by WWT Partnership.

THE WIZARD OF ID   Brant parker and Johnny hart

By permission of Johnny Hart and Creators Syndicate, Inc.

The best way to do this is to take separate stories to one person at each newspaper. Decide where each story would most appropriately appear or who on the paper would most likely be interested. If it is a column item and more than one newspaper is involved, you should determine which columnist would be most likely to use the piece and plant it there—only there.

News media should also be able to trust you to have cleared publicity pictures submitted to them by securing a release from those who posed. They should also be able to trust you to protect them from copyright complications and libel and lottery laws that can be violated in publicity copy.

When you supply news to the media, you are bound, ethically and morally, just as they are, by the codes to which their members subscribe. By the same token, the news media owe public relations practitioners a responsibility to honor agreed-upon release dates and times (so-called "embargoed" releases). Most do. If a story breaks earlier than designated, try to discover why. Often it is an accident. However, if a publication frequently has "accidents," don't give future stories to that publication until there is no jeopardy to your client. Do this quietly, without any warning and certainly without threats. It won't take the publication long to figure out what is happening and why.

Crisis situations are the most trying for relationships because both sides are under pressure and both sides are generally frustrated. Journalists accuse PR people of misrepresentation and covering up information. PR people accuse reporters of bias

and inaccuracies. Part of the problem resides in how the "truth" appears to each side. PR commentator and practitioner David Finn has observed:

> One of the most disturbing discoveries public relations people can make about themselves is that learning "the facts" doesn't always tell them what they should believe. As citizens and readers of newspapers and television viewers, they have opinions on as many things as anybody else.
>
> But sometimes their convictions run counter to positions held by a client. Then they study "the facts" and listen to what their client's experts have to say, and those passionate convictions become surprisingly less convincing. They see another point of view and find it more persuasive than they imagined.
>
> The first time this happens, public relations people don't mind admitting they might have been wrong. But when it happens again and again they begin to wonder whether any point of view can be supported by a given set of facts and a particular group of experts. And they fear that a lifetime of listening to all the experts who support their clients' positions weakens their capacity to make independent judgments.[66]

The question of corruption of judgment is a serious one for public relations people. Often the heart of a dispute is not over facts but over the interpretation of facts and over conflicting value systems. In these situations, the best guide for the PR person is to return to the formula for socially responsible public relations decision making. Who are the publics? What are the interests of each in the decision or situation? How will an institution's policy, position or action affect each of these publics? What social values are involved? What values are in conflict? What will the effects be? Can the effects be defended? The PR person who loses the public's perspective has forgone public responsibility and become the persuaded instead of the persuader.

POINTS TO REMEMBER

■ Ethics are founded on moral principles that are themselves grounded in effects.

■ Judgments about an organization's standing are made in three areas: ethics, social responsibility and financial responsibility.

■ Ethics and responsibilities are public relations concerns on two levels. We have to consider the behavior of the individual practitioner and that of the institution she or he represents. Public relations is often called the "conscience" of management, but can't be if top management has none.

■ Top management sets the ethical tone in an organization, and the challenge for internal and external PR people is to guide those who hire them to responsible actions that are founded in integrity.

■ Although extremely complex, the study of ethics falls into two broad categories: comparative ethics (sometimes called descriptive ethics), the purview of social scientists, and normative ethics, generally the domain of philosophers and theologians.

■ Decisions about what is right or wrong some hold to be absolute; others say the situation is a factor.

■ Part of the complexity in ethical decision-making for public relations practitioners is that they are hired to be advocates; they play a role as educators, but also as persuaders.

■ Two theoretical paradigms help in understanding the ethical conundrums practitioners face: Habermas's on-going dialogue in the public sphere aims to reach consensus so that the actions of an organization gain legitimacy; Luhmann's negotia-

tions between systems aim, less ambitiously, to maintain functional interaction, resolve conflicts, and establish trust.

■ Both paradigms have "blind spots" and both put public relations practice in the conflict zones between the different rationalities of societies. In one, the practitioner is acting as an individual promoting consensus, and in the other as a system's representative of a special interest.

■ Some truths are verifiable and commonly accepted, but others are actually perceptions. Furthermore, beliefs and personal values influence how "truth" is defined. Thus ethics is inseparable from values.

■ Page's management principles stress conducting public relations as if the whole company depended on it. It might, because the belief that publics hold in organizations validates their organizations' existence.

■ Responsibility has two facets: social and financial. People's perception of how well an organization is fulfilling these gives the organization legitimacy.

■ Social responsibility means producing sound products or reliable services that don't threaten the environment, and it means contributing positively to the social, political and economic health of society. It also means compensating employees fairly and treating them justly.

■ Financial responsibility includes how the organization interacts with investors and investment advisers.

■ The fact that PR works to change people's views causes the individual practitioner's ethics to be closely entwined with the organization's social responsibility.

■ Political PR people often find themselves caught in the middle of conflicts resulting from use of news media by public officials and vice versa.

■ Conflicts often arise over interpretation of social and financial responsibility in a global setting.

■ Most professional PR practitioners recognize that they and their organizations have ethical responsibilities to at least ten different publics: clients, news media, government agencies, educational institutions, consumers, stockholders and analysts, community, competitors, critics and other public relations practitioners.

■ Ethical problems that must be resolved in public relations research include how to collect the data, how to accumulate and store information and how to use research.

■ As a consenting agent of attitude change, you need to consider what you are trying to change, and you must ask whether the attitude change is one that will benefit the involved publics.

■ Public relations practitioners are constrained in their efforts to influence management by at least four factors: (1) lack of access to management; (2) restraints on information collection; (3) roadblocks to dissemination of timely, accurate information; (4) a narrow definition of the role of public relations. Of these, the first two pose the most serious problems.

■ Senior executives are sometimes accused of talking about ethics but failing to follow through. Practitioners who see themselves as "team players" may be swept up in a bad ethical environment and jeopardize their own credibility.

■ To be a professional maintaining the standards embodied in a code of professional ethics often takes courage, as well as a strong set of personal values.

■ Ethical conflicts among multinational corporations include issues of the status of women and children, hiring practices, job descriptions, conditions for promotion, treatment of animals and contracts or agreements with suppliers or the government. Working directly for foreign governments poses even more ethical questions.

■ Responsibility in advertising and sponsorships includes assuming personal responsibility in protecting the client and the customer regarding products and in political issues.

■ The PRSA Code of Professional Standards for the Practice of Public Relations requires conduct-

ing business in the public interest, dealing fairly with the public, adhering to standards of accuracy and truth and not knowingly disseminating false and misleading information or corrupting the integrity of the channels of communication.

■ Responsibility in publicity means being honest and faithful as a source of information, as a supplier of illustrations and as the funder of information and space or other considerations.

■ The problem for public relations people involved in politics is that people tend to see all campaigns as "public relations" efforts, regardless of who actually runs them.

■ Increasing criticism has been voiced about junkets—all-expenses-paid excursions for movie reviewers, travel editors, fashion editors and real estate editors.

■ Political Action Committees (PACs) are clearly identifiable, legal organizations registered and incorporated in states to raise money for politicians whom they favor.

■ The media's right to know is related to the public's right to information. The Freedom of Information Act has given individuals access to certain types of information, and the media derive their right to that information from the public's right.

■ Promotions can have a significant impact on public opinion about the organization. Be sure the impact is a positive one.

■ Ultimately the ethical, responsible practice of public relations is a personal choice.

NOTES

[1] Ivan Hill, *Common Sense & Everyday Ethics* (Washington, D.C.: American Viewpoint, Ethics Resource Center 1), p. 5.

[2] John A. Koten, "Moving Toward Higher Standards for American Business," *Public Relations Review*, 12(3) (Fall 1986), p. 3.

[3] Christine Wicker, "SMU's Ethics Center Exploring 'Conflicts of Culture,'" *Dallas Morning News* (November 3, 1996), p. 37A.

[4] Amitai Etzioni, "Money, Power and Fame," *Newsweek* (September 18, 1989), p. 10.

[5] Associated Press, "Students Given Coupons For Not Cheating" (February 28, 1997).

[6] Tamara Henry, "Many Leading Students Say They've Cheated," *USA TODAY* (October 20, 1993), p. 2D.

[7] Steve Stecklow, "Cheat Sheets, Student Applications For Financial Aid Give Lots of False Answers," *Wall Street Journal* (March 11, 1998), pp. A1, 14.

[8] Sonia L. Nazario, "Schoolteachers Say It's Wrongheaded to Try to Teach Students What's Right," *Wall Street Journal* (April 6, 1990), p. B1.

[9] Hugh M. Culbertson, "How Public Relations Textbooks Handle Honesty and Lying," *Public Relations Review*, 9(2) (Summer 1983), pp. 65–73 (especially pp. 67, 68, 72).

[10] Sissela Bok, *Lying: Moral Choice in Public and Private Life* (New York: Pantheon Books, 1978).

[11] Susanne Holmstrom, "The Inter-subjective and the Social Systemic Public Relations Paradigms," *Journal of Communication Management*, 2 (1) (1997), pp. 24–39.

[12] Serge F. Kovaleski and John Mintz, "NRA Executive Uses Phony Identity To Get Pro-Gun Essays Printed," *Fort Worth Star-Telegram* (July 30, 1995), p. A5.

[13] Scott M. Cutlip, "The Tobacco Wars: A Matter of Public Relations Ethics," *Journal of Corporate Public Relations*, (1992–3). Northwestern University, Chicago, IL.

[14] Arthur W. Page, "The Page Philosophy" (Arthur Page Society, Inc., Room 19A, 225 West Randolph St., Chicago, Illinois 60606).

[15] Marvin Olasky, "Public Relations vs. Private Enterprise: An Enlightening History Which Raises Some Basic Questions," *Public Relations Quarterly*, 30(4) (Winter 1985–1986), pp. 6–13.

[16] "Doing What's Right Pays Off On Bottom Line Despite Gripes," *pr reporter* (March 31, 1997), p. 4.

[17] Wendy Bounds, "Critics Confront a CEO Dedicated to Human Rights," *Wall Street Journal*, (February 24, 1997), pp. B1, 7.

[18] Hadley Cantril, *Understanding Man's Social Behavior* (Princeton, N.J.: Office of Public Opinion Research, 1947), p. 60.

[19] Earl Babbie, *The Practice of Social Science Research*, 8th ed. (Belmont, Calif.: Wadsworth, 1998) pp. 438–46.

[20] Rick Wartzman, "Information Please, A Research Company Got Consumer Data from Voting Rolls," *Wall Street Journal* (December 23, 1994), p. A1, 12.

[21] John Koten, "IRS Use of Mail-Order Lists Concerns Market Researchers," *Wall Street Journal* (March 8, 1984), p. 29. See also Michael W. Miller, "Data Mills Delve Deep to Find Information About U.S. Consumers," Wall Street Journal (March 14, 1991), pp. 1, A12.

[22] Cynthia Crossen, "How 'Tactical Research' Muddied Diaper Debate," *Wall Street Journal* (May 17, 1994), pp. B1, 8.

[23] Michael Ryan, "Organization Constraints on Corporate Public Relations Practitioners," *Journalism Quarterly*, 64(2 & 3) (Summer–Autumn 1987), pp. 473–82.

[24] Ibid.

[25] "Study: Senior Execs Get Lowest Ethics Marks in the Org'n," *pr reporter* (March 30, 1998), p. 2.

[26] For a discussion of personal responsibility in professional PR ethics, see Dean Kruckeberg, "Ethical Decision-Making in Public Relations," *Public Relations Review*, 15(4) (1992), pp. 32–37.

[27] For an interesting alternative view of the bribery problem in international business, as well as numerous cases highlighting other conflicts in overseas business (and PR) see Henry W. Lane and Joseph J. DiStefano, *International Management Behavior* (Blackwell, Basil), 1996.

[28] Andy Pasztor, "Lockheed Pleads Guilty to Conspiring to Violate Anti-Bribery Regulations, *Wall Street Journal* (January 30, 1995), p. A15B.

[29] "Is Corruption an Asian Value," *Wall Street Journal* (May 6, 1996), p. A14.

[30] For articles discussing these issues, see *Public Relations Review* 19(1), (Spring 1993).

[31] Philip Lee, *Review of Reports on Media Ethics in Europe*, ed. Kaarle Nordensteng (University of Tampere, Finland, 1995), in *Media Development*, 2 (1996), pp. 40–41.

[32] Patrick M. Reilly, "Virginia Slims Gets its Own Record Label," *Wall Street Journal* (January 15, 1997), B1, 6.

[33] Eben Shapiro, "Molson Ice Ads Raise Hackles of Regulators," *Wall Street Journal* (February 24, 1994), p. B1, 5.

[34] Ibid.

[35] Leon E. Wynter, "White Firm Berated for Using Black Symbols," *Wall Street Journal* (February 25, 1994), p. B1.

[36] Richard B. Schmitt, "Can Corporate Advertising Sway Juries?" *Wall Street Journal* (March 3, 1997), p. B1, 8.

[37] G. Bruce Knecht, "Hard Copy, Magazine Advertisers Demand Prior Notice of 'Offensive' Articles," *Wall Street Journal* (April 30, 1997), p. A1, 8.

[38] William M. Bulkeley, "Censorship Fights Heat Up on Academic Networks," *Wall Street Journal* (May 24, 1993), B1.

[39] Martha T. Moore, "Political Ads: The Camera Can Tell Lies," *USA TODAY* (May 23, 1996), p. 6A.

[40] Lisa Leiter, "Tough Decisions: College Papers Struggle with Holocaust Ad Question," *Quill* (October, 1992), p. 45.

[41] Hearings Before the Presidential Commission on the Assassination of President Kennedy, Vol. 18, Exhibit 1031 (Washington, D.C.: U.S. Government Printing Office, 1964), p. 835.

[42] Public Relations Society of America, *Code of Professional Standards for the Practice of Public Relations: An Official Interpre-*

tation of the Code as It Applies to Political Public Relations, Precepts 1 and 2.

[43] Ibid., Precept 3.

[44] Ibid., Precept 4.

[45] Michael Waldholz, "Controversy Builds Over Threat of Common Chemicals," and Cynthia Crossen, "Clamorous Pro and Con Campaigns Herald Book's Launch," *Wall Street Journal* (March 7, 1996), pp. B1, 10.

[46] Kelley Griffin, "Calcium Supplements: Boon or Boondoggle?" *Graduate Woman* [newsletter of American Association of University Women], 81(6), p. 12.

[47] "Post-It Scam Continues to Strike," *pr reporter* (March 4, 1996), p. 4.

[48] Hazel Warlaumont, "Blurring Advertising and Editorial Photographic Formats," *Visual Communication Quarterly* (Summer, 1995), pp. 4–10.

[49] David Lieberman, Fake News, *TV Guide* (Feb. 22–8, 1992), pp. 10–16, 26.

[50] Doug Levy, "What Kids Read About Smoking," *USA TODAY* (October 11, 1994).

[51] William L. Rivers, *The Adversaries* (Boston: Beacon Press, 1969), pp. 157–64.

[52] "Doctored Images Now Common," *pr reporter* (April 10, 1995), p. 1.

[53] Tom Wheeler and Tim Gleason, "Photography Or Photofiction, An Ethical Protocol for the Digital Age," *Visual Communication Quarterly* (Winter 1995), pp. 8–12.

[54] Shiela Reaves, "The Unintended Effects of New Technology (And Why We Can Expect More)," *Visual Communication Quarterly* (Winter 1995), pp. 11–15.

[55] Mac Seligman, "Travel Writers' Expenses: Who Should Pay," *Public Relations Journal* (May 1990), pp. 27, 28, 34. See also Ed Avis, "Have Subsidy, Will Travel," *The Quill*, 79(2) (March 1991), pp. 20–25; Eric Hubler, "Freebies on the Tube," *The Quill*, 79(2) (March 1991), pp. 26–27.

[56] Betsy Wiesendanger, "Morley Safer versus Public Relations," *Public Relations Journal*, 50(6) (June/July 1994), p. 6.

[57] William B. Blankenburg, "The Adversaries and the News Ethic," *Public Relations Quarterly*, 14(4) (Winter 1970), p. 31.

[58] James McGregor, "Chinese Journalists Learn Value of PR, and Foreign Firms Use the Opportunity," *Wall Street Journal* (October 21, 1991), p. A17.

[59] Alecia Swasy, "Commercial Tie-ins Muddy Earth Day Observance," *Wall Street Journal* (April 15, 1991), p. B1.

[60] Ginny Carroll, "Green for Sale," *National Wildlife*, 29(2) (February–March 1991), p. 24.

[61] Frank Edward Allen, "McDonald's to Reduce Waste in Plan Developed with Environmental Group," *Wall Street Journal* (April 17, 1991), pp. B1, B6.

[62] Ralph T. King, Jr., " Charity Tactic by Genentech Stirs Questions," *Wall Street Journal* (August 10, 1994), pp. B1, 2.

[63] Amanda Bennett, "Doing the 'Right' Thing Has Its Repercussions," *Wall Street Journal* (January 25, 1990), p. B1.

[64] Amar Bhide and Howard H. Stevenson, "Why be Honest if Honesty Doesn't Pay?" *Harvard Business Review*, 67(5) (September–October 1990), pp. 121–29.

[65] Joseph L. Badaracco, Jr., "The Discipline of Building Character," *Harvard Business Review* (March–April 1998), pp. 114–19.

[66] David Finn, "Medium Isn't Always the Message," *Dallas Morning News* (May 21, 1981), p. 4D.

Selected readings, activities and assignments appropriate to this chapter can be found in the *Instructor's Guide* or on InfoTrac if you are using the InfoTrac College Edition.

CHAPTER 9

PR AND THE LAW

Law: a mousetrap easy to enter, but not easy to get out of.

FRANCIS MAITLAND BALFOUR

The law is the last result of human wisdom acting upon human experience for the benefit of the public.

SAMUEL JOHNSON, *MISCELLANIES*

You are public relations director for a toy company that has its own line of electronic educational toys with a very distinctive character called "cyber cadet" used in the promotions. One of your staff members tells you that the local library in the city where your corporate headquarters is located is using the cyber cadet figure on its Web page. Is this illegal? Should you talk with the corporate attorney about filing a lawsuit?

As your PR firm's account executive for a pharmaceutical company client, you are working on a competitive strategy to respond to another company's new product. You learn that this product is expected to be approved soon by the Food and Drug Administration. When that occurs, it will seriously challenge your client company's product. Your boss tells you to run your strategy by the client's in-house attorney because that way it will be "privileged" information and thus not ever publicly disclosed. Is that the case?

You are the staff public relations person for a school district that has just bought a new fleet of buses and vans in which to transport students. The manufacturer sends you some information about the safety of the buses and the adaptability of the vans for use with handicapped students. Your employer encourages you to put this in the school district's newsletter. Is this a good idea? Would the school district be responsible if some safety problems later appeared?

You've been asked to write a publicity release that downplays your organization's financial crisis. Can you do that?

One of your clients spent a lot of money for a distinctive logo that you promoted with stories in the trade press describing its development. Now you find an advertisement in the *Wall Street Journal* for an organization with a logo very similar to your client's. What can you do?

You've been asked to write the script for an infomercial (a program-length commercial) that mimics a talk show program to the extent of simulating "commercial breaks." You don't know anything about the product or the doctor being "interviewed" on this infomercial—other than information you've been given by your boss. Can you write the script?

Your lawyer client calls to tell you that she's just completed a week of special seminars and received a certificate. She wants to know if she can add the certification to the letterhead of the stationery you helped design for her. What do you tell her?

You're trying to create a full-page ad for a special newspaper section that will call attention to the annual outdoor sports event you handle. Thus, you need a photo of people attending an event that has yet to occur. Last year's news coverage included a good picture of a couple inflating a raft. Can you use the picture?

Your organization's human resources person calls to ask if you have model releases for the pictures of employees used in the last magazine. One of those pictured doesn't work for your organization any more. You don't have a release. Is this a problem?

These are all legal questions that PR practitioners encounter. Because such questions will sometimes catch you unaware, it's wise to have a close working relationship with your organization's attorney. Indeed, most public relations practitioners in independent practice have their own attorneys. Of course, sometimes the legal difficulties PR people encounter are of their own making.

In the late 1980s, the president of PRSA was accused of insider trading, and the first PR firm in history was charged with the same offense. PR people are faced with countless temptations, and the practice of public relations is a legal minefield.

THE LIABILITIES OF PRACTICING PR

PR practitioners are more conscious than ever of their legal exposure. An Oklahoma City counselor says he now buys malpractice insurance, a business expense he never considered until the mid-1970s. The policy is his response to three areas of exposure identified by attorney Morton Simon: (1) *normal legal exposure*, like that encountered by any other person, encompassing civil and criminal matters, including conspiracy; (2) *work-oriented legal exposure*, such as that found in the course of normal PR or publicity activities; (3) *extraneous legal exposure*, including everything from testifying as an expert witness to getting sports event tickets for a client to lobbying without registering as a lobbyist or reporting income and expenses from such activities. This third category also includes allowing the corporation to use the public relations office as a conduit for illegal corporate political contributions and, in the international arena, allowing it to use the PR office as the locus for bribes or other illicit activities.[1]

Liabilities have increased as out-sourcing has become more common. Organizations always have been responsible for anything done by their contract workers. The "work for hire" is considered the same as "in-house" work. If a photographer hired by the company failed to get permission to take someone's picture, that always became the company's responsibility once the photo was published. But now the photographer may be giving the picture to a PR boutique that is producing the brochure, magazine or newsletter for the company. The company is still responsible for the results, but monitoring the process is a lot more difficult.

PR consultant and educator Marian Huttenstine says public relations itself has its functional roots in commercial speech, advertising, traditional speech and the press, and as a result, statutory and case law for public relations is constantly evolving in all of these areas.[2]

PR developed in the USA largely because of the social, economic and political climate, and the last of these depends heavily on constitutionally protected freedom of speech and of the press. Huttenstine notes that some of the laws governing public relations practice would not be in place if First Amendment guarantees had not been found to apply to commercial speech.[3]

Legal Problems: Civil and Criminal

Civil suits involving PR practitioners may occur in relation to communication activities—for example, copyright infringements—or physical activities, such as accidents during plant tours. In addition, the practitioner may incur statutory and administrative liability in connection with dealings with government administrative agencies (SEC, FTC, FDA, ICC and others). A publicity release, for example, may violate SEC regulations, cause the company's stock to be closed for trading and result in court action. A carelessly worded ad can result in fines and perhaps court action. The statutory responsibilities are substantial. Sometimes a civil case results from failure to do something required as a matter of compliance (such as obligatory disclosure of certain information), rather than from doing something wrong—failing to disclose information, for example. Or it might be an entirely internal matter, such as a letter to employees advocating management's position on a unionization effort. The NLRB takes a dim view of persuasive communications that sound coercive.

More so than ordinary citizens, PR practitioners are also exposed to many opportunities for *criminal actions* such as bribery, price fixing, mail fraud, securities manipulation and even perjury. To yield to these opportunities, however, is to risk criminal charges, particularly for conspiracy. It is imperative, therefore, to understand the PR person's legal standing as the agent of the client. As Morton Simon explains:

Whatever the PR practitioner does, he usually does by reason of his retainer by his client and in concert with

the client. Joint or multiparty action is therefore almost indigenous to the PR function. This is the root of the conspiracy charge.[4]

Simon lists five situations in which a PR practitioner may be subjected to a conspiracy charge. These occur when the practitioner (1) participates in the illegal action; (2) counsels, guides and directs the policy behind it; (3) takes a large personal part in it; (4) sets up a propaganda agency to fight enemies of it; or (5) cooperates to further it.

A civil suit and a criminal prosecution can and often do grow out of the same legal situation. Protection from double jeopardy, being tried twice for essentially the same infraction, no longer covers defendants facing both civil and criminal action. In 1997, the Supreme Court ruled that defendants who contend that they have already been sufficiently punished by a civil suit now must offer very clear proof that their civil penalty is the equivalent of a criminal penalty. (See Hudson vs. U.S.) When a company is fined in civil court it isn't always likely that its executives will also face criminal action. However, parallel civil and criminal proceedings are becoming common because Congress has provided for a number of different types of civil penalties in cases involving securities regulations, banking, environmental codes, government fraud and drug laws. The government may prosecute and try to impose regulatory fines, order forfeiture of property or keep a company from doing business with certain entities.[5]

Legal Cases

Simon suggests that PR practitioners are usually involved in four specific kinds of cases: the big case, the human interest case, the routine case and testimony. The *big case*, as he describes it,

. . . may be antitrust action directed at [a company's] entire marketing program, a labor relations hearing involving thousands of employees, suits involving product liability—especially those which deal with basic safety or acceptability of a product—minority stockholders' actions charging mismanagement or fraud, and other litigation basic to the continued success of the company.[6]

The *human interest* case may not involve much money, but by its nature it has a particular appeal to the news media. Simon lists the following examples:

> . . . a minor civil rights charge, a local zoning conflict, a right of privacy suit by a "glamour name," air or water pollution charges, suits against a company by a retired employee seeking a large pension, and myriad other kinds of litigation which may concern either an individual or some community interest.

The *routine* types of litigation are commonplace results of being in business. They include "actions for breach of contract, workmen's compensation claims, tax refund matters." Routine suits rarely involve such public relations activities as the preparation of documents, publicity releases or media conferences for executives. Therefore, most routine litigation is unlikely to need staff PR involvement or the PR firm's help (if the company is a client). Of course, the PR person who owns a firm or works as a consultant is subject as such to all the routine and normal potential litigation of being in business.

Cases calling for a PR person's *testimony* typically involve his or her participation in the company program at issue in the legal action or his or her status as an "expert" witness. These may vary from "cases growing out of preparation of the company president's statement before a congressional committee to a $200 supplier claim for tables and chairs used at a company picnic." Cases may also involve a high-profile client or a company executive accused of some illegal act.

The potential now for any case—not just the ones Simon calls "big" or "human interest" cases—to attract attention is greater due to litigation journalism. Carole Gorney, the public relations educator who defined the term in an article in the *New York Times* in 1992, says *litigation journalism* is the use and/or manipulation of the news and information media to advance the positions of plaintiffs in civil lawsuits and/or to promote the practices of trial lawyers by attracting new clients for class action litigation.[7] This promotion also has occurred in high-profile criminal cases.

◼ Litigation Journalism/Public Relations

What Gorney identified as "litigation journalism," also has been called "litigation public relations" because the situation is one in which lawyers simultaneously act as both lawyer and publicist/spokesperson for their clients. One of the best known for this practice is Robert L. Shapiro, who represented O. J. Simpson in his murder case. "When we are retained for these high-profile cases, we are instantly thrust into the role of a public relations person," Shapiro wrote in a 1993 article, "Using the Media to Your Own Advantage." While Shapiro does not recommend lying to the news media or making up facts, he does say that the calculated manipulation of the news media is essential for a defense attorney to counter what he (as a defense attorney) considers the natural advantage of the prosecutor.[8]

Prosecutors also have used litigation journalism. Thus, a case may be tried in the court of public opinion at the same time it is being tried in the courts. The consequence is a conflict between the First and Sixth Amendments, the latter of which protects a defendant's right to a fair trial. Using public relations practitioners for high-profile cases is not new. The joint practice by lawyers of public relations and law is.

With regard to civil suits, legal concerns have grown for PR practitioners in connection with what Marian Huttenstine calls the duty or legal obligation for clear and accurate communications, detrimental reliance (ill effects of depending upon someone to keep confidences), vicarious liability and respondeat superior (being responsible for the action of others) and fair use.[9]

Duty is the civil legal obligation to act in a way consistent with what might be expected of a "reasonable person," as assessed by a judge or jury. Problems in this area generally have had to do with risks and warnings or misleading communications. The determination hinges on the interpretation of whether the reader or listener acted on the message "reasonably." The consequences of reliance have to be something detrimental (and quantifiable in terms of money damages) for the case to be actionable.[10]

Detrimental reliance may occur when relied-on information is faulty or when a promise is broken. One example consists of relying on information from others such as research and development people supplying product information for publicity and advertising that proves to be less than entirely accurate. Another involves using or distributing information from a supplier that later turns out to the flawed. Detrimental reliance also may occur if a PR person is a source for information to news media or others on the basis of a promise of confidentiality which later is broken and the results are damaging to the source.[11]

Being responsible for the acts of others under contract to your organization has always been a legal obligation. But now there is more of a responsibility on the part of the organization to be sure that those working for the organization either directly as employees or indirectly as contractors don't do anything illegal. Organizations today have greater difficulty meeting this obligation because whole tasks are contracted out and because those under contract often subcontract for special services. An example would be a contractor engaged to do the weekly newsletter who then subcontracts for art or distribution. For anything the subcontractors do, the organization for which they are ultimately doing the job—not just its contractor—is responsible.[12]

The fair use aspect of copyright law has become increasingly complicated because of the use of electronic transmissions.[13] We examine this question in some detail later in this chapter.

■ Working with Legal Counsel

Most large institutions, businesses and news media have legal counsel. If your client retains legal help, use it. The client's own counselor is as eager to stay out of trouble as you are. One word of caution, though. Some attorneys are not knowledgeable in communications law, and their instinct is to have a client or the organization say nothing. This is usually not the best public relations response. You need to know where to go for specialized legal counsel.

Many practitioners have also built up libraries of cases and regulations relating to both public relations and their clients. In addition, many PR firms have prepared manuals for their employees to alert them to legal trouble spots. Clients, too, may have manuals; the PR person should ask for them and examine them carefully for areas where misunderstandings might create problems.

The public relations person within a corporation needs to establish a liaison with the corporate attorney, advises Morton Simon. Simon suggests that some CEOs ask PR practitioners to do "Machiavellian" things because they don't understand what a PR person is supposed to do, because so many "loose" descriptions of the PR job are floating around and because PR activities are difficult to define.[14]

Another reason is the top PR person now holds a seat within inner management councils, helping to formulate policy that will affect the organization's various publics, with special concern for how that policy will be understood and accepted by those publics. Therefore, the corporate PR person is in a good position to assist corporate counsel in planning strategies and suggesting how the various publics are likely to receive legal actions.[15] The PR person also needs legal counsel's help, especially in reviewing financial materials. For these reasons, the relationship between the two needs to be complementary, not adversarial.

The relationship may not be privileged, either, in the legal sense. Public relations practitioners discussing a situation with an attorney could make a dangerous assumption that because a lawyer is present, there is *attorney-client privilege*. That's not necessarily the case. Some courts have ruled that if the discussion is a mix of business and legal topics and is not primarily a discussion of legal concerns or if substantial non-legal concerns are discussed, the discussion is not privileged and thus could become public. The key seems to be whether the attorney's motivation is to assess the legal position and to give legal advice.

Also, simply routing communications and documents through an attorney does not make them secure under attorney-client privilege either.

These documents may later be disclosed. Even documents prepared by in-house lawyers may not be secure if they contain advice to management that is strategic but is essentially non-legal in nature. The material must be primarily legal advice for it to deserve attorney/client privilege from disclosure.[16]

■ Ways to Stay Out of Trouble

Maintaining a good relationship with the organization's attorney is one of the best ways to stay out of trouble, but attorney Morton Simon identifies five others:

1. Recognize your individual responsibility for your actions—none of this "I only did what the boss said." The law won't look at it that way.

2. Know your business.

3. Ignore the vague lines between advertising and PR, because the law often does.

4. Decide how far you are willing to go to run a risk of jail, fine, a cease and desist order or a corrective order.

5. "Know your enemy," especially which government agency is likely to go after you. It helps to get on the agency's mailing list and read all speeches its administrators give. Often these provide the first hint of troubles for your company or industry.

Recognizing Troublesome Areas Can Keep You Alert to Potential Problems Simon notes three general types of legal involvements. The first consists of meeting federal, state and local government agencies' regulations on everything from antitrust matters to building permits.

The second consists of *government-related activities*—activities that hinge on laws or regulations such as those governing libel and slander; right of privacy; contempt of court; ownership of ideas including copyright, trademarks and patents; publicity; political views, registering political activity as lobbying and representing foreign governments; contract disputes; stockholder actions; fair trade problems; use of photos of individuals and groups; preparation of publicity releases, advertising copy, games and giveaway promotions; and financial collections.

The third type consists of contracts with clients and suppliers of goods and services. These deal with such matters as who owns the music for a commercial jingle if the client moves his or her account from the agency that created the commercial and what recourse you have if the photographer you hired to make enlargements messes up the color negatives you provided.[17]

In any of these three types of cases, a PR person *outside* the situation is likely to be called by either side as an expert witness. When this occurs, you must devote considerable time to research—gathering facts in the case, not just relying on what you are told. (Most PR testimony consists of fact finding, in the discovery part of litigation.) Additionally, most PR people alert their own attorneys, who can advise them of any legal traps or personal jeopardy. Litigants generally pay fees for expert witnesses. However, excessive fees tend to invalidate the testimony. (The opposition generally tries to get the precise sum made public, usually as a part of the deposition.)

Danger Zones The greatest legal danger zones to a PR person are business memos, letters and proxy fights; use of photos; product claims; accusations that might be ruled libel or slander; promotions involving games; publicity that might result in charges of misrepresentation; and political campaigns. You should keep handy a checklist of laws covering areas such as contracts, releases, statements of responsibility and rights of privacy.

Most important, don't guess. Get legal assistance. Talk with the organization's legal counsel. Work closely with media and organization attorneys. The New York Stock Exchange encourages calls and other inquiries. Query any government body involved, and get a statement of legal precedent or request an informal ruling.

Getting government advice and assistance won't work, though, with one of the biggest sources of difficulty for an organization—lawsuits initiated by an employee, a "whistle blower" who has called attention of authorities, usually government regulators, to some legal problem. Laws at the federal, state and local level constrain communications in "whistle blower" cases, so normal strategies may not work. For example, federal laws place a 60-day secrecy on the existence of a whistle blower. In some cases, an organization can be under investigation for a year or more before the situation is made public, and then it is usually the government entity involved that makes the announcement. All PR communication, then, can be only reactive. The same is true if information about the case is "leaked." Leaks may originate outside the organization from someone knowledgeable about the situation, but there is always a court seal on such cases affecting both the organization and the whistle blower.

At the national level, whistle blowers get their power from the U.S. Federal False Claims Act which allows citizens to "blow the whistle" on an organization's misdeeds, to start sealed lawsuits on the government's behalf, and to get 25 percent for themselves of what the government collects. At the state and local level, the government's primary role is to protect the whistle blower from some kind of retaliation, usually getting fired. Whatever branch of government joins the whistle blower's suit, the organization is in a default position. The government has both authority and power behind it, and public opinion often supports the whistle blower who is seen as the responsible citizen calling attention to organizational wrongdoing.[18]

GOVERNMENT REGULATIONS

As a practitioner, you may find yourself working with any of hundreds of government agencies. Of this multitude, five are particularly important: the Postal Service, the Securities and Exchange Commission (SEC), the Federal Trade Commission (FTC), the Food and Drug Administration (FDA) and the Federal Communications Commission (FCC).

Postal Service

Postal Service regulations prohibit dissemination by mail of obscene materials, information about a lottery (two important elements: consideration and chance) and material that would incite riot, murder, arson or assassination. A 1975 law exempts newspapers and broadcast stations from prosecution in publicizing state-operated lotteries. However, newspapers may not carry information on another state's lotteries in editions that are mailed.

Certain state laws prohibit the circulation of magazines carrying particular types of advertising, so space buyers have to beware. Furthermore, although substantial specifications exist for inserts in second-class magazines, the total reference to the subject in the *Postal Service Manual* with respect to controlled-circulation publications is one sentence: "Enclosures are not permitted."

All mailing pieces face multiple regulations regarding size, weight, thickness and where an address may appear. It is best to have the design of a piece checked by the post office, or to use standard shapes and weights already approved.

A sender's freedom to reach publics by direct mail has been limited by a 1970 decision in a U.S. District Court, which has been upheld by the U.S. Supreme Court.[19] Senders may be compelled to delete an address from their mailing list and may be prohibited by law from sending or having an agent send future mailings to an addressee at the addressee's request.

The case began when a mail-order business challenged a California regulation stating that the recipient has a right not to have to receive "a pandering advertisement which offers for sale matter which addressee in his sole discretion believes to be erotically arousing or sexually provocative." If a violation occurs, the addressee may report it and the Postmaster General will inform the sender, who then has an opportunity to respond. An administrative hearing is held to see whether a violation has occurred. The Postmaster General may request the U.S. Attorney General to enforce compliance through a court order.

Three points here are significant:

1. The law allows a person absolute discretion to decide whether he or she wishes to receive any further material from a particular sender. (The material need not be erotic.)

2. A vendor does *not* have a constitutional right to send unwanted material to someone's home. A mailer's right to communicate must stop before the mailbox of an unreceptive addressee.

3. The law satisfies the due process rights of the vendor who sends the material. It provides for an administrative hearing if the sender does violate the prohibitory order from the Postal Service, and a judicial hearing is held prior to issuance of any compliance order by a district court.

As a result, the Postal Service now provides two relevant forms. Form 2150 is directed to a particular sender and is usually requested when a person has received obscene or sex-related materials in the mail. Form 2201 is a request that a person's name be removed from *all mailing lists.* In an effort to counteract legislation that might be directed toward controlling unsolicited mail, the Direct Marketing Association has asked that all persons who wish to be removed from the lists of their members send their name and mailing address to the DMA (6 East 43rd Street, New York, New York 10017). The DMA then contacts individual mailers and asks that they delete the name. (The DMA in 1998 merged with Association of Interactive Media, a leading cyberspace trade group that is now operating as a subsidiary of DMA.)

Securities and Exchange Commission (SEC)

Public corporations (those whose stock is publicly traded and owned) have to be concerned with SEC regulations, and all corporations must be aware of and sensitive to personnel and financial information that might be released. The larger the company, the more likely it is to let something escape

that should not have. This is particularly true when the corporation must coordinate its information dissemination with one of its clients (especially in the case of companies with government contracts) or when releases are prepared by an outside firm.

It is wise to have a procedure for clearing news releases so that no one is confused about what to do and (it is hoped) so that no one jumps the gun and releases a story before it has been cleared (see Example 9.1). Some institutions release only the information required, but a case can be made for using releases as early warning signals (such as for possible bankruptcy filing) and as timely announcements of good news. Taking the offensive in takeover battles became a PR tactic. However, financial abuses of the 1980s pushed the SEC to take a more active role in policing disclosures.

Some suggested guidelines for disclosing information have been prepared by the American Society of Corporate Secretaries, after conferring with SEC representatives, to assist officers and employees responsible for disseminating corporate information to financial analysts and the investment community (see Example 9.2). Some companies have developed internal checks, and some advocate going beyond what is required (see Example 9.3).

The annual report and the 10-K are two documents that PR staff or firms must prepare. Annual reports have become promotional tools used by investment brokers and the company itself in presenting the company to all members of the financial public, from banks to analysts. When annual reports are distributed, a news release summarizing the main points and announcing the report's publication is also sent out (see Example 9.4). An effort to make the annual report an integrated document didn't work too well, so the SEC uses the 10-K as the best way to integrate management messages with financial reports (see Example 9.5).

In annual reports and the news releases that accompany them, the SEC does allow speculative claims. These are called "forward-looking statements" and must be identified as such in the report and the release.

EXAMPLE 9.1

Procedures for Clearing News Releases

HANDLING OF PRODUCT NEWS RELEASES

1. First draft of copy to primary sources for preliminary approval.

2. Draft of release to Corporate Secretary for approval.

3. Revised copy to Legal Department for approval.

4. Draft to division General Manager for approval in certain instances. (Group Public Relations Manager should make judgment in this instance.)

5. Copy of approved news release is then mailed to the company handling news releases, along with media selection sheets for distribution.

6. Media covered will depend on the nature of the product, its importance to the various markets and industries and the marketing philosophy behind the development. (Distribution should be as broad as possible without covering media that would obviously not be interested in the development.)

7. Internal distribution of the news release to be determined by the Group Public Relations Manager.

APPROVAL CHAIN FOR AGENCY-PREPARED RELEASES

1. Clear with primary source at division.

2. Send cleared draft to Group Public Relations Manager for corporate clearance.

3. Following approvals at corporate level, distribution may be made through agency channels.

4. Copies of completed release to all involved in clearances. (News releases that must be approved at the corporate level include features, case histories,

new product releases and any other product-oriented information released to magazines or other news media.)

HANDLING OF PERSONNEL NEWS RELEASES

1. First draft of copy to individual named in release to check accuracy of facts.

2. Draft of release to source requesting release.

3. Draft of release to division General Manager or individual's immediate superior at corporate level.

4. Draft to Corporate Secretary and Legal Department for legal clearances.

5. Draft to Group Vice President in cases of key promotions at divisional level. In instances of key corporate promotions, the Chairman, President, Executive Vice President, General Counsel, and appropriate Group Vice President must clear release.

6. Media coverage should include plant cities, corporate headquarter's city, the individual's home town, association publications and appropriate alumni publications, as well as trade magazines covering industries served by the division or group with which the individual is associated.

7. Internal distribution determined by Group PR Manager and, in cases of key corporate promotions, by Public Relations Director.

8. Copies of news release should be sent to everyone included in the chain of approval.

Note: These procedures depend on the organizational structure and policy. Each organization will develop its own clearance procedures.

Timely and Adequate Disclosure of Material Information The timely and adequate disclosure of *material* corporate information—information affecting investment decisions—is a principal purpose of the Federal Securities Acts, as well as the stated policy of all national stock exchanges for publicly held companies. In addition to the SEC, which administers six major federal statutes in this area, other federal agencies important to financial institutions include the Federal Deposit Insurance Corporation (FDIC), which insures bank deposits, and the Federal Home Loan Bank

EXAMPLE 9.2

Guidelines for Dealing with Financial Analysts and the Investment Community

A. PRINCIPLES OF PUBLIC DISCLOSURE

1. The basic rule for corporate officials, when dealing with financial analysts and other members of the investment community, is that no item of previously undisclosed material corporate information should be divulged or discussed unless and until it has been disclosed to the public by a general press release or by an equivalent public statement. Material information as defined most recently by the [SEC] is "of such importance that it could be expected to affect the judgment of investors whether to buy, sell, or hold . . . stock. If generally known, such information could be expected to affect materially the market price of the stock." Considering the facts of the cases decided to date, material information in each instance consisted of information about the corporation or its securities, which, if disclosed, could be expected to have a reasonably prompt and substantial impact on the market price of the securities involved, i.e., resulting in a market price change perceptible in excess of the usual day to day or week to week fluctuation of the stock in question.

2. The New York Stock Exchange has recommended that corporations observe an "open door" policy in their relations with the investment community. It is appropriate to communicate with stockholders, financial analysts, trust officers, investment counselors, etc., either individually or in groups to answer their questions or to volunteer information, so long as undisclosed material information is not privately divulged. It is important that information should not be given to one individual or group which the corporation would not willingly give to any other individual or group asking the same question. In other words, preferential treatment of any class of community

members with regard either to fullness of discussion or to disclosure is to be avoided.

3. If it is expected that any material information, previously undisclosed, is to be revealed at a meeting or interview, a press release should be prepared in advance and publicly released to the financial press and wire services prior to or concurrently with the meeting, unless the press itself is adequately represented at the meeting. If material information is inadvertently disclosed at a meeting a press release must immediately be issued.

4. Further explanatory information within the context of a previous public disclosure may be given to financial analysts and others. Any new material information, however, should be given only in accordance with the procedures set forth in Paragraph 3.

5. Estimates of future earnings may be dealt with by either of the following methods, depending upon the policy of the individual company:

   a. Those companies which make it a practice not to issue any projections of earnings are frequently asked by financial analysts to comment on estimates made by them with respect to a future period or periods. Some companies do not comment on such estimates; others respond that such a projection is or is not "within the ball park." It may be necessary under certain circumstances to emphasize that the "no comment" implies neither an approval nor disapproval of the estimate. If, however, an independently arrived at estimate is deemed to be unreasonably high or low for the period in question in the light of responsible projections made by management, it may be appropriate to indicate that such estimate is "too high" or "too low" in order to prevent widespread dissemination of a substantially

(continued)

EXAMPLE 9.2 *(continued)*

incorrect earnings projection within the investment community.

b. Companies desiring to issue projected earnings, which are responsibly prepared and appropriately qualified, should do so only by public disclosure. Once such disclosure has been made and the projection remains materially unchanged, the company may discuss with individuals or groups the background and details of such projection. Such projection can also be compared with earnings for prior periods. If a publicly issued earnings projection becomes materially inaccurate, a new correcting public disclosure should be made.

B. PROCEDURES AND PRACTICES

1. It is suggested that the following procedures be utilized to implement the Principles of Public Disclosure set forth in Section A:

a. Only certain designated officers or employees be authorized by the corporation to speak before or with members of the investment community;

b. One or more of such designated individuals (referred to hereafter as "the designated offi-

cial") be given the responsibility for approving, in advance, commitments for speeches or interviews with the press on financial matters;

c. Press releases and texts or outlines of speeches to be reviewed in advance by the designated official to insure, among other things, that they are not misleading, i.e., are accurate, balanced, and do not emphasize facts disclosed out of proportion to their actual importance when considered within the overall context of the corporation's business;

d. Answers to probable questions on sensitive matters be prepared in advance of meetings with the press or members of the investment community.

2. While it is impractical to categorize what constitutes material information, public disclosure should be considered for the following subjects prior to discussion with individuals or groups:

a. Total sales, sales by product groups, or percentage of total sales by product groups, for any period;

b. Earnings;

Board (FHLBB), which is responsible for savings and loan associations.

Major court cases have shown that corporate officials and employees must understand the legal obligations of proper corporate disclosure.[20] This is particularly true of the corporation's relationship with financial analysts and the investment community. In the *Texas Gulf Sulphur* case,[21] a federal District Court ruling that the U.S. Supreme Court let stand, an *insider* was defined as anyone who has access to information that, if disseminated, might influence the price of a stock. A PR person who writes a news release, then, could be considered an insider. A PR firm must therefore disclose in its news releases that it is acting on behalf of an issuer

and is receiving consideration from the issuer for its service (see Example 9.3). Richard S. Seltzer, former SEC special counsel, writes:

The SEC apparently believes that fraudulent schemes initiated by corporate insiders may be facilitated by the action—or deliberate inaction—of outside professionals: the accountant who "stretches" generally accepted accounting principles; the lawyer who is willing to "overlook" material disclosures; and even the public relations practitioner who seeks to portray a convincing, but inaccurate, picture of corporate events.[22]

Ignorance of the legal requirements, of course, is no excuse, as the Carnation Company found out

c. Profit margins;

d. Plans to borrow funds or to sell additional equity securities;

e. Proposed changes in dividend policy or rate, stock splits, or stock dividends;

f. Proposed acquisitions or joint ventures;

g. Proposed major management changes;

h. Contemplated major management changes;

i. Any other important development such as sale by the company of any significant asset, major contracts, pending material litigation, etc.

3. The following subjects are among those which, in the absence of special circumstances, are not ordinarily regarded as constituting material information requiring public disclosure prior to discussion with individuals or groups:

a. Total project capital or research and development expenditures;

b. Plans for construction of new plants or expansion of existing plants not falling under Paragraph 2(g) above;

c. Existing or planned inventory levels;

d. General trends of sales or other operating conditions for the industry as a whole;

e. Estimates of the corporation's effective tax rate and investment tax credit for the current and future years;

f. Depreciation policy and estimated depreciation rates;

g. General information concerning the company's business, prospects for various product groups, etc.

4. It may be in a company's interests to prepare a memorandum of each meeting or conversation with financial analysts or other members of the investment community, stating the names of the persons involved, the date of the meeting or conversation, and the items discussed. In addition, a complete record should be kept of all public disclosures.

5. Stricter limitations in addition to the foregoing Suggested Guidelines may apply in the event a public offering is pending or in process.

Source: "Corporate Reporting Requirements," *Public Relations Journal,* 36(4) (April 1980), pp. 25–47. Reprinted with permission of the Public Relations Society of America.

in 1984. Then Chairman of the Board H. Everette Olson and then President Timm E. Crull negotiated a sale of Carnation to Nestlé but did not tell Carnation's treasurer or the head of corporate relations because they didn't want to "compromise" those executives in their dealings with the financial press and general media. When leaks of the sale occurred and were denied by the two officers who had no knowledge of the negotiations, the SEC called their denials false and misleading. Wall Street lawyer John Ruhnka and law professor John Bagsby commented:

Disclosure decisions—what to disclose, when to disclose and how to disclose significant nonpublic information—have become potential minefields for publicly held companies. No simple guidelines protect them from subsequent liability. But executives can reduce the possibility of mistakes if they know the requirements, current legal or regulatory issues and the kinds of problems that regularly arise, [and] then adopt some practical responses. To consult with your legal counsel is natural, but not always enough.[23]

Another federal court decision also affected financial PR significantly. Pig 'N' Whistle, a Chicago-based restaurant and motel chain, was headed by Paul Pickle, who had previously been sentenced to three years in prison for misapplication of federally insured funds. Pig 'N' Whistle was

EXAMPLE 9.3

Discretionary Disclosure

The argument is made here for using a preliminary disclosure release as an early warning or advance information system. The release is not a forecast but an announcement. The risk is that management might abuse this technique, using it to manipulate its publics, with a resulting loss in credibility.

Mr. X, chairman of the board of Ajax Company, said today that the company's board of directors intends to increase the annual cash dividend payment on the company's common stock for the coming year to $2 per share from $1.75. The company issues the release three full months before the board actually increases the dividend as described.

Issuing such an anticipatory statement creates a number of potential benefits for the company:

■ The issuing company can control the timing of the announcement, an important consideration for companies that have learned through bitter experience that their dividend action, no matter how newsworthy, gets lost in a massive table with dividend action of many other companies. It also allows a company to give an accurate and valuable signal to investors when the timing may be right to do so.

■ A company can show the cause-and-effect relationship linking two corporate events. For example, the above example could be linked with a report of higher earnings for the year, sale of a problem division, or even a change in control of the corporation.

■ A corporation can respond to shareholder demands without imprudently putting itself at financial risk too early.

■ The impression may grow that a company is well managed; the company thinks ahead, says what it plans to do and then does it.

Source: Robert W. Taft, "Discretionary Disclosure," *Public Relations Journal*, 39(4) (April 1983), pp. 34–35. Used by permission of the Public Relations Society of America.

brought before the SEC in February and March of 1972 to answer charges of having distributed two untrue and misleading press releases concerning stock transactions and acquisition of property in 1969. The firm was also charged with illegal stock registration.[24]

The two releases, one made on September 8 and the other on December 30, contained untrue or misleading statements about the purchases of the Mary Ann Baking Company and the Holiday Lodge near Lake Tahoe. Pig 'N' Whistle stock shot up to $18 per share after the two releases—which came from Financial Relations Board, Inc., a public relations company—were printed. Pig 'N' Whistle had been a client of Financial Relations for eight weeks in 1969.[25] The statements released by Financial Relations were handled by only one member of the firm. The president of Financial Relations stated

that Pig 'N' Whistle had not provided the firm with proper SEC registration papers for the stock. The PR firm was told by Pig 'N' Whistle lawyers that immediate disclosure of the purchase made by Pig 'N' Whistle was necessary to comply with SEC disclosure requirements.[26] Thus, the releases couldn't wait for registration papers to be filed.

The SEC investigated the actions of both Pig 'N' Whistle and Financial Relations and ruled that Financial Relations had not exercised due caution in establishing the truth about the information furnished by Pig 'N' Whistle. The SEC said that Financial Relations should have done independent research before allowing any release to leave its offices. As a result, Financial Relations established within thirty days new procedures for reviewing the credentials of any new clients and for verifying the facts given to it for publication. This verification of facts covers any information that might affect investment decisions by stock purchasers. The SEC also ordered Financial Relations to cease any contact with Pig 'N' Whistle.

In the 1970s, following the Pig 'N' Whistle case, the SEC began reviewing possible new disclosure regulations designed to protect the stock purchaser. The most important outcome of this, from the point of view of public relations, is that the kind of information released has to be more detailed and exact. Statements must be registered and must include a budget and cash flow projection for the company.[27] It is an SEC violation to issue a false and/or misleading release, whether or not a profit is realized as a result.

Public relations practitioners have to provide more information and be more certain now than in the past that the information is true. Further, the people who do the research and write the releases now assume the same liabilities as does the company about which the releases are published. The information the public relations department or firm releases—the financial operations, history, future outlook, management and marketing structure of the company for which it is working—must therefore be carefully considered. The SEC has placed a heavy burden on public relations practitioners by holding them accountable. The agency has also left PR firms up in the air about how specific and detailed their information must be. The problem comes down to a matter of opinion and to the legal interpretation of "reasonable" or "ordinary care."[28] Financial releases must also be considered in the context of *other* public information put out about the company. This underscores the need to speak with one voice, to ensure that no information is misleading.

Initial Disclosures The basic principles of public disclosure are given in the guidelines in Example 9.2. The following points are critical:

1. Unless trade secrets or competitive data are at risk and would justify a delay, publicly held companies must announce all important developments promptly. The 8-K reports must be filed within fifteen days of the event, such as an unfavorable

> ## EXAMPLE 9.4
> ### SEC Requirements for Annual Report Interpretive News Releases
>
> The SEC has furnished guidance regarding the text of the discussion of financial condition and results of operations, known as Management's Discussion and Analysis of Operations (MD&A) section of the annual report, the Interpretive Release (33-6835; 34-26831; IC-16961; FR-36/May 18, 1989). Specifically, the release highlights the following areas of concern:
>
> - long and short-term liquidity and capital resources analysis;
> - material changes in financial statement line items;
> - required interim disclosure;
> - MD&A analysis on a segment basis;
> - preliminary merger negotiations.
>
> Separately, financial institutions are directed to disclose information regarding their participation in certain high yield financings and highly-leveraged transactions, whether as an originator, lender, purchaser or syndicator of secured high-risk debt.
>
> In addition to the historical overview, the release refers to a prospective or forward-looking discussion of operations and finances. This should address known trends, demands and commitments, as well as any uncertainties that are reasonably expected to have material effects on the financial condition and results of operations. Moreover, any industry-specific information which will further describe the particular nature of the company's markets should be included. Note that the SEC's "safe harbor" rule protects companies from liability if such required statements are made on a "reasonable basis" and in "good faith." Underlying assumptions, if disclosed, are also protected.
>
> Source: Reprinted with permission of Gavin Anderson Doremus & Co.

court ruling in a lawsuit, a sale of significant assets or an acquisition.

2. A timely news release must be issued to report any event that is likely to affect the price of stock. The exchanges will stop trading in a stock when a

EXAMPLE 9.5

SEC Requirements for Annual Reports

SEC REQUIREMENTS

Audited Financial Statements

- Consolidated balance sheets (2 years)
- Consolidated statements of income (3 years)
- Consolidated statements of cash flow (3 years)
- Consolidated statements of shareholders' equity, or footnote disclosure (3 years)
- Notes to consolidated financial statements
- Report of independent public accountants

Supplementary Financial Information

Selected quarterly financial data (2 years):

- Net sales
- Gross profit
- Income (loss) before extraordinary items and cumulative effect of any change in accounting policies
- Per share data based upon such income (loss)
- Net income (loss)
- Disagreements on accounting and financial disclosure matters

Selected Financial Data for Five Years

- Net sales or operating revenues
- Income (loss) from continuing operations (in total and per common share)
- Total assets
- Long-term obligations and redeemable preferred stock (including capital leases)
- Cash dividends declared per common share
- Additional items that will enhance understanding and highlight trends in financial condition and results of operations

(Such data may be combined with the five-year summary information on the effects of inflation and changing prices if required by FASB Statement No. 33, as amended by Statement No. 82.)

Management Discussion and Analysis of Financial Condition and Results of Operations

Discuss financial condition, changes in financial condition and results of operations; provide other information believed necessary to an understanding of the Company's historical, current and prospective financial condition. The areas to be covered include Liquidity, Capital Resources and Results of Operations; they may be combined whenever the three are interrelated.

Generally, the discussion shall cover the three-year period covered by the financial statements.

- Liquidity: Identify any trends, demands, commitments, events or uncertainties that will materially increase or decrease liquidity. If material deficiency is identified, indicate course of action to remedy the situation. Identify and describe internal and external sources of liquidity; briefly discuss any material unused sources of liquid assets.
- Capital Resources: Describe material commitments for capital expenditures as of end of latest fiscal period; indicate general purpose of such commitments and anticipated source of funds needed. Describe any known material trends, favorable or unfavorable, in capital resources. Indicate any expected material changes in mix and relative cost of such resources. Discussion shall consider changes between equity, debt and any off balance sheet financing arrangements.
- Results of Operations: Describe any unusual or infrequent events or transactions, or significant economic changes, that materially affected reported income from continuing operations. In each case indicate extent to which income was affected. Also describe any other significant components of revenues or expenses that would enhance an understanding of results.

The discussion should use year-to-year comparisons or any other format that will enhance a reader's understanding. Where trend information is relevant, reference to the five-year selected financial data may be necessary. Known trends, demands, commitments or uncertainties that are reasonably likely to have material impact on sales or revenues, income and financial condition must be described. Any events that will cause a material change in the relationship between costs and revenues (cost increases in labor or materials, or price increases or inventory adjustments) must be disclosed. If there are any material increases in net sales or revenues, provide narrative discussion of the extent to which such increases are attributable to price increases in the volume or amount of goods or services sold, or to the introduction of new products or services.

Review the impact of inflation and changing prices on net sales and revenues and on income from continuing operations.

Discuss any uncertainties regarding the impact of recently adopted legislation.

Industry Segment Breakdown for Three Years

- Revenue (with sales to unaffiliated customers and sales or transfers to other industry segments shown separately), operating profit or loss, identifiable assets, capital expenditures and depreciation attributable to industry segments and geographic areas for three years. Classes of similar products or services, foreign and domestic operations, export sales.

Financial Reporting and Changing Prices Information

- Five-year summary: effects of inflation and changing prices; may be combined with Selected Financial Data

Information on the Market for Common Stock and Related Security Holder Matters

- High and low sales prices of stock for each quarterly period in last two years
- Frequency and amount of dividends paid
- Principal market(s) in which the company's securities are traded and stock symbols.

Identity

- A brief description of the company's business

Directors and Executive Officers

- Name, principal occupation, title, employer's principal business

Litigation

- Cite significant cases; include any in which civil rights, ecological statutes or ethical conduct of directors or executive officers are involved.

Form 10-K

- Offer of free copy of Form 10-K in annual report or proxy statement in boldface type (not required if annual report is incorporated by reference into the Form 10-K and is filed with the SEC in satisfaction of disclosure requirements).

Type-Size Requirements

- Financial statements and notes—Roman type at least as large and legible as 10-point Modern; if necessary for convenient presentation, financial statements may be Roman type at least as large and legible as 8-point Modern; all type leaded at least 2 points.

Distribution

- Distribution of annual report to all stockholders, including beneficial owners underlying street names, analysts, brokers, press.
- Annual report must precede or accompany proxy statement if proxies are solicited in connection with an annual meeting.

Significant Accounting Policies

The SEC requires that these subjects be reported in accordance with generally accepted accounting principles:

- Principles of consolidation, summary of accounting policies, changes in accounting principles
- Inventories: valuation method
- Property, plant and equipment: depreciation policy
- Lease commitments
- Translation of foreign currency transactions
- Effects of changing prices and general inflation
- Long-term debt agreements, short-term borrowings
- Pensions: accounting and funding policies

DELIVERY OF REPORTS

Following are the delivery requirements of the annual report to your shareholders, based on where your securities are listed or traded.

(continued)

EXAMPLE 9.5 (continued)

NYSE

15 days before annual meeting: not later than 90 days after close of your fiscal year.

AMEX

10 days before annual meeting; not later than 120 days after close of your fiscal year.

OTC

No delivery of annual report to shareholders is necessary unless there is an annual meeting for which proxies are being solicited. State laws governing corporate activities should be checked to determine how many days before your annual meeting the annual report must be delivered.

ADDITIONAL CONSIDERATIONS

FASB Statement No. 96

New Financial Accounting Standards Board (FASB) rules will require companies to use the liability method to record deferred taxes. Such deferred tax expenses and liabilities must reflect future announced statutory rates beginning in 1988.

1986 Tax Reform Act (TRA) Effects on Earnings

Between 1987 and 1989, there were a variety of options for adopting the new GAAP tax rules. Companies that did not adopt the new rules in 1987 are required by a new SEC ruling to disclose the potential impact of the new rules on company earnings.

Pension Accounting

The FASB's new pension accounting rules issued in 1985 became mandatory in 1987. These rules govern determination of domestic U.S. defined benefit pension plan costs and the disclosure of pension plan assets and liabilities.

Cash Flow Statement

A Cash Flow Statement has replaced the Changes in Financial Position Statement.

Accountant's Report to Shareholders

Beginning in 1988, the Accountant's Report to Shareholders replaced the Audit Opinions.

The AICPA has clearly told auditors that they (1) are to actively search for fraud and (2) are required to evaluate whether or not there is substantial doubt about a company's ability to survive.

The Shareholder Communications Act

Since January 1, 1986, broker-dealers have been complying with SEC rules designed to help companies communicate with their beneficial shareowners.

Commercial banks, which account for about 75 percent of stocks held in "street names" including most of the beneficially owned shares of institutions, must also comply, effective December 28, 1986, with the provisions of similar SEC rules by furnishing, upon request, the names and addresses of beneficial owners.

However, bank obligations in connection with obtaining and forwarding proxy material to beneficial owners were deferred until July 1, 1987, in order to give banks sufficient time to establish workable procedures for the implementation of this system.

The Commission also adopted an amendment that changes from three to five business days the time in

leak occurs, but only briefly. (The New York Stock Exchange's maximum delay is three hours.)

3. A business judgment to withhold must be made in good faith—that is, not to defraud—and management must be able to demonstrate that it used reasonable care in identifying and evaluating facts in making the decision. In any case, announcements issued cannot be false and misleading. Texas Gulf Sulphur got into trouble by postponing a news release about a mineral find so that it could buy more land in the area of the discovery. The court found no fault with the company for withholding information about the find while it bought additional acreage, but the court found that issuing a release that downplayed the find was false and misleading.

4. There must be no delay in reporting good or bad news.

which a bank is to execute an omnibus proxy and provide notice of that execution to respondent banks.

The following amendments to the Shareholder Communications rules became effective in 1988:

Exclusion of specified employee benefit plan participants from the operation of the proxy processing and direct communications provision of the shareholder communications rules. The exclusion would apply only with respect to securities held by an employee benefit plan established by the issuer of the securities, or, at the option of the issuer, by its affiliate. Under the amendments, registrants would be required to cause proxy materials to be furnished in a timely manner to plan participants excluded from the operation of the proxy processing provisions.

The Commission also adopted an amendment to the definition of employee benefit plan, for purposes of the shareholder communications rules, to include those plans that are established primarily for employees but also include other persons, such as consultants.

Summary Annual Reports

A January 20, 1987, Securities and Exchange Commission ruling gives publicly-owned companies the option of issuing summary annual reports to shareholders without including the complete financial data previously required by the SEC.

However, the ruling stipulates that if a company uses the new format, every shareholder must receive in the proxy statement or in a 10-K all of the financial information before the annual meeting and in accordance with previously established rules.

The response to the issuance of summary annual reports has been underwhelming. In a 1988 study of nearly 300 corporations, many respondents expressed concern that the effort to limit the data would be viewed negatively by shareholders and securities analysts.

Other Postemployment Benefits

The Financial Accounting Standards Board (FASB) has a new standard on Employers' Accounting for Postretirement Benefits Other Than Pensions. The standard on other postemployment benefits (OPEB) requires recording the present value of these future costs as current liabilities. The required provisions took effect in 1992.

Financial Instruments

The FASB is expected to shortly issue a standard regarding information on certain financial instruments. Specifically, companies will be required to disclose the face amount, nature and potential accounting loss for financial instruments issued for fiscal years ending after June 15, 1990. Additional information is required regarding those financial instruments that have concentrations of credit risk.

Note: Another addition in the 1990s was the SEC requirement of an "online" filing. The "dry run" was in 1993. It became the required way to file financial reports in 1994. This increased pressure for earlier deadlines.

Source: Reprinted with permission of Gavin Anderson Doremus & Co.

---

5. Companies have what the SEC calls an implied duty to report material information between quarters so the financial markets will not be misled.

6. Formal disclosures (detailed financial documents that the SEC calls 10-K, 10-Q or 8-K) or informal disclosures (news releases) must be sufficiently accurate and complete that the information does not mislead, although every known material fact does not have to be communicated.

(The Ronson Corporation was charged with misleading those who read its formal 10-Q and 10-K reports for not revealing that it was losing an important customer that accounted for 15 percent of its revenues.)

7. News releases are as important as formal reports. The SEC concluded that Fidelity Financial Corporation's year-end release was misleading because it didn't point out that the company's

auditors had said they might need to include a "going concern" qualification on its 1981 financial
statement because it was losing money at such a
fast rate. The SEC said the release gave the impression of "business as usual."

Follow-up Disclosures Additional disclosure is
necessary under four circumstances:

1. New information must be updated when new
events make previous statements misleading.

2. Responses to outside reports must be made if
these are misleading and come from people in a position to have had the information approved by the
company, such as an underwriter, director or large
shareholder.

3. Trading of shares held by executives and all insiders, including the company itself and company-
managed pension plans, must be reported unless all
material information about the stock's value already has been made available to the public. (The
company is liable if it has given material nonpublic
information to outsiders.)

4. Acquisition and merger information must be
disclosed when negotiations reach agreement in
principle.

Executive Compensation Disclosure The SEC in
1992 changed policies regarding disclosure of compensation for senior executive officers in proxy
statements. This includes the CEO and the four
most highly paid senior executive officers who earn
more than $100,000 per year in salary and bonus
and requires details of other kinds of compensation
awards and payouts such as stock options. The SEC
also now requires disclosure in proxy statements of
employment and severance agreements of payments exceeding $100,000 for senior executive offi-
cers. The statements must also identify standard
compensation arrangements for directors and information on interlocking directorships. In the proxy
report, the SEC requires inclusion of a chart showing the total return of stock to shareholders (stock
price appreciation plus dividends) in comparison
with the returns on a broad market index, such as

the Standard and Poor's 500, as well as with a peer
group index, depending on the company's line of
business. Other changes in the proxy rules involved
unbundling proxy proposals so votes can be taken
on separate issues, reporting the number of yes and
no votes and allowing dissident stockholders to
nominate their own candidates. Complete voting
results have to be printed in the annual report and
the 10-K.

Rumors and Leaks When you are faced with rumors or leaks, you have three options: you can admit and disclose; you can make no comment or
deny; or you can dodge and mislead. Courts have
disagreed over where to draw the line clearly between exploratory preliminary talks and serious negotiations.[29] The former may be reported in a
relatively leisurely manner, but the latter should be
reported quickly because information about them
almost always leaks. Two bills introduced into
Congress in 1987 would have amended the SEC
Act of 1934 on this point. One would have required a yes or no response in talks about a tender
offer. The other would have made misleading statements illegal but would not have outlawed the "no
comment" response, which could cause speculative
buying.

Insider Information It is just as important to understand the SEC's view of information to which
there is "equal access." People who have knowledge that others do not have access to are called *insiders*. Thus, an insider, viewed broadly, is anyone
who has information "everyone" else doesn't have
(for example, information not generally available)
that would give that person an advantage in buying
or selling a company's stock. The court's rather
narrow definition in the *Texas Gulf Sulphur* case
stipulated that an insider is an "officer, director or
beneficial owner of 10 percent of any class of equity
or security." This definition has never been accepted by PR people, who looked with horror at
headlines like "Press Release Goes to Court."

PRSA's interpretation of financial PR in the
Code of Ethics was adopted in 1963 and amended
in 1972 and 1977. PRSA president Tony Franco

would have been charged by the organization with violating this code in 1986, had he not resigned from PRSA. Franco pleaded *nolo contendere* (which means "no denial but no admission") to the SEC charge in the case.[30]

Insider trading means using inside information to buy or sell securities or to buy puts, calls or other options on securities. This is considered insider trading whether the action is taken in the name of the person initiating the transaction or in the name of someone else. The U.S. Supreme Court upheld lower-court insider trading convictions of former *Wall Street Journal* reporter R. Foster Winans and two co-conspirators on November 16, 1987. The SEC viewed the ruling as an affirmation of its efforts to halt insider trading, efforts that had become very aggressive in the 1980s. The Court's opinion upheld the convictions of the former reporter for securities, mail and wire fraud. The Court refused to reject the misappropriation theory, which holds that information may be misused no matter how it is obtained. (In this case, the reporter had obtained it in the course of writing his "Heard on the Street" column.) The misappropriation theory strengthens the SEC's broad interpretation of insider trading.

The SEC's interpretation is expected to cover the gray areas of the insider trading law, including informed tips received directly or indirectly from or through associates; from raiders; from overheard conversation; or from prepublication access to news stories.

Even before the ruling in the Winans case, however, the SEC had charged a PR firm with insider trading. That case involved Ronald Hengen of R. F. Hengen, Inc., a financial public relations firm hired by Puritan Fashions Corporation (which was later bought by C. K. Holdings, Inc.). Andrew Rosen, Puritan's president in 1983, had issued an earnings projection of $3.25 per share on annual sales of $300 million. The SEC said in its complaint that both Rosen and Puritan's chief financial officer knew that the projection would not be met and so did Hengen, who told a stockbroker, who told another stockbroker. The two brokers allegedly engaged in $2 million worth of trading in Puritan stock before the public announcement that the earnings and sales projections were incorrect.

In 1998, the SEC's rule on insider trading got some criticism from the courts. The Eleventh U.S. Court of Appeals ruled that in insider trading cases, the SEC must show that a corporate insider "used" material, non-public information when trading. The SEC's stance is that "knowing possession" of such information is enough. Proof of use is more difficult, and the court recognized that in saying that the SEC could make "knowing possession" a rule so this would become a standard in judging such cases.[31]

Handling Timely Disclosures and Insider Trading

One specialist in investor relations summarized the insider and timely disclosure rulings as, "Tell as few people as possible anything, and then tell everyone everything," although it's not quite that simple, of course. Curtis Anders is more specific:

1. Remember, internal corporate communications channels are not always effective, so include internal notification in the disclosure plans.

2. Since decisions must be made in advance, it is important for the PR person to have continuing access to facts, and he or she must work closely with other PR people involved (as in a merger or other type of acquisition situation, for instance). Contingency plans should be made, on the assumption that a leak will indeed occur.

3. Keep the stock exchange notified or consult it if something unexpected occurs or if an exchange ruling is not clear.

4. Notify the appropriate official in the stock exchange by telephone either before or simultaneously with the release of the information to the news media.

5. Make the announcement on the broad tape [stock exchange tape] and give the release to Dow Jones, the public relations and business news wires, national wire services and any foreign news services that might be especially interested. This is about as close as you can get to telling everyone at once.[32]

Anders offers the following advice to ensure that a company will comply with the New York Stock Exchange's *equal access policy:*

1. *Make a comprehensive survey of the totality of information regarding the corporation, then establish a clear distinction between what can and should be made freely available to the public, including the facts that must be withheld and protected by the most stringent security provisions.*

2. *Designate certain executives to act as official spokespersons and insist that all contacts with the press, security analysts, and others be channeled through them. The corporation must speak with one voice to all.*

3. *Provide systems that will keep designated spokespersons informed at all times of what can and what must not be disclosed.*

4. *Avoid all situations that will tend to create the impression that the corporation is willing to give confidential information to anyone, or that it is willing to disclose any information to some recipients that it is not equally willing to provide to others or to the public generally at the same time.*[33]

If new stock is to be issued, there is a registration period during which two types of publicity are forbidden: *any estimates* (dollars or percentages), even in broad or general terms, of *earnings* or *sales* for the industry or any product lines, and *any predictions of increases* in *sales* or *earnings from any* source.

Federal Trade Commission (FTC)

While the Securities and Exchange Commission looks out for the rights of investors, another equally alert agency, the Federal Trade Commission (FTC), looks out for the rights of both investors and consumers. On the investor side, it monitors compliance with antitrust legislation and has been very aggressive in monitoring proposed mergers that impinge on antitrust laws. On the consumer side, the FTC's scrupulous surveillance has resulted in charges of false claims relating to publicity releases as well as to advertising. As in advertising, both the client making the assertions and the PR department or firm disseminating them

are legally liable. This can fall under the previously discussed area of duty and detrimental reliance. The only protection is to take prudent precautions.

Consequently, the publicist should seek some verification for product or service claims before publicizing them. One suspicious (or cautious) publicist insists on trying a product before he writes the release. "If it works, and works well, I write a better story. If it doesn't work, I don't write it!" This is fine if the thing to be publicized is tangible, but often it is not. Services must be carefully explored, too. Some professionals, such as lawyers, have been sued for deceptive ads. Since the writer is legally responsible, some PR writers, especially those in independent firms (as opposed to corporate staff), require notarized statements from research and development staff of product attributes.

The conscientious publicist is less concerned with the action of government agencies than with consumers' wrath or loss of confidence, but he or she should still be aware that fraud or misrepresentation, as it applies to advertising, is watched over by the FTC, the local Better Business Bureau and state and local law enforcement authorities. And the PR person should certainly be aware that payola and similar illegal promotional activities are grouped by the law in the category of "bribes."

Among the promotional activities monitored by the FTC are infomercials—program-length commercials that are scripted to simulate standard entertainment or educational features. The FTC now has guidelines for infomercials. Instead of attempting to prosecute the producers of the products (miraculous aging cures) or services (making $1 million in real estate), the FTC has decided to go after the producers of the infomercials. The FTC guidelines require that the infomercial producers have "reliable, scientific evidence" before making any claims for a product's efficacy or safety. The FTC also requires disclosures that the infomercial is a paid commercial if it runs longer than fifteen minutes. These disclosures have to appear at the beginning and end of the program, as well as before any ordering information.[34]

The FTC has also made some infomercial production companies more cautious. TV Inc. of Largo, Florida, says that it will no longer create infomercials for anything that has to be ingested, whether foods or medicines.[35]

The Federal Trade Commission also has a policy that holds celebrities accountable for the statements they make in advertising. The first example of that FTC policy was a consent agreement of May 11, 1980, with singer Pat Boone. Boone was a spokesman for Acne Statin, a skin preparation manufactured by Karr Prevention Medical Products, Inc. The FTC accused Boone of making false claims that the product cured acne, that it was superior to competitive products and that some members of his family had used the product with good results. Boone agreed to contribute to any restitution the FTC might order, but he didn't deny or admit the charges.[36] Under the Reagan administration, the Federal Trade Commission became less aggressive, and Boone was even quoted as saying he would go back on the air to support the product. But while Boone had personal knowledge of this particular product, many celebrities endorse products without knowing anything about them; their only contact might be in having the product shipped free to their home or office (see Example 9.6).

Food and Drug Administration

Like the FTC, the Food and Drug Administration (FDA) is active in protecting consumers. For instance, the FDA developed guidelines for consumer advertising initiated by drug companies. The first prescription drug advertising in the fall of 1983 appeared on cable TV shows aimed at physicians, but there is no way to exclude the lay public from exposure to the same advertising.

In September 1987, Sandoz Pharmaceuticals placed twenty-five full-page ads in newspapers nationwide to call attention to its antiallergy medicine Tavist-1. The *Wall Street Journal* noted, "the Sandoz ads are the first to mention a prescription drug by name in general-interest publications."[37] The Food and Drug Administration reviewed the Sandoz ads and proclaimed them legal. The FDA requires that ads mentioning a drug by name be balanced and contain the sort of prescription infor-

mation doctors get about side effects and possible problems.

Physicians have expressed some concern that ads such as this will show only the advantages of the product. Nevertheless, the marketing, promotion and advertising of prescription drugs already has the drug companies' PR people heavily involved.

In 1991, the FDA told doctors who serve as paid agents of the drug industry that they too would be targets of FDA surveillance. At the same time a warning went out to the pharmaceutical industry to stop touting (in promotional brochures and articles) FDA *unapproved* uses for products. The FDA is developing its guidelines for what the agency considers "appropriate" promotional activities.

But the FDA doesn't just watch advertising. News releases can get you into trouble, too. Nutrasweet's fat substitute was introduced by Monsanto in 1988 at a highly publicized news conference. The company said that, because the product was made with all natural ingredients, it didn't need FDA approval. But Monsanto found out differently: the product was held up by the FDA. The lesson here is that the government agency should be included in the news release screening (preapproval) loop, because it can rule that a news release is misleading or does not give fair balance; alternatively, it can say that the product hasn't been approved, either at all or for a specific use.[38]

Federal Communications Commission (FCC)

In 1981, the Federal Communications Commission (FCC) deregulated broadcasting—an action that primarily affected its public affairs programming requirements and the fairness doctrine for television and radio. In 1987, the FCC did away with the fairness doctrine altogether, as discussed in Chapter 8.

The deregulation has made it more difficult to get public service time. And the demise of the fairness doctrine has made broadcasters more hesitant to accept issue advertising in any form, whether purchased time or public service announcements,

EXAMPLE 9.6
FTC's Policy Toward Deceptive and Unsubstantiated Claims

Advertising claims that come to the attention of the FTC staff are evaluated on the basis of the criteria contained in this protocol.

A. CONSUMER INTERPRETATIONS OF THE CLAIM

1. List the main interpretations that consumers place on the claim recommended for challenge, including those that might render the claim true/substantiated as well as those that might render the claim false/unsubstantiated.

2. Indicate which of these interpretations would be alleged to be implications of the claim for purposes of substantiation or litigation. For each interpretation so indicated, state the reasons, if any, for believing that the claim so interpreted would be false/unsubstantiated.

B. SCALE OF THE DECEPTION OR LACK OF SUBSTANTIATION

3. What is known about the relative proportions of consumers adhering to each of the interpretations listed above in response to Question 1?

4. What was the approximate advertising budget for the claim during the past year or during any other period of time that would reflect the number of consumers actually exposed to the claim? Is there more direct information on the number of consumers exposed to the claim?

C. MATERIALITY

5. If the consumers do interpret the claim in the ways that would be alleged to be implications, what reasons are there for supposing that these interpretations would influence purchase decisions?

6. During the past year, approximately how many consumers purchased the product* about which the claim was made?

7. Approximately what price did they pay?

*Throughout, "product" refers to the particular brand advertised.

8. Estimate, if possible, the proportions of consumers who would have purchased the products only at some price lower than they did pay, if at all, if they were informed that the interpretations identified in response to Question 2 were false.

9. Estimate, if possible, what the advertised product would be worth to the consumers identified by Question 8 if they knew that the product did not have the positive (or unique) attributes suggested by the claim. If the claim can cause consumers to disregard some negative attribute, such as risk to health and safety, to their possible physical or economic injury, to specify. If so, estimate, if possible, the annual number of such injuries attributable to the claim.

D. ADEQUACY OF CORRECTIVE MARKET FORCES

10. If the product to which the claim relates is a low-ticket item, can consumers ordinarily determine prior to purchase whether the claim, as interpreted, is true, or invest a small amount in purchase and then by experience with the product determine whether or not the claim is true? Does the claim relate to a credence quality, that is, a quality of the product that consumers ordinarily cannot evaluate during normal use of the product without acquiring costly information from some source other than their own evaluative faculties?

11. Is the product to which the claim relates one that a consumer would typically purchase frequently? Have product sales increased or decreased substantially since the claim was made?

12. Are there sources of information about the subject matter of the claim in addition to the claim itself? If so, are they likely to be recalled by consumers when they purchase or use the product? Are they likely to be used by consumers who are not aggressive, effective shoppers? If not, why not?

E. EFFECT ON THE FLOW OF TRUTHFUL INFORMATION

13. Will the standard of truth/substantiation that would be applied to the claim under the recommendation to initiate proceedings make it extremely difficult as a practical matter to make the type of claim? Is this result reasonable?

14. What are the consequences to consumers of an erroneous determination by the Commission that the claim is false/unsubstantiated? What are the consequences to consumers of an erroneous determination by the Commission that the claim is true/substantiated?

F. DETERRENCE

15. Is there a possibility of getting significant relief with broad product or claim coverage? What relief is possible? Why would it be significant?

16. Do the facts of the matter recommended present an opportunity to elaborate a rule of law that would be applicable to claims or advertisers other than those that would be directly challenged by the recommended action? If so, describe this rule of law as you would wish the advertising community to understand it. If this rule of law would be a significant precedent, explain why.

17. Does the claim violate [an industry] Guide or is it inconsistent with relevant principles embodied in a Guide?

18. Is the fact of a violation so evident to other industry members that, if we do not act, our credibility and deterrence might be adversely affected?

19. Is there any aspect of the advertisement—e.g., the nature of the advertiser, the product, the theme, the volume of the advertising, the memorableness of the ad, the blatancy of the violation—which indicates that an enforcement action would have substantial impact on the advertising community?

20. What, if anything, do we know about the role advertising plays (as against other promotional techniques and other sources of information) in the decision to purchase the product?

21. What is the aggregate dollar volume spent on advertising by the advertiser to be joined in the recommended action?

22. What is the aggregate volume of sales of the advertised product and of products of the same type?

G. LAW ENFORCEMENT EFFICIENCY

23. Has another agency taken action or does another agency have expertise with respect to the claim or its subject matter? Are there reasons why the Commission should defer? What is the position of this other agency? If coordination is planned, what form would it take?

24. How difficult would it be to litigate a case challenging the claim? Would the theory of the proceeding recommended place the Commission in a position of resolving issues that are better left to other modes of resolution, for instance, debate among scientists? If so, explain. Is there a substantial possibility of whole or partial summary judgment?

25. Can the problem seen in the ad be handled by way of a rule? Are the violations widespread? Should they be handled by way of a rule?

H. ADDITIONAL CONSIDERATIONS

26. What is the ratio of the advertiser's advertising expense to sales revenues? How, if at all, is this ratio relevant to the public interest in proceeding as recommended?

27. Does the claim specially affect a vulnerable group?

28. Does the advertising use deception or unfairness to offend important values or to exploit legitimate concerns of a substantial segment of the population, whether or not there is direct injury to person or pocketbook, e.g., minority hiring or environmental protection?

29. Are there additional considerations not elicited by previous questions that would affect the public interest in proceeding?

Source: Elizabeth J. Heighton and Don R. Cunningham, *Advertising in the Broadcast and Cable Media*, 2d ed. (Belmont, Calif.: Wadsworth Publishing, 1984), pp. 310–11. © 1984 Wadsworth, Inc. Reprinted by permission.

because avoidable controversies can hurt advertising revenues.

The fairness doctrine required a station to provide reply time to any person or group who thought the presentation of a controversial issue had either attacked them or not presented their point of view. Still in force is the ballot rule, which requires stations to sell time to the opposing side if they sell advertising time to one side when both are represented on an election ballot. However, many stations erroneously think they don't have to do this any longer and have refused to sell time to an opposing point of view.

Many people forget that the FCC also regulates telecommunications, including telephone and computer networks and satellite communications. The newest technology to be regulated integrates voice, data, text and video into a single global network. Integrated Services Digital Network began by expanding and digitizing existing telephone networks; then data and text services were added to voice communications, with further plans to add video capacity. By using its fiber-optic cables, AT&T (which owns the largest number of telephone lines) can transmit not only telephone calls, but also television signals and other service signals directly into the home. The interest of telephone companies in the television market continues.

In 1988, the FCC opened the way for high-definition television (HDTV). Current policy requires HDTV broadcasts to be compatible with conventional television receivers, a policy similar to the one that required color broadcasts to be compatible with black-and-white sets.

COURT RULINGS AND LEGAL RESPONSIBILITIES

Many aspects of PR are affected by court rulings and a variety of civil and criminal laws. Here we will touch on those that seem particularly important. One aspect of almost all of the legal responsibilities resulting from these is the presence of truth as a required element. Johnson & John-

son's Tylenol was the subject of a civil suit settled in May 1987.[39] Actually, what was being contested was Johnson & Johnson's slogan for the product: "You can't buy a more potent pain reliever without a prescription." The slogan was not true, said Judge William C. Conner, and he accused Johnson & Johnson of false and misleading claims in its advertising for Tylenol that exaggerated its superiority over other pain relievers. The judge reviewed all of Tylenol's ads and said the case pointed out five good lessons for consumers and advertisers:

1. Don't be fooled by headlines and pictures.
2. Beware of every word, even the smallest ones.
3. Numbers don't mean much, even the big ones.
4. Know the ingredients behind the product.
5. Repeating a slogan doesn't make it true.

Another interesting example of a company's legal responsibility comes from a 1978 case. In that year a Minnesota court ordered the Ford Motor Company to pay for repairs to a buyer's pickup truck. Ford had advertised the vehicle in a TV commercial that showed it being driven over very rough ground. When the buyer drove his truck over similar ground, he did $500 worth of damage to the cargo box. The judge ruled that Ford's advertising became an implied part of the warranty, since it led the purchaser to believe the truck could be operated as it was in the commercial. The judge did not say Ford was guilty of false advertising. However, another judge found that the makers of Listerine mouthwash were. Listerine had been advertised as a cold remedy for fifty years, but in 1978 it had to mount a $10.2 million advertising campaign publicizing the fact that the claim was not true. The advertising had to say, specifically, "Listerine will not help prevent colds or sore throats or lessen their severity."

A 1990 case involved a special event. Volvo had spent twenty-four years building a favorable image of its cars as the safest and strongest on the road. The special event was a monster truck contest in San Antonio, Texas, one aspect of which involved driving the monster trucks over several cars, including a Volvo. The other cars caved in, but the Volvo stood tall, and was hardly affected. The reason, brought to light later, was that Volvo's advertising agency, WPP Group, had had steel reinforcing pillars placed inside the Volvo and had weakened the other cars' tops with cutting torches so they would collapse.

Footage of Volvo's "successful" performance was used in commercials. When the truth became known, however, WPP Group's actions for Volvo cost them the account, Volvo suffered a serious loss of credibility, and other public relations problems resulted from this deceitful action.

Special events have also captured the attention of the Internal Revenue Service. A 1991 IRS ruling would tax, at the rate of 34 percent, donations that nonprofit organizations receive from corporate sponsors. Athletic events got the first warnings, but also liable are cultural events that enjoy corporate sponsorship. The ruling was directed at Mobil Oil Company for the Mobil Cotton Bowl and John Hancock Insurance for the John Hancock Bowl. The potential reach of the ruling rallied all nonprofit groups to seek exemptions. The repercussions of the IRS ruling are indeed broad, extending even to universities that name endowed chairs or buildings for donors.

Another area to watch is the increasing number of discrimination and bias suits being filed by both employees and customers. One of the highest profile cases was the suit filed against Texaco after internal tape recordings of conversations that denigrated African-American employees were made public. To the company's credit, Texaco Chairman Peter Bijur publicly stated that this was unacceptable behavior, and an "equality and tolerance task force" was given "extraordinary powers" to change personnel policies and practices.[40] Race issues continue to create problems in the workplace as minorities challenge discriminatory practices. In some cases, such as a suit against Circuit City, complainants are finding it more difficult to offer the kind of admissible evidence that will support their case in court.[41] In addition to the issue of race, gender continues to be a problem with some women working in very uncomfortable environments where sexual harassment is accepted behavior. Mitsubishi Motors in 1998 agreed to pay $34 million to settle claims filed by female workers who claimed that they were insulted and groped on the job. High profile cases in these areas not only cost firms financially, for fines and recompense, but also make it more difficult for them to attract qualified employees. Some actions may even inspire boycotts which keep the issue alive in the court of public opinion.

Investor relations is another area of growing importance, especially in terms of public confidence in a company. For example, ValueJet was already suffering from a decline in public confidence after a May 11, 1996, crash in the Florida Everglades when it was hit with a shareholder lawsuit alleging that it deceived investors about its operations and maintenance.[42] In the case of Fundamental Service Corp., the regulatory arm of the National Association of Securities Dealers leveled the highest fine ever for misleading mutual fund advertising. In addition to the fines, it suspended three executives held responsible for the ads which, according to NASD, "overstated the fund's stability and safety and understated its risks and potential volatility."[43]

■ Free Speech and the Organizational Voice

Whether or not you, as a PR practitioner, are involved in preparing your organization's advertising, you share responsibility for maintaining the organization's credibility. This is especially true in relation to handling the publicity resulting from any lawsuit, because it is bound to have some impact on both consumers and investors. Such situations are exactly what public relations practitioners have in mind when they argue for speaking with one organizational voice and coordinating all communication efforts.

The freedom of that organizational voice may be jeopardized by legal actions, primarily against some forms of marketing and advertising. And while all courts have long recognized that organizations, like individuals, have a "voice," some Supreme Court decisions have restricted commercial freedom of speech in ways that have threatened to muffle organizational or institutional voices.

In recent decades court rulings on commercial speech have gone up and down, some favorable, some restrictive. A positive case in 1977 distinguished between strictly commercial advertising and newsworthy advertising that served the public interest. That same year lawyers got the right to advertise, and in 1980 a New York regulation that prohibited an electric utility from advertising was struck down. Other decisions in the 1980s were not so positive. But in Puerto Rico in 1993, it was determined that magazines could be distributed from free-standing racks on public property. Also that year, broadcast lottery advertising was allowed in states that had lotteries, although it was still banned nationally and in non-lottery states. In 1995, the courts determined that brewers may not be forbidden to publish alcohol content on labels.[44] (The result, though, had ethical implications, as with the iced beer advertising discussed in Chapter 8.)

Restrictions The first major restriction on institutional voices involved the banning of tobacco advertising on television. (There are efforts now to ban the advertising of all tobacco products in all media.) The free speech counterargument is that, as long as the product is legal, producers should be permitted to advertise it. (In fact, farmers are subsidized to grow tobacco. There seems to be some inconsistency in government policy, at least.)

The same sort of ruling appeared in a 1986 Supreme Court decision upholding Puerto Rico's prohibition against advertising gambling to local citizens, even though gambling is legal in the Commonwealth (which is associated with the United States). In 1990, the Court ruled that college students who wanted to hold a Tupperware party at a campus of the State University of New York could not do so because of a university ban on such "commercial" enterprises.[45]

In 1995 lawyers were restrained from "ambulance chasing" by mail for 30 days. In that ruling, standards from the 1980s *Central Hudson Gas & Electric Corp v. Public Service Commission* were applied. Basically, these are: the speech must be accurate and not misleading; the government must establish a substantial interest in regulating the speech; the regulation must advance the government's interest; and the regulation must be narrowly written so as not to trample unnecessarily on other rights.[46]

The early 1990s saw a flurry of legal action against artists and arts organizations—much of it centered on the National Endowment for the Arts, which had funded some exhibits and artists that provoked controversy over obscenity. The NEA was not the only focus for challenges to First Amendment rights. The rap group "2 Live Crew" was arrested while performing, and some record and tape store owners were arrested for selling the group's recordings, in both cases because the lyrics were alleged to be obscene. The eventual legal decisions in all of these most recent cases came out in favor of free speech, but the controversy is not over.

Observers see a threat to individual freedom in another case, involving a suit by the Attorney Registration and Disciplinary Commission of Illinois against a lawyer who listed his certification by a trial lawyers' group on his stationery. The American Advertising Federation filed a brief in court supporting the lawyer, saying that the certification mention doesn't constitute advertising, and even if it did, the restriction is far too broad. In any case, the federation urged, restrictions can't validly be placed on speech unless the speech is misleading.[47]

Contempt of Court Contempt may occur when you comment on a case that is pending before a court in such a way that it can be construed as an attempt to influence a jury or prospective jurors. When a case is in its pretrial stages, you should avoid putting your argument in advertising or publicity. A company with its case in court can't take it to the public by issuing releases or buying ads explaining its position. It can't send out a mailing if the judge has ordered that no public comment be made on the trial. If the news media's coverage of a trial erodes public confidence and hurts the company, it still can't respond. Failure to comply may result in a contempt citation. Even issue advertising can cause problems. Aetna Insurance's ads about damage suits running up the cost of insurance created problems subsequently in choosing a jury that had not been "exposed."

Just how much advertising can influence juries is the issue, and research findings are on the side of those who say it does. (Recall the Chapter 8 discussion of Dow's argument for First Amendment freedom in the silicone breast implant case.) But even if influence can be shown, does this necessarily impair the plaintiff's right to a fair and impartial hearing? Judges have not always agreed. In Maryland, a state court sided with Keene Corp., which bought a full page newspaper ad on the eve of a big asbestos trial criticizing the litigation as "lawyer-inspired." That judge said careful instructions to the jury would avoid any ill effect on the proceedings. A Los Angeles judge, on the other hand, ordered Northrop Corp. to stop running ads promoting its quality controls in making fighter jets the week before the company was to stand trial on criminal fraud charges that it falsified test data on jet parts.[48]

Many companies, nevertheless, see the need to launch defensive action in the face of the litigation journalism/public relations mounted by plaintiffs. In one case, Sony mounted a campaign to counter adverse publicity stemming from its sale of blank videocassettes, which consumers might use to create "pirated" versions of prerecorded tapes. However, this campaign didn't begin until the case was on appeal. A lobbying effort to change the copyright law was going on at the same time Sony was arguing that current law permitted its videotapes to be made, sold and used by the public. The Supreme Court upheld Sony's position. However, the fight to change the copyright law's treatment of videotapes continues.

Publicizing Political Views State laws cannot prevent firms from publicizing (or advertising) their position on political issues that materially affect their property, business or assets. In 1978 the Supreme Court found unconstitutional a Massachusetts state law that prohibited companies from making contributions to support a political viewpoint.[49] Thus, on referendum issues, corporations, like individuals, have the right to convey information of public interest, whether or not the issue directly affects the company.

The Supreme Court has not ruled on whether corporations can support candidates. However,

since corporate campaign contributions are illegal in most states, corporations have developed political action committees (PACs), which can gather funds and do have some impact. Recently, controversy has arisen over the power of these groups, and future regulations may limit their current freedom.

In 1988, the Supreme Court ruled unconstitutional a District of Columbia code provision that had made it unlawful to display within 500 feet of any foreign embassy any sign that would bring a foreign government into "public odium or public disrepute." It also found unconstitutional a lower-court ruling that protesters could not congregate within 500 feet of a foreign embassy. The ruling came after the Soviet embassy had been picketed with signs saying "Release Sakharov" (the physicist and human rights activist), and after a group outside the Nicaraguan embassy had carried signs that said, "Stop the Killing."

In another case of free speech, *Hustler* [magazine] v. *Falwell*, the Supreme Court ruled that, as a public figure, Jerry Falwell could not recover damages from an ad that was an obvious parody. The court ruled that public figures are not entitled to recover even for emotional distress unless the publication contains a false statement of fact made with actual malice.

■ Individual Practitioners' Responsibilities

Public relations practitioners must register with the U.S. government when they represent a foreign government or act as a lobbyist, and they are personally legally liable for the accuracy of statements they write for advertising and publicity—regardless of who directed them to write the material. They are also responsible for material and information they provide as a news source.

Registering Political Activity Public relations practitioners representing foreign governments must be registered with the U.S. government as foreign agents. (When the Justice Department took the PR man for the French-made Concorde SST to court for failing to register, he responded by putting a "foreign agent" identification on his Christmas cards.)[50]

Lobbyists functioning at all levels of government usually have to be registered, although laws vary. For example, New York City requires registration of anyone who attempts to influence city legislation or is responsible for "articles or editorials designed or intended to influence directly or indirectly any municipal legislation."[51] On the federal level, lobbying activities consist of (1) payment to a legislative agent of $500 or more in a given calendar quarter to lobby; (2) making twelve or more oral lobbying communications per quarter through paid officers, directors or employees with senators or representatives from districts other than those in which the principal place of business is located; (3) reporting all lobbying expenditures, including loans, of $10 or more.

Product Liability and Publicity and Advertising

Calling consumers' attention to a product that later harms them raises liability concerns among public relations writers and advertising copywriters who handle publicity. Many writers now ask for certification of product reliability before writing news releases and ad copy, as assurance that the product will perform as claimed and will not cause harm. Agency managers and in-house managers who were previously reluctant to ask for such protection for their ad and publicity copywriters might reconsider now that many media are doing so. Media have been characterized as "conduits" for harmful product or service information in judicial proceedings, and they don't like the idea of facing expensive lawsuits.[52]

■ Complying with Consumer Rights

People have sought legal means to obtain information that will help them make rational decisions about their lives.

Freedom of Information Act The FOIA brings much government-held information within the reach of the news media and the public in general, including reams of data provided by corporate executives to meet the regulatory requirements of various government agencies, commissions and bureaus. The public relations corporate staff officers should know what information is filed with these various government offices, to anticipate any that might cause problems if released under an FOIA request.[53]

Corporate lawyers will advise you about what confidential material is protected under the law, but generally the only types of information exempted from disclosure under the FOIA are trade secrets (narrowly defined) and confidential, commercial or financial data obtained from outside government. Competitive disadvantage is a legitimate argument for protecting confidentiality, but it must be proved; the mere possibility of harm to a competitive position is not adequate. Some portions of otherwise protected material still may have to be released if, after critical portions are eliminated, the basic confidentiality is protected. Another way to justify confidentiality is to show that release of the information will make it difficult for the government to get the same type of information in the future.

Right to Know Many states have enacted "right to know" laws patterned on the Freedom of Information Act. These make information available to the public regarding the presence of hazardous substances in the environment or other social threats. Some of the information becoming available under such laws is being released as a result of court rulings in favor of company management against regulatory agencies such as the Occupational Safety and Health Administration (OSHA).

Open-meeting Laws PR people need to be aware of which of their organization's meetings must be announced and open to the public. "Sunshine laws" require that almost all government meetings, except those dealing with personnel matters, be open. Very unfavorable publicity can result from violations.

In many states, it is impermissible to say only "personnel matters" or "closed" on the notice of a meeting. The matters to be discussed must be specifically listed on the agenda, even though that part of the meeting may be closed. Federal law requires that governmental bodies keep a tape recording of any executive session that is closed to the public. However, anyone who makes that tape recording or a portion of it public is subject to civil and criminal penalties. (Guides to different states' access laws are often published in *Quill*, the magazine of the Society for Professional Journalists.)

In their role as a news source, PR people often respond to calls from media representatives or initiate calls to share information that may or may not be about their client(s) or organization. If their statements are false or misleading, they may find themselves involved in litigation—even if confidentiality has been promised by the media.

■ Copyright Laws

Copyright laws protect a creative work, both in form and in style, from publication in any manner.[54] Before quoting from copyrighted works, you must ask for permission. There are some exceptions to this general rule, however.

If artistic efforts (writings, art, graphics, photos or other creative work) are done on company time by an employee using company resources, the material belongs to the organization (the person's salary constitutes his or her compensation). In some cases, an organization will make an arrangement for one-time use and permit the artist to earn extra money by subsequently selling the work elsewhere. However, the artist can only sell work done on company time when a prior agreement exists between employer and employee.

If the organization wants to use other work by the employee that is not a part of his or her regular duties or that doesn't qualify as "work made for hire," permission must be obtained. An example would be a piece of art produced by an employee privately and on his or her own time that is to be used on a company Christmas card.

When work is purchased from an outside person (as supplier), there can be confusion later unless an agreement is drawn up. Most PR people either buy file rights or one-time rights (which are

nonexclusive). But even then you should make sure there is a written agreement when the work is ordered (see Examples 9.7 and 9.8).

A Supreme Court decision issued in 1989 said that written agreements between a freelancer and the commissioner of the work are valid only if the work fits under one or more of nine definitions found in the law: work created within the scope of employment; collective work (ads); part of an audiovisual work; a translation; a supplementary work; a compilation; instructional text; a test or answers to a test; or an atlas.

The transfer of ownership of the copyright is defined as an assignment—a transfer of exclusive license to reproduce the work, to prepare a derivative from it, to distribute copies by sale, rent, lease, loan or transfer of ownership, and to perform or display the work in public. A written assignment has to be filed with the Library of Congress, just like copyrights the originator would file.

Extent of Protection Copyrights cover written and recorded (audiovisual and photographic) work, and are an intangible property right that begins when an original work is created. Copyright protects the specific expression of the idea. A person who wishes to copyright an original work must use the copyright symbol (©) on a substantial number of copies that are publicly distributed. In addition, two copies must be sent within three months of publication or recording to the Copyright Office of the Library of Congress, with a request for an application for registration for copyright. The fee can be as low as $11, but it varies with the size of the work being copyrighted. The copyright owner has exclusive rights of reproduction, adaptation, distribution, performance and display. Copyrights that were secured prior to January 1, 1978, are protected for twenty-eight years and may be renewed during the twenty-eighth year for an additional forty-seven years.[55] Copyrights secured after January 1, 1978, are good for fifty years after the author's death. Company publication copyrights are good for seventy-five years from the year of first publication or for one hundred years from the year of its creation if it is never published.

EXAMPLE 9.7

Sample Copyright Authorization Form

COPYRIGHT AUTHORIZATION

Date: _____

A. Name of work (property): _____

B. Use (brief description of use: e.g., annual report, press kit, feature story, speech, presentation):
_____
_____

C. Ownership of copyright (check as appropriate):

☐ 1. We (user of form) own, because it is

    ☐ Work-for-hire because it was made by our own employee(s).
       Name of employee: _____

    ☐ Work-for-hire because:
       (i) It is a commissioned work, and there is a writing signed by the creator to that
          effect.
          Date agreement signed: _____
          Name of creator: _____
                           - and -

       (ii) The work is one of the following:

☐ a contribution to collective work	☐ a supplementary work	☐ a test
☐ a part of audio-visual work	☐ a compilation	☐ answers to a test
	☐ instructional text	☐ an atlas
		☐ a translation

☐ 2. We do not own, but we can use because:

    ☐ We have assignment of all copyright rights by written transfer, signed by copyright owner,
       that has been recorded with Register of Copyright in U.S. Library of Congress.
       Date of assignment: _____
       Name of creator: _____

    ☐ We have one or more of the following five exclusive licenses:
       ☐ 1. to reproduce (make copies)
       ☐ 2. to prepare a derivative work (sequel or prequel)
       ☐ 3. to distribute (sell) copies
       ☐ 4. to publicly perform
       ☐ 5. to publicly display
       Date of signing license: _____
       Name of copyright owner: _____

    ☐ We have the following nonexclusive license in writing and signed by copyright owner
       (briefly describe nonexclusive right; e.g., the use of photo as cover of annual report, use
       of statistical table in annual report):
       _____
       _____

    ☐ We have purchase order, unsigned by copyright owner, but received by copyright owner
       and containing the nonexclusive license thereon and paid pursuant thereto:
       Name and date of purchase order: _____
       Date of payment of purchase order and check number: _____
       Nonexclusive license (describe): _____
       _____

Source: Reprinted with permission of the Institute for Public Relations Research and Education.

EXAMPLE 9.8

Letter of Agreement

This letter will confirm agreement between _____

(contributor)

and _____ regarding the contribution of

(author)

_____

(photographs or problems or artwork, etc.)

to the work titled _____

by _____

(author)

in return for _____

(acknowledgment in the preface, money, etc.)

The material described above has been specially ordered, requested, or commissioned for use as a contribution to an instructional work or as a supplementary work, and the undersigned parties agree that the material so described will be considered a work made for hire and the property of _____

_____

(author)

Please sign, date and return all copies of this letter to _____

_____

(author)

_____   _____

Contributor's Signature   Author's Signature

_____   _____

Date   Date

Source: Used with permission of Wadsworth Publishing Company.

When copyrights expire, the works they covered enter the "public domain" and become available to all for any of the previously restricted purposes.

In 1983–1984, news media contended that videotapes of news broadcasts constitute a copyright infringement. Some companies regularly supply clips of television exposure to clients, and other PR people capture their own. Implicated in the same issue was the legality of home videotaping with videocassette recorders (VCRs). The issue was resolved in 1984 when the Supreme Court ruled that Sony was not directly contributing to copyright infringement by making and selling VCRs, since VCRs have substantial noninfringement uses.[56]

Copying or "copycatting" is a common problem in advertising; but because *ideas* cannot be copyrighted, there is seldom a legal case in this area. The form that ideas take, not the ideas themselves, is entitled to copyright. However, a 1989 Supreme Court decision enables advertisers to copyright individual ads separately from the copyright that covers the publication in which they appear. If an advertiser brings a previously composed ad to a newspaper for publication, the advertiser owns the copyright unless there is an explicit agreement to the contrary. However, if the staff of the newspaper or magazine prepares the ad, the periodical owns the ad and can copyright it. Such an ad can't be published elsewhere without permission from (and compensation to) the publication that created it. Of course, for the copyright to be enforceable, the published ad must carry a copyright notice.

Fair Use Violation of any copyright is an infringement, but one defense against infringement is fair use.[57] This includes use of one or more parts of the work in criticism, comment, news reporting, teaching, scholarship or research. Many publishers filed suit against Kinko's Copies because of copyright violations in preparing "textbooks to order" for professors. Most Kinko's outlets are now extremely cautious about checking copyrights and asking professors to get permission, in writing, from the copyright holders before they will copy such materials.

Although the application of laws to the Internet is uncertain at best, copyright holders have been vigilant in surfing to discover infringements. The Internet poses a different kind of threat to copyright holders because it can disperse an endless number of free copies of all sorts of material from software to songs and everything in between. "To lose control over the material can be death," said Eileen Kent of Playboy Enterprises, which found students posting its photos on the Internet using their university accounts. Some companies like Sony Music Entertainment send notices to fans who use Sony images on their Web pages, and give them licenses to use the images as long as they don't change the images in any way.[58]

To reduce confusion about copyright on the Internet, there has been a push for changes in copyright law that would define digital transmission as a form of publication, and that would allow an electronic encoding of copyrighted material that would alert copyright holders when it is being used.

Public relations people might be tempted to send published information to people they think need to see it as attached documents in e-mail. This could be a violation. Texaco, for example, found itself in court because it had been copying articles from scientific and technical journals to use in the collection of research data. The legal case centered on one researcher who had made single photocopies of eight complete articles from a research journal in the Texaco library and put these copies in his personal files. Texaco had paid for three subscriptions to this journal at the institutional subscription rate. Texaco claimed this was fair use. The Court disagreed, ruling that the researcher made the copies for commercial reasons, to improve profitability, and cited the number of articles copied, each in its entirety. The Court also found that the plaintiff, the Copyright Clearance Center, had lost revenue under its photocopy licensing system, so it accepted the publishers' argument that they had suffered substantial harm.[59]

Abuse of copyright should not be confused with plagiarism. Plagiarism is the use and passing along as one's own original work someone else's created material which may or may not be copyrighted. A student taking term papers off the Internet and submitting them as personally created work is plagiarizing, but may or may not be violating an established copyright. A nonprofit group trying to publish a cookbook of recipes from performers who had appeared at its theater found an abundance of situations of plagiary, some of which were also copyright violations. The same discovery was made by writer Anne Fadiman, who noted that, "The more I've read about plagiarism, the more I've come to think that literature is one big recycling bin." Of course, the frequency of plagiary, even in established literary works, does not make it legitimate.[60]

Since so much public relations work is farmed out to freelancers, public relations freelancers should realize that they don't own works they were paid to produce. This includes work produced by employees within the scope of employment and work commissioned for use as a part of a collective work, if the parties agree that it is work "for hire."[61]

Copyright infringement applies also to music, which explains why more and more songs for everything from sales meetings to commercials are being written "for hire." Unless music is in the public domain, it may not be used. Even if the music itself is not copyrighted, the words may be. With regard to music, copyright infringement means using music, words or both—or similar-sounding versions—without express permission. And although permission may have been given to use the composition and the words, an additional copyright may exist on the specific arrangement or version of the composition. If you want to use a recording, you may have to pay for performance rights. You can't just choose music you like and use it. Furthermore, if you are determined to use a particular piece, be prepared for long negotiations for clearance and sometimes very costly permission fees, especially if you are going to broadcast it. The term *broadcast* has its own definition, which does not necessarily include using mass media. For example, sponsors of any form of public dancing in an entertainment establishment that uses records instead of live music have to pay the copyright holders a fee, and musicians who perform have to pay to use the compositions they perform in public or for recordings.

Nonprofit organizations can usually obtain permission to use music in a public relations campaign either free of charge or by paying a small fee. However, they still have to get permission.[62]

Fair use means occasions when copyrighted material can be used without permission. The nature of the copyrighted work and the proportion of the work used always have been important; thus, quoting a single verse of a long poem or a few lines from a song constitutes acceptable fair use, but reproducing most of the poem or song does not. Use for nonprofit purposes generally has been permitted. However, the accessibility of copy machines and the ability to "publish" electronically by putting something (words or art) into electronic computer networks (usually through bulletin boards) have generated more restrictive interpretations. One major key in recent interpretations of the law is the effect of use of the copyrighted material on the market value of the original. Another is use for commercial purposes, now defined not just as making money but as profiting through "appropriating" someone else's creative effort.

In the fall of 1994, the federal government issued a draft report updating the law on intellectual property. Motion picture, software, songwriters' and publishing groups supported the draft, while electronic computer services such as CompuServe and other commercial on-line services opposed it because it holds them responsible for what some subscribers might put on line.[63] One proposal to counteract this would hold the electronic services accountable for a copyright violation on their system only after they have been notified of it.

Confusions: Patents and Trademarks Patents are often confused with copyrights. *Patents* are government grants that offer protection for inventions and novelties; *trademarks* are distinctive, recognizable symbols (word, design or a combination of the two) protected from infringement, previous claim or use without permission. In this sense, trademarks are like a company's brand name or identification (logo). To use a patent or trademark, you must check with the government registry and ask the owners for permission to use. The Patent Office of the U.S. Department of Commerce administers laws dealing with patents and trademarks.

Is a trademark infringement really an infringement if you can't see it? Maybe, if it's on the Web. Web masters have been implanting trademarks in their sites with invisible coding so that visitors to the site don't see the trademark, but it is identified by search engines which then guide the unknowing Web user to the site. The first court ruling on this occurred in 1997 when a San Francisco federal judge ordered invisible coding of Playboy magazine to be removed from two adult-oriented Web pages. The suit was filed by Playboy Enterprises when it was discovered that the two sites were located by search engines whenever they looked for "Playboy" or "Playmate." This may turn out to be more than trademark infringement. Other cases suggest it may involve unfair trade practices in that it is considered unfair to pass on someone else's business as your own.[64]

■ Defamation: Libel and Slander

There are two kinds of libel: civil and criminal. Libel (written or otherwise published defamation) was originally confined to statements made in the print media, but it now applies to statements made in the broadcast media as well. The courts have interpreted libel as a more serious offense than slander (spoken defamation).

Civil Libel *Civil libel* is defined as tortious (that is, noncriminal) defamation of character by malicious publication tending to blacken the reputation of a living person so as to expose him or her to public hatred, contempt or ridicule. It also means injuring the person in his or her trade or profession. Use of "alleged" or other subtle qualifications offers no protection. Civil libel law encompasses all forms of defamatory communication about a person's character, including headlines, tag lines and all art work (photographs, cartoons and caricatures). It also applies to errors that may result in libel, such as incorrect initials or the wrong name with the

wrong photo. If the defamation occurs in an accurately quoted statement that contains a libelous statement, the person or medium publishing the statement may still be held responsible.

In libel cases involving public officials and public figures, "actual malice" must be proved. But don't count on plaintiffs' being held to that standard of proof. Definitions of all three designations—*libel, malice* and *public figures*—remain subject to individual interpretation in the courts.

Publication in libel suits is defined as dissemination of more than one copy. Consequently, office memos, letters, telegrams and broadcasting scripts are all subject to libel laws, just as newspapers, newsletters and brochures are. Anyone who takes part in the procurement, composition and publication of libelous material shares responsibility for the libel, although the original publisher is not responsible for subsequent publications by others. Even persons who bring the matter to the attention of anyone connected with possible publication are subject to being sued for libel (see Example 9.9 for a guide to determining what is libel). Copying and distributing a libelous piece can result in additional action against the person or persons responsible in the organization.

Slander is spoken defamation. It does not always apply to broadcast defamations, however, because multiple copies of a script may have been produced; thus, even though the copy is eventually spoken, the offending scripts constitute publication and are therefore libelous, not slanderous.

Criminal Libel *Criminal libel*—breach of peace or treason—involves inciting to riot or some other form of violence against the government or publishing an obscenity or blasphemy. Charges of criminal libel are rarely pressed, and one writer suggests that such a prosecution might be unconstitutional.[65]

Defense Against Libel Charges There are three traditional defenses against charges of libel:

1. *Truth:* substantial proof that is admissible in court.

EXAMPLE 9.9

A Guide to Libel

Is it Libel? Libel is the culpable (careless or knowing)
publication of false information damaging to a person's reputation.

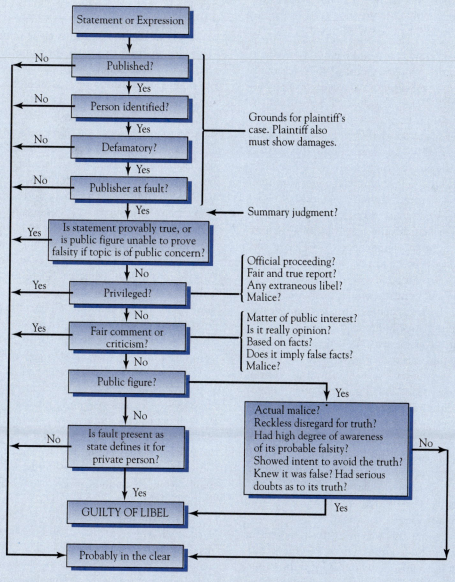

Source: Albert Skaggs and Cleve Mathews, "Is This Libelous? Simple Chart Helps Student Get
Answer," *Journalism Educator* (Autumn 1982), pp. 16–18. Revised chart (1992) reprinted with
permission of Cleve Mathews.

2. *Privilege:* a fair and true report of a public, official or judicial proceeding.

3. *Fair Comment:* statements made in an honest (albeit erroneous) belief that they are true; also, statements with some element of exaggeration or irony in them that nonetheless do not overstep the bounds of reasonable civility; however, it is up to the jury to decide the issue of "fairness."

A constitutional protection, if not a defense, is provided by the Supreme Court's 1964 decision in *New York Times* v. *Sullivan,*[66] which involved publication by the *Times* of a political advertisement that made various (false) allegations about a sheriff. The newspaper evidently did not attempt to verify the substance of these allegations prior to publishing the ad. The Supreme Court's opinion in the case held that a public official must prove malice in a libel suit, rather than some form of negligence. The trial court decides the question of "malice," but basically it involves an intent to harm. The primary significance of the *New York Times* v. *Sullivan* case lies in its implication that the Supreme Court may look at libel judgments to make sure that constitutionally guaranteed freedoms have not been denied. In addition, because the defamatory statements in the case were contained in an advertisement, the court's decision signaled that the standard of proof it was imposing applied to commercial speech as well as to noncommercial speech. Finally, the Supreme Court said it was limiting the power of all states to award libel damages for statements about public officials. In the court's opinion, *actual malice* was defined as either knowledge that the libelous statement was false or a reckless disregard for whether it was true or false. Thus, what the writer thinks about the truth or falsity of the statement becomes a central question in assessing its actionability.

A subsequent case extended this requirement to "public figures" other than government officials—that is, to anyone who has put him- or herself in the public arena, such as a United Fund chairperson. However, in a 1974 decision,[67] the Supreme Court held that information conveyed by the press that falsely maligns a person—such as by leveling unprovable accusations—is still subject to a jury determination of negligence, regardless of the public figure's status or voluntary involvement. What this means to PR people is that careless overstatements in a news release can be costly.

A Duluth, Minnesota, state court ruling, if reinstated by the U.S. Supreme Court, could make it even more costly. The case involved a public figure about whom all the statements made in the *Duluth News-Tribune* were true, but the plaintiff claimed that he had been defamed by implication—that is, by a false impression. The Minnesota Supreme Court overturned the lower state court's ruling in May of 1990. In February 1991, the U.S. Supreme Court declined to hear the case.[68]

The U.S. Supreme Court has ruled that public figures must prove statements false, defamatory and published with knowledge that they were false or with reckless disregard for their truth or falseness.

Private figures in most states must prove negligence to recover actual damages; and all plaintiffs, whether private or public figures, must prove reckless disregard for the truth or calculated falsehood to recover punitive damages. Since releases typically go into more than one state, you have to assume that a private plaintiff will only need to prove negligence to recover actual damages. However, the writer of the release might be in one of a few states that imposes a higher standard of proof.

The standard itself is interpreted differently in some states. Some use the "prudent person" standard, while others use the "prudent publisher" (which applies the standard of care set by the media).[69] One defense to an action filed by a private individual is that if the person has read and approved an article about himself or herself before its publication, he or she cannot later claim to have been libeled.

Another limit to libel charges is the *statute of limitations,* which provides that a person cannot be sued after a certain period of time has elapsed. (States have varying periods of from one to five years.) In the past, if the defamed person died, the suit would often be dropped, on the theory that the dead could not be harmed by false reports. But more courts are now accepting libel suits (and slander suits) on behalf of the dead, reasoning that their name or reputation could be defamed even if they themselves could not be materially injured.[70]

Fair comment has been interpreted in the past to apply to opinion pieces such as editorials, commentaries and reviews of all kinds. A 1990 Supreme Court decision rejected the idea of a distinction between fact and opinion, ruling that statements of opinion can be libelous if they contain false facts.

A 1994 case tested that ruling. The case involved a review of Dan E. Moldea's book about football called *Interference*. When it was panned by a *New York Times* reviewer who said that it involved "sloppy journalism" and contained "unfounded insinuations," Moldea demanded a correction or at least publication of a letter to the editor from him. When the newspaper refused, he sued. A federal district court judge in Washington, D.C., threw the case out; but a federal appellate court reinstated it, saying that criticism isn't protected from libel suits.

According to a *Wall Street Journal* article on the situation, people in the news media are unhappy at the prospect that a new area of libel litigation may open up, and book publishers are afraid that newspapers will simply get rid of book review sections.[71] Many public relations repercussions are involved, and these not limited to book reviews—especially if all opinion pieces with factual errors are found to be actionable.

Three rather spectacular cases in the 1990s put some different twists on suits against the media. In 1995, beleaguered by what appeared to it to be war against the tobacco industry, Philip Morris sued ABC for its "Day One" television magazine story that claimed cigarettes were "spiked" with nicotine to make users addicts. The very aggressive response by Philip Morris resulted in an apology by ABC, because the process of taking out nicotine, combining it with alcohol, and then putting it back in for flavoring could not be accurately characterized as "spiking." Philip Morris ran full-page ads touting the apology in 700 publications.[72]

Another widely-touted media apology followed an NBC "Dateline" story that showed footage of a General Motors pickup exploding in flames after a side-impact collision. Painstaking research on the part of GM proved the footage to have been rigged by attaching toy rockets to the fuel tank creating an explosion that would not otherwise have occurred. GM won the libel lawsuit. NBC apologized, paid GM's legal bills and fired three "Dateline" producers.[73]

A third case might have been a libel case, but wasn't, and that's what makes it interesting. ABC's "20/20" news magazine had employed undercover investigative techniques to report improper handling of food by Food Lion. In response, Food Lion accused ABC not of libel but of civil fraud because the two field producers who went undercover as employees had lied on their job applications. Food Lion also accused the two of breach of duty and of loyalty that employees owe employers, and trespass for getting into the supermarket under false pretenses. Without a libel suit, Food Lion couldn't ask for compensation for damages to its reputation. Food Lion did win a $5.5 million jury award, but that was overturned by a federal district judge who ruled that the award was out of proportion to the actual harm done on the basis of the suit. To collect the larger damages to reputation, Food Lion would have had to sue for libel under the Times v. Sullivan rule and prove the story false. The grocer never tried to do that.[74]

Because of the freedom of the Internet, gossip columnist Matt Drudge had been getting by with much more than traditional media could hope to until he libeled Sidney and Jacqueline Jordan Blumenthal. The couple filed a $30 million defamation lawsuit when Drudge reported an untruth: that White House recruit Sidney Blumenthal had a spousal abuse past that had been covered up. The Blumenthals were public figures. Drudge made no pretense to check the truthfulness of his material and he was a known detractor of President Bill Clinton. Within 24 hours Drudge apologized and took the item off his Web site. But what about America On Line which carried the column on their service? Is AOL a common carrier like a phone company? If so, it has no responsibility. Is it a publisher? The Blumenthals think it is. It might even be argued that AOL is an employer since it pays Drudge and promotes his site.[75] The new medium is making new rules.

The Internet is also enabling traditional media to evade some rules. Many news media are putting "hot" stories, for which all of the verification is not quite there, on their Web sites before using them on the air or printing them. Many media declare that they do this to "protect the free flow of information." They are afraid to risk a court injunction that would restrain them from using the information. Such was the case when the *Dallas Morning News* chose to publish the purported confession of Timothy McVeigh, later convicted in the Oklahoma City bombing. Other newspapers noted that this was an interesting use of the newspaper's Web site and that in the future, a U.S. medium might even bypass a judge's order by passing the story off to a foreign counterpart who could post the story on the Internet.[76] Many laws will change as a result of the Internet, including that governing privacy.

◼ Right of Privacy

The right of privacy applies only to people, not to organizations. Violations of it take four forms: (1) intrusion into solitude; (2) portraying someone in a false light (making the person appear to be someone or something he or she isn't); (3) public disclosure of private information; (4) appropriation (using a person's name or likeness for commercial purposes without the person's consent).[77] Unlike the other three, appropriation does not have to breach decency or cause mental anguish or ridicule. It is the privacy violation that causes most PR problems. Model and photo releases are usually obtained in order to avoid these problems.

A picture, letter or name of a living person cannot be used in advertising or publicity without his or her consent. For instance, a cereal company once used an artist's representation of a woman that showed her pregnant. Because the real woman was neither pregnant nor married, she sued.

Photos taken at an event for publicity purposes may later be used innocently or ignorantly in a brochure about the event. The photo might even be used in an ad, perhaps because it just happens to be available. Using such photos in an ad can lead to legal problems. Furthermore, even in a publicity situation, people may not be aware that their picture is being taken and for any number of reasons may not wish to have their photograph used.

Most attorneys for public relations people advise that releases should always be obtained. In most states, consent is the best defense; typically, newsworthiness is a more difficult rationale to defend. For example, employee pictures and names can be used internally; but if distribution is external, newsworthiness is lost as a legal defense. Even photos for internal use must be germane to the job—for example, giving information about promotions—or an employee who has not given consent may sue for invasion of privacy. Furthermore, use of an employee's name or image must end when the person leaves the organization's employment (refer to Example 9.8).

Employees must be treated both as employees and as private individuals who should not be forced to pose for annual report pictures if they don't want to. The company doesn't have the right to use their photos without permission. Furthermore, if they leave the organization and have not signed a permission form for the use of their picture, using it anyway can create a serious legal problem.

In one privacy suit, a photo became part of the product. A photograph of a prominent Chicago-area nun, Sister Candida Lund, chancellor of Rosary College in River Forest, showed her in nun's attire and seated in a chair. The photograph appeared on a greeting card produced by California Dreamers, Inc., of Chicago. The words above the photo, which does not identify Lund, say, "It's all right if you kiss me." Inside the card are the words, "So long as you don't get in the habit." The Dominican nun does not know where the card company got the photo, which certainly was used without her permission. She charged that the card demeaned her morals, violated her exclusive property rights (by using the picture without permission) and embarrassed her and the college. Apparently Rosary College alumni had seen the card in gift shops from Alaska to Texas.[78]

The courts have upheld the use of celebrity look-alikes under the First Amendment privilege, as long as it is clear that the real celebrity is not involved. A "false light" invasion of privacy suit in 1986 was ruled to state a claim similar to a suit for libel. The particular case (*Eastwood* v. *Cascade Broadcasting et al.* in the Washington State Supreme Court) was subject to the two-year statute of limitations for filing on libel.

The availability of information on line has created serious concerns about privacy. America On Line permits users to have aliases when using their service, but when faced with a subpoena, they will comply by supplying names and information about subscribers. Critics maintain that while a criminal subpoena leaves no recourse but to respond, civil subpoenas should be resisted. AOL says it notifies subscribers when court requests are pending so they may fight it if they wish. And while subscribers' names may not be protected, AOL says their e-mail is.[79]

Another Internet privacy issue arose over a database of personal information operated by Lexis-Nexis called P-TRAK. The database is used by the legal community to find litigants, heirs and others involved in a case. Some have claimed that it gives more information than just name, address and phone number, that it also gives social security numbers. That was originally intended to be part of the service, but was disabled shortly after P-TRAK was put in place due to complaints. It is still possible, though, to dial in a social security number and see to whom it belongs. In response to criticism, Lexis-Nexis does permit people to have their names removed from the database.[80]

■ Contracts and Consents

A PR practitioner need not get involved in a lot of permission forms and contracts, but he or she ought to know about at least five such forms: the model release, the employee contract, the photo agreement, the work for hire (usually writing) and the printing contract.

Major elements of a consent release (see Example 9.10) are identified by Frank Walsh as *written consent of all parties* (employer, employee and parent of employee if a minor); *consideration* (something of value exchanged, like $1); *scope of the use defined* (as photo used in brochure only); *duration* (a set time period, not forever); *words binding* (heirs also have to be considered after death of person giving consent); and *no other consideration* involved (such as some sort of inducement or promise).[81]

Contracts with celebrities should spell out exactly what the celebrity is to do and what aspect of the public personality will be used. The following considerations are significant:

1. Is endorsement for the client by the public personality a factor?

2. Does the public personality expect to be paid for the use of his or her name?

3. Are the public relations activities on behalf of the client proprietary?

4. Are there any relevant contractual provisions?[82]

Model Release Serious legal problems can arise from failure to get a person's permission before using his or her photograph or other likeness in publicity or advertising. The photographer should always have the model sign a photo release form. Pads of model releases are available in most photo or stationery stores. If pictures of minors are used, the permission of parents or guardians must also be obtained. The contract shown in Example 9.11 was used by a photographer taking pictures of a group of youngsters. Notice that the permission for use extends to publicity for the organization only. This guarantees that the pictures will not be used to endorse a product or to further any other unspecified purpose.

Employee Contract A client has a right to expect loyalty and confidentiality from a practitioner. Some large PR firms have their employees sign a restricture covenant—and that means everyone, from the account executive to the file clerk (see

EXAMPLE 9.10
Model Consent Release

EXCHANGE OF VALUE	In consideration of the sum of _____ dollar(s), the receipt I hereby acknowledge, I certify I am
PROPER PARTIES	twenty-one years of age and hereby give [organization's name], its successors and assigns and those acting under its
	permission or upon its authority, the unqualified right and
SCOPE	permission to reproduce, copyright, publish, circulate or
	otherwise use photographic reproductions or likenesses of me
	and/or my name. This authorization and release covers the
	use of said material in any published form, and any medium of
DURATION	advertising, publicity or trade in any part of the world for a
	period of ten years. Furthermore, for the consideration above
WORDS BINDING	mentioned, I, for myself, my heirs, executors, administrators
ON PERSONAL	or assigns, transfer to the organization, its successors and
REPRESENTATIVES	assigns, all my rights, title and interests in and to all repro-
	ductions taken of me by representatives of the organization.
	This agreement represents in full all terms and considerations
NO OTHER	and no other inducements, statements or promises have been
INDUCEMENTS,	made to me.
STATEMENTS	
OR PROMISES	
PROPER PARTIES	

_____   _____

(Signature)   (date)   (Signature-organization)   (date)

NOTE: Consent is written, but does *not include* any reference to minors or agents; nor is it a part of a broader agreement.

Source: Used with permission of Frank Walsh.

Example 9.12). Ted Baron, president of a New York firm, recommended this "because they have access to insider information and documents, some of which your clients' competition or others would love to get hold of."[83] What are the penalties for breaking a covenant? Any sort of punishment management decrees—even firing, if the breach injures a big client or causes the company to lose clients unnecessarily. A covenant is a moral commitment as well as a psychological one (for, of course, you are less likely to do something if you publicly say you won't).

Employers need to be especially careful with insider information, since "tippers" as well as "traders" are penalized for using any material nonpublic information.

EXAMPLE 9.11
Photo Release for a Minor

I _____ parent/guardian of _____
        (Signature)   (Name of minor)

do hereby grant permission for all photographs taken of _____
                                                (Name of minor)

during _____
             (Time schedule, which included on-site location)

may be used by _____
                 (Name of organization)

for either publicity or advertising for _____
                              (Name of organization)

Photo Agreement This is a contract between a PR practitioner or firm and a freelance photographer who is being hired to work on an assignment (see Example 9.13). Make sure that your agreement with the photographer spells out the limits of use for photographs. (Charges are usually higher when the photos will be used in ads than when they will be used in publicity.) You may want to use the photo more than one time or in different ways. Some photographers are willing to specify future use in one agreement. Many require one agreement per use. Remember that copyright protection begins for the photographer when the film is exposed. This will affect the agreement you draw up.

Work for Hire Occasionally a public relations practitioner in an organization (profit or nonprofit) or in a firm will hire a writer or artist for a specific job. It's common for a writer to be hired to handle an annual report, for example. The "work for hire" letter of agreement sets the terms of the employment arrangement (see Example 9.14).[84]

Printing Contract In making a printing agreement, remember that no two situations are exactly

alike, so the suggestions that follow will not always be appropriate. However, they may help you develop your own contract or agreement. In addition to the contract, you will need to furnish the printer with specifications identifying how you want the publication to look. The following suggestions are often relevant for making a printing agreement:

1. *Dummy* a typical issue of the publication, showing the number of columns, widths of columns, number of pages and estimated ratio of advertising to editorial matter (if you intend to have advertising). Ask the printer for a quote on the price for a fixed number of copies of a certain number of pages. Ask for the price per hundred for additional copies. You also need to know how much it will cost to add pages or additional color.

2. *Deadlines* for the publication must be reasonable for you and for the printer. You might vary deadlines for certain pages in a large publication like a magazine, especially if the pages have color or a great deal of statistical matter (such as charts or graphs). But make sure the deadline for the final product, as in delivery date and time, is firm.

EXAMPLE 9.12

Employee Covenant

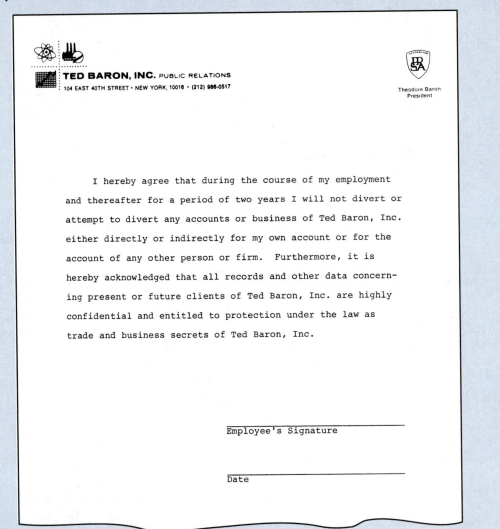

TED BARON, INC. PUBLIC RELATIONS
104 EAST 40TH STREET · NEW YORK, 10016 · (212) 986-0517

Theodore Baron
President

I hereby agree that during the course of my employment and thereafter for a period of two years I will not divert or attempt to divert any accounts or business of Ted Baron, Inc. either directly or indirectly for my own account or for the account of any other person or firm. Furthermore, it is hereby acknowledged that all records and other data concerning present or future clients of Ted Baron, Inc. are highly confidential and entitled to protection under the law as trade and business secrets of Ted Baron, Inc.

_____
Employee's Signature

_____
Date

Source: Reproduced courtesy of Ted Baron, Inc.

3. *Corrections* can be costly. The printer must agree to furnish galley proofs on all copy and advertising. Usually there is an extra charge for making corrections on page proofs.

4. *Makeup* troubles are often the reason for corrections. Make sure you provide the printer with legible dummys, correctly marked, and with copy you've checked for accuracy.

EXAMPLE 9.13

Photo Agreement

PHOTOGRAPHIC AGREEMENT FORM

This form will constitute our agreement with you for the services which you will render as a photographer for (Name) Corporation ("Company"). The specific terms and conditions under which you will render such services are as follows:

1. You will act as an independent contractor and will not be an employee of the Company.

2. Your duties will include photographic assignments for the _____ [corporate divisions] in _____ [countries]. You will perform your photographic assignments under the direct supervision of the Director of Public Relations of the Company or his appointed representative.

3. For each day that you render your photographic services to the Company as set forth above, the Company will pay to you the sum of _____ for your services, plus all reasonable food, lodging, and traveling expenses incurred by you in the performance of your assignment. Upon return from the countries set forth above, you will prepare and submit an expense report and the Company will reimburse you for such expenses. The Company also will pay the cost of all film and shall pay all photograph developing charges incurred by you in the performance of your assignments hereunder.

*4. All photographs taken by you in the performance of your assignments hereunder shall be and remain the property of the Company, including prints and negatives. In addition, the Company shall have the right to use all photographs taken by you in the performance of this agreement in any manner whatsoever, without limitations or restriction.

5. This agreement will become effective on _____ [date] and shall remain effective until you have completed your photographic assignments for the _____ [corporate divisions]. This agreement may be terminated by either party at any time upon notice to the other party. Termination of this agreement shall in no way affect the terms and conditions set forth in paragraph 4 above.

If the above terms and conditions are acceptable to you, please execute the enclosed copy in the space provided and return that copy to me.

(Name) CORPORATION

By _____
Director of Public Relations

Accepted this _____ day of _____

*This may not be agreed to by the photographer, who will want to retain copyright.

Source: From *Public Relations Manual*, Eaton Corporation. Reprinted by permission.

EXAMPLE 9.14
Work-for-Hire Form

Wadsworth Publishing Company

FREELANCE LETTER OF AGREEMENT

This letter will confirm the Agreement made _____, 19_____

between _____, the

"Illustrator," and WADSWORTH PUBLISHING COMPANY, the "Publisher," for the work entitled

_____

_____ by _____.

The Publisher agrees to pay the Illustrator _____

_____.

The Illustrator agrees that this compensation will be complete payment for all services the
Illustrator performs, that any material the Illustrator submits is assigned to and will become the
property of the Publisher, and that the Publisher will have the sole and exclusive right to
reproduce and publish the material in this or any other work, to make alterations or corrections
to the material, or to use the material for any purpose whatsoever. The Publisher also retains
the right to assign its interest, property, and liabilities under this Agreement.

Nothing in this Agreement will be construed to effect an employee-employer relationship. It is
understood that the Illustrator is an independent contractor. While the Illustrator will control
the means and methods of production, the Publisher will be the sole judge of the acceptability of
the material submitted by the Illustrator.

The Illustrator should sign and date this Letter of Agreement, add his or her social security
number, and return all copies of this Letter of Agreement to the Design Department, Wadsworth
Publishing Company, 10 Davis Drive, Belmont, CA 94002. A copy of this Letter of Agreement
will be returned to the Illustrator after a representative of Wadsworth Publishing has signed it.

_____   _____

Illustrator's Signature   Wadsworth Publishing Company

_____   _____

Social Security Number   Date

_____

Date

Source: Used with permission of Wadsworth Publishing Company.

5. *Paper* is sometimes a problem. You and the printer must agree on the type and quality of stock you will use, and you should insist on a guarantee of continuity of supply (and price, if possible).

6. *Art* charges are usually specific. Get a list of art charges from the printer, and go over with the printer the types of art you are likely to use. Keep the information sheet on charges for reference in planning individual issues.

7. *Printing technique* is a basic decision and usually a primary one, since few printers can handle both rotogravure and offset. In deciding on a printing technique, consider the quality of the job. If you have color covers, for example, with delicate shades, all the covers will not look alike when printed unless you pay extra for special handling— that is, for cleaning the press periodically to maintain color consistency. Don't put yourself in the position of demanding, after the fact, something you didn't arrange (and pay) for in the contract.

PR Services and Taxes

In some states, services such as home repair and maintenance are not subject to sales taxes. Although Florida repealed its controversial sales tax on advertising when revenues began to plummet and boycotts were invoked, service industries are growing in an economy that is no longer heavily industrial. As tax bases are sought, efforts surely will be made to tax the service sector, including professional services such as those offered by accountants, lawyers and advertising and public relations practitioners. Watch for state laws in this respect and, of course, the laws of other countries if you do business abroad.

Working Across Borders

Communication technologies often make working across borders appear to be seamless, but it's far from that, especially where the law is concerned. For example, while bribes are tax deductible in some countries, the USA has for years been virtually alone among major economies in making the paying of bribes illegal.[85] The USA has been working to level the playing field, and finally members of the top industrialized nations, through the Organization for Economic Cooperation and Development, have agreed to criminalize bribery by companies of foreign officials. They resolved to adopt this agreement as national law in each country, but that takes time.[86] Additionally, some customs die a very slow death, even in the face of new laws.

Economic rules also are different from country to country, and although we talk of global markets, these really belong to countries. The decision of Glaxo Welcome PLC to merge with Smith Kline Beecham PLC came after Glaxo had been talking about merging with American Home Products Corp. However, under London Stock Exchange rules, if a company's share price moves "significantly" on a true rumor, the company must make a decision. There's some speculation that this is what forged the merger and left American Home out of the deal.[87] Knowing a country's investment and banking rules is critical in doing business abroad.

Working abroad also means understanding how that nation's law enforcement agencies deal with terrorists. In the USA, the FBI strongly urges no cooperation with terrorists; in Russia, a USA systems analyst said if you don't pay off these criminals, you get blown up.[88] In some countries, kidnapping is so routine that it's almost like a criminal collection agency.

Laws affecting advertising are different too. Many companies ignore copyrights in countries where these are not usually enforced. Such a slip caused Procter & Gamble to sue Colgate-Palmolive in 1996 over toothpaste advertising in China. P&G says the Colgate ad using a seashell to illustrate the benefits of floride is the same ad that P&G used in 1989 only the shell was an egg shell. The suit was filed in New York, and both companies are USA-based, but usually the opponent or copycat of the copyrighted ad is from another country where the laws are different.[89] Knowing the law might have kept Philip Morris out of trouble in France where the company launched ads that claimed passive exposure to cigarette smoke is no more a health threat than drinking milk or eating cookies. The case was brought by a cookie manufacturer. The judge's decision pleased the French anti-smoking lobby.[90]

You will be concerned mostly with laws in the country where your public relations operation is based. The laws in this chapter have dealt almost exclusively with the legal structure in the USA. When you are working in other countries, you must know the government and media systems well, and how the legal system relates to them. In many nations, the government owns and operates the media.

You'll need resident legal counsel if you are working in other countries. If you are doing only some of your work abroad, you can get reliable information at U.S. missions to those countries, especially the consulates. The U.S. Chamber of Commerce can be helpful, too, as can the State Department and the Department of Commerce. You can use many other resources to help stay out of legal trouble, such as affiliating with a resident PR firm or working with resident professional public relations associations. There also are books and current business journals to help keep you informed.

The important thing to remember is not to assume that a government that seems similar to the one you are familiar with has laws that are the same or even close. Assumptions can get you into serious legal difficulties.

REVISITING THE HYPOTHETICALS

To close this chapter, let's try to answer the questions posed at the beginning of the chapter. Although the Internet is still relatively free from the imposition of laws, one that does seem to be working in that environment is the copyright law. Since it's the library that is using "cyber cadet," a nonprofit, what you might want to do first is write a letter calling the infringement to the library's attention and ask for change. Otherwise you look like the corporate heavy threatening the poor little library.

The issue of drawing up a strategy to respond to another company's product is something you need to write with the idea that it may be made public at any time. Running it by the in-house attorney is not likely to make it qualify as privileged unless there's a substantial amount of legal advice that comes back to you based on what you suggested. Just having the attorney take a look does not make it safe under client/attorney privilege.

Regarding the school buses, it's probably not a good idea to repeat in the school's newsletter information from the manufacturer touting the buses' safety and the vans' adaptability without obtaining verification of that information from one or more independent testing agencies. This is because you will be held legally responsible for checking out such claims before passing them on. Ignorance is no excuse for transmitting misleading information on which others may rely.

No, you can't write a publicity release that downplays the organization's financial crisis—unless, that is, you don't mind going to jail. You, individually, are responsible, regardless of who told you to do it. Moreover, it is not unthinkable that the person who approached you might, when faced with a lawsuit, deny having done so. Where does that leave you?

How you handle the question of the "copycat" logo depends on whether you registered your logo as a *trademark*. If you did, you can protect it better than you could if you had only copyrighted it. If you did nothing, you can count on a good logo's being copied. If you didn't do anything and you see something similar in the *Wall Street Journal* that might confuse people, you might have a case anyway. But if a significant difference exists—say, the organization is in another field of business altogether—you don't have much of a chance.

With regard to the infomercial that you've been asked to script, you can't make it appear so much like a program that the audience is likely to be misled. The inclusion of quasi "commercial breaks" within a larger commercial presentation is not approved by the Federal Trade Commission. Again, you'd better check to make sure that the product/service being promoted in the infomercial can do all the things you are being asked to say it can do in the script. Remember, the writer and the producer are the ones risking jail time, not the people who are offering the product/service for sale. Get a notarized statement from the marketer specifying what the product/service claims; and check with an attorney experienced in dealing with the FTC to see what your potential liability might be.

In the next hypothetical situation, if your lawyer client wants to include her certification on her letterhead, it could be interpreted as "advertising." Announcing a specialty is widely approved in medicine, but not in law, even though it is approved in some states. In fact, in some states you will find attorneys listed by state board certification of specialization in the telephone book's business section (yellow pages).

The photo you are thinking about using in the special section for the outdoor sports event may not be usable, because most news photographers don't get model releases when they take pictures. But they do get names and addresses—or they are supposed to. If you know the models' names and addresses, you can use the photo if you obtain their permission in the form of a signed release. Another reason to be careful about using such photos, even if you already have a release, is that one of the persons pictured might have died in the intervening period. You don't want to cause distress to the family by using the photo. When you have your own photographer shooting pictures during a special event, give the photographer a package of release forms to have the models fill out as the pictures are taken. This solves a lot of questions about use, and it helps with identifications, too.

The question from human resources about pictures of employees in the last magazine should always be answerable with a "Yes, there is a model release on file." In this instance, you could be in trouble since there isn't one. You should always get model releases when you take employee pictures, because you don't know how you might use the picture later, and you don't know how long each employee photographed will be with you. If you have a publication in production, and a person whose picture you've taken leaves the company, it

could cost a great deal to change the picture. In this case, since the magazine picture amounts to publicity, not advertising, you probably don't have a serious problem. But in situations like this one, a quick call to the organization's attorney is in order—to let the attorney know of a possible problem and to check the risk.

POINTS TO REMEMBER

■ The litigious climate in which public relations practitioners work means that any case, civil or criminal, can draw media attention.

■ Normal involvement with law for PR people falls into three general areas: normal legal exposure that any business might have, work-oriented exposure (or something peculiar to the client or organization's business) and extraneous legal exposure (such as testifying as an expert witness).

■ Legal involvement for public relations has increased due to out-sourcing, which generates much more contract work for which the organization is held responsible.

■ Public relations has its functional roots in commercial speech, advertising, traditional speech and the press, and most of its freedom would not be available if some First Amendment guarantees had not been found to apply to commercial speech.

■ Civil suits involving PR people most likely have to do with their communication activities, physical activities such as events, and interactions with government regulatory agencies.

■ PR practitioners are more likely than the average citizen to get involved in criminal conspiracy charges, such as for bribery, price fixing, mail fraud, securities manipulation and perjury.

■ Four kinds of cases are likely to typify a PR person's legal involvement: the big case that can threaten the organization's existence, the human interest case that will capture media attention, the routine case that grows out of contract disputes and such and the case in which the PR person testifies as an expert witness.

■ Litigation journalism means that many trial lawyers and prosecutors are trying their cases in the court of public opinion as well as in the court of law, with or without public relations counsel.

■ Increasing attention is being turned to the obligation for clear and accurate communications and the ability to depend on keeping confidences.

■ PR people need to work closely with lawyers and seek out those experienced in communications law for advice.

■ PR conversations with legal counsel may not fall under the attorney/client security that keeps them from being made public, and simply having an attorney review documents without specifically getting legal advice also provides no protection from having them made public.

■ Watch danger zones and take individual responsibility because you personally are legally liable.

■ One of the most difficult legal issues is the whistle blower suit because the PR response can never be anything but reactive.

■ The key government regulatory bodies that PR practitioners are usually involved with, in addition to those specifically regulating the client's or organization's business, are the U.S. Postal Service, the Securities and Exchange Commission, the Federal Trade Commission, the Food and Drug Administration, the Federal Communications Commission and the Internal Revenue Service.

■ Recipients of mail can refuse to receive unsolicited mailings, that is materials sent using mailing lists, and they can file with the postal service if they have received obscene or sex-related materials in the mail.

■ Publicly held companies must comply with requirements about disclosure of their business operations as designated by the Securities and Exchange Commission.

■ If public relations people have knowledge of the publicly held company's business, they are considered "insiders" and may not trade on information that has not been made publicly available.

■ The Federal Trade Commission watches very closely claims for products that are made in advertising and publicity, and these must be supported by verification. Again, the PR person who prepared the copy is legally liable, as is the company.

■ The Food and Drug Administration's job is to protect consumers. It monitors advertising, news releases, brochures and labels for material that could be deceptive. The FDA watches for any claims or even indications that a product is FDA-approved, when it isn't; or if it is approved for one use, they'll watch for claims about other uses.

■ The FCC regulates broadcasting and telecommunications, including telephone and computer networks and satellite communications.

■ The major defense for legal difficulties is provable truth.

■ Another area to watch are discrimination and bias suits filed by both employees and customers. High profile cases can do a good bit of damage to a company's reputation, not to mention costly fines.

■ Investor relations is another area of increasing importance, and this is where class action suits or action by regulatory bodies can be very damaging.

■ Court rulings on commercial speech have gone up and down, and while most recent cases are in favor of expanded commercial speech, there are important restrictions. Organizations don't have the broader constitutional freedom the First Amendment gives individuals.

■ Case law on organizational freedom of speech is not clear, but any organization attempting to influence the outcome of a trial is likely to be cited for contempt of court by the judge, probably at the suggestion of the opposition—a special problem for organizations involved in litigation journalism.

■ Influencing juries—although it may bring contempt charges or cause other difficulties at trial—is exactly what some companies think needs to happen because litigation journalism/public relations on the part of the plaintiffs has portrayed them in such an unfair light.

■ Organizations or groups of people are not restrained from expressing political views, although the role of PACs is being reconsidered.

■ As individuals, PR people are responsible for registering their own activities as lobbyists and for vouching for the truthfulness of whatever they present in publicity or advertising.

■ PR people also have to be sensitive to other consumer rights such as access to information through state and federal freedom of information acts and open-meeting laws.

■ Areas of special legal vulnerability for PR people are defamation, invasion of privacy and misuse of copyrighted materials.

■ The organization a PR practitioner works for should protect its own materials through copyrighting, and it must take particular care not to violate the copyrights of others (which is now easier to do because of electronic transmission of messages).

■ The Internet has created some confusion about the absolute protection of copyrights and trademarks, but most companies are pursing these infringements aggressively.

■ "Invisible" trademark use on the Internet is also an infringement.

■ Copyright infringement and plagiarism are not the same thing. The uncopyrighted work of another can be passed off as one's own, and that is plagiarism.

■ Saying or writing anything that could injure the reputation of another is especially risky, even if that person is a "public figure"; and individual rights of privacy must be considered in all publicity and advertising.

■ The Internet has been a place of free-flowing information, but individuals are increasingly pursing libel claims for material on the Internet.

■ Contracts and releases protect both the organization and those it works with, including employees, from legal wrangles over ownership of creations and rights of privacy.

■ Working across borders means understanding all the laws that govern the business you are involved in outside of your homeland. Disobeying another nation's laws can have serious consequences.

■ Although many international laws are being forged, such as agreements about criminalizing bribery and not dealing with terrorists, this is really up to individual nations to put in place and customs are slow to change even after the law does.

■ The most important protection for the PR practitioner consists of recognizing the danger signals and working with competent legal counsel to get through dangerous or potentially dangerous situations.

NOTES

[1] Morton J. Simon, speech to North Texas Chapter of the Public Relations Society of America, Dallas, Texas, August 29, 1978.

[2] Marian Huttenstine, "New Roles, New Problems, New Concerns, New Law," *Southern Public Relations Journal* 1(1) (Spring 1993), p. 5.

[3] Ibid.

[4] Morton J. Simon, *Public Relations Law* (New York: Appleton-Century-Crofts, 1969), pp. 16–17. Also see Joseph F. McSorley, *A Portable Guide to Federal Conspiracy Law: Developing Strategies for Criminal and Civil Cases* (Washington, D.C.: The American Bar Association, 1996).

[5] Edward Felsenthal, "Justices Rule People Fined by U.S. Also Can Be Criminally Prosecuted," *Wall Street Journal* (December 11, 1997), p. B14.

[6] Simon, 1969, pp. 16–17.

[7] Carole Gorney, introductory remarks, Symposium on Litigation Journalism, Austin O. Furst, Jr., Series at Lehigh University, Bethlehem, Pennsylvania, May 5, 1994.

[8] Jaxon VanDerbeken, "A Lawyer's Media, Simpson's Attorney Follows Own Strategy in Manipulating News Coverage," *Fort Worth Star-Telegram* (June 26, 1994), p. A6.

[9] Huttenstine, "New Roles," p. 5.

[10] Ibid., pp. 5–7.

[11] Ibid., pp. 7–8.

[12] Ibid., p. 8.

[13] Ibid., p. 10.

[14] Morton J. Simon, speech to North Texas PRSA.

[15] David H. Simon, "Lawyer and Public Relations Counselor: Teamwork or Turmoil?" *American Bar Journal*, 63 (August 1977), pp. 1113–16.

[16] "PR Communications Not Privileged, Can End Up in Court," *pr reporter* (July 21, 1997), pp. 1, 2.

[17] Morton Simon, *Public Relations Law*, pp. 16–17.

[18] "The ABCs of Dealing with Whistle-Blower Suits," *tips and tactics* of *pr reporter* (May 27, 1996), pp. 1, 2.

[19] *Rowan v. Post Office Department*, 397 U.S. 728 (1970), appeal of U.S. District Court for Central District of California, January 22, 1970, decided May 4, 1970.

[20] Two major cases are *SEC v. Texas Gulf Sulphur*, 344 F Supp. 1983 (1972), and *Financial Industrial Fund v. McDonnell Douglas*, 474 F. 2d 514 (1973).

[21] *SEC v. Texas Gulf Sulphur*, 344 F. Supp. 1983 (1972).

[22] Richard S. Seltzer, "The SEC Strikes Again," *Public Relations Journal*, 28(4) (April 1972), p. 22.

[23] John Ruhnka and John W. Bagsby, "Disclosure: Damned If You Do, Damned If You Don't," *Harvard Business Review*, 64 (September/October 1986), pp. 34–40.

[24] *SEC v. Pig 'N' Whistle Corp.*, 359 F. Supp. 219 (1973).

[25] Ibid.

[26] *SEC v. Pig 'N' Whistle*, CCH Fed. Sec. L. Rep. (1972), pp. 34–38, 42–43.

[27] For additional information, see Bryon Burrough, "SEC Bid for Full Merger Disclosure Begs Question: What Is Disclosure?" *Wall Street Journal* (August 12, 1978), p. 17.

[28] Alan J. Berkeley, "Stand by for Change: The Future of Investor Relations: Ripeness and the Disclosure of Significant Corporate Events," speech to Texas Public Relations Association, Houston, Texas, August 1987.

[29] See *Greenfield v. Heublein*, 742 F. 2d 751 (1984), a decision that did not settle the matter of whether boards of directors have to approve agreements in principle prior to the announcement. The failure to settle caused a class action lawsuit in 1985 over the RCA–GE merger. Compare *Levinson v. Basic, Inc.*, 786 F. 2d 741 (1986), where the court ruled that meetings occurring over a couple of months (during which time the company issued releases insisting it didn't know why trading was heavy) on a possible merger *were* material and should have been disclosed. The current Supreme Court rule is that materiality depends on the *probability* that the transaction under consideration will be consummated. (99 L. Ed. 2d 220)

[30] Frank Walsh, "Public Relations Firm Charged with Insider Trading," *Public Relations Journal*, 42(5) (May 1986), p. 10.

[31] Paul Beckett, "Lack of SEC Rules Irks Appeals Courts," *Wall Street Journal* (April 14, 1998), p. B11.

[32] Curtis L. Anders, "The New Guidelines for Corporate Information," *Public Relations Journal*, 25(1) (January 1969), p. 14.

[33] Ibid.

[34] Joanne Lipman, "FTC Zaps Misleading Infomercials," *Wall Street Journal* (June 19, 1980), pp. B1, B6.

[35] Ibid.

[36] *Facts on File* (September 15, 1978), p. 22.

[37] Michael Waldholz, "Prescription-Drug Maker's Ad Stirs debate over Marketing to Public," *Wall Street Journal* (September 22, 1987), p. 39.

[38] Joe and Losana Boyd, "Prescriptions for Preapproval," *Public Relations Journal*, 44(4) (April 1988), p. 14.

[39] William Power, "A Judge Prescribes a Dose of Truth to Ease the Pain of Analgesic Ads," *Wall Street Journal* (May 13, 1987), p. 31.

[40] Peter Fritsch, Allanna Sullivan and Rochelle Sharpe, "Texaco to Pay $176.1 Million in Bias Suit," *Wall Street Journal* (November 18, 1996), pp. A3, 6.

[41] Evan Ramstad and Louise Lee, "Race Issues Create Divide in Corporate Cultures: Circuit City Suit Shows Problems in Proving Bias," *Wall Street Journal* (November 18, 1996) pp. B1, 7.

[42] "ValueJet Holders File Suit Alleging Carrier Deceived Investors," *Wall Street Journal* (June 25, 1996), p. B7.

[43] Charles Gasparino with contributions from Deborah Lohse, "NASD Fines Firm, 2 Executives in Case of Misleading Ads," *Wall Street Journal* (February 20, 1996), p. B9.

[44] Sandy Davidson, "Supreme Court Strengthens Commercial Speech Protection, Media Law Notes," newsletter of the Association for Education in Journalism and Mass Communication, 23(3), (Spring, 1996), p. 10.

[45] Joanne Lipman, "Court Case Fans Firms' Worries About Commercial Free Speech," *Wall Street Journal* (September 12, 1989), p. B6.

[46] Rosalind C. Truitt, "The Cases for Commercial Speech," *Presstime* (March 1996), pp. 29–31.

[47] Ibid. For a good discussion of the issue, see Catherine A. Pratt, "First Amendment Protection for Public Relations Expression: The Applicability and Limitation of the Commercial and Corporate Speech Models," in Larissa A. and James E. Grunig, eds., *Public Relations Research Annual*, vol. 2 (Hillsdale, N.J.: Lawrence Erlbaum Associates, 1990), pp. 205–17.

[48] Richard B. Schmitt, "Can Corporate Advertising Sway Juries?" *Wall Street Journal* (March 3, 1997), B1, 3.

[49] *First National Bank of Boston v. Bellotti*, 435 U.S. 765. Supreme Court ruling, Attorney General of Massachusetts is No. 76-1172, argued Nov. 9, 1977, decided April 26, 1978.

[50] "Washington Wire," *Wall Street Journal* (January 2, 1976), p. 1.

[51] *Public Relations Society of America National Newsletter* (April 1974), p. 4.

[52] George E. Stevens, "Newspaper Tort Liability for Harmful Advertising," *Newspaper Research Journal,* 8(1) (Fall 1986), pp. 37–41.

[53] Advice and policy guidance on FOIA is available through the Executive Branch's Office of Information and Privacy. The FOIA Counselor service can respond to inquiries at (202) 514-FOIA. Additionally, the Justice Department can make available a list of all the principal FOIA administrative and legal contacts at all federal agencies that deal with FOIA matters.

[54] For a monograph on the implications of the interpretation of copyright law for public relations, see Harold William Suckenik, "Copyright Rights Just Changed Forever—Do You Know What You're Buying and Why?" from the Institute for Public Relations Research and Education, University of Florida, POB 118400, Gainesville, FL 32611-8400, email iprrc@grove.ufl.edu. The American Society of Journalists and Authors' Code of Ethics and Fair Practices has a position on work for hire and on model agreement. Society's address: 150 Broadway, Suite 302, New York, NY 10036.

[55] Write the U.S. Government Printing Office for copies of the copyright law that went into effect January 1, 1978, and for interpretations of the new applications. See also Kent R. Middleton, "Copyright and the Journalist: New Powers for the Freelancer," *Journalism Quarterly,* 56(1) (Spring 1979), pp. 38–42. Information on the World Wide Web is a mix of copyrighted work and work that is in the public domain. Just because it is available on the Web doesn't mean it can be used. For some assistance in checking on copyright restrictions, see the list of Web sites with information that appears in the *Instructor's Guide* for this text.

[56] *Sony Corporation of America et al v. Universal City Studios,* U.S. Law Week 52 LW 4090. Supreme Court case No. 81-1687 was argued Jan. 18, 1983, and was decided Jan. 17, 1984.

[57] *Harper & Row Publishers, Inc., v. National Enterprises,* 105. Supreme Court case No. 83-1632 was argued Nov. 6, 1984, and was decided May 20, 1985.

[58] Ross Kerber, "Vigilant Copyright Holders Patrol the Internet," *Wall Street Journal* (December 13, 1995), pp. B1, 5.

[59] Nicole B. Casarez, "Penny-Wise, Pound-Foolish: What Public Relations Professionals Must Know About Photocopying and Fair Use," *Public Relations Quarterly* 42(3) (Fall, 1997), pp. 43–47.

[60] Anne Fadiman, "Nothing New Under the Sun," *Civilization* (February/March 1997), pp. 86–87.

[61] Marshall Leaffer, "An Overview of Copyright Law for Journalists and Other Media Artists," speech to Association for Education in Journalism and Mass Communication, San Antonio, Texas, August 1987.

[62] Ibid.

[63] Junda Woo, "Government Paper on Copyrights in Cyberspace Vexes Some Firms," *Wall Street Journal* (September 2, 1994), p. B3.

[64] Ann Davis, "'Invisible' Trademarks on the Web Raise Novel Issue of Infringement," *Wall Street Journal* (September 15, 1997), p. B12.

[65] Robert Sack, *Libel, Slander and Related Problems* (New York: Practising Law Institute, 1980). The new edition of this volume is Robert D. Sack and Sandra S. Baron, *Libel, Slander and Related Problems* (New York: Practising Law Institute, 1994).

[66] *New York Times v. Sullivan*, 376 U.S. 254 (1964).

[67] *Gertz v. Robert Welch Inc.*, 418 U.S. 323 (1974).

[68] Amy Dockser Marcus, "'False Impressions' Can Spur Libel Suits," *Wall Street Journal* (May 15, 1990), p. B1. This case is Diesen v. Hessburg, SCM 455 N.W. 2d. 446. U.S. Supreme Court citation for this case is SCUS 498 U.S. 1119, Feb. 25, 1991.

[69] Susan Caudill, "Choosing the Standard of Care in Private Individual Defamation Cases," *Journalism Quarterly,* 66(7) (Summer 1989), pp. 396–434.

[70] Kyu Ho Youm, "Survivability of Defamation as a Tort," *Journalism Quarterly,* 66(3), pp. 646–52.

[71] Paul M. Barrett, "Author Who Sued over Scornful Review Is Now Scorned by the Publishing World," *Wall Street Journal* (April 17, 1994), pp. B1, B2.

[72] Alex M. Freedman and Amy Stevens, "Philip Morris is Putting TV Journalism on Trial in Its Suit Against ABC," *Wall Street Journal* (May 23, 1995), pp. A1, 14.

[73] Paul Holmes, "An Extension of Public Relations by Other Means," *Reputation Management* (March/April 1996), pp. 10–17.

[74] Scott Andron, "Scratched Car Saves ABC," *Quill* (September 1997), pp. 14–15.

[75] Linton Weeks, "Testing the Legal Limits of Cyberspace," *Washington Post National Weekly Edition* (September 8, 1997), p. 29.

[76] Evan Ramstad, "Putting News on Internet First Seen as Protective," *Wall Street Journal* (March 5, 1997), p. B8.

[77] Sondra J. Byrnes, "Privacy vs. Publicity," *Public Relations Journal,* 43(9) (September 1987), pp. 46–49.

[78] "Nun Not Laughing at Greeting Card," *Fort Worth Star-Telegram* (August 12, 1985), p. 7A.

[79] Constance Johnson, "Anonymity On-Line? It Depends Who's Asking," *Wall Street Journal* (November 24, 1995), pp. B1, 10.

[80] Thomas E. Weber, "New Lexis Database of Names Sparks Outcry on Privacy," *Wall Street Journal* (September 19, 1996), p. B2.

[81] Frank Walsh, "Elements of a Consent Release," *Public Relations Journal* (November 1983), p. 8.

[82] David M. Coronna, "The Right of Publicity," *Public Relations Journal* (February 1983), pp. 29–31.

[83] Ted Baron, "Legal Protection for the PR Agency," *Public Relations Journal* (September 1971), p. 33.

[84] For additional examples of model releases as well as copyright and trademark registration forms, see Roy L. Moore, Ronald T. Farrar and Erik L. Collins, *Advertising and Public Relations Law* (Mahwah, New Jersey: Lawrence Erlbaum, 1998).

[85] Dana Milbank and Marcus W. Brauchli "How U.S. Concerns Compete in Countries Where Bribes Flourish," *Wall Street Journal* (September 19, 1995), pp. A1, 14.

[86] Neil King, Jr., "Bribery Ban is Approved by OECD," *Wall Street Journal* (November 24, 1997), pp. A14.

[87] Steven Lipin and Sara Calian, "Did U.K's Strict Rules Spur Deal?" *Wall Street Journal* (February 2, 1998), pp. C1, 16.

[88] Patrick M. Reilly and Joann S. Lublin, "Should Businesses Negotiate with Terrorists?" *Wall Street Journal* (September 20, 1995), pp. B1, 5.

[89] Raju Narisetti, "Where's a Good Place to Put Toothpaste? On Seashells or Eggs?" *Wall Street Journal* (December 5, 1996), p. B5.

[90] Matthew Rose, "French Court Blocks Philip Morris Ads that Liken Passive Smoke to Cookies," *Wall Street Journal* (June 27, 1996), p. B3.

Selected readings, activities and assignments appropriate to this chapter can be found in the *Instructor's Guide* or on InfoTrac if you are using the InfoTrac College Edition.

CHAPTER 10

PROBLEM-SOLVING STRATEGIES: THE MANAGEMENT OF PR WORK

Don't just sell yourself and your ideas; sell the concepts of public relations as a top management function—then prove that it works.

JOHN W. FELTON, RETIRED VICE-PRESIDENT FOR CORPORATE COMMUNICATIONS, MCCORMICK & COMPANY, INC., NOW PRESIDENT OF THE INSTITUTE FOR PUBLIC RELATIONS AND LECTURER AT THE UNIVERSITY OF FLORIDA

Gone are the days of women succeeding by learning to play men's games. Instead the time has come for men on the move to learn to play women's games.

TOM PETERS, MANAGEMENT CONSULTANT

Strategic management applies to public relations in two important ways. The first is the public relations department's role as part of the management team in developing problem-solving strategies for the entire organization. The second has to do with the public relations department's own efforts to integrate and coordinate its work with that of the organization.

PR'S ROLE IN OVERALL ORGANIZATIONAL PLANNING

Any organization's public relations efforts exist to support the overall mission of the organization. For that reason, any public relations department's development of an annual plan, either for the organization or for the PR department, has to start with the organization's mission statement or organizational purpose. The way it develops from there often depends on the nature of the organization, but the elements of the public relations plan remain the same.

One role of the public relations department is to assist with the evaluation of an organization's mission. This may include revising and rewriting or perhaps conceptualizing and writing a mission statement. In any case it must be done as part of PR's policy-making role as counsel to management.

Mission, Descriptive and Identifying Statements

Most organizations develop their mission statement early in their existence; but at least once every five years, the statement deserves a careful and systematic review by internal and special external publics. While calling for a mission statement review is the prerogative of top management, the PR department is responsible for organizing and planning the review. One outcome of mission statement review is likely to be a rewritten or modified statement. Even if the mission statement is kept intact, internal publics and critical external publics must agree on this outcome of the review. The mission statement review is generally followed by a review of the long range objectives by which the organization intends to implement the mission.

Mission statements set the tone for the organization, establish its character and define the parameters of its activities. They may be long, philosophical commentaries on the nature of the enterprise—as most university mission statements are—or they may consist of one or two simple paragraphs.

In addition to the mission statement, organizations write *descriptive statements* about themselves. These are more subject to change than a mission statement, but essentially they interpret that statement. As an example, look over some of the literature your university admissions office sent to you when you were considering attending the school. The way the university describes itself tells you something about its self-image. The descriptive statements of publicly held companies appear in their annual reports, on the inside front cover—

usually in a box. These same statements appear in reports from analysts and brokers when you inquire about the companies' stock.

Because mission statements and descriptive statements tend to be long, most organizations also write a short, snappy *identifying statement* that can be used in connection with the organization's name. These are usually not more than one sentence long. Many organizations use these as the last paragraph in news releases, knowing the copy-editor will often delete the last sentence but that sometimes it will appear. The idea is for repetition of this identification to help reinforce knowledge of the organization's role. Look for this in the last paragraph of stories about nonprofit organizations in your local newspaper.

Objectives and Goals

Organizational objectives are always tied to the mission statement, and they must be consistent with the view of the organization projected by the descriptive and identifying statements.

Depending on its type, an organization may have several sets of objectives, fitting like concentric circles. The farthest circle out represents objectives ten years away; the next, objectives five years away; then three years away; and then one year away. Some organizations, especially nonprofit ones, develop elaborate books explaining these long-range plans. Generally they have to rely on these to raise money for the projects listed in the long-range plans, while the next year's objectives fit into an already established budget.

Unlike the mission statement, with its interpretations in the descriptive and identifying statements, objectives should have definite outcomes but remain unspecified as to time or degree. Early "management by objectives" work in the late 1950s confused goals and objectives, or used them interchangeably. Later works sorted out the two, assigning different qualities to each.[1]

Some dictionary definitions of *objective* use *goal* as a synonym. A thesaurus is likely to offer the following synonyms: goal, objective, purpose, aim, target, intention, destination, end. For planning purposes, it's better to treat an objective as the destination—where you want to go, analogously to a city on a road map—and goals as the achievements or incremental steps marking progress along the way—stopping points on the road map, taking you there. The goals are smaller, shorter-ranged, and easier to measure. Each one describes a set task to be accomplished within a given time period and to a specified degree.[2]

You can design and implement research to measure specific goals and to monitor your progress as you go.

Publics and Positioning

One aspect of planning for an organization involves identifying and describing all of its publics (see Chapter 4). You can then determine which are the primary publics under most circumstances—the ones you can expect to deal with directly on virtually a daily basis. You will work with secondary publics, too, but less frequently. Certainly both primary and secondary publics come into consideration in all aspects of planning. An organization's publics say something about what it is and what it does, just as surely as a person's friends and associates indicate what kind of a person he or she is and what he or she does.

The way these various publics respond to goals and objectives set by the organization directly contributes to the organization's level of success in accomplishing them. To build support for each public, you need to develop a realistic general message statement about how you'd like that group to view your organization. For example, employees are not likely to see management as "benevolent and kind," but "fair and honest" may be a reasonable view to strive for—provided that management really is, of course.

The way the organization wants to be seen by most of its primary publics, as reflected in its descriptive and identifying statements, is called *positioning*. Positioning is thus similar to the marketing strategy of differentiation, which involves emphasizing the ways in which a product or service differs from its competitors. A positioning statement communicates how the organization wishes to be viewed by all of its publics.

Determining how to express a position and how to advance the idea the position represents to each public is central to the planning done by the organization's public relations department.

Programs and Activities

Some of an organization's programs and activities are the primary responsibility of the public relations department, but many are not. With respect to these, the public relations department serves both as a source and resource. But when some of the organization's communications activities fall outside the responsibility (and authority) of the public relations department, most public relations directors feel they lack control. The least they would hope for is a "flow-through" pattern, in which all communications decisions cross their desk, even though these decisions may not be alterable. Most desirable is a consulting role in all such decisions. The role of the public relations department is often based on corporate tradition, on how management sees the public relations function and on the talents and abilities of the public relations staff, especially its leadership.

Monitoring and Evaluating

Even when many activities and countless forms of communication occur within an organization, the public relations department usually occupies the best position for monitoring what is or isn't happening and for evaluating how different publics are responding to various actions, messages and representatives of the organization.

Like other units in the organization, the public relations department is responsible for evaluating the results of its own efforts. At budget time, someone will always ask, "What did you do? How much did it cost? What did we get for the investment? How cost-effective was it? How did it contribute to the bottom line?" In its evaluations, however, the public relations department is more interested in answering questions along the lines of: "What do our publics think of us? How does this match with what we think of ourselves? How are events, situations, attitudes, etc., going to affect us in the future?" Both types of monitoring and evaluation need to go on, and both help the organization's leadership plan and give day-to-day direction to the organization.

Several commercially available computer software programs can be used to conduct a public relations situation analysis—setting objectives, writing a budget, developing a strategy, deciding on tactics and then evaluating results.

PLANNING AND MANAGING PUBLIC RELATIONS WORK

Public relations' role in developing an organization's formal planning is significant. PR advisers help develop a mission statement for the organization—counseling on publics and on strategies to reach objectives, as well as on environmental monitoring—as part of determining the organization's one-year, five-year and ten-year goals and objectives. In addition, the public relations department must develop its own communication goals and objectives.

Some PR communication plans are tied directly to the organization's plans. Even if an organization does not have periodic plans, the public relations department still must have a generic communications plan that fits into the organization's annual activities. In addition, the public relations department needs a crisis communication plan, or at least specific guidelines for dealing with crises. Like other communication activities that rely on the cooperation of other divisions in the organization and on the blessings of top management, however, crisis management plans must be developed jointly with other departments in the organization and must be approved by top management (see Chapter 15). Public relations managers have "vertical" jobs, in management terms, because they must function directly with all parts of the organization and at all levels.

PR is difficult to plan and manage because of high expectations, uneven levels of demand and the creative element. It calls for flexibility and entrepreneurship, often in environments that don't reward either. Many public relations problems arise from the failure of public relations practitioners to manage an internal situation, and this often turns on lacking approval to do whatever is necessary to accomplish the job. One PR practitioner whose publications were heavily criticized in a professional workshop complained that she knew what to do but couldn't convince her boss. A public relations manager for a presidential candidate resigned because, among other things, he couldn't get advance copies of the candidate's speeches. Ridiculous? Of course, but it happens all the time. Invitations to a major benefit arrived a scant four days before the event because a mailroom manager decided to send the hand-addressed envelopes third class after she opened one and saw that everything inside was printed. PR people often find it difficult to avoid drowning in details, but *not* watching the details is just as disastrous.

Strategic Planning

Strategic planning is used because traditional planning depends on a reasonably predictable environment; but due to the global nature of politics and economics, a predictable environment no longer exists. Management consultant Peter Drucker wrote:

> Planning as a rule starts out with the trends of yesterday and projects them to the future—using a different "mix" perhaps, but with very much the same configuration. This is no longer going to work. The most probable assumption in a period of turbulence is the unique event which changes the configuration. Unique events cannot, by definition, be "planned." But they can be foreseen. This requires strategies for tomorrow, strategies that anticipate where the greatest changes are likely to occur and what they are likely to be, strategies that enable a business—or hospital, school or university—to take advantage of new realities and to convert turbulence into opportunity.[3]

Planning for the PR Function

The plan for the PR unit or department begins with its own mission statement, describing how it sees itself, its role and its contributions to the organization. This statement is necessary because the public relations department is often called on to do things or to respond to possible opportunities that constitute temptations unrelated (or even counterproductive) to its central mission.

The mission of the PR unit helps define the job description for the whole unit—what it does in and for the organization. Changes in top-level management can cause discomfort with what the public relations department is doing unless the department can point to something that describes the department's activities and offers a clear rationale for them. New management may still want to make some changes, but it may nonetheless benefit from a better understanding of what the public relations function has been or should be—particularly if management comes to the top from another organization or from an unrelated area within the organization, such as engineering.

The public relations department also needs to set its own objectives and goals with respect to managing the department. For example, one long-range objective may be for the department to produce its own presentation slides and graphics in-house. A goal for the year could be to obtain equipment, or perhaps only software, that would make such an objective more achievable.

Next, the public relations department needs to prioritize its own publics. This differs from maintaining a database on the organization's publics, which might include description (demographics and psychographics), data (addresses, for instance), analysis (attitudes toward the organization and its products or services) and prioritization by issue or event. The PR department's own publics may include top management, other important sources of information within the organization, media personnel and special trade or government publics. The department needs to understand clearly who these publics are and what their special relationship to the unit is.

The department's relationship to the organization should also be spelled out in its own position statement, describing itself as "counsel to management" or "communications center" or whatever it intends to be within the organization.

Then the public relations department needs to schedule and prioritize the activities that traditionally fall within its sphere of responsibility. This is very important because sometimes, when special requests come or opportunities appear, other duties may not get done or may have to be postponed. The department's "calendar" of activities helps it plan its time effectively. Perhaps, too, some things the department has been doing just because "we've always done it" need to be replaced on the schedule by other, more centralized activities.

Finally, the department needs to continually monitor everything it does to see whether the planned activities are being done correctly and whether they are eliciting the desired response. Monitoring the department's activities as they occur saves some of them from being ultimately unsuccessful and makes end-of-year reporting easier. The result of each activity should be scrutinized to determine what worked and what didn't, and recommendations should then be offered for the next year. The department must also perform a year-end review and evaluation, either as part of its overall management review or as part of the budget-making process. In any case, the public relations department's activities reports resemble those of other departments except that most of its activities support the organization as a whole or other specific units within the organization, rather than the department itself. This sometimes means that the department fails to get the recognition it deserves.

Along the way, the public relations department's plans for itself and for the organization may be interrupted by the need to develop special problem-solving strategies.

Problem-solving Strategies

One of the oldest formulas for problem-solving is John Marston's R-A-C-E formula—an acronym for

EXAMPLE 10.1

What Do You Do When There's a Problem?

What is the procedure for handling a problem? Where do you start?

1. Assemble readily available facts and background material. Have everything at hand relative to the problem; analyze and discuss these with executives. Background materials include four areas: organizational/client, opportunity/problem, audience, research.

2. Determine which publics are involved or affected.

3. Decide if additional research is needed to properly define the problem and evaluate its scope.

Where do you go from here?

4. Once the problem is defined and the publics determined, formulate a hypothesis, Assemble facts to test the hypothesis, and revise it if the hypothesis is disproved.

5. Elements to consider in this initial planning:

a. What is the objective of the PR effort—what specifically do you want to accomplish? Be able to state this in concrete terms.

b. What image of the organization do you want to present? (This should be a projection of the mission statement, but specifically adapted for this situation.)

c. Which publics are targets? Why?

6. Who are other audiences whose opinions matter?

Now that you know whom you want to talk to and what image you want your actions to reflect, what do you say to accomplish that?

7. What message do you have for each public? These messages should have a particular slant for each audience, but they should convey the same basic theme and information.

8. What media can you use to carry these messages? Which media for each group are received and are credible? Will these media carry your message? If not, what other media can you use? Can you use conventional channels of communication (magazines, newsletters, closed-circuit TV, etc.) for internal audiences?

9. What response do you want from each audience?

Research, Action, Communication and Evaluation.[4] But the concept is found earlier (without the acronym) in Scott Cutlip and Allen Center's 1952 edition of *Effective Public Relations:* find the facts; establish a policy and/or plan a program; communicate the story; and get feedback from internal and external publics to help determine modifications or future planning.[5] A modification (with another acronym) appears in Jerry Hendrix's *Public Relations Cases:* R-O-P-E.[6] Like Marston, Hendrix begins with research (R) but then he moves to objectives (O), of which he sees two: output objectives and impact objectives. Output objectives are communications the public relations effort seeks to generate over the target period. Impact objectives have three divisions: informational objectives (message exposure, comprehension and retention);

attitudinal objectives (creation, reinforcement and change); and behavioral objectives (creation, reinforcement and change). The P in Hendrix's formula stands for programming. The final step, once again, is evaluation (E).

The problem-solving procedure offered by Glen M. Broom and David M. Dozier is more complex.[7] The ten steps begin with defining or identifying the problem (1), followed by performing a situational analysis that involves assessing background information and data and examining internal and external factors and forces (2). Problem identification and situational analysis are followed by setting program goals (3). [Broom and Dozier use the term *goals* instead of *objectives.*] The next steps are to identify publics—who is affected and how (4)—and then to set program objectives

10. What budget can you use for this—regular allocated budget or a special fund?

11. What is the best timing for actions? Develop a schedule and tie-in with other events to make news when appropriate or to avoid it if news coverage might prove detrimental.

12. Review problems or obstacles that might arise and make contingency plans for these.

13. Build in monitoring devices so you'll always know how you're doing.

Once it's all over, how do you know what happened?

14. Plan for evaluation.

15. Evaluate all aspects of the situation—the impact on and response from all audiences. Evaluation includes (1) impact—informational, attitudinal and behavioral—and (2) output (media efforts and results).

16. Communicate results.

In brief:

1. Find the central core of difficulty.

2. Check your total list of publics and note all of those who are involved in the problem, both centrally and peripherally.

3. Determine the problem's status in terms of potential harm to the organization.

4. List the related difficulties to be considered.

5. Explore the alternatives.

6. List the desirable objectives.

7. See how the solution fits into the long-range plans that are shaped toward what you see as the mission.

8. What are the immediate plans, and how do these fit with the long-range plans? Short-term solutions that don't fit long-range objectives and are not consonant with the mission statement are wrong. Don't do them. Start over.

Procedure for handling the problem internally:

1. Detail the plan and submit it to the policy executive for approval.

2. Get approval in writing.

3. Keep all people who are directly involved informed on a continuing basis throughout the move toward solving the public relations problem.

---

(5) and plan action programs (6) for each public. Then each public's communication program—message and media strategies—is determined (7). These steps are followed by program implementation—in which responsibilities, schedules and budget are assigned (8)—evaluation (9) and finally, feedback (10).

The Broom–Dozier process may not be as easy to remember, but it constitutes a more complete approach to problem solving. The approach taken by one of the authors of this text is presented in Example 10.1. Any problem-solving plan should take into consideration intervening situations: how others will react (especially within the existing power structure); how the organizational culture affects the approach to problem solving; and how those who are not intended publics for

messages—the nimbus groups—may interpret or respond to them.

■ Intervening Situations

Some difficulty in handling public relations problems may occur because of differing perceptions of the problem and of existing situations. The perceptions involved may be yours or others'. One way of understanding barriers to solving problems appears in Example 10.2. Robert L. Katz sees five major barriers: (1) information you don't know; (2) effects of the way you look at the problem; (3) limitations you face (that is, restrictions on the choices the situation offers); (4) your own personal limitations (or management's); (5) problems associated with upsetting the equilibrium of the organization

EXAMPLE 10.2
Barriers to Problem Solving

These barriers to arriving at a solution to a problem illustrate the complex inter- and intrapersonal difficulties you are likely to encounter.

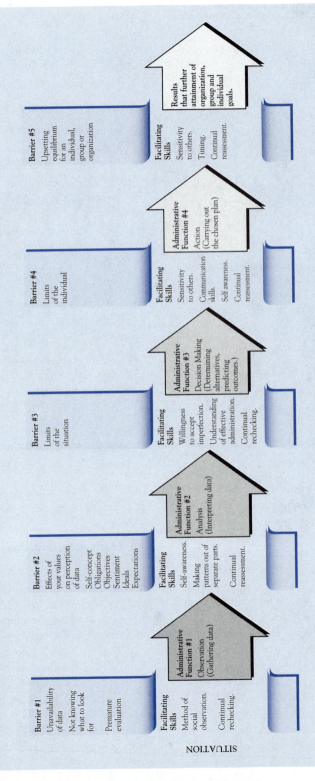

SITUATION

Barrier #1
Unavailability of data
Not knowing what to look for
Premature evaluation

Facilitating Skills
Method of social observation.
Continual rechecking.

Administrative Function #1
Observation (Gathering data)

Barrier #2
Effects of your values on perception of data
Self-concept
Obligations
Objectives
Sentiment
Ideals
Expectations

Facilitating Skills
Self-awareness.
Making patterns out of separate parts.
Continual reassessment.

Administrative Function #2
Analysis (Interpreting data)

Barrier #3
Limits of the situation

Facilitating Skills
Willingness to accept imperfection.
Understanding of effective administration.
Continual rechecking.

Administrative Function #3
Decision Making (Determining alternatives, predicting outcomes.)

Barrier #4
Limits of the individual

Facilitating Skills
Sensitivity to others.
Communication skills.
Self awareness.
Continual reassessment.

Administrative Function #4
Action (Carrying out the chosen plan)

Barrier #5
Upsetting equilibrium for an individual, group or organization

Facilitating Skills
Sensitivity to others.
Timing.
Continual reassessment.

Results that further attainment of organization, group and individual goals.

Source: Adapted and reprinted by permission of *Harvard Business Review*. An exhibit from "Human Relations Skills Can Be Sharpened," by Robert L. Katz, July/August 1956, p. 64.

or of others. Each barrier not only threatens to block your efforts to arrive at a solution, but holds out the prospect of making the problem worse.[8]

The problems that your own biases contribute are detailed in Example 10.3, which shows how difficult it is to attempt an "objective" view of a problem, much less an "objective" presentation of the problem to others.[9] Difficulties of perception can affect the way issues management is handled, for example.

The way various stakeholders see a problem can cause an organization to modify or change its reaction to problems. Stakeholders may not define the problem the same way management does, for example, and they may not appreciate the organizational purpose because it doesn't match their own perspectives. Furthermore, they may not understand or be able to comply with the process offered as part of the proposed solution. In that case the proposed solution may not even strike them as reasonable.

The way various individuals within the organization perceive the problem affects the organization's responses, too (see Example 10.4). Some of this has to do with power structures, and some with organizational culture. Power structures are a frequent source of resistance to responses. Sometimes that power resides in top management; sometimes it rests with departments within the organization that influence management decisions in certain situations. In dealing with environmental issues, for example, management is likely to turn to engineering to see what is possible and how much it will cost.

Sometimes influence comes from power structures outside the organization. One powerful group is large stockholders—organizational investors such as insurance companies or pension plans—which influence decisions about dividends. Certainly institutional ownership of large blocks of stock has affected the attention paid to quarterly reports; some observers say that this has caused businesses to focus on short-term (rather than long-term) solutions to problems.

Another major factor in how an organization responds to a problem situation is the organization's corporate culture. The stronger the corporate culture is, the less flexibility the organization has in adopting solutions that are out of the ordinary or are not within the normal range of the expected behavior of the organization.[10]

The way the decision-making groups function together also affects problem solving. This is less likely to follow any specific decision-making model, however, than it is to be related to the initiative of members of the group who are making the decisions, to their interpretation of their choices and to the effects of those choices (contingency factors).[11]

Public relations people are involved in problem-solving situations almost constantly, and a good many of the eventual solutions to these problems are arrived at by groups. Occasionally, these groups include some people from outside and some from inside the organization; but most are arrived at internally, with much of the effort being exerted by the public relations department or outside PR counsel to the organization.

PR DEPARTMENTS AS SOURCES AND RESOURCES

Resources available in the public relations department are often needed by other divisions of the organization. PR can supply information on the organization's publics, on the socioeconomic and political climates in which the organization functions and on media.

Working with top-level executives means, as one PR practitioner explained it, juggling "the roles of seer, guru, confessor, follower, mentor, listener, disciplinarian, friend and confidant."[12] The practitioner James E. Lukaszewski, noted that "good, straightforward counsel is often hard to find at the top, and CEOs often are frustrated by the inability of those around them to offer strong and positive advice."[13]

Longtime McCormick Communication Vice President, now President of The Institute for Public Relations, John W. Felton described another role besides adviser—that of educator. He helped management understand the different attitudes represented by the mix of age groups in the workplace so

EXAMPLE 10.3
Personal Perceptions and Problem Situations

The way we look at a problem situation determines our approach to solving it. The complexity of our view is shown here. Other intervening factors arise when we attempt to communicate our perception—including how we want others to think of us.

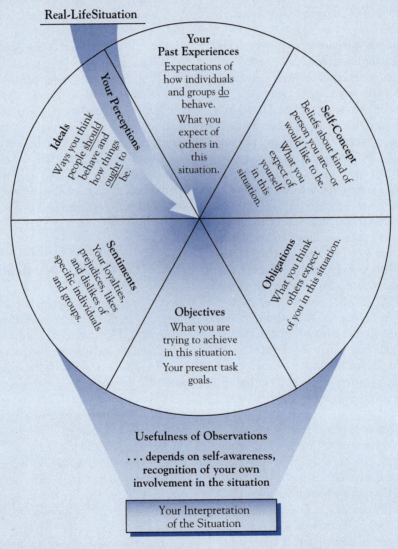

Real-LifeSituation

Your Perceptions

Your Past Experiences
Expectations of how individuals and groups <u>do</u> behave.
What you expect of others in this situation.

Self-Concept
Beliefs about kind of person you are—or would like to be.
What you expect of yourself in this situation.

Ideals
Ways you think people <u>should</u> behave and how things <u>ought</u> to be.

Obligations
What you think others expect of you in this situation.

Sentiments
Your loyalties, likes, prejudices, and dislikes of specific individuals and groups.

Objectives
What you are trying to achieve in this situation.
Your present task goals.

Usefulness of Observations
. . . depends on self-awareness, recognition of your own involvement in the situation

Your Interpretation of the Situation

Source: Adapted and reprinted by permission of *Harvard Business Review*. An exhibit from "Human Relations Skills Can Be Sharpened," by Robert L. Katz, July/August 1956, p. 67. Copyright © 1956 by the President and Fellows of Harvard College; all rights reserved.

EXAMPLE 10.4

Difficulties with Perceptions in Solving Problems

As the Account Executive
Explained It

As the Writer's Copy
Described It

As the Art Director
Illustrated It

How the Production Department Got in
All the Copy Changes After Final Layout

How a Research Focus
Group Perceived It

What the Client Wanted

MORAL: Asking Questions Is a Sign of Strength

that management could communicate with them more effectively. To do this, McCormick represented generational attitudes as reflected in their life-styles and developed a chart for management based on a comparison of attitudes represented by trends in the 1950s, 1960s, 1970s, 1980s and 1990s. This helped management recognize the complexity of the values held by their workforce so that plan-

ners could anticipate employee reactions to messages and policy decisions.[14]

Lukaszewski says that, to work as a close counsel to top management, you must have the following ten characteristics: (1) be someone who listens; (2) have the intuition to advance ideas and interpret events; (3) have the courage of your convictions; (4) give both factual and feeling feedback;

(5) be able to inspire; (6) be trustworthy; (7) have insight; (8) be a complete thinker (which means being able to identify the problem, analyze it, forecast outcomes, recommend a range of ideas and then test specific options); (9) be a pragmatist; (10) understand the dollar value of time.[15]

He also recommends that you keep ego involvement out of problem solving and recognize the difference between influencing people and controlling them. Usually someone else, not the PR person, must take the recommended action, which the PR person then supports.

Knowing how to get members of management to use your abilities and counsel is part of making them aware of the public relations department as an integral organizational resource. Offering advice and counsel to other managers also develops their awareness of public relations as a valued part of the organization and builds a constituency. The research on publics that the public relations office does in its monitoring and evaluating should be extremely useful to sales and marketing as well as to research and development, for example. Many PR departments train other managers in media relations, especially if they are in jobs that occasionally (at least) put them in contact with mass or specialized media.

Much of the information public relations works with is stored electronically and can be put into a format so that other departments can use it. At one time, departments depended on public relations primarily for media contacts, news stories and publications. Technology, however, has turned every office and department into a center for sending messages by fax or e-mail, and most have the capability for desktop publishing. A public relations director said that getting a handle on what is being communicated through the different departments is more challenging now, as is controlling the number and type of departmental publications. The result is more communication policy making on the part of the public relations department to preserve the integrity of its organization's communication system.

A number of publications for the organization as a whole must be prepared by the public relations department. One such publication is the manual that determines how the organization's name and logo will be used by all of its departments and by anyone outside the organization, such as when it is used in cooperative promotions (see Example 10.5). In addition to having written descriptions that set out color, size, type, format and permission procedures, most organizations keep slicks and disks available for easy use by their own divisions and by others. Another publication that public relations departments produce is the organization's staff or employee handbook, which sets forth various procedures that employees must follow. This publication also helps instill the corporate culture and standardizes many day-to-day activities.

Depending on the organization, there may be several other publications, usually dealing with processes or procedures. These include a safety handbook, a guide to handling crises, and a style manual for handling corporate letters, memos and the like.

PR often acts as the publishing division of the organization. As a result, other departments make numerous publication requests of it. Since PR is usually a profit center in most large organizations, these projects are charged to the requesting department. PR wants the business, even if it has a number of projects in progress, because it wants to control and coordinate the organization's publications so that they all seem to belong to the same "family" and to "speak with one voice." The family look of all public images reinforces the organization's identity and helps PR build the corporate image. The growing tendency of departments to send projects to outside suppliers or to do the job themselves with desktop publishing equipment makes the manual governing the use of logo, colors and corporate style increasingly important.

In addition to acting as the publications division, the PR department usually serves as the presentations division, too. This means writing speeches and making slides, electronic visuals or full-blown videos for internal and external use.

Internally, the unit may produce or coordinate video news releases and (if nonprofit) public service announcements for radio and television. It

EXAMPLE 10.5

American Heart Association's Logo and Guidelines

To improve the consistency of its image, the American Heart Association first issued a Graphic Standards Manual in 1983. In updating its image, AHA issued another, more complete manual to explain how the logo, with the slogan, should be used. The manual also includes the style for material, including tone and manner of graphics and audio and editorial content, the names of all of AHA programs and the media the AHA uses to deliver its varied messages. The page reproduced here lists acceptable uses for the logo and slogan.

Signature Uses

Consistency is important in creating a clear, well-defined and recognizable brand identity. The following examples show proper and improper signature uses. They demonstrate how to improve our communications through stronger product branding by avoiding interference with the signature and inconsistencies in application.

We cannot list all improper uses on these pages. If you identify a use that you are not sure is proper, please contact the National Center Design Studio for further guidance.

Acceptable Uses

Slogan printed in the same color as the symbol and logotype.

Printing the signature on a subtly patterned background such as a lightly screened graphic or photograph. Take care to place the signature in an area of the photograph that will not interfere with clear definition of the signature.

Printing the signature on various colored backgrounds. (See Color, p. 1.6.)

The heart-and-torch symbol may be printed as a graphic element on some internal organizational guides and manuals. (See Internal Publications, p. 3.9.)

may also be in charge of setting up satellite coverage of events or handling teleconferences or other meetings that need to be scripted and videotaped, such as the annual meeting.

While the "clients" for these presentations are generally management or principal officers, the calls may come from a subdivision of public relations or related departments such as investor relations, public affairs, consumer relations, industrial relations, labor relations or—in the case of universities and some other nonprofit organizations—development (fundraising); alternatively, they may come from marketing, human resources (usually for training videos or presentations of benefits changes) or any special unit of the central organization or its subsidiaries. Requests from public relations subdivisions and other departments may be for production only, but requests from other divisions generally involve research as well as production, and they carry the possibility of extensive revision because of communication problems that often arise between the specialists and the communicators.

Charging for PR Services

Public relations departments in organizations must figure out how to charge for what they do for other units against the budgets of those other units. The tasks that the PR unit has as its primary responsibility are paid for out of the PR budget, but funds for service projects for other units are not built into this budget. Consequently, service projects can drain away resources (people and money) from the department's own budgeted needs unless the costs (for both people and operations) are charged back to those who requested the services.

Two systems are commonly used to handle this cost. In the first, the public relations department gives an estimate to the requesting unit, and that unit determines how elaborate it can afford the production to be and still stay within its own budget. Then, generally, funds are transferred from the other unit to public relations by accounting. No money actually changes hands. If the public relations department has to go outside the organization

for some services, these bills are submitted directly to the other unit for payment. (Occasionally, the public relations department may want to pay these bills and ask for reimbursement because, if the other unit doesn't pay promptly, it can damage the relationship between the PR department and a supplier it works with on a continuing basis.)

The second system involves having the public relations division function as a profit center for management. In such cases, the unit may be elaborately equipped, but it is expected to earn money. For that reason, it takes outside jobs—either from the organization's subsidiaries or even from other organizations. Thus the public relations division, although internal, functions like an agency; and strict accounting of time, talent, supplies and other resources becomes critical. If the public relations division doesn't turn a profit, it may find itself "out of business," regardless of how much the organization itself may have used the PR function. Often when this type of arrangement is used, management sees the PR function as being oriented less toward counseling and more exclusively toward communication.

Setting Fees   Most of the costs of a PR person, firm or department are for personnel time. Thus, systematic ways must be developed to keep track of the time spent and to charge for it. Three basic methods can be used for determining client charges:

1. The *fixed fee*, seldom used now because it is a bit risky, sets a specific fee in advance for all work and expenses on a particular project.

2. The *fee for services plus out-of-pocket expenses* is a more popular form of billing. Out-of-pocket costs include such items as travel for a client, hotel rooms and meals, taxis, gratuities, telegrams, long-distance phone calls and entertainment.

3. The *retainer* covers counseling, supervision, profit and overhead. Overhead costs include all indirect expenses of doing business: utilities, secretarial and clerical costs, office supplies, amortization of equipment and so on. Additional charges are made for services at hourly rates that reflect payroll costs plus out-of-pocket expenses. Many firms charge a retainer that covers counseling, supervision and profit, with an additional charge covering payroll and overhead expenses. All out-of-pocket costs are extra and are billed as such.

In all three cases, any estimate you submit as a quote is subject to a 10 to 15 percent variance, and most clients understand and expect this. Any larger change needs approval in writing with the client's signature.

Firms The cost of staff time spent on a project is measured in staff salaries, usually prorated to the nearest hour of time spent. The cost of executive time and supervision depends on the size of the agency: large agencies have executive oversight; small ones include the executive in the staff portion of the time.

A PR business incurs chargeable and nonchargeable expenses. The following time and expenses can be charged to a client: (1) meetings with clients to prepare account material; (2) interviews, surveys and placement of materials; (3) supervision of mailing and distribution of releases, photograph assignments and other visual material prepared for the client; (4) travel time, including going to and from client's office, as well as time spent in off-hours (evenings and weekends) with client personnel on client matters. Nonchargeable expenses include the following: (1) keeping up contacts with media representatives; (2) meetings with office and staff and other group conferences related to PR business; (3) new business solicitation and preparation of materials for potential clients; (4) professional activities such as seminars, meetings and time spent on professional/firm matters; and (5) leisure time spent away from home in hotels, as well as purely social activities with clients, whether or not these occur in the evening or on weekends. Example 10.6 shows a typical budget.

This type of cost accounting makes it necessary for employees and executives to keep an accurate record of time spent on a project. Time segments are broken into small sections, such as five minutes or fifteen minutes. To simplify matters, clerical, secretarial and mailroom salaries are ordinarily billed as overhead. This means that only the executives have to keep detailed records of how much of their time is spent for a specific client. To facilitate this, most executives keep diary sheets (see Example 10.7) and weekly expense reports. A number of software systems are available to firms that want to computerize the monitoring and reporting of these records.

Most companies determine their profit objectives before setting hourly wages. *Small firms* do a lot of networking and rely on outside suppliers for advice, skills and services. They also rely heavily on freelancers and other contract workers. The highest fees these firms earn are for counsel and for strategy sessions, which are usually handled by the principal. Lower fees are paid for writing and producing materials. These tasks are most often farmed out. Most firms count on a 20 to 75 percent return before taxes, based on a 70 to 75 percent billable portion of a 7.5-hour day and a 1,550- or 1,660-hour year, including vacations and holidays. Higher fees are generally charged for emergencies, special projects and delinquent accounts. Most give their retainer clients quarterly reports, with charges for extra services or credit carried over to the next quarter.

Medium-size firms set aside a specific amount from profits to attract new business. Most hire people only when they get a new account. They use teams to work on accounts, but generally use only part of a team member's time for a specific account. Sometimes a new businessperson is hired just to get new accounts and is paid a commission to do so. Many of these firms are made up of generalists who rely on specialists to handle certain accounts.

Large firms are generally organized into groups composed of people who have the special expertise needed to handle a particular client's requirements. Larger firms normally have departments, such as media relations, that serve all groups. Groups usually make their own presentations, so the firm's principals are less in demand by the client than they are in the smaller and medium-size firms.

E X A M P L E 1 0 . 6

Typical Budget

Expenditures:	Jan	Feb	Mar	Apr	May	Jun	6 Mo. Totals	Jul	Aug	Sep	Oct	Nov	Dec	12 Mo. Totals
Staff:														
Salaries														
Benefits														
Expenses														
Part-time help														
Office:														
Rent or space allocation														
Utilities														
Equipment:														
Maintenance & Repair														
Purchases														
Rental														
Communications:														
Telephone														
Telegraph, TWX, Telecopier, etc.														
Messenger service														
Postage														
Production:														
Design services														
Typesetting														
Photography														
Printing														
Media space														
(Other)														
TOTALS														

Source: Reprinted with permission by Jim Haynes, "Organizational Budgeting Techniques," in Carol Reuss and Donn Silvis, eds., *Inside Organizational Communications* (New York: Longman, 1981), p. 72.

EXAMPLE 10.7
Executive Weekly Time Report/Diary Sheet

Burson·Marsteller Weekly Time Report

Week Ending Sunday (or the 15th)

Employee Name   Employee Number   Office Name   Group Name   Month Day Year 19

	Client Number	Division Number	Job No.	Client Name	Mon	Tues	Wed	Thurs	Fri	Sat	Sun	Total Hours
1												
2												
3												
4												
5												
6												
7												
8												
9												
10												
11												
12												
13												
14												
15												
16												
17												
18												
19												
20												
21												
22	9 9 9 9 9			New Business								
23		0 3 3		Administrative								
24		0 3 4		Company Meetings (Non-Client)								
25		0 3 5		Outside Meetings, Conventions, etc. (Non-Client)								
26		0 3 8		Company Promotion								
27		0 9 0		General								
28		0 9 1		Absence								
29		0 9 2		Vacation/Holiday								

Total Items   Total Hours

For Accounting Use Only: Batch Control #:   Date Input: Input By:

Source: Reprinted with permission of Burson-Marsteller.

Large firms hire generalists and specialists and are more likely to hire outstanding people and then find work for them. New people are usually tested at skills-level jobs (such as writing releases or managing a news conference) to see what they can deliver, before they are given the chance to try management jobs.

The Small Client Making small accounts profitable is sometimes a problem. One difficulty you are likely to encounter is that, because smaller companies have little experience in using public relations services, they often make unreasonable demands and expect extraordinary results. It helps if you concentrate your efforts where you are most likely to get demonstrable results: trade publications, weeklies, locally produced Sunday supplements and other regional media. See if the client has a feature appropriate for a local television "magazine" program. You will probably have to do a better selling job to the print and television media on such features because of their limited scope and appeal.

Be sure all your efforts are related to the client. Tell every success story to the client, even if it is just a column item. Help the client develop programs that will generate publicity. You may want to help the client start a simple internal communications program, like a newsletter. Help the client use advertising economically. Small clients need the effectiveness of a paid-for message. Watch the client's costs carefully. Small budgets can't absorb things like printing overruns or expensive mass mailings. Probably most important, be sure you have a contract that spells out obligations and provides for prompt payment, such as ten days after billing. If you are dealing with a new client you don't know much about, it is not a bad idea to require some prepayment.

The Large Client Large clients can be habit-forming. They supply needed capital and often prestige. But if they pull out, your financial health and your credibility can be damaged. Diversification offers the best defense against such damage. You need to guard against relying too much on one account. At the same time, that account may give the firm a great deal of expertise in one area, such as public affairs, or in one industry, such as investments or fashion or automobiles. You can't ethically handle competing clients at the same time, but if you lose one account and have built a reputation in a field, it makes sense to find other clients in that same field to match your expertise. Large clients often demand involvement by the principals in the firm, and they sometimes consume more time than you can reasonably bill for if you're not careful.

Personalities are always important in client relations, but they are critical with a superclient. You need to be sure of the people skills of those working on the account who are in close contact with the client. You may be dealing with the client's middle-level management, whose power to make critical decisions may be quite limited. You may have to work with someone who is out of the policy mainstream and who may therefore mislead you concerning top management's wishes. This can cost you the account. Sometimes when a budget gets very large, expectations grow unrealistically high.

■ Budgeting a PR Operation

In a PR office, salaries and fringe benefits amount to approximately 80 percent of the total expenses, leaving 20 percent for profit, new business development and company (as opposed to client) costs. Thus, 20 percent of the costs cannot be billed out. Since some of these costs are discretionary, it occasionally works best to have a set budget for them so that no misunderstandings ensue over travel and entertainment allowances, membership dues, long-distance phone calls and other nonbillable expenses. The other company expenses are usually predictable, since they involve rent, insurance and utilities. Such variables as office supplies and postage have to be estimated roughly.

The amount to invest in seeking new business must also be calculated rather roughly, based on the rate at which the firm desires and needs to grow. PR practitioner Alfred G. Paulson, author of articles on fiscal planning, suggested that a 20 percent anticipated or planned annual growth rate is not realistic and might prove taxing for a company that already handles a large volume of business.[16] The costs of attracting new business and of acquiring the staff to handle it are real considerations. If too rapid an expansion takes place, problems with limited facilities might also enter the picture. However, Paulson warned that an anticipated growth rate of 10 percent or less would be too low to stimulate the action and enthusiasm needed to develop new business contacts and clients. A growth pattern of roughly 15 percent, he said, allows a realistic profit return expectancy of 25 percent before bonuses, profit sharing and taxes.

You may think that charging the media for supplying information is an odd twist, but lawyers apparently think it's a good idea. With the prevalence of litigation journalism, some lawyers are billing clients for the time they spend talking to the news media. This is not a widely approved practice, and some lawyers with large firms record it as an unbillable line item, according to a *Wall Street Journal* story whose reporter was charged for one call he made to a lawyer. That lawyer, Gloria Allred, a Los Angeles plaintiffs' lawyer, said she doesn't bill her clients but does charge media. According to the news story, she frequently holds press conferences and appears on television interview shows instead of responding at no charge to media inquiries.[17]

Some attorneys say that they only bill clients for direct media relations work such as offering advice on media strategy or conducting a press conference.[18] Presumably, such charges to an organization from its attorney could be charged against the public relations budget.

In an organizational setting, PR department budgets vary dramatically depending on management's perception of the importance of the function. Nonprofit organizations value the PR function more highly than do many commercial enterprises, since so much of the total organizational operation is PR-related. PR budgets can therefore account for from .5 to 1 percent of the nonprofit's total budget. Corporate PR budgets are anywhere from 0.1 percent to 1 percent of the total budget, although a few are as high as 3 percent. Many corporate PR departments keep slim staffs and farm out many jobs to suppliers. In any case, as prices change and costs increase, you will have to defend your budget decisions and campaign vigorously for additional money simply to continue functioning at current levels. Consequently, you will have to prove the effectiveness of your function. Although your budget must conform to the organization's for accounting purposes, you have some leeway within those limits. Jim Haynes, a seasoned practitioner and educator, offers a series of guidelines for developing a budget. Remember, Haynes says, to add in overhead, which is what the organization charges back to you as your portion of operating costs for space plus the services of the people who work there plus equipment purchases and maintenance.

Haynes says:

Everything that's worth doing costs money, just as everything that's not worth doing costs money. The trick is to decide what is worth doing. List those things in order of importance, and do only those important things you can afford to do. Simple, right? Perhaps not, but it's the most logical approach to budgeting I've ever heard of, since it's based upon what needs to be done, rather than "what we did last year."

How do we do that?

After you have studied your organization's objectives and determined how communication can assist in their accomplishment, do the following:

- *List all your audiences in order of importance, with the most important at the top of the list.*
- *For each audience, list the communication media you plan to use during the next 12 months to reach that audience.*
- *Put a price tag on what it costs to use that medium one time.*
- *List the number of times during the next 12 months you plan to use the medium. (How many newsletter issues will you print? Etc.)*
- *Multiply the number of times by the unit cost to reach a total cost for the year for each medium.*
- *Do the same thing for each communication medium, audience by audience.*
- *Add up the total cost for the year for each audience, dropping out the costs for media that repeat from one audience to the next. (For example, a newsletter might be distributed to several different audiences, but include its cost only once, the first time it appears.)*
- *Add all the totals for all the audiences. That's your desired communication budget for the year.*
- *If the total is too big, you have two choices:*
  - *Eliminate audiences, starting at the bottom of the list with the least important audience.*
    (or)
  - *Eliminate media, starting at the bottom of the list for each audience.*
- *Add to your total the cost of overhead expenses which cannot logically be appropriated to the cost of communicating with individual audiences.*

Overhead items will vary from organization to organization but might include such expenses as rent, utilities, equipment, supplies, salaries, etc.

■ *Be sure to make a comparison with present expenditures. Many organizations have never prepared an overall communication budget and they are frequently surprised to find out how much money they're spending on ineffective materials!*[19]

If the advertising/marketing unit reports to your public relations department, your budget must include a line item for advertising. How much you budget for advertising is a subjective management decision. However, some variables have been identified by the Strategic Planning Institute of Cambridge, Massachusetts, which has compiled these variables into a database, Profit Impact of Market Strategy (PIMS). The Cahners Publishing Company commissioned a study using PIMS to identify the factors most frequently considered in determining product ad budgets. These "decision rules" are (1) setting the ad budget as a percentage of total industry sales; (2) raising ad budgets to get or sustain a high market share; (3) increasing ad budgets in faster-growing markets; (4) increasing ad budgets for lower deliverability (that is, lower plant capacity); (5) spending more for advertising at lower unit prices; (6) spending more for advertising if customers typically spend less of their income on the product; (7) planning to spend more for advertising for the very highest-quality products; (8) spending more for advertising if there are many products in the line; (9) diverting more advertising dollars to standard products.

If you are not dealing with the product line but are handling corporate or image advertising, you need to follow these additional decision rules:

1. Spend more if your organization is new to the field or if you need to clarify your image because of a name change, a merger or a previously low image in the field.

2. Spend more if you have *no* consumer products or services.

3. Spend more if you wish to increase recognition as an industry leader.

4. Spend more, and certainly not less, in a recession when product or service advertising is reduced in order to hold market identity and market share.

5. Spend more for before-and-after research to pretest and to evaluate product impact.

Sometimes the PR department is responsible for an organization's philanthropic efforts (usually for publicity or goodwill). Corporate giving and sponsorships, as well as cause-related marketing, have to be evaluated at the outset for consistency with the donor's organization mission. A way must be devised to measure the efforts' impact in publicity or goodwill. Unobtrusive measures (such as number of applicants for a grant or scholarship) and formal evaluations (such as surveys for recognition of donor and gift) may be used for this purpose.

■ Defending the Budget

The same research you use to evaluate the effects of public relations efforts can be used to defend the budget and to ask for increases. In addition, as in all other units, equipment has to be repaired, updated or replaced, and this calls for budget documentation of the equipment's usefulness to the public relations department in achieving its own goals and in furthering the organization's goals.

Budget officers want evidence of cost effectiveness, but success with people is difficult to document, and much of what public relations departments and firms do involves people. You have to find creative ways to make your case for success.

You'll also have to defend the public relations talent in your department, and you may have some difficulty in explaining how you use people there. Many creative people are not interested in being promoted to management tasks. In fact, in some cases, such promotion would be a disaster for them and for the department. They need to be compensated, however, and they need to receive salary increases to encourage them to stay in the department. You have to find a way to explain the value of what they do, without changes in title or job description.

"Benchmarking" can be an effective method of demonstrating the value of public relations and defending PR budget proposals. Benchmarking is an ongoing systematic measurement of a public relations department's work, comparing it with that of higher performing and world-class public relations departments. According to Craig S. Fleisher and Sara Burton, it generates knowledge and action that can lead to performance improvement, and it can provide practitioners with useful information about roles, issues, functions, processes and practices.[20] H. Lawrence Smith adds that benchmarking compares performance against "best practices" within a peer group.[21]

Managing PR People

To manage PR people effectively, you must first recognize that they are creative people who work under continuous pressure and face criticism from all fronts for whatever they do. Next you must realize that they are individuals with professional attitudes that tend to make them more committed to their field than to the particular place where they may be working. Finally, although most PR people are highly trained communicators, they often don't communicate as effectively with their colleagues as they do when they are working either with other departments or with outsiders at a communications task.

An organized and systematic plan is necessary to accomplish tasks, but PR employees are generally less tolerant of inflexible rules and routines than other employees. They often face criticism from other employees who don't understand the nature of public relations jobs but do know that PR people come and go with more freedom than many other employees. In addition, other employees know that PR people work with the (often unpopular) media. Perhaps worst of all, PR people are spokespeople for management.

Cultivating personal growth and keeping PR employees from getting bored with routine chores are challenges for PR managers. PR managers must also see to it that their employees learn the organization's business thoroughly. They also must see to it that their employees keep up with developments in their own field.

You will probably not have management responsibility right away; but while you are laboring at lower levels in the hierarchy, consider keeping a list of things to recall when you do assume management responsibilities. The newer *peer review* management evaluations through which employees evaluate their bosses can be a good learning tool for you, for example. Remember, employees look to the manager or supervisor for leadership and for knowledge of the rules. The manager is expected to provide a good working environment for employees and to support them in their dealings with top management. Employees look to the manager for counsel (sometimes even on personal matters). They expect the manager to listen, to do more than they do and to do it better. Finally, they expect the manager to help gain recognition for them and for the department. Employees are the public relations "frontline" of any organization, and that holds especially true for the PR department's own employees.

Cultural Values and Social Conflict in a Global Society

With the internationalization of business, some of an organization's public relations employees may be sent abroad, either for brief periods or to live and work in another culture. Large public relations agencies have offices all over the world, and these tend not to be staffed entirely by nationals of the country where the office is located. Consequently, PR people need to consider how the cultural values of the parent organization can cause conflict in the resident culture.

Accompanying employees on foreign assignments is some of the organization's own culture—often called *corporate culture*, although it exists in nonprofit organizations as well. While this culture often helps give the organization a recognizable identity and an implicit "code of conduct," it also conveys a value system. *Value* is used here in its sociological sense: societal ideals, customs, institutions and traditions that the people of that society hold in high regard. Some organizational cultures are responsive to their environment, assimilating quickly by adapting to the resident culture while maintaining some of their own culture. This happens most readily when the employees are able to assimilate and when the parent company allows offices in the foreign community to adapt to the resident culture.

Value conflicts can occur over such concepts as time, status of women, regard for animals and ecology. All of these can put the organization at odds with its environment and can be sources of misunderstanding and resentment.

An organization may not be willing to compromise on some values, such as cleanliness, education, personal freedom and egalitarianism. Moreover, some ways of doing business in other parts of the world may conflict with laws governing the parent company—anything from standard bribes or kickbacks to the subordinate status of women to the employment of children. In these situations, some understanding must be reached with the host nation, and this can only be accomplished when the organization's employees act with flexibility and sensitivity. While the organization faces unique challenges abroad, it also gains opportunities to learn and to incorporate new ideas from the host culture. Particular care must be exerted to ensure that internal publications and audiovisual presentations—some of which may be prepared at home but distributed to offices abroad—don't offend or violate cultural norms.

Of course, you don't have to go abroad to get into trouble by offending a cultural group. The stereotyping of people in any medium is likely to cause trouble, even when it's intended to be amusing; and language can offend, as General Motors discovered at home. GM's situation involved nimbus groups—unintended recipients of a message. Often this occurs internationally when mass media (publications and broadcasts) cross borders to reach publics who are not intended recipients. In the GM case, an internal video—and not the video's effect on its intended (internal) public, but its effect at second hand on external publics who learned of it through news reports—caused the problem.

The video, presented by GM's Chevrolet Division at an internal marketing show in Detroit during September of 1990, contained interviews with customers who explained why they preferred the Chevrolet product. At one point the video showed a foreign competitor's product while one of the customers referred to it as "that little faggot truck."

News reports of the video reached the city of San Francisco, which has a politically powerful gay community. The city threatened to rescind its contract with GM to buy about $500,000 per year in cars and trucks unless GM showed how it would avoid discriminating against gays in the future. The city's officials were acting under a city ordinance that bans discrimination against homosexuals.

GM's response was to issue a corporate directive barring discrimination or insults against homosexuals, and GM Chairman Robert C. Stempel sent a letter of apology to the city of San Francisco. The company included a notice about the directive in its December 1990 company newsletter. Although the company already had an anti-discrimination policy, the new directive extended its protection to cover sexual orientation.

The nationwide directive issued on November 29, 1990, to GM managers stated that each employing unit would be responsible for implementing the policy. San Francisco officials wanted to see how GM implemented the policy before they agreed to lift their boycott, and they wanted GM to donate to a national organization that fights discrimination against gays.[22]

As GM discovered, problems often arise not out of carefully considered situations but out of careless, off-handed ones. Every word, every gesture, every representation of the organization is important.

POINTS TO REMEMBER

■ The PR department helps plan, write and disseminate the organization's mission and strategy as well as its own communication plans.

■ Public relations people use the mission statement to develop descriptive and identifying statements for the organization to use repeatedly to establish how it sees itself.

■ It is important for the PR department to determine how the organization wants to be seen by all of its publics.

■ The PR department helps management develop and interpret the organization's objectives and goals, and the PR department plans programs to help the organization achieve those objectives and goals.

■ The degree of involvement of PR in these activities depends on how management sees the public relations function.

■ PR departments are involved in identifying and solving strategic problems for the organization, a multiphase activity that begins with the perception of the problem by management, by the PR department and by others.

■ Solving the problem means recognizing the resources of the organization, the power structure, existing decision-making processes in the organization and the corporate culture.

■ The most crucial role for public relations is acting as counsel to management; but to do so, public relations practitioners must understand the problems and needs of management and must win management's trust and confidence.

■ In addition to fulfilling its support role to the organization, the public relations department must develop its own mission statement, prioritize its own publics and develop plans for its role as a department in the organization.

■ The department needs to monitor and evaluate its own activities as well as those of the organization because it must develop and defend a budget.

■ Many PR departments not only are resources to the organization, but also are expected to be profit centers, some even accepting outside clients.

■ Fees for public relations work are figured in any of three ways: as fixed fees, as fees plus expenses or as a retainer.

■ It's crucial to keep strict account of how people's time is used because that's where the PR firm's (or department's) greatest expense is.

■ PR firms often accrue unbillable expenses and consequently look for large clients to help meet expenses.

■ Too much dependence on one large client can force a firm into financial difficulty, and too many small clients can cost a firm more than they return in fees.

■ Of importance with setting and living within a budget is defending that budget to chief financial officers and clients who look for dollar value in PR services.

■ People are PR's greatest cost and its greatest asset; however, since they are usually creative types, they are not always easy to manage.

■ Many creative PR people do not want to be moved into management slots, but they need to be compensated on an increasing scale to keep them doing the same job well.

■ Adding to the challenges of managing PR people are the problems of maintaining offices abroad. PR managers must consider how their own cultural values can lead to conflicts in the resident culture.

■ Culture conflict can also occur at home. Avoiding culture clashes in the workplace and in PR practice requires both strategic planning and sensitivity.

NOTES

[1] Russell L. Colley, *Defining Advertising Goals for Measuring Advertising Results* (New York: Association of National Advertisers, 1961).

[2] The widely used Colley DAGMAR process clearly positions goals, separating them as measurable. See also Michael L. Ray, *Advertising and Communication Management* (Englewood Cliffs, N.J.: Prentice-Hall, 1982) for a complete discussion of the *measurable* goals principle.

[3] "Developer of 'The Strategic Management Process' Questions Traditional Planning: Sees Limitations, Need for Line

Management Involvement," "tips and tactics," *pr reporter*, 23(6) (April 15, 1985), p. 2.

[4] John E. Marston, *The Nature of Public Relations* (New York: McGraw-Hill, 1963), pp. 161–73; also in his *Modern Public Relations* (New York: McGraw-Hill, 1979), pp. 185–95.

[5] Scott M. Cutlip and Allen H. Center, *Effective Public Relations* (Englewood Cliffs, N.J.: Prentice-Hall, 1952), p. 87.

[6] Jerry A. Hendrix, *Public Relations Cases* (Belmont, Calif.: Wadsworth, 1998), pp. 5–6.

[7] Glen M. Broom and David M. Dozier, *Using Research in Public Relations* (Englewood Cliffs, N.J.: Prentice-Hall, 1990), p. 25.

[8] Robert L. Katz, "Human Relations Skills Can Be Sharpened," in *People: Managing Your Most Important Asset* (Boston: Harvard Business Review, 1990), p. 67.

[9] Ibid., p. 61.

[10] C. A. Bullis and P. K. Thompkins, "The Forest Ranger Revisited: A Study of Control Practices and Identification," *Communication Monographs*, 56(4), pp. 304–5.

[11] Marshall Scott Poole and Vonelle Roth, "Decision Development in Small Groups V Test of a Contingency Model," *Human Communication Research*, 15(4) (Summer 1989), p. 588.

[12] James E. Lukaszewski, "How to Coach Executives," *IABC Communication World* (June 1989), p. 38.

[13] Ibid.

[14] John W. Felton, Schranz Lecture, "A Generation of Attitudes," Oct. 20, 1994, Ball State University, Muncie, Indiana.

[15] Lukaszewski, "How to Coach Executives," pp. 39–41.

[16] Alfred G. Paulson, "Cost Accounting in the Public Relations Firm," *Public Relations Quarterly*, 16(3) (1972), pp. 14–15. See also "Budgeting in the Public Relations Agency" and "Accounting Reports in Public Relations," *Public Relations Quarterly*, 9(4) (1972).

[17] Amy Stevens, "Lawyers and Clients," *Wall Street Journal* (April 29, 1994), p. B10.

[18] Ibid.

[19] Reprinted with permission of Jim Haynes, public relations counselor, Dallas, Texas.

[20] Craig S. Fleisher and Sara Burton, "Taking Stock of Corporate Benchmarking Practices: Panacea or Pandora's Box?" *Public Relations Review*, 21 (1) (Spring 1995), pp. 1–20.

[21] H. Lawrence Smith, "Accountability in PR: Budgets and Benchmarks," *Public Relations Quarterly*, 41 (1) (Spring 1996), pp. 15–19.

[22] Jim Carlton, "An Apologetic GM Bars Discrimination, Insults Against Gays," *Wall Street Journal* (December 31, 1990), pp. 3, 28.

Selected readings, activities and assignments appropriate to this chapter can be found in the *Instructor's Guide* or on InfoTrac if you are using the InfoTrac College Edition.

CHAPTER 11

COMMUNICATION CHANNELS AND MEDIA

The sharp drop in the credibility of most U.S. institutions means that the message must be designed with the background of a specific public in mind, so that it will be fully understood. It means also that the real questions in the minds of those publics must be solicited—and answered.

CARL HAWVER, FORMER PRESIDENT, PUBLIC RELATIONS SOCIETY OF AMERICA

In my opinion, the best prevention and the most effective form of communication is behavior itself!

STEPHEN A. GREYSER, PROFESSOR OF BUSINESS ADMINISTRATION,
HARVARD BUSINESS SCHOOL

Channels of communication are public or private paths for messages to and from various publics. Media are conveyances for messages in those channels. Public channels are dominated by mass or specialized media available to anyone who chooses to subscribe or tune in. Private channels are more commonly used by media directed to a particular chosen individual or group. It's important to remember that, while a medium may be a person, media generally are either print or electronic.

The frequently used classification of print and electronic media into internal and external types is somewhat artificial because it focuses on the medium's intended audience or public, not on the medium itself. As we noted in Chapter 4, however, publics don't necessarily accept those categories. Some members of external audiences, such as stockholders or university alumni, may see themselves as internal. And parts of the Internet, such as e-mail, are more private than public.

Another distinction frequently made in public relations regarding media is between controlled and uncontrolled types. When a medium is said to be controlled, there is some guarantee that the message crafted for that medium will be delivered to the audience as created, without modification, barring some kind of technical failure or human error. But with global access to messages through electronic technology, many messages now reach audiences for which they were never intended. For example, the commercials that accompany television programs are beamed by satellite to audiences all over the world; but in most cases, these were designed for audiences in the country of origin, with virtually no regard to their international exposure. Information available on electronic data banks is another example: most of it was prepared with a specific audience in mind. Now many unintended audiences are receiving and using messages in ways the preparers never imagined.

The challenge today is to think of media as recognizing no borders and of messages as having the potential to reach unintended audiences who may misinterpret them. Given that general guideline, the public relations practitioner must still try to design public-specific messages and media.

CHOOSING THE MEDIUM

All public relations efforts should have a specific objective. That objective, together with the audience, the message itself, the element of timeliness and your budget, should determine your choice of media. Generally, a mix of media is used, and one important consideration in this regard is the choice between controlled and uncontrolled media.

A billboard is an example of a controlled medium. You have complete control over its content and its appearance. Television, on the other hand, is an uncontrolled medium, since—even when you control the content of a message (because it is an ad or PSA)—you do not control its context (what spot is shown immediately before or after it, and what content the surrounding program will have). Still, an advertisement or public service announcement does constitute a controlled communication because the creator generally has control over the message. Other forms of communication are uncontrolled. For example, a news conference or a groundbreaking ceremony that receives TV coverage is an uncontrolled communication, since the PR person has no assurance that the cameras will film the event or focus the coverage in the desired way.

Of course, an element of uncontrollability lurks in every aspect of communication. There is no guarantee that the audience to whom a message is directed will pay attention to it or respond to it. You must carefully weigh the advantages and disadvantages of each medium before investing time, creativity and money in it. However, avoid the temptation to consider *production costs* instead of *cost-effectiveness*.

You should consider three questions in selecting the proper medium for your message:

1. What audience are you trying to reach, and what is its credibility rating for each medium?

2. When do you need to reach this audience, and by what date does it need to receive a message in order to respond to it?

3. How much do you need to spend, and how much can you afford to spend?

After you have answered and evaluated these questions, you need to ask four additional questions:

1. Which medium reaches the broadest segment of your target audience at the lowest cost?

2. Which one has the highest credibility, and what is its cost?

3. Which medium can you count on to deliver the message within the necessary time constraints for the message to be effective?

4. Should a single medium be used? If a media mix is desirable, which media should be used to complement one another?

To make effective use of the media selected, you must know enough about the mechanics and technology of each medium to prepare the copy properly. Most students are surprised by the amount and different styles of writing demanded of PR practitioners. PR professors are not surprised, however, because in recommending students for jobs after graduation, they find the most frequently asked question is "Can they write?" The question implies "for all media." In preparing messages for all media, you must consider the differences and the advantages and disadvantages of various media (see Examples 11.1 and 11.2).

EXAMPLE 11.1

Principal Media: Advantages and Disadvantages

TELEVISION

Advantages

1. Combines sight, sound and motion attributes
2. Permits physical demonstration of product
3. Believability due to immediacy of message
4. High impact of message
5. Huge audiences
6. Good product identification
7. Popular medium

Disadvantages

1. Message limited by restricted time segments
2. No possibility for consumer referral to message
3. Availabilities sometimes difficult to arrange
4. High time costs
5. Waste coverage
6. High production costs
7. Poor color transmission

RADIO

Advantages

1. Selectivity of geographical markets
2. Good saturation of local markets
3. Ease of changing advertising copy
4. Relatively low cost

Disadvantages

1. Message limited by restricted time segments
2. No possibility for consumer referral to message
3. No visual appeal
4. Waste coverage

MAGAZINES

Advantages

1. Selectivity of audience
2. Reaches more affluent consumers
3. Offers prestige to an advertiser
4. Pass-along readership
5. Good color reproduction

Disadvantages

1. Often duplicate circulation
2. Usually cannot dominate in a local market
3. Long closing dates
4. No immediacy of message
5. Sometimes high production costs

NEWSPAPERS

Advantages

1. Selectivity of geographical markets
2. Ease of changing advertising copy
3. Reaches all income groups
4. Ease of scheduling advertisements
5. Relatively low cost
6. Good medium for manufacturer/dealer advertising

Disadvantages

1. High cost for national coverage
2. Shortness of message life
3. Waste circulation
4. Differences of sizes and formats
5. Rate differentials between local and national advertisements
6. Sometimes poor color reproduction

Source: Leon Quera, *Advertising Campaigns: Formulation and Tactics* (Columbus, Ohio: Grid, 1973), pp. 71–74. Used by permission.

EXAMPLE 11.2

Supplemental Media: Advantages and Disadvantages

DIRECT MAIL

Advantages

1. Extremely selective
2. Message can be very personalized
3. Little competition with other advertisements
4. Easy to measure effect of advertisements
5. Provides easy means for consumer action

Disadvantages

1. Often has poor image
2. Can be quite expensive
3. Many restrictive postal regulations
4. Problems in maintaining mailing lists

POINT-OF-PURCHASE DISPLAYS

Advantages

1. Presents message at point of sale
2. Great flexibility for creativity
3. Ability to demonstrate product in use
4. Good color reproduction
5. Repetitive value

Disadvantages

1. Dealer apathy in installation
2. Long production period
3. High unit cost
4. Shipping problems
5. Space problem

OUTDOOR POSTERS (ON STATIONARY PANELS)

Advantages

1. Selectivity of geographical markets
2. High repetitive value
3. Large physical size
4. Relatively low cost
5. Good color reproduction

Disadvantages

1. Often has poor image
2. Message must be short
3. Waste circulation
4. National coverage is expensive
5. Few creative specialists

TRANSIT POSTERS (ON MOVING VEHICLES)

Advantages

1. Selectivity of geographical markets
2. Captive audience
3. Very low cost
4. Good color reproduction
5. High repetitive value

Disadvantages

1. Cannot be employed in all theaters
2. Waste circulation

CHOOSING THE MESSAGE— ADVERTISING OR PUBLICITY

Confusion about what is advertising and what is publicity is natural because lines are blurring between the two. Furthermore, while consumers of information may intellectually know the difference, they seldom remember whether the source of information was advertising or publicity unless the presentation was particularly memorable. For the discussion in this chapter, though, it is important to separate the two.

The major distinction is *economic*. Advertising has its own space and time in print and broadcast media. That space and time is for sale. So, *advertising is time or space that is paid for.*

3. Surroundings may be disreputable

4. Few creative specialists

MOVIE TRAILERS

Advantages

1. Selectivity of geographical markets

2. Captive audience

3. Large physical size

4. Good medium for manufacturer/dealer advertising

Disadvantages

1. Cannot be employed in all theaters

2. Waste circulation

3. High production costs

4. No possibility for consumer referral to message

ADVERTISING SPECIALTIES

Advantages

1. Unique presentation

2. High repetitive value

3. Has a "gift" quality

4. Relatively long life

Disadvantages

1. Subject to fads

2. Message must be short

3. May have relatively high unit cost

4. Effectiveness difficult to measure

PAMPHLETS AND BOOKLETS

Advantages

1. Offer detailed message at point of sale

2. Supplement a personal sales presentation

3. Offer to potential buyers a good referral means

4. Good color reproduction

Disadvantages

1. Dealers often fail to use

2. May have a relatively high unit cost

3. Few creative specialists

4. Effectiveness difficult to measure

COMPUTERS

Advantages

1. Highly personalized

2. Creativity and flexibility

3. Home, office and remote site use

Disadvantages

1. Restricted group of users

2. Costs high

There are two exceptions to this. One occurs when a medium uses its own time or space to promote one of its own products. A newspaper might advertise its own Web page. It looks just like an ad, but it is for the same organization and no money has changed hands. In broadcasting, you recognize these commerical messages as "promos," or promotional announcements for something special in the programming, usually for that day or something later in the week. Another exception is when *the media give time or space* in their commercial slots *to nonprofit organizations* for messages which are prepared just like commercial messages. These messages are called *public service announcements*.

Publicity, on the other hand, *is news about a client, product or service that appears in the time or* space that media reserve for "copy"—news, features or editorial content—or "programming" in broadcasting.

Most programming is not wholly paid for because advertising is sold around the programs. However, some television stations do carry what is identified in viewing guides as "paid programming" or "infomercials." In that case, the entire program is really an ad. Print versions of that situation are special sections that may look like the rest of the paper, but are really advertising, and a disclaimer is printed on the section that says "Paid Advertising."

TYPES OF ADVERTISING USED IN PR PRACTICE

Three types of advertising are most common to public relations practice: house ads, public service announcements and institutional advertising used for issues, advocacy and identity. Three other types are used less often, but do occur: specialty, cooperative and professional advertising.

House Ads

A house ad is what an organization prepares for use in its own medium or in another medium controlled by the same owner. For instance, a newspaper that is part of a chain of print and broadcast media might promote a special subscription offer or announce a new "Lifestyles" section by running an ad or promo on the chain's television stations. No money is exchanged, although space allotments or "budgets" are established.

Public Service Announcements

PSAs are sales or promotional pieces—not news stories—in the form of announcements. Generally, broadcast stations give unsold air time for PSAs, which are prepared just like commercials, from organizations such as the United Way, the American Heart Association or the local symphony. No money is exchanged, but the station may send the nonprofit organization an invoice for the amount

of air time given, listing the number of hours and the commercial rate and bearing the notation "paid in full."

One word of warning if you work for a nonprofit advertiser: Just because your free public service time leaves some money in your advertising budget, don't splurge on sizable ads in print media. Broadcasters can read. If a station is running your spots free of charge on public service time and you buy sizable ads from a print space salesperson, you are likely to get a bill instead of a complimentary credit slip from the broadcaster.

PSAs have also found their way into cable systems.

The release of radio PSAs on compact disks (CD) appears to be an effective format, according to News/Broadcast Network's president Mike Hill. Hill said his firm released a PSA to 3,000 radio stations and found wide acceptance, since most radio station libraries have now converted to CDs. The lower CD production cost makes the format more affordable, Hill said.[1]

Print PSAs are generally, but not always, found toward the back of magazines and occasionally in newspapers. Leftover space is made available for free display ads (see Example 11.3).

Commercial partnerships with nonprofits are not new, but they have increased dramatically as advertising costs have accelerated while the ability to reach audiences has dropped. These partnerships are sometimes confused with public service announcements. The intent is to serve the public, but the commercial partnership takes the message statement out of the realm of public service announcements and into the area of cooperative advertising and promotion.

Institutional Advertising

The objective of some institutional advertising is to convey a particular message. *Issue ads* are used by an organization as a forum for its views on a topic or problem. When the issue affects the organization directly, the advertising almost amounts to "position" statements directed to the public. Mobil Corporation uses these ads often on issues such as

EXAMPLE 11.3
American Heart Association's Public Service Announcement

Reproduced with permission. "Research gave him a future," PSA, 1995. Copyright American Heart Association.

support for multinational companies. These ads are often called "advertorials" in print media and sometimes "infomercials" in broadcasting, although infomercials are usually longer than a 60-second spot on an issue. Another type of longer infomercial, the "intermercial," appears on the Internet; it includes dialogue and motion video and may last up to four minutes. Their name comes from "interstitials" which are the ads that pop up while a browser is downloading a page from a site.

Companies seeking public support for corporate policies and programs have begun to invest more in *advocacy advertising*. Advocacy ads are a form of lobbying to influence public opinion. They go beyond offering a general comment on issues to urging support for a position that benefits the organization specifically. At one time, advocacy advertising in the broadcast media was known by the sobriquet *advertorials,* but the latter term now is applied to long magazine supplements as well. The long copy provides more information about a product or service and generally appears in magazines carefully chosen to reach audiences likely to be interested in learning more about the organization than a single-page ad could convey.

Corporate advocacy advertising often looks like editorial copy, although it may be clearly identified as an ad. Some corporate advocacy is done in partnership with a nonprofit organization and becomes a form of cooperative advertising.

Another type of institutional ad, which functions less as a persuasive message than as a reminder, is the type some companies call *sustaining* or *image ads.* Image ads are often used by companies seeking to modify their public image. They may present a redesigned logo or a change in policy.

The image ad is also used by monopolies that wish to represent themselves as public servants. Companies frequently use this type of advertising to win favorable public opinion.

Nonprofit organizations, especially trade and professional organizations, may use image advertising, too. Because of an image ad's tone and content, it may be mistaken for publicity.

Some image advertising looks like product advertising and vice versa. A company may relate image to product if it is important to the company's reputation that its name be associated, in the public's mind, with a certain product. When image ads are not used, the company may begin to suffer a decline in public approval and market share; after two years, the decline is quick and dramatic. If image ads are stopped when money is tight, the results can be disastrous.

A device similar to image ads is the *identity ad*, often used by nonconsumer product companies, or by consumer-oriented companies when takeovers or spinoffs have blurred public recognition.

Commercial Advertising by Nonprofits

Not all advertising that nonprofit organizations do is public service advertising. Much is paid-for time or space. The *Wall Street Journal* carried a story about a campaign by the Episcopal Church to get people to return to church. The television commercials were created by the St. Louis office of D'Arcy Masius Benton & Bowles for the Episcopal Radio-TV Foundation, a nonprofit Atlanta-based group that produces programming under the auspices of the Episcopal Church.[2]

While many churches (Episcopal included) run ads around traditional religious holidays, this campaign in four states (Georgia, Tennessee, Ohio and Iowa) was aimed at getting people to return to the Episcopal Church on a regular basis. The target public was women between 25 and 45 because research showed these were more likely than other population subgroups to return to church and to bring their families. Other research, however, indicates that a much older generation is likely to attend church services on a regular basis. The investment was necessary to help reverse declining

membership, according to the Rev. Canon Louis C. Schueddig of the Episcopal Radio-TV Foundation. He was quoted in the *Wall Street Journal* article as saying, "Materialism isn't the option it was five years ago."[3]

Creating Problems and Solving Problems with Advertising

Advertising can sometimes do more harm than good. For example, a spot on Peruvian television showed Africans ready to devour some white tourists until they are offered Nabisco's Royal Pudding instead. Peruvians saw it as fanciful and funny, but when when the television show Inside Edition attacked the ad in the USA, Nabisco said the ad was inconsistent with the company's values and was a "mistake." Adapting sales pitches to foreign markets without offending home audiences is essential. Although many companies depend on local agencies to appeal to that market, some guidelines need to exist.[4]

One of the first considerations for global advertising is usually language, but it's also important to be sensitive to cultural preferences. Culture may be a more important consideration than language. In fact, often when English will work as a language, the culture is so different that the art or graphics or even "tone" of the writing won't be effective. Advertising that creates a public relations problem is not money well spent. This is where research about publics is more than worth the investment.

Even in domestic settings, more thorough research wouldn't hurt. In fact, it's the lack of research that dooms most corporate image ads. Most of the image ads are so "fact free" that they fail to persuade. This is especially the case among people like investors who read the *Wall Street Journal*, where many such ads appear. Many of these corporate ads are not test marketed for potential impact on stock price. What corporate image ads should be doing is building confidence.[5]

Ads are more often used successfully to do just that in time of crisis. Getting a message out about a problem is usually best in a controlled format that advertising offers. Ads showing 800 numbers for people to call are often notices of some sort of difficulty or problem, and access to the company is critical to bolster confidence or, in some cases, to offer information.

Advertising in Other Formats

Sometimes the artwork for a print ad can be used in other formats. The most common of these is the *poster,* which in smaller form is called a *flyer,* and in larger form a *billboard.* Mail inserts are another type of format. Other versions are *transit* or *in-store* advertising. Some versions, usually of flyer size, are even sent as *fax* advertising. Fax advertising, which is usually from suppliers or service industries, has encountered some problems because the receiver pays for the paper on which the unsolicited message is printed.

There should be continuity between poster or billboard art, the packaging for a product and the store displays. An opera association, for example, may have a table flanked by posters set up in the lobby at performances to sell cups, tote bags, umbrellas and other items bearing the opera's logo. The purpose in this case is to raise money for the nonprofit organization. Some of these items, like pens with the opera logo, are the types of materials that profit-making organizations give away as advertising specialties.

Specialty Advertising Without looking, can you recall the company whose name is on the pen you use or on your desk calendar? Advertising specialties are useful, inexpensive items, such as pens or calendars, imprinted with an organization's name, logo or message. These items are given away to customers or perhaps as souvenirs to those who attend a special event.

Cooperative Advertising Cooperative advertising offers almost as many advantages as advertising placed by a single organization. When one advertiser shares a message with another—such as when a cheese dip manufacturer combines with a potato chip manufacturer to buy advertising space and time—it also shares the production and space/time costs. This enables each to participate in both the production and the exposure. Sometimes creative

compromises are necessary, but it still is a controlled situation.

Cooperative advertising can involve commercial–nonprofit partnerships. One example is the actual endorsement of a product by a nonprofit organization in exchange for part of the proceeds of the sale. The first to do this was Johnson & Johnson's aspirin, which teamed up with the Arthritis Foundation, and the partnership was touted in the ads and on the product's bottles.

A more traditional partnership exists between the National Cancer Institute (NCI) and the Kellogg Company. The cereal company wanted health identification for a new All-Bran fiber cereal, and NCI was trying to get more attention for its Cancer Prevention Awareness Program, which emphasizes a low-fat, high-fiber diet. NCI did not specifically endorse Kellogg, and Kellogg was careful not to make any such claim in its advertising. NCI did let Kellogg publicize its research on the value of bran, however, and Kellogg benefited from NCI's credibility as a federal agency. The combined effort involved both a consumer campaign and a professional campaign, the latter directed toward dietitians and general practitioners. The messages appeared on All-Bran boxes and in magazine ads for the product.[6]

The partnerships can be between nonprofits, too, as when the American Heart Association, the American Cancer Society and the American Lung Association combined their efforts to combat smoking. Another arrangement is exemplified by a joint effort of the National Spa and Pool Institute (an industry trade group), the Consumer Product Safety Commission and the American Red Cross to develop a campaign on pool safety.[7]

Advertising by Professionals

Both advertising agencies and PR firms are now learning to deal with advertising and promotion by lawyers, dentists, doctors and other professionals, who used to be prohibited by their professional codes of conduct from engaging in such commercial activities. As these professionals began putting their names in print and their faces on television, a new market for public relations practitioners opened.

In 1975, after the Federal Trade Commission began attacking advertising restrictions on lawyers, doctors and dentists, self-promotional advertisements began to appear—particularly in local newspapers and on local television. Several Supreme Court decisions supported this trend among the professional groups. Although some PR practitioners are understandably pleased by the development, others consider handling some professional clients to be ethically questionable. The most recent ethical problem has arisen over testimonial ads for lawyers—especially televised testimonials. Although such ads are growing in popularity, many lawyers feel that they are in poor taste and may be misleading.[8]

Some law firms are hiring their own public relations directors, and some are hiring marketing directors. Their expectation in doing so is that the person hired will improve the bottom line through getting new clients and maintaining good relationships with existing clients, as well as by creating an identity for the firm.

■ Languages and Advertising

In the USA, advertisers are targeting their ads more frequently by using languages other than English. There are language-specific media—print and broadcast—and neighborhoods where the language of preference is not English. In the latter case, mail to these zip code addresses and billboards and posters placed in these areas are not in English, but in the preferred language (see Example 11.4).

ADVERTISING AS CONTROLLED/ UNCONTROLLED COMMUNICATION

■ Controlled Advertising

One significant advantage of using paid advertising is that the advertiser nearly always has *total control*—over the message itself, over the context in which it will appear (size, shape, color) and over the medium in which it will run. And, of course, the advertiser knows approximately *when* an audience will receive the message. In addition, the advertiser has access to media research about the medium's audience, indicating *who* will receive the message and *how often* the audience will be exposed to it. Finally, media research will tell the advertiser the typical *impact* an ad schedule will have on the target audience's behavior.

■ Uncontrolled Advertising

Uncontrolled advertising consists of PSAs prepared for use on radio and television stations. The message is controlled, but the delivery time is not.

Only nonprofit organizations qualify for free public service time. But because such time is scarce, the United Fund and local symphony season ticket drives must compete for it just as fiercely as any business competes for dollars. National organizations like the American Heart Association and the American Red Cross send stations highly professional tapes, usually cut with a celebrity's voice. These are mailed far enough in advance to give station personnel time to find good slots in the daily programming for the announcements. In contrast, local organizations are more likely to put in a frantic call the day before a local blood drive asking the station to run some announcements starting immediately—with no tape and probably not even any copy. Or someone drops by with a dozen slides and two pages of copy and does not understand why this can't be aired. Remember, however, that any PSA is used only if the station has time available to give, and even this slot may be sold and the PSA bumped at the last minute.

The amount of time and space for PSAs decreases as commercials and the media's own advertising—house ads and promos—fill up the vacancies. In broadcasting, this has occurred to such an extent that FCC Chairman Reed Hundt chastised broadcasters in 1997 for "self promoting at the expense of PSAs."[9] His comments occurred at a time when both the Executive and Legislative branches of government were revisiting the issue of requiring additional public service responsibilities in exchange for their digital TV licenses.

Many people imagine that the stations already are required by the Federal Communications Commission to devote a certain percentage of each broadcast day to PSAs. But a station is not compelled to do so by law. Furthermore, an FCC action in 1984 erased a guideline for TV that recommended devoting 10 percent of airtime to nonentertainment programming. The corresponding guideline for radio was abolished in 1981.

Station policies on PSA time are so diverse that they defy any general description. The effective practitioner simply learns and then meets the demands of the stations.

PREPARING ADVERTISING MESSAGES

A person writing advertising copy needs more than a list of details from marketing and sales describing what is supposed to be pushed. The copywriter must also know the purpose of the ad or commercial, the media it will appear in and its audience.

Copywriters must clearly define an ad's purpose. Is the purpose to *inform*? Is it to introduce a new product, attract a new market, suggest a new use for a familiar product, give a corporate identity to a conglomerate or familiarize an audience with a new trademark? Is the purpose of the ad to *persuade*? Should the ad or commercial try to get its audience to think or do something? The following ad from a laundry company appeared in a British newspaper; its purpose is quite clear: "Strong, fat women who wish to lose weight wanted for hard but well-paid work."

Sometimes an ad's purpose is "positioning." Advertisers developed this technique as a way of finding a foothold in the marketplace, and publicity strategists are now borrowing it. Positioning attempts to isolate a segment of the market in a highly competitive field by creating a unique image for a product that is fundamentally the same as its competitors. Thus, this technique artificially segments the audience.

After determining an ad's purpose, the next consideration is which media to use. Most ads go into a media mix, so the way the material can be interpreted for all sorts of media is important in crafting the message and planning the visuals.

Even if you hire others to write and produce the ads, you need to know a great deal about the media in which these ads will appear so that they will fit each medium's audience. In every case, you need to know about costs and estimated impact in order to make a useful presentation. You have to plan how to allocate resources so that you make the most of your budget.

Because advertising is so expensive, most organizations turn over actual ad development to a group of professional writers and artists. However, these people don't know the organization and the publics as well as someone who works with them all of the time. You need to help them convey the right tone in the ad, and you also have to get absolutely correct information to people who will be developing the ad, commercial or PSA. If a mistake winds up in an expensive production, and it's your mistake, the people who developed the ad don't have to make good on it. They will do it again, of course, but it has to be paid for again. Also, advertising deadlines are often tight, and there may not be time if the mistake is a major one. What happens then—when the media space or time is bought and there's no ad for it? Someone may be out of a job.

A special consideration in evaluating ads before they are approved for distribution is to reexamine the ad that has been produced in light of the purpose that was defined earlier. Sometimes ads are designed to win awards, and they often do. But the recognition for the award benefits the producer of the ad more than the organization paying for it. Award winning ads are not always message-effective. The interests of the client compel you to keep the purpose in focus. Your responsibility is to evaluate carefully the best way to deliver your message within the constraints of time and budget.

UNCONTROLLABLE PROBLEMS

One of the biggest problems you will face in using advertising is that, if you get a good idea, it's likely to be imitated. Christian Brothers created a very successful ad campaign for its beverages using

EXAMPLE 11.4
Advertising Brochure for Service Protection Plans in Two Languages

InLine and InLine Plus services provide repair and replacement of Inside Wire rendered defective by reason of ordinary wear and tear, simple negligence, and partial destruction of the Inside Wiring by reason of fire, lightning, wind, or casualty.

InLine service also includes the modular mounting cord that extends from your telephone set to your jack receptacle or connecting block associated with Inside Wire. A cord will be given to any InLine or InLine Plus subscriber when it is determined the trouble is in the modular mounting cord.

What is NOT included in the InLine® services?

Excluded from coverage of InLine services are Inside Wire rendered defective by reasons of flood, earthquake, acts of war, fire, lightning, wind, or other casualty requiring a substantial reconstruction of the premises. (The preceding exclusions do not apply in Kansas.) Also excluded from coverage of InLine services are Inside Wire rendered defective by gross negligence, willful damage, or vandalism. Inside Wiring that did not work when the service was ordered or that does not meet our installation practices or technical standards is not covered by InLine services. Outside wiring or a detached structure on the same premises is not covered by InLine services. For example, aerial or buried wire from your home to a tool shed or barn is not Inside Wire, and thus is not covered by InLine. Inside Wire inside the detached structure, however, is covered by InLine.

If damage to Inside Wire occurs in connection with other physical damage to a portion of a residence or business premises, repair or replacement of it normally is provided so long as continuous telephone service is provided at the premises. If destruction of a residence or business premises is so severe that telephone service must be disconnected and subsequently re-established, the installation or replacement of Inside Wire is not provided by InLine services. (Usually, your fire or homeowner's insurance policy will reimburse you for the cost of replacement of wiring damaged by fire and other insured risks.)

Inside Wiring is not covered when we are prevented from accessing it, for example, by the owner of the property, by government or military authorities (i.e., the Customer lives on a military base), or by your landlord.

Customer's Responsibility

If the work you request requires conduit, cutting and patching of finished walls, floors and ceilings, or structure modifications, you are responsible for arranging to have such work performed by other persons.

After each repair or installation visit, you have the responsibility to reestablish the connection or verify proper functioning of any telephone transmitting, dialing or answering equipment connected to your Inside Wire, such as automatic dialers, fire and burglar alarms, meters, sensors, answering devices, and telephones. It is also your responsibility to reprogram any telephone numbers or codes that have been extinguished as a result of the line or any equipment being disconnected during our tests of the functioning of your Inside Wire or the central office network access line.

You are also responsible for obtaining repair of any of your telephone equipment determined to be defective, for obtaining a replacement telephone, and for the proper and timely return of any loaner telephone provided to you as a subscriber to InLine Plus.

Charges and Taxes

By requesting InLine or InLine Plus, you agree to pay our current charges for such services, as well as any taxes and fees assessed against either you or Southwestern Bell on the charges for the service.

Cancellation of Service

You may cancel the service at any time by calling our service center. Charges are prorated to the date service is canceled, except that, for the first month, there is a minimum of one month billing. There is no charge for canceling the service. We may cancel the InLine services upon a customer's failure to timely pay the charges for InLine services or in instances where there has been an abuse of the service. An abuse of service occurs when a customer repeatedly uses or permits damage to occur to Inside Wire. If InLine or InLine Plus is reordered after cancellation, there is a 30-day waiting period before the service becomes effective.

Limited Warranty

Identification and isolation of the cause of trouble in an electronic network, like the telephone system, is sometimes difficult and time consuming, especially if the trouble is from multiple causes or is intermittent. Our sole responsibility under InLine and InLine Plus is to use reasonable skill, procedures and equipment to locate and fix the trouble, or isolate it to specific customer Inside Wire or telephone equipment. Except as otherwise provided in this Agreement, if we are not successful in identifying or eliminating the problem, or if we do not perform a repair or replacement correctly, so long as you continue to subscribe to InLine services, we will return to your premises to correct the repair or replacement at no additional charge. No other warranty or guarantee, expressed or implied, is given for InLine or InLine Plus. The warranty for loaner telephones purchased by InLine Plus Customers is governed by warranty documents included with the telephone set delivered to you.

DISCLAIMER OF WARRANTY

WE HEREBY EXPRESSLY DISCLAIM ALL AND ANY IMPLIED WARRANTY OF FITNESS FOR A PARTICULAR PURPOSE, OR ANY IMPLIED WARRANTIES NOT EXPRESSLY GRANTED IN THIS CONTRACT.

LIMITATION AND EXCLUSION OF LIABILITY

Southwestern Bell shall not be liable for delays or failure to perform Inside Wire repair or installation service due to circumstances beyond our reasonable control, i.e. labor strikes, natural catastrophes, civil disturbances, weather, material shortages, and unusual work loads.

Southwestern Bell's liability for damages caused by or arising out of our failure to perform or ineffective performance of InLine services, or our failure to provide an InLine Plus loaner telephone or radio interference filter, in a proper and timely manner, shall in no event exceed the lesser of (i) $100, or (ii) the actual cost to repair, replace or install the Inside Wire, or (b) the actual cost to provide a loaner telephone equipment, incurred by you during the first 30 days after we have made a service call to your home or business, if you were an InLine services subscriber at the time of the repair.

Southwestern Bell shall not be responsible or liable for defacement or damage to customer premises occasioned by drilling of holes, or in the attachment and removal of wiring and equipment with standard screws, staples, hooks, fasteners and adhesives when performed in a workmanlike manner.

SOUTHWESTERN BELL SHALL NOT BE LIABLE UNDER ANY CIRCUMSTANCES FOR ATTORNEYS' FEES, INCIDENTAL OR CONSEQUENTIAL DAMAGES, INCLUDING BUT NOT LIMITED TO LOST PROFITS OR ANY OTHER EXPENSE, LOSS OR DAMAGE, DIRECTLY OR INDIRECTLY ARISING FROM THE PERFORMANCE OR INLINE PLUS SERVICES OR FROM THE MALFUNCTIONING OR NON-FUNCTIONING OF APPARATUS CONNECTED TO YOUR INSIDE WIRE, SUCH AS AUTOMATIC DIALERS, FIRE AND BURGLAR ALARMS, METERS, SENSORS, ANSWERING DEVICES AND TELEPHONES.

Prices

For current prices for any services described in this Contract, call our service center.

Amendment of Contract, Increases in Prices, and Termination of Offering

We reserve the right to discontinue offering InLine and InLine Plus, or to amend the terms and conditions, including increasing the prices, by giving InLine and InLine Plus Customers at least one month written notice of the contract amendment, change in the charges, or discontinuance of the offering. This notice may be in the form of a notice included with or as part of your monthly phone bill. By paying the monthly charge after the effective date of the notice, you agree to be bound by the amendment or change in charges.

Important Additional Information for the Customer

Our Customers experience a wide variety of need for Inside Wire repair. On average, 1.5% of our residential and single business line subscribers obtain some form of Inside Wire repair each month. Your repair experience may be significantly higher or lower. The following is a partial list of factors that may affect your need for repair: weather conditions in your area, age and condition of your home or business location, number of telephone users in your home or business, equipment in your home or business, the presence of pets or animals, and other variables. You are in the best position to decide whether this service is a good value based on your own experience with telephone service and repair.

ENTIRETY OF AGREEMENT

NO REPRESENTATIVE OF SOUTHWESTERN BELL HAS AUTHORITY TO MAKE ANY REPRESENTATION, PROMISE, GUARANTEE, OR WARRANTY TO YOU OTHER THAN THAT STATED IN WRITING IN THIS CONTRACT. IF SUCH STATEMENTS HAVE BEEN MADE TO YOU, PLEASE CALL OUR SERVICE CENTER LISTED IN YOUR SOUTHWESTERN BELL TELEPHONE DIRECTORY IMMEDIATELY, INASMUCH AS SUCH CONDUCT CONSTITUTES A VIOLATION OF COMPANY POLICY. THIS CONTRACT CONSTITUTES THE COMPLETE AGREEMENT AND UNDERSTANDING BETWEEN SOUTHWESTERN BELL AND YOU CONCERNING THE PROVISION OF INLINE AND INLINE PLUS SERVICES. THIS CONTRACT IS INTENDED BY SOUTHWESTERN BELL AND BY YOU AS THE FINAL EXPRESSION OF OUR AGREEMENT FOR PROVISION OF INLINE AND INLINE PLUS SERVICES, AND IS A COMPLETE AND EXCLUSIVE STATEMENT OF ITS TERMS. THIS CONTRACT MAY NOT BE SUPPLEMENTED OR MODIFIED EXCEPT IN WRITING, WHEN SIGNED BY AN AUTHORIZED REPRESENTATIVE OF SOUTHWESTERN BELL.

Courtesy of Southwestern Bell.

EXAMPLE 11.4 (continued)
Advertising Brochure for Service Protection Plans in Two Languages

WHAT IS IT, HOW WILL IT BENEFIT YOU, AND WHAT DOES IT COST?

Southwestern Bell Telephone Company handles millions of telephone calls for its customers each day. Of those calls, 99.9% go through on the first attempt.

On occasion, you may experience a telephone service problem. The problem could be in our network, in the wiring that connects your telephone to our network, or in your telephone set. This booklet tells you about your phone service and about two helpful service protection plans – InLine® and InLine® Plus. But first, here is some basic information on how your telephone service works so you will know your options if something goes wrong.

Overview of Your Phone System

There are three parts of your telephone service that you need to know about to understand what your costs may be if something goes wrong:

1. Outside wiring – is the network that brings telephone service to your home or business. If something goes wrong with outside wiring, we will repair it free of charge – whether or not you subscribe to InLine.

2. Inside wiring, jacks and cords – are the wiring inside your home or business which connect outside wiring to your wall jacks and the cord from those jacks to your telephone. If something goes wrong in your wire, jacks or cords, you are generally responsible for having it fixed, and

3. Telephone equipment – is the phones or other telecommunication equipment in your home or business. If something goes wrong with that equipment, most often you must pay the cost of replacing or fixing it.

Your need for inside wire repair will depend on your circumstances. Generally, inside wiring does not often need to be fixed. When it does, however, you may have to pay $78 – $116 or more for a single visit by a technician to decide what is wrong and fix the problem, unless you have InLine or InLine Plus.

How Can We Help You Keep Down Costs If Something Goes Wrong with Your Telephone Service?

We want to help you avoid unexpected costs. That's why we are offering you two service plans: "InLine" and "InLine Plus." You can choose either plan to cover inside wiring and jacks in your home or business, but you do not have to sign up for a plan. These are optional services that you do not need to continue basic phone service. You can cancel at any time without a disconnect charge.

What Do You Get If You Sign Up For InLine?

As a subscriber to either InLine or InLine Plus, if you have a problem with your telephone service, just call us. We will diagnose the trouble and, if the problem is with your inside wire, jacks or cords, we will repair the trouble at no additional charge. InLine Plus also offers you more. If the problem is with your telephone, we will loan you a phone to use for up to sixty (60) days. If you wish to purchase the loaner phone, you may contact our service center. Our repair technician will see to it that you are supplied with a loaner phone so that you don't miss important calls. InLine Plus also provides simple radio-interference filters in certain instances. Please see the actual contract terms that follow.

What Kinds of Problems are NOT Covered by InLine® and InLine® Plus?

While Southwestern Bell provides a great variety of service and protection through its InLine and InLine Plus service plans, it does not cover every conceivable type of damage to your inside wiring, jacks or cords. For example, InLine service does not cover problems with your inside wiring due to intentional damage or wiring that does not meet installation or equipment standards adopted by Southwestern Bell. For further information concerning exclusions, please see the actual contract terms that follow.

If you are renting your home or place of business, your landlord rather than you may be required to pay to fix inside wiring. Check with your landlord to see who is responsible for fixing inside wiring. Even if your landlord will fix your wiring, you may prefer the convenience and peace of mind of InLine – the choice is yours.

How Much Do InLine® and InLine® Plus Cost?

If you sign up for InLine or InLine Plus, you will pay a few dollars per month for each telephone line you have in your home or business. InLine Plus costs a bit more than InLine. The prices are subject to change and may vary from state to state. Please call our service center listed in your Southwestern Bell telephone directory for the present price in your state.

READ CAREFULLY

INLINE® AND INLINE® PLUS SERVICE CONTRACT TERMS AND CONDITIONS

InLine® and InLine® Plus sometimes jointly referred to hereinafter as "InLine services") are offered by Southwestern Bell Telephone Company (hereinafter, "Southwestern Bell" or "we" or "our") to residence and business single-line local exchange telephone service customers (hereinafter, "Customers" or "you"). Read this Contract thoroughly before you pay your first bill which includes a monthly charge for InLine or InLine Plus services. By paying for one of these services, you agree to everything written in this Contract.

For a flat monthly fee, InLine provides trouble isolation service and repair service on inside telephone wire, jacks and cords. Inside Wire is that wire on the customer's side of the network interface device, which is usually a box located on the outside of your home. Unless specified otherwise, the term "Inside Wire" or "Inside Wiring," when used in this Contract, shall include inside telephone wire, jacks and cords connecting the jacks to your telephone equipment.

For a flat monthly fee for InLine Plus provides the same service InLine provides, and provides the use of a loaner telephone set for up to sixty (60) days and a radio interference filter, as necessary.

InLine and InLine Plus are optional services that are not required for you to subscribe to or continue local telephone service.

InLine and InLine Plus become effective thirty (30) days after your order is received (effective immediately in Arkansas), except that the service will become effective for Customers ordering new telephone service on the date of installation, and for Customers ordering InLine or InLine Plus at the time of a paid repair or installation visit, on the day after the premises visit.

InLine and InLine Plus are also offered for trouble isolation and repair of Inside Wire used in connection with certain other two-wire telephone service such as single line wide area, foreign exchange in specific limited territories, and foreign central office.

InLine and InLine Plus are not offered for repair of complex Inside Wire associated with multiple lines that use common equipment such as telephone stations that are a part of a key or PBX system, nor are they offered in connection with Centrex type service or lines connected to coin telephones.

If you have more than one single line telephone service at one location, e.g. two telephone numbers, and you wish to order one of these optional InLine services, you must subscribe to one of the InLine services for each telephone number or service at the same location,

If you live in rented/leased facilities, military housing, condominiums or cooperative dwellings, you should first determine whether you are responsible for repairs to your telephone Inside Wire prior to subscribing to the service.

If something goes wrong with your Inside Wire, you have several choices. You can fix it yourself. You can also call a third party, such as an electrician, to fix it. Alternatively, you can call Southwestern Bell, and we will fix it. We will charge you for time and materials in fixing the problem, unless you have one of the InLine services.

What is included in the InLine® services?

When you report trouble that interferes with the proper functioning of telephone service, we will test the line to determine if the trouble is on our side of the telephone network interface (demarcation point between our responsibility and your responsibility) or on your side. If the trouble is on our side of the telephone network interface, the trouble will be repaired at our expense as part of our local telephone service obligation. If the trouble is on your side of the network interface, we will test the line to determine if the trouble is in your Inside Wire or in your telephone set. If the trouble is in your Inside Wiring, we will repair or replace the defective Inside Wiring. If the trouble is in your telephone set or other associated equipment, such as a separate ringer, transformer, lights, speaker telephone, or answering device, we will isolate the problem.

If you have InLine Plus, you will be offered the temporary use of a substitute telephone set for up to sixty (60) days (without cost to you) and informed of the procedure for returning the loaner telephone. In most instances, your loaner phone will be delivered by a commercial carrier, or mailed to you, within three (3) days after we identify the faulty telephone instrument. You have free use of the loaned telephone set for sixty (60) days. You have fifteen (15) days after the sixty (60) day period in which to return the set to us. If we do not receive the loaned set within a total of 75 days, we will bill you for the retail price of the loaner set. (Call our service center for the current price for the telephone set.) If you experience electrical noise or radio interference, InLine Plus will provide a simple filter without charge. If the filter does not eliminate the noise, you will have to obtain and pay for repair service from Southwestern Bell or another repair service.

At our discretion, we determine the manner in which repairs will be made, and the color and specifications of replaced wire, jacks and connecting blocks. Surface mounting is the standard for replaced wiring and jacks. Requests for replacement with concealed wiring requiring extra work will be subject to time and material charges.

IMPORTANT LIMITATIONS AND EXCLUSIONS EXIST TO THESE SERVICES. YOU SHOULD READ THE FOLLOWING CONTRACT TO UNDERSTAND ALL TERMS AND CONDITIONS. THE PRECEDING PORTIONS OF THIS BROCHURE ARE MERELY ILLUSTRATIVE AND ARE NOT A CONTRACT.

(continued)

EXAMPLE 11.4 *(continued)*

Advertising Brochure for Service Protection Plans in Two Languages

CÓMO ENTENDER

Los Servicios InLine®

¿Qué son?
¿Qué beneficios brindan?
¿Cuánto cuestan?

Su amable compañía
local de comunicación global™

Southwestern Bell

¿Qué es lo que NO cubren los servicios InLine?

Los servicios InLine o InLine Plus no cubrirán Alambrado Interior considerado como defectuoso debido a inundación, terremoto, actos de guerra, incendio, rayo, viento u otro que requiera de la reconstrucción sustancial de bienes propiedades. (Las restauraciones anteriores no se aplicarán en Kansas) Asimismo, se excluye de la cobertura los servicios InLine, el Alambrado Interior considerado como defectuoso a causa de negligencia total, daño intencional, o que no funcione al momento que se haya ordenado el servicio debido a que aquél no satisfizo nuestras prácticas de instalación o estándares teóricos, o cuando no exista en la residencia Alambrado Interior del tipo cubierto por el Alambrado Interior de alguna clase de estructura separada de la residencia o edificio. Por ejemplo, no se considerará como Alambrado Interior, el alambrado arriba subterráneo, o el que use fuera de una casa y hasta un cobertizo o cuarto para herramientas, granero o establo, por lo tanto, InLine no lo cubrirá. Una vez que ocurriera abuso del servicio, el alambrado telefónico interior dentro de la estructura separada, si lo cubriría InLine.

Cualquier daño que ocurriera al Alambrado Interior asociado a otros daños físicos de la residencia o propiedad comercial, así como la reparación o reemplazo, se proporcionarán regularmente en la medida en que se proporcione al Cliente los servicios InLine. En el caso de que la residencia o propiedad comercial sufriera destrucción muy seria y que fuera indispensable que el servicio telefónico tuviera que desconectarse para posteriormente reconectarse, la instalación o reemplazo del Alambrado Interior no estará cubierto por los servicios InLine. (Generalmente, no aplica para detectar y reparar la falla, o para aislar el problema del Alambrado de algún procedimientos y equipo para detectar y reparar la falla.) Cliente en particular o de algún equipo telefónico. Excepto, cuando otros daños en forma del Alambrado Interior tengan éxito en identificar o eliminar el problema, es si no desempeñamos correctamente la reparación o el remplazo, mientras usted continuar suscrito a los servicios InLine o InLine Plus no otorgará otras garantías, ya sean expresas o implícitas. La garantía para los teléfonos comprados de Southwestern Bell se provee a los Clientes de Alambrado Interior o InLine Plus con respecto a los documentos de garantía que se incluyen en los equipos telefónicos que se le entregaron a usted.

Responsabilidad del Cliente

Usted será responsable de contratar a las personas necesarias para hacer el trabajo que su propiedad requiriera, como por ejemplo, instalación de cortina y plantación de árboles/arbusto terminados, pisos y cielos rasos, o modificaciones a las estructuras.

Después de que nuestro servicios técnicos terminen la reparación o la instalación, usted tendrá la obligación de restablecer la conexión o de verificar el funcionamiento apropiado de cualquier transmisión telefónica, marcación o equipo para contestar conectado a su Alambrado Interior, tales como marcación automática, alarmas de incendios o robo, medidores, sensores, máquinas contestadoras y teléfonos. Además, usted será responsable de reprogramar todos los números telefónicos y códigos que hayan quedado a raíz de que la línea o cualquier otro equipo se haya desconectado durante nuestras pruebas para revisar el funcionamiento de su Alambrado Interior o de la línea de acceso a nuestra red telefónica central.

Asimismo, usted será responsable de contratar a quien repare su equipo telefónico que se haya determinado como defectuoso, de obtener un teléfono para reemplazar el suyo, y de estar al pendiente del plazo para la devolución de cualquier teléfono prestado que le proporcionara a los suscriptores del servicio InLine Plus.

Cargos e Impuestos

Cuando usted solicita InLine o InLine Plus, estará conviniendo en pagar los cargos actuales por dichos servicios así cuando todos los impuestos y cargos actuales que se le aplicaran a Southwestern Bell o a usted sobre las cuotas del servicio.

Cancelación del Servicio

Usted podrá cancelar el servicio en cualquier momento, sólo tendrá que llamar a nuestro departamento de servicio al cliente, y que cargos se le seguirán aplicando por el servicio se cancele, excepto que, para el primer mes, se necesitará una facturación mínima de un mes. No se le cobrará por la cancelación del servicio. Nosotros podemos oportunamente los cargos por el servicio o en aquellos casos en los que ocurriera abuso del servicio. Ocurrirá abuso del servicio cuando el cliente ocasione o permita repetidamente que se cause daño al Alambrado Interior o InLine Plus, después de la cancelación de los servicios InLine o InLine Plus, el Cliente solicitara la reinstalación de éstos, tendría que esperar 30 días.

Garantía Limitada

Algunas veces es difícil y se requiere tiempo para identificar y aislar la causa del problema de alguna red eléctronica, como la del sistema telefónico, especialmente cuando el problema se debe a causas múltiples o es intermitente. Nuestra única responsabilidad bajo InLine e InLine Plus es el caso de la habilidad razonable, de procedimientos y equipo para detectar y reparar la falla, o para aislar el problema del Alambrado Interior de algún Cliente en particular o de algún equipo telefónico. Excepto, cuando otros daños en forma del Alambrado Interior tengan éxito en identificar o eliminar el problema, es si no desempeñamos correctamente la reparación o el remplazo, mientras usted continuar suscrito a los servicios InLine o InLine Plus.

DENEGACIÓN DE LA GARANTÍA

NOSOTROS POR ESTE MEDIO DENEGAMOS DE MANERA EXPRESA TODA O CUALQUIER GARANTÍA IMPLÍCITA DE ADAPTACIÓN O FUNCIONAMIENTO PARA UN PROPÓSITO EN PARTICULAR, AL IGUAL DE CUALQUIERA OTRAS GARANTÍAS QUE NO SE OTORGUEN EXPRESAMENTE EN ESTE CONTRATO.

LIMITACIÓN Y EXCLUSIÓN DE RESPONSABILIDAD

Southwestern Bell no será responsable por las demoras o incumplimiento en la reparación o instalación del servicio a causa de circunstancias ajenas a nuestra voluntad, ya sea por huelgas, manifestaciones populares, calamidades naturales, clima, escasez de materiales y cargas de trabajo mensuales. La responsabilidad de Southwestern Bell por los daños causados o en el desempeño indebido de los Servicios InLine o InLine Plus, en facilitar un teléfono prestado InLine Plus o un filtro para radiointerferencias, en una manera oportuna y apropiada, y en ningún caso excederá la cantidad que sea la menor del la suma de $100, (útiles) el costo actual de la reparación, reemplazo, o instalación del Alambrado Interior, o el costo actual para adquirir un equipo telefónico prestado, en la que usted ha incurrido durante los primeros 30 días posteriores a la fecha en que hayamos hecho la visita de servicio a su casa o negocio y usted fuera suscriptor de servicios InLine al momento de la reparación.

Southwestern Bell no será responsable por el deterioro o daño ocurrido a las propiedades de clientes al perforar agujeros, al unir o remover alambrado y equipo con tornillos en su casa o negocio, en aquellos casos, cuando estas labores no se desempeñen en forma competente.

SOUTHWESTERN BELL, BAJO NINGUNA CIRCUNSTANCIA, SE RESPONSABILIZARÁ POR LOS HONORARIOS LEGALES, DAÑOS INCIDENTALES O CONSECUENTES, INCLUYENDO PERO NO LIMITADOS A LA PÉRDIDA DE UTILIDADES O CUALQUIER OTRO GASTO, PÉRDIDA O DAÑO, DIRECTA O INDIRECTAMENTE SURGIDO DEL DESEMPEÑO DE O DE LA FALTA DE LOS SERVICIOS InLine O InLine PLUS O DEL MAL FUNCIONAMIENTO O FALTA DE ÉSTE EN APARATOS CONECTADOS A SU ALAMBRADO INTERIOR, COMO POR EJEMPLO, MARCACIÓN AUTOMÁTICA, ALARMAS DE INCENDIOS Y ROBO, MEDIDORES, SENSORES, MÁQUINAS CONTESTADORAS Y TELÉFONOS.

Precios

Para los precios actuales de cualquiera de los servicios descritos en este Contrato, comuníquese con nuestro departamento de servicio al cliente.

Enmiendas al Contrato, Incrementos de Precios y Terminación de la Oferta

Nos reservamos el derecho de descontinuar la oferta de InLine e InLine Plus, o de enmendar los términos y condiciones, incluyendo los incrementos en precio, dándole a los Clientes de InLine e InLine Plus, al menos con un mes de anticipación, notificación escrita de cualquier enmienda al contrato, cambios en las cuotas, o sobre la descontinuación de la oferta. Una notificación podrá ser en forma de aviso que se incluya en el recibo telefónico mensual del Cliente, o como parte de dicho recibo. Al pagar mensualmente el cargo después de la fecha efectiva de la notificación, usted estará conviniendo y se sujetará a la enmienda o al cambio de cuotas.

Información Adicional Importante para el Cliente

Nuestros clientes experimentan una amplia variedad de necesidades que suscitan reparaciones del Alambrado Interior. En promedio, un 1.5% de nuestros suscriptores residenciales y pequeñas empresas obtienen, en algún forma, reparaciones mensuales del Alambrado Interior. Tal vez su experiencia en reparaciones del Alambrado Interior podrá ser significativamente alta o baja. A continuación le ofrecemos una lista parcial de factores que podrían afectar su necesidad de reparaciones del Alambrado Interior, las condiciones climatológicas de su zona, fecha de construcción y condición de su casa, ubicación de su negocio, número de usuarios del teléfono en su casa o negocio, años de instalación y condición del alambrado telefónico, presencia de su casa o negocio, de animales domésticos o mascotas y otras variantes. Usted está en la mejor posición para decidir si el servicio InLine la vale en base a su propia experiencia con el servicio telefónico y reparaciones.

TOTALIDAD DEL CONTRATO

NINGÚN REPRESENTANTE DE SOUTHWESTERN BELL TENDRÁ AUTORIDAD PARA EFECTUAR REPRESENTACIÓN DE TIPO ALGUNO, PROMESA, GARANTÍA, DISTINTA DE LA QUE SE DECLARE POR ESCRITO EN ESTE CONTRATO. SI TALES DECLARACIONES SE LE HAN HECHO A USTED, POR FAVOR COMUNÍQUESE INMEDIATAMENTE A NUESTRO DEPARTAMENTO DE SERVICIO AL CLIENTE USTED EN SU DIRECTORIO TELEFÓNICO DEBIDO A QUE TAL CONDUCTA CONSTITUYE UNA VIOLACIÓN A NUESTRA POLÍTICA EMPRESARIAL. ESTE CONTRATO NO PODRÁ SUPLIRSE O MODIFICARSE, EXCEPTO QUE SE DECLARE Y SE ESPECIFIQUE, CUANDO TOTALIDAD ENTRE SOUTHWESTERN BELL Y USTED CON RESPECTO A LA PRESTACIÓN DE LOS SERVICIOS InLine E InLine PLUS. ESTE CONTRATO SE CELEBRA ENTRE SOUTHWESTERN BELL Y USTED, SIGNIFICANDO LA EXPRESIÓN FINAL DE NUESTRO CONVENIO PARA LA PRESTACIÓN DE LOS SERVICIOS InLine E InLine PLUS, Y ES UNA DECLARACIÓN COMPLETA Y EXCLUSIVA DE SUS TÉRMINOS. ESTE CONTRATO NO PODRÁ SUPLIRSE O MODIFICARSE, EXCEPTO POR MEDIO DE UN ESCRITO QUE OSTENTE LA FIRMA DE ALGÚN REPRESENTANTE AUTORIZADO DE SOUTHWESTERN BELL.

EXAMPLE 11.4 (continued)

Advertising Brochure for Service Protection Plans in Two Languages

¿QUÉ SON? ¿QUÉ BENEFICIOS BRINDAN? ¿CUÁNTO CUESTAN?

Southwestern Bell Telephone Company administra diariamente millones de llamadas telefónicas de sus clientes. De estas llamadas, el 99.9% se realizan en el primer intento. En ocasiones, usted podría experimentar algún tipo de dificultad con su servicio telefónico. El problema podría estar en nuestra red telefónica, en el alambrado que conecta su teléfono a nuestra red, o en su equipo telefónico. Este folleto le instruye acerca de su servicio telefónico y de dos planes útiles de protección para éste: InLine® e InLine® Plus®. Pero antes que todo, a continuación le presentamos información básica acerca del funcionamiento de su servicio telefónico. De esta forma, usted estará enterado de cuáles serían sus opciones cuando algo no llegara a funcionar bien.

Conformación de su Sistema Telefónico

Su servicio telefónico consiste de tres partes y usted debe conocerlas para un mejor entendimiento de los gastos que usted tendría que hacer cuando algo se descomponga.

1. **Alambrado exterior** - es la red que lleva el servicio telefónico a su casa o negocio. Si el alambrado exterior no funciona correctamente, nosotros lo repararemos sin cargo para usted - nosotros lo reparamos sin costo alguno para usted - usted no es suscriptor de InLine.

2. **Alambrado interior, enchufes y cordones telefónicos** - es el alambrado telefónico dentro de su casa o negocio. Cuando este equipo no funciona bien, la mayoría de las veces usted deberá pagar el costo de reemplazarlos o repararlos.

La necesidad de la reparación de su Alambrado Interior se basará en sus circunstancias, y generalmente, este alambrado no requiere de reparaciones frecuentes. Sin embargo, cuando se llegaran a necesitar, usted tendría que pagar de $78 a $110 o más, solamente por una visita del personal técnico que localizará la falla y que le indicará cómo corregir el problema, a menos que usted tenga los servicios InLine o InLine Plus.

3. **Equipo Telefónico** - está compuesto por los teléfonos y otros equipos de telecomunicación de su casa o negocio. Cuando este equipo no funciona bien, la mayoría de las veces usted deberá pagar el costo de reemplazarlos o repararlos.

¿Cómo Podemos Ayudarle a Mantener sus Gastos Bajos Cuando Algo No Funciona en su Servicio Telefónico?

Nosotros deseamos evitarle gastos inesperados. Por esta razón le ofrecemos dos planes de servicio: InLine® e InLine® Plus®. Usted podrá elegir cualquiera de los dos planes de cobertura para su alambrado telefónico interior y escoger quién es responsable de las reparaciones interiores del alambrado interior. Incluso, si su arrendador tuviera obligación de reparar el alambrado, tal vez usted preferiría la comodidad y tranquilidad que InLine brinda - la decisión es suya.

¿Qué beneficios le brinda InLine?

Cuando usted contrata cualquiera de los planes InLine o InLine Plus, toda dificultad o problema que tenga en su servicio telefónico, sólo llámenos. Nosotros determinaremos el problema, y si éste se localiza en su alambrado interior, enchufes o cordones, nosotros nos encargaremos de la reparación, sin cargo para usted. InLine Plus le ofrece más aún reparaciones sin cargo para usted - nada que usted desea comprar el teléfono prestado, deberá comunicarse con nuestro departamento de servicio al cliente. Nuestros técnicos en reparaciones asegurarían que se le facilite a usted un teléfono en préstamo para que no pierda llamadas importantes. También en algunos casos, InLine Plus le proporcionaría filtros simples para radiointerferencias. Por favor lea los términos actuales del contrato que se mencionan más adelante.

¿Qué tipo de dificultades o fallas NO cubren InLine® e InLine® Plus?

No obstante que Southwestern Bell ofrecer una amplia variedad de servicios y protección amparados en los planes de servicio InLine e InLine Plus, es imposible cubrir todo tipo de daño imaginable que le suceda a su alambrado interior, enchufes o cordones. Por ejemplo, los planes no cubre problemas del alambrado interior causados por daño intencional o alambrado interior que no satisfaga los están-

dares de instalación y equipo de Southwestern Bell. Para mayor información acerca de las exclusiones, por favor lea los términos actuales del contrato que se mencionan más adelante.

Si usted alquila su casa o el lugar de su negocio, quizá su arrendador, y no usted, tendría que pagar por la reparación del alambrado interior. Verifique con su arrendador sobre quién es responsable de las reparaciones interiores del alambrado interior. Incluso, si su arrendador tuviera obligación de reparar el alambrado, tal vez usted preferiría la comodidad y tranquilidad que InLine brinda - la decisión es suya.

¿Cuánto cuestan InLine® e InLine® Plus?

Cuando usted se suscribe a InLine o a InLine Plus, pagará unos cuantos dólares mensuales por cada línea telefónica de su casa o negocio. InLine Plus cuesta un poco más que InLine. Los precios están sujetos a cambios y podrían variar de estado a estado. Por favor llame a nuestro departamento de servicio al cliente, listado en su directorio telefónico de Southwestern Bell y obtenga los precios actuales para su estado.

LEA CUIDADOSAMENTE

TÉRMINOS Y CONDICIONES DEL CONTRATO DE SERVICIO INLINE® E INLINE® PLUS

Southwestern Bell Telephone Company (que en lo sucesivo se denominará "Southwestern Bell", "nosotros", "nuestra/s", "nuestros") ofrece a los Clientes residenciales o pequeñas empresas (que en lo sucesivo se denominarán "los Clientes" o "Usted") suscribirse al servicio telefónico local de línea individual, la contratación del InLine o InLine Plus que en ocasiones y en adelante se denominará conjuntamente como los "Servicios InLine"). Lea detenidamente este Contrato antes de que pague su primer recibo; el cual incluye el cargo mensual por los servicios InLine e InLine Plus. Al pagar por alguno de estos servicios, usted estará de acuerdo con todo lo escrito en este Contrato.

Por una cuota fija mensual, InLine proporcionará servicios de aislamiento de problemas y de reparación del alambrado Interior, enchufes y cordones telefónicos. [3] Alambrado Interior es el alambrado colocado en el exterior de su casa. A menos que se especifique de otra forma, el término "Alambrado Interior" de la red del cliente; esos cordones, y el término "Alambrado Interior" dependiendo de su uso en este Contrato, deberá incluir el alambrado telefónico interior, enchufes y cordones que conectan los enchufes a su equipo telefónico.

Por una cuota mensual fija, InLine Plus proporcionará el mismo servicio que InLine, así como equipo telefónico prestado para que usted lo use hasta que un período máximo de sesenta (60) días y un filtro para radiointerferencia, si fuera necesario.

InLine e InLine Plus son servicios opcionales, no requeridos para que usted se suscriba o continue con su servicio telefónico local.

InLine e InLine Plus entrarán en efecto en un plazo de treinta (30) días a partir de la fecha en que su orden se recibió (en Arkansas entrarán en vigencia inmediatamente). Se exceptuará la anterior cuando los Clientes ordenen su nuevo servicio telefónico a la fecha de instalación de éste, o cuando los Clientes ordenen InLine o InLine Plus al momento que nuestro personal técnico realice reparaciones pagadas o instalaciones. En este último caso, la contratación del servicio deberá efectuarse al día siguiente de que nuestros técnicos hayan efectuado la visita a la propiedad.

InLine e InLine Plus se ofrecerán también para casos de aislamiento de problemas y reparaciones del Alambrado Interior, aplicado en conexión con otros servicios telefónicos de dos alambres (en líneas individuales diseñadas para la transmisión de voz de servicio residencial o de negocio en oficinas centrales extranjeras con territorios específicos limitados y en oficinas centrales extranjeras.

InLine e InLine Plus no se ofrecerán para reparaciones complejas del alambrado interior o equipo telefónico múltiples (por ejem equipo común, como por ejemplo, estaciones telefónicas que usen parte de un sistema telefónico principal o central telefónica privada, ni tampoco cubre la extensión con servicio tipo Centrex o líneas conectadas a teléfonos públicos.

¿Qué incluyen los servicios InLine®?

Cuando usted nos reporte alguna dificultad o problema que interfiera con el funcionamiento apropiado del servicio telefónico, nosotros probaremos la línea para definir si tal dificultad o problema reside en nuestra interface de la red telefónica (punto de demarcación entre nuestra responsabilidad y la de usted) o en su alambrado. Si el problema está en nuestra interface de la red telefónica, el problema se repararía sin cargo para usted ya que es nuestra obligación como compañía prestadora del servicio telefónico local. Si por el contrario, el problema está en su alambrado o la interface de la red, nosotros probaremos la línea para establecer si la falla está en su Alambrado Interior o en algún equipo telefónico específico. Si el problema reside en su Alambrado Interior, nosotros repararíamos o reemplazaríamos el Alambrado Interior que esté asociado con éste, como por ejemplo, en un timbre operado, transformador, baro, teléfono con altavoz o máquina contestadora, nosotros aislaríamos la dificultad.

Cuando usted contrata InLine Plus, se le proporcionaría el equipo telefónico prestado si sus teléfonos sucum hasta por un período de sesenta (60) días (sin costo alguno para usted) y se le informará el procedimiento para la devolución de ese teléfono prestado. En la mayoría de los casos, usted recibiría su teléfono prestado a través de alguna compañía comercial de fletes, o por correo, dentro de los tres (3) días siguientes de que nosotros hayamos identificado la falla en el instrumento telefónico. Usted podrá usar gratis el equipo días. Después de que se cumplan esos 60 días, usted tendría quince (15) días más para devolvernos el equipo. Si no recibimos el teléfono prestado en el plazo completo de 75 días y al por menor (llame a nuestro departamento de servicio para que se le proporcionen los precios actuales del equipo telefónico. Si usted no observara problemas eléctricos o radiointerferencias en la línea telefónica de la red, es decir si no filtro no elimina el ruido, usted tendría que contactar a Southwestern Bell u otro servicio de reparación.

Queda a nuestra discreción determinar la forma en que se harían las reparaciones y/o especificaciones del alambrado a reemplazarse, enchufes y bloque de conexiones. El montaje en la superficie sería del tipo puns, only to see J&B, a competitor, launch a similar campaign.

Another seemingly uncontrollable problem that advertising campaigns frequently encounter involves the undesirable placement of ads in a newspaper or magazine relative to the adjacent copy. The same thing can happen in broadcasting, although it's fairly standard to have standing "kill" orders for, say, an airline commercial when the evening news carries the story of an airline crash. Most media try to avoid placement errors because it makes advertisers unhappy and can result in demands for compensation.

Yet another difficulty has to do with campaigns that attack the competition. These may take the form of a product-to-product confrontation, like soft drink taste tests, or one politician lambasting another. Some companies don't consider it much of a problem if the competition mentions their name in an ad. They reason that consumers will forget which product was supposed to be better. They seem to respond like composer George M. Cohan, who said to a newspaperman in 1912, "I don't care what you say about me, as long as you say *something* about me, and as long as you spell my name right." But anyone who has watched some of the battles among the fast-food chains might question the legitimacy of such a view.

Election campaigning in the USA and elsewhere (perhaps due to either direct or indirect U.S. influence) is increasingly negative. One perceived effect of this is lower voter turnout due to disgust with the whole affair—a rather dangerous trend in democracies. Some evidence suggests that negative advertising works for the attacker if a decision is forced within a time frame, as happens in the case of elections. But the decision to use negative advertising, either in an attack or in a counterattack, demands careful consideration because of its longer-term public relations costs, some of which may be intangible.

Myths are the source of two other problems advertising must face. The first is the notion that one ad campaign can be effective across national boundaries and cultures. Evidence from an experienced agency, Gray Advertising, Inc., indicates that global campaigns only work when three conditions exist:

1. The market developed the same way from country to country.

2. Consumer targets are similar.

3. Consumers have the same wants and needs around the world.

If even one of the conditions does not exist, a global campaign will not work. For example, Gray says that Kellogg's Pop-Tarts failed in Great Britain because toasters aren't widely used there. The General Foods Corporation positioned Tang in France as a substitute for breakfast orange juice, but it subsequently found that orange juice was not popular among the French and that they drank almost none at breakfast.

The second myth is that a single advertising design or concept will work within a culture. Psychographics indicates the need for different appeals that might not be apparent from demographics. Whether the format is movie ads or paperback covers, it's important to adjust the advertising appeal to the audience. In many cases, different appeals must be designed to sell exactly the same product to different audiences.

TYPES OF PUBLICITY USED IN PR PRACTICE

A second major category of messages placed in various media by PR practitioners is publicity. What is publicity? Is it a column item in a local newspaper? A cover story in a national magazine? Thirty seconds on the 6 p.m. television news? A bit of chatter by a radio disk jockey? The mention of the company's name once or twice in a long story about the industry? A single photo in a newspaper or magazine? A 2-inch item in an association publication? An annual report? A house publication? A film? Postings on a Web page? It is all of these and more.

Publicity is information about an organization that is carried as editorial (not advertising) content in a publication or news medium. Often it's news, but it can also be a sales or promotional message.

Candidates for public office who make frequent speeches and expect these to be reported in the news are selling two things: themselves and their ideas. They hope you will buy them at the ballot box. Other publicity, of course, may be strictly informational. Most of a daily newspaper's business pages are filled with publicity releases and stories based on publicity releases. Here PR people function as reporters, and what they write about their organization or client is hard news.

Reporters who cover a certain area—for instance, public affairs—rarely get to talk with the top officials and executives in their field. Consequently, they must rely on public relations people who know what the news media want, need and will use. The PR people must know their own organization thoroughly, have access to the top echelons (where they can get the information they need) and prepare it in a form that the news media can use (see Chapter 12). The news media also depend on PR people because they never have enough reporters on a staff to cover everything going on in a metropolitan area. Much of the information the news media use comes to them from public relations sources. These are facts they did not have to gather, stories they did not have to write and pictures they did not have to take. But public relations representatives who expect to remain effective must justify the trust of the news media by being accurate, truthful and reliable.

Although much of the publicity information that PR people provide to the news media is "packaged" as news tip sheets or news releases, many other publicity tools are used to reach nonmedia publics. These include publications, films and video productions, speeches, various employee media, Web pages and other special media. Chapter 12 discusses tactical details of "how to do it."

▮ Publications

Three broad categories of publications carry publicity directly to audiences: organizational, industry and trade or association.

Organizational Publications Organizational magazines, sometimes called *house publications*, are dis-

tributed to employees and perhaps to stakeholders of a company. The distribution is usually vertical: copies go to everyone in the organization, from top to bottom. Occasionally in a very large organization a publication may go to just one type of employee and thus get horizontal distribution—for example, a publication for supervisors. Some organizations' publications are intended for external audiences such as Aramco World. Others like ASPCA's Animal Watch are for financial/stakeholder audiences and still others are primarily internal.

The oldest continuously published external corporate magazine is *The Furrow* published by John Deere & Company since 1895. The magazine has evolved from a tabloid-size periodical published on newsprint to a four-color magazine published in 18 overseas markets in 11 languages. The magazine is directed to Deere's farming customers all over the world, and its purpose is to provide them with information they can use to do their jobs most effectively.[10]

Industry Publications A company or even a nonprofit organization may be a member of an industry organization. Such groups often publish periodicals aimed at bettering the entire industry. Industry organizations' magazines often gain wide distribution. They are received not only by industry executives but also by business editors, financial analysts, economics specialists, government officials and anyone else who has a particular interest in the industry.

Trade or Association Publications Also distributed horizontally are trade or association publications—magazines, newsletters, newspapers or annual reports published at the national headquarters of a group whose members share common goals or interests. Among them are labor union publications, religious magazines and newspapers, and fraternal and professional publications.

Other media include corporate, industry or association films, which are supervised (though rarely produced) by the organization's public relations staff.

Sponsored Magazines Both profit-making and nonprofit organizations may publish sponsored magazines. They are a costly venture, however, and some profit-making organizations have quietly folded their efforts, while others accept outside advertising for support. One magazine going to court personnel and attorneys in a large Southwestern city focuses on issues that often underlie court cases (domestic violence, delinquency and the like) and is being published for a nonprofit, human-services organization.

Sponsored magazines published by profit-making companies may accept outside advertising, but charge less than newsstand magazines. Some companies seek cosponsors because the venture is so expensive. These magazines differ from a company's own service magazines, although the latter are costly, too. Examples of service magazines include various airlines' in-flight publications and American Express's *Departures*, which goes to its platinum card holders. Sponsored magazines are "custom-published" by major media companies that want to expand their business. However, companies may find it impossible to sustain them during an economic downturn, because they are so expensive to produce.

Newsletters Newsletters can be internal, external or both. Some external newsletters are income generators, because their audiences pay for them through subscriptions.

Internal newsletters offer an effective means of communicating with employees. A newsletter should not be a collection of trivia, but it should contain items of interest. Many newsletter items later become subjects of fuller treatment in the institution's magazine. One company newsletter editor describes her publication as a "circulating billboard." In other companies it is much more, containing short articles, bits of humor, important announcements and notices. Some are also promotional. The Associated Press uses its broadsheet newsletter to sell its services and features to members.

External newsletters are also a publicity vehicle. Some are used for addressing issues. Others are created for and subscribed to by members of the public. Subscription to a newsletter can come through membership in an organization or through direct subscription, like a regular commercial magazine. The paid newsletter business is a big one. More than 10,000 subscription newsletters exist, and most cover highly specialized subjects and are obviously intended for a particular target public. Generally, they enjoy a high readership.

Desktop publishing has made newsletters of all kinds more attractive as a means of communication and has enabled them to resemble publications more than "letters."

Technology has solved one big newsletter problem—the inability to include photos. Lightweight digital (filmless) color cameras store high-resolution photos on a chip for direct transfer to a computer through a cable. Connecting the cable to the computer enables you to look at the photos in the camera, choose the ones you want to use and transfer these to the hard disk. Software enables the user to edit or crop the photos, which can then be used in several ways with graphics and in either page-layout or word-processing programs.[11]

Some newsletters are delivered electronically. One, designed for "news junkies," is published by CPC Communications of New York. InfoWire is a daily 10-page evening newsletter that can be received over a fax machine. Subscribers can forward the telephone number for their fax machine on the road, so the newsletter follows them to each destination when they go on a trip.[12]

Handbooks One major employee publication that PR departments produce is the employee handbook, which functions as both a reference work and an effective orientation tool. It should provide a definitive statement of what is expected from employees and what the organization offers them. The handbook should thoroughly explain policies, rules and regulations, and it should indicate how management helps to further the education and career development of the employee. The handbook should also detail how and under what circumstances the corporate name and logo can be used. Inclusion of a management organizational chart with the names of individuals whom employees need to know about or contact in various departments is essential. Workers at all levels should be made aware of the way to get questions answered and problems solved. Most corporations find it necessary to produce handbooks annually in order to keep the information current.

Some organizations also publish handbooks for external use. Organizations with specialists, such as universities, often publish a guide identifying those who are knowlegeable and willing to speak to media and others about their area of expertise. Their names are also generally forwarded to ProfNet, a subsidiary of PR Newswire. ProfNet's Experts Database gives reporters profiles of professors seen as leading experts by their institutions so a reporter can get an immediate comment when needed for a breaking news story.

■ Film/Video

As audiences become increasingly oriented toward graphics and audiovisual presentations, PR practitioners cannot afford to ignore films and videos as informational and publicity vehicles.

Sponsored Films One type of film to consider is the long feature, or *sponsored film*. This is a film without stars put out by an organization or corporation and distributed free of charge. Such films can be produced for as little as $15,000 or as much as $500,000. Most fall in the $40,000-to-$50,000 range. Large companies may have their own film-producing units, but most hire independent film producers. The customary audiences for sponsored films are schools, community organizations, television stations and (in some cases) movie theaters.

Feature Fillers Another type of production to consider is the one- to five-minute film clip, usually on videocassette. Such clips generally serve as fillers for feature programs, talk shows or local sporting events. To win acceptance, fillers must be newsworthy and timely, must show activity and must have only one mention or plug for the sponsor. They are generally presented in a news magazine format.

Corporate Videos for External Use Various companies are making corporate videos with a message especially for classrooms; most of these videos are distributed by Modern Talking Picture Service, Inc., which reports that 64,000 of the estimated 110,000 public and private schools in the United States have shown students at least one of its 3,600 titles from 120 corporations in a recent 18-month period.[13]

Some of these do draw criticism. Exxon Corporation's videotape created for high school science classes asserts that the Valdez oil spill did not destroy Alaska's wildlife. A Monsanto Company video discusses the uses of pesticides in increased farm productivity and Union Carbide Corporation's video says chemicals add to more comfortable living.[14] Some educators and environmental groups have challenged these messages, which usually look like documentaries. Corporate spokespeople counter by saying that the environmentalists are using the classroom, too. Indeed, some educators have used the videos as teaching tools, showing the corporate video and then one sponsored by an environmental group on the same issue. Despite the attendant criticism, companies and special-interest groups evidently deem the videos sufficiently serviceable to justify their continued production and dissemination.[15]

Corporate Videos for Internal Uses Although some internal videos—such as video "newsletters" for employees—use the news magazine format, other formats are borrowed from television—such as MTV-style videos and game-show spoofs.[16] The videos are used to communicate the corporate culture, to inform employees about corporate resources available for dealing with such problems as substance abuse, to instruct and train employees in new techniques or new jobs and to give employees the organization's side of controversial public issues in which it may become involved.

The reasons for using videos to reach internal audiences start with the fact that most employees now are products of total television immersion: they get most of their news from television, and they use VCRs for home entertainment.

Employee information (training) remains the primary use for corporate videos, but they are also being used in employee relations (benefits) and crisis communication (informing employees of the organization's side of a controversial issue so that they can pass that view along to external audiences).

Some corporate videos are directed toward a combination internal/external audience such as investors who "own" the company but don't work there. Some crisis communication videos are specifically designed to reassure such audiences. Other videos deal with investor relations and address "recommenders" of corporate investment such as brokers and analysts.

Videos focusing on community or environmental issues may be produced originally for internal audiences, but then may be adapted for special external audiences. The flexibility of the medium, which allows minor adaptations to be made on basically the same video, renders it especially useful for targeting messages to special audiences.

Teletext and Videotex Teletext is a one-way system of information transmission that is delivered via a regular TV broadcast signal; subscribers to the service are given a decoder (similar to a cable television converter) that allows them to read the text on the TV screen at any time. Videotex is a two-way system of information transmission that can be delivered via a cable TV system or telephone lines and can be received on a TV set or a personal computer monitor; subscribers to videotex services can request specific information from these sources.

Intranet Just as the Internet is the major new channel for global communication, computer systems within organizations make use of closed electronic systems. These Intranets are used for all sorts of internal communication such as e-mail, meeting notices and newsletters.

■ **Speeches/Meetings**

Speeches are also publicity. When the president of an organization speaks to the local Monday club,

the result is publicity, whether or not the local media cover the speech. This is because a person is also a medium. The PR person usually gets the job of researching and writing speeches. To be well received, the remarks must be tailored for that particular group. The speech writer must also remember the personal characteristics of the speaker delivering the speech: the speech has to sound like the speaker, not like the writer.

Speeches are often published as brochures and sent to special audiences. This extends their usefulness as publicity tools. Sometimes, a copy of a speech is sent with just a special card (not a business card) attached. In other cases, the speech consists of a reprint with additional information. Occasionally, the speech is packaged as a publication—for example, a brochure. More unusual is a package that shows the visuals of the presentation—useful if charts and graphs are important.

Meetings often generate publicity, too, whether they are for internal or external audiences. Increasingly, meetings are used for external audiences as a proactive device to share concerns about an issue or environmental situation, and these are often covered by media. Internally, meetings are used to enable management to interact with employees and to gain feedback. Small group meetings are seen as an effective management tool,[17] and they often generate publicity in internal publications.

■ **Other Promotional Messages**

Another category of public relations messages used to promote organizations and individuals appears neither as editorial content nor as news in media. Examples of those promotional messages include exhibits and characters identified with the organization (Mickey Mouse appearing for Disney; the Cookie Monster from Sesame Street appearing for PBS). Other forms are books, multimedia presentations and closed-circuit television appearances. Other new media being used include material on CD-ROMs and information being made available 24 hours a day on special television networks. One

example is HealthNet from the David Sarnoff Research Center, which also makes material available in video format for CD-ROM.

Many presentations, like the ones this book's publisher puts on, occur at trade shows or conventions. Some organizations invest in videotapes or slide tapes that can be used at display areas or meetings with little support from organization representatives. Your college's admissions office probably uses such a traveling exhibit to recruit students.

Closed-circuit television is used a great deal in investor relations. Top executives can give a report on the company and then be interviewed by investment analysts. Reuters Information Services, Inc., owners of the British news service, uses "Reuters TV 2000" to transmit corporate presentations directly to analysts, giving them a chance to phone in questions. Paine Webber, a stockbrokers' group, broadcasts a radio program to its 250 offices around the world on its global network.

In addition to using high-tech communications such as satellite broadcasts and computer networks, companies can rely on the old standby: print. Examples of self-promotion books abound— of historical note are Lee Iacocca's *Iacocca: An Autobiography*, Stanley Marcus's *Minding the Store*, John F. Kennedy's *Profiles in Courage* and Richard Nixon's *Six Crises*. A book gives prestige to the subject and can be worth the time invested in producing it. Organizations usually save this device for an anniversary or other special occasion. Some

books miss being connected to an organization because they are written by a well-known author commissioned to prepare the manuscript. When a political figure, celebrity or executive's name is on the book as author, the chances are that a ghost writer was employed. Much of the writer's time is devoted to tracking down elusive information, validating information given as fact and searching for illustrations. Nevertheless, a sincere effort, well done, often proves to be an asset.

Organizations also take advantage of their history by opening museums. Museums are gradually replacing plant tours, which sometimes raise legal problems. (Kellogg and Gerber have quit offering plant tours.) Coca-Cola opened a museum in Atlanta in 1990, but it's a latecomer to the museum business. BMW and Mercedes Benz both have automobile museums in Germany. Some companies put a mini-museum on tour or establish small displays in historical districts (such as at a country store among a group of restored homes).

Books and museums have their limits. Much more pervasive are postal stamps. What could be better than getting people to stick a symbol of the organization on their mail, and pay to do that? The postal service in the USA has created a plethora of commemorative stamps in recent years. There's everything from opera stars to cartoon characters, but an organization can't just ask and have it happen. Proposals go to a panel that approves each suggestion. Some organizations go to considerable lengths to impress the selectors because the identification would represent invaluable publicity.

Symbols of all kinds give recognition to a product or company. For the 1997 Super Bowl, General Mills sent two employees, each carrying a suitcase of flat Wheaties boxes, one with the New England Patriots and the other with the Green Bay Packers, to the game. After it became apparent that Green Bay was going to win, Packers boxes were given to the television news crews. Consequently, the box appeared on Fox, the network carrying the game, CNN, ESPN and a number of local stations.[18] Less obtrusive but very effective publicity resulted when a PR practitioner had pictures made of children using milk cartons with the tops cut off as modeling clay forms. The publishers of a national children's educational book accepted the photo as showing an example of the creative application of everyday household items. The photo of the cartons subsequently appeared in the book, with the name of the milk company clearly visible. Such pictures, with the product in the background or foreground, are often used. If you ever wondered why hotels always have speaker's rostrums clearly labeled with the hotel's name and insignia, now you know.

An entire industry has developed around making sure that identifiable brand-name products are used in television shows and in movies. As a viewer, you may have noticed that you can read the label of a star's soft drink, or that a billboard is clearly visible in a street scene or that a particular make of car is used. These are not accidental choices of the prop department.[19]

PUBLICITY AS CONTROLLED/ UNCONTROLLED COMMUNICATION

Determining where to place publicity demands an objective look at what is likely to happen to it, from creation to delivery. This means considering how much control you can exert over the delivery of the message by the medium.

■ Controlled Media

Many specialized media, such as company, industry, trade and association publications, are under *their* editors' control. If you are the editor, it is a controlled publication; but if you are the PR director for a company submitting publicity to an industry or trade publication, your submissions are subject to editorial discrimination and revision. Thus, if you are not the editor, specialized media fall into the uncontrolled category. Another person decides whether and how to use your material. On the other hand, magazines, brochures, newsletters and videos you produce and distribute are controlled, because you decide when, where and how to deliver the message. And this is certainly true of that mixed advertising/publicity medium, your Web page.

■ Uncontrolled Media

News releases may be exceptionally well written; but once they are in the hands of an editor, anything can happen and you can't do much about it. An editor may run a release as you wrote it, give it to a reporter to rewrite, give it to a reporter to use as a take-off point for an independently researched story or junk it entirely. Trade publication editors discard 75 percent of the releases they receive, and radio news people discard 86 percent. Most discarded PR material, however, richly deserves such an end. The news media treat a professionally prepared release from a trustworthy source with respect, although it still may not be used if there is no space or time for it that day.

Editors get news releases from public relations wire distribution sources, from faxes, from e-mail and through the mail. They may also get picked up from an organization's Web page, but this usually occurs when a news tip has gone out (unless reporters happen to be following the organization for a particular reason). News tip sheets alert editors to possible news or feature stories. In addition, "calls for coverage" or queries may be used to elicit media coverage of PR events—a presidential press conference, the arrival of Santa to open a store's Christmas buying season, ribbon cuttings and

groundbreakings. Whether these get any attention is up to the editors, who decide whether or not to assign reporters. Of course, even when reporters are assigned, they may not cover the event as the PR person would have wished. But if the event is well planned, the coverage will reflect it.

PREPARING PUBLICITY MESSAGES

Some publicity messages go directly to audiences as controlled communications; others go to members of the news media, who constitute an intermediary audience.

Direct Publicity for Audiences

Public relations offices frequently prepare material for audiences directly in print, electronic and video formats. It is quite common for newletters and magazines to be developed by PR people, while most video production is done outside the organization.

Publications PR practitioners encounter two principal problems in putting out institutional publications, beyond the problem of justifying its existence to some dollars-and-cents-minded person in accounting. The first involves finding out what is going on in the organization. The second problem involves the tendency of management to view the publication as a propaganda organ for telling readers what it would like them to believe rather than what they would like to know.

Gathering information inside an organization is similar to what news reporters do—finding and cultivating sources. People who can be relied upon to provide timely and accurate information are priceless. It often helps to distribute forms which give people guidance in the type of information that would be useful. Within organizations, most PR publications people depend on meeting regularly with department heads, watching internal bulletins for newsworthy events in the making and talking to a lot of people.

Finding good information is not an easy job, and the second problem can make it more difficult. Management is justified in wanting to use publications to communicate, but the audience is often less interested in what management wants to say than in getting answers to problems they are encountering. What they want to know will usually make better copy than what management wants them to know. Surveys and readership studies give some guidance in determining what makes a publication worth its place in the budget.

Annual reports are still done in-house by some companies. Although they only represent a small part of the communications that go to the investors and analysts of a publicly held company, they are very important as public relations tools. Of all the publications produced by a company, the annual report is seen as the signature piece. For that reason, many privately held companies and some nonprofits also produce annual reports for institutional identity.

Electronic Communication Some companies have almost no paper publications. In such companies, almost all communication is electronic and usually over an Intranet. Departments may have their own publications, and task forces may be working together electronically without ever meeting. Chat rooms exist for discussion of issues. There's heavy dependence on Listservs for getting the correct distribution of notices to people, and reliance on people reading and responding to their e-mail. Sophisticated electronic information users have systems managers who maintain these communication channels and create useful links of databases. For many companies, all of this internal electronic communcation has become an integral, daily part of getting a job done.

Problems with these changes occur in organizations that have many unskilled workers who are likely to be excluded from the employee communications because they are not comfortable with computers. However, this problem will decrease as new generations enter the workforce, since children are becoming computer users at much lower ages.

Videos are increasingly used for instructional and motivational jobs within organizations, and some companies have their own closed-circuit television. The medium is successful partly because of its familiarity, and in part because it is the closest thing to face-to-face communication. Satellites have increased the range of the video format, and some U.S. businesses have developed their own corporate networks. Even some annual reports have gone out as videos. And although most companies still publish an annual report, investor relations now depend heavily on electronic communcation in general.

■ Publicity Through Mass Media

In contrast to both advertising and publicity prepared directly for audiences, publicity prepared for the mass media generally is totally uncontrolled, both as to the delivery and as to the message. Infor-

mation about an institution, product or person that appears as news in newspapers or magazines or on radio or television is used at the discretion of news editors. Thus it may be used in any context or not at all.

Print Publicity Information reaches the news media through many routes, but three are basic: news releases, coverage of an event and interviews. To be acceptable, a *news release* must be written in the style used by the particular medium, and it must be presented in a form suitable to the technology of the medium. Awareness of the technological demands of each medium is also important if you expect *coverage of an event*. A speech may be an event, and certainly a news conference is, but an *interview* is not. The public relations person may formally arrange for a reporter to interview someone in a position of authority. Or the reporter may interview the PR person as representative or spokesperson for the institution. This informal situation—it may be a phone call or a visit by news media representatives—can be an organization's most significant source of publicity. Generally it is the source used most often by the media, which often ignore events and throw away publicity releases.

More and more often, media interviews are handled by the chief executive officer (CEO) with the aid of the PR person. The PR person's job therefore extends to preparing the CEO to be an effective, efficient spokesperson. Some PR agencies, notably Burson-Marsteller, have become specialists in providing such training for their clients.

Much of the bad publicity an organization gets can be attributed to errors by management: poor planning, ineffective communication or bad policies. Not getting any publicity at all, however, is probably the fault of the publicist. Newspeople say they throw away 80 to 90 percent of the news releases they get, because they are not usable. "Not usable" may mean the stories are incomplete (full of holes), inaccurate, not timely or just don't fit the news need. (See Examples 11.5 and 11.6.)

Getting information to news media in a timely way now often means delivering the news electronically. It also means that the material in the release had better agree with other information on the same topic available to the editors on-line. To avoid bad publicity and nonpublicity, you should always observe the following six rules:

1. Make sure that the information you offer is appropriate to the medium in content and style, and is timely.

2. Check all facts carefully for accuracy, and double-check for missing information.

3. To deal with any questions that may arise, give the name and phone number of the person newspeople should contact.

4. Include on photographs the name, address and phone number of the supplier, stamped or written in felt-tip pen on the back margin, so the ink won't soak through; attach captions with rubber cement (not glue, paper clips or Scotch tape); and most importantly, make certain the captions are there.

5. Never call to find out why a story or photo did not appear; and certainly don't ask, as you submit an item, when it will appear.

6. Do not send out a note with mailed releases asking for clippings. Newspapers do not run clipping bureaus.

Another mistake that publicity release writers commit involves failing to pay attention to the medium's audience. Trade publications often receive more general "mass media" releases that can't be used because they are not tailored to the publication. Some general media publications, although not technically trade publications, are by specialization much like trade or industry publications. One example is *TV Guide*, the largest-circulation magazine in the United States. (*Readers Digest* is second.) Another is the magazine *Country America*, published by the Nashville Network with a primary focus on country music.

Some organizations would do well to pay attention to another type of specialized media—the so-called alternative media—especially if they need to reach activists and special interest groups. Examples of alternative newspapers include the *Boston Phoenix*, the *San Francisco Bay Guardian*, the *Chicago Reader*, Phoenix's *New Times* and the

LA Weekly. These are often better read and have higher credibility (especially among activists) than traditional newspapers. Other relevant media are activist networks like PeaceNet, Public Data Access in New York City and the WELL in San Francisco; each such network is run by grassroots activists concerned with civil rights, feminism, peace, ecology or some other issue. The opportunities are endless for public relations practitioners to reach their audiences if they think "micro" rather than "macro" in terms of publicity, and if they target releases especially for the audience of the medium selected.

Connecting an organization to hard news can work if there is really something to contribute. Organizations often "stretch" when trying to tie their organization to something that has occurred and can look opportunistic. For example, while some organizations had a legitimate reason to issue a public statement on the death of Britain's Princess Diana in 1997 or to take some specific actions such as naming a memorial fund, others simply rushed to be included. The result can make an organization look very self-serving and risk criticism.[20]

In different parts of the world, handling the news media varies so widely that a local practitioner is often needed for guidance. Customs such as giving out free samples varies, and the style of the presentation in the releases is different too. In many cases, English language releases work well, but even if the country uses English, it's not likely to be American English. Spellings and word meanings may be different, even when the language is the same. Having releases available in the local language is good, as long as you are confident about the translation. This is especially critical with important documents such as the releases that go with annual reports or other financial matters.[21]

Broadcast Publicity You need a sophisticated knowledge of the medium to be able to prepare broadcast-quality publicity. Television generally uses videotape cassettes with sound or satellite "feeds," but it can also use either sound or silent 16-mm color film. Although TV news directors prefer to use their own staff's material or something from another news source, they increasingly use

EXAMPLE 11.5

News Release Format by Organization for Individual to Use

**United States
Information
Agency**

WASHINGTON DC 20547-0001

NEWS RELEASE

USIA

**FOR IMMEDIATE RELEASE
DATE**

FULBRIGHT AWARD

_____ has been awarded a Fulbright grant
to _____,
the U.S. Information Agency and J. William Fulbright Foreign Scholarship Board announced
recently.

_____ is one of approximately 2000 U.S. grantees who will travel abroad
for the 1998/99 academic year through the Fulbright Program. Established in 1946 under
Congressional legislation introduced by the late Senator J. William Fulbright of Arkansas, the
program is designed "to increase mutual understanding between the people of the United States
and the people of other countries."

The Fulbright Program, America's flagship educational exchange program, is sponsored
by the U.S. Information Agency, an independent foreign affairs agency within the executive
branch of the U.S. government. USIA promotes mutual understanding among nations and
peoples through a number of educational exchange activities. It explains and supports U.S.
foreign policy through a wide range of information programs.

During its 51 years, the Fulbright Program has exchanged nearly a quarter of a million
people -- more than 70,000 Americans who have studied or done research abroad and more than
130,000 people from other countries who have engaged in similar activities in the United States.
Thousands of high school teachers from around the U.S. also have been exchanged with foreign
teachers through the Fulbright Program.

Fulbright alumni include President Fernando Cardoso and First Lady Ruth Cardoso of
Brazil; NATO Secretary General Javier Solana; U.S. Senator Daniel Patrick Moynihan; Nobel
Prize winner Milton Friedman; historian John Hope Franklin; college president Ruth Simmons
and presidents emeritus Hanna Gray and Derek Bok; writers John Updike, Eudora Welty, Joseph
Heller; musicians Aaron Copland and Anna Moffo; business leaders Alberto Vitale and Kathy
Waldron; and journalists, Roger Rosenblatt, Georgie Anne Geyer, and Hedrick Smith.

A recent independent study of the Fulbright Program undertaken by the National
Humanities Center in North Carolina found that "(The) Fulbright (Program) remains a vital
force, all the more critical to American interests as the peoples of the world struggle with rapid
change and the dynamics of a global economy."

###

The United States Information Agency is an independent foreign affairs agency within the executive branch that explains and supports U.S. foreign policy and national security interests abroad through a wide range of information programs. The agency promotes mutual understanding between the United States and other countries through a series of educational and cultural exchange activities.

For media inquiries about the Fulbright Program, contact:

> United States Information Agency
> Office of Public Liaison
> 301 4th Street, SW
> Washington, DC 20547
> Telephone: (202) 619-4355
> Fax: (202) 619-6988
> E-mail: lhermann@usia.gov

For public inquiries or general information on the Fulbright Program, contact:

> United States Information
> Office of Academic Programs
> 301 4th Street, SW
> Washington, DC 20547
> Telephone: (202) 619-4360
> Fax: (202) 401-5914
> E-mail: exchange@usia.gov

EXAMPLE 11.6
Wild Art: Photo Publicity

An emperor in training

The Associated Press

An emperor penguin tends to his newly hatched chick at Sea World of California. The San Diego site is the only zoological facility in the world to successfully breed emperor penguins. The chick is the 16th hatched at the facility and will remain on its father's feet for the first few weeks of life. It was hatched Sept. 17.

publicity videos. VNRs (video news releases) usually cover hard news, not features, and may be transmitted by satellite.

VNRs and B-roll (sent along so that news directors can create different versions of the piece) are so widely used now that the video distribution industry has grown. Media distribution agencies will send advisories to television news directors by newswire, fax or one of the computer networks and transmit the VNR by satellite to all the stations at once. Most production companies are able to provide the uplinks. The media distribution companies will also provide verification of station use. Some cassettes are still sent too, but it's cheaper to use the satellite.

One way to contain costs is to partner with another company. These co-op VNRs spread production and distribution costs, and can result in a video with a broader appeal. Issues and events, such as holidays, are especially good for co-op VNRs because they can explore trends, offer different aspects or provide research information. In one example, a major producer of notebook computers cooperated with another electronics manufacturer to talk about home electronics during the Christmas buying season.[22] Some VNRs have been successfully used to support marketing campaigns, but this only works if the VNR precedes the commercial message.[23]

One use of VNRs can be to provide television stations with background they couldn't get and with quotes from experts not accessible to them. That's what happened when the Journal of the American Medical Association began offering VNRs on various topics, called JAMA Reports. Their producer, On the Scene Productions, says that if the story has broad consumer appeal, good production quality and an unbiased approach, then the opportunities for the videos to be used are good. When the report can be tied to a breaking story, of course, it's even more valuable to news directors.[24]

Educational TV often uses PR-produced feature videotapes and films if they contain no commercialism, and on rare occasions so does commercial TV. Frequently television stations show a short feature film or videotape offered by a group. These are usually 90 seconds long, but some are three minutes long; most are entertaining, light and informative. Local stations use these most often on weekends, when news is slow and they have time they can fill with non-network shows.

Publicity never supplants spot news—news recorded at the time an event occurs (usually by journalists)—but it is the best way to tell an advance story. However, such a videotape or film is just as subject to editing as a written news release is, and it too may not be used at all. This is definitely an uncontrolled area—nearly as uncontrolled as the spot coverage of news that results when a television crew is alerted to an event.

Sometimes an organization or profession is the subject of a television documentary. The PR practitioner can cooperate with those who are researching, writing and filming the documentary, but that is all that the PR person can do: help and hope for the best.

A form of television publicity that cannot be overlooked is the talk show. Daytime and evening talk shows continually present people promoting their latest book, movie, song or persona. Most local stations have a format that allows for local bookings. In such events, the PR person should be sure of three things: (1) that the show fits the PR objective; (2) the organization or sponsor gets credit; and (3) that the spokesperson is well coached or skilled in television appearances. Some interviews also may be sent by a news distribution service like MediaLink via satellite. However, most stations still tape the "send" for later use.

One of the myths that haunts public relations people is the notion that television exposure is critically important. This is not so. Television exposure is so fleeting and the audience is so fragmented that, unless all networks use the information, the impact will be minimal. Most of the impact from local coverage comes from documentaries or news features.

Just as the possible benefits of being on television or in newspapers or magazines are exaggerated, so is the damage caused by negative stories. But some balanced stories that tell both sides of a story are seen within an organization as being "negative" because they say something against the organization. You can't avoid that, but you can be sure you tell the organization's side of the story successfully.

TRADITIONAL HYBRIDS: DIRECT MAIL AND 900 PHONE NUMBERS

Direct mail is a hybrid of publicity and advertising. In certain instances (such as newsletters from politicians), direct mail can be considered publicity. On the other hand, direct mail that seeks magazine subscriptions, for example, most certainly is advertising. Direct mail is a form of controlled communication: the message can say anything that does not violate a law; it can be any size or shape the postal service will accept; and it can be sent any time its sender chooses. Mailing lists are available for almost any audience you might wish to reach (if not, you can send it to "Occupant" at a particular address). However, just because the envelope arrives does not mean the message will be received.

The latest form of direct mail is electronic mail (e-mail). Many associations now list, along with members' office and home addresses, their fax and e-mail addresses. These systems are excellent for "perishable" messages that need instant delivery and a prompt response.

Traditional direct mail has a high mortality rate, which is why so much is invested in designing appeals and in doing multiple mailings. The hope is that at least one effort will reach its intended audience.

The seven cardinal rules governing direct mail are as follows:

1. Know what the objective of the mailing is, and concentrate on it.

2. Use the correct mailing list. Remember that December through February is a significant job-change period; if you don't have time to check the accuracy of your list, mailings at this time should go to the title and not to the person.

3. Write copy that explains what the product or service does for the recipient.

4. Design the layout and format to fit the image of the product or service you are presenting.

5. Make it easy for the prospect to take the action you want taken.

6. Tell the story at least three times, and repeat the mailings two or three times.

7. Research all direct mail by testing the offer, package and list. Test to see if the offer is attractive to target audiences. Use alternative offers to make sure you have the best incentive. Test the package (presentation). Make sure respondents know what to do with the offer, and keep the directions simple and clear. Test the list with a sample mailing to ensure that it's accurate. Test the mailing even if it is as little as 1,000 pieces. Don't ever drop untested pieces in the mail.

Example 11.7 shows a direct-mail piece, in multiple languages.

Three important considerations go into planning a direct mailing: recency, frequency and monetary matters. The *recency* of a direct mailing is significant in evaluating response; stories of delayed-action response are rare. *Frequent* mailings increase your chances of response by providing reminders. The *monetary* aspect—what you can afford to spend—influences the design and outcome of a direct mailing.

Usually direct-mail investments more than pay their way. The key to success is the mailing list you select. *Occupant* lists—lists organized by addresses—are easy to find and inexpensive but very impersonal, and often inaccurate. If you are mailing to a limited geographical area, you can make up your own list from the crisscross, or city, directory. *Specialized* lists are available according to age, income, educational status and almost any other kind of breakdown you want. Many organizations sell lists of their membership, and you can buy other lists from direct-mail list companies. Some base their lists on auto registrations, others on phone directories and others on complex sampling strata. Direct-mail services already have about 80 percent of U.S. households located, but about 6 percent of all third-class mail still goes undelivered.[25]

The price you pay for use of a list entitles you to use it only once. To protect its list, the mailing house actually sends out the material for you. It is important to remember that 23 percent of a general list, 22 percent of a business list and 35 percent of a business executive list go bad in a year. Planning a periodic check of your list is the best way to safeguard the integrity of your basic mailing file. The U.S. Postal Service will help. If your address list is on a diskette, you can send it in and the post office will standardize addresses, make sure cities match zip codes, validate the zip codes and add four extra digits to each code. Your post office also will report any addresses that can't be coded.

Remember that every piece of correspondence going out of the office is an image maker or breaker. Careful attention to spelling indicates that you care about the recipient. Typographical errors suggest that the message was not important enough to command the writer's attention, and the person receiving the letter might wonder why it should deserve his or hers. Accurate spelling and syntax also imply knowledge and authority. Perhaps the most compelling reason for making every piece of copy perfect is that your letterhead is your signature.

Every bit as personal as a note bearing your letterhead is a telephone call. The promotional tool 1-900-Telephone charges calls to the customer. The voice information system offers callers access to a prerecorded message or other public relations information, if they have a touchtone telephone. Callers can be charged anything from 50 cents to as much as $50 per call and may be billed at a flat rate or at a cost per minute.

The 900 numbers have been used for fundraising, for offering live or prerecorded messages, for promotions and for marketing games. In the 1980s, Johnson & Johnson set up a 900 line during the Tylenol tampering crisis so that callers could get immediate information.[26] During the 1991 Persian Gulf "Desert Storm" war, AT&T set up a 900 line for the USO so that stateside callers could talk to troops involved in the conflict.

NEW HYBRIDS, NEW CHANNELS

Digital technology has created a whole new way of conveying information and interacting with publics. Some of you may be taking your public relations principles class on-line where you have assignments electronically delivered and returned, enjoy topical discussions in a "chat room," have graphics to illustrate text and get your academic counseling for the class in personal responses to your e-mail messages to your instructor. You'll be doing your academic research on-line, and your personal research too, such as finding the cheapest tickets for a trip home or a break from school and buying them on-line as well.

You may be using a CD-ROM with the class. Although not a new technology, more public relations people are using CD-ROMs now instead of brochures or in place of whole presentations such as media kits. There's more space for information and the quality of the video is superb. You can use a CD-ROM or the Internet to deliver VNRs.

Computerized touch-screen kiosks offer interactive displays at trade shows. If you are selling an expensive item such as a house or car, prospective buyers can look at different options, select what they want and go as far with the transaction as the company allows, electronically.

The Internet offers Web sites that provide 24-hour-a-day, global sources for news media. Reporters are likely to go to a Web site first for information and may or may not try the telephone or fax. All kinds of consumers of information use Web sites, and the news media have their own Web sites where users expect to find the latest information being processed by the news medium.

The Internet

Organizations of all kinds, profit and nonprofit (including government), have Web pages, and when you access those pages, especially those of profit-making organizations, you are likely to get

EXAMPLE 11.7
Direct Mail in Multiple Languages

Service mark of AT&T

9-1-1 SPEAKS YOUR LANGUAGE

9-1-1 HABLA SU IDIOMA

9-1-1 Nói Tiếng Của Quý Vị

9-1-1 번에서도 한국말로 합니다

能說您的語言

СЛУЖБА 9-1-1 ГОВОРИТ НА ВАШЕМ ЯЗЫКЕ.

VIETNAMESE
Việt Ngữ

QUÝ VỊ CẦN LÀM GÌ KHI GỌI 9-1-1?

Khi quý vị cần giúp đỡ:

1. Gọi 9-1-1.
2. Đừng cúp máy.
3. Báo cho 9-1-1 biết trường hợp khẩn cấp của quý vị cần:
   - CẢNH SÁT (POLICE)
   - CỨU HỎA (FIRE)
   - XE CỨU THƯƠNG (AMBULANCE)
   (Cố gắng học những từ này trong Anh ngữ)
4. 9-1-1 có thể đưa vào một thông dịch viên. Đừng cúp máy. Cứ giữ máy thoại.
5. Báo cho 9-1-1 biết ngôn ngữ của quý vị.
6. Nên bình tĩnh.
7. Cho 9-1-1 biết những tin tức của quý vị:
   - tên
   - số điện thoại
   - địa chỉ nơi đang cần giúp đỡ
8. Trả lời tất cả mọi câu hỏi.

9-1-1 chỉ được dùng cho các trường hợp khẩn cấp.

Ví dụ:
   - hỏa hoạn
   - tội ác
   - bị thương cần xe cứu thương
   - nguy hiểm đến tính mạng và tài sản

9-1-1 **không** phải là nơi hỏi tin tức.

Nếu có gì nghi ngờ, gọi 9-1-1.

SPANISH
ESPAÑOL

¿QUE DEBE HACER CUANDO LLAME AL 9-1-1?

Cuando necesite ayuda:

1.) Llame al 9-1-1.
2.) Manténgase en la línea.
3.) Dígale a 9-1-1 cuál es su emergencia:
   - POLICÍA (POLICE)
   - INCENDIO (FIRE)
   - AMBULANCIA (AMBULANCE)
   (Trate de aprender estas palabras en inglés).
4.) 9-1-1 puede agregar un intérprete a la línea. Escuchará un sonido de "click". No cuelgue. Manténgase en la línea.
5.) Dígale a 9-1-1 qué idioma habla.
6.) Mantenga la calma.
7.) Debe a 9-1-1 su:
   - nombre
   - número telefónico
   - la dirección en donde se necesita la ayuda
8.) Conteste todas las preguntas.

9-1-1 es sólo para emergencias.

Por ejemplo:
   - incendio
   - crímenes
   - herido que necesita ambulancia
   - peligro para la vida o propiedad

9-1-1 **no** es un número de información.

En caso de duda, llame al 9-1-1.

RUSSIAN
РУССКИЙ ВАРИАНТ

ЧТО ДЕЛАТЬ, КОГДА ВЫ ЗВОНИТЕ 9-1-1?

Когда вам нужна помощь:

1) Звоните 9-1-1.
2) Дождитесь ответа.
3) Укажите диспетчеру службы 9-1-1 характер чрезвычайной ситуации:
   - ПОЛИЦИЯ (POLICE)
   - ПОЖАР (FIRE)
   - СКОРАЯ ПОМОЩЬ (AMBULANCE)
   (Постарайтесь выучить эти слова на английском языке).
4) Служба 9-1-1 может подключить к разговору переводчика. В этом случае вы услышите щелчок. Не вешайте трубку. Дождитесь ответа.
5) Скажите диспетчеру службы 9-1-1, на каком языке вы говорите.
6) Сохраняйте спокойствие.
7) Скажите диспетчеру службы 9-1-1:
   - ваше имя
   - ваш номер телефона
   - адрес, по которому требуется помощь
8) Ответьте на все вопросы.

Звоните 9-1-1 исключительно в случае чрезвычайной ситуации.

Например, в случае:
   - пожара
   - преступления
   - телесного повреждения, требующего скорой помощи
   - опасности для жизни или собственности

Служба 9-1-1 не является информационной службой.

В случае сомнения, звоните 9-1-1.

EXAMPLE 11.7 (continued)
Direct Mail in Multiple Languages

ENGLISH

WHAT TO DO WHEN YOU CALL 9-1-1?

When you need help:

1.) Call 9-1-1.
2.) Stay on the phone.
3.) Tell 9-1-1 what your emergency is:
   - FIRE
   - POLICE
   - AMBULANCE
4.) 9-1-1 may add-on an interpreter. You will hear a clicking noise. **Don't** hang up. Stay on the phone.
5.) Tell 9-1-1 the language you speak.
6.) Be calm.
7.) Give 9-1-1 your:
   - name
   - phone number
   - address where help is needed
8.) Answer all questions.

9-1-1 is for emergencies only.
For instance:
   - fire
   - crime
   - injury needing an ambulance
   - danger to life or property
9-1-1 is **not** for information.
If in doubt, call 9-1-1.

KOREAN
한국말

LAOTIAN
ພາສາລາວ

CHINESE
中文

ARABIC
اللغة العربية

both advertising and editorial messages. That makes the Web page one of the most versatile of the new hybrids.

There are several ongoing tasks that are important for maintaining interest in a Web site. These include: offering substantive content, keeping it updated and fresh, making it easy to use, providing a good word presentation for those who turn off graphics to save loading time, having all of the "basic" data such as you would expect to find on organizational "fact sheets," as well as the newsworthy items that would attract all of your publics, not just media.[27]

For that to happen, you might consider microsites for a number of functions, such as new campaigns, special offers, crisis communications and on-line sales. Although you can use a link from a home page, if special items aren't easy to find and use, people will give up. Microsites work in reverse. People put up special sites with their own address and the site then offers a link to the home page. The micro-sites typically don't last very long.[28] Their flexibility makes them an especially good publicity and promotion tool and a place reporters depend on for information.

The Internet is also turning out to be a reliable source for video news as well. While probably not the best way to distribute VNRs, on-line video is interesting not just to news people. While TV producers are not likely to pull a VNR off the Internet, they may get story ideas there where they can see what is available. Also, Video Monitoring Services is able to send clips to subscriber clients electronically.

One creative use of the VNR occurred when Orbis Broadcast Group decided to offer a public service to television viewers who wanted more information about their health-care VNRs. The firm let viewers know on television where more information could be accessed, and once at the site, viewers could participate in chat sessions with physicians and find other consumer information from leading health care organizations.[29] The two-way interactive aspect is what makes the Internet so attractive as a new communication channel. Example 11.8 shows how one company uses its newsletter to bring publics to its web sites.

▉ Benefits and Disadvantages of Interactive Audio/Text/Video

The Internet has dramatically changed public relations practice in that publics can be defined more clearly and targeted more precisely. Furthermore, the interactive nature of the Internet allows for more reliable monitoring and evaluating. The down side to this change is that bad news may be instantly global, and e-mail and chat room conversations can spread rumors and even pretend to originate from organizations. Organizations can also be attacked outright by rogue sites that mimic theirs. It is much more difficult to contain a crisis, but easier to respond.

Web sites are often created and then abandoned, reflecting badly on the organization. Some Web sites are simply too complex to use efficiently, and people don't return to them unless they find the technology intriguing. (For some good Web-sites selected by *Reputation Management* magazine, see Example 11.9.)

A stand-alone unit for interactive use, such as a kiosk, can be a good teaching tool, and an intriguing draw at a meeting or show. However, unless well conceived, they can be simplistic and boring as well as not really providing any information about the user.

▉ Virtual Reality

Virtual reality experiences in cyberspace, available now in some malls as entertainment, rely on computer-generated images. The user must wear goggles and gloves (or hand attachments) that electronically create the illusion of a three-dimensional experience. The simulations vary from walking around inside a patient who has a tumor so a surgeon gets a good look at it and all the surrounding organs before making an incision or planning radiation therapy, to looking inside a storm system so a meteorologist can get a better view of the storm's potential. It could also be used to let a potential customer "fly" a plane—perhaps one not yet built—or to enable a user to explore an underwater site as a "dry" scuba diver. Virtual reality seems

EXAMPLE 11.8

Utility Company's Mailer and Web Site Connections

FLAME TIPS

CUSTOMERS ASK

I'm having a hard time paying my winter bills. Can you give me any help?

We place great emphasis on assisting customers who are having difficulty paying their winter gas bills due to unforeseen financial difficulties.

If it appears you will have difficulty paying a large winter bill, let us know immediately. We may be able to put you on our Extended Payment Plan, allowing you to pay large bills over an extended period of time.

Another source of help might be the Budget Payment Plan, which allows monthly budgeting by averaging your gas bill payments over the year.

Our representatives can provide information on all services offered by Oklahoma Natural and others who may be of help. We may be able to direct you to local, state, and federal programs that provide aid at certain times of the year. And, privately funded fuel aid programs such as Share the Warmth can sometimes help.

PURE FACTS

Low-input pilots on new gas water heaters save energy and money.

A leaky faucet that fills a cup in 20 minutes wastes 3,200 gallons of water a year.

140°

Set water temperature at 140°F. with a dishwasher or clothes washer. Otherwise, 120°F. is sufficient.

ON THE WEB

ONEOK Inc.
NYSE-OKE

OKLAHOMA NATURAL GAS

- CORPORATE INFORMATION
- FINANCIAL INFORMATION
- RECENT NEWS
- FLAME TIPS
- CUSTOMER SERVICE
- INDEX

Customers and other interested net surfers can now read **Flame Tips** on the Internet through our home page on the World Wide Web. There, you

will also find information about ONEOK Inc., parent company of Oklahoma Natural.

Find us on the Internet at the following address:

http://www.ONG.com or **http://www.ONEOK.com.**

Oklahoma Natural Gas Company   *February 1996*

PRINTED ON RECYCLED PAPER

Source: Reprinted with permission of ONEOK, Inc.

EXAMPLE 11.9
Good Web Sites to Visit

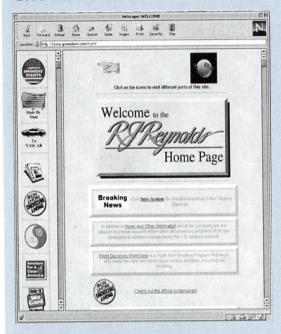

Reynolds Tobacco Company tackles tough
public affairs issues online.

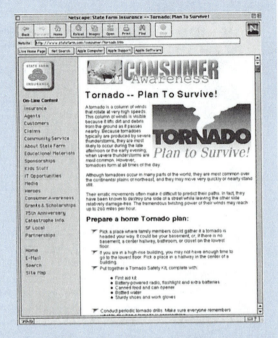

State Farm provides helpful information
on disaster preparedness.

capable of creating countless artificial worlds for people to experience.[30]

POINTS TO REMEMBER

■ Channels of communication are public or private paths by which messages travel through media.

■ Public channels are for the mass media, and private channels apply to the print and electronic media of organizations.

■ The two principal types of public relations communication are advertising and publicity, both of which may take many media forms.

■ In planning a public relations strategy, the practitioner chooses channels and media based on the purpose of the communication, the intended audience, the message to be delivered, the resources available and the credibility of the medium chosen to carry the message.

■ A media mix is generally used, and media can be categorized as controlled or uncontrolled.

■ Public relations uses many types of advertising in various formats, which means that PR practitioners have to know how to prepare, place and evaluate ad copy.

■ Creating most advertising messages of any kind —public service announcements or commercial messages—is a costly process, and evaluations of effectiveness are limited.

■ Advertising can create problems as well as solve them. Especially in a global environment, ads must be watched for their suitability in terms of language and culture for the intended audience as well as the unintended audience which may be exposed to them.

■ Using ads may be especially important when a problem occurs, because it is a controlled format.

■ Uncontrollable problems with advertising include unfortunate placement, imitation of good advertising ideas and the ill effects of negative advertising.

■ Two myths associated with advertising are that a single concept can be used globally and that a single concept can work with all audiences within one culture.

■ Messages that are not advertising generally are referred to as *publicity*—some form of news or information about the organization.

■ Publicity can go directly to audiences or can be sent through mass and/or specialized media.

■ Organizations generally produce publications such as magazines, newsletters and annual reports, and at least the last two are being made available electronically, usually through a Web page.

■ Publications may be done in-house or outside. Most film and video work is produced by outside specialists unless the organization is large enough to support an in-house facility.

■ Videos are used for external and internal audiences.

■ Other forms of electronic messages are videotext, teletext and Intranet.

■ Meetings and speeches are also a form of media, and speeches may be mailed for additional exposure.

■ Other media for promotional messages include exhibits, characters identified with the organization, multimedia presentations, closed-circuit television, books, commemorative stamps and even cartoons.

■ Publicity in the mass media and in specialized media outside the organization is uncontrolled and demands careful preparation to meet the demands of the medium.

■ Fewer news releases are being used in print media now, whereas use of video news releases (VNRs) is increasing.

■ Traditional hybrids (combinations of advertising and publicity) are direct mail and 900 telephone numbers. The success of direct mail depends on research to keep target audiences identified.

■ Digital technology has created a whole new way of conveying information and interacting with publics. CD-ROMs and Web sites offer opportunities for profit and nonprofit organizations to send direct messages to specific publics.

■ Web sites on the Internet provide sources of information and video for news media seekers as well as others.

■ Along with the many benefits of the Internet, there are some down sides, such as the global spreading of bad news and rumors and outright attacks by rogue Web sites and misleading e-mail.

■ New technologies such as virtual reality hold a lot of promise for public relations use.

■ The effectiveness of all communication depends on the appropriate and inventive use of existing channels of communication and their media.

NOTES

[1] "News/Broadcast Network Studies Usage of PSAs on Compact Disc," *PR News* (October 23, 1993), p. 5.

[2] Laura Bird, "And They're Very Good at Praying for Success," *Wall Street Journal* (October 15, 1993), p. B1.

[3] Ibid.

[4] Leon E. Wynter, "Global Marketers Learn To Say No to Bad Ads," *Wall Street Journal* (April 1, 1998), p. B1.

[5] Terry Haller, "Corporate Ads Doomed," *Ad Age* (January 25, 1982), p. 47.

[6] Steve Rubin, "Pooling Resources Builds Public/Private Partnerships," *Public Relations Journal*, 48(10) (1992), 32–33. Also see a consumer advocate concern, Laura Beil, "Stamp of Approval," *The Dallas Morning News* (April 20, 1997), pp. J1, 10.

[7] Ibid.

[8] Ellen Joan Pollock, "'I Love My Lawyer' Ads May Spread to More States," *Wall Street Journal* (December 7, 1990), pp. B1, B4.

[9] Heather Fleming, "PSA Slice Shrinks as Commercial Pie Grows," *Broadcasting & Cable* (March 31, 1997), p. 19.

[10] "Reaping What They Sow," *Inside PR* (February 1994), pp. 20–21.

[11] Walter S. Mossberg, "Apple's Camera Is a Computer Gizmo a Boss Will Love," *Wall Street Journal* (May 19, 1994), p. B1.

[12] Ibid.

[13] Suzanne Alexander Ryan, "Companies Teach All Sorts of Lessons with Educational Tools They Give Away," *Wall Street Journal* (April 19, 1994), p. B1.

[14] Ibid.

[15] Ibid., p. B2.

[16] Adam Shell, "Reaching Out to the TV Generation," *Public Relations Journal*, 46(11) (November 1990), pp. 28–32.

[17] Zoe McCathrin, "The Key to Employee Communication, Small Group Meetings," *Professional Communicator* (Spring 1990), pp. 6, 7, 10.

[18] Kevin Helliker, "Old-Fashioned PR Gives General Mills Advertising Bargains," *Wall Street Journal* (March 20, 1997), pp. 1, 6.

[19] Fen Montaigne, "Name That Chintz! How Shelter Magazines Boost Brands," *Wall Street Journal* (March 14, 1997), pp. B1, 8. Also see Mary Kuntz, Joseph Weber with Heidi Dawley, "The New Husksterism, Stealth Ads Creep Into A Culture Saturated With Logos and Pitches," *Business Week* (July 1, 1996), pp. 76–84.

[20] Joshua Harris Prager, "Death of a Princess, Birth of a Thousand Press Releases," *The Wall Street Journal* (September 16, 1997), B1, 6.

[21] Aimee Stern, "Overseas Sales Hype," *International Business* (February, 1993), pp. 64, 66.

[22] Judy L. Roberts, "Co-op VNRs Distribute Messages and Costs, *Tactics*, PRSA (June 1997), pp, 20–21.

[23] Douglas Simon, "VNRs Support Corporate Image Campaigns," *Tactics*, PRSA (June 1997), p. 26.

[24] Sally Jewett, "Health Care VNRs—Alive and Well," *Tactics*, PRSA (June 1997), p. 23.

[25] Michael W. Miller, "Post office's Planned Address List Raises Privacy Jitters," *Wall Street Journal* (December 13, 1990), pp. B1, B6.

[26] Adam Shell, "1-900-A-PR-Tool?" *Public Relations Journal*, 46(9) (August 1990), p. 9.

[27] David Gumpert of NetMarquee Online Services, "Challenge for Web Site Managers: Now That You're A Publisher, What Will You Publish?" *tips & tactics*, supplement of *pr reporter* 35(2) (February 24, 1997); and see "Planning Powerful Electronic Publications, *tips & tactics*, supplement of *pr reporter* (October 27, 1997), 35(14).

[28] Greg Hansen of Cyberactive Services, "Smaller May Be Better for Web Marketing," *tips & tactics*, supplement of *pr reporter* (December 8, 1997), 35(16).

[29] Adam Shell, "The Wired World of Video PR," *PRSA Tactics* (June, 1996), p. 23. Also, see entire issue of Inside PR's magazine *Reputation Management* (November/December 1997).

[30] Doug Stewart, "Through the Looking Glass into an Artificial World—via Computer," *Smithsonian* (January 1991), pp. 36–45.

Selected readings, activities and assignments appropriate to this chapter can be found in the *Instructor's Guide* or on InfoTrac if you are using the InfoTrac College Edition.

TACTICS AND TECHNIQUES: DETAILS THAT MAKE PR STRATEGY WORK

By speaking out you can control to some extent . . . perhaps to the only extent . . . the way in which you are perceived, and if you are both candid and cooperative with the press, they will give you an even chance and the benefit of the doubt . . . and that . . . is all you should expect in today's world.

ANTONIO NAVARRO, SENIOR VICE-PRESIDENT, W. R. GRACE & CO.

Corporations are wise to accept the premise that it is better to dine on 50 percent of a large, plump turkey than 100 percent of a sparrow.

TRANSLATED BY *WASHINGTON JOURNALISM REVIEW*

We have to recognize that the magnitude of communication possible through the advent of technology will add to the din, making it even more difficult, not easier, for messages to get through undistorted. In essence, the method of communication will become so deceptively easy that it could mislead practitioners as to the effectiveness of their activities.

JOHN F. BUDD, CHAIR AND CEO, THE OMEGA GROUP

Public relations work is somewhat like a giant jigsaw puzzle: there are many pieces, and each must fit perfectly with the others to make the whole picture. In Chapter 10, you learned strategies to help you develop the picture. In Chapter 11, you surveyed the communications channels PR practitioners use as the framework for that picture. In this chapter, you get a look at the pieces. Have you ever worked a jigsaw puzzle by first separating what appeared to be ground from what looked like sky? Well, you can divide the major sections of the public relations puzzle—advertising and publicity—in the same way. In trying to sort out puzzle pieces by "sky" and "ground," however, you may sometimes have found pieces that included parts of both, and others that looked like one but were actually the other. That's also the case with advertising and publicity in public relations.

ADVERTISING

Advertising has been defined as paid-for time or space, except in the case of public service announcements (PSAs) where the time and space are donated to a nonprofit organization. But in some situations, advertising looks a lot like publicity. Usually when advertising takes on the appearance of publicity, there is no intention to deceive the careful viewer. Ads are supposed to be clearly labeled as such, but they can be labeled and still look very much like editorial copy. Sometimes when a newspaper publishes a special section on something like the opening of a hospital, the reader may not be aware that almost all of that section—even the news columns—consists of advertising.

The tendency of some public relations people to view public service announcements as publicity, because no money changes hands, is confusing to most students and mystifying to others. Clearly, though, print PSAs look exactly like ads, and broadcast PSAs sound exactly like commercials. Moreover, they are handled through the advertising departments of print media and through public service or public affairs directors at radio and television stations. Publicity, on the other hand, is handled by media news staffs and must compete for time or space with staff-generated news material. Perhaps the most clearcut difference, however, is that PSAs, like other advertising, are controlled communications whose precise content is dictated by the originating organization. In contrast, publicity is subject to whatever revisions or editing the news media see fit to impose.

Ads as News Lookalikes

Ads sometimes look like publicity. Although the copy is clearly marked as advertising, it may resemble a news feature and may be read as one by read-

ers. These ads frequently appear in local publications and highlight products and services offered by local businesses. Some types of product advertising done by specialty houses look like a feature story or column. The line between advertising and publicity will blur further as traditional media are used in more and more exotic ways. All such stories are promotional pieces, however, and wouldn't pass muster as a news column if submitted to an editor.

Sometimes public relations people have difficulty with ads that closely resemble publicity releases, because unsophisticated managements don't know the difference between the two. Often, as in the "Homes" sections of Sunday newspapers, whole sections of copy may be involved, all consisting of display advertising (see Example 12.1). In addition, newspapers sometimes run special sections—whole sections devoted to a special topic or event and built around the advertising that is sold.

The editorial copy in such a section is essentially written for those who have taken out ads. The amount of space purchased determines the length of the stories, as well as the amount of illustration material (art) that accompanies them. The only "free" copy in the section is what you write about the event or the topic itself, such as a historical feature, a current "what's going on" news item, profiles of people from previous events and photos related to the topical content of the section. The copy in most special sections, other than the Sunday real estate sections, looks like news but is not straight news.

Special sections may appear in many different forms. One on health care, for example, may look like a regular newspaper section, as might a *single advertiser* supplement for a new store. Alternatively, a store may use a magazine format to be inserted within a newspaper. A chamber of commerce annual report may look like a Sunday tabloid insert similar to the *New York Times Book Review* section (which is editorial matter, not advertising). Advertorials—magazine advertising supplements—often look like special features. Broadcast advertorials, or infomercials though, look like editorials and deal with ideas or issues and not with products or services. Another area that invites confusion is

EXAMPLE 12.1

A Full-Page Advertisement That Resembles Publicity

This ad, placed by the Pakistan Tourism Development Corporation, is written almost like news copy. But it is an ad because it appeared in paid-for space.

Reprinted with permission.

broadcast news promos (the broadcast equivalent of house ads). These often sound like actual news soundbites and can mislead the viewer or listener.

To maintain credibility with the news media, you have to know the differences in their styles of copy but be able to write appropriately for all.

Print and Broadcast PSAs

Public service announcements are examples of publicity-generating ad copy that are similar to special sections and display advertising. In all of these forms, you do *not* work with the publication's editorial staff in placing them. With print PSAs, you will probably deal with newspaper or magazine designers and layout artists in the publication's advertising department, who position ads and editorial matter. You might also work with a newspaper's advertising director to get a drop-in ad placed in a regular advertiser's space, with that advertiser's permission. Or you might work with a large regular advertiser to sponsor your space. Regular advertisers usually agree to do this only for nonprofit organizations or in conjunction with special civic events that are open to all, such as a Fourth of July fireworks celebration.

If your message is for the broadcast media, you will deal with public service directors who are usually partial to general interest subjects like health and safety or to specific social problems like substance abuse or child molestation. You can sponsor a PSA if you represent a profit-making organization as long as you are delivering a nonprofit organization's message that does not directly benefit your own organization. A classic example in the USA is AT&T's sponsorship in the 1980s of a PSA on illiteracy for the Assault on Illiteracy program, a nonprofit organization. AT&T's corporate advertising district manager explained why the company sponsored the ad: "We wanted a subject related to information and communications because that's the business we're in. We also wanted the public to know that, while we are a gigantic corporation, we are committed to performing deeds in the pub-

lic interest." The AT&T spot went to 400 TV stations, was aired 1,374 times on 296 stations and made an estimated 682,280,000 audience impressions.[1]

When you are planning a PSA, you first need to consider its purpose. Then you must consider the budget, the amount of money you have to spend and the amount you can get from donations. You must also try to foresee problems you are likely to encounter in shooting, including actors, location, permissions, music and sound. Example 12.2 provides a quick reference for planning time.

For just the reasons stated by AT&T's ad director, a profit-making organization may sponsor a whole campaign or a portion of one.

Preparing Successful Ads

Your most important consideration in preparing any type of advertising copy is effectiveness—achieving your purpose. The purpose must be clear because it's difficult for even the best copy to create awareness, convey specific information, get action and affect attitude. You must decide where the public is in relation to the product or service (including a nonprofit organization's service) and go from there. The fact that memory is multidimensional means that, in order to be able to measure your ad's effectiveness with some degree of reliability, you have to know exactly what you wish to achieve and how prepared a specific public is to receive your message.[2]

Decisions about effectiveness include whether or not to use humor, whether to make comparisons and whether to use negative comments. Again, what you decide depends on what you are trying to accomplish and whom you are trying to reach. Humorous ads seem to get attention (see Example 12.3), but they convey less information and don't always ensure recall of the advertiser.[3] There's a risk in comparative ads too, especially in credibility. Credibility also can be at stake in negative advertising, but you can usually count on recall. And while most people say they don't like negative ad-

EXAMPLE 12.2
PSA Preparation Schedule

Task	Time Required	Task	Time Required
Choosing a cause or topic	4 to 12 hours	Shoot day (on set)	8 to 14 hours
Script research	3 to 8 hours	Music selection	1 to 3 hours
Finding a nonprofit sponsor	12 hours to 3 days or more, depending on your persuasiveness	Casting narrator	1 to 4 hours
		Recording narrator at sound studio	1/2 to 1 hour
First-draft script	2 to 6 hours	Choosing takes and editing (digital)	5 to 8 hours
Script rewrites	1 to 3 hours	On-line edit to finished master with title	4 to 9 hours
Script approvals	3 to 8 hours, depending on the number of drafts		
Location scouting	5 hours to 2 days		
Casting	5 to 8 hours		
Prop shopping	3 to 5 hours		
Setting up shoot (crew) plus meeting with camera crew	2 to 4 hours		

Source: Adapted from Margie Goldsmith, "How to Get Results with PSAs," *Public Relations Journal* (January 1986), p. 34. Copyright January 1986. Reprinted by permission of *Public Relations Journal*, published by the Public Relations Society of America, New York, NY.

vertising, they do respond to negative political advertising that seems to offer insight into an issue or an opponent's personal characteristics.[4]

One of the most memorable parts of any ad is the organization's logo, designed not only for high recognition, but also for a positive attraction or reaction. According to one study by Frank Thayer, "Successful corporate symbols will be those which effectively evoke the positive and powerful responses already present in the mind of the subject and those which were learned at a much earlier stage of their cultural education."[5] The latter point suggests that, as organizations become involved in global communication, these logos should be pretested abroad to ensure that they meet with cultural acceptance. Organizations often change their logos so that these "grow" with the organization and reflect a more modern look or encompass appreciation and understanding by a more diverse array of people. Sometimes logos change for a special occasion (see Example 12.4). Other organizations cling to an established logo for high recognition.

PUBLICITY AND PUBLICATIONS

Just as some advertising resembles publicity, some publicity and promotional pieces look like advertising. This is particularly true of brochures, which are as likely to be sales pieces as to be news or information pieces.

Brochures are one type of publication that organizations regularly produce themselves. Desktop publishing has increased the number and decreased the expense of such in-house publications. Except for brochures, house publications generally follow a magazine format, although some are designed as megapapers—oversized newspapers that are folded for a magazine or newsletter look.

One of the most important magazine-format publications an organization produces is its annual report. Although only publicly held companies are required by law to produce annual reports for their stockholders and for the Securities and Exchange Commission, many nonprofits publish

EXAMPLE 12.3

House Ad Using Humor

Everyone knows that children and dogs always attract attention. Furthermore, anyone who has ever owned an Irish Setter (as one of the authors has) appreciates the validity of this illustration. The illustration is memorable and is closely tied to the message and the source.

Source: Reprinted with permission of Dow Jones & Co., Inc., publisher of *The Wall Street Journal.* Copyright 1991.

EXAMPLE 12.4

Logos

The Audit Bureau of Circulations has been monitoring the circulation of print media since 1914 and has changed its "look" or logo several times over the years to modernize. The newest logo, introduced in 1989, coincided with ABC's 75th anniversary.

Reprinted with permission.

annual reports for their stakeholders as well. But nonprofit organizations are less likely to produce quarterly reports. Publicly held companies must do so, and these often take the form of brochures of variable size and format. Sometimes speeches by top executives and reports by researchers are produced in brochure or magazine format and are sent to stakeholders as publicity.

Publicists often get extra mileage out of their newspaper and magazine stories by reprinting them for their own mailings.

Producing Brochures and House Publications

Publishing is a highly technical part of public relations activity. It is full of traps for the unwary—and unfortunately, mistakes are very tangible and easily noticed. With desktop publishing, more materials like brochures and house publications are now computer-generated, but not all of these are prepared by the PR department. Thus, the public relations practitioner may have to publish some guidelines for the publications' physical appearance so that they look as though they belong to the same organization, no matter who produces them. Publications from an organization should appear to belong to a "family." If you don't control this, the organization's image will suffer fragmentation.

Brochures The first decision you have to make in producing a brochure is to determine its purpose and its *audience*. This will suggest not only the number of copies to print, but also the distribution method to use. Distribution is critical to planning and can determine the brochure's format—for instance, whether it will be mailed as a self-mailer or whether it will need to fit into an envelope.

Brochures can come in all shapes and sizes, but these are virtually predetermined if the piece has to be mailed. If it is going in the mail, you must decide whether to enclose it in an envelope at additional expense or to send it as a self-mailer—that is, a folded piece with a tab or staple closing and part of the surface reserved for the recipient's name and address. In either case, it is important first to check with the Postal Service, particularly if your piece requires a specially designed and irregular envelope, since there are regulations governing acceptable envelope size. There are also regulations about sealing and addressing self-mailers and about sending a bulk mailing. Finding out all this in advance is important because it affects brochure design, including the choice of paper stock. Postal Service workers are invariably friendly and helpful in explaining postal limitations because they want your publication to conform to their regulations.

After determining the physical properties of the brochure and its envelope (if there is to be one), use a folded piece of paper as a mockup. Visualizing helps. Make sure the size exactly matches that of the finished piece.

Next decide what is to be said and how. Figure out what can be said with illustrations. Brochures usually succeed or fail with readers on the strength or weakness of their graphics, so it is important to begin working early with an artist. The artist responsible for the design must know the concept and the purpose, as well as the distribution method and how it affects the design. Together you must reach some decisions about color (ordinarily a financial, rather than an aesthetic, decision) and about the method of reproduction. Most printing today is offset. Ask for rough layouts, and ask the artist to offer a choice of several different ideas.

Once you have approved the design, you must decide on the exact paper stock, finish, weight and color; the precise color of ink; and the kind and size of type for each portion of the layout. Paper suppliers, printers and typesetters usually have samples, which many artists also keep on hand. Choose the printer carefully, because even an attractive layout that is clumsily executed is unusable. The number of brochures printed affects their cost: the more printed, the lower the cost for each.

The artist can go ahead with production after all details are settled, copy has been written and supplied and either illustrations have been supplied or artwork has been approved.

Copyfitting and layout may fall to the artist or another person skilled at layout, but public relations people should also master these techniques. Since the advent of desktop publishing, it is generally accepted that the PR person can write the

CHAPTER 12 / TACTICS AND TECHNIQUES

copy, design the format and produce a camera-ready piece. If you do not produce the piece on a computer, you will send out the copy, marked for type sizes, to be set by a typesetter. After the type has been set and proofread, the finished art readied and everything pasted up, it is time to begin work with the printer. Be sure to arrange with the printer to check proofs before the entire printing is run. Mistakes can happen. Instructions on the layout can be misunderstood or stated incorrectly. Proofing is your last chance. Take it.

When a large printing run is complete and the folding is done, it may be worthwhile to have the stuffing and mailing handled by a mail service. Such firms offer different services, but nearly all will work with a mailing list and either charge for labeling or use your labels. Since most operations are computerized, it is best to provide a mailing service with a printout of the addresses on mailing labels.

After the mailing, be sure to keep enough brochures on hand to meet additional requests. Keep at least five as file copies. You may need them for reference.[6]

Some brochures are costly pieces, like one for a construction company that took the form of a paper house when unfolded, or the Honda Accord brochure whose headlights came on when it was opened, or a music company's brochure that played a tune. The limits are set not by creativity but by cost.

House Publications When you are producing a house publication, all other decisions depend on who the audience is. Since a house publication goes to employees or members only, it is likely to have quite a different design from a publication that receives broader distribution. What type of publication, then, is most likely to be accepted and read—a newsletter, a tabloid newspaper format or a magazine? This decision is usually influenced by the budget allotted, which sometimes makes such a question academic.

The next decision involves frequency of publication. Frequency usually depends on the public relations department, and monthly issues are about all most PR departments can cope with.

Some produce quarterly publications, while others publish simple and inexpensive daily or weekly "news sheets."

The method of distribution is another consideration. If it is entirely internal, with distribution either in pick-up boxes or by supervisory personnel or in-house mail service, you need not be concerned about mailing regulations and labeling. However, many companies have found it advantageous to send the publication to the recipients' homes. Then employees won't read it "on company time" and won't throw it away at work because they are busy there. Furthermore, home delivery encourages other family members to read the publication. When home delivery is used, it is important to keep up with address changes, which the human resources department should have in the employee records, and it is critical to consult with the mailroom so that delivery can be worked into a reasonable schedule, with consideration given for the mailroom workers' other duties.

Once these policies are decided, content deserves the most careful attention. Enlightened management knows that what the employees want to know about the company is more important than what the company wants to tell the employees. Built into the publication should be ways to convey information and allowances for two-way communication—perhaps through letters to the editor or a response column that answers questions of general concern. Many employee publications give an Intranet address also. The tone of the publication—which includes writing style, layout, artwork, type choice and general design—greatly affects the attitude the employees adopt toward it: whether they perceive it as their publication or as an authoritarian management tool.

To help determine content, and even type and frequency of publication, PR staffs have used questionnaires to find out what employees might like in the way of employee publications. The difficulty here is that some employees have no idea of what is possible. Choosing among unknowns is a bit of a problem. What seems to work better is to get a sample of house publications from others (not necessarily in the same type of company), and select a representative panel to meet on company time and discuss the type of employee publication that might be effective and that could be produced within budget, time and talent restrictions.

It is a good idea to retain the panel even after the publication appears, since panel judgments provide a check on whether the publication is being read, what part of it is best liked and what is missing.

Develop a dummy or mockup suggesting design and general type of content. Estimate how much copy and artwork will appear in each publication and approximately how many pages each will be; then determine how the publication will be printed. Learn what kind of presses will be used, because the number of pages (excluding cover) might have to be multiples of eight or at least four. Also, you will need to decide whether you want a self-cover or a separate cover.

Larger organizations may have in-house printing plants; if you need to choose an outside printer, however, make sure to get bids from several. The printer will need to see the dummy, know how many copies are needed and know how often the publication will appear. Printers also need to know whether the publication will be coming to the shop camera-ready or on computer disk or whether the printer will be responsible for setting type and preparing the art. Together with the printer, you have to decide on paper stock for the cover and inside pages and also headline and body type. The printer will have a price list for artwork and special effects, to help in estimating the cost of each issue. Remember, the printer with the lowest bid might not provide as high-quality work and might have more expensive "alteration costs" for changes you might make as the process of printing proceeds.

Staff is a major concern in starting a house publication. Who will write and edit? Where can help and talent be found and put to work? Writers, photographers and artists are all important to the success of a house publication, and some reasonable assessment of potential must be made before a publication can be launched. Again, budget is a factor in deciding how much talent can be bought. In the case of an employee publication, however, ego appeals, esprit de corps and gentle persuasion often work in lieu of remuneration.

A "beat" system and network of news correspondents for gathering information and preparing it for publication on schedule must be developed. Deadlines must be set for all art and photos, as must specifications for the way material is to be submitted. Some successful operations use reporting sheets, which are handled by a person in each department. These are turned over to the editor and help in gathering news. Some departments ask that news be sent by e-mail to an editor. Longer articles are generally determined by editorial/administrative decision and worked out on an assignment basis. Some editors plan a whole year's content; others plan one issue at a time, working only two or three months in advance on major stories.[7]

Some publications are prepared by institutions to be a customer or client service, offered at no charge. These bonus publications, from institutions like insurance companies, are designed to make the customers feel good about the organization. The publications act as subtle ads suggesting that the company cares about its customers. Often the publications do not call attention to their sponsorship. An example is a fitness magazine sent out by a hospital group.

Some organizations produce magazines that compete with consumer periodicals. Examples are *Smithsonian* (the Smithsonian Institution's magazine) and *Audubon* (an environmental club magazine that holds its own well against independent commercial environmental magazines).[8]

Some organizations have abandoned their printed house publications in favor of videotaped "magazines" that are shown to employees at their worksites. Still others use CD-ROMs.

Producing Annual Reports

Responsibility for the annual report should be shared by two key people, according to William Ruder and David Finn: a communications specialist responsible for deciding the *character* of the report; and a high-level management representative (generally the chief financial officer or the chief executive officer) responsible for the *content*.[9] The design and the language of the report should be the province of the communications specialist, who should not have to yield to the style preferences of persons whose expertise lies in different areas.

To give these two individuals the authority they need, all key management personnel should be informed about who has the responsibility for the report and should be involved in contributing to the point of view the report ultimately reflects. Through meetings, a consensus may be reached on theme and approach.

The communications expert should prepare the first draft, working with content supplied by the other key person, and this document should be circulated for comment and contributions. Its impact on all audiences should be weighed, but specifically its *effect* on priority publics should be determined. For example, many annual reports contain copy that touts diversity in the workforce and professes a commitment to teamwork, but then these reports show disdain for employees in the illustrations or have pictures that clearly reveal power resting in the hands of a few white males. Annual reports going to many different countries must be carefully checked for culture clashes. In addition to being sensitive to such representations while the report is being planned, the communications expert should suggest to other members of management how the published report might be used to communicate with various publics, because this could have some bearing on the presentation adopted.

Annual reports used to be almost synonymous with complex and obscure prose, but some are now down-to-earth and occasionally even entertaining. The *Wall Street Journal* quoted Wisconsin Securities Company of Delaware as once describing one of its ventures as a "a flop," and the same annual report contained enough additional candor for the *Journal* writer to comment, "Now that's telling it like it is."[10] New Hampshire's Wheelabrator-Frye, Inc., has aimed its annual report toward youngsters. The educational effort—to tell fourth through sixth graders about the free enterprise system—consisted of a twenty-page cartoon report telling what this manufacturer of environmental and energy systems did with its money that year.

Not only did the company get publicity from the circulation of the report among youngsters (whose parents and teachers also were exposed), but the report's novel approach generated a lot of publicity. Several companies have bought enough pages in magazines like *Time* to present the entire annual report to an audience of millions.

"Millions" may represent overkill, but to make the most of the published report, it does need to be in the hands of all interested publics. Again, the communications expert should suggest to other departments the most effective use of the published piece.

Some annual report planning begins nearly a year in advance. It is common to begin at the end of the first quarter, and certainly work should commence no later than three to six months before the close of the fiscal year. The wise public relations person builds some padding into any schedule, and the annual report is the publication most likely to need it, since it is such a significant document (and for publicly held companies, it is legally required, with firm deadlines for its distribution). After all, it constitutes the organization's most comprehensive statement about itself.

The annual report is a process as much as it is a publication—a comprehensive review of the past year. Because approvals and participation are so important and because the report must be produced on a deadline, the schedule needs to be structured so as to prevent delays. You'll have to work with outside auditors, who are responsible for the financial content, and have the entire report reviewed by legal counsel as well as the company's audit committee of its Board of Directors. The chief financial officer generally has oversight of the annual report, as does the investor relations practitioner, who usually reports to the CFO and who may or may not be in the public relations department (see Example 12.5).

Every annual report normally contains the same kind of information, but reports differ from company to company as to their order or their headings. Most contain the following five elements: (1) a letter from the chairman; (2) the auditor's report; (3) financial statements; (4) a longer

EXAMPLE 12.5

Production Timetable for Annual Reports

Conception, copy and design for a calendar year annual report should begin shortly after midyear. A production schedule should be developed early, and a firm delivery date established. Working back from this date to set week-by-week goals can help avoid confusion and save time and money.

WEEK 1:

Start analysis of previous books; develop goals/ themes: contact division/department heads for ideas/copy. Circulate timetable with delivery date.

WEEK 2:

Begin rough design exploration. Begin copy outline.

WEEKS 3–4:

Continue design and copy outline.

WEEK 5:

First design review and copy outline.

WEEK 6:

Start photography. Develop copy and comprehensive design.

WEEKS 7–8:

Continue developing copy and comprehensive design.

WEEK 9:

Begin production and type estimating.

WEEK 10:

Final review of comprehensive with photos. Copy review.

WEEK 11:

Start retouching. Develop charts, illustrations and typesetting, if possible.

WEEKS 12–13:

Typesetting and mechanicals.

WEEK 14:

To printer, check blueprints.

WEEKS 15–17:

Printing and binding.

WEEK 18:

Delivery.

Source: Reprinted from Doremus, *Public Relations Checklist for 1989–90 Annual Reports.*

---

section narrating pertinent facts about the past year's operation; (5) photos and charts.

Shareholders also get quarterly reports, and some companies package these attractively as newsletters. Others use a brochure format or create packages that resemble thick statement stuffers. (Chapter 9 discusses SEC requirements for the annual report and the 10-K quarterly reports.)

Ever since the SEC began requiring that a company publish its 10-K and go on-line with it, the annual report has ceased to serve primarily as a financial document and has instead become primarily a public relations piece.

Even though annual reports have taken on a different significance, many remain hard for the shareholder (who may not be a financial expert) to understand. To many CEOs, therefore, the idea of an executive summary, or shortened version of the report, has seemed a good one. In 1987, the Financial Executives Institute devised the summary format, according to which financial information is relegated to the 10-K and to the annual meeting proxy statement. Since then, businesses have come to use the executive summary format routinely, in addition to the annual report, although not all companies favor it.

Speeches as Publicity or Publications

For all the time and trouble that goes into preparing an executive's speech, you need to get more out of it than just one-time media coverage at the event. That's likely to be limited at best, even if the speaker is important. When George Bush became a candidate for president of the USA in 1988, his campaign managers asked CBS to send a television crew to cover his first campaign address following the announcement of his candidacy. CBS declined, but CNN showed up, and his campaign managers said they thought the cable network's coverage might actually have been preferable, since it was an all-news network and was therefore likely to give the story more time and to repeat it more frequently on succeeding newscasts.

Presenting a speech is one of many types of meetings that an organization may hold and use for further publicity (by sending speech texts or meeting transcripts to the news media). These events are often videotaped as an additional way to generate publicity. Some videotapes are made expressly for such publicity.

Most organizations reprint major addresses in brochure format and mail them to their special publics with a printed notice or a business card attached. Remember also to send copies to publications like *Vital Speeches of the Day* and *Executive Speeches*. These prestigious and often-quoted periodicals review and analyze the speeches sent to them and reprint the best ones in their own pages.

You need to circulate copies of the speech internally as well. Remember that your employees are PR's front line. What would their response be if someone told them about a major speech by your organization's president that they were unaware of? Employees need facts to help you. You might even consider videotaping the speech for internal use

over closed-circuit TV or over other internal audio-visual communication systems. You can also refer to the videotape the next time you write a speech for that person, to ascertain what gestures the individual is comfortable with and what idioms she or he is likely to use. The question-and-answer session after a speech is especially helpful in these areas (see Example 12.6).[11]

Special Events

While a speech can be a special event, other events such as an open house are really just occasions or celebrations. Then there are big events like a celebrity visit; a convention; or a trade, commercial or consumer show.

Sometimes you may plan for a celebrity's visit, and the celebrity fails to come; but if you think creatively, you can have the event anyway. Stanford University did when president of the former Soviet Union Mikhail Gorbachev was unable to make a planned appearance at the Hoover Institute. The Institute had spent a frantic 21 days preparing for his visit on short notice. But in three weeks, it had created media packets for the anticipated 1,500 reporters, assembled 4,000 presentation folders, written eight facts sheets, disseminated three news releases and prepared prints of 1,000 special photographs from the Institute's Soviet archives.

The official reason given for the cancellation was "time constraints," but no one is sure about this explanation, since Gorbachev spent two hours at Stanford University and spoke to 1,700 faculty, staff and students. The Hoover Institute's staff didn't let three weeks of planning go to waste, though. They exhibited Russian archival material, released the commemorative poster planned for the exhibit and opened the Institute's doors to the news media, with scholars available to respond to questions. While they hoped until the last minute that Gorbachev would make an appearance, they also took the initiative and had former Secretary of State George Schultz, a Hoover Institute Distinguished Fellow, present Gorbachev with a 1921 Russian pro-literacy poster (a rare item from the collection), and that event was covered by television.

EXAMPLE 12.6
Meeting or Speech Checklist

This is perhaps the most common arrangement asked of PR people and one that is often carelessly handled. The following detailed list may be adapted to suit particular situations.

1. Set up a day in advance when possible; if not, set up at least two hours before the program. Check the *podium* for proper height (short or tall speakers); test the podium light and microphone.

2. Find out what activity will be going on in the *room next to your speaker*; you don't want the speaker to have to yell to make him- or herself heard. When planning for a large group, it is important to see whether the hotel or restaurant expects another large group and, if so, what that group is. If your group consists of retired schoolteachers, they may not enjoy being housed in a hotel with a group of boisterous rodeo riders.

3. Check out the *sound system*, amplifiers and speakers. Find the cutoff for piped-in music.

4. Find access to the *lighting* controls.

5. Check access to *electrical outlets*. Have spare heavy-duty extension cords ready for broadcast media.

6. If visuals are to be used, check out the *projection system* for equipment being used, i.e., VCR, computer and extra cables and cords. Test the proper distance for projection for VCR or computer. Make sure a table for the projectors is set up at the proper distance. Run two projectors, one on blackout so that it's ready if the other fails. Test the powerbook or computer being used.

7. Have the proper number of *chairs and tables* on hand, and have them placed correctly. It may be desirable to cover the tables with cloths. Arrange the tables so that they are as close to the speaker as possible without crowding. However, a smaller room with some crowding is preferable to the yawning cavern of a big hall if attendance is light. If you get early enough warning about impending light attendance, most hotels can use screens to help "shrink" the room space.

8. Make arrangements for *water and glasses*; also, for coffee or other refreshments. Be sure there is a firm understanding about the *service*: when delivered, replenished and removed, and in what quantity.

9. Locate a *telephone*. If one is in the room, be sure to arrange for an immediate answer if a ring should interrupt the speaker.

10. Make out *name tags* and have additional blank tags on hand. Remember that women guests may not have pockets for the pocket insert tags. Use pressure-sensitive tags, clips or pin-ons.

11. Set up a table for *guest registration* and name tags.

12. Maintain a *list of guests* invited, marked for those who confirmed their acceptance and for those who sent their regrets.

13. Have *place cards* or attendants to help guests to their seats.

14. Prepare a *program* of activities for the speaker and for guests, too, if possible.

15. Have *writing materials*, including cards, available in case the speaker wants to make last-minute notes.

16. Have *information kits* to give to guests.

17. Have an easy-to-read *clock* or stopwatch for timing.

18. Be sure all computer components are compatible.

Then the staff put out news releases on that presentation, which resulted in over 100 newspaper stories and more than 50 radio and television news items.[12] Thorough planning for special events is the key.[13] Event planning software is available, and some firms do nothing but special events for organizations.

■ Setting up for Events

There are nine steps or stages in planning for meetings or special events such as dedications, open houses and plant tours:

1. Start planning early. Depending on the size of your event, a year in advance is not too soon.

2. Make a blueprint and a timetable. Plan every detail, no matter how minor, and assign people responsibility for each. Have alternates selected as "backups." These can be one or two extras—people without specific assignments but involved in planning so they can step in if necessary. Once you have all details listed, "walk through" the event mentally as a participant. That way, you will find what you overlooked.

3. Form as many committees as you deem feasible. By involving management and employees in this event, you spread the workload and get the employees enthusiastic and knowledgeable.

4. Use company professionals wherever possible: artists, design personnel, copywriters, exhibit specialists and the like.

5. Provide special attractions to ensure attendance and to make the event memorable. Examples: prominent personalities, parades, concerts, dances, films, exhibits of historical materials, citations or awards, prizes and drawings, product demonstrations and tours of the plant in operation.

6. Provide giveaways and souvenirs (they need not be expensive) for everyone. There should be different souvenirs for different target audiences. Personalize all items and tie them to the event. (Advertising specialty companies have catalogs filled with suggestions.)

7. To ensure smooth flow of traffic, arrange for parking; if the plant is some distance from the population center, provide bus transportation from points of departure. Train guides to conduct tours for visitors, and have knowledgeable employees positioned at strategic points to provide information and answer questions. Use signs and printed maps to direct visitors.

8. Publicize the event well in advance through all possible channels. Use all available controlled media to keep employees and other publics informed. Use the mass media for a broad appeal. If necessary, use advertising.

9. When the event is over, thank everyone who helped and participated. A successful dedication or open house requires the services of many—and hard work by quite a few—and their efforts should be gratefully acknowledged (see Example 12.7).

◼ Handling Visual Presentations

Public relations practitioners frequently plan presentations that involve the use of visual materials—a presentation to financial analysts, for example, or one to employees explaining a new benefits package.

Visual Devices You will be using various devices for visual presentations. Easel pads, overhead projectors, PowerPoint computer projection and slides are described here.

Easel Pads An easel holding a chart pad or other visual aid can be the best tool for helping executives generate ideas and reach conclusions in the shortest time possible. It can stimulate group interest, help organize discussion, help explain or clarify and help summarize and review. Be sure to keep a supply of markers and masking tape on hand so you can tape torn-off pages onto a wall for a review. (Don't tape directly onto wallboard, though, or the paint will peel off.)

Overhead Projectors Overhead projectors are simple to set up and use, but make certain you understand how to operate the projector. The most common use of projectors is with transparencies which you can make on a copier. Power point is presentation software that also is projected. If you are using the projector in connection with a computer you can project directly from the computer screen to the overhead projector screen.

Increasingly, presentation rooms are equipped with interactive computers linked to wall-mounted high-resolution screens. Texts from laptops on the conference table can immediately be shown on the screen for all to see, and items for discussion can be quickly arranged categorically as participants generate new ideas. Always be careful not to clutter your presentation with too much material. The information put on the overhead must be clear and

EXAMPLE 12.7

Checklist for Facilities

Organization is essential to ensuring that significant details are not overlooked. One of the easiest ways is to make a checklist far enough in advance—so that you can add those "middle of the night" thoughts to it in plenty of time to plan for and implement them.

One Week Before	Day Before	Day of Event	Following Week
Complete media kits, including speeches, bios and photos, with event timing indicated for broadcast news.	Have kits available for news media on request.	Meet with news media representatives, distribute kits.	Send follow-up letters to news media represented.
Advance release out.			
Find out what special facilities news media will need, and make arrangements to accommodate these needs. Order all supplies and equipment for newsroom or media use area. Check lighting, sound levels, electric outlets and so on.	Set up media area. Check out all equipment and special facilities. Check all visual displays and logos.	Recheck news media area to be sure all supplies and equipment are ready for use.	
Draft final guest-acceptance list.			
Prepare guest information kits including program, brochures and the like.		Distribute guest information kits with badges.	
Prepare media, guest and host badges.	Set up physical facility and procedure for badge distribution.	Check badges and be sure badge issuance is recorded.	
Make arrangements definite. Be specific and agree on contingency plans. Plan cleaning of site and arrange for any special decorations. Remember logos, displays and so on.	Check eating area and order. Be sure time of service, place and cleanup are clear. Check site, grounds and all facilities.	Check food preparation, delivery and service.	

EXAMPLE 12.7 (continued)

One Week Before	Day Before	Day of Event	Following Week
Complete speeches and get adequate number of copies for kits, requests and files.	Have kits available for news media representatives who cannot attend.		
Assign hosts for VIPs.	Check with VIP host to confirm schedules.	Be sure all VIPs' needs are met.	Mail thank-yous.
Arrange for any citations or presentation materials.	Check to be sure special presentation materials are on hand.	Be sure persons making presentation have materials.	
Communicate individual responsibilities clearly and accurately			
Detail any necessary safety precautions. Outline plan for emergency situation. Anticipate and be sure to communicate all emergency planning to all who might be involved.			
Arrange for message board for media and guests. Have local airline schedules, taxi numbers and hotel and restaurant lists, with times and phone numbers available.			
Make final transportation and hotel arrangements for guests. If remote, plan transportation and hotel accommodations for news media also.			

easy for anyone in the room to read. It should be the type of material that would be difficult to capture in words only and should include graphs, charts and statistics.

Slides Not everything can be made into a good slide. Poor color choice, intricate diagrams, cluttered charts and wrong-size type or lettering can leave your audience red-eyed and discouraged. Slides must have good color contrast, clear details that are kept to a minimum and type or letters of an appropriate size. You may want to provide handouts of the slide material for audiences to follow along with or take away.

A good four-step rule of thumb that almost always works can help you evaluate whether a given piece of material can be translated into a slide:

1. Measure the widest part of the material being considered for a slide.

2. Provide a reasonably wide border, and measure the border on both sides.

3. Add items 1 and 2 together.

4. Multiply the total by 6, giving you a total distance in inches (or feet, as the case may be) from your eyes or from the eyes of a person with 20/40 vision to the material. This is important. If someone with 20/40 vision can read the material easily and see all the pertinent details, then the material could make a good slide. If the material can't be easily read, it must be modified until it does pass the test.

Artwork prepared for 3 × 4-inch slide projection should be prepared in a 3 (high) to 4 (wide) proportion, because the image should be masked down in photography and slide binding to 2¼ × 3 inches, which is a 3 to 4 proportion. Artwork for 35-mm double-frame slides (2 × 2s) should be prepared in the proportion of 2 (high) to 3 (wide); and art for a 35-mm filmstrip should be prepared in a proportion of 3 (high) to 4 (wide). The use of these proportions is very important. If they are not used, effective space on the slide is lost.

Slides also can be computer-generated. Your own organization may have this capability. If not,

you can buy the service. Such slides can be very simple, or they can be so elaborate that they give the impression of movement, resembling the animated art used in cartoons.

When you plan a slide presentation, you need to consider its eventual development into another format such as a videotape or CD-ROM. This is especially important if you intend to present it often. A videotape presentation requires more slides and more consideration of visual "bridges" established by transition slides. A CD-ROM has similar requirements but the images must be digitalized. Both benefit from the addition of audio.

Dos and Don'ts of Visuals Computer technology has simplified the process of making visuals and has increased their technical quality. However, some general dos and don'ts remain important for practitioners who want to achieve effective visual communication. The function of a visual is to illustrate a point, to clarify and to fix a fact or image in the minds of the audience. It should correlate with the spoken narrative, whether it is a recorded sound track or a live presentation. People retain more information when it is presented to them in a combination of sight and sound than they do when only one of these two senses is employed.

A good visual must have simplicity. It must be capable of being instantly absorbed by the mind. Variables that influence simplicity include color choice, design elements, typeface and lettering and how photos are used. Following are a few common pitfalls to avoid in order to retain simplicity in visuals.

Backgrounds Never use black type on a dark background. This is so elementary you might think that it is never done. Yet people who should know better, such as qualified commercial artists, make this mistake every day. The usual error involves black type on a blue background that never seems to photograph as light as the designer thought it would. Blue is never a good color for background use with black type. If the blue is light enough to contrast strongly with the type, it invariably washes out and produces a weak visual. Similarly, white letters should never be used against a pastel background.

Overloading The use of a visual with too much detail is another common mistake. Don't use too many design elements or too many shapes—circles, triangles, rectangles, square blocks—in planning a visual. A design may be made so "arty" that the message is lost in a maze of shapes, curlicues and clashing colors. Better to be simple than sorry. For the same reason, don't use too many typefaces in a single visual, and don't overload a visual with too many words. It is better to break up a statement or a thought into two or three slides, and let the audience take it in short bites. Similarly, bear in mind that script type is about 50 percent harder to read than simple, uncluttered Roman letters.

Color At the other extreme, don't make the mistake of having too much white space in a visual either. Remember, white means clear film, 100 percent light transmission and an overpowering glare from a white screen. If you must show a white form, photograph only the essential areas, and cover the rest with color-aid paper that has cutouts to allow the important areas to stand out on the screen. Your visual will be much more effective. This is easier to achieve with computer generated slides because the colors can be controlled electronically. These also can be projected directly to a screen. Make sure that the slides maintain consistency of format, color and placement of material.

Conflicting Messages Visuals should complement the audio portion of your presentation. They should not fight each other for supremacy. The word or words on the screen should be identical to the words to be spoken. Don't say one thing visually and something else orally. The mind simply cannot accept two conflicting statements simultaneously.

Putting a Show Together The sequence of events in developing a slide production consists of nine steps: (1) set your objectives; (2) work out a budget; (3) prepare the conceptual plan (an artistic development of the idea); (4) write the script; (5) test the concept and script on an audience; (6) shoot the visuals; (7) produce the visuals; (8) edit the visuals and script; (9) complete for presentation (record the script and synchronize, add music and so on). The show should capture the mood of the message as well as provide visual content. If the intent is to create a CD-ROM, the music and images must be digital.

Adding Sound If you are a production expert, you can add sound effects and musical themes from suppliers such as audio archives (Films for the Humanities and Sciences, Box 2053, Princeton, NJ 08543-2053). They can provide anything from a convoy of diesel trucks to an orchestra tuning up. However, many large metropolitan areas also have professional sound studios and sound suppliers. Hire a professional if you aren't one.

■ Handling Audio Presentations

A sound system can make or break a presentation. To avoid major breakage, you must pay attention to four key areas of sound system preparation: sound reinforcement; rented or company equipment; simple equipment; and choosing components.

Sound Reinforcement Never accept the word of a hotel that adequate sound reinforcement will be provided. Few hotels own acceptable professional equipment. The electronic rostrums, microphones and portable loudspeakers they provide vary widely in age, quality and condition. Frequently the parts are not physically or electronically compatible with one another.

Do not check the sound item off your list until a dry run—held in the meeting room—has established that every component in the system functions properly. Make certain that any assistant who must operate the equipment knows exactly how it works, knows the location of all switches and controls, knows the proper volume and tone-control settings and knows how to operate auxiliary equipment such as phonograph turntables, tape recorders or additional microphones. It exasperates both the audience and speaker to have to break the bond of communication between them in order to give mechanical instructions to an equipment operator.

Check out the loudspeaker systems. Adjust their volume level to a point slightly higher than you would normally set it—recognizing that the room, when filled with people, will be much more sound-absorptive than when it is empty.

Rented or Company Equipment   If you cannot rely on the hotel sound equipment, you can rent suitable gear from a nearby audio rental facility. Or you can bring it in and have your own firm set it up (subject to local union regulations and hotel convention requirements). The last approach is probably the most reliable—and the most economical.

Simple Equipment   When selecting the equipment you will use, remember the auto mechanic's maxim: you'll never have trouble with the accessories they *don't* include. A bewildering array of microphones, loudspeaker systems, amplifiers and accessory equipment are available for highly specialized uses and for startling effects. But keep your equipment basic and simple.

Choosing Components   The technical information you need to make a wise choice regarding components is not great, and most manufacturers furnish helpful literature that even a novice can readily understand.

It's a good idea, nevertheless, to choose components to suit your individual needs. Microphones, for instance, are available in a great many types and prices, but no other element is so vital to the sound system. However good the other components are, they cannot compensate for a poor microphone. Be sure it is suited to the use for which it is intended. Price is no index to suitability.

Numerous evils commonly associated with poor sound reinforcement are actually side effects of unsuccessful attempts to offset microphone deficiencies. Amplifier hum or background noise may be caused by a microphone with a low output, inadequately compensated for by turning up amplifier

gain (volume). Ear-splitting treble emphasis often occurs because an amplifier's treble control was turned up to overcome a loss of articulation at the microphone. When amplifier gain is held so low that the audience must strain to hear, the microphone is often to blame. In this case, if the gain were turned up, intolerable feedback would result because of the microphone's inability to distinguish wanted from unwanted sound.

For a worst-case example, consider this true account of Murphy's Law. It comes from the experience of Chuck Werle, now of Werle & Brimm Ltd. of Chicago, from a time when he was with the Leo Burnett Company. He and his colleague Richard Criswell were giving a presentation before the Florida Public Relations Association:

> My collaborator had told me by phone that he was bringing a reel of 16 commercials. Turns out he said 60—not 16. That was the first thing. We asked for an overhead projector. It never showed up. I asked for a slide projector. It jammed. We asked for a video-cassette recorder. The first one came late, then didn't work. The second one did work . . . until we stopped it to make a point and then it never started again. After all these horrendous problems, I went to pick up a rental car. It was in stall 1311 and it stalled two blocks from the airport. This all happened on Friday the 13th.[14]

Producing Institutional Videotapes and Films

Some annual reports are now published on videotape as well as in print. The videotapes are often used to introduce the firm to new audiences, such as security analysts who have not previously followed the firm, communities in which the firm has not previously operated, large groups of new employees hired for specific tasks or successful job candidates who have been hired for high-level positions. Much post-production video work is shifting to digital. With digital editing, a video story can be edited the same way you use a word processing computer to edit text.[15]

Companies and nonprofit institutions—including the U.S. government—make considerable use not only of videotape cassettes but also of 16-mm film. Beginning in the early 1970s, the trend was to make these films in 35 mm, and then reduce them to 16 mm. Technology has lowered the cost of this type of treatment, and the larger film gives higher quality and increases potential use, including possible distribution to movie houses. The life of a film is usually about seven years, with potential audiences in the millions. The technique of using clips from the film or taking clips from the outtakes for corporate advertising distributes the costs over a broader marketing range. Furthermore, the unit cost per public impression must be considered.

When considering whether to produce a film or video, the first decision to make is what your message is and for what audience it is intended. Then you must consider how much it will cost, and who is going to produce it—an in-house unit, an outside commercial studio or both? Only a few corporations have in-house production units, but their size and capacity varies, and even large units occasionally farm out a large undertaking, at least in part. Although many commercial studios exist, only a few are known for award-winning films and videos. Some commercial studios are just producers; others are producers and distributors.

You'll need to be very specific in describing your film or video needs to whomever will produce it. Many in-house and commercial producers use standard project proposal forms. (see Example 12.8)

The following is a checklist for critiquing films and videotapes:

Before looking at the film or video, be sure you know its subject, purpose, and the nature of the audience it purports to reach. Only then can you judge whether it meets its goals, or is suitable.

As you look at the film or video, rate it on each of these ten points:

1. Attention Span: *Is it "gripping," or "interesting," or just plain able to hold the audience's attention throughout? This is critical: if it is boring, nothing else really matters!*

2. Subject: *Does the film or video adequately cover the subject in a clear way, and fulfill its expressed purpose? Is it too long? Or (seldom) not long enough?*

3. Audience Suitability: *Does it clearly address the audience it's aimed at . . . or the group you plan to show it to?*

4. Visuals: *Are the pictures in focus? Properly exposed? Are the colors true? If there are graphics, do they help to clarify and explain, or are they just there for effects?*

5. Timeliness: *Are the visuals up to date? (Nothing turns off an audience faster than an old-fashioned haircut or clothing style, or any printed matter on screen that shows the age of the film.)*

6. Talent: *Are the participants or actors real, and natural? Do you believe them? Can you hear and clearly understand what they're saying?*

7. Sound: *Are the sound effects and/or music appropriate to the action? Is there proper balance among words, sound effects and music, so that the message gets across in the most effective way?*

8. Editing: *Does the story flow naturally? Is the editing pace good, so the story neither drags, nor moves too fast? Are you jolted by unusual angles, jumps in action, scenes that are too short or too long, or by bad sound?*

9. Script Content: *Someone once said (or wrote) that the best script for a film is one with the fewest possible words. A well-done informational film should rely heavily on visuals to tell the story. Words should fill in, adding information that cannot be seen. Most films have too many words. And words should be simple. Long words or cumbersome phrases are distracting.*

10. Believability: *Is the film "professional," in the sense that it moves along smoothly, in a logical fashion, and you're not distracted by the mechanics of the medium? In summary, did you find the film or tape honest and believable?*[16]

■ Handling Celebrity Appearances

The presence of celebrities almost guarantees publicity, so luring them and making them glad they came is important. Arrangements for a celebrity's appearance may be made through an organization with which the celebrity is involved—for example, as the national chairperson of a charity. Or if the celebrity is a columnist or television star, contact may be made through his or her syndicate or network, using a local publication or network affiliate station as a starting point. Ultimately, though, you

EXAMPLE 12.8

Videotape Proposal

Client _____ Dept./Co. _____

Project _____

Address _____ Mail Code _____

Telephone _____ Fax _____ E-Mail _____

• What is this tape expected to accomplish?

• Who is the target audience?

• After viewing the program, what should the audience:

Know

Think

Feel

• What is their present knowledge toward the topic?

• Essential content (facts/ideas that must be included):

I.

II.

III.

IV.

V.

VI.

will probably deal with the celebrity's agent. It is important to remember that this person is a *business* agent.

Once you have the celebrity scheduled, you should request updated biographical information from his or her agent or public relations person and 8 × 10-inch glossy photographs of at least two different poses. The biographical data will give you a start in preparing the advance publicity. It is helpful if you can also get a telephone interview to fill in details, since vita sheets are sometimes outdated or incomplete. Further, personal information and a personal contact offer insight into the celebrity's

likes and dislikes and give some indication of what type of promotion would be best. It is important to determine what that person likes to do and does best because this is where he or she will perform best for you. Recognize that some celebrities have unusual demands—for example availability of multicolored candy with all the pieces of certain colors removed from the dish.

In planning the celebrity's schedule, you will probably work with the agent or with a person charged with scheduling. Make sure your communications with this person are clear, concise and definite. Your dependence is mutual, so you should

- Non-essential content (not critical but "nice to know")

  I.

  II.

  III.

- Video completion date _____ • Production begins _____ • Video length _____

- Presentation environment:

  Where will the video be shown?

  How many people will be in the audience?

  What type of equipment will be used (tape format, screen size)?

- Subject experts (names/titles/phone numbers) and other information sources:

- Budget _____ • The final script will be approved by _____

Time Line (to be completed by coordinator & client after review of Video Proposal Form)

	Date:	Duty:	Approved by:
• Script Outline	_____	_____	_____
• Script Draft 1	_____	_____	_____
• Script Draft 2	_____	_____	_____
• Final Script	_____	_____	_____
• Shooting begins	_____	_____	_____
• Rough Cut Edit	_____	_____	_____
• Final Edit	_____	_____	_____

Signatures/Date: Client _____   Coordinator _____

TPC 9/96

Source: University of Northern Iowa, Office of Public Relations. Reprinted by permission of University of Northern Iowa Office of Public Relations.

try hard to establish rapport. Get off to a good start in your first contact by providing the following information: (1) travel arrangements, including who will be meeting the celebrity (and whether an airport arrival interview is planned); (2) where the celebrity will be staying; (3) what provision has been made for transportation; (4) what financial arrangements have been made (Get this ironed out early!); (5) what the schedule of appearances is; (6) what other group appearances have been scheduled and what special events the celebrity will participate in. Make multiple copies of the schedule so your staff and the celebrity's staff have

contact information. Include phone numbers at various locations.

Give the celebrity as much background as possible, not only on relevant groups and people, but also on the city. Personalize by tying the information into the celebrity's own background, career or special interests. This will help prepare the celebrity for the questions that he or she will have to field, and it will also make him or her feel comfortable and welcome rather than exploited.

Be sure all newsmaking events on the schedule are covered by your own staff reporter and photographer. In fact, don't go anywhere without your photographers. Some of the best picture possibilities can be missed if you depend on news media photographers working only on assignment. Moreover, the celebrity may want pictures, and these are easier to get from your staff than from the media. Someone in the office should keep a log of television appearances and clippings to present later to the celebrity, or to the accompanying PR person or agent.

Media information kits should be prepared and distributed in advance of the celebrity's appearance, but keep extra ones with you at all times. If reporters assigned to the story have not seen the kit, they may ask you numerous questions that are already answered in the kit.

Arrangements should not only reflect the celebrity's star status, but also be personalized. One television actor found that the PR director at an affiliate station had keyed everything, even the fruit in his room, to the TV series in which he portrayed a teacher (the fruit was, of course, apples). For another celebrity, who was an art lover, pictures in the hotel suite were replaced with valuable paintings on loan from the local art museum.

The red-carpet treatment begins at the airport, where most major airlines maintain luxurious VIP rooms suitable for interviews. It may be the best place to have an initial press conference and have the celebrity greeted by a city official. Make arrangements through the airline's local public relations representative. Most airlines will also expedite baggage handling. The hotel's PR department is also eager to cooperate in seeing that the star's room is specially prepared with flowers or fruit. You should check the celebrity in before arrival and have the room key in hand, to make this a smoother operation.

For transportation, a chauffeured limousine is almost a must for important celebrities; if this is impossible, try to get a new car on loan, say a demonstration model from a promotion-conscious dealer. Get a courteous driver who understands time schedules and knows the city. Be sure the celebrity knows how to contact the limousine service or driver in case of an emergency or a change in plans. One solution is to put up the driver in the same hotel as the celebrity so that immediate access is possible. Cellular phones—or at least a pager for the driver—can be helpful here.

Assign someone who is understanding and sympathetic to be with the star throughout the schedule. This person should be able to handle special requests like hairdressers at 6 A.M. or filet mignon at midnight. Be sure it is someone with patience, tact and diplomacy who also understands the significance of keeping on schedule. After a celebrity appearance is over, this person can probably suggest the best way to say thank you.

Take care of all departure details such as checkout, bills, airline flight confirmation and baggage check-in. Attention to the celebrity cannot be relaxed just because the itinerary is closed. The farewell remarks of a celebrity are usually recorded and remembered, too. One thought to keep in mind is that celebrities talk to other celebrities. A public relations director who was having difficulty getting a particular celebrity happened to mention it to another celebrity who had once been the organization's guest for the same event. To the PR person's surprise, the celebrity said, "Well, I'll just call and tell her she needs to be here. It's a good promotion vehicle, and you people know how to do things right."

Some celebrities you may be responsible for handling are relatively new at public relations appearances. For example, the book publishing business is so highly competitive that authors are frequently sent "on the road" to garner sales for their books. Some of these new celebrities may be more difficult to handle than more seasoned people because, while they are less likely to have high expectations of recognition, they are more likely to expect some "privacy" or time for themselves.

Some celebrities are extraordinarily generous with the demands of self-promotion. The *Wall Street Journal* tells of author Ken Follett's willingness to be the prize in a contest advertised in bookstores promoting his novel, *Pillars of the Earth.* Follett's novel is about the building of a medieval cathedral, and the contest prize was a free trip to England with the author and a guided tour by him of Westminster Abbey. Not only was Follett willing to be a tour guide, he also agreed to write for *Good Housekeeping* a romantic short story called "The Abiding Heart," set in the same cathedral he described in his novel. In exchange, Follett's publisher, a division of Penguin USA, got two full pages in the magazine to advertise the trip and tour contest.[17]

While some authors like Follett may be accommodating and may see promotions as opportunities, many others may resent the time spent doing such mundane things as going to television stations to give interviews, making guest appearances in bookstores or speaking to various clubs and organizations. You must build some personal time into their schedule, and you must handle them in such a way that you preserve their dispositions for the public appearances.

Preservation of talent may be necessary if the celebrity is a performer. Some performers are asked to make a number of appearances and play, sing or do whatever they do either too close to their performance schedule or in conditions that might jeopardize their being able to perform—soloists singing outside in cold night air, for example. You may be responsible for the schedules of some celebrities who are traveling without their own staffs, and you need to think of their needs in planning their appearances.

PUBLICITY THROUGH THE MASS MEDIA

Good working relationships with media personnel are always important for smooth functioning, but they are particularly crucial when they can facilitate, impede or even destroy a public relations program. The secret of success in placing publicity is to develop a good working relationship by *knowing and anticipating the needs of the media.* Your PR efforts in handling publicity are usually a two-part operation: providing the information you want to convey to that medium's public; and responding to inquiries. Your contacts are valuable as a source for placing stories or story ideas and as a resource for

keeping you advised of media changes in personnel or procedures.

Fortunately, some things never change, and among them are the standards by which publicity is measured. Publicity is ranked by editors and TV news directors for news value. Publicity should meet three criteria:

1. Is it important to this medium's audience (readers, listeners or viewers)? For local media, it must be of local significance to be considered (that is, it must have a local angle).

2. Is it timely? It must be news—something that just happened, is happening now or is scheduled to happen in the near future—not something the beat reporter had three days ago.

3. Is it accurate, truthful and complete?

One PR person, who had heard a newspaper's assistant metropolitan editor chew out an unfortunate publicist for offering copy with "more holes than a sieve," was later asked by the editor if the reaction had been too harsh. "Not at all," he replied. "Sloppy copy just makes it harder for the rest of us."

Strict news value is one yardstick of value. Another is human interest, a story or picture with humor, drama or poignancy. Humorous stories, especially, have an edge because so much of what editors must print is serious. A publicity piece that is genuinely funny or appealing is usually given good display.

In handling publicity, you are concerned with offering news releases to mass and specialized media, both print and broadcast. Your primary task is to interest the media in story and picture ideas they might cover. In doing this job, you must prepare materials that tell about the institution, such as newsletters, brochures and pamphlets, television and radio spots, slide presentations and perhaps films. When necessary, you must arrange for the media to talk directly to management in interviews and conferences. Therefore, you must master the styles of all media and develop working relationships with professionals in all of these fields.

A PR person must know, for example, the exact copy deadlines for all local media and the approximate deadlines for state and national media. If you are involved in international PR, you must be prepared to work late (in some cases very late) to reach your contacts abroad during their working day, because of time differences.

Knowing the media's working schedules will save you a great deal of grief. And it might be wise to call a sports, business or other section editor periodically to check on the possibility of new deadlines. Such attention to details separates the professional from the inept amateur.

Knowing whom to contact at the various media with your news is also essential. You need to make sure your releases get to the reporter or editor who covers your organization. Since media people change jobs and assignments frequently, your current media contact may not be the same person you dealt with last week.

If it is someone you need to call after normal working hours, be sure you have the bypass or after-hours phone number or you'll get stopped by a recording.

■ Technology and Public Relations

A PR person must keep current in the area of new technology for mass communications, and this knowledge must extend far beyond a knowledge of desktop publishing. Computer developments of particular significance to public relations include (1) the use of computers for storing, sending, receiving and printing information and art; (2) the growth of satellite transmission and cable video; (3) the growth of specialized PR services, including broadcast monitoring services to catch publicity (a parallel to the print media clipping services); (4) computerized graphics design services.

Typesetting and Printing Processes Public relations practitioners began to feel the impact of new technology in the newsrooms early in 1973, and it has increased continuously since then. All news releases that came in used to be "processed" with all other newspaper copy, including stories generated by the staff. Often a good publicity release would be checked over by a reporter (who would often call

the person who had issued the release to ask for additional information or clarification) and then go to the copy desk for editing. It thus had a reasonably good chance to survive and get into the paper.

However, when newspapers converted to photo-offset printing and began using video display terminals (VDTs) to put stories directly into their computers, publicity releases then had to be rekeyed by an editorial clerk, unless electronically transmitted to the newspaper by the PR practitioner. The chances of hard copy PR releases being used have decreased considerably, and the chance of a release's being used "as is" is almost nonexistent. For releases to escape being discarded, both staff and agency public relations practitioners must submit electronically acceptable copy.

PR Wire and Video Services Specialized wire and video services carry public relations news directly into the world's newspaper and broadcast newsrooms. This capability is especially important since the PR newswires provide copy from computer to computer so it can then be called up on a terminal for editing and subsequent direct transmission to the typesetting equipment. First begun in 1954, the publicity wire concept began to catch on as a result of the technological advances of the media. Its use was further stimulated by the U.S. Supreme Court's simultaneous disclosure decision in the *Texas Gulf Sulphur* case (see Chapter 9).

The increasing importance of television has heightened the need for video releases. Satellite transmission has made the world's broadcast stations readily accessible to such releases. Many public relations media services provide a complete publicity package of video news releases and satellite transmission.

The privately owned publicity services offer simultaneous transmission of news releases and provide a rather efficient national network. Although they are membership organizations and charge for their services, they are run much like news bureaus, and their editors may reject copy as they try to exercise some judgment about what to send.

These PR suppliers provide journalists (via computer) with news releases, facts sheets, graphics and other information that PR people pay to have sent. Such publicity services charge clients an annual fee and then charge for each release. The price depends on the distribution ordered. A surcharge is usually added for larger-than-average releases (more than 400 words) and more complex ones with photos, graphics, spread sheets and audio. Video rates are more expensive. In addition to publicity, clients may send advisories and invitations, such as notifications of news conferences.

One particular advantage public relations wire services have for practitioners is the resulting national and international coverage now available for clients of a practitioner working from a single base. Before these services appeared, many practitioners tried to make arrangements with agencies in other cities to help handle out-of-town releases. It was a Rube Goldberg operation at best, and it depended greatly on the PR contacts or affiliations the practitioner had in other cities. Now releases are available 15 minutes after transmission and can be placed on the client's Web site as well as sent to news media. This strictly business arrangement is easily structured and has predictable results. Additionally, the wire services archive news releases for one year.

Another advantage to the practitioner is editorial acceptance of the PR sources. Because copy is carefully checked before it is moved (even though the practitioners supplying the material are "clients"), news media are assured of a double check on details, timeliness and other elements that often make PR copy unacceptable. To preserve their own reputations, the PR news bureaus won't move inferior or inaccurate copy. One service even reminds clients: "Write to wire style and member newspaper computerization [constraints]. Following AP style and keeping computer specifications in mind are marks of communications professionalism that improve your release's chances. Again, we'll be glad to help whenever you need us." The company has built a reputation for reliability with the media it services.

Yet another advantage of public relations wire services is that they are already in the newsroom. Many metropolitan dailies have a PR news wire feeding their computers right along with the Associated Press, Reuters and other services' wires. Copy is pulled from that source and considered for use on its merits. Broadcast releases are often a direct feed, after an advisory is wired. In contrast, many mailed releases (print and videocassette) that reach reporters are never even opened. In addition, mail service may be delayed by lack of weekend delivery or by holiday closing. For all of these reasons, a newswire service is a good investment when broad coverage is desired, timing is significant and the budget allows.

Computer technology helps outside the newsroom as well. Reporters use laptop computers to cover news outside the office. At a special event, they can use a computer billboard service to keep up with what's going on from their hotel room. They can download a news conference release and work their stories from that information, if they wish, and then send the stories directly to the newspaper's computer. Steve Lee, President of Quick Silver, a high tech firm, who spent a lot of time in London servicing a major client, says that he experienced good acceptance of computer releases sent to media at the cost of a long distance telephone call. Direct radio and television feeds, of course, are not viewed as unusual by the broadcast media. Most take a direct feed, after an advisory is sent.

A side benefit of PR distribution services like MediaLink is that most also supply basic news data banks for storing releases and published stories. These data banks can give a news story a longer shelf life.

Most of these services, as well as specialized clipping and monitoring services like Burrelle's, Luce and Video Monitoring Services of America, provide an accounting of media use. Some users complain that the services (particularly some of the video services) are not exhaustive, but inflated figures are probably more of a concern than underreporting. Many organizations supplement their data services by hiring at-home workers to monitor video releases for them.

Video tracking uses two primary technologies. One places an invisible time-and-date tag in the tape that appears on two separate lines of the TV signal's "Vertical Blanking Interval." Decoders at Nielsen Media Research scan broadcast signals in their respective markets, searching for these time-date codes. The time, date, broadcast duration and location of airing are then sent to the video producer. Another company's tracking system uses Video Encoded Invisible Light (VEIL) technology, which is placed directly into the video picture. Pulses of light create computer-readable bits of information. Collection points in each market report confirmed TV broadcast usages.[18]

Following up on news releases yourself is more difficult, because you won't have the list of media that a service uses. Distribution and clipping services do maintain up-to-date media lists, because that's the heart of their business, but you will be given a copy of only a general distribution list.

You'll probably develop your own limited media directories. Lists of media abroad are now more readily available, with international directories.

Now software packages also offer solutions to building and maintaining media lists and measuring results.

You'll also keep lists of where you placed your advertising, of course, and the monitoring services will trace your advertising as well as your releases if you want to purchase that additional service. The services will also perform an analysis of both. Television services that handle production for your public service announcements sometimes monitor the use of your PSAs, too. But even the best services won't catch everything. They may misreport or misinterpret events. Use information from these services as a monitoring device; use your own research to measure results.

Media Electronic Systems   When a PR person gets a story of regional or national interest in a local paper, there is a good chance that the story will receive regular newswire service attention. The Associated Press wire service uses an "electronic carbon"—a computer-to-computer hookup that allows newspapers to send copies of their local stories instantly into local AP bureau computers. The increased flow of stories from member papers to the bureaus increases the use by other

papers of PR-generated stories of regional or national significance.

Another AP computer advance offers greater control over laser photos, so that photo editors can crop, enlarge, reduce, brighten, darken or otherwise improve the quality of photos sent. By 1986, the technology had developed to the point where it was possible to send an image and get a color photograph of it without a negative.

Newspapers' electronic information delivery systems (EISs) are copy cannibals—devouring vast amounts of incoming material and immediately relaying facts, breaking news, sports scores, recent stock reports and such. EISs have enlarged the medium's "news hole" of available space for news. Cable is another cannibal, using programming 24 hours a day. Much of cable's programming gives PR practitioners special opportunities to reach some TV audiences with long video productions.

In-House Electronic Systems   Material that organizations can offer news media and other publics is much more sophisticated now. In particular, PR agencies and departments are finding that computers make preparing graphics much easier. Computer graphics programs permit instant call-up of common illustrations such as bar charts and pie charts. The artist works on a computer having a lighted display board. The programs contain different designs and type sizes so that, to create a pie chart, for example, the artist simply types the percentages of the various pie slices to be drawn and the computer does the work. The pie can even be tilted for a three-dimensional effect. The system also allows slides to be produced for meetings and publications. The rule for using charts, especially if you are sending them with news releases, is to keep them simple (uncluttered) and clear (no artsy gimmicks that confuse or distort meaning).[19]

Computer graphics for three-dimensional color designs can be made either with an electronic pen or directly by a computer. Laser graphics require more technical skills but also provide movement and three-dimensional effects. Laser artwork can be entered into a computer graphics console and synchronized for incorporation into slide, film and computer presentations. These graphics can represent the special effects of movement to a multi-image presentation.

Computer-delivered photos are also available from digital cameras. These have built-in LCDs so images can be viewed as soon as they are shot, and with a direct connection to a computer, the images are immediately available for editing, processing and integrating into presentations.

■ PR & the Internet

It is virtually impossible to effectively practice public relations today without using the Internet and its World Wide Web (referred to as "the Web"). Not too long ago, the Internet was a text-based system that only connected academic institutions and government agencies; it was no more than a government-supported utility. With the arrival of Mosaic, the Web was able to feature graphics as well as sound and video content, and it quickly gained commercial attention. The Internet has grown into a "network of networks" that nobody owns or manages. The Internet includes well over 100,000 networks in more than 100 countries. Connections to other networks allow e-mail to be sent to about 180 countries. Many journals and other media as well as all types of businesses and organizations now maintain a Web presence, and proudly announce their Web addresses in their promotions and advertisements.

What do public relations practitioners need to know about the Internet and the World Wide Web? As much as possible, and many mid-career and senior-level practitioners who never had a computer course in college are now experts who are enthusiastically trying to learn more. If you know nothing about the Internet and your organization wants a Web page, the best choice might be a Web marketing design company. Knowledgeable staff will work with you to create a Web page that will attractively feature your organization to an estimated 31 million Web users; will use their server to connect you to the Web; will customize and register a domain name for your organization, e.g., *http://www.uni.edu*; and will provide e-mail addresses, e.g., *Dean.Kruckeberg@uni.edu*. Such a consulting firm will also promote your Web site to

search engines, browsers and a range of Internet guides as well as link your organization's site to other Web sites. Audio and video also are commonly featured on Web sites. A Web site is available 24 hours a day seven days a week, and can be a lot cheaper than many forms of comparable advertising and promotion.

Of course, your organization can install its own server and then design its own Web page and hire a "Web Manager" ("Webmaster" is now an ancient term). However, many public relations practitioners are learning HTML (Hypertext Mark-up Language) and are using economical software to create and regularly update their organizations' Web pages.

Companies are using their Web pages to accept customer orders 24 hours a day seven days a week, with no personnel needed to answer the phone. Orders can be sent, credit cards checked directly, and the order goes straight to the shipping department. Furthermore, question-and-answer pages result in satisfied customers, and operations manuals on the Web save a lot of printing costs. People are also attracted to giveaways and promotions.

What makes a good Web page? Ben Schneiderman offers eight "Golden Rules of Interface Design": 1) strive for consistency; 2) enable frequent users to use shortcuts; 3) offer informative feedback; 4) design dialogs to yield closure—e.g., provide sequences with a beginning, middle and end; 5) offer error prevention and simple error handling; 6) permit easy reversal of action; 7) support internal locus of control; and 8) reduce people's short-term memory load.[20]

Computer scientist Christopher Akers recommends an organized page that follows a chronological thought process. Explain in users' own language where links go. He urges Web managers to use pleasant colors, not those that will result in headaches for the viewers, and to not clutter the pages. Background shouldn't stand out and take focus away from the subject, he says. "Compress" images and sound effects so they won't take forever to download, or use software to "stream" the downloading a little bit at a time. There should be a happy medium between "breadth," which makes a page too long with too much information, and "depth," i.e., tree linkages. And, says Akers, link the Web page to e-mail so the viewer can communicate with you easily.

Gerald Anglum, associate director of public relations at the University of Northern Iowa, never had a computer class in college. However, he is a knowledgeable and skilled Web manager who uses the Web effectively in his public relations responsibilities. Anglum doesn't want frequent users to ever see a repeat of the UNI Web page (see Example 12.9). He may change the page every day. Pages can be structured so that students, parents, alumni and other specific publics can quickly access the information they want. An important advantage of a Web site for PR practitioners, Anglum said, is that corrections can be made in five minutes and at no cost (as opposed to a glaring error in a publication that had a 15,000-copy press run).

However, Anglum notes that a Web page can be "horrible" if it advertises that your organization is "out of touch," and appears poorly organized. He says information that can be downloaded in one two-hundredth of a second with the Ethernet on campus can take someone with a small modem 2.13 seconds, which adds up to an unreasonable amount of time in large downloads. And don't forget the simple information, such as the address and telephone number of the organization, he reminds public relations practitioners.

Today, creative users of the Web can even access distant television and radio stations. The Web is only in its infancy, and Anglum recommends that students learn as much about the Internet and the World Wide Web as possible. A lot can be learned just using the Web, Anglum said.

■ Preparing to Work with the Media

Because you must constantly sell ideas in stories or pictures to the media, you have to do advance work in gathering ideas and information.

Preparing the Story You should have some basic training as a reporter; this is because, in order to write about news, you have to be able to recognize it when you see or hear it. In a large institution, where people may be too busy to bother giving you

"news tips," you must be enterprising enough to search out the news yourself. One way to encourage news cooperation in a large organization is to tell people exactly what you need and how and when to get it to you. Of course, once you have the information, you are often expected to make banner headlines with it.

Sometimes, a PR person's news sense becomes dulled by spending too much time reading company materials and too little time perusing outside news and newscasts—not to mention talking too much to company people instead of to newspeople. When this happens, he or she is likely to produce a three-page story in response to the boss's suggestion for a "great news story," when in fact the story deserves only three paragraphs. Although you should listen to the suggestion carefully (never discourage any news source), you should assess the story from a news editor's perspective, not from a company perspective. Is it really worth three pages, is it simply a column item, or does it deserve no exposure at all? Maybe the idea is good but the medium is wrong. Maybe the idea is good for the company publication but lacks appeal outside the institution. A publicity person must keep his or her sense of news value finely honed.

In gathering information for a release, a publicity writer must act the way a reporter would with the same access. Start with secondary sources, finding out if the company files contain anything written about the subject—any research or sales reports, any memos. Then seek out the primary sources, interviewing people to learn everything they know and are willing to share.

A good publicist keeps a basic file of the following:

- Statistical information
- Governmental information—regulatory and other
- Basic reference books for the field of interest and for related fields
- All legislation on problems—pending or proposed
- Trade association data
- Trade union literature—each union, and how it operates

E X A M P L E   1 2 . 9
Using the Internet for Publicity

http://access.uni.edu/acal/   Northern Iowa Calendar   Thursday, October 15, 1998

University of Northern Iowa
Calendar of Events

This calendar is a partial listing of University of Northern Iowa events. All times are Central Standard, unless noted otherwise, and are subject to change.

List by Date

Today	Tomorrow
This Week	Next Week
This Month	Next Month
All Upcoming Events (up to 2 yrs)	

List by Category

Academic	Administrative	Alumni
Art, Exhibits, Films, Lectures	Athletics (Varsity)	Budget Development
Career Placement	Conferences, Workshops, Camps	Financial Aid
Meetings	Music & Theatre	Special Events
Student Organizations	UNI Museum and Marshall School	

Custom Searches

1. Date Range Search

From: [January ▼] [1 ▼] [1998 ▼]

To: [January ▼] [1 ▼] [1998 ▼]   [Search]

2. Full Text Search

Search for text: [_____] Restrict search to above date range.

NOTE: This searches all the text of every event in the calendar. The text you search for cannot contain any punctuation marks - any punctuation will be treated as a egrep-style regular expression.

Other calendars and schedules of interest:

- ITS Training - Technology Workshop Schedule
- KUNI/KUNY Programming Schedule
- Placement and Career Services
- Wellness and Recreation Services

Contributions to this calendar are made through the WWW by various authorized people across the campus. To inquire about authorization for your organization, contact the Data Access Team of Information Technology Services. Organizations with a

(continued)

EXAMPLE 12.9 *(continued)*

Information & Directories

Campus Update

Admissions & Financial Aid

Student Life & Services

Colleges & Departments

Administration & Support

Outreach & Partnerships

Alumni & Foundation

University of Northern Iowa

What's up at UNI

The University of Northern Iowa invites everyone to celebrate a "Panther Reign" Homecoming, with a week of activities Monday, Oct. 12, through Saturday, Oct. 17. For a schedule of events, click here.

If you'd like to see video clips of UNI in Motion, follow this link.

Quick Links

Welcome from President Koob

Phone and E-mail Directory	FAQ
UNI Calendar	Places to visit
Campus Map	Academic Departments
Athletics	About this WWW Space
Access UNI	
World Wide Wisdom	Great Teaching

UNI Net Search

General Information | Campus Update | Admissions & Financial Aid | Student Life & Services | Colleges & Departments | Administration & Support | Outreach & Partnerships | Alumni & Foundation

The University of Northern Iowa is located in Cedar Falls, Iowa.
The general address is 1227 West 27th Street, Cedar Falls. IA 50614.
When mailing to this address, please note "Attention to:" so that the item can be routed properly.
For individual phone, e-mail and postal addresses, please use the "Phone and E-Mail Directory"
Quick Link on this page.

Maintained by The Office of Public Relations.
Designed for Netscape Navigator or Microsoft Internet Explorer.

EXAMPLE 12.9 *(c o n t i n u e d)*

University of Northern Iowa Office of Public Relations News Release Directory

Thursday, October 15, 1998

University of Northern Iowa Office of Public Relations
News Release Directory

10/14/98	• UNI WILL HOST THE UNI-DOME COLLEGE FAIR MONDAY, NOV. 2 • STUDY ABROAD OFFICE HOSTS STUDENT MEETING TO TO DISCUSS FINANCIAL MATTERS • NEW AQUATIC LEARNING CENTER AT UNI BIOLOGY GREENHOUSE
10/13/98	• LUX SERVICE AWARD RECIPIENTS AND FINALISTS TO BE HONORED AT THE UNI HOMECOMING FOOTBALL GAMEON SATURDAY, OCT. 17 • UNI PARENT ASSOCIATION BOARD ORGANIZES FOR THE 1998-99 SCHOOL YEAR; NEW COMMITTEE FOR PUBLIC SAFETY CONCERNS
10/12/98	• REGENTS' INSTITUTIONS TO HOLD RECEPTION FOR ALUMNI, LEGISLATORS AND LEGISLATIVE CANDIDATES IN MASON CITY TUESDAY, OCT. 13 • INTERNATIONAL SERVICES WILL BEGIN HOSTING INTERNATIONAL COFFEE HOUR AT UNI
10/9/98	• UNI AWARDS DEGREES TO 453 SUMMER GRADUATES • JOHN 'JERSEY' JERMIER WILL SERVE AS GRAND MARSHAL OF THE 1998 UNI HOMECOMING PARADE, OCT. 17 • NOTED RESEARCHER TO SPEAK AND TEACH AT UNI DURING THE WEEK OF OCT. 19-23 • UNI DEPARTMENTS OF MODERN LANGUAGES AND HISTORY, AND THE WOMEN'S STUDY PROGRAM, AUSTRIAN LECTURER
10/5/98	• THERE'S HELP AVAILABLE TO HELP TEENS MAKE CAREER CHOICES • CHILEAN EDUCATORS WILL OBSERVE PRICE LABORATORY SCHOOL CLASSROOMS AND MEET WITH UNI SCIENCE EDUCATORS DURING INSERVICE
10/1/98	• AREA TEACHERS AND EDUCATIONAL PROFESSIONALS PARTICIPATE IN LEADERSHIP INSTITUTE CONFERENCE AT UNI • STUDENTS SERVE IN THE STUDENT ALUMNI AMBASSADOR ORGANIZATION AT UNI • FOUR UNI ACCOUNTING GRADUATES AMONG STATE'S TOP FIVE, NATION'S TOP 120 HONOREES FOR PERFORMANCE ON MAY CPA EXAM
9/30/98	• THE INTER-AMERICAN STUDIES COMMITTEE WILL PRESENT THE CANADIAN FILM SERIES AT UNI • UNI TO HOST NATIVE IOWAN JACK BENDER FOR PHI ALPHA THETA/DEPARTMENT OF HISTORY LECTURE, OCT. 14 • UNI WELLNESS RECREATION CENTER WILL SPONSOR 'CAR-FREE DAY' ON THURSDAY, OCT. 8 • U STUDENTS PARTICIPATE IN THE NATIONAL STUDENT EXCHANGE PROGRAM • UNI FORENSICS PROGRAM HOSTS TOURNAMENTS
9/29/98	• CHILDREN MOVE THROUGH DEVELOPMENTAL STAGES OF SPELLING, TOO • INTERIM ASSOCIATE DEAN, DEPARTMENT HEADS BEGIN WORK THIS FALL AT UNI
9/25/98	• NECHANICKY FAMILY NAMED 1998 FAMILY OF THE YEAR FOR UNI

(continued)

EXAMPLE 12.9 *(continued)*

University of Northern Iowa Office of Public Relations
News Release

Date: 10/14/98

NEW AQUATIC LEARNING CENTER AT THE UNIVERSITY OF NORTHERN IOWA BIOLOGY GREENHOUSE

CEDAR FALLS–Students can now learn the workings of an aquatic biosystem at a new facility on the University of Northern Iowa campus. Located in the biology greenhouse, the aquatic learning center houses a 1,000-gallon pond, a fast-moving stream, a waterfall and tanks that resemble stagnate ponds.

The pond has a variety of fish, algaes and mosses, aquatic plants that grown in, on and under the water, and bog plants. Due to the dormancy of native plants during the fall, tropical plants have been added to the aquatic learning center.

"There's something for everybody," said UNI Biology Greenhouse manager, **Ron Camarata**. "We have a hydroponics display. We have tanks where we can grow things in uncirculated water—which is like stagnate ponds. Then we have the pond, the fast-moving stream, the bogs, and the tanks with the marginal plants, like cattail.

The stream supports the growth of moss and other organisms on and between rocks, while the pond water is circulated in order to make it clean for fish and other organisms, according to Camarata. "When you have a pond like we have, you need circulating water and a number of different plants to keep the water stable. By that, I mean free of algae and suitable for fish," said Camarata. "I think students will start to understand the importance of clean water, and perhaps have a better appreciation for fish and plants, and the role they play in our environment."

Construction of the pond began in October 1997 and was completed by January 1998. The pond was filled and stable for plants by February. Some visitors to the center will remember the room, built in 1934 with tanks installed for aquatic use, was used from the 1950s through the 1970s as an animal room, housing everything from a five-foot alligator to armadillos, prairie dogs, turtles and salamanders, according to Camarata. After the Biology Research Building was built, the animals were removed and cacti were brought in before making it into a learning center.

There are plans for biology department professors to use the center for research after the pond stabilizes. Many classes have begun using the aquatic learning center, including Plants for Human Use, Activity Based Life Sciences and General Biology. The center has also become a part of the UNI tour for school children.

"And, I'm sure when you go in there, you have no preconceived ideas about it," Camarata said. "You've probably visited many places and really enjoyed the surrounding beauty of the place, but didn't think about what's in the water or what's happening in the water. I think students will start to understand.

"I think they'll have a better understanding of how the fish depend on certain things in their environment and how the plants depend on the fish to a certain extent, and how it all plays a part in keeping the environment clean."

Private donations funded the project for the Biology Department at the University of Northern Iowa. Local businesses making donations include: lumber from Barnes Builders, concrete from Benton's Concrete, reinforcement rod from Gross Ornamental Steel and park benches from Earl May. Labor was provided by the UNI Physical Plant.

STUDY ABROAD OFFICE HOSTS STUDENT MEETING TO DISCUSS FINANCIAL MATTERS

CEDAR FALLS–The Study Abroad Office will host a financial information meeting on Wednesday, Oct. 28, at 10 a.m. in Baker Hall, room 59. Topics of discussion will cover scholarships, loans and other financial matters.

Special loans and scholarships are available to students who plan to study overseas. Application forms and additional information can be picked up in the Study Abroad Office.

Study Abroad Coordinator Judith McConnaha also advises students in several other areas of the overseas experience, such as visas, health issues and insurance, travel options, and managing money while abroad.

For more information, call the Study Abroad Office at 273-7652.

UNIVERSITY OF NORTHERN IOWA WILL HOST THE UNI-DOME COLLEGE FAIR ON MONDAY, NOV. 2

CEDAR FALLS–The University of Northern Iowa will host the 1998 UNI-Dome College Fair in the UNI-Dome on Monday, Nov. 2, from 9 to 11 a.m.

EXAMPLE 12.9 *(continued)*

http://www.uni.edu/pubrel/newsrel/101498.html	News Releases for October 14, 1998	Thursday, October 15, 1998

(High School) has been invited to have students attend the College Fair and visit with representatives from post-secondary institutions.

The College Fair will host more than 90 post-secondary institutions to visit with students from the high schools in attendance. The institutions will include representatives from 2-year, 4-year, public, private, technical and cosmetology schools, plus the armed services. A browsing format will be used at the College Fair with special information sessions (sp:addressing financial aid and career counseling.

HIGH SCHOOLS INVITED TO 1998 UNI-DOME COLLEGE FAIR

Alden Community High School Independence High School

Aplington/Parkersburg High School (Parkersburg) Janesville High School

Cedar Falls High School Maquoketa High School

Clarksville High School Nashua-Plainfield High School (Nashua)

Columbus High School (Waterloo) Northern University High School (Cedar Falls)

Denver High School Tripoli High School

Dike/New Hartford High School (Dike) Union High School (La Porte City)

Don Bosco High School (Gilbertville) Walnut Ridge High School (Waterloo)

Dunkerton High School Wapsie Valley High School (Fairbank)

East Buchanan High School (Winthrop) Washington High School (Vinton)

East High School (Waterloo) Waverly-Shell Rock High School (Waverly)

Expo High School (Waterloo) Wellsburg-Steamboat Rock High School (Wellsburg)

Greene High School West High School (Waterloo)

Grundy Center High School West Delaware High School (Manchester)

Hudson High School GED–Hawkeye Community College (Waterloo)

Back to the news release directory.

- Records of the organization—a file copy of *all* your own publications
- File of ads run
- File of speeches by organization officials
- Clippings of all information about the company, with publication name and date for each
- List of individuals and organizations interested in the company, including civic groups appealing for contributions
- Biographies of top executives
- Pictures of stores, plants, products and other activities
- Lists of editors and publications
- People in all media, to contact as potential recipients or sources of releases or information
- File on major competition and antagonists and their efforts
- Timetables of occasions for publicity, with some code for indicating news releases
- Material that you are likely to need quickly— should be available electronically.

Like a reporter, you should never begin work with some predetermined idea about the length of the story. Find out everything you can, since you must have complete information before you can properly condense it—and otherwise news people won't later be able to get answers from you regarding questions you never anticipated (which they will ask). In doing your research, you may find that you have accumulated information for not one but several stories. You may find that, with a different emphasis, the story could be used by the newspaper, the local city magazine, an industry publication and your company's own house periodical. If your story focuses on a person, there may be even more opportunities for publication, because (again with a different emphasis) the story may be used in professional, religious or other publications of organizations in which that person is active. Research represents your principal investment in time. Make it pay off for you.

You should be familiar enough with the medium to which you are submitting copy to be absolutely certain the writing style you used pre-cisely matches the style of the medium. For instance, it is important to know whether a newspaper has an "up" or "down" style—that is, whether it uses capital letters frequently (up) or seldom (down). Find out and accommodate. Beware especially of writing the way people from whom you got your information talk, because they often use jargon (business, professional, educational, governmental or whatever) that is unintelligible to outsiders. Don't write what someone says, write what the person means. Of course, this is impossible if you don't understand it yourself, so never be afraid to say to a source, "I'm sorry, that is out of my area. You'll have to explain. I don't understand." They probably don't know anything about communications either, so you're even. Most PR people emphasize the need to be creative and conceptual—to be able to see the "big picture." Although they agree with that idea, experienced PR people will tell you it is the details that matter.

News Releases Public relations people are news managers, whether they are dealing with news releases that they initiate (and subsequently distribute, mail or put on PR wires) or whether they are issuing responses to media inquiries. Sometimes these inquiries result from leaks of information that the PR person was trying to "manage." At special events, PR-sponsored newsrooms facilitate both news releases and response releases because a PR newsroom manager is on duty who either has the information or knows where to get it promptly. The newsroom manager also knows the needs and schedules of the news media.

Whatever the circumstances, you have to be sensitive to media schedules. Your news schedules have to be worked out to fit the media served in each case. *Deadline* means just that. It is the *last* minute for handling new information, not the *preferable* time for doing so. When you are initiating news, you should let editors know your plans in advance, if possible, so that they can put your story on their schedules or in their "futures" books. One way to offer easy access to your organization's news releases is to offer them through your Web site.

Each story for newspaper and broadcast news should be prepared in a style and form appropriate to the particular medium. You must use the inverted pyramid or modified inverted pyramid format for news releases and accepted formats for features. In all cases, you must write the story as if you were a reporter. (Formats for news releases and news tips appear in the *Instructor's Guide* as well as information on deadlines.)

Planning Publicity Photos and Illustrations A publicity story generally has a better chance of being accepted by a news medium if you can offer an illustration (line art or photos) to go with it. Many newspapers prefer to shoot their own photos, and the wire services almost always do. In such cases, you must work in advance of the day the newspaper intends to use the story to preserve its timeliness and still allow the editor to schedule a photographer at a time when you can set up the picture. You should have all the elements of the photo assembled—people, things or both—before the photographer arrives. But how the photographer arranges or uses the subjects is his or her business. Don't interfere.

If you have hired a photographer to take the picture for you, you may have to offer substantial guidance, depending on the photographer's background. If the photographer has news experience, you can probably trust the person's news judgment. But if he or she is a commercial photographer with no idea of newspaper requirements, you must make sure that the following five guidelines are observed: (1) keep the number of subjects down to four or less; (2) get high contrast and sharp detail suitable for publishing in print media; (3) avoid clichés (people shaking hands or receiving a plaque); (4) position your subjects close together; (5) keep the backgrounds neutral.

Make the most of the photographer you have hired and get the photos you need—not only for one particular story but for other possible versions of the story for different media. Once you have good photographs, you can use them in a number of ways. It is a good investment of your time to go

with the photographer to ensure that you get the shots you want and to confirm spellings of names and other cutline information.

In ordering photographic prints, be sure to get some for your own files. Keep your photographic files up to date, so you aren't caught offering an old photo to a news source when a news opportunity occurs. The news media often pull photos out of their own libraries to use, but they expect to get something new from someone seeking publicity— even if they initiate the request. Anticipate this with adequate photo files. In addition, do not give competing media the same picture, even if it is only a person's photograph.

Try to arrange with a photographer for your organization to buy the negatives or disks. This is particularly important for high-cost assignments that involve color or aerial photography. Get a written contract. Otherwise, because of copyright law, the pictures belong to the photographer, and you have only bought specific rights. If the photographer will not sell the negatives or sign releases on "work for hire," you must anticipate all future uses of the photos you order for the file (publicity, ads, promotional materials) and identify those uses in the contract. If you own the negatives, you may for convenience ask the photographer to store them for you at his or her studio so that additional prints can be made later.

The same is true for other artwork and film. If you plan to invest in elaborate schematics, maps, charts or graphs, make sure they become yours. Similarly, when you hire someone to shoot film or videotape to use in releases to television (although most TV stations and all networks prefer to shoot their own footage), it is all right to let the company that processes and duplicates the film or videotape keep the master, because they have the temperature-controlled environment to preserve it; but be sure you own that master. Although all you may have planned at the moment is a short segment for a news clip or news feature, you might need that footage later. Make sure everyone knows and understands who the owner is and how much reprints cost.

News photographers do not have time to develop and print film other than their own or to make extra prints for you; neither do the wire services. Both newspapers and wire services have photo sales departments to take care of reprint requests. Television stations have commercial operations that develop film. Be prepared to pay for whatever you ask for. If you ask for videotape to be prepared at a station or for illustrations to be handled by a newspaper's art department—whether it involves photo retouching or designing the cover for a special section—get your checkbook out. The news media are businesses.

When you hire a photographer or when one is assigned by a publication to cover some event, try to think of an original pose to replace unimaginative stock poses. Make sure all the people and the props the photographer will need are ready well before the time for the shot. Action shots are best because they help tell a story, but a "portrait" character study of a person whose face shows deep emotion is also desirable, especially when that person is in an interesting environment that relates to the accompanying story.

You should have at least two specific shots (including camera angles) in mind before "shooting" the event. Discuss these with the photographer beforehand. Consider publication needs in terms of horizontal or vertical shots, the number of people to be included in the pictures and whether you need color or black-and-white photos. You also need to consider the event from the standpoint of the photographer, including how close the photographs can be taken. In some cases, the photographer needs to be unobtrusive. For that reason, many PR directors insist that their staffs have first-hand knowledge of photography, to understand lens openings and lighting. When you have a picture in mind, look through the lens to be sure it is there. If it isn't, work toward what you want. The more professional the photographer, the less direction he or she needs. Allow for travel time and rest periods while shooting, and be prepared to pay half or all the agreed-upon fee if you must cancel at the last minute.

Video News Releases Some organizations prepare their own video news releases, but most out-source this form of release. Many public relations services will handle video news releases for you, transmitting them worldwide by satellite. They also can monitor use of your video news release.

Initially, video news releases met with some resistance from news directors who felt they had less control over packaging news stories that came in this form from an outside source. However, it's so easy to edit videotape cassettes that few news directors balk any longer at accepting a video release, especially when they have B-roll to use. Public relations services that produce and distribute video releases make it their business to know what the trends are, and they keep up with the preferences of network, cable and major station news directors.

Promotions

The notion that media attention follows good promotions is not new. Edward L. Bernays said that the idea is to make news—to create really newsworthy events. One news photo that has come to symbolize white resistance to the civil rights movement of the 1960s shows the late former Alabama Governor George Wallace standing at the door of the University of Alabama confronting the first two blacks who sought admission. That was a true media event, according to both Wallace and Macon L. Weaver, who was at that time the U.S. attorney responsible for enforcing the federal court's mandate:

> Few people knew, but those two black students were already officially registered before George Wallace stood in the schoolhouse door for the benefit of press and television. The students had been registered by the Alabama dean of admissions inside the library of a federal judge. . . . Everything was coordinated [among Wallace's office, the university and the federal government] . . . the route for the students . . . the circle for the press. . . . His standing in the schoolhouse door was a charade. He got some publicity out of it. He got his wish.[21]

Wallace later said he stood at the schoolhouse door only because, without a symbolic protest, Klansmen and other extremists would have stormed the campus.

Pseudo-events have earned some "bad PR" for promotions. And, of course, promotions themselves often earn a bad name for PR. In promotions, you see PR's closest ties to marketing—so close that some observers have called promotions "marketing PR." You are even likely to hear a component of marketing described as "advertising, selling and public relations."

Sometimes you have to sell an idea or concept in order to sell a product, as Bernays promoted the "American breakfast" of bacon and eggs to sell his client's product. Similarly, film competitors Kodak and Fuji engaged in big-time selling at the 1986 celebration of the restoration of the Statue of Liberty. Kodak promoted itself through its American Family Album, a permanent exhibit of portraits of American individuals and families. Rival Fuji promoted itself by entering a blimp adorned with its logo in the Great Blimp Race that ended at the Statue of Liberty. Why? People take pictures at big events, according to Ted Fox, spokesman for the Photo Marketing Association.[22]

Selling an image along with a product doesn't work, though, when the product isn't there to sell. At the America's Cup, the world's premier yachting event, RayBan sunglasses, a division of Bausch & Lomb, wanted to keep the French company Vuarnet from cutting into its market. Obviously, people watching such an event wear sunglasses. So during the races at Newport, Rhode Island, RayBan sponsored a boat-ferry system, known as RayBan launches, and distributed a newsletter about the yacht races and other Newport activities. All of these activities proceeded under the direction of the sports division of Hill & Knowlton, later part of Hill & Knowlton's marketing communication unit. But local stores had not stocked anything but their normal supply of RayBan sunglasses, and thus RayBan couldn't deliver enough of the product its promotion had created a demand for.[23]

When you see an ad that focuses on an event or a problem, look for the publicity. And when you see the publicity, such as stories about champagne around New Year's or exotic recipes using particular fruits in newspapers and magazines, look for the advertising. Sometimes there is also direct contact with the product itself, such as food samples in grocery stores. It's all promotion.

Often the only place you have to look is up. The skies are crowded with blimps, including ones you can see at night. The familiar Goodyear dirigible, a 195-foot ship, has smaller competitors, the 123-foot long Lightships that American Blimp Corporation began building in 1990. The design staff works on computers to build the airborne

EXAMPLE 12.10

Floating Ad

American Blimp Corporation is a relative newcomer to the business of building and using blimps as airborne billboards to advertise brand names.

Source: Reprinted with permission of the artist, Hai Knafo and Mr. James Thiele.

billboards that are lighted from inside. The new ships compete with the three Goodyear ships which the company made, a Fuji ship made in England and a Florida blimp builder's ship leased to H. P. Hood, a New England dairy products company.

At sporting events, the ships have camera platforms for network crews and the networks also insist that the blimp sponsor buy air ad time. The floating ads are becoming increasingly popular, although certainly not for all products. A Miami corporate image consultant observed that you'll probably not see one advertising Weight Watchers.[24] (See Example 12.10).

Image Marketing An image is the impression of a person, company or institution that is held by one or more publics. An image is not a picture; that is, it is not a detailed, accurate representation. Rather, it is a few details softened with the fuzziness of perception.

Marketing reaches out to publics and tries to build a relationship beyond the product or service, but usually related to it. Shell worked with the National Safety Council and the American Trauma Society to develop a booklet to help motorists who happen upon a roadside accident and want to help. The magazine ad for Shell had a sample from the booklet inserted. There's also a note on the insert that says for nonmedical roadside emergencies help is available from its Shell Motorist Club, a membership organization, also a relationship building effort. (See Example 12.11a and b.)

Sometimes customers develop their own relationships, and it's not always what the company had in mind. Examples are the nicknames customers give products or companies. For years Coca-Cola resisted being called "Coke." Its advertising even urged, "Call for it by full name. Nicknames encourage substitution." But, by the 1940s, it had given up and decided not only to live with "Coke," but to endorse it. In 1982 the company's new low calorie drink was introduced as "Diet Coke." Another nickname, that was first resisted and then adopted is "FedEx." However, "Mickey D's" for McDonalds, is still not exactly what the company prefers, but it is the way some customers have personalized their experience. If the nickname is negative, it may be best to ignore it, as Neiman-Marcus has done with "Needless Markup," and the abbreviated "Neiman's," which the company doesn't like either. Stanley Marcus noted that "you give it more publicity by fighting it than by ignoring it."[25]

Publicity Spin-Offs Coverage of the spat is what occurs from any conflict a company might get engaged in, and that's likely to be negative publicity. A more desirable publicity spin-off occurred when Revlon, Inc. introduced a new stock offer at the New York Stock Exchange. The company invited in cover girls Cindy Crawford and Claudia Schiffer. The supermodels first toured the trading floor then went to the press gallery for interviews with the likes of the "Today" show among others. One stock trader told *The Wall Street Journal* that "Guys had their suits pressed, they got new shirts, they put on cologne." The traders also were wearing lapel buttons with a photo of the models. The

"spin-off coverage" was in the *Journal*, and a number of other publications as well as on television.[26]

Celebrity Spinoffs Promotion planners often look for a "big name" to attract media attention. It's not a novel idea, but sometimes it can result in negative publicity that has nothing to do with the product. For instance, the celebrity's private life may make the news in a way that hurts the promotion, such as when athletes are involved in drugs. Advertising has used celebrities frequently enough to have a long history of good and bad experiences. Although celebrities can increase recognition, they can't rescue a product, and the wrong celebrity, such as one exposed in compromising circumstances, may actually harm it.

These risks dictate that care be taken in choosing the celebrity. If you don't know much about them personally, you may need to contact a major talent agency or one of the national services that tracks celebrities—where they have appeared, how they have been received and how they have behaved. You want to find a celebrity who is a good "fit" for your event, and you want to be sure you have a contract that covers all that you will want the celebrity to be involved in.

Celebrities' names and pictures are often used in the pre-promotion of a special event. Be sure you have the celebrity's specific, written permission before using his or her name and picture in any advertising. Some who may agree to come to an event will not let their names or photographs be used in advertising because of previous advertising contracts for products or services. You must also make sure that any prior advertising association of the celebrity will not conflict with the image you want to create for your organization.

In using a celebrity for promotion, you may encounter the same problem that advertisers have when they use celebrities: people remember the celebrity, but not the message. You should also be aware that the celebrities are less concerned about the promotion than you are, and they are not under the same control in a publicity event as they are in producing a commercial. Don't expect them

EXAMPLE 12.11

Relationship-Building Ad

Shell teamed with the National Safety Council and the American Trauma Society to advise motorists how to help at the scene of traffic accidents, building relationships among motorists and all three organizations.

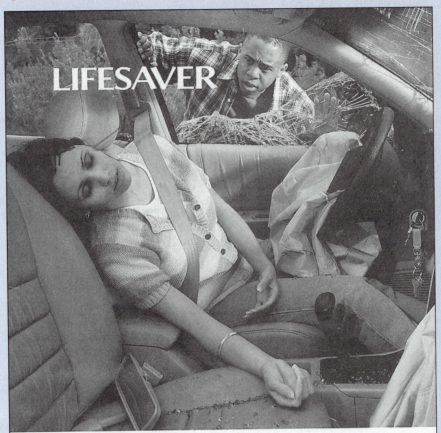

Source: Reprinted with permission of Shell Oil Company.

EXAMPLE 12.11 *(continued)*

Each year, thousands of drivers and passengers die in the few minutes *after* an auto collision. Many of them could be saved if the first people on the scene— people like yourself—knew how to respond quickly and correctly.

Move well beyond the wreck, and park out of harm's way. Use your flashers, raise your hood or trunk, and watch for traffic, fuel and wires.

Q. I've just seen a bad collision. What can I do to help?
A. *First and foremost, don't make things worse.* Pass *well beyond* the wreck before signaling and pulling off of the road, out of harm's way. This keeps you from blocking the view of the collision to oncoming traffic, and it gives emergency crews room to work. Turn on your emergency flashers and raise your hood to call attention to yourself.

Then carefully approach the wreck, avoiding dangerous situations like wires, fires or hazardous materials. *Next, turn off the ignitions of all vehicles* to reduce the risk of fire. This simple step could keep a bad collision from becoming much worse. Remember, check for spilled gasoline or downed power lines before getting too close. And don't move an injured driver to get to his keys.

Now call for help if possible. Be sure to stay on the line until the emergency dispatcher hangs up. If you're needed to administer first aid, assign the call to someone else and be specific: "You in the red jacket — call 9-1-1!" Consider carrying a cellular phone in your car. Many

Reduce the risk of fire by turning off a wrecked car's ignition. Just don't move a driver to get to the keys.

of today's models have emergency numbers programmed into them.
Check for injuries. Are victims awake and responsive? If so, encourage them not to move. If they don't respond, verify that they are breathing. Then attend to those with severe bleeding (wear latex gloves if possible). And remember:

NEVER MOVE A VICTIM UNLESS THERE IS AN IMMEDIATE, LIFE-THREATENING DANGER SUCH AS FIRE, LEAKING FUEL OR RISING WATER.

Q. Should I always stop?
A. Whatever the situation, your intervention might help save a life.

Wouldn't you want to be helped if you were the one trapped or injured? Also, if you were involved in the collision, you *must* stop. All states impose severe penalties on drivers who don't stop in such cases. Remember, you can be "involved" in a collision without actually hitting anything. If you contribute to a crash in any way, you're obligated to stop.
If the fear of making a mistake keeps you from stopping, be aware that most states have "Good Samaritan" laws to protect individuals from liability if they stop and, in good faith, administer first aid. The

If emergency crews are racing to a crash ahead of you, pull over to let them safely pass. And don't assume the first ambulance or police car you see will be the only one. Watch for other emergency vehicles following closely behind the first. The last thing you want to do is pull out and cause another collision.

scope of protection varies, so check your state's laws.

Q. What's my first step in treating the injured?
A. Before beginning any first aid, check to see if any victims are awake and responsive. This may help you assess the level of care each victim needs. A conscious victim's responses will often help you evaluate the extent of his injuries. "What hurts?" may reveal broken bones, bleeding or internal injuries. "Can you wiggle your fingers or toes?" could help you assess potential spinal damage. And no response at all might mean a victim isn't breathing.

Q. I don't think she's breathing! Now what?
A. *First, make sure breathing has stopped.* Is the victim completely nonresponsive? Is her chest rising and falling? Can you feel breathing? Hear it?
If the victim is not breathing, open her airway. Gently move the

head into its normal, "eyes front" position and lower the jaw.
Listen for gurgling or gagging. Both are signs of a blocked airway. If you hear either after opening the mouth, gently clear it of any obstructions.
If the victim is still not breathing, begin artificial respiration. Pinch the victim's nose shut. Open your mouth wide, take a deep breath, and put your mouth tightly over the victim's (you may wish to carry a pocket mask or mouth barrier for such emergencies). Blow a full breath, then watch for the victim's chest to rise and fall. If she doesn't start breathing on her own, blow one full breath every five seconds. Do this for at least one

To control severe bleeding, apply constant pressure to the wound with a bandage or a thick, clean cloth. If possible, wear latex gloves.

minute. Be sure to breathe yourself — you don't want to hyperventilate!

Q. How do I control severe bleeding?
A. Press firmly against any wounds with some sort of bandage, preferably a thick pad of clean cloth. This will absorb the blood and allow it to clot. (If possible, place a barrier — several layers of cloth, latex gloves, a plastic bag — between you and the victim's blood.) If blood soaks through the dressing, *don't remove it.* That could open the wound further and make bleeding worse. Instead, add more layers of cloth and apply pressure even more firmly. If possible, get someone else at the scene to help you tie the bandage in place.

1. Is the victim awake and responsive? Are you sure breathing has stopped?

2. If the victim is not breathing, gently straighten her head into the normal, "eyes front" position.

3. Lower the victim's jaw.

4. Gently clear her mouth of liquid or debris.

5. Check for breathing once again.

6. If the victim still isn't breathing, begin artificial respiration.

to be. Things that you didn't plan for can and do happen.

Publicizing Special Events

A special event may be any newsmaking situation—from a corporate open house to a freeway ribbon cutting to the preview of an exhibition of rare paintings. The publicity for each event requires its own unique handling, but a few basic rules apply to virtually every case.

The Mechanics   First, you must establish a timetable because so many events have to dovetail. The timetable should include the dates for the first announcement, which must be coordinated with any special invitations and advertising. Second, mailing lists must be prepared for both special activities and the news media. You must start early and set restrictive policies on handing out news media credentials. (You should not invite your PR colleagues to any media-day function, unless they had an active part in the planning.) Third, the promotion campaign itself must be planned in detail, with a theme selected that will carry through all advertising, publicity, letterheads, invitations and posters.

A media kit should be prepared for the event, and it should be one of the most carefully thought out pieces of the entire promotion. Media kits are mailed in advance to people who may not attend the special event but who may write something about it. They are also handed out at the event itself.

Because the kits must serve a variety of media—specialized and mass, print and broadcasting—parts of the kits differ.

Media kits have to be tailored to each occasion; if mailed, they should also include a cover letter that briefly explains the event. The contents are as follows:

Some news distribution services will prepare media kits for you and will coordinate their delivery. But you must provide the information the service needs to prepare the kits, along with any special instructions that you want them to have.

For example, some have found it especially effective to put the guidance heads (suggested headlines for news releases) on the front of envelopes going to the news media. If you want something special like this, you have to tell the distribution service.

Setting up a Newsroom   The next most important planning should go into arranging the media facilities during the event. Find out from the local media what they will need, and then plan for the out-of-town reporters.

Setting up and maintaining a newsroom or media facility for a convention, meeting or any special event requires planning and constant attention. You will need three to four weeks for phone installations, although in a crisis, you can get a portable phone bank installed at considerable extra cost. The phone lines are helpful for electronic transmissions. Most reporters will have cell phone and laptops. The facility you set up is for people responsible for gathering the news and getting it out, so it must operate efficiently. When a newsroom is cramped, badly located or understaffed, it can result in poor coverage. The following elements are essential for a smooth-running operation.

First, have a sign-up sheet in the newsroom. Provide space for each representative's name, the medium that he or she represents and the local telephone number and address where the person can be reached.

Second, use a rack or display stand to keep media kits from falling apart and to let you know when supplies are running low. Have a separate place for the "news tips of the day," pick-up schedules, new facts sheets and new news releases. Daily news releases should list the day's events and summarize results of the previous day's events. All information must be easily available to media representatives. This means accessibility of news information, background material and releases, illustrations and people to be interviewed.

Third, select for the newsroom staff an experienced crew who are cognizant of the need to be helpful and friendly and who know the importance of media deadlines. The number of staffers depends on the size of the event and the expected news coverage, as indicated by past occasions. The importance of having one well-qualified person in charge cannot be overemphasized. That person is an "anchor" who should always be available during regular hours and should be replaced by another "anchor" at other times. (When you have international coverage of an event, you have to run a 24-hour newsroom.) This person should be able to handle emergencies and opportunities and should know how to deal with delicate press and personal relations. Leaving the goodwill of an organization up to an inexperienced person can be damaging. Give all staffers pagers or cellular phones. You and other key people associated with the event should also wear pagers or carry beepers. In some situations key people may need ear attachments so they can get messages instantly.

Fourth, separate the newsroom from the traffic of the convention or meeting.

Fifth, provide separate interview rooms for print and broadcast reporters. It is advisable to have an interview "set" for television coverage, another area for radio interviewing and a third location where newspaper and magazine reporters can talk with people. There should be plenty of wall plugs and extension cords for lights and other electronic equipment.

Sixth, plan for special equipment needs. Mini-cams and TV vans have made coverage easier for TV reporters, but large doors must be available nearby to allow equipment to be brought into the newsroom area. Get information in advance about electrical outlets and other essentials that the TV crews require. Murphy's Law almost guarantees that someone will blow a fuse or trip a circuit-breaker. At large news conferences, risers are usually necessary in order for each camera to have a clear shot.

Seventh, be aware that most print journalists now use laptop computers to send their stories directly to the newsroom. These devices function most efficiently over plug-in telephones and *single* telephone lines, so make sure that phone jacks are available. The telephone company has to be notified that an FCC-registered device is going to be used. During some special events, you may be dealing with more than one telephone company. Be sure to check this situation in advance and clear it with the companies.

Eighth, make certain that the newsroom has the following supplies: (a) telephones for local and long-distance calls, plus metro lines so that surrounding cities can be dialed free of toll charges, voice transmission equipment for broadcast newspeople, telephone directories, modems and direct lines that are always kept open; (b) copy machines; (c) computers and printers; (d) bulletin boards and pins or tacks and boards with erasable markers and erasers; (e) individual desks or tables with comfortable chairs and good lighting; (f) coat hangers and space to hang coats; (g) wastebaskets; (h) paper for the printers and copiers, shorthand spiral notebooks, envelopes and pencils; (i) drinking water in bottles and paper cups for hot and cold liquids; (j) paper towels; (k) an extra camera with a flash unit and film if not digital, batteries of all types, computer cables, jewelers' tools for quick repairs and basic tools such as hammers, pliers and regular and Phillips-head screwdrivers in assorted sizes. Ideally, you would have an electrician available. The building may have one. If so, make special pay arrangements for the help you might need, and then be prepared to pay by the hour for actual work.

Ninth, darkroom facilities should be provided for people not using digital cameras and who may or may not bring their own portable labs. This space needs electrical outlets, running water and blackout curtains. You don't want to have to commandeer a restroom. Building supply rooms with sinks sometimes can be temporarily converted if you clear it with the building manager and alert the cleaning crews. When you make these arrangements in advance with the building people, they generally cooperate, but they don't like surprises. If they seem possessive about the building, it is because they are held responsible for its condition. You may have to sign a contract and put up a deposit to cover major (temporary) adaptations of the existing facilities.

Tenth, providing food in the newsroom is practically a must. Food is worth the cost because reporters expect it, and it keeps them from wandering away from the site. How elaborate the food table is depends on the budget and generosity of the organization operating the newsroom. The basic requirements are coffee with donuts or rolls in the morning, sandwiches for lunch, and coffee and soft drinks throughout the day. Parties, however, should be held elsewhere. The distinction between working newspeople and partying newspeople is important to maintain. Never call a news conference unless it is a working session; never have a party for newspeople and expect them to work. However, it is customary at large conventions to have a cocktail hour or reception for the reporters at the end of the working day and to provide free tickets for evening meals. If lunchtime includes a regular session of the program, a media table should be set up in the eating area.

Eleventh, be sure restroom facilities are nearby and that they are kept locked, but keep several keys in the newsroom. Check periodically on restrooms' cleanliness and on the availability of supplies. Arrange for building maintenance people to help, and be prepared to pay them. It is useless to know that you need towels if you can't get to a supply.

Twelfth, to protect the equipment, secure the newsroom for use only by authorized media representatives. It cannot be a social lounge for curiosity seekers, people looking for a cup of coffee (or other nourishment) and registrants to the meeting, who always seem to prefer the newsroom but get in the way. Visitors and unaccredited persons—regardless of who they may be—should be handled firmly and not admitted to the news area, where they interfere with the news-gathering process and are resented by the working newspeople.

Thirteenth, to ensure a good news operation, put yourself in the place of the reporter or editor. Update your Web page regularly and post news releases as well as other updates. Evaluate what you would need to cover the meeting properly, and then plan from that point. If your newsworthy event didn't get the proper coverage, it may be because the PR people didn't put the time, money and staff into a sincere effort.

Other Special Event Considerations The day before the event, call local media as a reminder; you can check on their technical needs again at this time. If you have arranged for something like one of the blimps as a symbol of publicity, you don't want to miss getting coverage.

Plan tie-ins to the special event. Motels and businesses around town are usually willing to display special messages on their marquees, especially if the event is an annual attraction or has some civic interest. Exhibits and displays can be developed and placed with institutions such as banks, utilities, schools and libraries. The chamber of commerce usually has a list of simultaneous conventions and meetings, and a special offer might be made to the sponsors to show your exhibit or display at these, if attracting crowds is one purpose of the special event.

Gimmicks Some public relations people plan newsmaking gimmicks that will attract attention to their clients. At a groundbreaking for the SPCA (Society for the Prevention of Cruelty to Animals), two trained dogs manipulated the shovel. Airplanes are available to tow banners over large crowd assemblies, such as football games and music festivals. Helium balloons, painted with logos, can be rented to float over the event. Even squadrons of aircraft that puff smoke on computerized command (called sky typing) can be obtained, and there are always biplanes to do classic skywriting.

Stunts of this type are clever and are accepted for their general interest. Any stunt that misleads, however, or creates a hazard—such as a human fly who walks up the side of a building, tying up traffic and rescue forces from the police and fire departments—is not generally regarded too highly by the news media.

Extending the Publicity Coverage To get as much mileage as possible out of your publicity, you can send clippings and stories to special publications, such as trade magazines and newsletters, as well as to other media that serve special publics. If possible, it is always newsworthy to get a mayor, governor or state legislator to issue a proclamation to mark the event. (See Example 12.12)

You can also produce your own magazines and books for a special event, such as a corporate

EXAMPLE 12.12

Proclamation

Association of Women in Communications arranged for the governor of Oregon to issue this proclamation at the time of its 1996 convention in Portland.

OFFICE OF THE GOVERNOR STATE OF OREGON PROCLAMATION

WHEREAS: The Women In Communications International Conference on Information and Technology will be held in Portland; and

WHEREAS: The conference will bring together national and international communications professionals in marketing, journalism, advertising, public relations, graphic design and more; and

WHEREAS: Women In Communications is a professional association that promotes excellence across all communications disciplines by developing the potential of women; and

WHEREAS: Women In Communications functions to support, train and serve communications professionals and assist them in achieving their career goals.

NOW, THEREFORE, I, John A. Kitzhaber, Governor of the State of Oregon, hereby proclaim October 4-5, 1996 to be

WOMEN IN COMMUNICATIONS 1996 INTERNATIONAL CONFERENCE DAYS

in Oregon and encourage all citizens to join in this observance.

IN WITNESS WHEREOF, I hereunto set my hand and cause the Great Seal of the State of Oregon to be affixed. Done at the Capitol in the City of Salem in the State of Oregon on this day, September 30, 1996.

John A. Kitzhaber

John A. Kitzhaber, Governor

Phil Keisling

Phil Keisling, Secretary of State

anniversary or a merger. Banks and newspapers have been known to commission books from historians for their anniversaries, but most often the job falls to a public relations writer. Whenever possible, give the job to a historian. You will probably have many disagreements along the way, but the historian's reputation and desire not to compromise her or his scholarship will bring a credibility to the publication that cannot be purchased. Management may not appreciate the historian's "warts 'n all" approach, however; and management may also dislike the fees that will have to be paid.

Sometimes "extended coverage" of promotions and events is neither favorable nor desirable. Promotions that are tied to sales often turn negative, for several reasons. The promises stated or implied in sales promotions may result in some disenchanted consumers whose complaining can create negative media attention. Furthermore, business editors are likely to look for the bottom-line consequences of sales promotions, which are increasingly seen as unprofitable. (Some sales promotions are not intended to be, especially when the product is new and the purpose is to introduce the product.)[27]

Sometimes news coverage can be negative in near-disastrous ways. For example, after journalist Ward Bushee wrote an editorial criticizing the dangers of ceremonial jet flyovers, he was invited to fly with a National Guard pilot. Special permission for a civilian to go along had to be cleared through the public affairs office at the Pentagon, so this wasn't a casual invitation. Nevertheless, the plane that Bushee was in collided with another, and his pilot had to push the eject button to save both of their lives. Fortunately, the journalist was not critically injured, and the Iowa National Guard said the accident wouldn't affect its policy on public relations flights.[28] But the episode is something to consider.

ON THE JOB WITH MEDIA PEOPLE

Successful publicity is often closely tied to the relationships you form in getting and disseminating information. Four groups are especially important to the publicist: (1) newspeople; (2) production people; (3) other PR people; (4) freelance writers. You need to know whom to turn to first in all four categories. Next you need to know the level of their skills, either by examining their work (when possible) or by checking their reputations (second best, but everyone seems to know everyone else in the media). Remember, you too will quickly become known by your degree of trustworthiness and by the quality of your work.

Relations with Newspeople

A good PR practitioner knows newspeople's jobs almost as well as they do, and is courteous and considerate toward newspeople. The PR professional also knows the importance of getting to know the newspeople, and therefore initiates contact. One of the best ways is to hand-carry news releases to all the local media. It is time-consuming, but by regularly hand-delivering releases, the PR person establishes a working relationship with the media that permits extra consideration when the institution he or she represents may be under attack. Take the release to the particular editor or reporter who should receive it. Make sure no questions are left unanswered. Visits should not be long, and you must be alert for hints that you should leave. Minutes to a newsperson are precious. Don't engage in extended conversation unless the newsperson invites it (say, by offering you a cup of coffee), and then be sure to take the time. Plan a delivery schedule that gives you the needed flexibility but still allows you to get the releases to other media with deadlines. You probably will find that you have to call ahead to get in. Most media now have security checks, so you can only get in to see someone if the person knows you are coming.

Include on your list of local media not just the daily metropolitan newspapers but also television and radio stations and suburban newspapers. Include ethnic and alternative media, too.[29] If it is necessary to translate the release into a different language, call on the faculty of commercial language schools and local college or university language departments or on one of the relatively new firms of language specialists that handle business and industrial translations. (Be sure the translator knows current idiomatic use of the language.)[30]

An illustration of fractured media relations appeared in the *Business Wire Newsletter*. According to the newsletter, the San Francisco bureau chief for *Business Week* received in the mail a seven-page feature sent by a local public relations person to the magazine's New York office. New York had kicked the story back to the San Francisco bureau; and in checking, the bureau chief found that the "leapfrogging" of his office in favor of New York was a product of simple ignorance. The PR person did not know that *Business Week* had regional offices, including one in San Francisco. In sending releases to national publications, be sure to check whether they have local offices or representatives; if so, deal directly with those closest to you.

On the other hand, you do need to know what national offices are doing, what the headlines are and what these may mean. For example, the Dallas bureau chief of the *Wall Street Journal* says that, if your (local) release is issued before the Dallas office opens at 8:30 A.M., you need to wire it to New York WSJ offices, too, so it will make the Dow Jones ticker.

When special events attract newspeople from outside the local area or members of the specialized media such as travel or outdoor publications, be sure to make personal contact while the opportunity is there. Contacts make smoother one of the more effective PR efforts—alerting news media to stories that might interest them. Usually this is a personal, individual effort, but some organizations have had success by publishing collections of news tips or story ideas for the state and national media.

If you are sending out many releases a week to the local media, you obviously cannot hand-deliver all of them, but it is important that you see all local newspeople on your mailing list at least once a month; there are no "little" or insignificant newspeople.

Most importantly, *be available*. PR people not only should not have unlisted telephone numbers, they should deliberately list their home phone numbers (as well as business phones) at the top of each release. A story may be processed after 5 P.M., and if you want it on the 10 P.M. news or in the morning paper, you should be available to answer questions. Often the caller is not an editor but someone from the copy desk who wants to check the spelling of a name in your story or to get some background to flesh out the story. You should immediately oblige them. The need comes at the time of the request, not later, when it is convenient for you.

In working with news photographers, never tell them how to take their pictures, since they know what their editors expect. But remember that, as the PR practitioner, you know the event, the institution and the people, so you may be able to think of other pictures that might be newsworthy and *suggest*—the word cannot be too strongly emphasized—them to the photographer.

This additional advice comes from a corporate manual:

> When you think you have a story that rates a picture, call the city editor, the business editor or reporter and present your idea. If the editor thinks it has merit, you will usually find it gets coverage. If you're turned down, there's probably a good reason for it. Try again, but come up with a better idea next time. Unless the picture possibility comes up suddenly, give the paper several days' notice. You'll have a better chance of scoring.
>
> Don't try to get an iron-clad promise from a paper for photo coverage of an event days in advance. An important news break may occur which will prevent the photographer from taking your picture at the last moment. [If you are simultaneously visited by several competing photographers, be sure you do not suggest the same pictures to each.]
>
> Newspapers will accept and publish well-executed pictures by photographers other than their own staff members. There are a number of excellent freelance press photographers whose services can be acquired at reasonable cost.
>
> Ask other PR people for recommendations and look at their work. Tell the photographer what type of pictures you need, how they will be used and the format. Unless you negotiate, the photographer owns the negatives. Also be sure to let the photographer do the "directing" of the subjects.

In working with television journalists, think and talk in 10-second sound bites, and remember the visual aspect of the coverage.

Relations with Production People

PR people need to work effectively with two types of production people: those in the media and suppliers. In the media, much of the technical work is handled electronically. However, knowing the production staffs and understanding production processes make it easier for you to avoid problems with the material you supply and to unsnarl problems that do occur. You need to know what is and is not technically possible in the various media, and it helps to be familiar with the terminology.

Knowing the terminology and production processes can be critical when you are dealing with suppliers. Technical suppliers produce your printed pieces, color separations for your artwork, slides, videotapes and sound. You have to know what you want, and you have to appreciate and be able to pay for quality (or accept less if you don't have the budget). More importantly, your directions will be followed by the producers. If you have scaled a picture wrong, failed to fit the copy correctly or, worse, misspelled a word, you will be charged for your mistake when it is corrected. Just as with other craftspeople, if the mistake is the suppliers', they will correct it at no charge; but if it is your error or change of mind, they will charge for "alteration costs." Mistakes always cause delays, and the ones you make can be costly to fix. A PR project can go over budget quickly if it encounters technical problems.

When production people contribute to a nonprofit effort, as production houses and printers often do, you are likely to get a credit slip, like the ones you receive from broadcast stations after your PSAs have run. A gracious "thank you" certainly is in order.

Relations with Other PR People

On occasion, you may work with PR people from other firms. It may be in a cooperative promotion; it may be because you've hired the firm to help with a special event; or it may be that you have a long-standing relationship with an advertising agency.

Fiascos have occurred when a practitioner who is supposedly directing the agency's efforts has suddenly felt threatened by them and has withdrawn his or her support and cooperation. To avoid such trauma, be sure to spell out in the beginning who has final approval over copy, and make sure deadlines and timetables are worked out to preserve your long-established relationships with the media. Then relax and manage. It is your job to supply the major source of information to the firm or agency, and to see that work is expedited, that deadlines are kept and that quality is maintained. It should be a rewarding experience from which all participants benefit.

Relations with Freelance Writers

Although it may be time-consuming, you should try to cooperate with freelancers who may be using your PR department as a source of information for a story they hope to sell or for a book they are writing. The freelancer may have a contact you lack, and the writer's status as a free agent lends credibility to the material.

Of course, freelancers can also waste your time, especially if they are really nonwriters or writer "hopefuls" on a fishing expedition. There are a couple of ways to check, without offending them. One is to ask them what and for whom they have written, and then look up the articles in the *Readers' Guide to Periodical Literature*. Another way is to ask them if they have sent a magazine or newspaper a query on the article idea and received a response; if they say they have, you can call the editor for confirmation. (To make it seem like less of a "corroboration" check, you can suggest to the editor that you certainly are willing to cooperate but that perhaps you could help the writer better if you knew what direction the story was to take and whether art might be needed.) Most editors will tell you immediately if the writer is working on assignment or on speculation. You should not dismiss the writer working without assignment, however; on the contrary, you may be able to help an inexperienced writer.

Many magazines use staff for stories or assign writers. Working with a magazine's experienced people usually increases your own appreciation for what you are publicizing and is a pleasurable, albeit time-demanding, experience. One news bureau director and university magazine editor, contacted by a nationally syndicated Sunday supplement about a story on the university, found that three weeks' work with the magazine writers produced not only national coverage but a handsome reprint she could use as the primary portion of one of her magazines.

Sometimes a writer has malicious intent, but an experienced PR person can take the offensive to advantage. As one practitioner says, "I give them the straight stuff, and I try to keep them busy. Every time I say something, I try to think how it could be distorted, contorted, twisted beyond recognition, and if it still seems to shake out okay, I spit it out. One thing I do know, while they are talking to me they are not talking to the opposition or gathering facts against us." The key here is to anticipate how the truth might be used against you.

If a story seems unfair or distorted, employers are likely to blame the PR person, but the PR person cannot pass the blame on to the media without aggravating the situation. Most professional public relations people have never registered a complaint with any news medium in their entire careers. The standing rule with respect to the media is to call only if they have made a substantial error. If the story is libelous, let your institution's lawyer make the call. On the other hand, some PR practitioners think talking back gets attention, consideration and corrections.

Protecting Relationships: Contracts and Deadlines

One way to establish some understanding about what is to occur in PR–media relationships is to sign contracts and to keep to your written and unwritten obligations.

Contracts Trouble with some media arrangements, such as exclusive cover stories or special TV appearances, can be avoided through contracts. Contracts have enormous value as preventives. The PR person also arranges contracts with suppliers of services. You should consider having contracts with an outside agency or studio, with a printer, with models and with any artists or photographers, even if they are your best friends or relatives. If your close friend, the photographer, has a contract, you can say, "The boss wants one of those color prints for his office," and your friend can say, "Well, it's not in the contract. How much do you think we ought to charge him for it?" A contract gives you the chance to suggest a fair price or say, "Forget it!" Bad feelings resulting from unexpected charges can be avoided if things are spelled out—in friendly but specific language.

Deadlines Meeting deadlines is essential to a smooth operation. Allow enough flexibility in planning for mistakes—yours and others'. Once you have promised copy to the artist or typesetter or ads to the media, you *must* make that deadline. This is an unforgiving business, and either you function within the framework of allotted time segments or you don't function at all. Remember the significance of both contractual agreements and deadlines. The former may be invalid if the latter are not observed. Make sure that you get the ad or commercial to the proper person at the agreed time in a form usable to the medium.

Direct Contact: Client or Boss and Newsperson

Public relations people usually have to prepare top management for an interview situation with the media. It may be one-on-one in the office of the executive, or it may be a news conference on familiar or unfamiliar ground with many reporters. In some instances, there may be a series of interviews on a "media tour," where the executive spokesperson is taken to different media that have accepted "bookings" (that is, made arrangements) for the executive to talk with editors, specialized reporters or representatives of special-interest publications. The tour may also include visits with news departments of broadcast stations and perhaps appearances on talk shows. On the latter, the executive may appear alone or as part of a panel or as the guest of an on-air personality. In any event, the success of the interview depends less on the interviewee's personality (although that is certainly important) than it does on his or her preparation for the interview situation. The most efficient media "tours" today are by satellite since it saves time for the interviewee and the media.

Some problems occur when the executive being interviewed has not done the necessary homework and is not fully prepared for questions. The interviewee must not only be consistently ready with a brief, concise, clear and honest response, he or she must also be aware of the interviewer's style and personal background. One exasperated PR executive said it was a problem to get his company's spokesperson to remember even an interviewer's name, much less his or her background and style. As a consequence, this PR person insisted on a role-playing exercise for the executive before any scheduled appearance. Although the executive was not ecstatic about submitting to the PR person's aggressive interviewing rehearsal, the spokesperson did prefer preparing in this manner to "reading all that dry stuff." Even if an executive is willing to prepare, however, it helps to have a run through, with someone playing the devil's advocate and asking provocative questions. It is also important to have the executive listen carefully to the questions asked—a skill that can be learned in rehearsal.

In planning for an appearance, the executive and the PR director should develop some quotable material—ideally something carefully researched to appear fresh and newsworthy. Remember, the reporter is looking for a story, and it is wise to be able to offer one. If the reporter gets into a sensitive area, it is a mistake to mislead or skirt the truth, since most good reporters can spot such devices quickly and then they move in for the kill. Rarely should one try to go "off the record" (although this is possible in certain circumstances with print media). It is usually better to say something, rather

than "No comment." It is also a good idea to ensure that the reporter has followup access to the executive in case he or she needs to clarify something (see Example 12.13).

The best way to get an accurate representation in the news media is to give a good performance. Does that mean a mistake-free performance? No, but it means correcting any mistakes immediately, according to former ABC affiliate broadcaster Dan Ammerman. Ammerman pointed out both the importance of television as a medium and the significance of getting your message straight by relating the story of Gerald Ford's slip during his televised debate with Jimmy Carter in the 1976 presidential campaign.

Ammerman said that Ford lost the presidency of the USA by failing to correct his mistake *immediately*. During the debate, Ford declared that Eastern Europe was not under Soviet domination, and despite being given three chances to correct his mistake, he did not. Ammerman said Ford could have said, "I'm sorry, I didn't phrase that correctly, what I meant to say was" and then say what he meant. Had he done so, according to Ammerman, the slip would not have made headlines the next day. Furthermore, Ammerman quoted Ford's campaign strategists as determining that they had to convert 174,000 voters each day from the day their candidate was nominated to the day of the election. This would have assured Ford a slim victory. For two weeks following the crucial debate, however, no voters were converted. A Gallup poll taken after the election led George Gallup to state that "to the best of my ability to judge," President Ford lost to Jimmy Carter on that one misstatement in their debate. If the strategists had been able to acquire 174,000 voters per day for the fourteen days between the debate and the election, Ford would have beaten Carter.[31]

The role of the PR person in the interview is that of preparer, facilitator and clarifier. The public relations person who tries to inject him or herself into the process during the actual interview is asking for a hostile reaction. The role of clarifier includes interpreting facts and technical language, offering background information, reminding the

E X A M P L E   1 2 . 1 3
Conducting Media Interviews

The element of control that is present with written communications is far less so in an interview situation. As a consequence, the danger of looking bad in print is far greater when news is provided through this method. Certain ground rules, however, can make the interview more manageable and less burdensome to the person being interviewed. Following are guidelines for public relations people and executives to follow in conducting media interviews.

RULES FOR PR PEOPLE

1. Select the place for the interview, one preferably on the home ground of the person being interviewed.

2. Be sure to allow sufficient time for the interviewer to complete an assignment.

3. Know the topic of discussion, and have supporting material at hand.

4. School the person interviewed beforehand as to what questions to expect. Be prepared to handle touchy questions.

5. Know your reporter's habits, etc., and give the person being interviewed a verbal sketch. At the same time, make sure the reporter is completely aware of the person being interviewed—background, hobbies and so on. These things can help establish rapport in preliminary conversation.

6. Set ground rules for the interview, and make sure both parties understand them.

7. Avoid off-the-record remarks. If it's off the record, keep it that way. Exceptions might occur if the reporter is known and trusted.

8. Help the reporter wind up the story in one day.

9. Make sure the reporter gets the story sought. In agreeing to do the interview, you have said in essence that you will give the reporter the story.

10. Stay in the background, and do not try to answer questions. If the question is one that requires an answer contrary to company policy and the person being interviewed starts to answer, remind him or her it is not policy to disclose that information. Or if the interviewee wants to hedge on a question that is perfectly all right to answer, say it is OK to answer.

11. Offer to answer further questions later.

12. Do *not* ask the reporter when the story will run or how big it will be.

RULES FOR EXECUTIVES BEING INTERVIEWED

1. Know the topic you are to discuss.

2. Anticipate touchy questions.

3. Be completely honest.

4. Answer questions directly. If you cannot answer the question, say you cannot.

5. If you don't know an answer, say so and offer to get one. Follow up on this offer.

6. Keep the meeting as cordial as possible even in the face of bantering and pushing.

7. Avoid off-the-record remarks unless you know and trust the reporter. Explain that the information is not for public disclosure and politely decline an answer.

8. Be sure to answer questions that are matters of public record or not against company policy.

9. Use the personality that helped get you into a management position, and look professional.

10. Offer help later if the reporter needs it.

---

interviewee of questions that might have been overlooked and perhaps extending the interview if necessary.

Phillips Petroleum once printed "golden rules" for handling newspeople on 3 × 2-inch plastic cards and gave them to executives who took the company's media training class. The flipside of each card listed the company's public relations contacts, with home and office numbers. Among the seven rules was the admonition to "*be brief and to the point*. Be pleasant even when the reporter is hostile. Answer the question, then shut up. Dead air isn't your problem. Correct misstatements." Another rule states, "*Never answer hypothetical questions. These get you into trouble with speculation.*" And still another good piece of advice: "*Never use expert talk. Sharks are sharks, not marine life.*"[32]

To these rules, Jim Blackmore and Alex Burton add, "Never say 'never' such as 'that never happened here before'"; and they advise tape-recording the interview yourself. They also advise correcting an inaccuracy or misrepresentation immediately.

You can hire a professional coach from a good firm like Audio-TV Features or the Executive Television Workshop to help prepare the executive to be interviewed. Some agencies like Burson-Marsteller and Hill & Knowlton also prepare their clients for these experiences and for others, such as appearing as an expert witness or giving government testimony. People who are going to give depositions or appear on the witness stand can benefit a great deal from role-playing sessions in which they are questioned aggressively and challenged, because that's what's going to happen to them.

Some top executives haven't been seriously challenged face to face, much less insulted, in years. They may need some training in proper reactions and responses under verbal fire. They also may need to be reminded of the different types of audiences who will respond to their remarks. These audiences include news media, employees, other industry or association people, consumers and various others. They need to think through responses to see how each sensitive public is likely to react.

Other recommendations include the following:

1. Go to the location prior to the presentation, if possible, and get an idea about the physical setting.

2. Go early to get a seat so you can hear and see before you appear or before your client or boss appears. Get a seat for the person who will be interviewed.

3. If prepared testimony is to be given and if it is longer than two pages, attach a summary statement to the front.

4. Bring extra copies of the testimony and of your news release about it for the media's table at the hearing.

5. Know how to address the person in charge.

6. Dress conservatively and in your best outfit.

7. Be courteous and respectful, but stand your ground.

8. Thank the person presiding for giving you an opportunity to speak when you begin and when you finish.

9. Have an adequate supply of business cards to give reporters.

10. Plan your schedule so you will have time to meet with reporters afterward.[33]

When the client or the boss comes into direct contact with the news media, both sides probably have some misperceptions of the other. But the greater misperceptions probably are held by the client/boss. Most have had limited contact with newspeople, and some have had bad experiences. Your job is to see that all encounters are productive, if not altogether positive, experiences.

Again, two steps you can take will help you accomplish this. First, prepare your client or boss for the experience by going over the issues that are likely to come up, whether or not these are the main topics to be discussed. Be sure she or he understands how responses are likely to be interpreted and reported. Second, make sure you are there to see what happens and to follow up with information, interpretation, pictures or whatever else is needed.

News Conferences and Results In general, don't call a news conference if you can avoid it, and never call one unless you are sure that what is to be said is newsworthy. But especially if there is a controversy, call a news conference in such a way that the organization doesn't appear to be hiding something. Call a news conference if you have a celebrity whose time is severely limited, and you believe many newspeople would want to meet her or him. If you can, separate print and broadcast media by holding two news conferences; however, you may not be able to. If you do separate news conferences, be sure that deadlines do not give one medium an unfair advantage. Some general rules to follow are these:

1. Choose a convenient (to the news media) location with adequate facilities. Try to choose a site that makes sense for the story—unless it's miles away from all central facilities.

2. Choose the right day and time, if you have a choice. Monday is good for coverage, and in some metropolitan locations Sunday is acceptable because news crews are working.

3. Plan to have the news conference covered for your own organization (videotape, audio—in addition to and separate from the sound-on tape—and still photography). You need to be sure what was said, and you may be able to use some of the material later in your own followup story.

4. Take all of the background information on the person and the organization that you will need. Assign someone to get the names of reporters and media they represent, with phone numbers for call-backs.

5. To news media who didn't make it, offer a story and pictures (sound bites and videotape release when possible). Give them the same background material you prepared for those who attended. You should provide media kits for all news conferences.

6. Rehearse your spokesperson and be as aggressive in your drill as you can possibly be. Play devil's advocate.

7. Evaluate with your spokesperson the results right after the conference and again when the stories are in. Show him or her how the news media used what was said.

Media Tours: Print and Broadcast Although you can hire a PR news service or an agency to arrange a tour, you must be aware that, while your client or boss is providing information, he or she is also creating an image. A national business publication described an interviewee—an author on a book promotion tour—as looking like a "wrung-out pol-

itician." A newspaper columnist told how another interviewee asked him what day it was; this person, a film star riding the circuit to promote a new movie, did not know what city he was in either. The agenda is rigorous: one-night stands in major market cities talking with entertainment columnists, appearing on TV talk shows, opening new buildings and being the guest celebrity for special events in places like shopping malls. The name of the game is *exposure*. Winning national exposure is a bone-wearying job. It requires a lot of calls and a lot of small efforts to create some momentum toward major recognition.

Politicians use the personal appearance as a media event to help create exposure. Candidates develop a message (called The Speech by media who travel with them) and present it as often as a dozen times in one day to different audiences. The most skillful emphasize some portion of it for a particular audience. The result of this single-message presentation is that the news media stop reporting on the speech and begin to report instead on audience reaction to it or on trivia of the campaign. One gubernatorial candidate, capitalizing on the scarcity of things to report once his campaign was underway, had media kits constantly updated with "The Campaign to Date," his own version of the varying emphasis he gave his speech in different towns or to particular audiences. A political columnist who was a member of the opposing political party admiringly called the update "useful to us and damn smart politics." What is being sold in tours by personalities is the image of the individual.

The satellite media tour is easier on the individual involved because the person can stay in one location and reach stations all over the nation. Here are some rules for on-the-road media tours to get the best results:

1. Become thoroughly familiar with the people you will meet on the schedule. Know their medium. Be familiar with their work.

2. Be sure all physical arrangements are firm, and confirm these by letter. Call your office or agency daily to get changes and messages.

3. Take plenty of money and letters of credit. You may have to charter a plane to keep on schedule.

4. Be sure your person keeps on schedule and fulfills all commitments. Take advantage of any "down" time to make phone calls to let people know you are in town. Watch the person's health and personal appearance. Anyone going through this ordeal needs help and attention to his or her personal needs such as rest and diet.

5. Keep up with props, supplies of media kits, luggage and so forth.

6. Make notes at stops of what followup is needed. If some of it can be done by the office, pass along instructions in your twice-daily calls to staff.

7. Keep clippings if you are in town long enough to get them. In any case, take notes of who attended all sessions.

8. Be responsive and sensitive to both sides. Keep your client or boss from getting depressed or burned out.

More Informal Contact Trade shows are in the category of special events, as are most PR parties. The problems that can arise from these are due to the less controlled circumstances involved and the consequently increased opportunities for Murphy's Law—what can go wrong will go wrong—to operate. At trade shows, you must be alert to the presence of media people from specialized publications. Many feel that they deserve special attention, and they should get it. They certainly shouldn't be ignored.

GOOFS AND GLITCHES

Today world markets are the only markets, and translating materials is therefore a commonplace task. Perhaps in the future PR offices will consider as standard equipment the hand-held computer that translates words and phrases into any of thirteen languages, with the help of the appropriate tape cassette. Actually, few agencies handle their own translations, with or without language computer assistance. The problem involves the nuances of a language.

For example, a PR and advertising agency director in Mexico City tells about the agency's U.S.-based affiliate, which insisted on sending them billboards ready to put up for a client, Parker Pen. The Mexico City agency had wanted to handle the art and translations. When a billboard of twenty-four-sheets arrived, a secretary in the office opened one package of poster duplicates of the billboards, gasped and began laughing. The Spanish translation had not taken into consideration local usage—and it was advertising that its new product would help prevent unwanted pregnancies! The Mexico agency's experience is not unique. Otis Engineering Company displayed a poster at a Moscow trade show saying that its oil well completion equipment was effective in improving one's sex life. Ads for "rendezvous lounges" on an airline's flight in Brazil startled and offended patrons, because "rendezvous" in Portuguese translates as a place to have sex. In Southeast Asia, a promise by Pepsodent to brighten teeth was not impressive. Chewing betel nuts is common, as are the discolored teeth that the practice causes.

Countless such goofs have occurred. When Dr Pepper, the soft drink manufacturer, designed its logo for the Middle East, where its product was to be bottled for the first time, it could have used some expert help. In July 1978, the Dallas-based beverage company took a copy of its new logo for the Middle East production to the *Dallas Morning News*, where Aziz Shihab, chief editor of the newspaper and former editor of the *Jerusalem Times*, noticed a problem. Shihab explained that Arabic has no letter *p* and that Arabs consequently often confuse the letters *p* and *b* when reading English. The Arabic symbol that is used for *p* in translated works is the Arabic letter *b* with three dots, instead of the usual one, under it. The company was thus alerted to the problem, and the *News* shared the story with its readers (see Example 12.14), showing both the incorrect (right) logo, which spells "Dr Bebber," and the corrected (left) version.

EXAMPLE 12.14
Dr Bebber—Something Lost in Translation

Source: Reprinted with permission of *Dallas Morning News.*

If not language, cultural differences can cause problems. In a promotion for Damavand refrigerators, the 18,000 foot Mount Damavand over Tehran seemed the perfect image, especially with the line, "Only nature makes cold like Damavand." The Iranian government which is ruled by Islamic law didn't think it was such a good idea. The government told the company that refrigerators could not be compared to nature because that was God's territory.[34] If you are advertising in Iran, according to *The Wall Street Journal,* you need to know that "Iranian ads can have no women, no English, no celebrities, no jokes, no product claims and no hints, whatsoever, of sex, aristocracy or America."[35]

But you don't have to go abroad to get into trouble with sensitivities. In promoting its mouthwash, Scope, Procter & Gamble just before Valentine's Day announced a list of "least kissable" celebrities, using names gathered from a survey. One of the least kissable was Rosie O'Donnell, who then repeatedly said "Only dopes use Scope" on her popular talk show. Rival Listerine not only donated bottles of its product to the celebrity and the show's audience, but also sent $1,000 to For All

Kids Foundation, her favorite charity, each time she kissed a guest celebrity on her show.[36]

Adding to the list of questionable judgments was the decision of America West Airline to turn back a planeload of paying passengers on their way to Phoenix. The plane had been in the air from Dallas-Fort Worth International Airport for an hour when it was ordered back and the 50 passengers dumped so the plane could take home the California Angels baseball team. The team, last in the American League West, had just lost to the Texas Rangers. The excuse for turning back a plane already in the air, according to America West, was that the Angels' chartered America West plane had been grounded for mechanical work and the airline didn't have another plane available to meet its contractual obligation. After the bad publicity, the airline acknowledged there probably was a better solution to the problem.[37]

Perhaps the worst goofs occur because of complacency, arrogance and "head-in-the-sand" denial that small problems can become big problems. Organizations are learning that they must continually monitor these little problems, and that's what is creating a market for services such as eWatch,

EXAMPLE 12.15

The International Language of Gestures

On his first trip to Naples, a well-meaning American tourist thanks his waiter for a good meal well-served by making the "A-Okay" gesture with his thumb and forefinger. The waiter pales and heads for the manager. They seriously discuss calling the police and having the hapless tourist arrested for obscene and offensive public behavior.

What happened?

Most travelers wouldn't think of leaving home without a phrase book of some kind, enough of a guide to help them say and understand "Ja," "Nein," "Grazie" and "Où se trouvent les toilettes?" And yet, while most people are aware that gestures are the most common form of cross-cultural communication, they don't realize that the language of gestures can be just as different, just as regional and just as likely to cause misunderstanding as the spoken word.

Consider our puzzled tourist. The thumb-and-forefinger-in-a-circle gesture, a friendly one in America, has an insulting meaning in France and Belgium: "You're worth zero." In parts of Southern Italy it means "asshole," while in Greece and Turkey it is an insulting or vulgar sexual invitation.

There are, in fact, dozens of gestures that take on totally different meanings as you move from one country or region to another. Is "thumbs up" always a positive gesture? Absolutely not. Does nodding the head up and down always mean "Yes?" Not in Bulgaria!

To make matters even more confusing, many hand movements have no meaning at all, in any country. If you watch television with the sound turned off, or observe a conversation at a distance, you become aware of almost constant motion, especially with the hands and arms. People wave their arms, they shrug, they waggle their fingers, they point, they scratch their chests, they pick their noses.

These various activities can be divided into three major categories: manipulators, emblems and illustrators.

In a manipulator, one part of the body, usually the hands, rubs, picks, squeezes, cleans or otherwise grooms some other part. These movements have no specific meaning. Manipulators generally increase when people become uncomfortable or occasionally when they are totally relaxed.

An emblem is a physical act that can fully take the place of words. Nodding the head up and down in many cultures is a substitute for saying, "Yes." Raising the shoulders and turning the palms upward clearly means "I don't know," or "I'm not sure."

Gestures, called illustrators, in semantics are physical acts that help explain what is being said but have no meaning on their own. Waving the arms, raising or lowering the eyebrows, snapping the fingers and pounding the table may enhance or explain the words that accompany them, but they cannot stand alone. People sometimes use illustrators as a pantomime or charade, especially when they can't think of the right words, or when it's simply easier to illustrate, as in defining "zig-zag" or explaining how to tie a shoe.

Thus the same illustrator might accompany a positive statement one moment and a negative one the next. This is not the case with emblems, which have the same precise meaning on all occasions for all members of a group, class, culture or subculture.

Emblems are used consciously. The user knows what they mean, unless, of course, he uses them inadvertently. When Nelson Rockefeller raised his middle finger to a heckler, he knew exactly what the gesture meant, and he believed that the person he was communicating with knew as well. . . .

In looking for emblems, we found that it isn't productive simply to observe people communicating with each other, because emblems are used only occasionally. And asking people to describe or identify emblems that are important in their culture is even less productive. Even when we explain the concept clearly, most people find it difficult to recognize and analyze their own communication behavior this way.

Instead, we developed a research procedure that has enabled us to identify emblems in cultures as diverse as those of urban Japanese, white, middle-class Ameri-

EXAMPLE 12.15 *(continued)*

cans, the preliterate South Fore people of Papua, natives of New Guinea, Iranians, Israelis and the inhabitants of London, Madrid, Paris, Frankfurt and Rome. The procedure involves three steps:

- Give a group of people from the same cultural background a series of phrases and ask if they have a gesture or facial expression for each phrase: "What time is it?" "That's good." "Yes." And so on. We find that normally, after 10 to 15 people have provided responses, we have catalogued the great majority of the emblems of their culture.
- Analyze the results. If most of the people cannot supply a "performance" for a verbal message, we discard it.
- Study the remaining performances further to eliminate inventions and illustrators. Many people are so eager to please that they will invent a gesture on the spot. Americans asked for a gesture for "sawing wood" could certainly oblige, even if they had never considered that request before, but the arm motion they would provide would not be an emblem.

To weed out these "false emblems," we show other people from the same culture videotapes of the performances by the first group. We ask which are inventions, which are pantomimes and which are symbolic gestures that they have seen before or used themselves. We also ask the people to give us their own meanings for each performance.

The gestures remaining after this second round of interpretations are likely to be the emblems of that particular culture. Using this procedure, we have found three types of emblems:

First, popular emblems have the same or similar meanings in several cultures. The side-to-side head motion meaning "No" is a good example.

Next, unique emblems have a specific meaning in one culture but none elsewhere. Surprisingly, there seem to be no uniquely American emblems, although other countries provide many examples. For instance,

the French gesture of putting one's fist around the tip of the nose and twisting it to signify "He's drunk," is not used elsewhere. The German "good luck" emblem, making two fists with the thumbs inside and pounding an imaginary table, is unique to that culture.

Finally, multi-meaning emblems have one meaning in one culture and a totally different meaning in another. The thumb inserted between the index and third fingers is an invitation to have sex in Germany, Holland and Denmark, but in Portugal and Brazil it is a wish for good luck or protection.

The number of emblems in use varies considerably among cultures, from fewer than 60 in the United States to more than 250 in Israel. The difference is understandable, since Israel is composed of recent immigrants from many countries, most of which have their own large emblem vocabularies. In addition, since emblems are helpful in military operations where silence is essential, and all Israelis serve in the armed forces, military service provides both the opportunity and the need to learn new emblems.

The kinds of emblems used, as well as the number, vary considerably from culture to culture. Some are especially heavy on insults, for instance, while others have a large number of emblems for hunger or sex.

Finally, as Desmond Morris documented in his book *Gestures*, there are significant regional variations in modern cultures. The findings we describe in this article apply to people in the major urban areas of each country: London, not England as a whole; Paris, not France. Because of the pervasiveness of travel and television, however, an emblem is often known in the countryside even if it is not used there.

Source: Paul Ekman, Wallace V. Friesen and John Bear, "The International Language of Gestures," *Psychology Today* (May 1984).

which tracks comments that are being made on the Internet's thousands of electronic forums and discussion groups.

Intel's experience is a classic example of what can happen when a company ignores a "small" problem. In early 1995, word of a flaw in that company's Pentium processor chip spread throughout the Internet. Intel failed to act quickly enough before issuing an Internet-wide message addressing concerns about the chip. *Advertising Age* reported that the company's credibility was nearly destroyed by its failure to respond to what appeared to be a minor public relations problem.[38]

As you can see, goofs and glitches have a way of creating problems, some of them serious. Sometimes you only find out about them when you get an early morning phone call, "Have you seen the morning paper?" or "Do you have the news on (radio or TV)?"

TALKING BACK AND CORRECTING

The PR edict for years was "suffer in silence" when the news media made a mistake in their coverage. There was reason for such a decision: "You can't fight with a pen people who buy ink by the barrel." There were also adages such as "Why spit in the wind?" and "I was taught not to kick jackasses."

Today, for most PR people, the idea of talking back is still limited to demanding and getting their side of the story presented. Some, however, launch a campaign.

Ronald Rhody of Rhody & Company, Inc., offers several observations and postulates for responding to media, which he calls the Ben Franklin approach to the problem because they are based on this Franklin quote: "A little neglect may breed mischief: for want of a shoe the horse was lost; for want of a horse the rider was lost; for want of a rider the battle was lost; for want of a battle the kingdom was lost."[39] The following are Rhody's principal postulates of the Ben Franklin approach:

1. No contest was ever won from the sidelines. Be players, not spectators.

2. The public has a right to accurate and balanced information about your operations.

3. The public's right to know is as much your responsibility as it is the responsibility of government or the media.

4. Fear of controversy or criticism is a luxury no institution in today's society can afford. Silence never swayed any masses, and timidity never won any ball games.

5. Take the initiative in all circumstances, whether the news is good or bad.[40]

Rhody thus disputes the conventional wisdom that is employed when dealing with this constituency (namely, remember that the news media represent a public). The only caution he considers appropriate in taking on the news media is the same one you would exercise with any other public: making sure you have documentable facts on your side.

Most PR people now endorse the notion that you can get substantial errors corrected—preferably editorially, and if not, by advertising. If redress seems necessary, file a lawsuit.

POINTS TO REMEMBER

■ Advertising is paid-for time or space, except in the case of public service announcements (PSAs), where the time and space are donated to a nonprofit organization or cause. Usually when advertising takes on the appearance of publicity, there is no intention to deceive.

■ PSAs are handled through the advertising departments of print media and through public service directors at radio and television stations. Publicity, on the other hand, is handled by media news staffs and must compete for time or space with staff-generated news materials.

■ The purpose of advertising must be clear because it's difficult for even the best copy to create awareness, convey specific information, get action and affect attitude.

■ One of the most memorable parts of any ad is the organization's logo, which is designed for high recognition and positive attraction.

■ As organizations become involved in global communication, logos should be pretested abroad to ensure that they meet with cultural acceptance.

■ Except for brochures, house publications generally follow a magazine format. Some, however, are designed as megapapers: oversized newspapers in format that are folded for a magazine or newsletter look.

■ The first decisions to make in producing a brochure are to determine its purpose and its audience.

■ Since a house publication goes to employees or members only, it is likely to have a different design from a publication that receives broader distribution.

■ What employees want to know about a company is more important than what the company wants to tell employees. A house publication should make allowances for two-way communication.

■ Although only publicly held companies are required by law to produce annual reports, many nonprofits publish annual reports for their stakeholders.

■ Responsibility for the annual report should be shared by two people: a communications specialist responsible for the character of the publication, and a high-level management representative responsible for the content.

■ Most annual reports contain the following five components. (1) a letter from the chairman; (2) the auditor's report; (3) financial statements; (4) a longer section narrating pertinent facts about the past year's operation; (5) photos and charts. Some annual reports are now produced on videotape as well as in print.

■ Visual presentations include easel pads, overhead projectors and slides, PowerPoint and other computer projections and slides projected directly from the computer to the screen. Not everything can be made into a good visual, however. The function of a visual is to illustrate a point and to clarify and fix a factor or image.

■ A film video should have an objective—a specific, stated purpose. It cannot "tell the whole story."

■ The secret of success in placing publicity is to develop a good working relationship with journalists by knowing and anticipating the needs of the media. Efforts usually have two parts: providing the information you want to convey to that medium's public, and responding to inquiries.

■ Specialized wire and video services directly link public relations news to the world's newspaper and broadcast newsrooms. The privately owned publicity services offer simultaneous transmission of news releases and national or even global networks.

■ PR people use the Internet for external publicity and Intranets for internal communication. Posting information and news releases at a Web site makes it available 24 hours a day, and allows for instant updating.

■ The Associated Press wire service uses an "electronic carbon"—a computer-to-computer hookup that allows newspapers to send copies of their local stories instantly into local AP bureau computers.

■ Computer graphics for three-dimensional color designs can be made either with an electronic pen or directly by a computer; laser graphics provide movement and three-dimensional effects.

■ In-house PR use of technology includes access to data banks, word processing, computer generation of art, desktop publishing and communication by videoconferences and electronic mail systems.

■ Public relations people are news managers when they deal with news releases they initiate and when they issue responses to media inquiries.

■ A deadline is the last minute for handling news information; when you are initiating news, let editors know your plans in advance so they can put your story on their schedules. Each story should be prepared in a style and form appropriate to the particular medium.

■ A publicity story generally has a better chance of being accepted by a news medium if you can offer an illustration to go with it.

■ Keep your graphic and photographic files up to date so you aren't caught offering old artwork to a news source when a news opportunity occurs.

■ You should have at least two specific shots in mind before going to "shoot" the event.

■ Don't call a news conference if you can avoid it, and never call one unless you are sure that what is to be said is newsworthy.

■ Words, emblems and gestures all have cultural connotations. Be aware of meanings, especially taboos.

■ For most PR people, the idea of talking back to media is limited to demanding and getting their side of the story presented. However, some PR people aggressively reply to media that they think have wronged them.

NOTES

[1] Jennifer Bingham Hull, "If the Doc's on TV, Maybe It's Because He Takes the PR Rx," *Wall Street Journal* (August 23, 1983), pp. 1, 16.

[2] Victor V. Cordell and George M. Zinkhan, "Dimensional Relationships of Memory: Implications for Print Advertisers," *Journalism Quarterly*, 66(4) (Winter 1989), pp. 954–59.

[3] Bob T. W. Wu, Kenneth E. Crocker and Martha Rogers, "Humor and Comparatives in Ads for High- and Low-Involvement Products," *Journalism Quarterly*, 66(3) (August 1989), pp. 653–61, 780.

[4] Karen S. Johnson-Cartee and Gary Copeland, "Southern Voters' Reaction to Negative Political Ads in 1986 Election," *Journalism Quarterly*, 66(4) (Winter 1989), pp. 888–93, 986.

[5] Frank Thayer, "Measuring Recognition and Attraction in Corporate, Advertising Trademarks," *Journalism Quarterly*, 65(2) (Summer 1985), pp. 439–42.

[6] For production details, such as copyfitting and scaling photographs to fit the designated space, see Doug Newsom and Bob Carrell, *Public Relations Writing: Form & Style*, 5th ed. (Belmont, Calif.: Wadsworth, 1998).

[7] For a full discussion of this topic, see Newsom and Carrell, *Public Relations Writing*, pp. 323–40.

[8] David Mills, "Publications at No Charge Are Subtle Ads," *Wall Street Journal* (August 5, 1983), p. 19. See also Rodney Ho, "Environmental Magazines Defy Slump," *Wall Street Journal* (September 10, 1991), p. B1.

[9] William Ruder and David Finn, *How to Make Your Annual Report Pay for Itself*, second booklet in *Management Methods*, a series on public relations by members of Ruder and Finn, Inc.

[10] N. R. Kleinfield, "An Annual Report Is No Comic Novel, but It Can Be Fun," *Wall Street Journal* (April 15, 1977), pp. 1, 29.

[11] "Formal Guidelines for Reviewing Information Films or Videotapes," *pr reporter* (February 23, 1982), p. 4. For information on writing scripts and speeches, see Newsom and Carrell, *Public Relations Writing*, pp. 375–88.

[12] Michele Horaney, "The Russian President Is Coming . . . No He's Not!" *Public Relations Journal* (August 1990), p. 11.

[13] Details by Jim Haynes on planning an event appear in the *Instructor's Guide* to this text.

[14] "Murphy's Law at Meetings Comes True, Has This Ever Happened to You?" *pr reporter*, 27(10) (March 5, 1984), p. 2.

[15] Jodi B. Katzman, "Interactive Video Gets Bigger Play," *Public Relations Journal*, 51(1) (May 1995), pp. 6–8, 10, 12.

[16] "Formal Guidelines for Reviewing Information Films or Videotapes," *pr reporter* (February 23, 1982), p. 4.

[17] Meg Cox, "Literary World Is Debating How Much of a Huckster a Book Writer Should Be," *Wall Street Journal* (August 2, 1990), pp. B1, B4.

[18] "How Videos Are Tracked," *Public Relations Journal*, 51(1) (May 1995), p. 8.

[19] For the ten pitfalls to avoid in supplying graphics, especially for newspaper use, see James W. Tankard, Jr., "Quantitative Graphics in Newspapers," *Journalism Quarterly*, 64(2&3) (Summer and Autumn 1987), pp. 406–15.

[20] Ben Schneiderman, *Designing the User Interface: Strategies for Effective Human-Computer Interaction* (Reading, MA: Addison-Wesley, 1998), pp. 74–75.

[21] Macon L. Weaver, quoted in Michael Leahy, "Thanks to TV . . . He'll Always Be Remembered for Standing in the Schoolhouse Door," *TV Guide* (April 4, 1987).

[22] Clare Ansberry, "Do People Really Buy Film Based on Entries in a Great Blimp Race?" *Wall Street Journal* (July 8, 1986), p. 33.

[23] Donna M. Lynn, "If the Shoe Fits: The Success of Sports Marketing Programs Seems to Depend on Matching the Right Sports to the Right Mix of Public Relations Objectives," *Public Relations Journal*, 43(2) (February 1987), pp. 16–20, 43.

[24]Bill Richards, "Bright Idea Has Business Looking Up for Ad Blimps," *Wall Street Journal* (Oct. 14, 1997), pp. B1, 8.

[25]Andy Dworkin, "Lighthearted Nicknames Have Serious Side," *Dallas Morning News* (March 15, 1998), pp. H1, 2.

[26]Patrick McGeehan, "Revlon Inc. Throws 'Model' Bonanza At the Big Board to Kick Off Its Stock," *Wall Street Journal* (March 4, 1996), p. 5, B5.

[27] Some negative financial aspects of promotions are detailed in two articles: John Philip Jones, "The Double Jeopardy of Sales Promotions," *Harvard Business Review* (September–October 1990), pp. 145–52; Magid M. Abraham and Leonard M. Lodish, "Getting the Most Out of Advertising and Promotion," *Harvard Business Review* (May–June 1990), pp. 50–60. The latter carries this observation: "Managers must cut back on unproductive promotions in favor of hard-to-imitate promotion events that directly contribute to incremental profitability. And they must use the new data to shape distinctive promotional efforts for specific local markets and key accounts." (p. 50).

[28] Associated Press, "Flyover Foe Gives Ride a Try and Nearly Dies," *Fort Worth Star-Telegram* (June 4, 1990), sec. 1, p. 3.

[29] Andrew Patner, "Papers Take Alternative Path to Success," *Wall Street Journal* (June 19, 1990), p. 31.

[30] Many U.S. publics do not recognize English as their language of choice, and the variety of languages in the United States alone can present a challenge. *PR News* reports that some 100 languages are spoken daily in the southern part of California alone. *PR News*, 66(46) (November 26, 1990), p. 3.

[31] Dan Ammerman, speech to the Texas Public Relations Association, Fort Worth, Texas, February 25, 1978.

[32] *pr reporter* (September 20, 1982), p. 3.

[33] John Martin Meek, "How to Prepare Your Client for Government Testimony," *Public Relations Journal* (November 1985), pp. 35–37.

[34]Peter Waldman, "Please Don't Show Your Lingerie in Iran, Even if It's For Sale," *Wall Street Journal* (June 21, 1995), pp. A1, 8.

[35]Ibid.

[36]Yumiko Ono, "Mouthwash PR Bad-Mouths Star And Other Zlutzy Campaigns," *Wall Street Journal* (Dec. 23, 1997), p. B8.

[37]H.G. Reza, "Flight Called Back to D/FW, Passengers Booted for Angels," *Fort Worth Star-Telegram* (Oct. 1, 1996), p. A10

[38]Wendy Marx, "PR Joins the Interactive Parade," *Advertising Age*, 66(16) (April 17, 1995), p. 15.

[39] Ronald E. Rhody, "The Conventional Wisdom Is Wrong," *Public Relations Journal* (February 1983), pp. 18–31.

[40] Ibid., p. 19.

Selected readings, activities and assignments appropriate to this chapter can be found in the *Instructor's Guide* or on InfoTrac if you are using the InfoTrac College Edition.

CHAPTER 13

CAMPAIGNS

Experience keeps a dear school, but fools will learn in no other, and scarce is that; for it is true, we may give advice, but we cannot give conduct.

BENJAMIN FRANKLIN, *SAYINGS OF POOR RICHARD*

Public relations must move forward from the realm of constructing corporate and institutional images to promoting debate and education on the great issues of our time.

FRANK VOGEL, FORMER DIRECTOR OF INFORMATION AND EXTERNAL RELATIONS, WORLD BANK

The interactions of organizations with their publics provide the setting for specific efforts such as public relations campaigns; such interactions also form the background against which all case studies must be examined. The study of campaigns and cases is more than a shared learning experience or the basis for developing a public relations repertoire; it is ongoing research into what gives an organization viability and credibility in a fluid socioeconomic and political environment that is global in scope. In this chapter we look at the planning, implementation and evaluation of campaigns. In Chapter 14, we look at case studies for analysis and discussion.

TYPES OF CAMPAIGNS

Campaigns are coordinated, purposeful, extended efforts designed to achieve a specific goal or a set of interrelated goals that will move the organization toward a longer-range objective expressed as its mission statement (see Example 13.1).

Campaigns are designed and developed to address an issue, to solve a problem or to correct or improve a situation. They accomplish these purposes by changing a behavior; by modifying a law or opinion; or by retaining a desirable behavior, law or opinion that is challenged.

EXAMPLE 13.1
Campaign Model

MODEL OF THE SUCCESSFUL ORGANIZATION

Begins with, and invests much energy in, a

1. Definitive Mission Statement (Values)
   - the distilled essence of the organization's reason for being
   - implies its positioning, goals, policies.

This is carried out by

2. Corporate Culture (Shared Values)
   - demonstrated by role models, heroes
   - reinforced by rituals, stories
   - the source of teamwork, morale, productivity.

This in turn lets the organization speak with One Clear Voice to penetrate the changing and competitive environment by building

3. Positive Public Relationships (Expressed Values)
   - more than marketing or communication
   - the source of loyalty, credibility, trust.

Over time this creates

4. Reputation (Understood Values)
   - generates latent readiness to like, accept, trust, believe
   - a serendipitous, self-powering force that lies at the core of all human interface
   - epitomized in the old Squibb motto, "The priceless ingredient of every product is the honor & integrity of its maker."

Source: "Opportunity '85: Bring Rigor and Process Management to Building Public Relationships by Creating an Easily Applied and Simple to Explain Conceptional Framework." Reprinted with permission, *pr reporter*, 28(1), (January 7, 1985), and Bob Thompson.

A campaign may be constructed around a *positioning statement*—an objective operating statement for the organization. For example, the American Heart Association decided in the 1980s "to be known as *the* source for information about cardiovascular disease in the U.S." This statement described the organization's central mission: to reduce death from cardiovascular disease. Communication planning is then structured to help the organization achieve its mission, in light of how the organization has positioned itself.

The term *positioning* is often used in marketing to refer to a competitive strategy—a way to identify a niche in the market for a product or service. Public relations people tend to talk about positioning in terms of the entire organization and to build a communications effort around a statement that describes the organization's positioning of itself. When the positioning is to set a new course, it calls for a campaign.

Of course, there are many other reasons for a campaign. Indeed, most organizations have more than one campaign going on at a time. But not all of these campaigns are so central to the organization as to change its positioning or alter its corporate culture.

Various types of PR campaigns exist. Six are described by Patrick Jackson, senior counsel and cofounder of Jackson, Jackson and Wagner, an international firm located in New Hampshire:

There are a number of public relations campaigns, in fact about six. First we have the skills to put on a public awareness campaign, to make people aware of something. School is starting again so please don't run over first graders on their way. Simple awareness.

Second, we have the skills to mount public information campaigns, to offer information along with awareness. Totally different than a simple awareness campaign.

Third, we have the skills to do a public educa-tion campaign, using the word education in the peda-gogical way, meaning that a person has encompassed the material sufficiently, and is emotionally and atti-tudinally comfortable enough with it that he or she can actually apply it to daily behavior. We have the skills to run those campaigns.

But there are other kinds of campaigns that we must also prepare. Fourth, sometimes we must reen-force the attitudes and behavior of those who are in agreement with our position. All they may need is a reminder of shared values.

And sometimes, fifth, we have to change or at-tempt to change the attitudes of those who do not agree with our position. This requires creation of cog-nitive dissonance and is much tougher.

Sixth, and finally, we have the skills today to carry out behavior modification campaigns. To convince people, for instance, that they ought to wear their seatbelts or that drunk driving is neither in their nor society's best interest. These are light years differ-ent from awareness or information campaigns.

These six types of public relations activity—and this is my list, of course; you should make your own and it may have five or eight types—are the process of our field. But note that each type attempts to moti-vate different levels of behavior. That's the reason we mount the campaigns. It's a little hard for us to deny, therefore, that behavior is the outcome we seek— not the thinking or feeling or even social interaction that precedes behavior. They are the means to an end.[1] *[Emphasis added.]*

CHARACTERISTICS OF SUCCESSFUL CAMPAIGNS

Regardless of how you categorize campaigns, expe-rience suggests that successful ones share some ba-sic principles and characteristics. Five principles of successful campaigns can be identified: (1) assess-ment of the needs, goals and capabilities of priority publics; (2) systematic campaign planning and pro-duction; (3) continuous monitoring and evaluation to see what is working and where extra effort needs

to be made; (4) consideration of the complemen-tary roles of mass media and interpersonal commu-nication; (5) selection of the appropriate media for each priority public, with due consideration of that medium's ability to deliver the message.

Studies of successful campaigns indicate that five elements or characteristics are always present. First is the *educational* aspect of a campaign. A cam-paign should always enlighten its publics—telling them something they didn't know or giving them a different perspective or way of looking at some-thing they already knew, or thought they knew.

The second element is *engineering*—a factor critical to behavior change, which is the objective of almost all campaigns. Engineering involves en-suring that the means are there (and convenient) for publics to do what you want them to do. Thus, if you want them to throw trash in containers in-stead of on the ground, the containers must be conveniently located. (One city put slanted barrels on the median at left turn signals so that drivers waiting for the green arrow could dump trash there instead of pitching it out the window.) Asking women in developing nations to have their chil-dren inoculated against disease can only achieve the desired result if the doctors and the serums are readily available—probably taken to women and their children in the villages. You can't expect a woman who works from daylight to dusk, and often beyond, to take a day off to walk miles carrying an infant to get a shot and then to walk miles back carrying the same, now unhappy, child.

The third element of successful campaigns is *enforcement*. There must be something beyond in-centive to underscore the significance of the cam-paign. Many automobile seatbelt campaigns went through the education and engineering phases but failed to elicit behavior change until laws approved fines for noncompliance. The same has been true for campaigns in favor of wearing motorcycle hel-mets, and in many developed nations for cam-paigns to inoculate children. Today children are not allowed to attend school until they can prove that they have had certain inoculations.

The fourth element in successful campaigns is *entitlement*, which is also a form of *reinforcement*.

Entitlement means that publics are convinced of the value of the appeals of the campaign and in a sense "buy into" the message. This helps with reinforcement, because it extends the message statement by having others outside the campaign give it voice. Such reinforcement is needed not only because people forget, but because new members of a public are added daily, and continuing messages have to be available for them. Those who are complying also need the reinforcement, so they will continue to do what they have been doing. The "Smokey Bear" campaign in the United States to prevent forest fires is one of the most successful information campaigns ever; it's more than 40 years old and still going, as the need for it remains as great as ever.

Evaluation of a campaign is the fifth significant element. In ongoing campaigns like Smokey, there are annual evaluations, as well as three- and five-year checks. The same is true for public health organizations like the March of Dimes, which looks each year at its "walk" to see what the focus should be and has changed that focus from time to time as a result of these evaluations. The evaluation is a campaign's report card. It identifies what kind of desired behavior change occurred, when and in which publics.

PLANNING A CAMPAIGN

As discussed in Chapter 10, the first task in planning a campaign is to look at the organization's mission statement in order to clarify the objectives and goals of the PR program (see Example 13.2). Within the limits of the organization's objectives and goals, you must set those for the PR program that your research suggests are needed. Define the objectives—what you want to accomplish—as precisely as possible and in long-range terms. Then attach measures to your short-range goals. A clear statement of goals means you will be able to evaluate the success of your campaign because you can measure how close you came to achieving them or by how much you surpassed what you expected.

Look critically at the goals you've set, and ask some probing questions. Are they compatible with the current PR program? Where are they headed, ultimately? Would any conflict with your institution's policy? Is there possible conflict with a major public? With any particular public? How significant is the conflict? Could it destroy a program? More pragmatically, how will you measure success along the way?

You must clearly delineate your publics before planning your strategy. The demographics and psychographics will give you insight into the tactics you should employ to make your strategy succeed. Demographics comprises objective, statistical data like age, sex, education and income. Psychographics comprises the value statements you can make about audiences, their lifestyles, their likes and their dislikes. Part of your strategy involves deciding the most effective way to reach each public. What do you want to have happen as a result of the communication? How far do you need to take a public to get that to happen? Since there are six steps in the persuasion process, a public is likely to be at *one* of the six levels. You have to reach them at that level and bring them along through the other levels to acting (see Chapter 7).

Setting Goals, Timetables and Budgets

Results can be identified on several levels. Suppose, for example, that you are in charge of public relations for the local public library system. Your first goal may be to get a bond issue for a new library passed. But you also want to increase awareness of library services in specific areas and, perhaps, to stimulate demand for more bookmobiles to serve more distant areas. You may lose the bond issue, but if results are positive with the other two objectives, you will have accumulated ammunition that can be used at future budget hearings to help increase services and to provide more bookmobiles.

Estimates or timetables for achieving results need be no more elaborate than a marked calendar, but the deadlines must be realistic, given the objectives involved. Allow for foul-up time, and

EXAMPLE 13.2
Organization's Mission Statement

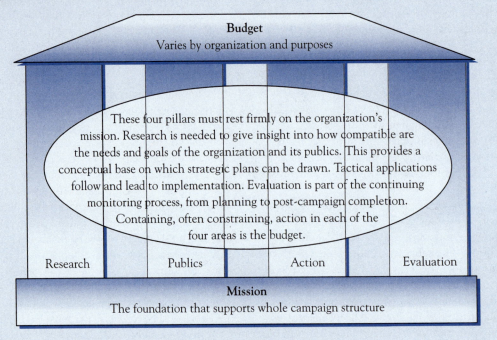

Budget
Varies by organization and purposes

These four pillars must rest firmly on the organization's mission. Research is needed to give insight into how compatible are the needs and goals of the organization and its publics. This provides a conceptual base on which strategic plans can be drawn. Tactical applications follow and lead to implementation. Evaluation is part of the continuing monitoring process, from planning to post-campaign completion. Containing, often constraining, action in each of the four areas is the budget.

Research   Publics   Action   Evaluation

Mission
The foundation that supports whole campaign structure

The organization's mission statement governs all action and functions as a foundation.

Initial *research* is a *situational analysis* of organizational strengths, weaknesses, objectives, product/service/idea being offered, publics (characteristics, segments, priority, behavior), opposition or competition, media (tools and tactics) and previous experience with communication elements.

Organizational objectives include the objectives of the organization's total program and how the campaign is to help achieve them.

Publics are considered by priority, in terms of the expected behavior for each segment and also by area and by time elements.

try to finish work ahead of schedule. Avoid the need to explain continually why you are behind. Contingency planning means deciding in advance who will pick up the ball if someone drops it and what effect the substitution will have. Downtime from mistakes can be reduced considerably if you have a realistic timetable. Don't crowd yourself or your staff. Consider how to integrate the project into the overall schedule of PR activities so it

won't conflict with regular duties such as writing the annual report or preparing for a stockholders' meeting. If necessary, allow for calling in extra clerical help when there is an overload.

You have to know at this point whether you are working from your department's regular allocated budget or from a special project budget. If it is a special project budget, you must know its size and be aware of whatever conditions or restrictions

Once the analysis is complete, and once organizational objectives have been studied in light of the analysis and publics studied, the size of the total communication campaign budget is reviewed.

A *tentative budget mix* is developed with proportions assigned to communication elements such as publicity, advertising, promotion, marketing—such as product or service trials or sampling, merchandising—including possible changes in presentation or packaging, monitoring of each element during the campaign and evaluation measures.

The *public relations budget* fits with other organizational resources such as marketing, human relations and information systems.

Action communication goals are set for each public in general terms and specifically for segments of priority publics.

Message strategy, positioning and format are created to present the organization the way it wants to be seen in the campaign by all publics.

Tactics are developed to use specific media for a message distribution plan that includes all events and all publics.

Budget allocations either are special allocations for phases of the campaign or are designated by categories such as publicity, promotion and special events.

A *timetable* is detailed to specify implementation by particular *action* and to identify the *person responsible* for seeing that it happens, and designated *reporting procedures* are outlined.

Evaluation is undertaken for control during the campaign and for a final assessment. There is continuous measurement of effects for all campaign aspects, adjustment as monitoring suggests by time, area and publics. The final evaluation of the campaign effects is set against the accomplishment of measurable goals and how these goals help the organization meet overall organizational objectives.

Source: Adapted from Michael L. Ray, *Advertising and Communication Management* (Englewood Cliffs, N.J.: Prentice-Hall, 1982) forepiece, and Russell H. Colley, *Defining Advertising Goals* (Association of National Advertisers, Inc., 1961), where Colley distinguishes between marketing *objectives* and the achievement of specific, measurable advertising *goals* toward that objective. This was the "management by objective" technique (MBO) (a much older concept) as applied to advertising. Public relations people were even later in adapting the MBO to PR.

are being placed on it. Alternatively, the budget may be a mixture of your regular budget plus specific additional amounts for specific purposes. It might also be that some money must be raised before your budget is complete. Accurate knowledge of your budget will allow you to see what extra help you can contract for, how creative you can get, which media you can use and how often you can go to them.

Setting Creative Strategy: Choosing Theme and Media

The success or failure of a PR campaign depends largely on your creativity—in deciding on the theme, in choosing the media and in using the media. Go back and ask what you expect to achieve. How will you monitor progress toward that expectation, and how will you measure results?

What does each public need to know? What is the best way to say it? What would be the most likely way to get that public's attention? This is where creativity—in use of words or symbols in an original approach to the medium—makes the difference.

The theme may be determined in a number of ways—from several persons brainstorming together, from one person's new idea or from adaptation of someone else's successful idea. It is important to entertain *all* ideas without passing judgment. Criticism kills creativity and may snuff out a potentially good idea at birth. Stimulate people to share ideas—no matter how wild—by offering encouragement and enthusiasm. A good theme won't save a poorly executed campaign, but well-oiled campaign machinery won't save a bad idea either. You also need to pretest ideas as well as completed materials, getting feedback from the publics.

Your choice of media depends both on the publics you want to reach and on the message you want to deliver. You should be able to make a preliminary decision as to which media are right once your goals are determined; however, the *creative choice* of media is something different. What is a unique way to reach a special public? What media have not been used before but could be? Someone, after all, was the first to use bumper stickers, skywriting and silk-screened T-shirts.

The *creative use* of media is also important. A media schedule that lists which media to use and when can be the key to a campaign's success—and also to its failure. Cereal companies that began advertising in the comics might have been laughed at by those who advertised in women's pages, but the comic-page advertisers knew who their real consumers were and how to reach them. A PR person has to be careful about the complementary use of advertising and publicity. Advertising is definite, scheduled communication that appears along with whatever planned activities it is designed to promote. Publicity is indefinite communication that cannot be guaranteed except in controlled media. If the planned activities are newsworthy enough, mass media attention may result.

In both advertising and publicity, you are presenting a message—information. People either seek information or just process it. If involved enough in the subject to seek information, they are not likely to turn to mass media, says PR researcher James E. Grunig.[2] Grunig found that only people with extra time to spend are exposed to mass media. The more active people are, the less time they spend with mass media. To reach the involved, you need to use specialized publications because that is where people actively seeking information on the subject go. However, if you are aiming for low public involvement and perhaps just want exposure to an issue, then a mass medium is appropriate, especially one like television that forces audiences to process information. Remember, though, that the public you most want to reach might not be there, and your effort (if publicity) or expense (if advertising) may be wasted.

Your budget has a great deal to do with how much flexibility you have in choosing media, and with how many publics you can reach effectively.

■ Contingency Planning

One cheerful PR person says his smile is the result of always anticipating the worst that could happen, and then being pleasantly surprised when it doesn't. Undesirable possible outcomes always have to be kept in the back of your mind. What if a billboard company confuses dates, and your ads don't go up on time? Can you use newspaper advertising and radio or TV commercials to take up the slack? What if your publicity is pushed off the news by a disaster or other breaking story? What if your TV time is preempted? Flexibility and contingency plans are needed.

A PR director can get help in contingency planning from his or her staff. Not only will the staff make creative suggestions and come up with good alternative proposals, but they will support the project, particularly when it is likely to consume a lot of their time. The director should evaluate accurately and honestly what each individual can best contribute to the project (and should think about individuals' talents rather than just about the jobs each has done before). After the project proposal is accepted by management, the director must write down everyone's duties and responsibilities to avoid misunderstandings over who does what and when.

Remember to allow for contingencies in the timetable, too. Build in some leeway, or one missed deadline will jeopardize the entire effort. Elasticity in the schedule will also allow you to take advantage of opportunities and make changes.

You will undoubtedly experience having some critical element in a project barely make it—programs delivered from the printers with the ink barely dry, artwork delivered only an hour before it is needed for production. But if a PR director allows this to happen often, his or her staff will find the work environment too harrowing and unpleasant, and the PR practitioner will risk his or her mental and physical health as well as job and reputation.

Setting Internal Strategy: Selling the Program Within the Organization

After you have set your goals, you must plan the strategy you will use to achieve them. One of your first tasks in mapping your strategy is to sell your plan to management. You do this with a carefully reasoned and well-designed presentation, based at least in part on what has received approval in the past.

People doing a job tend to get so caught up in their enthusiasm that they forget that others, including top management, may not know what they are supposed to be doing or why. In addition, some CEOs demand to know more than others, and some are more quantitatively oriented than others. Cultural differences can complicate matters, too. One U.S. employee in a Japanese company was excited by some successful promotions, but in reporting these to his Japanese boss, he had his enthusiasm considerably dampened by questions like: "How much are you going to spend? What are you going to accomplish? How much more are you going to sell next month, next quarter, next year as a result?" He resisted, but finally was pushed into putting numbers on the board for the demanding manager.[3]

The greatest danger in presenting a plan rests in failing to anticipate questions and challenges. Listen to opposing points of view, but maintain control and do not allow "a good plan to get nibbled to death," as one PR director put it, before you have a chance to test its effectiveness. One PR director who has to work in a hostile climate makes a practice of duplicating her presentations and circulating them to management instead of calling a conference, because she says people will approve ideas on paper that they would never approve in an open meeting. If necessary, show your plan to several important people first, so you can anticipate the reception it will get, before you actually present it formally. The whole process is not unlike caucusing in politics before calling for a committee vote. Much verbal battle can be eliminated by careful listening in the planning stages.

IMPLEMENTING THE CAMPAIGN

Implementing the project involves adapting and applying tactics to strategies while adhering to the timetable and budget, keeping people informed and solving problems positively.

Adapting and Applying Tactics to Strategies

The framework for your whole campaign must be suited to its institutional environment (either a closed or an open communication system), as determined by top management. This is not synonymous with proaction and reaction. A campaign *is* proactive. But some campaigns are mounted by closed communication organizations.

You will choose messages and messengers for *each* public, drawn from what your research tells you are the best choices. You will select a master communications strategy—a functional strategy based on differentiation, segmentation or modification. This, with other factors such as what your image research tells you is the goal to be achieved, will determine your campaign's emphasis—publicity, advertising and/or promotion. You will set persuasive strategies for your publics because you want to make sure that something happens.

You will use tactics to shape specific messages for delivery to each public in order to achieve the purpose you have determined. You have to keep on a schedule and within the budget in making these choices. If the publicity writer says it is impossible to get the information needed for a story in time for it to go into the media kit as scheduled, determine how long the delay may be, set an absolute deadline and make sure it is one you can live with. Most importantly, keep people informed of changes as well as of first plans. Most foul-ups occur because one person does not know the problems besetting another person whose work is related.

■ Keeping People Informed

There are many ways to solve internal communications problems. The head of one small PR firm, noting that his staffers headed for the coffeepot between 9:30 and 10:00 A.M., scheduled a coffee-break conference time with free doughnuts. In persuading his staff members to sit for a while and discuss their successes and problems, he helped them integrate their staff work. Staffers, hearing the problems of others, discovered how their own timetables were going to be affected.

The chief executive of a larger PR operation, after observing the most horrendous arguments among his staff over who was to blame for a delay, insisted that written communications be sent to everyone. Although he admits that sometimes snafus still occur, he says it is only because someone did not read a communique. Some companies use computer message systems so that memos are waiting when a terminal is turned on each morning. Faxes are useful too, not only in communicating but also in creating a "hard copy" record that can be filed and referred to when questions arise.

A multibranch operation has another alternative to written communication: a weekly loudspeaker telephone conference (telecon). Every week the advertising and PR staff of a Dallas company, for example, sit around a conference table

with a phone loudspeaker operation hooked up to their counterparts in branch offices in other parts of the country. Each person summarizes what he or she is doing and outlines travel plans. As a result of the conference, plans are frequently changed. It may be brought out that someone from Dallas and someone from Chicago are both heading for, say, a plant in Montreal. The PR corporate director, then, can tell the Chicago person to take care of both assignments, thereby reducing costs in travel expenses and staff. And videoconferencing is becoming increasingly common.

■ Solving Problems Positively

Still, even in the most carefully planned and well-managed effort, complications and confusion do occur. The important thing is to resolve each problem and get the job done successfully. Placing blame wastes time and energy and can damage working relationships. Good working relationships are imperative for smooth functioning any time, but particularly where personal relationships can facilitate or impede (or even destroy) the public relations program.

Whatever the PR projects, all internal publics should be kept informed. This is easy to overlook, especially when there is dynamic leadership. For instance, the director of a concert group that suddenly was given the opportunity to tour Europe was about to relay the story to the news media when someone suggested that the concert group's board of directors should be asked first to grant permission for the tour. Although approval seemed certain, and asking for it necessitated calling each of the twenty-three directors, the effort was worthwhile, because people in authority feel their status has been undermined when they learn of important actions first from the newspapers.

Pleasing everyone is impossible, but the PR practitioner who works according to policy—real policy, not "unwritten policy"—is usually safe. Unwritten policies may seem as compelling as written ones, but persistence and diplomacy can often change them—although this may be difficult if they represent the principal interests of the major stockholders. Written policy generally is much less flexible and should be followed carefully until changes are adopted. Policies can be changed by the bold, but you must first devise a strong justification for the change and then determine how to sell it to the publics involved, anticipating how they will perceive it.

EVALUATING THE CAMPAIGN

Two types of evaluations have to occur in a campaign: monitoring and postmortems.

■ Monitoring

You need an ongoing system for monitoring all major activities. Some measures can be unobtrusive, such as counting the number of color-coded tickets collected for an event, the number of gift certificates redeemed or the number of phone calls received. Other areas require the more careful monitoring of formal research (see Chapter 6). Monitoring is important in a campaign because you may need to change directions, reallocate resources or redefine priorities to achieve your objective. Monitoring makes it possible, for instance, for political candidates during a campaign to increase television exposure in an area where their name recognition or support is low or to arrange for an unscheduled appearance in the area.

Although results of such monitoring are less visible in other types of campaigns, the need to monitor remains. Think about it on a personal level. You wouldn't want to plan a party, send out invitations and not know if anyone was coming. You would be buying food or guaranteeing a certain turnout for a caterer. Before you did these things, you would certainly want to know how many people to expect.

■ Postmortems

Every PR campaign deserves a thorough and honest autopsy. What worked, what didn't and why? What was accidentally a success? What could have been done better?

Formal research is needed here. You need to uncover some solid evidence that objectives were achieved or not achieved. You need to establish what missed the mark and by how much. Anecdotal evaluation is useful and often insightful, but it does not make a good budget defense.

To make a postmortem successful, you must keep all analyses on a professional level; no witchhunts should be permitted. If something did not work, there is usually more than one reason for its failure and more than one person responsible. Use constructive criticism to suggest, "if we had attempted to do this, would it have worked better than what we did try?" Egos, especially creative egos, are fragile things, yet no one minds looking in the mirror unless she or he sees someone in the background pointing an accusing finger.

As mentioned in Chapter 6, you need to evaluate several results. These include the impact on publics; the effect on the organization's goals and mission; the effect on the attitudes of publics toward the organization and on their perception of the organization; and the effects on the organization's financial status, ethical stance and social responsibility.

The most effective evaluations are continuing programs—for instance, annual surveys of what audiences like or dislike, surveys of employee attitudes and measurements of consumer attitudes. Evaluations may also be done by reading letters and taking phone calls from happy and unhappy publics and by talking with various publics to ascertain their attitudes. These give you benchmarks against which to measure a campaign's effects. If you say after a campaign, "It's all over, we can forget it," instead of instituting an ongoing evaluation program, you will put yourself in the position of, as one astute advertising executive put it, "constantly reinventing the wheel."

Although this discussion has addressed campaigns mounted for a specific purpose and for a specific period of time, an organization should have an overall public relations program tied to its fundamental mission and goals. This should be a written program complete with rationale, policy support statements, listed priorities, identified publics and illustrations of the tools to be used. Most

Reprinted with special permission of North America Syndicate.

importantly, it should receive top management endorsement, just as budgets do.

In each campaign you need to look for the "self-interest" appeal being made to each target audience—the key to all effective communication. Search out the other communication strategies in message structure and media delivery that have proved successful (or unsuccessful) in informing and influencing the target audience.[4] Look beyond the specific strategies to find their base in some general concept that you can apply to other campaigns. Then plan your program by integrating all of these elements into a flexible and feasible timetable, and secure management and staff support. Select media that will ensure successful and on-time implementation of the program. Finally, evaluate the results or effectiveness of the program through formal post-program research and through less formal methods of responses from staff and publics. You are measuring for financial impact, ethical impact and social responsibility.

CAMPAIGN OUTLINE

Before narrowing our focus to the issue of changing behavior, let's review the steps involved in the whole process of developing and executing a campaign. In summary:

■ Define the problem. Set goals for the *campaign* within an organizational framework.

■ Evaluate the impact of the problem on publics and on the organization, and define clearly the issues involved in the problem.
■ Develop an organizational strategy consonant with the mission.
■ Determine a communication strategy to reach the stated goals.
■ Plan actions, themes and appeals to publics. In developing a functional strategy, plan where the emphasis will be—ads, publicity and/or promotion.
■ Develop an organizational responsibilities plan, with budgets and timetables.
■ Decide which tactics fit the strategy best and how you will monitor each aspect.
■ Evaluate the results or effectiveness of the program.

CHANGING BEHAVIOR

Public relations practitioners are often depicted as masters of manipulative techniques designed to get people to think or act in a certain way. And in fact most campaigns do strive to produce behavior changes. This is the case even when campaigns start at the awareness level, since the purpose of a campaign to create awareness (of a problem, of a product or service or of a person) is ultimately to get action. The same goes for "information campaigns" as well: what is desired is action, which may mean getting people to behave differently from how they usually behave.

The ethical question of the propriety of such campaigns is not always raised, especially when the campaign appears to reflect majority social values. But sources behind the campaign pay for it, and their values or "social agenda" may not match that of individuals who lack the means and (in some cases) the access to communicate through public and private media. Imbalances of means and access are part of the concern over development campaigns in some countries. These "public information campaigns" usually are handled by the government, which may not allow much input from those who are the objects of the campaign. All information campaigns, Charles T. Salmon says, represent weapons in conflicts of interest, and social intervention involves conflicts of values.[5]

A successful campaign—one that changes behavior—has three elements, according to the U.S. Forest Service: education, engineering and enforcement.[6] The educational part consists of telling people what you want them to do, which in the case of the Forest Service was to refrain from destroying the forest. The second step, engineering, enables people to accomplish what you are asking. To this end, the Forest Service built "fire-safe" camp sites and put up steel signs that were difficult to vandalize. The third step is enforcement, where the will of the people begins to get restricted. Laws were enacted to protect the national forests, and people who failed to obey the laws became subject to fines. Regulations also permit access to forests to be restricted if the Forest Service determines that the danger of damage to the forest is too high.

But laws can be overturned, or people can flagrantly violate them. What is it that makes people accept and obey? William Paisley says that, because the public in the USA accepts the notion of a "free marketplace of ideas," campaigns (even conflicting ones) are common. But to gain public support, a social issues campaign must get on the public agenda of issues, and the issue must be seen as having some public merit.[7]

Then, in addressing the merit of an issue, a fourth "E"—entitlement—is added to the list of campaign elements.[8] Some public issues are seen as obligations and others as opportunities, but entitlement involves laws, public policy and public acceptance. Laws can be upheld or changed, and laws tend to change with society's social agenda, as drinking age laws illustrate. Public policy becomes a part of the entitlement consideration when more than one group or agency claims a social issue; and certainly environmental issues of all kinds have multiple sponsors who usually carve out their own part of the issue and try to make the identification with it distinctive. The final part of entitlement, as Paisley sees it, is public acceptance. In the USA, the issue requires association with first-party stakeholders—those whom the issue affects directly—to have credibility and thus win widespread public support. The fifth "E" is evaluation.[9]

Who Is Entitled?

Whether the government should decide what's best for everyone or whether those who are governed should participate in the decision-making process is at the root of most social issues.

Getting Grassroots Involvement

Changing behavior works best when the people who are being asked to change are encouraged to participate in formulating the behavioral goals. Top-down information campaigns in most countries are doomed to failure. On the other hand, if members of the public become partners in the planning, they share ego involvement in the push for successful outcome; and self-persuasion is a major ingredient.

A good example is the campaign by the Crime Prevention Coalition, using McGruff the Crime Dog and the slogan "Taking a Bite out of Crime." The program has been implemented through local police departments, which handle the campaign materials—videos, brochures and other information on how to protect yourself from crime. These efforts, reinforced by a media campaign, show McGruff dressed in a fedora and trenchcoat. The dog is a favorite with children, who take messages home from school and also take part in the watch program. Neighborhood watch

EXAMPLE 13.3

MADD Billboard

For this billboard, Mothers Against Drunk Driving used the actual wreck of a car in which a man and his three young children were killed by a speeding pickup truck whose driver was drunk. The car's engine block had to be removed so the sign could support the wrecked frame; but five months after the accident, and with the help of five different agencies, the car was mounted on a billboard on a heavily traveled freeway between Minneapolis and St. Paul. It immediately caught the attention of national and international media, including Time and Newsweek magazines.

Source: Used with the permission of MADD, Minnesota State Office.

programs are a major ingredient of the campaign. The focus on community partnerships means that the program takes on a slightly different character for each community.[10]

Community involvement has always been a part of the MADD (Mothers Against Drunk Driving) movement, which has community chapters and state offices. MADD's Minnesota State office put up a billboard that included the actual car in which a man and his three children were killed (see Example 13.3).

The billboard was a shocker, drawing national and international media attention. The victims in the crash were a 36-year-old University of Minnesota agricultural researcher from Nigeria and his

three young children. All were killed instantly on September 28, 1989, when their Toyota was so crumpled when struck by a speeding pickup truck that the rear end of the car was pushed to within 6 inches of the dashboard. The accident scene was so hideous that rescue workers called to it had to undergo counseling later to overcome what they had witnessed. There were no skid marks from the pickup truck, which slammed into Ojobona Oju's car at 65 miles per hour. Its drunk driver had himself lost a leg to a drunk driver in 1981.

The idea for putting the crumpled car on the billboard came from a retired public relations director who felt it would send a strong message. Implementing the idea wasn't easy. The widow had returned to Nigeria, with her entire family in coffins in the plane's cargo hold. She had to be located to get a release. The car itself couldn't be released until after the driver, Brian Patterson, was tried and all criminal charges against him adjudicated. (He was sentenced to 63 months in prison and an additional 10 years of probation, during which time he must totally abstain from alcohol and nonprescription drugs.)[11]

The MADD billboard joins other dramatic and controversial signs of the times. One of the most controversial artists is Mark Heckman of Grand Rapids, Michigan. Many of Heckman's clients are private individuals who want to make a political statement. Sometimes his billboards are so provocative that they get a response from "the other side." When the Gannett outdoor sign company put up Heckman's billboard urging people to fight AIDS by wearing condoms, a Grand Rapids businessman threatened to cancel his own billboard. A Kalamazoo group later leased the same billboard for its message: "Abstinence! It beats AIDS."[12]

Billboards often play an important role in development communication campaigns, and they often rely on drama and symbols more than on words. That's important, given the communications problems of a high rate of illiteracy and/or a multiplicity of languages. Language problems make radio an important campaign medium, as well. Unfortunately, many development campaigns have depended on mass media and top–down message construction, with no development of infrastructures to make carrying out the messages possible. The result has been some information or education about what the government wants people to do, but not much in the way of "engineering" to see that it's feasible, and very little interactivity and feedback, although this is improving as governments realize that even authoritarian governments need "entitlement" to gain compliance.

One type of campaign that has received widespread mass media attention is the campaign for population control. Although various countries' experiences could be cited, the pattern is the same for many. Billboards and radio spots carry slogans

and jingles. In some countries, television is also used, especially soap operas. A few countries have tried taking folk media, puppets and plays to outlying villages.

These campaigns encounter at least two basic problems. First, the message of having few children appears to make little sense in a rural community where many hands are needed and mortality rates are high. Second, too few family-oriented clinics or health programs may be available for followup counseling and materials, and in any case the male typically makes most of the family-planning decisions. Women living in these societies could tell the planners why their messages won't work, but while many people might talk to them, few people ask them anything and even fewer listen.

One difficulty in getting useful interaction with or feedback from people in many countries relates to their social relationships. Recognizing this problem, Hernando Gonzáles has offered a revised interpretation of the interactive model that doesn't look at the flow of information up or down in situations where status and power are likely designators.[13] Instead, his model looks at the already established norms of interactivity, with a view toward building coalitions so that power can accrue to these groups, which can then act as representative voices.

One campaign that did seek help from its publics with message development was Family Health International's population control/health campaign in the Caribbean. FHI is a nonprofit organization. The campaign, "Condoms . . . Because You Care," was developed by AIDSTECH[14] with funding from USAID (see Example 13.4).

GOVERNMENT CAMPAIGNS

Most countries have some sort of government agency responsible for conducting campaigns for the country as a whole. These often deal with issues of population control in countries such as China and India, economic restructuring in newly democratized countries such as Romania and Bulgaria and tourism in Mexico and many island nations.

EXAMPLE 13.4

Public-Generated Messages for a Caribbean Campaign

"CONDOMS . . . BECAUSE YOU CARE"

The Creation of a Condom Promotion Campaign in the Eastern Caribbean, December 1990

The campaign button and the poster carry messages generated by their publics and the entire promotion was built on field research.

The condom promotion campaign was initiated on 26 November, 1990. Preliminary evaluation data (see chart) demonstrate changes in condom sales (83%) before and after campaign implementation from randomly selected outlets.

In addition, qualitative research (focus groups) with shop owners and members of the target audience indicate very high message recognition for all aspects of the campaign. For example, in initial campaign design, focus group participants were unable to recognize the condom "symbol" without the word "condoms" beneath it. One year later, focus group participants demonstrated high awareness of the campaign: symbol recognition without the defining word was high. In addition, familiarity with the poster (tested without the text) was also high, and responses to the graphics and text separately were equally positive.

Shop owners indicated that both condom sales and discussion about condoms in shops had increased noticeably and that people responded very favorably to the display boxes. Many shops requested that the artwork also be produced on the back of the box so that they can turn the box around if they wish to have the dispensing slot facing the shop clerk rather than the customer. Additional boxes were printed with artwork on both sides.

Response to the campaign was so positive that two additional steps were initiated to expand the program:

1. Installation of condom promotion materials and display boxes in all Ministry of Health clinics nation-wide as part of their condom distribution system.

2. Training of CBD outlet managers in condom sales and logistics strategies to further increase numbers of condoms purchased.

EXECUTIVE SUMMARY

A series of focus groups and interviews were conducted in Antigua and Dominica to pre-test several ideas for use in a condom promotion campaign that had been designed based on prior field research. The participants in the various aspects of the qualitative research provided input in the selection of the text for a condom promotion poster, as well as for the graphics and standardized condom symbol to be used as point-of-purchase materials in the community-based distribution outlets in the Eastern Caribbean. Interview participants, both men and women, responded most favorably to the poster text of **"It's not the end of anything. Its only the beginning.**

Condoms . . . Because You Care." Focus group participants—young men, older men, and young women—strongly favored the "Cool Man and Woman" visual (close-ups of man and woman on front of display box) for the point-of-purchase materials and made concrete recommendations for changes in the current design to make it more appealing and target-audience specific. Of the range of choices, condom symbol #4 was chosen (among the 5 options) as representative of the preferred style; the color preference, however, tended much more strongly toward the bright blues, greens and pinks. Recommendations, therefore, were made for the needed changes in the picture and the condom symbol.

E X A M P L E 1 3 . 4 *(c o n t i n u e d)*

"Condoms...Because You Care"
A Lifestyle Approach to Condom
Promotion in the Eastern Caribbean

Ostfield, Marc[*]; Fevrier, W[**]; Jagdeo, T[***]; Cole, L[*]; France, B[*].
[*]AIDSTECH, Family Health International, RTP, NC, USA
[**]Dominica Planned Parenthood Assoc., Dominica, West Indies
[***]Caribbean Family Planning Affiliation, Antigua, West Indies

Goal: To reduce the spread of HIV in the Eastern Caribbean by changing social norms about condoms in order to increase condom sales and use.

Methodology: This campaign uses an innovative approach to position condoms in a "lifestyle" format — associating condoms with the "good life," the things that the "in" people use, rather than linking condoms with AIDS, family planning, or general health messages. The campaign seeks to make it more comfortable for people to discuss condoms by altering social norms and reducing the stigma associated with condom purchase and use.

Strategy: The campaign uses a range of promotional and point-of-purchase materials to convey the carefully designed "lifestyle" message in Community-Based Distribution (CBD) outlets (such as shops and bars) in the Eastern Caribbean nation of Dominica (pop. 82,000): (1) a poster developed in conjunction with the Caribbean Family Planning Affiliation, (2) a display/ distribution box, durable enough for long-term use and easy to assemble, (3) a sticker with a condom symbol for CBD outlets to indicate "condoms available here," (4) a button with the "lifestyle" tag message for all CBD outlets.

Results: The promotional campaign was initiated 26 November, 1990. Data below demonstrate changes in condom sales before and after campaign implementation from randomly selected outlets. A dramatic increase (83.15%) occurred in average monthly condom sales across sites following campaign implementation in all CBD outlets.

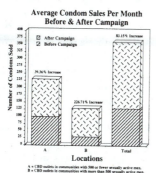

Average Condom Sales Per Month Before & After Campaign

A = CBD outlets in communities with 500 or fewer sexually active men.
B = CBD outlets in communities with more than 500 sexually active men.
(Number of sexually active men is based on an estimate of 25% of the total population).

Conclusion: Condom sales can be increased in Community-Based Distribution outlets, with a relatively small amount of promotional work using a "lifestyle" message in innovative ways to change social norms. The use of additional channels of communication such as radio or television, which were not utilized in this campaign, may significantly increase the impact of such a campaign on condom sales. Further evaluation will measure changes in non-CBD sales, reported usage, and campaign recognition.

Funding: Partial support for this project was provided by AIDSTECH/Family Health International with funds from the Regional Development Office/Caribbean of the United States Agency for International Development.

(continued)

EXAMPLE 13.4 *(continued)*

BACKGROUND

This project grew out of AIDSTECH's work in the Eastern Caribbean during the course of the past year. The staff at the Dominica Planned Parenthood Association and at the Health Education Office of the Ministry of Health, as well as in similar offices in other Eastern Caribbean nations, had requested assistance in effective ways to promote condoms that were being sold in their community-based distribution (CBD) outlets (bars and shops in villages throughout the country). Currently, all condoms sold in the CBD shops were sold directly from their white, A.I.D. boxes; as a result, they were not very visible in the shops and customers often did not know that they were even available. The shop owners were interested in promoting condom sales, both for health and financial reasons.

Simultaneously, AIDSTECH began negotiations with Dr. Tirbani Jagdeo, Chief Executive Officer of the Caribbean Family Planning Affiliation (CFPA), about the possibility of designing and distributing a regional condom promotion poster—one that was not specific to AIDS, STDs, or Family Planning. CFPA took a leading role in the design and distribution of positive, well-received posters to promote Family Planning messages throughout the Caribbean. AIDSTECH had been impressed with CFPA's work and track record and approached them about the condom poster idea. CFPA was enthusiastic about the project and arranged to work with AIDSTECH creative staff in the poster design.

The idea for this project grew out of conversations between AIDSTECH staff and Family Planning Associations in a variety of OECS nations in the Fall of 1989. Dominica was selected as the pilot country for this campaign because of its strong interest in the program and its well-organized CBD system and meticulous record-keeping detailing numbers of condoms sold in all CBD outlets throughout the country. AIDSTECH began its field work on this project in early 1990, with initial field research (including interviews with Family Planning personnel, shopkeepers, and MOH staff in several countries) conducted January through March of that year. Based on the data collected, a graphic artist was hired to begin production designs for use in the CBD distribution program, as well as for the condom symbol to be used throughout the entire campaign (CBD program and CFPA poster). In April, 1990, AIDSTECH sent a team to Antigua and Dominica to work with CFPA on the poster design, conduct interviews to pre-test poster messages, and run focus groups to pre-test CBD promotion ideas. The joint team made up of AIDSTECH staff and consultants with CFPA staff worked closely for several days to identify possible themes and messages for a "lifestyle" condom promotion poster. These themes, and accompanying ideas for visual images, were then pre-tested in both Antigua and Dominica.

Materials were produced by AIDSTECH and CFPA in the subsequent months; campaign materials (posters, boxes, buttons, stickers) were delivered to Dominica in early October, 1990 for distribution throughout the Family Planning Association CBD network and the initiation of the campaign.

OBJECTIVES

The goals of the campaign were to increase condom sales throughout Dominica's CBD outlets by increasing condom awareness and condom visibility. Based on principles used in advertising in many regions of the world and some preliminary research conducted in Mexico by AIDSCOM/Porter Novelli, the "lifestyle" approach was selected to be tested in this campaign. By increasing condom visibility in a fun, socially acceptable and relevant way, this campaign could set the stage for further education and information about condoms throughout the society, reaching marginalized populations at high risk. In addition, a highly visible, acceptable campaign could increase overall societal comfort levels in dealing with issues of condoms, sexual health and AIDS prevention. The campaign, from its inception, was designed to be a low-cost way to promote condoms and increase visibility and sales. Rather than using the tools of traditional condom social marketing, such as re-packaging and re-marketing the condoms themselves, this campaign sought to provide additional ways for NGO's and shop-owners to display and promote the condoms they were currently selling. Social marketing of con-

EXAMPLE 13.4 (continued)

doms had been effective in some countries (e.g., Zaire), but it is a very expensive means of increasing sales. In addition, social marketing campaigns focus on specific brands and may not have as much impact on overall condom sales and use. This condom promotion campaign, however, was not brand-specific and could contribute to the overall acceptability of all types of condoms and, presumably, condom sales.

The objectives of the qualitative research that supported this campaign were to:

- Outline the design of a condom promotion poster and select visual elements for use in the poster photo.
- Identify the most appropriate textual message for use on a condom promotion poster designed jointly by CFPA and AIDSTECH.
- Select the most appropriate promotional design for use in the CBD program for point-of-purchase materials.
- Pre-test and select the preferred condom symbol for use throughout the campaign.
- Identify shop-owners' concerns and needs regarding condom display/distribution boxes.

METHODOLOGY

To accomplish these objectives, the AIDSTECH team conducted a series of interviews and focus groups with target audiences in Antigua and Dominica. The qualitative research participants were segmented based on age and gender. The process was as follows:

Structured Interviews: The AIDSTECH team conducted a series of 23 interviews (14 men, 9 women) in St. John's, Antigua, to pretest the three possible messages developed by the CFPA-AIDSTECH team and the potential visual images to accompany them. Participants for the interviews were recruited from 5 different shops in downtown St. John's.

In addition, AIDSTECH staff conducted a series of interviews with shopkeepers and bar owners in six villages in Dominica to pre-test the artwork and structure of the condom display box. These interview participants were those who worked in or owned CBD outlets in Dominica.

Focus Groups: AIDSTECH staff conducted a total of four (4) focus groups in Dominica. Two focus groups took place in Roseau with women, and two in Grand Bay with men. Participants were recruited by the staff of the Dominica Family Planning Association. The data from these interviews and focus groups were used to determine visuals and text for the condom promotion poster and the artwork for the condom display box and condom symbol.

FINDINGS AND RECOMMENDATIONS

Condom Promotion Poster: In keeping with the idea of developing a "lifestyle" campaign, the CFPA-AIDSTECH team developed three possible sets of text for the poster to accompany the visual image.

Text: The text ideas that were developed and pre-tested were:

1. **I was strong enough to talk about it. We talked. We listened. Now we use condoms. Not for her. Not for me. But for both of us.**

2. **People who care use condoms. How about you?**

3. **It's not the end of anything. Its only the beginning. Condoms . . . Because You Care.**

Each of these sets of text was designed to convey a social message, one that positioned condom use in the context of people's relationships with one another, in much the same way that traditional advertising of soft drinks or other consumer goods does.

Visuals: The text above was to be framed against a backdrop of a social situation to emphasize the "lifestyle" aspects of the campaign. The possible options all involved public places that would not require showing someone's home (such as a party). The visual images that were pre-tested were:

1. **Beach scene**
2. **Sporting event**
3. **Restaurant scene**

Of the visual images, the beach scene was preferred overwhelmingly. When interview participants were asked what place they thought of when they were

(continued)

EXAMPLE 13.4 *(continued)*

EXAMPLE 13.4 (continued)

having fun, the most prominent and enthusiastic responses involved the beach. In addition, the beach was cited as the place to meet friends and possible boyfriends/girlfriends. In focus group discussions in Dominica, when participants were asked to describe the activities of a "fun day at the beach," the most frequently mentioned activities were having a barbecue or going on a picnic. Participants said that the people they were most likely to go to the beach with were friends and siblings. In addition, they often meet other friends at the beach.

The restaurant was cited as a friendly environment, but was perceived to be too formal—not as much fun. It was also less likely to be a place to go with a group of friends for the focus group participants.

Some of the men in the focus groups also mentioned football matches as "fun" environments; the women, however, indicated that, while they were a fun place, it seemed to be more so for men. So, if a site was to be chosen that was considered to be equally enjoyable for men and women, the beach was the most appropriate selection.

Based on these responses from the interviews and focus groups, the beach scene was selected as the most appropriate visual image for the poster.

For the text, the three ideas were presented in both the interview and the focus groups. Ideas #1 and 3 were most well received by all participants. Idea #2 was perceived to be too "weak." Focus group participants in Dominica (especially women) felt that it did not make the point about using condoms in a strong enough fashion. Among the men, in both interviews and focus groups, #2 was consistently liked least of all the choices. Idea #2 generated little discussion in the focus groups and minimal responses in the interviews.

Among the other ideas, there was much discussion. Many interview participants liked #1 for its literal message. Respondents pointed out that it was very clear about telling people what to do. When asked who was speaking, however, all respondents said that it was a man. The women in the focus groups, while they liked that the man felt "strong enough to talk about it," did not like the fact that, as they saw it, the man seemed to be the primary deciding factor. In the interviews, idea #1 was usually most well-received by

people who put the least time into thinking about the messages; thus, for those people who were interested in the campaign and took active part in the interviews, this idea received only a lukewarm response. For those interview participants who seemed to want to conclude the interview as quickly as possible, idea #1 was usually their first choice. The interview team felt that this was most likely because it was the most literal of the options; choosing it was easy and gave the respondents a feeling of having completed the interview quickly and easily.

Those who actively discussed each message overwhelmingly preferred #3 ("It's not the end of anything. It's only the beginning. Condoms . . . Because You Care"). Interview participants frequently commented that this one had a bit of mystery about it. Some asked the interview team what it meant; when the question was turned back to them to try and answer, they had a range of creative ideas. Those who came up with explanations for it always favored this text over the other options.

In the focus groups, this text generated by far the most discussion of the three options. Both women and men in their respective groups debated its possible meaning and, as one group rightly noted, **the fact that the phrase could generate so much discussion made it a very valuable tool for getting people to think about condoms.** In one focus group, a woman pointed out that it reminded her of a perfume advertisement, with a little bit of mystery attached. This notion was quickly echoed by the rest of the group. Both men and women felt that the slogan could refer to any of the following things (all of which were seen as positive kinds of condom promotion messages):

1. It's not the end of hope . . .

2. It's not the end of sex . . .

3. It's not the end of the day . . . (more chances to get to know other person)

4. It's not the end of romance . . .

5. It's not the end of the relationship . . .

6. It's not the end of fun . . .

(continued)

EXAMPLE 13.4 (continued)

In addition, women in particular felt that this message spoke to their concerns about relationships with men, not just sex. In other words, the message told them that having sex was simply the prelude to a relationship—and not an end in itself. For the women in the focus groups, this was a very significant positive attribute of the message.

Overwhelmingly, all respondents liked the "Condoms . . . Because You Care" tag line. Even for participants for whom #1 was preferable, many suggested concluding with this tag line as well. When asked why they liked this line, interview participants responded that it made them "feel good" and that it made them think very positive things about condoms. The caring referred to in the line, they felt, could refer to caring about your partner, caring about yourself, or even caring about people with AIDS. For virtually all respondents, these were seen as very important and powerful messages.

When this tag line was combined with the more "mysterious" feelings in the first part of #3, it was seen as a powerful combination that emphasized positive feelings and encouraged people to think about and talk about the issue of using condoms.

Given that this program seeks to increase awareness and use of condoms without promoting any kind of AIDS, STD, Family Planning, or health-specific message, it was felt that #3 best represented the ideas behind the condom promotion campaign: that it epitomized the "lifestyle" message by presenting somewhat ambiguous text that could lead people to think more about the poster and the issue in general.

Recommendations:

It's not the end of anything.

It's only the beginning.

Condoms . . . Because You Care.

Against backdrop of beach scene. [Frye's Point in Antigua discussed as possible option for shooting photograph.]

Condom Symbol: The campaign included a condom symbol for two reasons:

1. To help shopkeepers have a recognizable way of indicating "condoms available here."

2. To create a unifying theme for the campaign.

During the preliminary research phases of the campaign, AIDSTECH staff met with a range of people involved in AIDS prevention and condom promotion throughout the region to discuss the idea of a condom symbol. Early drawings were pre-tested in shops in Dominica, and it was found that respondents could not identify an abstract condom symbol (e.g., a circle in a square, like a condom in its package) without some kind of identifying label. During a second round of pre-testing in the region in March, 1990, another set of possible symbols were pre-tested. Interview participants expressed a strong preference for the more literal of the condom symbols. During the final pre-testing in April in Antigua and Dominica, focus groups strongly favored the most literal-looking of the possibilities presented. In addition, the word "condoms" was added to the bottom of the symbol to clarify its meaning. When the selected symbol was pre-tested with the additional textual label, its meaning was very clear for focus group participants. When asked what they would think about a shop that had this symbol and label on its door, the overwhelming response was that the shop sold condoms. The only other response given in the focus groups was that the shopkeepers were trying to promote condom use. The team conducting the research felt that this symbol was clearly understood by participants. The campaign

In addition to those major campaigns, different units of central governments may be involved in special efforts to correct problems or make improvements. In the USA, many government agencies form coalitions in areas where their interests coincide, and they often create alliances with non-profit groups that have similar purposes. Sometimes they are joined by corporations.

An example would be the annual "National 3D Prevention Month Coalition." The "3D" stands for "Drunk and Drugged Driving," and the coalition began in 1991. Participants include 52

EXAMPLE 13.4 *(continued)*

would eventually like to remove the label—when the symbol has achieved a sufficient level of recognition.

For the symbol's colors, all qualitative research participants favored very bright colors, particularly blues, greens, and pinks. Symbols in all three of these colors were printed after shopkeepers requested a variety of colors to use in their shops.

The final condom symbol is integrated into both the CFPA-AIDSTECH condom promotion poster and the condom display box to enhance the unifying theme of the campaign.

Condom Display Box: The purpose of the condom display box was to increase condom visibility in the CBD outlets. Prior to campaign implementation, all shopkeepers stored and displayed condoms in the white cardboard USAID boxes. Photographs taken during preliminary fieldwork conducted in March, 1990 indicate how the white boxes were virtually invisible in the shops. After speaking with a variety of shopkeepers and bar owners, AIDSTECH developed three different box design structures.

Needs for the newly designed box structure, as identified by AIDSTECH and the shopkeepers, included:

- Durable, yet resistant to heat and moisture
- Easy to assemble and lightweight for shipping
- Easy dispensing of condom strips
- Condoms dispensed from front or side so that boxes can be stored on top
- Wide enough to support other boxes on top
- Opaque, to prevent light from harming condoms
- Easy to change artwork
- Dark enough so that dirt does not show

The box designs that were pre-tested were developed by AIDSTECH in conjunction with an artist and packaging specialists to ensure that these needs were met. Three box designs were taken to Dominica and pre-tested with 14 shopkeepers and bar owners in six villages throughout Dominica. The box design chosen was the only one that reflected all the needs listed above.

For the front panel of the display boxes, a series of artwork ideas were pre-tested, all with a variation on a lifestyle theme. The interviews with shopkeepers revealed several main themes:

- The artwork needed to be large enough to be visible from a distance.
- Artwork showing faces rather than animals, blue jeans pockets, etc., were strongly preferred.

Among focus group participants, artwork with faces was also strongly preferred. In addition, groups expressed a strong preference for artwork in which the faces were looking out (toward the consumer) rather than at one another.

The condom symbol, when integrated into the box artwork, was preferred when positioned between the man and woman, rather than above or to the side. Focus group participants, especially women, felt that this drew attention to the reason for the display.

The artwork for the box is produced separately from the box itself. In this way, campaign themes and styles can be changed without requiring box replacements each time.

Source: Written by Lynda Cole, former Director of AIDSTECH, and used by permission.

separate member organizations. The hub of this wheel of groups is the National Highway Traffic Safety Administration of the U.S. Department of Transportation.

The 3Ds Coalition has its own Washington, D.C., office and each year works through the alcohol and drug prevention departments of all sorts of institutions, including colleges and universities. The 3D Prevention Month is a part of the overall campaign Safe and Sober.

National coalitions like this are mirrored in international campaigns such as conferences on population control and the environment. The United Nations is a focal point for many international efforts that benefit multiple countries.

GLOBAL CAMPAIGNS: DOES ONE FIT ALL?

The nations of the world always have engaged in a great deal of economic interaction, but something quite different happened after World War II. First, many national economies were shattered, and the USA invested heavily in the Marshall Plan to rebuild them. As the various nations began to recover their economic strength, they turned to the USA first as a marketplace for their goods and later as a place to invest their new wealth.

Along with the increase in international economic activity came the need for help in dealing with different governments, with the languages and customs of foreign and unfamiliar customers and with the effects of two new technologies—aviation and television. This need existed both in the USA and in the foreign countries. The USA was rapidly expanding its political and commercial involvement abroad, and the foreign nations were discovering the USA as an eager customer. The borders between countries seemed to vanish, and businesspeople talked of "jet lag." Later, the micronization of electronic technology and the advent of the computer made virtual face-to-face contact such as videoconferencing possible throughout the world.

From bankers putting together financial packages in Brussels or Paris, to loan participants coming from Caracas, Frankfurt, Tokyo and Madrid, to hospital administrators convening in Geneva, the world began to look more like a community, although a few neighbors would do battle from time to time over one issue or another. The vision that many people had held for the role of public relations in its 1950s growth period seemed on the verge of becoming reality. Expansion in the social sciences and in communication theory seemed to provide the needed support.

Companies that had waded into international waters early found many requests for their services, so they began to formulate public relations campaigns to reach their new-found publics. Some of these campaigns were product-oriented; some were political; some were service-centered; and some were professionally focused.

Going global is even more necessary today, but it is still a very untidy and uncertain business. The PR firms that got in early (in the 1960s and 1970s) are still at the top of the heap: Burson-Marsteller, Hill & Knowlton and Ogilvy & Mather. They control a campaign—"a seamless campaign" as Burson-Marsteller calls it.

Although PR firms and networks are available to do the job, some companies still handle their own PR/advertising/marketing/sales campaigns at home and abroad. Their PR and marketing people may or may not work together. A survey of service industries showed their PR departments to be small compared to their marketing staffs. And in most instances these departments reported to marketing, which in turn reported directly to the principal office.[15] This suggests that PR, at least in service industries, is being used for publicity and promotion. Certainly PR is not in a hierarchical position in these industries that facilitates interaction with management.

One of the most intensive global campaigns is the World Health Organization's AIDS campaign. In addition to experiencing the problems of any campaign (language barriers, government regulations and media), the AIDS campaign suffers from a lack of infrastructure—a problem not limited to nonindustrialized nations. Add to that the cultural taboos of many societies regarding any discussion of sexual matters, as well as the objections of social conservatives in all cultures who fear that sex education encourages promiscuity, and you have a real campaign challenge.

WHO has responded by creating basic educational materials that it furnishes to health authorities in various countries to adapt to their own cultures. Many countries have turned the development of their plan (and the funds to implement it) over to public relations firms. While many nations have taken aggressive action, others have not, perhaps because they face too many other issues that demand immediate attention. But the problem is global and involves essentially the same facts everywhere, so at some point the campaigns tailored for various countries and for the ethnic and cultural groups within those countries will offer a remarkable case study.

POINTS TO REMEMBER

■ Campaigns are designed to accomplish specific organizational objectives.

■ A campaign's foundation is the organizational mission, and its roof or containing factor is the budget. The elements are research, publics, action and evaluation.

■ Planning for a campaign involves setting goals, creating timetables and developing budgets.

■ Setting the creative strategy means choosing a theme and media to use in communicating with the designated publics.

■ Internal strategy is critical to establishing organizational support for the campaign.

■ Implementation has three major components: (1) adapting and applying tactics to strategies; (2) keeping people informed; (3) solving all problems positively.

■ While a campaign is in progress, all elements have to be monitored so goals are achieved. After the campaign, a review or postmortem to determine what worked and what didn't is important for future planning.

■ Governments conduct comprehensive campaigns to make improvements or to solve problems. Like other organizations, governments often conduct several campaigns at the same time. Some of these are handled by government departments.

■ Often campaigns are undertaken by coalitions.

■ Most global campaigns, even those for a product being sold around the world, do not work well across cultures. The cultural aspect is more important than are national borders or languages, although laws can affect certain campaign tactics.

■ Campaigns are usually built around a desire to establish, change or modify behaviors. The five *e*'s

of a successful campaign are education, engineering, enforcement, entitlement and evaluation.

NOTES

[1] Patrick Jackson, speech for Vern C. Schranz Distinguished Lectureship in Public Relations, Ball State University, Muncie, Indiana, 1984.

[2] *pr reporter* (May 29, 1978), p. 1.

[3] John E. Rehfeld, "What Working for a Japanese Company Taught Me," *Harvard Business Review*, 68(6) (November–December 1990), pp. 167–76 (p. 171).

[4] Ronald E. Rice and William J. Paisley, eds., *Public Communication Campaigns* (Beverly Hills, Calif.: Sage, 1981), p. 7.

[5] Charles T. Salmon, ed., *Information Campaigns: Balancing Values and Social Change* (Newbury Park, Calif.: Sage, 1989), p. 47.

[6] William Paisley, "Prologue," in Ronald E. Rice and Charles K. Atkin, eds., *Public Communication Campaigns*, 2d ed. (Newbury Park, Calif.: Sage, 1989), p. 17.

[7] Ibid., p. 21.

[8] Ibid., p. 23.

[9] Ibid., p. 23.

[10] "Campaigns Can Change Behavior If They Involve a 2-Step Process: 3 Examples Show How National Efforts Using Partnerships & Grassroots Programs Are Making Headway," *pr reporter*, 33(10) (December 10, 1990), p. 1.

[11] "Billboard Displays Powerful Message," *MADD in Action* (May–August 1990).

[12] John Pierson, "Political Statements Take Graphic Form," *Wall Street Journal* (September 24, 1990). p. B1.

[13] Hernando Gonzales, "Interactivity and Feedback in Third World Development Campaigns," *Critical Studies in Mass Communication*, 6 (1989), pp. 295–314.

[14] Lynda Cole, Associate Director of AIDSTECH, Research Triangle Park, North Carolina, furnished all of the materials on the Caribbean campaign reproduced in this example.

[15] Andreas Rossbach, "Marketing and Public Relations in the International and Domestic Markets of North American Service Companies: Partners or Adversaries," unpublished master's thesis, Texas Christian University, August 1987.

Selected readings, activities and assignments appropriate to this chapter can be found in the *Instructor's Guide* and on InfoTrac if you are using the InfoTrac College Edition.

CHAPTER 14

CASE STUDIES

Learning teaches how to carry things in suspense, without prejudice, til you resolve.

FRANCIS BACON, AUTHOR, STATESMAN AND PHILOSOPHER

That man is wise to some purpose who gains his wisdom at the expense and from the experience of another.

PLAUTUS, ROMAN POET AND PLAYWRIGHT

Some public relations practitioners and educators argue that case studies have been a major detriment to public relations theory-building. Critics say that case studies don't allow for a conceptual or theory-based framework to systematically analyze public relations problems. However, case studies can be valuable for those who recognize their inherent weaknesses, but nevertheless appreciate that much can still be gained from them.[1]

PR practitioners and educators use case studies in two ways. First, they may pose a PR problem and outline a possible solution according to specific guidelines, as suggested by an existing case. Second, they may dissect a historical case as a learning experience to determine what worked, what didn't and why. The historical case is generally referred to simply as a *case*. The existing situation in need of a PR solution is generally called a *problem*, which is why many PR courses use the title "PR Cases and Problems."

A PR firm keeps a special library containing files of the cases it has handled. These are often written as historical case studies and are not merely the final evaluation of PR action. The firm's new employees often are assigned to research these cases in the firm's library, which also serves as a resource center for the entire staff. Furthermore, examples of successful campaigns presented as case studies to potential clients can help recruit new business.

CASE ANALYSIS

An analysis of a historical case can be broken down into four parts. The first part should include a summary of the case—that is, an explanation of the nature of the problem or problems the campaign addressed and the problem background—and the research-based purposes of the PR actions taken to address the situation or problem, based on discovery research and remedial research.

The second part involves additional research into publics; an assessment of the impact of the problem, situation or proposed action; a prioritization of the publics; a discussion of the evolution of the problem, together with its probable causes; and an explanation of what was done to deal with the problem. In looking at the steps taken to solve the problem, you should pay special attention to research into the problem itself, how the publics were selected and what was learned about them. Study the techniques and tools used to reach these publics, and compare these with other possible techniques and tools. Study, too, the role of the public relations person in the solution, especially with regard to the interaction of PR with other departments. The solution should offer some evidence that it was a reasonable and workable way to handle the problem. Evidence may be available from the continuation of the program, from letters of endorsement, from evaluation research or from other data such as responses to the program.

The third part of the analysis should consist of a detailed description of the institution involved in the problem—what it does, what it is. Samples of all materials used in the program should be included: news releases to all media, special coverage, scripts, posters, advertising, letters, special publications and so on. Copies of progress reports should be examined and included in the analysis. Such reports are generally available if the PR problem was handled by a PR firm, because the firm must report to management periodically. Internally handled problems are sometimes less well documented, because there is some informal reporting. The action taken and all communications efforts made should be explained in detail.

The fourth part of the analysis should be a consideration and evaluation of what worked particularly well and what could have been improved. Especially valuable are thoughtful recommendations about how such a program might be handled better if a similar situation confronts the same institution in the future.

This type of dissection of a PR event is useful for students trying to develop approaches to PR problems, and the same careful, detailed study and documentation is also useful for practitioners after a campaign. Such a dissection is part of the evaluation discussed in Chapter 5.

Elements included in both the existing and the historical cases are basically the same (see Example 14.1).

Availability of Cases

Cases serve as idea resources for PR practitioners in solving problems and for PR scholars in building theory. The Public Relations Society of America each year solicits documented cases in 45 categories for its Silver Anvil competition. The structure of those cases generally follows the outline in Example 14.1, although the designations are Research, Planning, Execution and Evaluation. (You may recall from Chapter 10 two other sets of frequently used designations: Research, Action, Communication and Evaluation; and Research, Objectives, Programming and Evaluation. The elements of each set are much the same, although the emphasis may differ.) Case entries and two-page profiles from each PRSA competition are kept for two years and are available for review in the Professional Practice Center of PRSA's New York headquarters (33 Irving Place, New York, NY 10003-2376) by appointment. The phone number is (212) 460-1459; Web site is silveranvil.org.

Self-generated case studies that have won awards are also available from the International Association of Business Communicators (IABC). IABC's International Gold Quill Awards are published each year in a booklet that offers several hundred cases. These are available from IABC, One Hallidie Plaza, Suite 600, San Francisco, CA

EXAMPLE 14.1
Elements of PR Cases—Existing and Historical

Existing Case/Campaign Development	*Historical Case*
RESEARCH To help identify the problem and establish objectives.	To describe the nature of the problem and its background—the evolution and probable causes. To define the objectives involved in the solution. To consider other possible solutions and their consequences.
PUBLICS To designate publics and recognize which are target publics. To learn what they know and believe and how to reach them with available media.	To determine how priority publics were selected and how each was involved in the solution.
ACTION To plan ways of reaching publics in an effective, efficient manner within a flexible, feasible timetable. To develop a persuasive strategy. To get management and staff support.	To examine the tools and techniques used in terms of their effectiveness with the various publics. To look for evidence of management and publics' endorsement through continuation of the program or through other results that give evidence of a solution. To include samples of action taken—PR tools and techniques.
EVALUATION To evaluate the results or the effectiveness of the program as revealed by post-testing research or less formal methods such as responses from publics and staffs.	To recommend better ways to approach similar problems, should these occur in the same organization. To analyze lessons to be learned from the solution implemented.

94102. IABC's phone number is (415)433-3400. In 1998, there were 1,701 entries from 18 countries.

In addition, the Harvard Business School publishes various case studies, some of which address public relations problems. These are available from Harvard Business School Publishing, Boston, MA 02163. Unlike the PRSA cases, which are self-reporting for a competition, the Harvard cases are field studies performed by graduate students. Of course, the field studies are done with cooperation and consent of the companies being investigated. Harvard's Business School dean in 1908 began looking for ways to build theory in his newly established discipline and got the idea for case studies

from Harvard Law School. The first cases were a bit of a "hard sell," since the researchers tended to unlock closets that hid corporate skeletons; however, the Harvard case study approach now has a prestige factor attached to it.

Considerably more difficult to find are cases that document problem solving when culture is an issue. However, resources in other disciplines such as anthropology and sociology (including social work) offer some help. If you explore that literature, you need to be familiar with the social science approach, which is as follows: problem definition, purpose, problem *solver*, process and, finally, solution (usually with some evaluation). But whereas in social work the researcher usually becomes the problem solver, in anthropology the researcher looks at indigenous problem solvers who may be village elders or others of status.

Why look at such cases for guidance in addressing public relations problems? Here's one example. The object was to get health information to Indian tribes living in remote parts of Mexico who deliberately maintain their distance from the mainstream of Mexican affairs for fear of "cultural contamination." In that sense, they are much like the Amish in the USA, who preserve their own culture and traditions in "island communities." Members of the Indian tribes depend on a shaman for guidance and care in their physical and mental health. The shaman is therefore the key to getting the health information to the tribe. A more direct approach to tribe members might be possible, since many of them speak and read Spanish and their communities are accessible, but the results would be ineffective at best. A worst-case situation would be a serious domestic disturbance resulting from the effort.

The only reasonable solution, then, seems to be to "sell the shaman" on the health programs. But that's not easy either, since the shaman stays in the community. However, a village elder does have some connection to the larger Mexican society because he travels to other communities bringing goods to sell and then buys provisions to take back. (In these tribes, it's always a "he." The women and young people are never allowed out of the community.) The contact has to be made, trust established, and the representative granted access to the tribe's shaman. Usually this process takes months or even years. But it is the only way to deliver health information and to get any kind of compliance or adoption.

As public relations efforts continue in the global community, observations from anthropologists and case studies from the fields of social work and agriculture (which is the source of the diffusion process and resulting theory) will have increasing significance and bear careful study by PR practitioners and scholars.

Learning from Experience and Borrowing Ideas

RR practitioners who work in the public affairs area may be more familiar than those from the marketing/promotions area with the situation of having a priority public of one. Often a successful case depends on the support of one person—a key staff member of an agency or a committee chair. Often in such cases, the PR person will work with the organization's lobbyists. Ronald N. Levy offers the following suggestions, based on his experience, for helping your lobbyist win in such situations:

1. Get started early and use material from an executive's speech, because it already has been researched and cleared for release.

2. Use arguments people can relate to, ones that affect them.

3. Show what impact winning on your issue will have on the major concerns of the day.

4. Don't put all your arguments into one release (except for the trade publications). No one wants to know everything, at least immediately, and you need additional material to keep sending.

5. Present only your case, not the opposition's.

6. Don't engage in pejorative name calling. If you have to, refer to the other side as "less informed" or "well intentioned."

7. Keep in touch with the lobbyist to get feedback on which arguments seem to be working best.

8. Don't cover just the news media. Send information to important constituencies, too, so they will have information to reinforce their support.

9. Keep in mind that the key objective is to win, not to accumulate more clippings, interviews, editorials and photo layouts. Winning is the bottom line.[2]

Even with the best of help, though, things can go wrong, as the American Heart Association (AHA) found out in its public affairs campaign to put a seal of approval on foods that met AHA standards. After three years of planning and working with all regulatory agencies as well as industry, and just five days before the first labeled foods were to become available to consumers, the AHA got a letter from the Food and Drug Administration (FDA) threatening regulatory action to stop the program. At first, the AHA said it wouldn't cancel the launch of the first phase of its program: labeling of margarines, spreads, crackers, oils and canned and frozen vegetables (altogether, fewer than 100 labeled foods). However, the AHA did eventually fold the campaign. James S. Benson, acting commissioner of the FDA at the time, cited possible consumer confusion over the meaning of the labeling as grounds for intervening. Critics of the FDA's decision to intervene, however, argued that political pressure from beef and dairy producers provided a more plausible explanation for the FDA's behavior. The Department of Agriculture already had told the AHA that it would not support the program, but that agency had no regulatory power over the AHA's labeling program.[3]

Various supporters of the AHA plan felt that the campaign was stymied by three unavoidable problems. One was the power of some industries over the agencies that supposedly regulate them. A second was the fact that the AHA had previously attacked the tobacco industry, which now owns a number of food product companies, leading many observers to conclude (justly or unjustly) that these companies had objected to the program out of simple vindictiveness. A third problem was that the very existence of the campaign represented an affront (or embarrassment) to the federal government, which had done little in response to consumers' demands for information about what they were eating. The subsequent regulatory activity by the government mandating better labeling was viewed by some AHA supporters as confirming this last point.

Nonprofit organizations always have to be careful about their public affairs efforts. They are restricted in how much pressure they can exert on government, because direct lobbying may endanger their tax-exempt status. They have, therefore,

focused on promotions designed to compete for funding dollars, to convince people to take advantage of their services (so they can prove they need money) and to increase or maintain their image-share of the marketplace. The most competitive have been health organizations and organizations that represent the arts. In fact, their promotions have been called marketing/public relations.

Nonprofit institutions that emphasize the selling aspect of marketing without paying enough attention to their publics can encounter hazards. Marketing professor Alan Andreasen warned nonprofits to pay as much attention to their clients as they do to their products.[4] He pointed out that nonprofits are always in financial difficulties and really suffer when the economy is bad and the federal government makes substantial budget cuts in social services. Clients will remain loyal if they see themselves as part of the institution.

Loyalty of clients has become a national problem for MADD, which found itself the subject of a TV network investigative piece in March of 1991. The problem centered on the organization's distancing of itself from its founder, Candy Lightner, which caused some loss of identity. The organization has also been accused of spending too much of the money it takes in from donors on raising more money instead of on the cause. That accusation is not an unusual one to hear about fund-raising efforts. Some people who give to university appeals and then receive a package of expensive gifts in response wonder how much of their money goes to the real appeal. The national public broadcasting stations, which also use gifts in fundraising, have tried to get around this by offering a check-off option that enables the donor to relinquish the standard gift so that all of the money can go to programming. Many museums and other organizations will tell donors how much of their "membership" can be counted as an outright "donation." It appears that the Internal Revenue Service is as interested as consumers in how these donations are used.

Reports of the six-figure salary commanded by United Way's (now former) chief executive touched off a major flap in early 1992. Local groups affiliated with United Way scrambled to establish that they were abiding by the standard of spending no more than 12 percent of the contributions they received on administrative expenses, but published audits showed that in many cases they were over the limit.

As noted in Chapter 8, for two years during a racial discrimination suit, Texaco had "no comment" until a disgruntled executive leaked tapes purporting to show that executives were planning to destroy evidence. Negative headlines and a boycott resulted. Within 11 days, Texaco CEO Peter Bijur had not only apologized and suspended every individual involved, but he ended the original suit with a $176 million settlement. This shift in strategy resulted in the boycott being lifted, in media turning to other interests, and put an end to the financial cost of the incident. Some corporations have even learned the benefits of "pre-emptive confession." When a senior executive at CNA made offensive comments to female subordinates, the women took their complaints to another executive. Both men were ultimately forced to resign. The story broke when CNA's public relations division faxed an unsolicited news release to media.[5]

While no theory links corporate values and economics, Johnson & Johnson's former chairman Jim Burke thinks that his company's credo enabled it to take rapid and correct action during the Tylenol crisis. He commissioned a study of the financial performance of 20 U.S. companies that had written value statements for at least a generation. The study showed a net income for the 20 companies that increased by a factor of 23 at a time when the gross national product (GNP) increased by only 2½.[6]

Obviously, corporate values have to be accepted by the employees in order to be recognized by others, particularly consumers. As noted in Chapter 6, employees are PR's front line, and most of the concerns of middle management involve personnel. Thus, top management is often relieved of these chores. But unfortunately top management is where the attitude toward employees is set.

Middle managers adopt the corporate culture and treat their employees, generally, as they are treated and as they perceive their boss to be directing them. Some companies, aware of this interpretive problem, have developed management guides, which are especially popular with companies coping with mergers or diversifications.

You can borrow ideas from the experiences of others on your own. By all means, file every case study that you find. You may need it sometime. You'll have to create your own system for retrieving your collectibles. Some practitioners use a publics typology, like the one in Chapter 4. Others use a media typology, as in Chapter 11. Others use a less formal method and simply maintain a collection they label "gimmicks," or "good strategy." The following pages present two "collectible" cases you can put in your file for future reference.

CASES FOR STUDY

The first tells how the German automaker BMW promoted itself in the Middle East through a press photographers' competition. The second tells how a hospital in Iowa handled the international media attention being given to the birth of septuplets.

▌ BMW Gulf and Middle East Photography Event

This next case is about the "BMW Gulf and Middle East Press Photography Contest," a competition conceived and executed by the Middle East public relations firm Fortune Promoseven for its client BMW.[7] The original case study was prepared by that firm. However, the case was adapted during summer 1994 by Dean Kruckeberg, Badran A. Badran, Muhammad I. Ayish and Ali A. Awad for the textbook, *Case Studies in Public Relations,* as this project team helped prepare the new public relations degree program for the United Arab Emirates University.

CASE STUDY #1

BMW Gulf and Middle East Press Photography Contest*

FORTUNE PROMOSEVEN

Fortune Promoseven was founded in Beirut in 1968 by Akram Miknas, its president and chief executive. Fortune Promoseven performs services in public relations, advertising, publishing, media, direct marketing, TV and film production, still photography and creative and marketing support. Company literature describes the firm as the most extensive communications network in the Middle East, with an office in London and 12 offices in the Middle East in addition to its headquarters, including offices in Amman, Beirut, Bahrain, Cairo, Casablanca, Doha, Dubai, Jeddah, Kuwait, Muscat, Riyadh and Tehran. The firm has a combined staff of 350 people. Fortune Promoseven is affiliated with the U.S. agency McCann Erickson.

Fortune Promoseven has an impressive client list, including Lufthansa, BMW, Lockheed, Boeing, Coca Cola, L'Oreal and Upjohn.

Fortune Promoseven's public relations staff performs a variety of services, including external and internal communication, event management, direct marketing, government relations, consultation and recommendations, crisis management, media monitoring, evaluation, media relations, preparation of company literature and translations.

CLIENT BACKGROUND: BMW

German motorcar maker BMW, which was established more than 75 years ago and has built a worldwide reputation for upmarket cars, has more than five million cars and motorcycles on the world's roads today. Annual sales of BMW automobiles in 1995 is expected to be in excess of 600,000 units, equivalent to a world market share of 1.5 percent.

In the upmarket segment, BMW's share is, however, much larger at 10 percent. And in the topmost automobile segment (cars with 12-cylinder engines), every other car registered worldwide is a BMW.

BMW cars, motorcycles, engines and components are manufactured at factories in Germany, Austria, South Africa, and the U.S.A. BMW has also returned to the production of aircraft engines. Another new company, BMW Fahrzeugtechnik GmbH in Eisenach, Thuringia, manufactures tools for large industrial presses.

BMW's own sales subsidiaries and importers in more than 100 countries supply BMW products to the world's markets and are responsible for both service and parts. The company has some 4,400 authorized dealers throughout the world to ensure optimum service for its vehicles.

No other company outside Japan has grown as quickly in the last 20 years as BMW. The company is one of the very few that has made profits year-in and year-out for the past three decades.

BMW automobiles and motorcycles are characterized by their dynamism, elegance and future-oriented technology. In their quality and safety, they live up to the highest standards.

In early 1994, BMW purchased the Rover Car Company from British Aerospace, merging two of the biggest European auto makers.

For almost two decades, BMW has been actively involved in the cultural scene wherever the company is based as well as in international cultural promotion in general. Experiment and innovation are the topics BMW most commonly emphasizes.

RESEARCH

The client's request was that we prepare a public relations event throughout the Middle East to extend recognition in the region that BMW is actively involved in the cultural scene wherever the company's cars are sold.

The objectives were to:

■ Associate BMW with a cultural activity.
■ Familiarize personalities in the media with the BMW name.

*As submitted by Fortune Promoseven.

مسابقة BMW الرابعة للتصوير الصحفي لمنطقة الشرق الأوسط

ترسـل الاشـتراكات إلـى
بروموسـفن القابضـة
قبل ٣٠ سبتمـبر ١٩٩٥.

العنـاوين مذكـورة
فـي استمـارة
الاشـــتـراك.

(continued)

CASE STUDY #1 (continued)

■ Obtain for BMW extensive mention in the media in an activity unrelated to the manufacture and sale of cars.

Fortune Promoseven deliberated about BMW's requirement and proposed the "The BMW Gulf and Middle East Press Photography Competition," open to all regional press photographers and freelancers accredited to regional publications.

The first competition, held in 1989, was an outstanding success, achieving all objectives of participation and media exposure.

The second competition, which concluded in November 1991, also has been termed a resounding success. Participation and media interest in this event were substantially larger than in the first one. This interest is expected to grow progressively in the competition which is scheduled to be held every two years.

Before accepting the concept of a Middle East press photography competition, several other ideas were considered and examined. The press photography competition was decided upon after it was realized that this was a suitable means through which BMW could become involved in the region's cultural activity. By involving the press, the widest possible media exposure for the client and competition was assured; in addition, because most of the region's press are closely affiliated with government and government-managed radio and television services (there are almost no private radio and TV stations in the region), the agency also could involve prominent government media personalities, assuring coverage of the event in state media facilities, thereby linking the BMW competition with a cultural activity that could be perceived as having the support of both the state and the public.

Studies and investigations were undertaken to determine whether this planned competition would duplicate similar events and whether the region's press photographers would be responsive to the event. The findings were that:

■ The planned competition would be the only forum at a regional level for Middle East press photogra-

phers to display their work and to pit their skills and techniques against each other; and
■ Middle East photographers were very enthusiastic about the prospect of a regional competition.

On the basis of these findings, it was decided to:

■ Initiate a BMW Gulf and Middle East Press Photography Contest once every two years for a rolling trophy and other prizes.
■ Involve the participation of prominent regional media personalities as judges to maximize the event's prestige and media coverage.
■ Conduct the event over a period of six months, culminating in a grand awards presentation. (The extended duration would provide sustained media exposure over this period of time.)

Fortune Promoseven then updated media lists for the Middle East and collected the names and addresses of freelance photographers accredited to regional publications. The information was needed to send out individual invitations.

Eight Middle East countries in which BMW has an interest were targeted for the competition. These were: Egypt, Lebanon, Saudi Arabia, Kuwait, Qatar, the United Arab Emirates, Bahrain and Oman. Together, the countries have a population of approximately 76 million.

Fortune Promoseven's research revealed that, among these countries, there were about 40 major publications that had significant and substantial readership and that wielded influence. The majority of these were in the Arabic language, with about 10 printed in English.

As is the prevailing system in these countries, the major print media identified in each of the eight countries had close affinity with their respective state-owned radio, television and wire service agencies. Consequently, targeting these print media assured the competition some spill-over coverage in radio, television and wire services.

The competition was conducted in both English and Arabic, and all materials (press releases, print

CASE STUDY #1 *(continued)*

packages, etc.) were produced and distributed in these two languages.

PLANNING

Undertaking an event of this scale and scope required making preparations and arrangements for a large number of directly and indirectly connected activities. Since a similar competition had not been undertaken on a regional basis in the Middle East previously, planning for the very first competition in 1989 was both wide-ranging and detailed.

The target audience was the print-media photographers. Through their participation, the event was assured of the involvement of the print media itself, as well as associated media such as radio and television. Involving on the judges' panel highly respected regional government and private sector media personalities from throughout the Middle East provided the impression that this event was being supported by these private and government sectors.

Involvement of the state and private sector media and their subsequent coverage of the event assured the widest possible media exposure for the event throughout the six-month duration of the competition. Media exposure peaked at the culmination of the event with the announcement of the winners at an awards ceremony to which several VIPs and prominent personalities were invited.

The media strategy required an event that could run throughout a period of six months, culminating in an elaborate final presentation ceremony. Because their own staff were involved in the competition, the media would get caught up with the event and would be highly receptive to press releases issued about the progress of the event. This build-up would result in considerable media coverage in the Middle East for the culmination of the event, not only because of the event itself, but also because highly placed government and private sector personalities would be involved and invited.

The resulting publicity would broadcast BMW's association, not only with a cultural activity, but with respected and responsible media and media personalities and would associate BMW in the public mind with a concern unrelated with trade and commerce.

As events unfolded, the strategy worked itself out exactly as planned—both in the first competition in 1989 and in the second competition which concluded in November 1991. Achievement of objectives in the 1991 competition can be measured by the facts that:

- The competition has established itself clearly as a Middle East cultural event with a momentum of its own.
- It has associated BMW with what is now perceived as a scheduled cultural activity.
- The response to the competition was overwhelming (over 300 entries were received). Photographers from as many as 27 major and influential Middle East publications took part.
- Press publicity generated in English and Arabic was substantial, and the competition also received coverage on radio and TV.
- State support was made evident when the Ministry of Information, State of Bahrain, agreed to hold the awards ceremony under its patronage.
- State support was made further evident by the agreement to permit the awards ceremony to be held at the Bahrain National Museum. (This was the first commercially related event to be held on these premises.)
- The media coverage and attention assured that the event received significant public interest.

EXECUTION

From the very inception, an attempt was made to obtain the support for the competition from editors of all major Middle East publications. This support was achieved by maintaining personal contact with editors through the mail, fax and telephone and by keeping them constantly informed. The strategy familiarized the name of BMW among editors and helped the agency to become closely acquainted with these editors.

(continued)

CASE STUDY #1 (continued)

The print package for the competition included the following:

- Posters
- Invitations
- Banners
- A folder containing loose sheets with a biographical profile of each judge, together with his photograph, for distribution to the media
- Special letterhead
- An 18-page (including cover) brochure giving information on the first such competition as well as on the second competition.

Throughout the duration of the competition, the agency generated and issued nine press releases (in English and Arabic) together with related photographs. These received significant coverage.

A well-attended press conference was held on the afternoon of the awards ceremony to announce the winners to the media beforehand, thereby assuring that the evening's event would receive coverage in the next day's newspaper.

Midway through the six-month duration of the competition, a full assessment of progress was made, and the press photographers' response was reviewed in a report to the client. At that stage, it was felt that a renewed burst of publicity was needed, and this was provided through press releases and contact through the mail and telephone.

Judging Session

The following were produced, arranged for or accomplished:

- Forms for the judges to use at the judging session.
- Air tickets, visas and hotel accommodations.
- Short-listing of the entries and mounting them for judging.
- Dinner for the judges so they could meet with BMW officials.
- Gift for each judge.

Awards Ceremony

This required coordination and follow-up action for the following:

- Client
- Editors
- Press photographers
- Agency's regional offices.

It also required accomplishing the following tasks:

- Earning government approval and patronage.
- Obtaining permission for use of Bahrain's National Museum Exhibition Hall.
- Drawing up a VIP invitation list and sending the invitations.
- Maintaining liaison with BMW regional offices in the Middle East and arranging their representations.
- Identifying the chief guest and inviting him.
- Arranging tickets, visas and hotel accommodations for the first three winners to attend, and notifying their respective editors-in-chief of their success.
- Listing all publications from which photographers participated and producing a poster for exhibition at the awards ceremony.
- Mounting selected photographs, including the winning photos, and arranging their lighting for display at the awards ceremony and the subsequent one-week exhibition at Bahrain's National Museum.
- Producing certificates of merit for distribution.
- Preparing checks for cash prizes.
- Having the rolling trophy engraved.
- Preparing press kits for distribution at the awards ceremony.
- Preparing biographical sketches of winners.
- Sending out press releases.
- Organizing caterers.
- Hiring photographer and video cameraman to record the event.
- Inviting national press, television and radio.

CASE STUDY #1 *(continued)*

- Producing copies of winning photos for distribution to the media at the awards ceremony.
- Sending letters to all entrants thanking them for their participation and advising them of winners' names.
- Holding a press conference on the day of the awards ceremony.
- Organizing tours and other programs for the winners during their stay in Bahrain.
- Organizing/coordinating visits to chief editors and senior Bahraini officials by the BMW senior executives who were visiting Bahrain for the awards ceremony.

Video

A video was produced that incorporated the highlights of the initial 1989 event, explained the procedures followed for the 1991 competition and judging session and highlighted parts of the print package created by Fortune Promoseven. This video was shown to invitees of the awards ceremony. The awards ceremony and the exhibition were themselves videotaped, and a final video incorporating all elements of the competition was produced as a promotional tool for the client and for the agency.

Tour of Photo Exhibition

Finally, a selection of photos entered for the competition, together with the winning photos, would make a tour for exhibition at the premises of BMW importers in each of the Middle East countries. These exhibitions, too, would be promoted in each country in which they were being staged by sending out individual invitations to VIPs and other prominent personalities and by issuing press releases.

The touring exhibition involved:

- Preparing a proposal for exhibition of a selection of entries, including winning entries, at the premises of importers of BMW cars in the Middle East.
- Sending out the proposal and coordinating with importers who wanted to host the exhibition.

- Preparing and freighting the photographs to the importers under a decided time schedule for each Middle East country and for London.

EVALUATION

Fortune Promoseven and BMW consider the competition a success because of the following:

- The competition has firmly associated BMW's name with a Middle East cultural event that now has a momentum of its own.
- More than 300 photo entries were received.
- Photographers from 27 prominent and influential Middle East publications participated, as well as three freelance photographers accredited to major Middle East publications.
- Extensive press coverage in Arabic and English was received throughout the Middle East during the entire six-month duration of the competition.
- The event was covered by radio, and Bahrain TV also gave extensive coverage to the awards ceremony and interviewed the first three winners.
- No paid-for advertisements were purchased to promote the competition.
- Firm links were established between the Middle East media and Fortune Promoseven on behalf of BMW.
- The competition has taken on a significance and glamour of its own, which complements one of the facets of BMW's image—namely, prestige.

A final report to the client was made detailing the following:

- All media coverage received.
- Comparison with the 1989 event.
- Points of contention raised by the judges.
- Comments on print package.
- Recommendations for improving the next competition.

Source: BMW and Fortune Promoseven. Reprinted by permission of Fortune Promoseven.

CASE STUDY #2

The Public Relations Story Behind the Birth of the World's First Surviving Septuplets

Written by Kimberly Waltman, Iowa Methodist Medical Center public relations, and Lynne Yontz, Blank Children's Hospital public relations.

OVERVIEW

Prior to Nov. 19, 1997, two things were certain. Number one, no woman in the United States had ever given birth to seven babies at one time. Number two, there was no set of living septuplets anywhere in the world.

When the public relations staffs at Iowa Methodist Medical Center and Blank Children's Hospital in Des Moines, Iowa, were told in confidence that a patient was carrying seven fetuses, uncertainty became a driving force in the planning process. Since this was unprecedented, no references existed on handling a situation with such a variety of possible outcomes ranging from horrific to miraculous.

One strategy set the tone for the extraordinary event that awed physicians, defied science and wowed people around the globe: the patient's rights and wishes would always come first—the policy for all patients at Iowa Methodist and Blank Children's Hospital. In addition, the patient and her family would approve any public relations tactics prior to implementation.

BACKGROUND

Although the patient was not admitted to Iowa Methodist until Oct. 15, representatives from public relations, security, administration, nursing and the medical team began strategizing in late September. The public relations director and media relations manager from Iowa Methodist and the public relations coordinator from Blank Children's Hospital developed a "plant of action for media coverage" for the day of the births and for 24 to 48 hours after the births.

In addition to crafting a "plan of action," the planning process included educating key players, including the patient and her family and the physicians involved with the delivery and care of the babies. One member of the Iowa Methodist public relations team and one member of the Blank public relations team met with the patient and her husband to discuss the potential media coverage of the story and establish communication tactics between the public relations staff and the family.

Educating the family's perinatologists Paula Mahone, M.D., and Karen Drake, M.D., (a perinatologist is an obstetrician specializing in high-risk pregnancies) and the babies' neonatologists (a neonatologist is a pediatric sub-specialist who cares for sick and/or premature newborns) consisted of media training sessions with an outside agency. Media training focused on the media's mindset, editorial process and interviewing techniques. It was critical for physicians to understand the media frenzy that would more than likely occur and to foster the necessary communications skills to manage themselves in such an environment.

A very detailed call system was developed so members of all departments involved could be contacted 24 hours a day, seven days a week. Members of the Iowa Methodist and Blank Children's Hospital public relations staff carried pagers. Other department personnel were contacted via office, home, pager and cellular phone numbers.

MEDIA RELATIONS

On Oct. 29, the Iowa Methodist media relations manager received a call from a local television station. The station's assignment editor asked, "Do you realize you're sitting on a worldwide media story?" As previously agreed upon, the story was confirmed, but few details were given.

The station led their noon newscast with a reporter live in front of Iowa Methodist. The reporter conveyed that there was a woman pregnant with seven babies and that she could deliver them at any time.

CASE STUDY #2 *(continued)*

Source: © 1997 Time, Inc. Reprinted by permission.

(continued)

CASE STUDY #2 *(continued)*

Bobbi and Kenny McCaughey

CASE STUDY #2 (continued)

Within two hours of the breaking story, the public relations department was inundated with media calls. Reporters from around the country descended upon Des Moines anxiously awaiting the births. The first news conference was held at 3:30 p.m. on Oct. 29, confirming that a patient at Iowa Methodist was carrying seven fetuses.

A list of guidelines was distributed to each credentialed member of the media. Each of them was expected to comply with the outlined standards or face immediate loss of privileges. The guidelines stated that media must:

- Visibly wear credentials at all times while on hospital property.
- Limit time in the hospital to using the pay phones and public restroom facilities.
- Refrain from bringing cameras into the hospital at any time (except for news conferences and news briefings).
- Enter the building where the news conferences were held through one main entrance.

GOALS/OBJECTIVES

At this point, the public relations department focused on three objectives:

1. Obtaining the patient's approval of news conference contents.
2. Establishing the public relations department as the entity for media to acquire accurate and timely information.
3. Prioritizing media interview requests with priority given to local media followed by national, then regional.

News conferences were held throughout the next two days releasing statements from the patient and her family; information about the patient's care; and information regarding how the babies would be cared for at Blank Children's Hospital, which is on the same campus as Iowa Methodist.

Three days after the story broke, the patient and her family requested that no additional information be released by the hospital until after the babies were born. At that point, the public relations department faced one of the most challenging and difficult aspects of managing the situation. Local, national and international media awaited news of the births on the hospital's doorstep, and public relations staff continued to turn down media opportunities.

Because all interview requests were turned down, the media looked to physicians at competing hospitals as well as other healthcare organizations around the country for hypothetical information on the patient and the babies.

Although bothersome to watch experts who were not involved with the situation conduct interviews about topics surrounding the highly anticipated births, the key strategy set forth at the very beginning remained the top priority: the patient's wishes would always be honored and her interests protected.

While the media understood the hospital's strategy, they were persistent and creative when pitching story ideas to public relations. Oftentimes, they insisted their story ideas weren't "septuplet related." One local television station went so far as requesting an interview regarding the plans for snow removal in the lots where 14 satellite trucks were stationed even though less than one inch of snow had fallen.

PUBLIC RELATIONS PLAN

The three-week silent period turned out to be very beneficial. It not only allowed public relations to prepare for any possible outcome; it gave each team member time to feel comfortable and confident about every facet of the extremely detailed plan.

The following details were outlined and accomplished during the three-week period:

- An employee communication plan was established in order to communicate with one of the hospital's most important audiences.
- The "day of birth" plan was detailed and included assignments for each of the 12 public relations staff members and a telephone notification system.

(continued)

CASE STUDY #2 *(continued)*

- Determined the order and specific content of each news conference.
- Prepared media handouts such as hospital fact sheets and physician biographies.
- Devised a system to process media requests.
- Assigned a public relations staff member to each spokesperson to schedule interviews.
- Credentialed all news media which included producing and distributing media badges and media guidelines.
- Assembled a master media list complete with phone numbers for reporter's home or hotel, work fax, cellular and pager.
- Pre-programmed all media fax numbers into two machines in the public relations office.
- Worked with security to determine the needs of public relations as well as assist with media control.
- Devised a plan for updating the Web site (facts about the births were online 10 minutes after the initial announcement).

Exactly three weeks after the story broke, the wait ended. At 12:15 p.m., three members of the public relations staff contacted the three local television stations simultaneously to tell them that the patient's

As the days of waiting for the birth of septuplets wore on, the media turned to humor to pass the time.

medical team had been assembled. The long-awaited delivery was finally underway and the world was watching.

NEWS CONFERENCES AND NEWS BRIEFINGS

News conferences and news briefings were the two public relations tools used to disseminate information around the globe. These vehicles of communication brought to life the individuals intricately woven into the historical event. All news conferences and briefings were held in the same location for ease of media accessibility.

Among the fourteen official news conferences and briefings held, here is a glimpse of the more monumental moments:

At 2 p.m. the day of the births, the maternal grandfather and a hospital vice president announced the miraculous births. At that point, a situation brimming with uncertainty became a public relations dream: A crisis with a positive outcome.

The media's focus quickly shifted to Drs. Mahone and Drake. Following their first appearance during a news conference (the second news conference that day), media requests poured in from all corners of the country. All three networks wanted to lead their morning news programs with a live interview. Other media entities wanted them on the cover of their magazines or newspapers. The physicians continued to see patients during the chaos that followed the unparalleled delivery, making it difficult to meet all the media's requests.

The momentum of the astonishing event continued with a spontaneous news conference held by Iowa Gov. Terry E. Branstad announcing fundraising efforts to build the McCaugheys a new home in Carlisle, Iowa. Companies that had already agreed to donate various products and services were highlighted.

Due to increasing debate about the issue of fertility treatments, the patient's fertility specialist granted a news conference the day after the births. Katherine Hauser, M.D., made a statement regarding the pa-

CASE STUDY #2 *(continued)*

tient's treatment and answered a limited number of questions.

The highly anticipated debut of Dr. Hauser was followed by a news conference featuring staff and physicians from the Variety Club Intensive Care Nursery (the unit where premature infants are cared for, including the septuplets) at Blank Children's Hospital. They provided information about the unique delivery and the type of care received during the first 24 hours. The nurses' and physicians' personal stories of their involvement gave the world its first glimpse of what the babies were truly like.

Perhaps the most memorable and emotional news conference appearance occurred Nov. 21, when the patient was introduced to the world only two days after giving birth by cesarean section to seven babies. Her emergence brought a unique closure to the frenzy that descended upon the Midwestern city in America's heartland.

Following the last formal news conference, news briefings were held throughout the next few days to give an updated medical condition of each baby. One briefing was actually a diversion so the patient and her husband could leave the hospital unnoticed by the media.

The fury of media activity dwindled for Iowa Methodist with the patient's release from the hospital. Originally, the date of her release was going to be kept secret. However, the morning she was to be released, her father announced the much-anticipated event during a live television interview on Face the Nation.

24-HOUR INFORMATION LINE

The eyes and ears of reporters and the public shifted from the patient and Iowa Methodist to the magnificent seven, the team of neonatologists providing their care and Blank Children's Hospital where each baby progressed daily.

Once the media frenzy subsided around Thanksgiving, a 24-hour information line was established. This line provided updates on the babies' conditions three times a day throughout their entire hospital stay.

MILESTONES NOTED

The media, although no longer stationed in front of the two hospitals, continually sought milestones in the babies' lives. One milestone was the babies' one-month birthday. A news conference was held to

A series of news conferences were held by hospital administrators, physicians, nurses and staff to share accurate and timely information with the world's media.

(continued)

CASE STUDY #2 *(continued)*

accommodate the numerous requests Blank received for updates on the babies' conditions.

Curiosity about the babies' release from the hospital continued until March 1—the day the last two babies went home. Prior to March 1, nationwide faxes to notify the media were sent by Blank Children's Hospital public relations within one hour of a baby's release. To celebrate the last departure for members of the McCaughey family, the media was invited to cover the March 1 event.

STATISTICS AND MEDIA FACTS

The following statistics and facts illustrate the impact of this renowned event:

For a two-day period after the babies were born, the public relations department received 2,000 calls and averaged 25,000 hits per day on the hospital Web site. The highest number of hits was 36,000, when a photo of each baby was released. Prior to the septuplet event, the hospital Web site averaged 250 hits per day. Between Oct. 29 and Nov. 24, more than 200 media representatives were credentialed and 14 news conferences and news briefings were held.

The story made the cover of *Time, Newsweek* and *People* magazines. More than 4,000 clips were received via a clipping service from U.S. and Canadian newspapers. Physicians, clinical staff and administrators conducted more than 200 one-on-one interviews with print and broadcast media. According to the outside video monitoring service, the event had more than 10,000 mentions in the top 48 television markets through Nov. 22.

By 6 p.m. the day of the births of the world's only living septuplets, *The Des Moines Register*, Iowa's statewide newspaper, printed an extra edition with proceeds benefiting the McCaugheys.

EVALUATION

There were several ways to measure the success of this event, the most significant being the safe and healthy delivery of the septuplets.

From a public relations perspective, however, the evaluation process included a variety of facets such as positive feedback from members of the media and a self-evaluation.

More than 200 media were credentialed to attend news conferences and briefings at the hospital auditorium.

CASE STUDY #2 (continued)

Reporters from *The Des Moines Register, Newsweek* magazine and NBC News Today sent letters of commendation to the president of Iowa Methodist and Blank Children's Hospital. In addition, a *Time* magazine staff member told a public relations staff member that the staff's efforts were outstanding and better than some of the presidential events the magazine had covered.

The public relations staff made a list of "lessons learned" that would be a strong starting point if an event of this magnitude ever commands the efforts of a public relations team again. The following items were included on the list:

- Better equip the public relations staff room next to the media with additional fax machines and phones.
- Establish a room next to the media center for physicians, administrators and visitors separate from the public relations staff room.
- Take additional information on media request forms such as first choice interview, second choice interview and length of deadline.

- Establish better communication between the public relations staff room in the media center and the public relations main office where phone calls and media requests were answered.
- Designate one public relations staff person each day/night to be the main contact for administration (and others who need to know) to call for updates and other pertinent information.
- Have more people in the public relations main office to fulfill simple radio and print interview requests.

Managing the biggest news story of 1997 gave Iowa Methodist and Blank Children's Hospital public relations professionals a unique and unparalleled opportunity to showcase medical care while the world watched. The care provided in this event, however, is the same care provided every day for every patient served.

Satellite trucks and media vehicles lined the hospital driveway for weeks.

Source: Text and photos, Iowa Methodist Medical Center and Blank Children's Hospital. Reprinted by permission.

POINTS TO REMEMBER

■ Case studies demonstrate how campaigns to achieve specific public relations objectives are planned, implemented and evaluated.

■ Case studies may be used in two ways: (1) they may pose a PR problem and outline a possible solution according to specific guidelines, as suggested by an existing case; (2) they may dissect a historical case as a learning experience to determine what worked, what didn't and why.

■ The historical case is generally referred to as a *case*; the existing situation in need of a PR solution is generally called a *case problem*.

■ PR firms keep a special library containing files of the cases they have handled. These are often written as historical case studies.

■ An analysis of a historical case can be broken down into four parts: (1) a summary and the research-based purposes of the PR actions; (2) additional research into publics, an assessment of the impact of the problem, situation or proposed action, a prioritization of the publics, a discussion of the evolution of the problem, together with its probable causes and an explanation of what was done to deal with the problem; (3) detailed description of the institution involved in the problem; (4) consideration and evaluation of what worked particularly well and what could have been improved.

■ Cases serve as idea resources for PR practitioners in solving problems and for PR scholars in theory building.

■ Case studies are available from PRSA, IABC and Harvard Business School. Case studies in anthropology and sociology may discuss problem solving when culture is an issue, but the social science approach to case studies is somewhat differ-

ent. Case studies in agriculture are a source of information about the diffusion process and resulting theory.

NOTES

[1] Dean Kruckeberg, "Using the Case Study Method in the Classroom," in Lynne M. Sallot, ed., *Learning to Teach: What You Need to Know to Develop a Successful Career as a Public Relations Educator* (2nd ed.) (New York: Public Relations Society of America, 1998), pp. 221–233.

[2] Adapted from Ronald N. Levy, "How to Help Your Lobbyists Win," *Public Relations Journal* (August 1982), p. 31.

[3] Joanne Lipman, "AHA's Seal of Approval Dealt a Blow," *Wall Street Journal* (January 25, 1990), pp. B1, B4. See also Marian Burros's New York Times News Service story of Wednesday, February 7, 1990. It appears in the *Fort Worth Star-Telegram* of that date on page 1, section 6, under the headline, "Do Ya Gotta Have Heart?"

[4] Alan R. Andreasen, "Nonprofits: Check Your Attention to Customers," *Harvard Business Review* (May–June, 1982), pp. 105–10.

[5] Sydney Freedberg, Jr., "Run Away: The Business Cycle Meets the Spin Cycle. (Full Disclosure in Public Relations)," *The New Republic*, 216(24) (June 16, 1997), pp. 11–12.

[6] Rosabeth Kanter, "Values and Economics," *Harvard Business Review* (May–June 1990), p. 4. This same piece says, "Values should be inclusive—general enough to embrace diverse parts of the organization and diverse people. One company's attempt to spread a new management philosophy relevant to its traditional operations wing failed in a publicly humiliating way because the marketing group—mostly young MBAs—rebelled."

[7] Dean Kruckeberg, Badran A. Badran, Muhammad I. Ayish and Ali A. Awad, *Case Studies in Public Relations* (Al-Ain United Arab Emirates: United Arab Emirates University Press, 1994), pp. 19–28.

Selected readings, activities and assignments appropriate to this chapter can be found in the *Instructor's Guide* or on InfoTrac if you are using the InfoTrac College Edition.

CHAPTER 15

CRISES

Corporations have challenges that they have never faced before. This presents global opportunities for those who practice public relations.

HAROLD BURSON, BURSON-MARSTELLER

When the crisis occurs the research must be at hand . . . its facts understood . . . the communicators ready to go into action.

The modern PR person must know how to research any subject, do it quickly, and summarize it well and briefly.

FRANK W. WYLIE, FELLOW, PRSA, AND PAST PRESIDENT, PRSA

The crisis of all crises is supposed to occur on January 1, 2000, when we find out which computers have not been reprogrammed to identify the new year. Millions of computers all over the world may not be able to distinguish between 1900 and 2000 because of an old programming practice that expressed years as only two digits. Computers not reprogrammed will either produce inaccurate data or simply shut down. Since computers run everything from air traffic to banking, the total worldwide repair bill is estimated at $300 billion.[1] Consequences in just the USA of the information shutdown are expected to stifle economic growth and result in a recession.[2] One serious problem is the interactivity of computer systems which means a glitch in one of them affects all of them.[3]

Talk about crises creating crises—in May of 1998 airlines in the USA were busy pulling all Boeing 747s out of their fleets to inspect wiring bundles that might be worn enough to ignite fuel systems. Such a defect seemed to be the only answer to the mystery of why a TWA plane bound for France blew up shortly after take-off in New York during July 1996. Consequently, the USA's Federal Aviation Administration ordered all USA airlines to check for wear from chafing on insulation surrounding wires passing through wing fuel tanks, fuel-pump wires in planes with 30,000 plus flight hours and center pump wiring too, although these evidenced less wear.[4] TWA's loss of Flight 800 generated a 24-hour involvement in crisis communication with media, federal accident investigators, personnel and the families of victims for three weeks after the accident, and constant fol-low-up as various theories about the cause prolifer-ated, much of them on the Internet.

Crises never truly go away. Subsequent litiga-tion usually causes further media attention. For ex-ample, the 1993 World Trade Center bombing was back in the news in 1997 as the alleged master-mind, Ramzi Ahmed Yousef, went on trial in New York. He and Eyad Ismoil, who was accused of hav-ing driven the van carrying the bomb, were both found guilty in November and face life in prison. Another terrorist act, the Oklahoma City bomb-ing of the Alfred P. Murrah Federal Building in 1995, was back in the news too in 1997 and 1998 with the trials and subsequent convictions of both Timothy McVeigh, for murder and conspiracy, and Terry Nichols, convicted for conspiracy only. Their sentencing carried over into 1998. Memori-als and dedications also carry forward a crisis when lives are lost. Certainly that is true with the Okla-homa City bombing and the deaths that came in 1993 to a religious cult based near Waco, Texas when their facility burned after a 51-day siege be-tween the cult's leader, David Koresh, and USA federal agents.

Even without direct ties to other countries, as in the case of the World Trade Center, many of to-day's crises are global in their impact. Certainly that was true of the 1998 Asian economic crisis, and "mad cow" disease, which has been a problem in Britain since the mid-1980s.

Mad Cow Disease only became a crisis in 1996 when the food chain scenario showed that the dis-ease could affect humans who ate beef. In humans, the fatal illness is caused by Creutzfeldt-Jakob Disease (CJD); in cattle, it's bovine spongiform en-cephalopathy (BSE).[5] The source for BSE is ap-parently a disease that first affects sheep, called Scrapie. Parts of sheep are added to cattle food for protein. The European Union put a ban on British beef in 1996 and the EU plan calls for destroying British cattle over the age of 30 months, except those in the dairies. It was anticipated that 700,000 British cattle would be destroyed every year for six years. There was also a tougher requirement about how animal remains could be processed into bone

meal. Another problem for consumers lies in the number of other uses for beef beyond directly con-suming it as meat. Albumin from the blood is in moisturizing creams; gelatin from the bones is in desserts, yogurt, candies and adhesives for stamps; desiccated liver is used as a nutritional supplement; collagen from the inner layer of the hide is used in cosmetic treatments and wound balm; and tallow from the intestines is used in soaps, creams and cosmetics.[6]

Clearly, many aspects of the BSE problem carry the potential for widespread alarm. But beef producers are quick to point out the lack of a proven connection between BSE and CJD. There's also a lag time, five years in cattle and more than ten in people. Why the crisis, then? When scien-tists found people with a new variant of CJD that is similar to BSE, it was determined that eating in-fected beef was likely the cause. The culprit in both is something called a prion that acts like an infectious microbe (virus or bacteria) but is distinct from anything seen before.[7] In the USA, a big con-sumer of beef, the commodities market showed little effect, perhaps because USA beef are fed dif-ferently. However, once a CJD victim in Kentucky was identified, beef stocks took a tumble. Then, in a highly celebrated case, television talk show celebrity Oprah Winfrey responded to an audience discussion of the disease, saying that she "would never eat a hamburger again." She was sued by the beef industry. Taking her whole show to Amarillo for the duration of the trial, she was acquitted, and the beef industry didn't seem to win in the court of public opinion either.[8]

Crises come in many forms, but public rela-tions people for the most part deal with *public* crises. These can be described, categorized and usually (in general form at least) predicted.[9] Crises are like plays; there are only so many basic plots. Everything else is a variation. Two factors are always present: crises involve people and they in-terrupt the normal "chain of command."

Causes of crises are either physically violent or nonviolent. The physically violent ones come to mind immediately—earthquakes, fires, storms, plane crashes and terrorist acts, to name but a few.

The collapse of the Asian economies in 1998 is an example of a physically nonviolent crisis.

Each of these broad categories, *violent* and *nonviolent,* has subsets with more specific descriptors. Some violent crises are created by *acts of nature,* such as lightning that sparks a forest fire or a hurricane or typhoon that sweeps a coast. Some nonviolent crises, too are created by acts of nature—crises such as viral epidemics, insect plagues and droughts. These may take lives, but they are not cataclysmic or overwhelmingly violent. That factor alone calls for a different type of crisis management.

Some crises result from *intentional* acts committed by a person or group. Violent intentional crises are due to acts of terrorism that result in loss of life or freedom, such as hostage-taking. This category also includes product-tampering, when it results in loss of life or destruction of property. Nonviolent intentional crises include bomb and product-tampering threats, hostile takeovers, insider trading, computer viruses, malicious rumor and other malfeasance.

The third subcategory of crises includes *unintentional* events that are neither acts of nature nor deliberate acts of individuals or groups. This category includes violent unintentional accidents, such as explosions, fires and chemical leaks. On the nonviolent side are process or product problems, which often have delayed consequences such as stock market crashes, business failures or hostile takeovers. Example 15.1 provides an outline and summary of the various kinds of crises.

Whatever organization you are working in or with, you can predict and thus anticipate most possible crises. This means that you can plan for crises.

In responding to the notion that crises could be planned for, one corporate PR director said, "Research and planning sound great, but that's academic. I'm too busy fighting alligators to drain the swamp." Often such a response is a form of denial or simply an excuse—one that public relations counselors often hear, especially when they are called on a weekend and asked to put out a bonfire that had been smoldering for months. When the fire is either contained or extinguished, the alligator comment often follows. The problem for the PR person is that the CEO, whom the counselor is also dealing with, is asking how the fire got so big so fast. The key to good crisis management is anticipation.

IMAGINING THE WORST

Part of that anticipation is listing the kinds of crises your organization is most likely to face. Many crisis managers use a descriptive typology.[10] Once they have put a name to a type of crisis, such as "technological," it helps to think about the company in terms of the different types of problems in this area that could arise. Planning includes eliminating some risks by examining policies that might be put in place to prevent crises in that category.

One example of preventive policy resulted from Southwest Airlines' consideration of the matter of wheelchairs. An evaluation of the number of customers using wheelchairs raised concern about what would happen if a passenger came in with a personal, motorized wheelchair and wanted it shipped on the plane just like luggage. That "what if" started research into FAA regulations regarding what could be carried, exploration of what types of wheelchairs were being used, and inquiries of engineers about the capacity of the airline's planes to carry such cargo. The result was a "no wheelchairs" policy which is communicated to all passengers so there's no last minute decision to be made.

Others develop policies governing certain possible crisis situations using a more formal risk management strategy that involves a risk assessment process. Risk assessment comes from interpretations of data from a number of sources, much of it scientific, to determine safety levels. An example is evaluating risks from exposure to pesticides used on foods—processed or unprocessed. Research helps policy makers develop some risk assumptions and these govern policy, including government regulatory decisions.[11]

An important part of assessing any potential crisis is evaluating the vulnerability of the organization to the worst case scenario of that crisis. For

EXAMPLE 15.1

Crisis Typology

Source of Crisis	Violent: Cataclysmic—Immediate Loss of Life or Property	Nonviolent: Sudden Upheaval but Damages, If Any, Are Delayed
Act of nature	Earthquakes, forest fires	Droughts, epidemics
Intentional	Acts of terrorism, including product tampering, when these result in loss of life or destruction of property	Bomb and product-tampering threats, hostile takeovers, insider trading, malicious rumors and other malfeasance
Unintentional	Explosions, fires, leaks, other accidents	Process or product problems with delayed consequences, stock market crashes, business failures

very serious potential crises, many managers use simulations to test their vulnerability and the potential success of their crisis plans.

Crisis management is also immeasurably aided when top executives accept an integrated two-way symmetrical model of public relations. When that model is used with proactivity and symmetry—along with issues management, planning, prevention and implementation—resolving conflicts that a crisis might cause is likely to be easier, because the organization and its publics have been talking to each other all along.[12]

An organization confronted with a crisis is concerned with its own behavior and with the behavior of its members and of all its other publics. Some publics tend to be neglected in the planning process—unintended (often global) audiences of communication about the crisis. Such publics, known as "nimbus" publics,[13] often receive information about the crisis because of the global nature of technology. Every crisis plan needs to take into account the potential global impact of crises, even when these are viewed as being essentially domestic. Organizations experience a crisis, not as an isolated event or series of events, but as one or more occurrences that develop in the total environment of public opinion in which the organization operates. That total environment encompasses various

nimbus publics that the organization may not have recognized as being affected by the crisis and by the organization's response to it.

Sometimes a crisis creates the nimbus public, as in the case of Muslim reaction to USA bookstores' selling Salman Rushdie's The Satanic Verses after Iran's Ayatollah Khomeini condemned it. Other nimbus groups may be identified for the first time as a result of a crisis. An example is the anti-American activism in Mexico when the United States invaded Panama in 1990.[14] Handling such nimbus publics means considering the environment of public opinion in the planning process (see Example 15.2).

A crisis gets your attention and demands the immediate attention of top management. It may or may not come with preliminary hints or warnings. But whether the crisis involves violent or nonviolent dangers created by natural events, deliberate acts or accidents, it can be anticipated with good imaginative powers exercised through brainstorming. Various departments within the organization should participate.[15]

You need to hold brainstorming sessions with various departments because someone may be aware of a possibility that you couldn't imagine without having that person's special job-related knowledge. Look at all aspects of the organization.

EXAMPLE 15.2

Public Opinion Node in Crisis Management

The minimum objective of crisis management with respect to public opinion is to maintain the positive public opinion the organization enjoyed before the crisis and to limit negative public opinion, collectively or from any single public, to pre-crisis levels. The public opinion node itself contains all opinions (positive or negative) held by all members of a specific public.

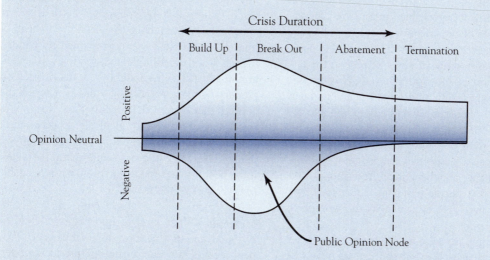

Source: David Sturges, Bob Carrell, Doug Newsom and Marcus Barrera, "Crisis Communication Management: The Public Opinion Node and Its Relationship to Environmental Nimbus," *SAM Advanced Management Journal*, 56(3) (Summer 1991), 22–27. Reprinted with permission.

What is rather dismaying about crises is that only 14 percent are truly sudden, accidental and unexpected, according to a 1996 study of more than 50,000 news stories by the Institute of Crisis Management. The remaining 86 percent were more or less predictable—the result of operational or organizational weaknesses, bad practices and other discoverable "bombs" waiting to explode.[16] This is the reason to involve as many people in the organization as possible because there's no other way to discover the potential problem. "The notion that one person, sitting atop a corporate hierarchy, can regu-

larly and successfully guide the daily actions of tens of thousands of individual employees is a pleasant confection . . ." says Lockheed Martin president Norman R. Augustine. He also says the one aspect of business in which a chief executive's influence is measurable is crisis management. "Crises tend to be highly formative experiences—watershed experiences, sometimes even life-threatening experiences for a business," Augustine says. He advises avoiding them when possible, but "once you're in one, accept it, manage it, and try to keep your vision focused on the long term. The bottom line of my own experience with crises can be summarized in just seven words: Tell the truth and tell it fast."[17]

The "imagining" process, Ian I. Mitroff of the University of Southern California's Center for Crisis Management suggests, is designed for top executives to put themselves in the role of an intelligent adversary and ask, "What is the most creative way I could wreck this company? . . . Then they have to ask, 'What is the most intelligent way we could respond?'"[18]

In looking at "wreckable" areas, Dow Chemical's corporate communications director in Sarnia, Ontario, suggests these potential targets: (1) *products or services* in terms of safety, effects on the environment and use of scarce materials; (2) *processes* such as manufacturing, transportation and finance; (3) *locales* of operation, including sending and receiving facilities; (4) *people problems*—officers and executives, their corporate and private lives and personnel policies, especially employment and separation policies and benefits.[19] You should add health to the people-problems category, since AIDS or some other epidemic in the workplace may cause panic.

While you are imagining the worst, consider the impact that each event you can identify will have on each public individually. When you do this, you can anticipate possible chain reactions—that is, for example, what an explosion that contaminates your product will do to your stock and how you are perceived by important publics (see Examples 15.3 and 15.4). The way you handle a crisis while it is occurring can lessen or increase its impact significantly. Planning can help you develop strategies out of the intensity of a crisis. It also helps you clarify or modify a management response, depending on whether management operates in a closed or in an open climate.

Planning

An organization's communication climate has a great impact on how management handles crises.[20] Of all the wrong decisions an organization can make in a crisis, deciding to shut off the flow of accurate information is probably the worst. Closed

and open communication systems have been described earlier; but in terms of crisis management, the open system is much the easier one in which to operate. Rumors are less likely to start when information is openly available and a residue of trust exists inside and outside the organization. You must always consider an organization's communication climate when you undertake crisis planning.

In planning for a crisis, you must always recognize that information is going to be in great demand. Unfortunately, you won't be able to get much information about the crisis itself ahead of time. You can make a crisis easier to handle, though, if you organize the information you *can* obtain in advance. You should collect information on products/services, processes, locales, people and the policies that govern the organization. Keep all of this information readily available to those most likely to need it, and keep it in a form that is most likely to be usable in a crisis. Information is useless if the people who need it don't know it is available or don't understand how to use it.

Materials   What kind of information should be gathered, and in what form should it be kept?[21] You need details and descriptions of products or services, product contents and product development processes or service processes, as well as a list of general operating procedures. You should also have current safety and instruction manuals, and copies of all recent inspection reports. In case of an explosion or a fire, you will have to describe contents and processes, with full awareness of potential danger areas—that is, the explosive nature of stored grains or the use of inflammable chemicals in a cleaning operation. You need a full description of all locations, including what is kept in surrounding areas and specifics such as acreage, street names, and the location of nearby homes, businesses or nonprofit organizations.

For every operation, you need a list of personnel and the times specific personnel are likely to be occupying an area. If the organization has clients or customers who are likely to be on the premises, you need that information, too. In 24-hour-operations—for example, mines, manufacturing plants, some retail stores, medical facilities and

EXAMPLE 15.3

An Organization's Operational Environments in a Crisis

The direct environment includes the publics central to the organization, as well as other publics most directly affected by the crisis. The indirect environment encompasses other readily identified publics that usually are involved in the organization's ongoing relationships with constituencies. The cloud around an organization's environment is its nimbus, consisting of groups that are not normally identified as being among the organization's publics but that become such publics as a result of the crisis.

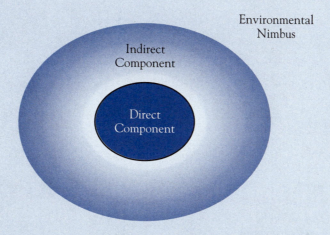

Source: David Sturges, Bob Carrell, Doug Newsom and Marcus Barrera, "Crisis Communication Management: The Public Opinion Node and Its Relationship to Environmental Nimbus," *SAM Advanced Management Journal*, 56(3) (Summer 1991), pp. 22–27. Reprinted with permission.

resident educational or care-giving institutions that operate with shift changes—you must set up a system with your personnel or human resources department so that you have at your fingertips an up-to-the-minute record of which employees are working where at what particular time. This information must be kept *remote* from the location. For example, at the time of a disaster, one mining company had to call all families and ask which family members were missing to determine who was trapped in a mine. This occurred because an explosion close to the opening of the mine blew up the shack in which miners had signed on for the shift. You should also keep a list of personnel benefits that employees receive in the event of death or injury on the job.

Keep separation policies on hand in the event that an employee or employees are responsible for the crisis. You should have policies and processes governing access to facilities, since many crises are caused by disgruntled employees or former employees. You also need access to as much information as your personnel office has on all employees and officers in the event of a crisis that involves them. You may not use all of the available information, for reasons of privacy, but the undisclosed facts

EXAMPLE 15.4
Stages of Public Opinion in a Crisis

Latent issues should be detected by environmental monitoring, but when a crisis occurs, groups tend to form in relation to the event and to responses to it by the organization and by other publics. The result may be public debate of issues, as occurred after the United States and its allies went to war in the Persian Gulf in 1991. As time lapses after an event, public opinion forms. It does so more dramatically if the crisis, like the Persian Gulf conflict, involves daily changes and additional events. The result of opinion formation is a form of social action—peace protests in the case of the Persian Gulf war. Then there is usually counteraction, followed by the eventual restoration of group norms.

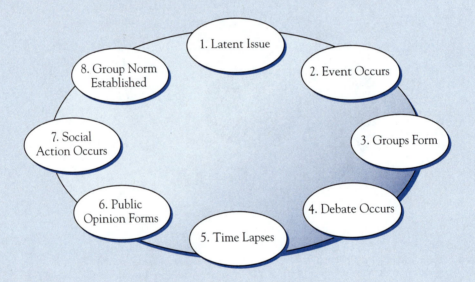

Source: David Sturges, Bob Carrell, Doug Newsom and Marcus Barrera, "Crisis Communication Management: The Public Opinion Node and Its Relationship to Environmental Nimbus," *SAM Advanced Management Journal*, 56(3) (Summer 1991), pp. 22–27. Reprinted with permission.

available to you may help you to put a situation into perspective.

Part of being prepared is routine and consists of maintaining current corporate facts sheets containing all necessary basic information in the files at all times. Such information should include the following:

1. Addresses of the home office and all branches or subsidiaries (if any) and all telephone numbers,

including the numbers of security people and night numbers that override the main control and put you through to the person on duty.

2. Descriptions of all facilities, in detail, giving layouts and square footage and the number of people in each area (very important facts in case of fire or cave-ins).

3. Biographical information on all employees, and long, in-depth pieces on key executives. Often called "current biographical summaries," these are useful for speeches and introductions, but here they might become standing obituaries, material ready to use with only the addition of cause of death.

4. Photos of all facilities and all principals (recent photographs; not the architects' rendering of the ten-year-old building or the CEO's favorite photo from several years past).

5. Statistics on the facilities and the institution: number of people employed now; cost of buildings and equipment; annual net (or gross) earnings; descriptions of products or services, or both if that is the nature of the institution; major contracts with unions and suppliers; details of lawsuits pending or charges against the institution; information on regulatory or accrediting agencies with some sort of oversight covering the institution, its products and its services (for instance, the Food and Drug Administration over products in that area or hospital accreditation over health-care institutions).

6. A history of the institution, including major milestones, prepared like facts sheet.

7. Emergency information such as nearest hospital, police and fire chief's direct numbers, best access routes, hazardous substances identification and potential threat, local government officials' direct numbers and numbers for contacts at regulatory agencies.

8. Ways to check personnel to see who might have been involved—a format for accounting for each member of the workforce.

Simply keeping all these materials up to date is a major undertaking, but it is vitally important. Most institutions handle them piecemeal, updating employee biographies annually, and photos less frequently, and gathering new and relevant facts once the base is established. A periodic review of these materials is essential. Make a checklist and use it, marking the date of the most recent check next to it.

The crisis plan itself should be a guideline rather than a heavily detailed process, for two reasons: ease of recall and flexibility. Both features aid in the creative handling of a specific crisis.

Communication Some crisis plans are thorough and comprehensive, but they are never communicated. Then, when a crisis occurs, employees either don't have a copy of the plan or don't know how to follow its instructions. A good plan should include an easy-to-use facts sheet and background information.[22]

You should hold regularly scheduled meetings with all managers and supervisors likely to have to deal with a crisis, to review crisis response procedures. "Regularly" really depends on an organization's structure. In an organization with high turnover, quarterly review meetings may be appropriate. An organization with more stable employment and a system for giving information to new hires may prefer annual reviews. Reviews not only renew familiarity with procedures, they also allow planners to review the procedures themselves to ensure that they are relevant. Reviews spaced more than a year apart court trouble.

One reason to discuss crisis planning in advance is to get management involved in handling various publics before a crisis occurs. You may be able to alter some management tendencies toward procrastination by offering hypothetical examples of the effects of such behavior and by encouraging role playing. In organizations such as hospitals and banks, employees should be crisis-trained for the possibility that they may either have to negotiate with a hostage-taker or survive as hostages themselves.

As dismaying as it might sound, from 50 to 70 percent of the largest profit-making organizations in the USA haven't made any disaster plans. The percentage is probably even higher for nonprofit organizations, primarily because they are less likely to have personnel trained to handle this area and are not likely to have a public relations firm on retainer to plan for them and to help them through a crisis.[23]

■ Communicating During a Crisis

Three key elements promote successful communication during a crisis: (1) the existence of a *communication plan* as a part of the overall crisis plan, taking into consideration that normal channels

"It's all according to your point of view. To me, you're a monster."

Reprinted with permission from Modern Maturity. © 1995, AARP.

may not be open; (2) the ability to assemble a *crisis team* when a crisis occurs; (3) the use of a *single spokesperson* during the crisis.

In developing a communication plan, remember that employees are going to talk to neighbors and to casual acquaintances whether authorized to do so or not. Consequently, your communication plan must include strong internal as well as external communication. Determine the best system to use: memos, closed-circuit TV, computer terminals, telephone. Identify people likely to be the principal participants in a communication plan, and develop a system for checking message statements before these are disseminated through the media.

The message statements will be generated by the crisis management team that you assemble from staff. This team will be instructed by outside PR counsel (when you decide to retain outside help) and by the organization's legal counsel. Isolate the crisis management team from normal day-to-day business affairs during the crisis. If day-to-day business is interrupted, the company will appear to be consumed by the crisis and unable to manage the situation. Management of communication

during the crisis is not the same as managing the crisis itself.

Designate members of the crisis team as fact finders—people who will dig out facts, organize facts, resolve conflicting data and control and direct the flow of information to the team members and the spokesperson. Designate a person to evaluate the effects of the crisis on all publics and to monitor how the messages from the organization are influencing various publics and the factions within these publics.

You must include legal counsel in all planning because, when a crisis occurs, legal advice and PR advice to top management often conflict. Legal counsel tends to advise "no comment," while PR counsel urges "openness." The reasons underlying both tendencies are justified by what occurs. Since the opposition seizes upon every word, lawyers understandably believe that it is better to say very little. Openness clearly creates more difficulty for lawyers who are trying to defend an organization. As a PR practitioner, you must accept that fact. But at the same time, the openness of an organization in a crisis also affects public opinion favorably.

Whether the situation involves a jury trial or a Supreme Court hearing, the proceedings occur within the climate of public opinion.

Philadelphia's gas and electric utility, PECO Energy, took full responsibility for an explosion early one December morning 1995. Two Norristown homes were destroyed, two people were killed and one was injured. In the 18 months prior to the event, PECO employees had been involved in values training which had turned the utility's focus from being process driven to being people driven. The decision to accept responsibility came from CEO Corbin McNeill who apologized to the victims' families and told the news media that taking responsibility was the right thing to do both morally and pragmatically. A response from the Associated Press noted: "The utility's decision to take immediate responsibility for Tuesday's deadly blast is uncommon in the business world, but may strategically defuse negative public opinion and even reduce damage in lawsuits. . . ."[24]

Another acceptance of responsibility, this from American Airlines when its jet crashed in Colombia in 1996, brought this observation from a *Dallas Morning News* reporter," It was an admission that was surprising for both its swiftness and its candor."[25]

The way the story is told is important too because it must be credible and acceptable. For that reason, public relations educator Robert L. Heath advocates using a narrative format while recognizing the news media need the who, what, when, where, why and how. Heath says, "First, people need to recognize that crisis response entails the telling of a story—the enactment of a crisis narrative. The next consideration is the critical and strategic selection of the specific narrative account for and report on that event. . . ." It is essential that the story be truthful, that key publics are able to relate to the story and that the narrative demonstrates that the organization has control of the situation for a successful resolution to the story.[26]

After developing a plan for responding to a crisis and making people in the organization familiar with it, the next most important part of dealing with a crisis is designating *the* (as in single) most credible spokesperson. Some authorities say that choosing the spokesperson is the most important part of dealing with a crisis, because that person sets the style for handling the crisis. It may or may not be the CEO. Frequently the CEO is involved in making critical decisions to resolve the crisis if that responsibility has not been delegated to someone else. In any case, the person designated should be someone who is perceived by the organization's publics as knowledgeable and who is kept up to date on all developments. The spokesperson must know all aspects of the crisis, must understand their implications and must have sole responsibility and authority for speaking in the name of the organization. The appropriate spokesperson may be different in different crises. When a university was dealing with a football scandal, the designated spokesperson was the coach. The same school when faced with an academic crisis used the academic vice-president. Each had been previously trained to deal with the news media.

The spokesperson is usually a member of the crisis team and functions as your key contact for all media. If for some reason (probably time pressures), you decide to use a different inside spokesperson for employees than for the news media, you must be sure that the two present *exactly* the same information. The only difference should be the inside slant that the spokesperson for employees gives. Using an inside slant does not mean presenting biased information; it means taking into consideration the special concerns of employees. You might also choose an inside person because that person has greater credibility with inside audiences. But the external spokesperson must be someone respected and highly credible to inside audiences as well, or you will damage the credibility of the inside person in the process. The spokesperson should not be an outsider, even if that "outsider" is a quasi-insider, such as a staff member from the public relations firm of record. The firm's role is not to play the wizard who waves a magic wand and makes all the trouble go away. Instead, its role is to work in partnership with the organization, fully realizing that the final decision is always the client's.[27]

Reprinted with special permission of King Features Syndicate.

Employees' Critical Role You must truly believe your employees are the front line in public relations to use them effectively in a crisis. They are the organization's most credible representatives to the people outside the organization with whom they come in contact; and when you think about it, those people constitute all the rest of your publics—from media to customers, from clients to suppliers. People will develop perceptions from the way employees respond to their questions and from their behavior. Unfortunately, most organizations in crises neglect their employees. This not only mistreats personnel, but also harms the organization.

Employees get depressed during a crisis. They worry first about themselves and then about the organization (see Example 15.5). They become overly dependent on internal networks fed by rumors and on the news media. Employees should *never* first learn something about their organization from the news media unless it is something that has just occurred, like a fire. "Employees may hold the key to the organization's ability to survive and then recover from life-threatening crises," according to two researchers who have looked at the stress that crises cause employees.[28]

Management's Behavior In planning for crises, you need to be able to anticipate the communication climate by predicting how management is likely to act and react as the drama of a crisis unfolds. Relying on case studies and Hazel Henderson's pattern for typical management responses to

problems, Bob Carrell has developed some guidelines for anticipating management reactions in the three stages of crisis management: (1) prior to the crisis during normal day-to-day operations; (2) at the moment some event triggers the crisis; (3) during the crisis situation that follows the event (see Example 15.6).[29]

Carrell acknowledges that the crisis management effort can be hampered by the following elements:

1. The extent of a crisis may not be known immediately.

2. Persons or audiences affected by a crisis may be difficult to identify.

3. The cause of a crisis may be difficult to identify, and its cause(s) may never be fully known.

4. A crisis is always traumatic to audiences affected directly by it.

5. Accurate and appropriate information about a crisis is an expectation—sometimes rising to unreasonable levels—of audiences, especially by those directly affected.

6. Information decisions are made under conditions of high stress.

7. Because the situation is a crisis, the credibility of the organization is suspect among audiences directly and indirectly affected by it.

8. A crisis incites emotional behavior by everyone related to it. Physical exhaustion also takes a toll on everyone involved.

EXAMPLE 15.5

Employee Crisis Communication Model

Employees personalize their organization's crisis, and if their needs are not attended to through appropriate communications, their responses to external publics and their interactions with each other can impede the organization's recovery from the crisis.

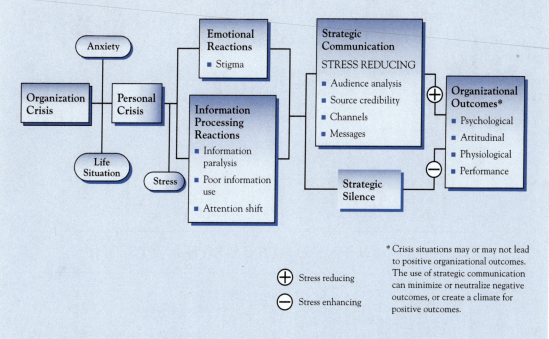

+ Stress reducing

− Stress enhancing

* Crisis situations may or may not lead to positive organizational outcomes. The use of strategic communication can minimize or neutralize negative outcomes, or create a climate for positive outcomes.

Source: Reprinted from J. David Pincus and Lalit Acharya, "Employee Communication Strategies for Organizational Crises," in *Employee Responsibilities and Rights Journal*, 1(3) (1988), p. 190.

However, Carrell notes that the tendency of management toward an open or closed communication style and the corporate culture that such a style creates have a great deal to do with the way the organization responds both internally and externally.

Crisis Constants Five communication elements that remain constant in any crisis help explain how people who do not directly experience the crisis will evaluate it. First, people learn about crises primarily from personal networks, if the situation is geographically close or if there is some relationship between the crisis and the network. An example would be an explosion in a nearby plant where employee networks carry the news to other employees faster than the mass media carry it. Second, people tend to interpret the seriousness of a crisis in terms of personal risk, or risk to people important to them. This perception may be based more on subjective than objective factors, so public and official perceptions of risk sometimes differ considerably. Third, government sources are relied on as the most authoritative. Fourth, the amount of mass media coverage indicates the significance of the

EXAMPLE 15.6
Toward a Matrix of Crisis Communication Management

CRISIS-TRIGGERING EVENT

	ON-GOING			SITUATIONAL			
	Assessment of Environment	**Development of Crisis Management/ Communication Plan**	**Pro-Action**	**Activate Crisis Communication Plan**	**Arrest Triggering Event**	**Recovery**	**Evaluation**
RESPONSIBLE MANAGEMENT BEHAVIOR LEVEL 4 (++)*	• Prudent evaluation of all categories of potential crises • Evaluates risks • Considers, prepares strategies and plans to prevent, minimize impact of crisis • Management is optimistic, confident, open-minded and aggressive	• Identify management team • Assign specific duties • Designate one person only to convey information to internal and external audiences • Train spokesperson, other members of crisis team • Plan viewed as positive way of meeting private and public responsibilities • Plan reviewed and revised regularly	• Implements, within capacity to do so, policies and strategies to prevent or minimize impact of crisis • Lobbies for government/public support for changes in laws and regulations • Aggressive, pro-active communication program to prepare audiences for crisis • Believes in principle of inoculation	• Spokesperson takes charge of communication function • Timely, consistent, candid information to internal and external audiences • Conveys information vital to public safety • Allays fears • Stifles rumors by supplying appropriate, factual information	• Inspires wholesome exchange of information with internal and external audiences • Seeks support as necessary • Makes adjustments in policies and strategies to arrest crisis	• Makes changes in policies and strategies to enhance recovery • Makes slight (if any) changes in organizational structure or personnel • Chances of recovery and turnaround are good	• Evaluates causes of recent crisis, responses to it, and outcomes • Reviews, revises crisis management/communication plan for future use in light of recent experience
RESPONSIBLE MANAGEMENT BEHAVIOR LEVEL 3 (+)*	• Evaluates some potential crisis categories, ignores others, myopic • Planning is spotty, myopic • Control systems questionable • Wants to prevent/minimize potential crisis but not fully committed to doing everything they can • Management often complacent	• Communication function regarded as defensive necessity • Communicates only as much and as often as required by internal and external pressure • Does some training but not much follow-up to keep plan current	• Selective implementation of policies/strategies designed to prevent/minimize impact of crisis, but could do more • Sporadic participant in lobbying programs • Little, if any, commitment to communication program to educate, prepare audiences for crisis	• Posturing messages with little substance • Face-saving approach • Rumors and propaganda often go on unchallenged or uncorrected • Group think creeps in • Grudgingly admits crisis but often denies culpability • Offers plausible excuses	• Exchanges only limited information with internal and external audiences • Fears ridicule • Makes policy and strategy changes only sufficient to arrest crisis, no more • Audiences view organization with skepticism	• May make changes in policies and strategies, but usually these are very few • May make some changes in personnel but organizational changes are rare • Chances of recovery and turnaround are fair	• May change crisis management/communication plan, but changes often do not taken very seriously
RESPONSIBLE MANAGEMENT BEHAVIOR LEVEL 2 (–)*	• Lip service to planning and preparation for crises • Management more concerned with sustaining power/status • Lacks sense of public responsibility	• Group think is common • Plan fully protectionist • Short-term solutions to long-term problems • Plan rarely reviewed and updated • Little or no training	• Does only what is demanded by law	• Often denies crisis exists • Rarely admits culpability • Places blame on others • Feelings of invulnerability are common	• Bunker mentality • Digs in and is often recalcitrant, inflexible • Communication channels are plugged up	• Reluctant to make changes in policies and strategies when changes made, usually are to conform to new public policies • In-fighting increases • Loss of confidence in leadership • Low morale • Loss of public confidence	• Existing plan remains unchanged • Rarely changes made in top management and in policies or strategies
RESPONSIBLE MANAGEMENT BEHAVIOR LEVEL 1 (– –)*	• Unable or refuses to recognize potential crises • Can't or won't develop a crisis plan	• Crisis management/ communication plan does not exist	• Grudgingly does what is demanded by law	• Self-postulating as victim of circumstances, incompetent personnel	• Ostrich syndrome • Admits nothing • Does nothing more than is absolutely necessary • Relies on short memory of audiences	• Searches for persons to be offered publicly as sacrificial lambs • Changes in policies and strategies are only those mandated by law • Chances for recovery are very poor	• Organization may collapse • Replacement of top and some middle management is probable • Restructuring is common

* (++) = Open; (+) = Mostly Open; (–) = Mostly Closed; (– –) = Closed

Source: Reprinted with permission of Bob Carrell.

crisis to a global public. Fifth, the availability of information in an open-communication environment reduces rumor and increases the accuracy of others' assessments of the situation.

Any crisis involves many more entities than just the organization that is experiencing the damage and is most responsible for the remedy. Developing an image that suggests the organization is successfully handling the situation depends on two factors: the reality of the organization's being able to cope with the problem; and how well the organization communicates its successful handling of the problem to those who didn't experience the crisis. An organization's inability to cope with a crisis or the perception that it is bungling its efforts to cope can dramatically damage its credibility.

One thing to remember is that the major issue is not so much when a crisis disappears but how it leaves that is the mark of success or failure. A corporate communications expert offers 10 guidelines. The first, again, is take responsibility, and the second is to recognize the difference between just some bad publicity and a real crisis and adjust your response accordingly. A third rule is to use research to determine how you are going to respond, not only for the facts of the situation, but also what major publics are thinking about the situation, and a fourth rule is to recruit some credible third parties to speak on your behalf. A fifth rule is to treat the news media as conduits of information, not enemies, and the sixth rule is assume you will be sued whatever you do, but openness may be a factor in your favor in litigation. Seventh, watch the Internet as closely as traditional news media to get some insight into how the situation is being perceived, and eighth, demonstrate empathy and concern. Rule nine is to take the first 24 hours very, very seriously because this is when the issues are framed and the company is judged by its response. The tenth rule is to begin now building corporate assets in the area of public opinion—corporate reputation—right away because you will need to draw on these in a crisis.[30]

There's good advice in watching the Internet carefully. Intel had ignored what one of its major publics, computer users, had been saying about its prized product, the Pentium processor. But the news media were monitoring the Internet. Therefore, Thanksgiving Day of 1994 found management unhappily trying to decide how to respond to a two-day-old story on CNN that said the chip did arithmetic wrong. Initially, their problem was they couldn't see that this really was a story, despite the fact that major news media were calling. The following week not only was it a major news story, but comedians were joking about it on television and the stock price had slipped dramatically.

In the past the Intel market had been primarily technical people who had been tolerant of flaws in new microprocessors and waited for the problem to be addressed with a new version. But this time, Intel found it had a broader range of customers from game players to those using it for complex math. Most of the users had little appreciation for "floating point divides" and "significant digits." The company did set up an 800 number so people could talk to technical experts, but often the answers were beyond the caller's level of expertise. Intel also counted on the mass media to get the story out. But, the timing and the level of its response made too many customers feel the company didn't care.[31]

Another company that should have known better, Wired Ventures Ltd., had a problem with a new stock offering. For this holding company of the profitable magazine, *Wired*, this was the second time an IPO (Initial Public Offering) had fallen through, and to make matters worse, what killed it was an e-mail message intended for employees that made its way on-line, a violation of the SEC's "quiet period" to keep the stock from being hyped.[32] The e-mail message somehow got into an on-line service called The Well with 10,000 subscribers. The publication of the memo by founder Louis Rossetto, Jr., was picked up by The Street.com, an on-line financial publication in New York. Although Rossetto clams everything in the e-mail memo was in the prospectus, nevertheless calling attention to it in the quiet period is not acceptable.[33] Some personal criticism came to Rossetto, whose authoritarian management style had supposedly alienated staff.

Arrogance also was attributed to some other CEOs who got themselves and their companies into trouble, such as Michael Milken of Drexel Burham Lambert, Inc. and Leona Helmsley with Helmsley Corporation. Both were convicted of misdeeds, Milken of securities fraud violations and Helmsley of mail fraud and income tax evasion.

The effect of CEOs' behavior makes for a compelling study. In 1992 the national chief executive of the United Way of America resigned after being accused of misusing funds. William Aramony, also said to be domineering and arrogant, was convicted in 1995 by a federal jury of 25 crimes, including fraud, tax evasion, conspiracy and money laundering. He had taken nearly $600,000 from the biggest charity in the USA. Two other executives were convicted too. The scandal broke in 1991, and although local United Ways tried to distance themselves from the national office, donations fell off rapidly and by 1995 had not yet reached the 1990 level of giving.[34] When CEOS are involved, the crisis is almost unrecoverable because of their leadership role. In other situations, good communications can help an organization recover its balance.

RECALLS AS CRISIS COMMUNICATION

The first Wednesday in January, 1994, the highest class of recall from the Food and Drug Administration went out in a joint announcement by the FDA and Copley Pharmaceutical, Inc. for Copley's Albuterol, a generic prescription drug used for breathing problems. It was being recalled due to bacterial contamination. Eight weeks after the class-one warning went out, it was apparent that many doctors were still uninformed, not to mention the patients. The problem, some said, was that Copley was not prepared to deal with the ultimate consumers of their drug because they are primarily wholesalers and distributors.

The public was not informed at the outset. Some contamination was found during the previous year, but since the bacteria was not likely to cause problems except in patients with immune system problems, cystic fibrosis or chronic obstructive lung disease, it wasn't thought the recall needed to be widely announced. The first limited recall was in December, but after the FDA elevated the recall status to a class one, Copley sent notices to 65,000 pharmacists and 223,000 physicians, notified the news media and set up an 800 line. Patients actually heard about it before their doctors, although some reported dissatisfaction with the responses they got when they called the 800 number. Some of the pharmacists were confused after the upgrade. Many patients went public with their stories, and Copley could only say that reports of deaths and illnesses were unconfirmed.[35]

That situation was reminiscent of the famous Tylenol crisis. In fact, in 1991, another pharmaceutical company (this time Burroughs-Wellcome of London) suffered a Sudafed product-tampering crisis like the one Johnson & Johnson and its laboratory had with Tylenol in 1982, when several people in Chicago died from taking Tylenol capsules that had been filled with cyanide. The two Sudafed deaths in Washington state during February of 1991 were only the fifth such poisonings with a consumer health product since 1982. Like Johnson & Johnson, Burroughs-Wellcome ordered a massive recall of the product. The deaths forced the entire industry to take another look at capsule pills. While industry officials want to protect consumers, they also hope consumers will be somewhat more vigilant.

The difficulty facing the companies in these crises was (and is) that consumers want their selections to be risk-free; unfortunately, says *Science* editor Daniel E. Koshland, Jr., that is "not only impossible, but intolerably expensive."[36] How does an organization communicate what it is doing to reduce risk, and how can it respond to crises like these?

Crises are evaluated in terms of the damage done or the risk of future damage. Evaluations not based on experience are based entirely on communication, and even people involved in a crisis rely heavily on communication in interpreting the crisis. Since many people depend on the mass media for information, those attempting to handle the crisis must try to get the most accurate information to the news media. This must be done not only to quiet rumors that exaggerate the situation and later damage credibility, but also to instill confidence in priority publics regarding the organization's ability to manage the crisis.

In the summer of 1993, Pepsi-Cola found itself involved in a tampering crisis. A syringe was reportedly found in a can of Diet Pepsi, and that report was followed by others. Pepsi's response to the call from the media about the syringe quickly identified the situation as tampering, not a problem with the canning process. Pepsi has specialists designated within the company for all areas of its business, so the production process could be cleared immediately. To offer proof, Pepsi brought the public into the plant with video news releases. Since the Food and Drug Administration is concerned about product safety, the agency was brought into the problem right away to help with copycat situations. Employees were briefed with bulletins twice a day, and company managers everywhere got a daily late afternoon bulletin. The four-day crisis was short because Pepsi was swift with its response and got the focus on tampering. Law enforcement and the FDA were kept informed and were responsive. Employees and media were kept up to date. The Pepsi team, headed by Public Affairs Vice President Rebecca Madeira, drew wide praise from public relations and media people for its handling of an incident that could have threatened long-term sales of the company's product.[37]

PR's Responsibility for a Crisis

When the advent of a crisis catches an organization unawares, this may bring criticism of public relations people. It is often seen as the PR person's responsibility to forewarn and prepare management. In some respects that's true. One invaluable contribution that PR makes is issues monitoring. (See Chapter 4 Publics and Public Opinion.) An-

other significant factor is the PR person's continuous monitoring of publics, which should again offer an opportunity for PR to be a bellwether of potential problems. If crisis anticipation is to remain a recognized role for PR, ignorance cannot be a good excuse. But even when warnings are given, PR does not run an organization; it is only a part of the management team.

When an organization fails to respond to a crisis in the making, it's often due to management's reaction to predictions or forewarnings. At least one response that usually causes trouble is *arrogance*. Arrogance leads to making some assumptions about the vulnerability of the company or the significance of the perceived problem. Ignoring nimbus publics is another difficulty that arises from arrogance, a feeling that some publics are just not important enough for consideration.

Another management mistake that causes trouble is the *failure to get objective information* from all publics that might be involved in a potential problem. Just asking a few people in a public won't work. If there is a potential problem, all of the publics involved need to be the targets of good information-gathering and listening. When a public has some misinformation that is causing the problem, a crisis might be averted by correcting misperceptions or misunderstandings before something erupts. This is often the case with employee relations issues or supplier problems or customer complaints.

Yet another cause for crises going undetected before they really develop is *using bad judgment*. An example of bad judgment that may be lethal is failing to alert employees to problems or potential problems. Even if employees can't be completely taken into confidence, they need to know enough to be helpful. One thing this accomplishes is making employees, especially line managers, aware of the public relations impact of events, actions and issues. They are then more likely to alert PR staff to potential or developing problems. They may become willing collaborators, because any crisis is seen as their crisis too. This kind of involvement also assures their support and cooperation when the unpredictable crisis does occur. They are even better equipped to anticipate and make decisions on their own that will be useful in responding to the crisis at their level.

Responding in a Crisis

Every crisis produces an initial management consultation that occurs face-to-face, by telephone conference call or through a satellite teleconference. It is important to keep comprehensive notes of this meeting. After the meeting, you should write a response release, clearing it first with top management and the organization's attorney. You need a recorded actuality simultaneously with the spokesperson's statement. Depending on the status of the crisis, you may need to call a news conference. If so, you must prepare a list of points you want to make; and of course, you must be prepared for the reporters' questions (see Chapter 12).

As news develops, you will issue bulletins to keep all publics informed. Some of these may be put on an electronic system, such as a Web page, e-mail, teletext or videotex; others will be written news briefs or taped actualities. All will quote the spokesperson.

If the situation attracts calls from media, employees or other publics (and most do), you must set up a telephone bank, train the responders and keep them supplied with updates of information and a list of people to call when they can't answer a question. If the situation involves consumers or large numbers of employees, not all of whom are located nearby, you may get an 800 number. When a large number of external publics, other than media, are involved, you may want to use a 900 number. Although this means that the caller must pay for the information, some callers will be glad to do so.

The telephone bank responders will direct some calls to the 800 or 900 lines. Media calls will be directed to yet another group of responders, preferably PR staff. Crises generate thousands of media calls a day, and a response system has to be developed, together with a method of recording who called when and with what questions.

Constraints of the crisis situation will keep you from communicating as freely as you would like, but all responders must understand that responses should never be misleading or deceptive in any way.

The Exxon Example Ineffective communication in a crisis can turn a difficult but manageable situation into a full-blown disaster, as Exxon discovered in 1989. When the supertanker *Exxon Valdez* ran aground on Bligh Reef in Prince William Sound off Alaska, many people in the oil industry said among themselves, "Thank goodness it happened to Exxon." It wasn't that they wished the company ill, and certainly no one was pleased about the accident, which promised to draw renewed scrutiny to past oil spills and the question of whether the industry's current safety measures were adequate. What the industry people had in mind was that Exxon had enough staff and crisis "know how" to handle the spill swiftly and professionally.

Such assumptions turned out to be unsound, however, because much of the infrastructure in Alaska and at Exxon for dealing with a crisis had been allowed to deteriorate over time since the original crisis planning was conducted. In addition, much of the research and development program had fallen behind.[38] Even so, Exxon could have fared better from a communications perspective if the company had firmly followed up the initial on-site response. The reaction of Exxon's chairman of the board, Lawrence G. Rawl, was to remain silent for two days and to stay in New York.

Exxon president William Stevens later conceded that some of what he and other company executives considered one-sided reporting of the accident was partly the organization's fault. Two news conferences a day were being held at Prince William Sound, but as Stevens notes, "we should have provided electronic linkage to the lower 48, with two-way question and answer capability. That way, both our people in Alaska as well as our executives and the reporters could have pursued the story more directly and simultaneously." Stevens said that the coverage from the reporters on-site was well-balanced and fair.[39]

Nevertheless, some question remains about how much more damaging than necessary the effects of the crisis were because of the following problems: (1) the unavailability of top management, which made them appear to be "stonewalling"; (2) management's focus on the employee error of the tanker captain Joseph Hazelwood and the pilot on duty, which looked like "scapegoating"; (3) the fact that the employee substance abuse rehabilitation policy, while admirable in other respects, lacked a monitoring element, enabling people with a history of problems to return in many cases to their jobs without having overcome their addictions; (4) the statements that the cleanup was over at the onset of cold weather in September, despite contemporaneous television coverage of still-suffering wildlife and ruined fishing businesses, which gave the cleanup effort the appearance of a half-hearted and ineffectual "whitewashing." (In fact, only a tenth of the spilled oil was cleaned up through the efforts of everyone—Exxon, Alyeska, the Coast Guard and volunteers.)

Even before the 1994 civil trial in which the jury awarded $5 billion in punitive damages to victims of the spill, Exxon had already paid $1.1 billion to settle state and federal criminal charges and spent $2.5 billion on the clean-up work. Furthermore, an appeal resulted in yet more bad public relations. A federal judge, in upholding the $5 billion award in a 1996 ruling, said that while he was sure the company would have difficulty getting an underwriter for the $5 billion bond, nevertheless he was concerned that Exxon would keep filing court petitions to delay paying damages.[40]

In U.S. District Judge H. Russel Holland's review of the case, he had become infuriated on discovering that Exxon cut deals in which seven Seattle-based fish processors were required to refund $730 of the $740 million of the punitive damages they claimed in the case. Holland called the arrangement an "astonishing ruse" to "mislead" the jury in the case and "negate its 1994 verdict awarding plaintiffs the $5 billion in punitive damages." Experts in legal ethics called it "an apparent fraud on the jury," and Geoffrey Hazard, author of the

American Bar Association's model code of ethics, said it was designed to "vitiate the legal effect of the jury's expression."

Because Judge Holland blocked Exxon's maneuver by deciding to throw out the punitive-damage claims by the fish processors, it might not be a factor in other legal cases still pending. Exxon paid $70 million to the fish processors in 1991 in return for entering into the agreement.[41] In addition to the processors, Exxon said others had signed away their claims so the company was trying to reduce overall its punitive damages by $240 million.[42] While no one would fault the company for trying to staunch the financial hemorrhaging, the way the effort was made resulted in further damaging the company's reputation.

With the *Exxon Valdez* disaster came public recognition that, assurances to the contrary, no organization has the capacity to clean up a spill of this size—11 million gallons or 240,000 barrels of crude oil, which at the time ranked it 30th among the largest spills in world history and first among U.S. disasters.[43] Subsequently, it was surpassed by the Persian Gulf spill engineered by Saddam Hussein in January of 1991. Yet, the *Exxon Valdez* disaster remains a landmark because it involved U.S. oil going to U.S. refineries for U.S. consumption—oil that was being carried in a U.S. tanker with a U.S. crew under the oversight of the U.S. Coast Guard and working in cooperation with a U.S. pipeline (Alyeska)—and because the wreck occurred in U.S. waters that were among the nation's most environmentally sensitive.[44] It also triggered a U.S. media blitz of the first order.

Dealing with the Media in a Crisis PR practitioners encounter a number of difficulties when working with mass media to communicate the reality of a crisis. One is the inclination of reporters to be more interested in the rare and unusual, especially in communicating risk. For example, a volcanic eruption, which is sudden and dramatic, may get more attention than dangerous water pollution, awareness of which often develops slowly and undramatically. In the latter instance, it may be difficult even to get access to communication channels.

Communication channels are usually disrupted by crises. The disruption may be mechanical (especially if the crisis is a natural disaster), or it may result from demands that the crisis makes on personnel who ordinarily would be taking care of the communication functions. In either case, extra efforts have to be made by the organization to get information to mass media.

Media representatives usually seek authoritative information about a crisis, primarily from government sources. When a crisis occurs, though, people in positions of authority are generally absorbed in helping solve the crisis. Therefore, they seldom see the value of setting aside time to communicate information about the crisis. In addition, those involved in solving the crisis may be a mix of government and nongovernment personnel, such as in a natural disaster or terrorist act, when law enforcement, fire and safety groups work with others from the government. These may also interact with nonprofit relief groups like the Red Cross. All must work with the organization at the center of the crisis, which may be a privately owned business.

Although each group involved may have its own traditional methods of dealing with the news media as a single organization, they are less effective in responding to media inquiries when forced to do so as a loosely organized unit brought together by the crisis. Lines of authority are blurred, and some of the personnel may be out of their usual geographic boundaries. Beyond that, even the best-prepared organizations—and there aren't many of those—can seldom cope with the demands of the news media for information once the media have been attracted to the crisis. The more experienced an organization is with handling crises, the better the response will be (see Example 15.7).

Another problem is the tendency to close down the normal communication channels discussed earlier in this chapter. Often the crisis is such a threat to an organization that either the organization itself or others with control over it, like the government, severely limit information about the crisis.

Even in the best of circumstances, a crisis generates contradictory information. So much occurs at the same time, and so many people have different pieces of information, that it is difficult to present a clear picture. The situation is even more complicated if the crisis is the result of an adversarial action such as a hostile takeover. In an adversarial situation, the crisis is complicated by counter-rhetoric that also helps to shape the reality for all publics. In such situations, the most credible source often wins the battle for public opinion.

Sometimes a crisis situation turns around for a while but then resurfaces because of an accident, investigative reporting or legal action. Some crises continue for years, so you need to plan for short- and long-term crisis management. The key is to maintain credibility.[45]

Credibility is always at stake. Public perception of an organization's honesty and openness in the beginning is essential. Observations in news reports that someone was unavailable or refused to comment erode confidence quickly. Failure of an organization to be prepared is also an issue. This is not easily forgiven in most cases where there was opportunity to discover the problem. Even in sudden and unpredictable situations, though, a company can still look bad. A good example is when cities fail to warn residents of impending natural disasters such as storms. Not anticipating such acts of nature and failing to prepare for them causes a loss of confidence and credibility. Responses from a company or organization that seem self-centered and devoid of sympathy for victims are among the most serious mistakes. How to find the proper emotion in a response to a given situation or crisis has been studied by academician and researcher W. Timothy Coombs, who developed a typology of responses. His guidelines are useful because he examines the crisis, considers the management - response strategy and looks at the various factors that influence the type of response, such as whether the organization is truly at fault or there is a misunderstanding.[46]

A model of mass media behavior in a crisis has been developed by Joseph Scanlon and Suzanne Alldred of the Emergency Communications Research Unit, Carleton University, Ottawa, Canada. Drawing on their research and experience, reporters respond to hearing of a crisis by trying to

EXAMPLE 15.7

Crisis PR: Media Headquarters in Emergencies

Your operation must contain two specific areas that serve as a central clearing point for reporters and company PR personnel in a serious emergency. These areas should be equipped with several telephones and with some place for the people to sit and write.

If the emergency is centered in the area of one of the headquarters, the alternate location should be used. Additionally, company employees should be informed of this fact so they are able to direct reporters to the area from which news will be forthcoming.

At least two secretaries should be made available to the staff member handling public relations if the emergency takes place during working hours, since there will be times when this individual will, by necessity, be away from news headquarters.

If no news headquarters needs to be established, all calls from news media should be directed to one or two designated lines. While the PR person is out assessing the situation, names and phone numbers of callers should be taken.

HANDLING PR IN THE EMERGENCY

1. Need for establishing the news headquarters will be determined by the PR person. News headquarters will keep all visitors to the site under control and out of the way of any emergency work being done. Also, having a news service indicates the company's desire to be cooperative. The size of the emergency will determine whether there is a need for a headquarters.

2. The person handling public relations will maintain contact with reporters, make sure they stay in approved locations while on plant property and provide as quickly as possible all information determined to be in the company's best interests.

3. The person handling public relations will check with a designated representative of management on the text of announcements and help formulate answers to questions.

4. The person handling public relations will be responsible for guiding reporters into the disaster area, if company management will permit such a visit.

5. The fundamental responsibility for which facts are to be given to the press and ultimately to the public

must remain with top management. It is the responsibility of the person handling public relations to operate with the approval of top management.

6. Maintain close contact with members of media. More often than not they will be able to tell you things you don't already know. This is a great way to stem the flow of false information.

7. Keep a log of all facts given out, with times they were released. This avoids duplication and conflicting reports, if new developments should change facts.

8. Do not release the names of victims until you know for a fact that the families involved have been notified. Tell the reporters that the name of the victim will be made available as soon as the next of kin has been told of the mishap.

9. When it is necessary to admit a fact already known to the press, be sure confirmation is limited only to definite information that will not change. If fire fighters carry a victim from the plant in a body bag and the reporter sees it, say only that one body has been recovered. DO NOT SAY that you "don't know how many are dead." Never speculate as to the cause of accidents, amount of damage, responsibility, possible down-time, delays in shipments, layoffs and so on.

In other words, say no more than to confirm what is already known, and yet give the reporters the impression the company will give all the assistance it possibly can. As facts that won't be harmful become known, clear them and give them to news media people.

QUESTIONS TO LOOK FOR IN EMERGENCIES

What Reporters Can Get from Other Sources If Forced To

1. Number of deaths.

2. Number of injuries.

3. Damage. (Fire chief will give estimate in dollars; give yours in *general* terms of what was destroyed as soon as known.)

4. What burned and/or collapsed.

5. Time.

(continued)

EXAMPLE 15.7 (continued)

6. Location within plant (paint locker, press room, etc.).

7. Names of dead and injured, following notification of relatives.

8. Their addresses, ages and how long with company, as well as occupation.

9. How many people employed; what activities.

Facts Desired But Not Necessarily Desirable to Give

1. Speculation about anything.

2. Any delivery delays or such. (Accentuate positive as soon as course is sure.)

3. How caused. (Let city officials release this; chances are story will die before report is completed.)

4. Specific damage estimate as well as what was destroyed. (This information might be extremely valuable to competitors.)

DEALING WITH THE MEDIA DURING EMERGENCIES

In meetings with the press at the scene of emergencies, several things should be remembered. Basic is the fact that the public is represented by the press, and this medium has a recognized right to information that may vitally concern the community, employees, their friends and families and the victims. It is also common knowledge that the best way to prevent the spread of false rumors and misinformation is through issuance of factual information. At the same time, the company must guard its own interests and insist on relaying factual information only in an orderly, controlled manner.

Remember

1. Speed in reply to a query is all-important. All reporters have deadlines to meet.

2. Keep cool. If reporters get snappy, chances are it's because they are under considerably more pressure at the moment than you. Try to cooperate to the extent possible.

3. If you don't know the answer, attempt to get it for the reporters.

4. Eliminate obstacles wherever possible. Most reporters agree that, the more obstacles they find in their way, the harder they will work to ferret out the real story—from any source possible. They will almost always use something they have uncovered, and you have no control over what they might uncover.

---

get information by "whatever ingenious or technical means are available, and use their background files to fill in the gaps."[47] In making the point that editors assign people so that the breaking story receives continuous coverage, to ensure that information is released as soon as it is gathered, Scanlon and Alldred note that the coverage consists of periods of high drama followed by lulls. Reporters often share information and attempt to fit it into a deadline-driven framework. Trends for coverage, the researchers say, are set by the prestige media, but while the national and international media cover the story only at its height, the local news media stay with it all the way through to resolution of the situation. The role of the public relations person is important (1) in conducting the delicate negotiations that have to go on between source and media about what to use and what not to use; (2) in providing enough opportunities, such as news conferences, for information to be given to the media; and (3) in educating as well as informing, so that reporters don't fall back on stereotyping to explain the incident itself or the people involved in it.[48]

When media are involved in direct coverage of a crisis, some slanting is expected due to the factors mentioned such as timeliness, deadlines and competition. Bias is likely to enter the reporting of crises in any case, something to keep in mind if your company is a multinational. The bias is likely to represent the political-economic position of the reporter's country. In cases of religious states, that

---

EXAMPLE 15.7 *(continued)*

5. Never ask to see a reporter's story. Time is usually a factor. If you feel the reporter may be misinformed, check back with him or her on the point to make sure.

6. There's seldom a reason why you should not be quoted by name. As a member of the management team and one charged with public relations, you are speaking for the company.

7. Never argue with a reporter about the value of a story.

8. Any information that goes to one source in the emergency is fair game to all. Don't play favorites. They listen to and read each other's copy anyway.

9. Never flatly refuse information. Always give a good reason why it isn't available. Be sure facts are, indeed, factual.

10. Always know to whom you are talking. Get the reporter's name and phone number in case you need to contact him or her later.

11. Never give an answer that you feel might not stand up. It can embarrass you later.

12. Never falsify, color or slant your answers. A reporter is trained to see a curve ball coming a mile away and has fielded them before. If a reporter thinks you are pitching one, he or she will remember it a

long time and tell colleagues and other members of the news media over coffee. This will also set him or her off quicker than getting no information at all.

13. Be especially alert about photographs. You have no control of photos taken off company property, but you have every right to control photos taken within the plant. Consider the possibility of pool photos and film/video where it is impractical to have several photographers on the scene at once. Remember, photos can be as harmful as words.

14. Be sure no time lag comes into play between the time you get information that can be put out and the time it is actually given to news media people.

15. Have safety, labor and employee records available for your reference if possible.

16. Be quick to point up long safety records and any acts of heroism by employees.

17. If damage must be estimated for the press immediately, confine statements to general descriptions of what was destroyed.

18. Always accentuate the positive. If your public relations is good, so are your chances of receiving an even break.

---

may also become an important factor. The amount of attention paid to a crisis and the approach to the story are both influenced by such bias. Some of the best evidence of this occurs in a study of earthquake coverage by the *New York Times* and the *Washington Post*. The better coverage of both natural disasters and nonpolitical news was given to countries perceived to be friends of the USA.[49]

Problems with Instantaneous, Global Coverage of Crises

"The New World Disorder" is the title of a commentary by journalist Daniel Schorr at the beginning of the *1994 Encyclopaedia Britannica Book of*

the Year. For the most part, it is a litany of crises created by people—people acting in the capacity of government officials. But was 1993 significantly worse than previous years, or does it just seem that way because we know more about what is going on in almost every nook and cranny of the world today?

There is a positive side to the exposure of previously sequestered parts of the world, unknown mostly because of their remoteness, but sometimes because of their repressive governments. Atrocities visited on people in those world nooks and crannies now draw international public attention to them. While that should result in public opinion bringing pressure to bear on those perpetrating atrocities, the results of the Bosnian situation indicate that this may not happen. Instead, the result may be, as Schorr suggests, a sense of international disorder and chaos that promotes despair. The closing words of his commentary are these:

> A paradox of 1993 was that leaders enjoying such high-tech capabilities for communicating their messages still seemed to be held, generally, in such low esteem. The "Information Highway," which broke into American consciousness in 1993, promised a new dimension of interactive communication. Whether leaders would have anything more inspiring to communicate remains to be seen.[50]

The problem with many of today's crises is that we watch them on television as they occur. And the media play a key role in this drama. In some situations, such as the accident that took the life of Britain's Princess Diana in 1997, the media monitor every move, although sometimes without much information. In other situations, such as in connection with some of the refugee crises around the world, media access is problematic and dangerous. Thus, the impression of witnessing crises at first hand through the media is simply a perception drawn from what the media choose to show or are able to show. People act on those perceptions—sending aid to crisis sites with sympathetic appeals or avoiding areas that appear to be dangerous due to natural or political crises.

In addition to problems of perception versus reality that instantaneous coverage creates, "crisis while it happens" coverage raises credibility problems because, in any breaking news situation, information is sketchy and conflicting. When the information is released without benefit of editing (which involves checking), it places a heavy burden of responsibility on the news staff providing the coverage.

When the crisis involves confidentiality, the difficulty of getting accurate information to the public through the news media is increased. The role of the public relations spokesperson becomes more crucial, and the spokesperson is often subjected to intense media criticism. The military spokespeople who handled briefings during the Persian Gulf crisis were subjected to intense

grilling. The U.S. government has, since the invasion of Grenada on October 25, 1983, maintained tight control over in-the-field coverage of military conflicts. The U.S. media, accustomed to the freedom that accompanied the earlier system of self-censorship of the editing process, have not responded favorably to the new controls. But despite government censorship and controls, the instantaneous coverage that is transmitted globally has circumvented the traditional editing process, and editing now is left to reporters who often don't have the luxury of time to check and confirm their information.

Instant coverage has always been a source of difficulty in terrorist attacks, which, because of mounting problems in the Middle East, have been elevated there to the level of constant risk from the lower level of isolated incidents. Some observers have criticized the news media's role in this situation. While researchers have failed to document the most frequent accusation—that news media coverage legitimates terrorist activities—evidence suggests that the news media do fail to explain the underlying objectives behind many terrorist activities.[51]

There is some evidence that the news media, like witnesses, are less likely than government sources to use sensationalist, judgmental or inflammatory words in describing acts of terrorism, although they do often use inflammatory characterizations of the perpetrators of terrorism.[52] Presumably the political nature of government sources influences them to characterize terrorism as political violence. When an organization (whether a nonprofit group or a company) is the victim of terrorism, especially in the case of hostage taking, witnesses should be made available to the news media, when possible, because they have credibility and are less likely than government sources to use inflammatory words. It is also important to try to control the tendency of news media (and often of government officials) to use the victims of terrorism as symbols.[53] For example, if the hostage is depicted as representing the USA or American citizens, the hostage's value to a terrorist who is acting out a protest against the USA or its policies increases. The same could be said for employees of financial institutions, taken hostage to protest economic disparities.

There is a very fine line between keeping a hostage from becoming a valuable symbol and projecting an uncaring attitude about the person's fate. The role of the public relations spokesperson in working with the news media in this situation is critical. The media's contribution in a crisis as interpreters and educators could be enhanced in many instances if they were dealing with adequately prepared and trained public relations spokespeople who could supply accurate background information.

Talking Back in a Crisis Organizations used to take their lumps in the news media silently when negative publicity occurred, especially if they had tried to be open and cooperative and the policy had backfired.

Hostility levels between business and the news media go up and down, and the PR person usually tries to ride the tide without drowning. Organization officers often admit that they rely on their PR person to handle all contact with the news media because their rage wouldn't permit civility. Of course, when PR people get along well with news media representatives—as they must—their internal loyalty sometimes becomes suspect. Nevertheless, the advice PR people gave for years to irate CEOs who wanted to talk back (or worse) to the news media was "let me handle them." And they handled them with kid gloves.[54]

However, the public relations stance is different now and more companies are talking back.

In 1993, for instance, when NBC's *Dateline* program decided to show the dangers of exploding gas tanks on General Motors trucks, the producers didn't get the kind of video they wanted. To get a better picture, they rigged their test vehicle's side-mounted gas tanks with toy rockets. But NBC didn't tell viewers that the source of the spark that set the test truck on fire was not a crash impact but the rockets. GM first complained to NBC about the *Dateline* show. This did not elicit the retraction GM wanted, so *three months* later the company

went to court. Furthermore, it held a news conference to announce the filing of the defamation suit against NBC.[55]

In watching the televised news conference, NBC executives learned things about the production of the show that their own internal investigations had not revealed. The following day, *Dateline* show anchors Jane Pauley and Stone Phillips apologized to viewers and to GM. Their statement was that NBC "does not dispute" that it used toy rocket engines as "igniters" in its staged crashes of GM trucks and that their report significantly understated the speed of the vehicle at the time of impact. Their apology also said that *Dateline* had reported erroneously that a fuel tank had ruptured in one of the test crashes.[56] The on-air retraction, which included the statement that the "unscientific re-enactment of a crash" was a "bad idea from start to finish," came just hours after a settlement was reached.[57]

The *Wall Street Journal* said, "GM has staged a brilliantly executed rejection of a highly public attack on its corporate reputation."[58] One of the *Journal*'s rare photos showed a picture of Harry J. Pearce, GM's general counsel, with the identifying caption, "who launched the auto maker's public relations counteroffensive during a Monday news conference."

The question of whose reputation remained free of dishonor might have been difficult for viewers (who were also watching news reports of a jury verdict of $105.4 million against GM in a suit involving the truck) to answer. Opinions of business executives and the news media, as reported by the *Journal* the day after the settlement and retraction, seemed divided about whether this was an isolated instance of media-created news or whether competition had driven the media to lower their ethical standards.[59] Probably, CNN owner Ted Turner was on target when he said that, whatever the situation, it wasn't good for the credibility of journalists.

The difficulty is that, as more aggressive action is taken, public credibility is severely strained. The idea that talking back to the news media is a recent phenomenon is not entirely correct, but it has been accelerating. The question that could be asked is the same as the question the GM story posed: Is it because the news media are being increasingly irresponsible, or have the companies under attack found that it pays to fight back?

Getting into the ring with the news media requires the PR counselor to be a heavyweight in the realm of ideas and to know how to handle the company's position politically, economically and socially. Further, crafting aggressive programs that take the offensive requires thorough knowledge of the industry as well as of all factors that affect the climate of public opinion. In some cases, as in Mobil's, it also means defending yourself within the profession.

Understanding Various Media Roles Some of the most serious issues that occur in reporting global crises arise from a conflict of opinion about the function, role and responsibility of the mass media. In some countries, news media are privately owned and function with few government restraints. In other countries, news media are under considerable government regulation and supervision. There are differences in government oversight among the media, with broadcast media being the most highly regulated, even in the USA. Media roles are interpreted differently, too, with some countries seeing them as representative spokespersons for the country. Even more controversial is the view of media "responsibility," which varies individually among journalists as well as collectively among media organizations and is closely tied to values.

The way news media representatives interpret the function, role and responsibility of the news media affects how they report a crisis, how they interact with news sources in a crisis and how their media offices present information from reporters to their audiences. Regardless of where these media are situated, technology has made their reports potentially accessible to audiences all over the world. Accounts of crises are evaluated for the timeliness and usefulness of the information they contain. That information is the result of cooperation between the news media and the spokespersons for the organization in crisis.

When the organization sees news media coverage as a threat and withholds information or makes it difficult for news media to obtain information, reports of the crisis are much more distorted and the organization's perceived ability to cope with the crisis is much reduced. Fear that disclosure will damage an organization's image virtually ensures that the crisis will be reported in greater depth, over a longer period of time and with added sensationalism, since media will turn to outside sources that often deliver speculation and rumor rather than facts.

Increasingly, electronic bulletin boards, which have no editors and are global with little regulation, are being used as source of information (with impact) and rumor. Intel Corporation's decision to recall its flawed Pentium chip in December 1994 was attributed to negative "public opinion" created on Internet. Cyberspace, too, is increasingly a conduit for information and rumor.

DEALING WITH RUMORS

If an emergency is long-term and serious, as in natural disasters, rumor headquarters must be set up and staffed. In the absence of fact, there will be fabrication. Because rumors feed on anxiety, emotional topics such as threats to physical or emotional well-being are always an integral part of them. And the people most distressed by the "news" are the ones most likely to pass it on (see Example 15.8). The following advice on handling rumors comes from communications specialist Walter St. John.[60] First, try to avoid situations like these, which encourage rumors to grow:

1. Authentic and official information and news are lacking.

2. Authentic information is incomplete.

3. Situations are loaded with anxiety and fear.

4. Doubts exist because of the existence of erroneous information.

EXAMPLE 15.8

How a Rumor Grows

He Said, She Said

As rumors are passed on through a network of people, they undergo typical changes:

THE ORIGINAL STORY
"Two boys and two girls were fishing when their boat capsized. Only the girls knew how to swim; they grabbed the boys and guided them safely back to shore. The boys' parents were very grateful."

EXAGGERATION
The details become vivid and sharper, often for the sake of drama:
"Some teen-agers were having a party at night on a boat when it capsized. One of the boys had a broken leg. Two of the girls were on the swim team and two other girls were lifeguards. They saved everyone else."

SIMPLIFICATION
As the story becomes rumor, it gets shorter and more concise as it is passed on; some details drop out altogether:
"Some boys and girls were in a boat that capsized. The girls knew how to swim and rescued the boys."

INTERPRETATION
The rumor is reinterpreted in terms of the world view of the teller, emphasizing stereotypes:
"The other night some teen-agers were drunk out on a boat, and it capsized. Two of the boys were on the swim team and two other boys were lifeguards. They saved the girls."

Source: Dr. Jack Levin/Northeastern University

5. People's ego needs are not being met (satisfaction from possessing the "inside dope").

6. Prolonged decision-making delays occur on important matters.

7. Personnel feel they can't control conditions or their fate.

8. Serious organizational problems exist.

9. Organizational conflict and personal antagonism are excessive.

The following strategies should be used to combat rumors:

1. Analyze the scope and seriousness of the nature and impact of the rumor before planning and engaging in any active correction.

2. Analyze the specific causes, motives, sources and disseminators of the rumors.

3. Confer with persons affected by or being damaged by rumors. Level with them and assure them of your concern and of your sincere attempts to combat the rumors effectively.

4. Immediately (and massively, if it appears advisable) supply complete and authentic information regarding the matter.

5. Feed the grapevine yourself with counter-rumors placed by trusted colleagues and confidants.

6. Call the key status and informal leaders, opinion molders and other influential people together to discuss and clarify the situation and to solicit their support and assistance.

7. Avoid referring to the rumor in disseminating the truth. You don't want to reinforce the rumor itself, *unless* it already is in wide circulation. In that case you *must* go public so that those passing on the rumor will be discredited.

8. Conduct meetings with the staff and others at the grassroots level to dispel the rumors, if necessary.

Once rumors begin to travel, they spread with considerable speed, and it is extremely difficult to stop them. The best way to combat rumors is preventively—restricting the need for them in the first place by keeping people promptly and accurately informed and by maintaining good two-way communication. But when rumors start, you need to act immediately to control them.

Three illustrations demonstrate the power of rumor and the difficulty in getting a rumor under control. The Walt Disney Co. found itself in the headlines with stories that its videos had embedded in them obscene subliminal messages. As an example, in "Aladdin," the title character is supposed to murmur so that it can scarcely be heard, "All good teenagers take off your clothes." One New York mother, who had bought almost all of the Disney videos for her children, was "tipped off" to the supposedly subliminal messages by a neighbor. Although she couldn't hear the messages, she said she felt she had entrusted her children to pedophiles and threw all of the tapes in the trash. Of course, by the time there was a newspaper story about the rumor, it was sufficiently diffused but many people had already reacted. Supposedly there were messages in "The Lion King," where dust supposedly spells "sex," and in "The Little Mermaid" as well as "Aladdin," and this "news" went around the world. TV ran the identified sequences in slow motion. Disney denied the charges, and the demonstrations were not clear. Nevertheless, it was the suburban myth of 1995.[61]

Just as difficult to dispel was the rumor in 1997 that donors to Bill Clinton's campaign had received burial plots in Arlington Cemetery. The source of the rumor was a story in the *Army Times* (also reported on WJLA-TV in the Capitol City) that the Clinton administration had granted a higher number of Arlington burial waivers than previous administrations, although an Army official told the *Army Times* that "no politics were involved." Paul Rodriguez covered the story for *Insight* Magazine, in which he said these were "allegations and suggestions." Nevertheless, a news release issued by Rodriguez was picked up immediately by radio talk show hosts Rush Limbaugh, Oliver North and G. Gordon Liddy. Their take was that such action had "defiled the sacred dead of the country."

The mainstream press couldn't resist the story, especially since Republican chairman Jim Nicholson called it "one of the most despicable political schemes in recent history," and White House advisor Paul Begala called it "the classic big line strategy" by the "Republican sleaze machine." After the story ran in traditional media, such as *The Washington Post, New York Times, Los Angeles Times, USA Today* and CNN, the White House defeated all of the charges by November 21, 1997, but failed to kill the rumor. Begala blamed the traditional media for giving credibility to the story. The media claimed that because people were calling and asking about the story, it was their responsibility to write about it.[62]

It was not widely known that rumors in the black community affected different products and manufacturers until the ABC network show "20/20" presented a program called "Black and White" on April 19, 1996. The prime time program showed how pervasive the rumors were, and how resistant to change even when people were confronted with the truth.[63] These rumors were the subject of a book, *I Heard It Through the Grapevine,* by Patricia Turner, professor of African-American studies at the University of California. Some companies lost enough market share to close; others bought space in black media to respond to charges and were successful because those media were credible to the ethnic community.[64]

Squelching a rumor proved impossible for Procter & Gamble Company. The corporate trademark of a man-in-the-moon face with a cluster of thirteen stars inspired a story that the company was part of a Satanic cult. The rumor first surfaced in the 1970s, but it peaked in July 1982, when Procter & Gamble received 15,000 complaint calls on its toll-free lines. The rumor was refuted in 1982 by leading TV evangelists and columnist Abigail Van Buren; in 1984 her sister, columnist Ann Landers, also refuted the rumor. Most disturbing to the $13 billion per year company, however, were fliers that revived the rumors in 1984, urging "good Christians" to stop buying Procter & Gamble products.

At that time, the Cincinnati-based company launched a direct-mail campaign. According to Public Relations Director Robert Norrish, the company would have sued if it had been able to determine whom to sue. Norrish said, "It's goofy. It's a ridiculous rumor. It's libelous. The whole thing is just absolutely without foundation. . . . It dignifies the rumor by denying that there's any truth to it."

Some people who had passed along the rumor retracted it, but others still felt there was "something to it." Attempts to pinpoint who was spreading the rumors failed, P&G's rumor tracker (and former FBI agent) James D. Jesse eventually gave up trying to find the originators, although he had even hired outside investigators to help, when he could "get them to stop laughing."

It was not a joke to P&G. The company finally removed the logo from its products, retaining it only on its corporate materials.[65]

RECOVERY AND EVALUATION

For help in recovering from a crisis, Bob Carrell, professor emeritus of advertising at the University of Oklahoma, suggests looking again at the first phase in his matrix of crisis communication management—a phase before the crisis event occurs. He makes these recommendations for getting a crisis under control:

1. Determine the cause(s) of the crisis. It is important to undercut rumors and speculation that may have been rampant.

2. Decide which strategies and policies can be developed that will prevent similar or related crises. Direct experience with a crisis, although painful, teaches more than even the best scenario ever could. A crisis is the most severe test of existing strategies and policies.

3. Ask whether the crisis plan itself worked and whether changes should be made in it.

4. Evaluate the performance of all personnel in the crisis situation. Any failures in the crisis plan may have been caused by faulty provisions in the plan or by poor execution.

Figuring out a good way to apologize for creating a crisis and selecting good timing for the apology are other aspects of recovery. Exxon's apology was more too late than too little, and the company is paying dearly for it. American Airlines didn't waste any time before apologizing for a ground crew's decision to order a change of pillows after a gay-rights group left one of its airplanes, and it probably saved itself some difficulties.

The problem with apologizing often involves the legal ramifications of such public statements. Lawyers prefer that their clients not admit any guilt, so the company may elect to plead "nolo contendere" if it is sued. As *Time* commentator John Rothchild recently observed, "Given the number of companies that take advantage of this opportunity, we could start a pretty good nolo mutual fund."[66] The other problem in a crisis is that lawyers for insurance companies don't even want employees to express too much sympathy for victims or relatives of victims in crises because it might cost the insurer more.

Rothchild discusses the problem Prudential Securities (which he characterizes as "the brokerage arm of the Rock of Gibraltar") had in 1994.[67] Ultimately, Prudential Securities paid $370 million to settle claims from investors who were sold limited partnerships that cost them big losses. The company's CEO, Wick Simmons, even said, "Certain limited partnerships were sold by our firm to some clients that lacked adequate information or were not suitable for their investment needs. That was wrong." In addition to using the word "wrong," which few companies are willing to do even when they should, Prudential mounted an expensive ad campaign using real brokers and other Prudential employees, including Simmons himself. The problem with the ad campaign was that it kept reminding people of the problem. Not only that, but one investor recognized a broker who was apologizing on air as the one who had sold him a limited partnership, and the customer got so angry that he filed another lawsuit. Thus, as Rothchild notes, there is some logic in the advice of attorneys to distance yourself from the damage.[68]

Some companies are looking ahead and attempting to establish a standing corporate policy about responding to crises. Sometimes this even involves responding to the crises of others. While some responses of companies in a crisis are seen to be altruistic, others recognize these as public relations opportunities. After yet another California earthquake in 1994, while others were sending money and supplies, Monsanto Company in St. Louis was saving its resources for the possibility that the 1995 spring rains might cause torrential flooding again. While this might seem selfish and opportunistic, actually Monsanto was looking after its own company's community relations. It has set aside $200,000 for possible use in two river towns where it has plants.[69]

Whatever the strategy a company decides on, it needs to have the following outcomes to be considered a success in crisis handling, according to two management theorists: early detection, incident containment, business resumption, lessons learned/policies implemented, improved reputation as a result of appropriate response, stakeholder resources readily available for response, and timely decisions made on the basis of facts.[70]

CASES THAT ILLUSTRATE THE TYPOLOGY OF CRISES

A brief recounting of some significant crises will illustrate each of the six typologies, and you can look for current examples in the news of the day. To show the persistence of crises, we will reexamine two important ones: Bhopal, an intentional violent crisis for Union Carbide India and Chernobyl, an unintentional violent crisis for the Ukraine.

Acts of Nature that were violent dominated the news in 1998, and most were attributed to the phenomenon called El Nino. This periodic atmospheric disturbance changes ocean water temperatures and causes considerable climate change. El Nino was blamed for **violent flooding** that resulted in homes sliding down mountainsides and into the sea in California, and also for causing droughts in places like Mexico and Central America. The **droughts** were in the **nonviolent** acts of nature category until the summer of 1998 when farmers burning their crops lost control of the fires, and smoke and haze moved north into the USA causing visibility to decrease to two miles in North Texas at some points during the crisis. This moved the situation into the **unintentional violent** category as lives and property were lost to the **raging fires.** A clearer illustration of the **Act of Nature, violent** category was the 1997 mud slide in Peru that buried the ancient villages of Cocha and Pumaranra taking as many as 300 lives.

In the **Act of Nature, nonviolent** category, a significant event was the spreading of the avian flu, which forced officials to destroy millions of chickens, geese and ducks in Hong Kong in an effort to control the situation. Heightened concern about mad cow disease also resulted in the destruction of whole herds of beef cattle in Britain. In the USA, an increase in the number of deaths caused by Escherichia coli (e-coli) bacteria resulted in government approval for the irradiation of meat products. As an epidemic, though, AIDs continued to dominate world concern.

The **Intentional, violent** crisis continues to be dominated by drugs and drug-trafficking. The 1997 World Drug Report estimated the annual turnover in drugs was $400 billion, or about 8 percent of total international trade. The nation with the highest drug-consumption rate remained the USA. In the **Intentional, nonviolent** category, Japan took the forefront when prosecutors there charged executives of major brokerages and other major corporations with having paid gangsters large sums of money to buy their silence at shareholder meetings. The gangsters had purchased large numbers of shares in the companies, and then threatened to disrupt the shareholder meetings by revealing damaging corporate information unless they were bought off. The scandal of such ties between big business and organized crime in Japan caused major problems with the country's financial industry.

In the **Unintentional, violent** category the accident that drew the most attention in 1997 was the one in Paris, France which took the life of Diana, Princess of Wales, (Diana Frances Spencer) and her companion Dodi Fayed, son of the owner of Harrod's Department Store in London and the Ritz Hotel in Paris. The tragedy had an international impact, and a marked influence on the way

the royal family related to its constituency. In April of 1997 in Mina, Saudia Arabia, at least 300 Muslims making an annual pilgrimage to Mecca died when fire erupted in a tent. More than 1,300 others were injured in the effort to get out. A gas cylinder used for cooking exploded and caused the fire. In the **Unintentional, nonviolent** category, the most significant event in 1998 was the collapse of the Asian stock market which sent ripples through the entire international economy.

Continuing Crises: Bhopal and Chernobyl

When reports first appeared of a lethal gas cloud leaking from Union Carbide's Bhopal, India, plant on December 3, 1984, people had no inkling of the extent of devastation involved. The gas eventually resulted in the deaths of as many as 2,300 people and in the painful injury of thousands more. The event, initially labeled an "accident," focused attention on the safety of chemical plants all over the world.

Although Union Carbide attributes the disaster in Bhopal to employee sabotage—a violent, intentional act—many people blame a failure of the plant's safety system, which had not been inspected for 31 months before the accident. A 1984 safety report had warned of problems at the plant. One of the publics affected most critically was a "nimbus" public: the squatters who had built homes just outside the plant.

It was the worst industrial disaster in the history of the world. The gas that escaped from Union Carbide India's pesticide plant in the province of Madhya Pradesh caused, by government count, 1,600 deaths at the time and 700 more from aftereffects. (Other reports estimate as many as 100,000 injured.) Many Bhopal residents still have illnesses related to their exposure. Many children were left orphans.

The chemical that caused the damage was methyl isocyanate gas, used in pesticides. The event received intensive media coverage during the first week of the tragedy for a number of reasons:

(1) the sheer numbers of human beings dead, dying and permanently injured; (2) the involvement of a U.S. company, although Union Carbide USA owned only 50.9 percent of the Indian subsidiary company and although the facility was entirely managed by the subsidiary and run by Indian nationals; (3) the existence of a "twin" plant in the USA in Institute, West Virginia.

The *Wall Street Journal* praised Warren M. Anderson, Union Carbide's chairman, for flying to India with a team of technical experts. Although he was put under house arrest along with the Indian plant manager and the chairman of Union Carbide India, he was released on bail and taken immediately to the airport. He never got to talk to the people in Bhopal. The Indian officials were kept in jail for ten days, leaving Union Carbide India leaderless. Even though Union Carbide USA was getting all of its information from the news media and couldn't get through on one of Bhopal's two trunk lines, the company decided to be open in all its communications.

Efforts by Union Carbide USA and Indian volunteers to help the victims have been thwarted by activists and by government action or inaction. Union Carbide USA offered to build a hospital and orphanage and was turned down. It had already gotten approval for a housing unit, but that approval was withdrawn. And a rehabilitation center outside Bhopal run by Arizona State University was closed after it was disclosed that Union Carbide had given the university $2 million for the center. Union Carbide also offered to convert the plant into a facility that made batteries, but the plant was closed. Then Union Carbide offered to turn the plant and its grounds, plus a nearby guest house and the research facility, over to the government to be used for medical facilities, a training center and a park. That too was refused.

The Indian government sued Union Carbide for $3 billion. Although there have been many efforts at settlement, none has been successful. The case was first tried in U.S. courts and then moved to Indian courts. Part of the problem may have been caused by U.S. lawyers who rushed to India to help people file suits against the company. Expec-

tations of huge settlements climbed. India's state and national governments have rejected any Union Carbide aid because they thought accepting it might taint their suit. However, about $5 million that was ordered to be paid to the American Red Cross by Union Carbide for Bhopal relief efforts was accepted. Only a portion of this amount was used by the Indian Red Cross. The Indian government's own relief programs have not been put in place. When the Red Cross offered to take over the government's entire child-care system at its own expense, it too was turned down.

The length of the crisis and the repeated frustration of the company's efforts to assist the victims, who were consequently left to suffer without help, caused a deterioration in the initially exemplary openness of management's handling of the crisis. The victims' continued suffering also turned more of India's people against the company. As one educator said, "We had considered Union Carbide a good neighbor until Bhopal."

Union Carbide's management also had to contend with more than one crisis. While the Bhopal situation was still very much in flux, the West Virginia plant had a minor crisis. But that was nothing compared to the attempted hostile takeover that developed when the Bhopal incident caused Union Carbide's stock to fall dramatically. To prevent a takeover, the company restructured, which caused another management crisis.

Union Carbide's public affairs officer at that time, Ronald S. Wishart, said the company is still paying the price for a decision made in March 1985 when

> . . . the short-term need to satisfy the media's uncontrollable lust for culprits overcame our great reluctance to suggest any criticism of the affiliate company in India. We made the decision consciously because that's what the facts at hand suggested. But we know now, after two more years of intense study, that the tragedy was the result of an act of sabotage by a disgruntled employee, and that act overrode all other considerations.

Evidence shows that the employee connected a water hose to the tank and added several hundred gallons of water. Wishart, who is now retired, says that the employee probably didn't anticipate the consequences. What he probably intended to do was to spoil a batch of the product and discredit a supervisor.

Wishart saw himself as "chief of staff" to then-chairman Anderson and saw his role as being

> to identify what our objectives needed to be, to prioritize them in each moment of time, in each situation we faced, to assemble the appropriate resources from the legal, financial, technical, commercial, industry, governmental and consulting communities, and to coordinate those resources to achieve the desired results. What we said, and how we said it, had to recognize the games being played, and the stakes involved in each game . . . [B]ut I'm afraid that our balancing act among objectives sometimes prevented us from scoring the points—short-term—that we would have liked to.[71]

The continuing coverage intermittently yields headlines, as usually happens with major crises. In 1992, the Indian government demanded that former chairman Anderson be extradited to India to stand trial for murder. A 1993 story in the national weekly edition of the Washington Post was headlined, "In Bhopal, a Relentless Cloud of Despair: Nine Years After the Deadly Gas Leak, Corruption and Inefficiency Are Delaying Aid to the Victims."[72] Union Carbide ended its relief efforts in 1989 when it paid the Indian government $470 million, to be divided among victims and their families. The settlement did not please many of those with claims, and the fact that claims courts in India were only set up in 1992, eight years after the disaster, has not helped. Whoever is to blame, the name Union Carbide is still associated with all of these problems.

As expected, the ten-year anniversary of the event, which occurred in 1994, was extensively covered—and with reason. Thousands of angry demonstrators denouncing India's involvement with foreign companies stormed the locked gates of the plant and some lay on the ground in shrouds representing those killed in the crisis. That event changed Union Carbide, which no longer manu-

factures pesticides, and affected the entire chemical industry.

The crisis came to the forefront again in 1995 when India asked a court to continue the case so that it could seek extradition of Anderson, now retired. But the Indian government has not asked the USA government to extradite Anderson. As many as half a million of those injured are still waiting for compensation.[73]

The Chernobyl nuclear disaster, which occurred on April 27, 1986, in the Ukraine, returned to the news in 1990 as the Supreme Soviet of the Soviet Union voted additional financial aid for parts of Belorus that had been affected by the accident. The region (now an independent state) had announced contingency plans to evacuate more than 100,000 people from two provinces where high cesium-137 levels had been discovered years after the accident. Increases in the birth rates of deformed farm animals had been reported, studies of plant and animal life had revealed other deformities and there were additional reports of human cancer—especially of the thyroid gland and lips.[74]

Chernobyl was again back in the news in 1993 after the World Bank determined that the Ukraine could afford to shut down the units still operating. But with Belorus not renewing its own nuclear power generation (which it abandoned in 1988), the Ukraine determined that it would not shut down the plant as planned. The decision brought warnings from the European Community and the International Atomic Energy Agency which is concerned about the safety of the Chernobyl reactors.

In 1995, the plant was back in the news as inspection teams examined the entombed nuclear reactor, which had cracks in it that allowed dust to come out. The Ukraine was seeking funds from the international community to close the plant entirely by 1999 and issue a final clean up. However, scientists and officials think Chernobyl will be the longest, most hightech and expensive environmental clean-up ever attempted. It could take billions of dollars and 100 years to complete. Plans call for a double-hulled shell, maybe 25 stories high, to encapsulate the reactor. Inside, a work-force of robots would break through the current tomb and remove the wastes in a highly radioactive environment. There's no decision yet about where these wastes would be stored. This is reactor 4. Reactors 1 and 3 are still working. Reactor 2 is damaged and closed. The whole plant could fall victim to a natural disaster or even an accidental one such as the collapse of a tower next to Reactor 4, which would shut off the cooling systems to Reactor 3 resulting in its meltdown, repeating the 1986 event all over again.[75]

The world learned of the original nuclear crisis on Monday, April 28, 1986. First indications of the Chernobyl disaster came the day before, however, when Swedish monitoring stations began recording high radiation levels. By 10 P.M. Sunday, readings at a Swedish monitoring station on the Finnish border had started to record hourly increases. But these recorders were not read until the next day. By 8 a.m. Monday, Sweden's Forsmark nuclear plant on that country's east coast was showing unusually high levels of radiation. Within thirty minutes, the Swedes issued an alarm and began to evacuate about 1,000 nonessential employees from their plant. They were afraid that their own plant had a leak somewhere.

Within four hours of the evacuation, Sweden's Nuclear Power Inspection Board was informed that an alarm had been declared at the Forsmark plant. In another four hours, news media were receiving information from the Swedish news agency Tidningarnas Telegrambyra. Two hours later, an Associated Press reporter was being told by a Swedish regional government official that the radioactivity was *not* coming from Forsmark, but from east of Sweden and Finland. He added, "If you know what I mean."

Within ten minutes of that statement to the AP, all news media organizations in Sweden were being briefed by Swedish Energy Minister Birgitta Dahl, who had called a news conference to say that the radiation was not from the Swedish plant, as authorities had first feared, but from somewhere else. The source was being investigated, she said, adding, "We are going to request complete information if there is proof pointing toward a certain country." It was 6 p.m. Monday in Sweden.

By now 26 hours had passed from the first detection of increased levels of radiation by the Swedish automatic monitoring stations. No word had come from any source but Sweden. At 9 p.m. Monday, three hours after the Swedish news conference, the then Soviet Union made its first public announcement. Tass News Agency in Moscow announced that "an accident has occurred at the Chernobyl atomic power plant, and one of the atomic reactors was damaged." Radio Moscow, the official broadcast source for the USSR, called the accident a "disaster":

> A government commission has been set up to investigate what caused the accident at the Chernobyl nuclear power station in the Ukraine where a reactor was damaged, and efforts are being applied to eliminate the consequences of the accident and to help the victims. The disaster was the first one at a Soviet nuclear power plant in more than thirty years. The use of nuclear energy for peaceful purposes is a vital necessity for humanity because of the gradual exhaustion of conventional fuels. Drastic measures are being carried out to guarantee the power reactor's reliability and safety.

Radio Moscow's broadcast was aired at 4 P.M. on Tuesday in the Ukraine, and it was heard early Wednesday morning in Europe. Victims of the Chernobyl disaster continue to be claimed in the 1990s, largely because people in the vicinity (including those who went in to help) were not told of the risks.

The Soviet authorities' performance did improve as the crisis continued following the accident. Ultimately, the Chernobyl accident resulted in the total destruction of a power reactor and the spread of radiation to a considerable portion of the globe. In the first few months, 31 people died and 300 others were hospitalized with acute radiation sickness. Another 18,000 were hospitalized with lesser symptoms, and 100,000 more are under long-term medical observation.[76]

POINTS TO REMEMBER

- Public relations people deal with crises, usually played out in the mass media, although more and more the "media" of cyberspace are becoming influential.

- Crises never truly go away. The way the company handled a crisis becomes a part of its reputation.

- Due to technology, word of a crisis is usually communicated globally.

- Two broad categories of crises are violent and nonviolent. Within each of these two are subcategories for acts of nature, intentional acts and unintentional events.

- Anticipation through imaging crises that could occur is part of planning. It is especially important to determine the vulnerability of the organization to different types of crises.

- The crisis may involve "nimbus" publics—publics that were not designated recipients of messages, activities or products/services of the organization.

- Crises can and should be prepared for both physically and in terms of the communication process.

- Many companies now are developing policies for responding not only to their crises, but to the crises of others.

- There are three key elements for dealing with a crisis: having a plan, assembling a team and using a single spokesperson.

- Employees are the most critical public in a crisis because they affect the way the crisis is interpreted by others.

- Some feel that dealing with crises openly is likely to create litigation, but you should expect to be sued anyway. If you've been open and honest in your communication, it probably will be an asset in litigation.

- The role of the CEO in a crisis is especially important. In crises where the CEO has been involved in or responsible for the crisis, the organizations have had greater difficulty recovering.

- Recalls of products are an important part of crisis communication, and the way they are handled affects public confidence in the organization.

- Some crises can be avoided through effective communication. All can be better managed. Good communication without action in dealing with the crisis, however, is not effective.

- In a crisis, the media will be there to cover it, but the organization's own channels of communication may be disrupted or difficult to reach.

- When possible, a unified message should be framed across organizational lines if many different groups are involved in the crisis, as they usually are.

- Logs need to be kept of who said and did what to whom and when, although this is a problem when the crisis demands a coping mechanism.

- PR people are sometimes blamed for a crisis, and there's some logic in that, because they are supposed to monitor issues and publics to forewarn and prepare management.

- However, management often chooses to ignore the warning because of arrogance or failure to listen to objective information from all publics. Sometimes it's just a case of bad judgment on the part of management. PR is a part of the management team, but not the ultimate decision maker.

- The credibility of an organization is always at stake, and that's why working with the news media is so critical. However, expect bias to occur in the coverage, which are often rooted in economic-political reasons, especially in global situations.

- The instant relaying of information in global crises adds to the need to frame the issue and to use responses that are seen as sensitive and empathetic.

- When wronged by the news media, see that corrections are made as soon as possible. When the media won't cooperate, it may be necessary to take legal action. However, be sure you are on solid factual grounds before doing so.

- Crises usually provoke rumors because there is a vacuum of information, and rumors can create crises that are difficult to quiet.

■ Rumors can only be counteracted with massive amounts of concrete, authentic information, which is usually difficult to get. Occasionally, using the grapevine is a more effective way of dealing with the rumor than going public, but this is not always the case.

■ Generally, unless the rumor is widespread, spokespeople should avoid repeating it as they disseminate the truth.

■ Once a crisis has passed, it's important to evaluate every aspect of what was done, to determine what might be a better approach next time—because there will be a next time.

■ Major crises never go away. They continue to turn attention to the organization and to recall the relationship of the organization to the crisis.

■ Knowing when and how a crisis is likely to appear or reappear is part of managing and coping with it.

NOTES

[1] Rajiv Chandrasekaran, "The Thousand-Year Glitch," *Washington Post National Weekly Edition* (May 11, 1998), pp. 6–7.

[2] Ibid.

[3] Ibid.

[4] "FAA Orders Wiring Checks On Additional Boeing 747s," *Wall Street Journal* (May 15, 1998), p. A6.

[5] Marilyn Chase, "U.S. Groups Move to Make Cattle Feed Safe for Food Chain," *Wall Street Journal* (April 1, 1996), p. A1.

[6] Daniel Pearl, "From Lipstick to Marshmallows, It's Got Some Cow in It." *Wall Street Journal* (April 3, 1996), p. B1.

[7] Robert Bonte-Friedheim and Stephen D. Moore, "Britain in Quandary on Mad-Cow Disease," *Wall Street Journal* (March 27, 1996), p. A15.

[8] Scott Parks, "Gracious in Victory, Oprah Praises Amarillo Residents," *Dallas Morning News* (February 27, 1998), http://www.dallasnews.com/oprah/oprah32.html.

[9] Doug Newsom, "A Crisis Typology," paper presented at the Latin American and Caribbean Communication Conference, Florida, February 5, 1988.

[10] Lerbinger describes crises as natural, technological, confrontation, malevolence, skewed management values, deception and management misconduct. He has a strategy for dealing with each. See: Otto Lerbinger, *The Crisis Manager: Facing Risk and Responsibility* (Mahwah, N.J.: Lawrence Erlbaum Associates, 1997).

[11] James D. Wilson, "Connecting Risk Assessment to Risk Management: the Center's Risk Analysis Program," *Center for Risk Management Newsletter*, Issue No. 9 (Winter 1996).

[12] Alfonso Gonzales-Herrero and Cornelius B. Pratt, "An Integrated Symmetrical Model for Crisis-Communications Management," *Journal of Public Relations Research*, 8(2), pp. 79–105. Also James E. Grunig and Larissa A. Grunig, "Toward a Theory of the Public Relations Behavior of Organizations: Review of a Program of Research," in Grunig and Grunig, eds., *Public Relations Research Annual*, vol. 1 (Hillsdale, N.J.: Lawrence Erlbaum Associates, 1989), pp. 27–61 (p. 60).

[13] David L. Sturges, Bob J. Carrell, Douglas A. Newsom and Marcus Barrera, "Crisis Communication: Knowing How Is Good, Knowing Why Is Essential," paper for Third Conference on Corporate Communication, Global Communications: Applying Resources Strategically, May 23–24, 1990, Fairleigh-Dickinson University, Madison, N.J.

[14] Ibid.

[15] Newsom, "A Crisis Typology."

[16] "'Smoldering Crises' Account for 86% of Business Crises," *pr reporter*, 38(9) (February 26, 1996), p. 4.

[17] Norman R. Augustine, "Managing the Crisis You Tried to Prevent," *Harvard Business Review* (November-December 1995), pp. 147–158.

[18] Nancy Jeffery, "Preparing for the Worst: Firms Set up Plans to Help Deal with Corporate Crises," *Wall Street Journal* (December 7, 1987), p. 23.

[19] Donald R. Stephensen, "Are You Making the Most of Your Crises?" *Public Relations Journal* (June 1984), pp. 16–18.

[20] Joanne Lipman, "In Times of Trouble, Candor Is Often the First Casualty," *Wall Street Journal* (December 15, 1986), p. 30.

[21] One of the most comprehensive crisis planning books is *The Emergency Public Relations Manual*, 3d ed. (1987), by Alan B. Bernstein, president of PASE, Inc., printed by PASE, POB 1299, Highland Park, N.J. 08904. Another is *Crisis Communications Planning Guide* by Skutski & Associates, Inc., 100 First Avenue, Suite 800, Pittsburgh, PA 15222. The Texas Public Relations Association's 1988 *Crisis Communications Management Plan* is in the *Instructor's Guide* to this text.

[22] Doug Newsom and Bob Carrell, *Public Relations Writing: Form and Style*, 5th ed. (Belmont, Calif.: Wadsworth, 1998), pp. 309–19.

[23] Jeffery, "Preparing for the Worst," p. 23.

[24] "Case: When You're Wrong, The Best Course Is To Say So," *pr reporter*, (January 15, 1996), 38(3), p. 1.

[25]Terry Mason, "Weighing the Financial Fallout of Speaking Out," *Dallas Morning News* (January 14, 1996), p. H1, 5.

[26]Robert L. Heath, "Telling a Story: A Narrative Approach to Communication during Crisis," Speech Communication Association Conference (now National Communication Association), San Diego, CA, 1996.

[27] James Wilson, "Managing Communication in Crisis: An Expert's View," *IABC Communication World* (December 1985), pp. 13–16.

[28] David Pincus and Lalit Acharya, "Employee Communication During Crises: The Effects of Stress on Information Processing," paper presented at the Association for Education in Journalism and Mass Communication, San Antonio, Texas, August 1987. Published as "Employee Communication Strategies for Organizational Crises," in *Employee Responsibilities and Rights Journal,* 1(3) (1988), pp. 181–99.

[29] Bob Carrell, "Predicting Ethical and Responsible Communication Behavior of Organizations in Crisis Situations," paper presented to International Association of Mass Communication Research, New Delhi, India, August 27, 1986.

[30]Harlan Teller, Hill & Knowlton Executive Managing Director of US Corporate Communications Practice, "Communicating During a Crisis Includes Research: 10 Rules of the Road," *tips and tactics, a supplement of pr reporter* 35(11) (September 8, 1997).

[31]Elizabeth Corcoran, "How to Win Friends and Influence People (Not), Intel's Handling of Its Pentium Problem May Have Made a Bad Situation Worse," *Washington Post Weekly Edition* (January 1, 1995), p. 21.

[32]Joan Indiana Rigdon, "Wired Reflects the Quirks of Its Founder," *Wall Street Journal* (October 28, 1996), pp. B1, 5.

[33]Deborah Lohse and Joan Indiana Rigdon, "Wired Kills IPO Amid Mishap With E-Mail," *Wall Street Journal* (October 25, 1996), pp. C1, 20.

[34]Anne Gearan, "Charity President Convicted of Fraud," *Associated Press* (April 4, 1995). Also see editorial, "The United Way After Mr. Aramony," *Washington Post* National Weekly Edition (April 17–23, 1995), p. 25; Jeffrey A. Tanenbaum, "Three Former United Way Aides Indicted," *Wall Street Journal* (September 14, 1994); Pamela Sebastian, "Unemployment and Unforgotten Scandal Work Against United Way Campaigns," *Wall Street Journal* (October 21, 1992), pp. B5, 10.

[35]Tom Knudson, "Copley Gets Strong Dose of Criticism for Its Drug Recall," *Wall Street Journal* (March 1, 1994), pp. B1, 4.

[36] Daniel E. Koshland, Jr., "Scare of the Week," *Science,* 244(4900), p. 9 (editorial, April 7, 1989). For the Sudafed story, see Michael Waldholz, "Sudafed Recall Shows Difficulty of Halting Tampering," *Wall Street Journal* (March 5, 1991), pp. B1, B4.

[37]Pepsi, *The Pepsi Hoax: What Went Right?,* brochure from the company published by Pepsi-Cola Public Affairs, 1993.

[38] Staff of *Management Review,* "The Alaskan Oil Spill: Lessons in Crisis Management," *Management Review* (April 1990), pp. 12–21.

[39] Ibid.

[40]Associated Press, "Judge Rejects Motion by Exxon to Avoid Bond in Valdez Case," *Fort Worth Star-Telegram* (August 8, 1996), p. C5.

[41]Charles McCoy and Peter Fritsch, "Exxon Defends Its 'Novel' Approach To Reducing Valdez Punitive Damages," *Wall Street Journal* (June 14, 1996), p. B2.

[42]Associated Press, "Judge Rejects Motion by Exxon," op. cit., (August 8, 1996).

[43]*Staff of Management Review,* "The Alaskan Oil Spill," op. cit., (April 1990).

[44] Ibid.

[45] Newsom and Carrell, *Public Relations Writing,* pp. 212–75 and 309–40.

[46]W. Timothy Coombs, "Choosing the Right Words," *Management Communication Quarterly* 8(4) (May 1995), pp. 447–76.

[47] Alan B. Bernstein, "Handling the Press Under Stress," *Enterprise* (October 1984), p. 2607

[48] Ibid.

[49]Flora Keshishian, "Political Bias and Nonpolitical News: A Content Analysis of an Armenian and Iranian Earthquake in the *New York Times* and the *Washington Post,*" *Critical Studies in Mass Communication* 14 (1997), pp. 332–43.

[50] Daniel Schorr, "The New World Disorder," In *The Encyclopaedia Britannica 1994 Book of the Year* (Chicago: Encyclopaedia Britannica, 1994), pp. 5–8.

[51] Tony Atwater, "Network Evening News Coverage of the TWA Hostage Crisis," Terrorism and the News Media Project, funded by the Gannett Foundation, sponsored by the Association for Education in Journalism and Mass Communication, Robert G. Picard and Lowndes (Rick) Stephens, directors.

[52] Robert G. Picard and Paul D. Adams, "Characterization of Acts and Perpetrators of Political Violence in Three Elite U.S. Daily Newspapers," Terrorism and the News Media Research Project, funded by the Gannett Foundation, sponsored by the Association for Education in Journalism and Mass Communication, Robert G. Picard and Lowndes (Rick) Stephens, directors.

[53] Jack Lule, "The Myth of My Widow: A Dramatic Analysis of News Portrayals of a Terrorist Victim," Terrorism and the News Media Research Project, funded by the Gannett Foundation, sponsored by the Association for Education in Journalism and

Mass Communication, Robert G. Picard and Lowndes (Rick) Stephens, directors.

54 Public affairs/PR people often differ from CEOs on issues. Some research indicates that the major factor is age, since people tend to become more conservative as they grow older, and the longer a person is in corporate public affairs, the more likely he or she is to reflect the interests of the CEO. These two factors are discussed, along with other research on the topic, in Fred J. Evans, "Business: Attacked from Without and Undermined from Within?" *International Public Relations Review* (November 1983), pp. 27–32.

55 Elizabeth Jensen, Douglas Lavin and Neal Templin, "Tale of the Tape, How GM One-Upped an Embarrassed NBC on Staged News Event," *Wall Street Journal* (February 11, 1993), pp. A1, A7.

56 Ibid.

57 Elizabeth Jensen, "NBC, in Settlement with GM, Disavows Its Re-Enactment in Truck-Crash Story," *Wall Street Journal* (February 10, 1993), pp. B1, B8.

58 *Wall Street Journal* (February 11, 1994).

59 "Top Executives Weigh Media's Fairness," *Wall Street Journal* (February 11, 1994), pp. B1, B8.

60 Walter D. St. John, *A Guide to Effective Communication* (Keene, N.H.: Department of Education, Keene State College).

61 Lisa Bannon, "How a Rumor Spread About Subliminal Sex in Disney's 'Aladdin,'" *Wall Street Journal* (October 24, 1995), pp. A1, A6.

62 Howard Kurtz, "The Story That Wouldn't Stay Buried," *Washington Post Weekly Edition* (December 1, 1997), p. 17.

63 ABC-TV Network, "Black and White," on "20/20" (April 19, 1996), 9 p.m.

64 Leon E. Wynter, "Word of Mouth Can Be A Weapon," *Wall Street Journal* (October 26, 1993), p. B1.

65 "Rumor About Trademark Bedevils Firm," *Fort Worth Star-Telegram* (October 24, 1984); and see Jolie B. Solomon, "Proc-

ter & Gamble Fights New Rumors of Link to Satanism," *Wall Street Journal* (November 8, 1984), p. 1.

66 John Rothchild, "How to Say You're Sorry," *Time* (June 20, 1994), p. 51.

67 Ibid.

68 Ibid.

69 Pamela Sebastian, "Firms Helping Disaster Areas Look to the Future," *Wall Street Journal* (February 18, 1994), p. B1, B8.

70 Otto Lerbinger, "Theorists Discuss Management Crisis Successes and Failures," *purview, a supplement of pr reporter*, No. 436 (March 9, 1998).

71 Otto Lerbinger, *Managing Corporate Crises* (Boston: Barrington Press, 1986), p. 16.

72 Compiled from newspaper reports; speech by Ronald Wishart to the Public Relations Institute at the University of Northern Iowa, Cedar Falls, April 10, 1987; transcript of May 3, 1987, "60 Minutes"; Union Carbide employee brochure, "Setting the Record Straight on Employee Sabotage and Efforts to Provide Relief"; and *Chemical Risks: Fears, Facts and the Media* (Media Institute, 1985).

73 Molly Moore, "In Bhopal, a Relentless Cloud of Despair," *Washington Post National Weekly Edition* (October 4–10, 1993), p. 17.

74 Mazhar Ullah, Associated Press, (January 7), 1995.

75 James Rupert, "The Cloud Over Chernobyl," *Washington Post Weekly Edition*, (June 26–July 2, 1995), pp. 6–7.

76 Compiled from various news reports of the time.

Selected readings, activities and assignments appropriate to this chapter can be found in the *Instructor's Guide* or on InfoTrac if you are using the InfoTrac College Edition.

GLOSSARY

ABC Audit Bureau of Circulations, an organization giving accurate circulation data on U.S. print media.

A-B rolling (1) Preparation of film for printing. All odd-numbered shots are put on the reel (A-roll), with black leader replacing the even shots. The even-numbered shots, with black leader replacing the odd shots, make up the B-roll. Both rolls are then printed together onto one film, thus eliminating splices. (2) Electronic A-B rolling means that on one film chain an SOF (sound on film) film is projected, while on the second film chain a silent film is projected. The films can be intermixed (A-B rolled) through the television switcher.

A-roll The portion of the video-news release (VNR) that has sound. This first clip in a double chain of video is used by television news directors who do not wish to edit the VNR.

academy leader A specifically marked film with numbers one second apart, used for cueing film in the projector.

accidental/convenience sampling A type of nonprobability sampling that involves the selection of happenstance, as opposed to planned, samples. Standing near the information booth at a shopping mall and asking questions of shoppers who happen to walk by is an example of using an accidental or convenience sample.

account A contract agreement with a client.

acetate A transparent plastic sheet used in layouts, called "cell" for cellulose acetate; it also serves as a base for photographic film and is used for magnetic tape too important to risk stretching. Acetate does not stretch and breaks cleanly.

across the board A show aired at the same time daily at least five days a week. Also called a strip show.

adjacencies Broadcast term referring to programs or a time period; usually means commercials placed next to specific programming.

---

*For a comprehensive book (668 pages) of communications terms (to 1990), see NTC's *Mass Media Dictionary*, by R. Terry Ellmore, 1991 (Lincolnwood, IL.: National Textbook Company).

advance News story about an event to occur in the future.

advertorial (1) In broadcasts, an organization's use of commercial time to state a point of view on an issue, often called an *infomercial*. (2) In print, a simulated editorial text with advertising content, usually run in consumer publications—product- or service-oriented copy.

aerial shot A photo taken from helicopter or plane. (In movie film production and printing, the term refers to a particular effect.)

affidavit A sworn statement, proof that commercials were aired at specific time periods.

affiliate A radio or TV station that is part of a network but is not owned and operated by the network.

AFM American Federation of Musicians, a union.

AFTRA A union whose membership consists of anyone who performs live on videotape. Filmed TV shows require membership in SAG—Screen Actors Guild.

agate Typographic term for 5½-point type, the standard unit of measurement for advertising lineage; fourteen agate lines to the inch.

air brush An artist's brush that operates with compressed air; it is used to retouch photos or create special effects in illustrations.

air check Tape made of a radio or TV program or a commercial when it is aired.

air time Time when a radio or TV program starts.

alignment (1) Straightness or crookedness of letters in a line of type. Also refers to the positioning of the elements in an ad for a desirable effect. (2) "Setup" of the head on an audio- or videotape machine.

alphanumeric A set of characters used in computer programming that includes letters, digits and other special punctuation marks.

AM May mean either a morning newspaper or standard radio broadcasting (amplitude modulation of 535 to 1605 kHz, soon to change to 1705).

angle Particular emphasis of a media presentation; sometimes called a slant.

animation Process of filming a number of slightly different cartoon drawings to create the illusion of movement.

annual report Financial statement by management, used as a communication to all stockholders, security analysts and other interested publics; required by Securities and Exchange Commission for publicly held companies.

answer print In 35-mm film, the first print off a negative (or in 16-mm, off a reversal) after the work print is completed; used to check quality.

AOR Designation for a type of radio station format, album-oriented rock music.

AP Associated Press, a cooperative or membership news-gathering service, dating from 1848, serving both print and broadcast media with stories and pictures. AP is international in scope and has its own correspondents, in addition to receiving material from member media.

Arbitron Ratings company and sales research organization for broadcasting (also known as ARB).

arc To move the camera in an arcing motion about a subject.

art General term for all illustrations in any medium.

art-type Adhesive-backed paste-on type used for special effects.

ASCAP American Society of Composers, Authors and Publishers—a licensing clearing house that sets fees and controls artistic performance activity. *See* BMI.

ASCII (Ask-ee) Represents American Standard Code for Information Interchange that makes the text easier to tranfer over networks.

ascender The element of a lowercase letter extending above the body of the letter, as in b, d and h. *See* descender.

aspect ratio TV picture measurement—three units high and four wide. Also used for film measurement, varying with the format.

assemble mode Adding shots on videotape in a consecutive order.

attitude A predisposition to behave in a certain way. People exhibit their attitudes by what they do or say; knowing someone's attitudes often helps predict how that individual will act.

audience Group or groups receptive to a particular medium.

audio Sound.

audio mixer (1) Control room technician who mixes sound from different sources. (2) Equipment for mixing sound.

audit In communications, a review analyzing perceptions of key publics (usually with an emphasis on internal publics), evaluating disparities between the two and formulating recommendations for improving the flow of communications.

author's alterations (AA) Typesetter's term for changes made on proofs by the author after type has been set. *See* printer's errors.

availabilities Unsold time slots for commercials.

back light (1) Diffused illumination from behind the subject and opposite the camera. (2) In three-point lighting, a light opposite the camera to separate the subject from the background.

back of the book In magazines, the materials appearing after the main editorial section.

backroom or backshop The mechanical section of a newspaper plant.

backtiming (1)In broadcasting, a method of determining the time at which various program segments must begin to bring a program out on time. (2) In a PR campaign, scheduling to determine completion dates for various component parts to climax.

B-roll Second clip in a double chain of video. News directors use B-roll footage to make their own versions of a video news release (VNR) that has been sent by a public relations practitioner.

backup (1) In newspaper assignments, a second reporter or photographer used as a backup in case the first does not or cannot complete the job. (2) In printing, when one side of a sheet has been printed and the reverse side is being printed.

backup lead-in A silent lead-in to a sound film or videotape recording when the original recording preceding the sound is uncut; lead-in sound may be blooped or faded out by audio mixer.

bad break In typesetting, an incorrect word division at the end of a line of type.

bank (1) Composing-room table for galleys. (2) A strip of lights.

banner Also called a streamer; a long line of type.

banner head Headlines set in large type and usually stretching across a page.

barter Paying for advertising through goods, rather than money, or airing programs with commercials or time availabilities without paying directly for the program.

BASIC Beginners All-purpose Symbolic Instruction Code—a common time-sharing and business computer language for terminal-oriented programming.

baud Channel speed for data transmission.

beat A reporter's regular area of coverage, such as "city hall beat."

beeper (1) Recorded telephone conversation or interview. (2) Device frequently attached to the telephone that "beeps" every 14 seconds as required by FCC to indicate that a recording is being made.

beep-tape Magnetic tape reproducing a continuous beep.

belief A conviction firmly grounded in the bedrock of one's value system.

Ben Day Process carrying its originator's name that makes possible a variety of shadings in line plates through photoengraving rather than the more expensive halftone.

bicycling Transporting film or audio or video recording from one station to another instead of making a duplicate.

bit Binary digit—either a "0" (zero) or "1" (one). Smallest unit of data handled by a computer, eight bits (a byte) stands for one text character.

black leader Also called opaque leader. (1) Black film used in editing. (2) Film used in 16-mm "A" and "B" rolls or checkerboard editing. The black film, without images, makes putting sequences together easier.

blanking out Breaking or separating forms and placing spacing material where lines or illustrations have been lifted, in order to print in different colors. Also called breaking for color.

bleed Running a picture off the edge of a page. Allow at least 1/8 inch additional on all bleed sides of an illustration to be sure it "bleeds" after trimming.

block programming Scheduling the same types of shows back to back; the opposite of magazine format, which is varied.

bloop To erase sound track—by degaussing (wiping out) if magnetic, or by opaquing (blocking out) if optical.

blow up To photographically enlarge the visual size of any item.

blurb A short promotional description of a story or article.

BMI Broadcast Music, Inc.—a copyright-holding organization from which permission for using musical selections may be received without asking individual copyright holders. Permission from BMI (or ASCAP) is obtained through a license fee. The copyright covers anything broadcast that exceeds four bars. Noncommercial stations get special consideration.

board The audio control board, which sends programming to the transmitter for broadcast or to the tape machine for recording.

body type Type used for text matter, as distinguished from display (headlines or headings) type.

boldface type (BF) Blacker, heavier type than the regular typeface, so it stands out from surrounding copy.

booklet A compilation of six-plus pages, printed with a paper cover and bound.

boomerang effect When a person affected by public opinion reacts oppositely from the expected way.

border The frame around a piece of typed matter.

box or boxed Type enclosed within printed borders.

bps Bits per second, how fast data can be moved.

break (1) Story available for publication. (2) Stopping point—may designate a commercial break.

breaking for color *See* blanking out.

break up To kill or break up a type form so it cannot be used to print from again.

bridge (1) A phrase or sentence connecting two stories. (2) In broadcasting, transitional program music.

bright Light, humorous news story.

broadside Message printed on one side of a single sheet no smaller than 18 × 25 inches, designed for quick reading and prompt response.

brochure A printed piece of (usually) six or more pages. More elaborate than a booklet, but without a backbone; differs from a pamphlet by its use of illustrations and color.

brownlines Lithographer's proofs.

browser Software such as Netscape Communicator or Internet Explorer used to "surf" the Internet.

BTA Best time available—commercial aired at the best time available for the station.

bulletin (1) Important news brief. (2) Wire-service message to kill or release a story.

burnish/burnishing Spreading dots in a halftone to deepen certain areas; also rubbing down to make paste-ups stick.

business publications Periodicals published by and/or directed toward business.

bust shot Photographic framing of a person from the upper torso to the top of the head.

busy Too cluttered, as in a print illustration, still photograph or TV scene.

butted slug Type matter that is too wide to set in one line on a composing machine; it is set on two slugs and butted together to make one continuous line.

B&W Black-and-white (monochrome) photograph (as opposed to color photo).

byline Reporter's name preceding a newspaper, magazine or broadcast story.

byte A set of adjacent bits considered as a unit. *See* bit.

cable television *See* CATV.

CAD/CAM Computer-aided design and computer-aided manufacturing—systems of special hardware and software used in architectural or mechanical design that produce working blueprints or drawings from which the structure or product can be manufactured.

cameo lighting Foreground figures are lighted with highly directional light, with the background remaining dark.

camera chain TV camera and associated equipment, including power supply and sync generator.

camera copy Copy ready for reproduction. Also called repros.

camera negative Original negative film shot by a film camera.

camera-ready Material for a publication or printed piece pasted up in final form, ready to make a plate for printing.

campaign An organized effort to affect the opinion of a group or groups on a particular issue.

caps Capital letters.

caption or cutline Editorial material or legend accompanying an illustration.

card image Computer language for the image of a punched card as represented by some other medium, such as a tape or disk.

casting off Estimating the space required for copy set in a given type size.

cathode ray tube (CRT) An electronic vacuum tube with screen, on which information, news stories, etc., can be displayed.

CATV Community antenna television, also called cable TV—a system in which home receivers get amplified signals from a coaxial cable connected to a master antenna. CATV companies charge a monthly fee for this service.

CCTV Closed-circuit TV—programs telecast not to the public but only to a wired network of specific TV receivers.

CD-ROM Compact disk, read only memory: electronic publication that makes much information available for research and offers an opportunity for publicity materials to be made available electronically.

cell or photocell Optical reader.

census Counting or asking questions of all elements or members of a population, rather than taking a sample of that population.

center spread Two facing center pages of a publication, printed on a single, continuous sheet.

central tendency The "average" direction or "middle ground" of data, usually expressed as the mean, median or mode.

CERP Confederation Europeenne Des Relations Publiques, based in Brussels, comprises four separate organizations: CERP consultants, CERP education, CERP PRO (public relations officers) and CERP Students, has consultative status with the Council of Europe and UNESCO and is recognized and supported by the European Commission.

chain *See* film chain, double chain.

channel (1) In broadcasting, a radio spectrum frequency assigned to a radio or TV station or stations. (2) In computer science, a path for electrical communication or transfer of information; an imaginary line parallel to the edge of tape along which lines are punched.

character Any single unit of type—letter, number, punctuation mark.

character generation Projection on the face of a CRT of typographic images, usually in a high-speed computerized photocomposition system. The series of letters and numbers appears directly on the television screen or is keyed into a background picture.

chase Metal frame around a type form.

cheesecake Photographs that depend for their appeal upon display of sexual images.

chroma key Electronic process for matting (imposing) one picture into another. Called "shooting the blue," because it generally uses the blue camera signal of color TV cameras, but it may use any color.

circular Flyer, mailing piece, free distribution item, usually one sheet and inexpensive.

circulation (1) In broadcasting, refers to the number of regular listeners or viewers of an area regularly tuned to a station. (2) In print, subscribers plus street or newsstand sales.

class publications Periodicals designed for well-defined audiences, with a focus limited to certain subjects.

CLC "Capital and lowercase" letters, used to designate a typesetting format.

client An institution, person or business hiring PR services.

clip (1) Newspaper clipping. (2) In broadcasting, a short piece of film or tape used as a program insert.

(3) To cut off high and low audio frequencies of a program. (4) To compress the white and/or black picture information, or to prevent the video signal from interfering with the sync signals.

clip art Graphic designs and illustrations sold with permission to use, so designers of advertising or publications don't have to create their own artwork. Some is sold as books of camera-ready line art, other types come suitable for electronic scanning or already in electronic form for computerized desktop publishing.

clipping returns Clippings, mentioning a specific subject, from newspapers, magazines, trade journals, specialized publications and internal publications. Commercial services supply clippings from numerous publications for a monthly charge and a per-clipping charge or for a flat rate per clipping. "Clips" also include TV.

clipsheet Stories and illustrations printed on one page and sent to publications. Offers a number of releases in one mailing; works best with small publications that cannot afford syndicated matter.

close-up (CU) An object or any part of it seen at close range and framed tightly. The close-up can be extreme (XCU or ECU) or rather loose (MCU) (medium close-up).

cluster samples Clusters or groups of elements in a population, such as particular cities or geographic regions, from which smaller samples are drawn. The population is first divided into clusters reflecting various traits; then a sample is drawn from each cluster.

coated paper Paper with an enameled coating to give it a smooth, hard finish suitable for best halftone reproduction.

cohort study Multiple samples drawn from the same population are studied longitudinally over time and then compared or contrasted.

coincidental interview Method of public opinion surveying in which a phone interview is conducted to gain information.

cold comp Type composition by various "cold methods"—from typewriter to high-speed computerized photocomposition systems.

cold light Fluorescent.

cold reading Broadcasting copy read by an announcer without prior rehearsal.

colophon (1) Credit line at the end of a book for the designer and printer; tells what typefaces and paper stock were used. (2) Publisher's logo. *See* logo.

color (1) "Mood" piece to go with a straight news story. (2) Lively writing. (3) Exaggerate, falsify. (4) Colored ink or art.

column rule A vertical line separating columns of type.

combination plate A halftone and line plate combined in one engraving.

commercial protection Specific time between competing commercials granted by a station.

community The immediate area affected by company policy and production.

community relations A function of public relations that involves dealing and communicating with the citizens and groups within an organization's geographic operating area.

compact disk (CD) Digitally encoded storage medium for sound or text, decoded by scanning with a laser beam (CD-I is an interactive disk).

composition (1) Typesetting and makeup. (2) Art arrangement of words into a stylistic format.

compositive or composite (1) In broadcasting, a sound track with the desired mix of sounds. (2) In photography, mixing elements from different negatives to create false image.

computer network Two or more interconnected computers.

computer program A set of instructions that, converted to machine format, causes a computer to carry out specified operations to solve a problem.

condensed Type that is narrower than regular face.

conservation Support of an existing opinion held by a public to keep it from changing.

console Part of a computer through which the operator or repair person communicates with the machine and vice versa. Normally it has an entry device such as a typewriter keyboard.

content analysis A research method that involves objective description or analysis of the language content of news releases, newspaper stories, speeches, videotapes and films, magazines or other publications.

continuity Radio and television copy.

continuity strip An ad in comic strip format.

control group Group composed of members chosen for particular characteristics or opinions. Used as a comparison to a *test group*.

control track The area of a videotape that is used for recording synchronization information (sync spikes), which is essential for videotape editing.

control unit In a digital computer, the parts that effect retrieval of instructions in correct sequence. The unit interprets each instruction and then applies proper signals to the arithmetical unit.

conversion　Influencing opinion away from one side of an issue toward another.

co-op advertising　Sharing costs of advertising between two advertisers. In broadcasting, it nearly always refers to a national/local share.

coppering　Revising old news to give it a feeling of currency.

copy　(1) Any broadcast writing, including commercials. (2) Any written material intended for publication, including advertising.

copy desk　The news desk at a newspaper, magazine, radio or TV station where copy is edited and headlines are written.

copy fitting　Determining how much copy is needed to fill a certain amount of space in a design or publication, or figuring how much space is needed to accommodate a given amount of text.

copyreader　A newsroom employee who reads and corrects (edits) copy and writes headlines.

core　(1) The "memory" of a computer. (2) A small hub on which film is wound for storage or shipping.

correspondent　Out-of-town reporter.

cost per thousand (CPM)　The cost to an advertiser to reach 1,000 listeners or viewers with a given message; figured by dividing time cost by size of audience (in thousands).

cover　(1) To a reporter, getting all available facts about an event. (2) Outer pages of a magazine—specifically, the outside front (first cover), inside front (second cover), inside back (third cover) and outside back (fourth cover).

cover shot　Shot of the scene used as a reserve if you miss the action with the first shot.

cover stock　Sturdy paper for magazine covers, pamphlets, booklets, tent cards, posters and other printed matter where weight and durability are important.

CPI　(1) In typesetting, characters per inch. (2) In computer science, the density of the magnetic tape or drum.

CPM　Cost per thousand (M means "thousand")—the ratio of the cost of a given TV segment to the audience reached (in thousands).

CPS　Characters per second—relates to paper tapes or typewriter speeds.

CPU　Central processing unit—the main frame of a computer, with circuits that control operations.

crawl graphics　Usually credit copy that moves slowly up the TV or cinema screen, often mounted on a drum (or crawl). More exactly, an up-and-down movement of credits is called a roll, and a horizontal movement a

crawl. Both the roll and the crawl can be produced by the character generator.

credits　List of people who participated in a TV or film production.

cropping　Changing the shape or size of an illustration to make it fit a designated space or to cut out distracting or undesirable elements.

cross-fade　(1) In audio, a transition method in which the preceding sound is faded out and the following sound is faded in simultaneously. The sounds overlap temporarily. (2) In video, a transition method whereby the preceding picture is faded to black and the following picture is faded in from black.

CRT　*See* cathode ray tube.

crystallization　Creating an awareness of previously vague or subconscious attitudes held by a public.

CTC or CTK　Copy to come.

CTG　Copy to go.

CTR　Computer tape reader—attached when needed to a phototypesetting device.

CU　*See* close-up; usually head and just below shoulders of a person in TV, film or still photograph.

cue　(1) In TV, film or radio, a signal to initiate action. (2) A mark in a TV script for technical and production staffs. (3) White or black dots on film indicating the end. (4) To find the proper place of a transcription.

cumulative audience ("cume")　The audience reached by a broadcast station in two or more time periods or by more than one station in a specific time period (such as a week).

custom-built network　A network temporarily linking stations for a special broadcast.

cut　(1) To delete part of some copy or to end a program suddenly. (2) A track or groove in a transcription. (3) In engraving, a metal plate bearing an illustration, either lined or screened, to be used in letterpress printing (with a raised printing surface made from a matrix). (4) Instantaneous transition from one film or video source to another. *See* engraving.

cutaway shot　A shot of an object or event peripherally connected with the overall event and neutral as to screen direction (usually a straight-on shot). Used to intercut between two shots in which the screen direction is reversed. Also used to cut between two takes with the same shot, avoiding a jump cut.

cutline　The caption or legend accompanying an illustration.

cybernavigation　An expression that means finding your way around through the electronic information accessible by computer such as locating IPRA Online, a part of CompuServe's Public Relations and Marketing Forum (PRSIG).

cyberspace The abstract location of the electronic information superhighway—that is, the transmission and reception of information available through computer technology.

daisy wheel A type head used in letter-quality printers that contains a font of type on a circular wheel.

data Information, often in numerical form and often obtained through systematic observation and surveys, that helps describe, explain or predict relationships, attitudes, opinions or behavior. *Data* is plural; the singular term is *datum*.

database/data bank A collection of data used by an organization, capable of being processed and retrieved.

dateline The line preceding a story, giving date and place of origin; usually only the location is printed.

deadline The time a completed assignment is due and must be delivered.

dealer imprint The name and address of the dealer printed on a leaflet, pamphlet, poster or similar matter, usually in space set aside for this purpose.

deck (1) Part of a headline. (2) A recording machine only (audio or video).

deck head A headline having two or more groups of type.

deckle edge A ragged edge on a sheet of paper.

delphi technique A research method that elicits an interactive exchange of ideas and information among a panel of experts to arrive at a consensus. Several rounds of questionnaires usually are involved, each incorporating and reporting responses from earlier rounds of questioning.

demographics Certain characteristics in the audience for any medium—sex, age, family, education, economics.

department Regular section on a particular subject in a newspaper or magazine.

depth of field The measure in which all objects, located at different distances from the camera, appear in focus. Depth of field depends on the focal length of the lens, the f-stop and the distance between object and camera.

DES Data Encryption Standard provides security for messages.

descender Bottom part of a lowercase letter that extends below the body of the letter, as in p, q and y. *See* ascender.

dirty copy Written material with considerable errors or corrections.

disk Record or transcription.

display type Type or hand lettering for headlines; usually larger than 14 points.

dissolve In TV or film, a gradual transition from shot to shot whereby the two images temporarily overlap. Also called lap-dissolve, or lap.

documentary An informational film presentation with a specific message.

dolly To move the camera toward (dolly in) or away from (dolly out or back) the object.

domain A part of Internet addresses, that which comes after the "@" sign and is separated by dots (periods).

donut A commercial in which live copy runs between the opening and close of a produced commercial, usually a singing jingle.

dope News information or background material.

dot-matrix printer A printer that forms type characters by arranging dots of ink in a grid, or matrix, pattern.

double chain A film story using two film chains simultaneously. *See* film chain.

double-page spread Two facing pages; may be editorial material or advertising, with or without illustrations.

double projection Shooting and recording sound and pictures separately for later simultaneous productions. Gives higher-quality reproduction.

double-spot Two TV commercials run back to back.

double system sound In film and TV, picture and sound portions are recorded separately and later may be combined on one film through printing (married printing).

double truck Center spread, or two full facing pages.

downlink To receive audio and video signals or digitized computer information from a communication satellite, which acts as transmitter.

download To feed a news release from the organization's computer directly into the medium's computer for typesetting, etc.

dress (1) The appearance of a magazine. (2) In broadcasting, a final "dress" rehearsal, or what people will wear on camera. (3) Set dressing, properties.

drive out In typesetting, to space words widely to fill the line.

driver A program that assists a computer with operating a device or interface.

drop folio In books and publications, page number at bottom of page.

drop-in ads Small advertising messages added to or "dropped in" regular advertisements of a different character; e.g., a 1-column-inch community-fund-drive ad in a department store's regular half-page ad.

dry A "slow" or "dry" news day when not much is going on.

dry brush drawing A drawing usually on coarse board made with thick ink or paint.

dry run A rehearsal, usually for TV, before actual taping or airing, if live.

dub Duplication of an electronic recording or an insertion into a transcription. Dubs can be made from tape to tape or from record to tape. The dub is always one generation down (away) from the recording used for the dubbing and is therefore of lower quality.

dubbing Transcribing a sound track from one recording medium to another, such as from film sound to audio tape.

dummy The suggested layout for a publication, showing positions of all elements. A hand dummy is rough and general. A pasteup dummy is proofs carefully pasted in position.

duotones Two-color art. Two halftone plates are made from a one-color illustration and etched to produce a two-tone effect.

dupe Duplicate proof.

ears Boxes or type appearing at the upper left- and right-hand corners of publications alongside the flag (newspaper nameplate).

easel shots or "limbos" Still pictures or models videotaped by a TV camera.

edge key A keyed (electronically cut-in) title whose letters have distinctive edges, such as dark outlines or a drop shadow.

edit To modify, correct, rearrange or otherwise change data in the computer.

editing Emphasizing important matter or deleting the less significant. (1) In live TV, selecting from preview monitors the pictures that will be aired, the selection and assembly of shots. (2) In print media, the collection, preparation, layout and design of materials for publication.

edition All identical copies, printed in one run of the press.

editorialize To inject opinion into a news story.

editorial matter The entertainment or educational part of a broadcast program or publication, exclusive of commercial messages.

EDP Electronic data processing.

electronic editing Inserting or assembling a program on videotape without physically cutting the tape.

electronic film transfer Kinescoping a program from videotape to film by filming the images that appear on a very sharp television monitor.

electronic newspaper A videotex or teletext system in which the individual becomes his or her own gatekeeper, selecting a tailored mix of news and other information.

electros or electrotype Printing plates made by electrolysis from original composition or plates. Made from wax or lead molds, they are much cheaper than original and duplicate photoengravings; used when long runs or several copies of plates or forms are required. If the expense of shipping is an additional cost factor, mats or flongs should be used instead of electros.

em The square of any given type body, but usually refers to the pica em, which is 12 points square. A common method of measuring type composition is to multiply the number of ems in a line by the number of lines.

embossing Making an impression by pressing a piece of paper between two metal dies so that it stands above the surface of the sheet.

en Half an em, a unit of measure in typesetting. Equal to the width of a capital "N" in the particular size of typeface being used.

enameled stock *See* coated paper.

end rate The lowest rate for commercial time offered by a station.

engraving ("cut") Zinc or copper plate that has been etched, generally with acid, to get a raised surface that, when inked, will print on paper. Engravings are reproductions of either line illustrations or halftones (screened); also called photoengravings, because they are made by being brought into contact with film negatives of illustrations. In commercial usage, *engraving* refers almost solely to letterpress printing, although in the past it referred to the intaglio processes.

essential area The section of the television picture, centered within the scanning area, that is seen by the home viewer, regardless of masking of the set or slight misalignment of the receiver. Sometimes called critical area.

establishing shot An orientation shot, usually a long shot with a wide angle giving a relationship of place and action; sometimes called a *cover* shot.

ET Electrical transcription—like a record but produced only for broadcast stations.

etching proofs Sharp, clean proofs from which zinc etchings can be made.

ETV Educational TV.

evaluation Measuring the relative success of a program or activity in terms of the goals and objectives set for it. Evaluation is a form of research, and may use various research methodologies to answer two basic questions, "Did we do what we set out to do? How well did we do it?"

exclusive A correspondent's report or story limited to a single station, network or periodical.

experiential reporting The sense of participation through computer-generated reality. One method is an interactive program with audio and video being used for armchair "tours." Another is cyberspace—a system of virtual-reality experiencing that requires wearing electronic "glasses" and hand-held devices or "gloves."

extended or expanded Extra-wide typeface.

external publication Publication issued by an organization to people outside its own employee or membership groups, such as to customers, the local community and the financial world.

extra condensed Compressed, very thin type.

face The printing surface of type. Also used to identify one style of type from another, such as plain face, heavy face.

fact sheet Page of significant information prepared by PR people to help news media in covering a special event.

fade (1) In audio, the physical or mechanical decrease of volume, either voice or music, to smooth a transition between sounds. (2) In video, the gradual appearance of a picture from black (fade-in) or disappearance to black (fade-out).

family Complete series of one typeface, with all variations (bold, italic, small caps, etc.).

fax Slang for "facsimile." Exact reproduction of printed matter (words and photos) by telephone or radio transmission; also used to refer to TV facilities.

FCC Federal Communications Commission, the government regulatory body for broadcasting.

feature (1) To play up or emphasize. (2) A story, not necessarily news; usually more of human interest.

feed Electronic signal, generally supplied by a source such as a network from which a station can record. Also, what one station sends to another station or stations.

field study Observation or experimental study in a natural setting.

file To send a story by wire, Telex, etc. In computer language, information on a related record, treated as a unit.

fill (1) In broadcasting, additional program material kept ready in case a program runs short. (2) To fill out for timing or space.

fill copy Pad copy. Relatively minor material used to "fill out" a broadcast or page.

filler A short, minor story to fill space where needed in making up the pages of a publication. Copy set in type for use in emergencies.

fill light An additional direction light, usually opposite the key light, to illuminate shadow areas.

film chain A motion picture film projector, slide projector and TV camera, all housed in single unit called a "multiplexor," used to convert film pictures and sound or still pictures mounted on slides into electronic signals.

film clip A short piece of film.

film counter A device used to measure film length while editing.

film lineup A list of films in broadcast order.

film rundown A list of cues for a film story.

financial relations A function of public relations that involves dealing and communicating with the shareholders of an organization and the investment community.

fixed position A spot delivered at a guaranteed time.

fixed service Short-range TV transmission on the 2,500-megacycle band; generally used for closed-circuit TV.

flack Slang for a press agent or publicist, primarily those in the entertainment fields; apparently first recorded by writer Pete Martin in the April 1, 1950, issue of *Saturday Evening Post*. Martin defined the term in a May 5, 1956, issue of the Post with these words, "And since 'flack' is Hollywood slang for publicity man. . . ." This word has a few meanings from obsolete provincial English usage: As a verb: to palpitate, to hang loosely, to beat by flapping. Also as a noun: a stroke or touch, a blow, a gadding woman. The word *flak* came into use during World War II and is an acronym for the German Flieger Abwehr Kanone, an aircraft defense cannon, literally translated to mean "the gun that drives off raiders." The Old English word and the military word may or may not have anything to do with the inspiration of its application to PR. Some sources say the entertainment industry's magazine, *Variety*, began using flack for publicist or press agent as a tribute to the motion picture industry's publicist, Gene Flack. This could account for the spelling since the German cannon was spelled flak. (Source: Wes Pederson,

Director of Communications and Public Relations, Public Affairs Council, letter to PRSA's *The Strategist*.).

flag (1) The front page title or nameplate of a newspaper. (2) A device to block light in film lighting.

flagship station The major network-owned station or the major station in a community-owned group of stations.

flighting Broadcast advertising technique for interspersing periods of concentrated advertising with periods of inactivity; usually six-week patterns help a small advertiser get impact.

flong *See* electros, matrix.

floppy disk A flexible disk on which computer-generated copy or graphics can be stored.

flyer *See* circular.

FM Frequency modulation—radio broadcasting (88 to 108 megacycles) with several advantages over standard (AM) broadcasting such as elimination of static, no fading and generally more consistent quality reception.

focus group A test panel of people, usually 20 or fewer at a time, selected and interviewed as representative of a particular public likely to have views and opinions on an issue or product.

fold Where the front page of a newspaper is folded in half.

folder A printed piece of four pages or a four-page, heavy-paper container for other printed materials.

folio Page number.

follow copy Instruction to the typesetter to set type exactly like the copy in every detail.

followup A story presenting new developments of one previously printed; also known as a second-day story.

font An assortment of typeface in one size and style.

form Pages of type and illustrations locked in a rectangular iron frame called a *chase*.

format (1) The size, shape and appearance of a magazine or other publication. (2) The skeletal structure or outline of a program, or even of the kind of programming a station does.

foundry proofs (1) Etching proofs. (2) Heavy borders of black foundry rules.

four-color process Reproduction of full-colored illustrations by the combination of plates for yellow, blue, red and black ink. All colored illustrations are separated photographically into these four basic colors. Four-color process is available to the letterpress, offset and gravure processes.

frame (1) A single picture on a storyboard. (2) A single picture in film footage. (3) $\frac{1}{30}$ second TV; $\frac{1}{24}$ second in film. (4) A command to camera operator to compose the picture.

freelancer An unaffiliated writer or artist, available for hire on a per-story basis or on retainer.

Freenet Free access network usually from some part of the community.

freeze frame Arrested motion, which is perceived as a still shot.

frequency discount A lower rate available to volume advertisers.

fringe time Broadcast time generally considered to be 5:30–7:00 P.M. and 10:30 P.M.–1:00 A.M., the early and late fringes bracketing prime time.

front of the book The main editorial section of a magazine.

front timing The process of figuring out clock times by adding given running times to the clock time at which a program starts.

f-stop The calibration on a lens indicating the ratio of aperture diameter or diaphragm opening to focal length of the lens (apertures control the amount of light transmitted through the lens). The larger the f-stop number, the smaller the aperture or diaphragm opening; the smaller the f-stop number, the larger the aperture or diaphragm opening.

fully scripted A TV script that indicates all words to be spoken and all major video information.

fund raising Working with donor publics to solicit funds, usually through benefits, for charitable groups.

futures research Research designed to anticipate and predict future events. Organizations often engage in futures research to help anticipate and prepare for changes in their political, social and economic environments.

gain Amplification of sound.

galley A shallow metal tray for holding type after lines have been set.

galley proofs Proofs reproduced from the type as it stands in galley trays before being placed in page form or (with cold type) as photocopied from the master print or repro.

gel or cell A sheet of transparent colored plastic used to change the color of a still photo, key light or graphic, or clear material used in film animation. (Inserted in front of key lights, on top of art.)

ghost writer A writer whose work appears under the byline of another.

gigabyte Data storage unit equivalent to about 1,000 megabytes.

glossy print A smooth shiny-surfaced photograph; the most suitable form for black and white reproduction in print media. Also called glossy.

government relations A function of public relations that involves dealing and communicating with legislatures and government agencies on behalf of an organization.

grain (1) Direction in which paper fibers lie, and the way paper folds best. Folded against the grain, paper is likely to crack or fold irregularly. (2) Unwanted silver globs in a photograph.

graphics (1) All visual displays in broadcasting. (2) Art, display lettering and design in print media.

gravure A form of intaglio printing. *See* intaglio printing.

greeking Pasting dummy, "pretend" text set in the desired typeface and size onto a layout. The type on the layout gives the appearance of what the finished publication will look like, even though the words or characters may be nonsensical.

gross rating points The combined quarter-hour ratings for a time period when each scheduled commercial for a single, specific advertiser was aired.

GUI Graphical User Interface, the icons or symbols that make interaction with a computer's system easier.

guideline Slugline—title given to a news story as a guide for editors and printers.

gutter The space between the left- and right-hand pages of a printed publication.

halftone A screened reproduction (composed of a series of light and heavy dots) of a photograph, painting or drawing.

hand composition Type set by hand.

handout Publicity release.

hard disk A piece of computer hardware capable of storing as much computer-generated copy or graphics as could be stored on 20 or more floppy disks.

hardware Physical equipment of the computer.

head The name, headline or title of a story.

headnote Short text accompanying the head and carrying information on the story, the author or both.

headroom The space left between the top of the head and the upper screen edge in a television display.

HDTV High-definition television, high definition electronic production or sometimes used to include any advanced TV system.

HDEP High-definition television, advanced television system with 1,125 scanning lines, 60 fields, an aspect ratio of 16:9 and a 90mHz bandwidth.

Helsinki Charter Union of IPRA, CERP and ICO to sign a charter agreeing on the quality and quality development for public relations.

highlight halftone A halftone in which whites are intensified by dropping out dots, usually by hand tooling.

hold News not to be published without release or clearance.

hold for release (HFR) News not to be printed until a specified time or under specified circumstances.

holdover audience Listeners or viewers inherited from a preceding program.

Home Box Office (HBO) A company that supplies pay TV programs to cable systems.

Home Information System (H.I.S.) A computer-based electronic information system that links the home to a variety of databases; the individual consumer controls the information mix delivered.

hometown stories Stories for local newspapers of individuals participating in an event or activity, usually written so the name and perhaps address can be filled into a general story.

horsing Reading a proof without the original copy.

host The server computer linked to the Internet.

house ad An ad either for the publication in which it appears or for another medium held by the same owner.

house magazine House organ or company magazine—internal publications for employees or external publications for company-related persons (customers, stockholders and dealers) or for the public.

HTK Head to come—information telling the typesetter that the headline is not with the copy but will be provided later.

HTML HyperText Markup Language, a name for formatting instructions and codes for interactive online Internet documents.

http Hypertext Terminal Protocol, used as a prefix to URLs (Uniform Resource Locators).

human interest Feature material appealing to the emotions—drama, humor, pathos.

HUTs Households using television—number with sets in use at one time.

hypertext Links documents to provide additional information about a topic.

ICO International Committee of Public Relations Consultancies Associations, based in London, represents more than 550 consultancies in Europe as follows by nation and initials of association: Austria (APRVA), Belgium (ABCRP/BGPRA), Czech Republic (APRA)

Denmark (BPRV), Finland (VTL), France (Syntec Conseil), Germany (GPRA), Greece (Hellenic PRCA), Ireland (PRCA Ireland), Italy (ASSOREL), The Netherlands (VPRA), Norway (NIR), Portugal (APECOM), Spain (ADECEC), Sweden (PRECIS), Switzerland (BPRA), United Kingdom (PRCA).

ID   Identification. In broadcasting, includes call letters and location in a 10-second announcement that identifies the station, usually in a promotional way.

impose   To arrange pages in a chase so they will be in sequence when the printed pages are folded.

independent station   A broadcast station not affiliated with a network.

indicia   Mailing information data required by the Postal Service.

industry relations   A function of public relations that involves dealing and communicating with firms within the industry of which the organization is a part.

infomercial   Advocacy advertising in the broadcast media that may be as long as program length. *See* advertorial.

initial letter   First letter in a block of copy, usually two or three copy lines deep; used for emphasis; frequently in another color.

inline   Letter with a white line cut in it.

input   Information entered in to a computer by typing, scanning, drawing, talking, singing or transfer from another computer.

insert   (1) New material inserted in the body of a story already written. (2) Printed matter prepared for enclosure with letters. (3) In film, a matted portion of a picture or an additional shot added to a scene.

institutional ads, commercials and programs   All productions planned for long-term effects rather than immediate response.

intaglio printing   A process in which the design is scratched or etched below the general level of the metal and filled with ink, so the transfer in printing will show only the design. Rotogravure is intaglio printing.

integrated commercial   A "cast"-delivered commercial incorporated into a show, or a multiple-brand announcement for a number of products by the same manufacturer.

intercut   TV film technique of cutting back and forth between two or more lines of action.

internal communications   Communications within a company or organization to personnel or membership.

internal publication   A publication directed to personnel or membership of a company or organization.

Internet   The home of thousands of electronic information networks—some of them begun by news media organizations for profit and by public relations people or by nonprofit organizations to provide instant information, some of them highly specialized—on a 24-hour basis.

Intranet   Internal network for organizations.

intermercials   Ads on the Internet that include dialogue and motion video and last up to four minutes.

interstitials   Web advertising that appears to a user while a browser is downloading a page within a site.

interval measures   In social science, constructed measures based on experiences with distributions, rather than a true zero.

interviewee   A person being interviewed.

interviewer   (1) A person who seeks information by asking questions either formally or informally. (2) One who asks respondents the questions specified on a questionnaire in an opinion or market survey.

interviewer bias   A form of survey error that occurs when the interviewer asks questions slanted to get a response to support a particular point of view.

investigative reporting   Searching below the surface for facts generally concealed.

IPRA   The International Public Relations Association, a global professional organization, based in London, representing senior practitioners in more than 70 countries.

ISDN   Integrated Services Digital Network offers voice and digital network services.

island   An ad surrounded by editorial material.

ISP   Internet Service Provider, an organization or a company such as America Online that provides gateway access to the Internet.

issues management   A function of public relations that involves systematic identification and action regarding public policy matters of concern to an organization.

italic   Type in which letters and characters slant.

item   A news story, usually short.

jingle   A musical signature or logo used for broadcast identification and as a vehicle for a message.

job press   A press taking a small sheet size, normally under 25 × 38 inches.

jump   (1) To continue a story from one page of a publication to another. (2) In film, to break continuity in time or space. *See* jump cut.

jump cut   Cutting between slots that are identical in subject yet slightly different in screen location. As a result, the subject seems to jump from one screen location to another for no apparent reason.

jump head   The title or headline over the continued portion of a story on another page.

jump lines Short text matter explaining the destination of continued text.

jump the gutter To continue a title or illustration from a left- to a right-hand page over the center of the publication.

justify To arrange type and spacing so that all type completely fills the line and is the same length as adjoining lines. Also called block style.

keying An electronic effect in which an image (usually lettering) is cut into a background image.

key light The principal source of illumination.

kicker (1) A short line over the source of directional illumination. (2) A headline. (3) A type of television light.

kill (1) To strike out or discard part or all of a story. (2) In films or TV, to stop production.

kinescope Film of a TV program film taken directly from a receiving tube. Also called a transfer.

LAN Local Area Network group of computers in close location connected by cable.

lapel Small microphone worn as a lapel button.

laser printer A printer that uses a laser beam of light to create the printed image at a level of quality often equal to that of mechanical printing and far superior to the output of a dot-matrix or daisy wheel printer.

lavaliere mike ("lav") A small microphone suspended around neck, worn on tie, collar, etc.

layout Dummy.

LC Lowercase (uncapitalized) letters.

lead ("led") Spacing metal, usually lead alloy, placed horizontally between lines of type to give more space between lines. Leads can be 1, 2, or 3 points thick. Ten-point type lines separated by 2-point leads are said to be "10-point leaded 2 points." See slug.

lead ("leed") (1) The introductory sentence or paragraph of a news story. (2) A tip that may develop into a story. (3) The news story of greatest interest, usually placed at the beginning of a newscast or in the upper right-hand corner of a newspaper, although some papers favor the upper left-hand position.

leaders (1) In print, dots used to direct the eye from one part of the copy to another. (2) In broadcasting, a timed visual used at the beginning of sequences for cues. See academy leader, black leader.

lead-in line A section of film, videotape or copy, such as the first sentence used by a newscaster, to cue the technical staff or news anchorperson.

leaflet A printed piece of about four pages, usually from a single sheet, folded.

leg Part of any network; usually a principal branch off the main trunk.

legend Cutline. See caption.

leg man A reporter who calls in information to a rewrite person.

letterpress A printing process in which raised type and plates are inked and then applied to paper through direct pressure.

letterspacing Putting narrow spaces between letters.

level (1) In audio, volume. (2) In video, number of volts.

lighting ratio The relative intensities of key, back and fill light.

light level Measured in foot-candles or in lumens.

light pen A penlike tube containing a photocell, which, when directed at a cathode ray tube display, reacts to light from the display. The response goes to the computer, and text in the data store can be deleted or inserted.

limbo Any set area used for shooting small commercial displays, card easels and the like, having a plain light background. The floor and the background appear to go on forever.

lineprinter A drum, chain or cathode ray tube printer that usually is capable of printing a complete line of characters in one cycle of operation. The whole line is composed in the computer.

linotype A typesetting machine that casts lines or letterpress type instead of single characters.

Listserv Internet mailing list.

lithographic printing Chemically transferring an inked image from a smooth surface to paper, as in offset lithography, offset printing or photo-offset.

lithography Printing from a flat surface.

live Performed at broadcast time.

live copy Copy read by station announcer, in contrast to electronic transcriptions or tapes.

live tag A message added to a recorded commercial by the announcer, usually to localize the spot.

localize To stress the local angle.

log A second-by-second daily account of what was broadcast.

logo Logotype or ligature: (1) A combination of two or more letters on the same body—e.g., *fl.* (2) A company trade name or product identification. (3) In broadcasting, a musical or sound signature used for identification.

long shot An object seen from far away or framed very loosely. The extreme long shot shows the object from a great distance.

loop (1) In audio, a technical way to keep up special sound effects or a background noise like rain by constant transmission from one spot of tape. (2) In video, loops used with videotape may replace kinescope pictures and sound recordings for national dissemination of TV programs. Loop feeds allow the affiliated local station's programs and news reports to be picked up by the network. Film loops permit continuous repetition of the picture.

LS　Long shot, as with a TV or film camera.

machine format　A broadcast format in which elements are not prefixed by time or relative position, but are varied. Opposite of segmented.

magazine format　*See* block programming.

mainframe　A large, fast computer usually programmed with several software packages and programming languages. Individual terminals may be linked to a mainframe for access to software and for manipulation or storage of data.

make good　When an ad or commercial is not run because of media error or when it is run with a misprint or malfunction, the offender must publish or broadcast it free at a later date.

make ready　To prepare a form on the press for printing.

makeup　(1) Getting type and engravings in printing form correctly. (2) Placing information and pictures on a publication's page. (3) Planning a group of pages. (4) In film, putting several films on one big reel.

manifest　In content analysis, the visible, surface content.

markup　Proof with changes indicated.

mass publications　Periodicals with wide appeal and large, general circulation.

master　The original of a film or videotape.

master positive　Positive film made from an edited camera negative and composite sound track with optical effects.

masthead　Name of publication and staff that appears in each issue of magazine or paper, usually on the editorial page in a box also giving information about the paper such as company officers, subscription rates and address.

material　In investor relations, a term applied to any event that is likely to affect the value of stock.

matrix or mats　A papier-mâché impression of a printing plate that may be used as a mold for a lead casting to reproduce the copy or art. Used for some ads and publicity primarily because of the economy of mailing, and used by small publications without engraving facilities.

matte　(1) Imposition of a scene or title over another scene, excluding background. Not a blend or a super.

(2) Name for a box placed in front of a lens to shade and hold filters and effects. (3) Dull finish needed for still photos used by TV so lights will not be reflected.

Mbone　Multicast (back)bone sends video over Internet.

mean　The mathematical "average" calculated by dividing the sum of values or scores by the total number of scores; one measure of central tendency.

median　The exact midpoint of an array of values of scores; one measure of central tendency. Half of the values or scores are above the median, and the other half are below.

media relations　A function of public relations that involves dealing with the communications media in seeking publicity for, or responding to media interest in, an organization.

Mediastat　A broadcast rating service.

medium shot　An object seen at medium distance, neither close up nor far away.

memory　Same as storage.

MICR　Magnetic ink character recognition—automatic reading by a machine of graphic characters printed in magnetic ink.

microwave relay　Use of UHF radio relay stations to transmit television signals from one point to another in a line of sight, usually about 25 miles.

midcourse evaluation　Evaluative research undertaken while a program or project is ongoing to determine whether any adjustments should be made in the original plan to account for changing public, media or environmental conditions.

milline　A unit of space and circulation used in advertising to measure the cost of reaching an audience. The milline rate is the cost per million for a one-column line of agate type.

MIME　Multipurpose Internet Mail Extensions that permits addition of non-text data such as video and audio to e-mail text.

minicam　A highly portable TV camera and videotape unit that can easily be carried and operated by one person.

minority relations　A function of public relations that involves dealing and communicating with individuals and groups of racial or ethnic minorities.

mixer　(1) Audio control console. (2) Person working this console.

mixing　(1) In audio, combining two or more sounds in specific proportions (volume variations), as determined by the event (show) context. (2) In video, combining various shots via the switcher.

mockup A scale model used for study, testing or instruction.

mode The most common or frequently found value or score in a data set; one measure of central tendency.

model release A document signed by a model allowing use of photographs or art in which he or she appears.

modem Modulator/demodulator—a device that translates computer signals for dissemination over a telephone line and vice versa.

monitor (1) To review a station's programming and commercials. (2) A TV set that handles video signals.

montage In TV and film, a rapid succession of images to give idea association. *See also* composite.

MOO Multi Object Oriented environment permits blending of texts, graphics and meetings (used for online instruction).

MOR Type of radio station programming that is "middle of the road."

more Written at the bottom of a page of copy to indicate that a story is not complete, that there is more to come.

morgue A newspaper library for clippings, photos and reference material.

MOS "Mitout sound"—film recorded without sound.

mouse A hand-held computer input device especially useful for applying features of graphics or desktop publishing software. When moved, it propels a pointer or cursor around the computer screen to select commands, functions or text.

movieola A device used to view film during editing.

MS Medium shot, as with a TV or film camera.

mult box A portable electronic box (usually resembling a large travel case) that allows dozens of tape recorders to be plugged in at once to record off the public address (PA) system so the speakers' remarks will be captured and transmitted to all simultaneously. *See* multiplexer.

Multigraphing A trademarked process for making numerous copies of typewritten or hand-drawn material. More closely resembles hand typing than does mimeographing.

multiplexer (1) A system of movable mirrors or prisms that takes images from several projection sources and directs them into one stationary television film camera. (2) An instrument for mixing signals.

must Written on copy or art to designate that it must appear.

NABET National Association of Broadcast Employees and Technicians—union for studio and master control engineers; may include floor personnel.

nameplate The name of the publication appearing on page one of a newspaper. *See* flag.

national rate A rate offered to advertisers in more than one market.

NET National Educational Television.

network Any link, by any technology, of two or more stations so they can each separately broadcast the same program.

network option time Broadcast hours when a network preempts on its affiliates and the stations it owns.

new lead Replacement for a lead already prepared, usually offering new developments or information. *See* lead.

newsprint A rough, relatively inexpensive paper, usually made from wood pulp, used for many newspapers and for other inexpensive printed material.

news release A news story written in print or broadcast style for use by a news medium.

news tip A news story idea not in story format given to a news medium for that medium's staff to write if the story idea is deemed to have merit.

news wheel A news show in which content is repeated with some updating.

Nexis Database.

NFS Network File System allows working on files from a remote host.

Nielsen The A. C. Nielsen Company—the biggest name in broadcast ratings. Reputations and shows literally live or die on their Nielsen ratings.

nominal measures Used in ordering data, these variables have attributes that are mutually exclusive or exhaustive.

nonparametric In statistics, a method or test that is not based on distributions.

nonprobability sample A sample selected in such a way that it's not possible to estimate the chance that any particular member of the population will be included in the sample. Using nonprobability samples results in the risk of over- or underrepresenting certain segments of the population.

NPR National Public Radio.

obituary News biography of a dead person.

OCR Optical character recognition—electronically reading printed or handwritten documents.

offset Lithographic process.

ombudsman/woman Someone who researches complaints and problems brought by individuals or groups against an organization.

online In direct communication with the computer CPU.

on the nose (1) On time. (2) Correct.

open-end   A recorded commercial with time at the close for a "tag."

open spacing   Widely leaded spacing.

opinion   An expression of an attitude, belief or feeling, usually in writing or orally, held at a particular moment.

optical center   A point equidistant from the left and right sides of a sheet of paper and five-eighths of the way up from the bottom.

optical reader   An electronic reader of copy.

opticals   In film, any variations to the picture achieved after or during filming, such as mattes or dissolves. May be done during filming or by control board when multiple cameras are used.

optical scanner   A visual scanner that scans printed or written data and generates their digital representation.

ordinal measures   Used in ordering data, these variables have attributes that can be rank-ordered.

orphan   In publishing, an indented opening line of a paragraph that appears as the bottom line on a page or column of type. To be avoided.

outline   The gist of a written article or program.

output   The information that comes out of a computer or other device, such as a printer, linked to a computer. Output may be in hard copy form on paper, or it may be digitized information stored on a floppy or hard disk.

outtakes   Filmed or taped scenes or sequences not used in the final production.

overdubbing   Recording separate channels on a multichannel tape separately; then adding and synchronizing so the original sound track is supplemented. This allows a few voices to become a chorus and a few instruments, an orchestra.

overline   Kicker.

overrun   Established printing trade practice that permits delivery of and charge for up to 10 percent more than the quantity of printed matter ordered.

overset   More type set than there is space to use.

pace   The overall speed of a show or performance.

pad   Fill.

page proof   A proof showing type and engravings as they will appear in the printed piece unless subsequently altered.

pamphlet   A printed piece of more than four pages with a soft cover. Differs from a brochure in its size, simplicity and lack of illustrations.

pan   Horizontal turning of the camera.

panel   (1) An area of type sometimes boxed but always different in size, weight or design from the text and partially or entirely surrounded by text. (2) In broadcasting and communication research, a group brought together to discuss one subject or several related subjects.

paper tape   A strip of paper on which data may be recorded, usually in the form of punched holes. Punched paper tape can be sensed by a reading head used to transfer the data. Each charge is represented by a pattern of holes, called a row or frame.

parametric tests   Tests of significance based on distributions that make different assumptions about the population from which the sample was taken.

participation spot   Shared time in a program for spot commercials or announcements.

pasteup   *See* dummy.

patch   (1) In broadcasting, a temporary equipment connection. Patch panels or patch boards are assemblies of jacks into which various circuits are permanently tied and into which patch cords may be inserted. They are essential at "on site" special events. (2) In publishing, a block of repro—usually one or more full lines—that is inserted in a mechanical in place of earlier material that contained an error or otherwise required updating.

PBS   Public Broadcasting System.

perforator   A keyboard unit used to produce punched paper tape.

personal   A brief news item about one or more persons.

photo composition   A photographic method of setting type to produce proofs on paper.

photoprint   Reproduction of art or a printed or written piece by one of many different photographic copying processes.

Photostat   A trademarked device for making photographic copies of art or text.

pica   Standard printing measure of 12 points. There are slightly more than six picas to the inch.

pied type   Type that is all mixed up.

PIQ   Program Idea Quotient—annual study by Home Testing Institute to get reactions to new program ideas. Ratings are on a 6-point scale from "favorite" to "wouldn't watch."

pix   Pictures.

place   Any type of printing surface, engraving or electrotype.

play up   To emphasize, give prominence.

plug   A free and favorable mention.

PM   Afternoon paper.

PMT (photo mechanical transfer)   A positive (as opposed to a negative) that can be printed by offset lithography.

point   Printers' standard unit of measure equal to 0.01384 inch. One inch equals slightly more than 72 points. Sizes of type and amounts of leading are specified in points.

poll Survey of the attitudes and beliefs of a selected group of people.

position Where elements in any publication appear; usually indicates relative significance.

postdubbing Adding a sound track to an already recorded (and usually fully edited) picture portion.

poster type Large, garish letters.

pot Potentiometer—a volume-control device on audio consoles.

power structure The socially, politically and economically advantaged.

PR Public relations.

precinct principle Organization of a campaign through delegation of local responsibilities to chosen leaders in each community. These may be opinion leaders and not necessarily political leaders.

preempt In broadcasting, to replace a regular program with a commercial or a news event of greater importance.

preemptible spot Commercial time sold at a lower rate by a station, which has the option of taking it back if it has a buyer at full rate, unless the first purchaser pays to keep it at full rate.

presentational TV performance format where camera is addressed as audience.

presidential patch Portable sound system with outlets for amplifiers to be connected; unity gain amplifier with numerous mike-level outputs used in pool remotes to cut down on the number of mikes needed.

press agentry A function of public relations that involves creating news events of a transient, often flighty sort.

pretesting Testing a research plan, any of its elements or any elements in a campaign before launching the entire program.

printer's errors (PE) Typographical errors made by typesetter.

privilege Constitutional privilege granted the press to print with immunity news that might otherwise be libelous—e.g., remarks made in open court.

probability sample A sample selected in such a way that the chance that any particular member of the population will be selected for the sample is known. Using a probability sample enables the researcher to calculate the chances that the sample accurately represents the population from which it was selected.

process plates and progressive proofs Each of the color plates printed singly, so they may be laid over each other for effect. In progressive prints, in addition to the single prints of each color, the colors are shown in proper color combination and rotation to suggest the final printed result.

program A set of instructions that make the computer perform the desired operations.

promo Broadcast promotional statement, film, videotape/recording, slide or combination.

promotion A function of public relations that involves special activities or events designed to create and stimulate interest in a person, product, organization or cause.

proof A trial impression of type and engraved matter taken on paper to allow the writer and publisher to make corrections.

propaganda A function that involves efforts to influence the opinions of a public in order to propagate a doctrine.

propaganda devices Specific devices—spoken, written, pictorial or even musical—used to influence human action or reaction.

PR wires Commercial wire services received by print and electronic media.

psychographics The attitudes and images held by media audiences.

public, publics Any group of people tied together by some common bond of interest or concern. *See* audience.

public affairs A function of public relations that involves working with governments and groups that help determine public policies and legislation.

publicity A function of public relations that involves disseminating purposefully planned and executed messages through selected media, without payment to the media, to further the particular interest of an organization or person.

public relations The various activities and communications that organizations undertake to monitor, evaluate, influence and adjust to the attitudes, opinions and behaviors of groups or individuals who constitute their publics.

public television Noncommercial broadcasting. Stations are financed by federal grants, private donations and public subscriptions.

puffery Unsubstantiated and exaggerated claims that appear in either advertising or publicity.

pulp Magazines printed on rough, wood-pulp paper, in contrast to "slicks"—magazines printed on coated or calendared stock.

punch To give vigor to the writing or editing process.

quads (1) Blank pieces of metal used to fill large spaces in a line of type. (2) A type of videotape recorder.

query A letter addressed to an editor that summarizes an article idea and asks if the piece might be considered for publication.

questionnaire The body of questions asked of subjects in a research effort.

Quicktime A computer-based video format for encoding and playing video files.

quoins ("coins") Triangular wedges of steel used in locking up a type form.

quote A quotation or estimate of costs.

RADAR Radio's All Dimension Audience Research—a survey conducted by Statistical Research Inc., for NBC, CBS, ABC and Mutual networks.

radio-TV wire (1) Broadcast wire. (2) The news services wire copy written in broadcast style.

ragged right (or left) In typography, when the left side of the text is justified and the right side varies in length. In ragged left, the right side is justified.

RAM Random access memory—a storage device in which the time needed to find data is not affected significantly by where the data are physically located.

random sample A sample in which each person or element of a population has an equal chance of being selected. A table of random numbers, sometimes generated by a computer, often is used to select sample members randomly from a population.

raster The scanned area of the CRT tube; line scans traced across the face of a CRT tube by a flying spot.

rating service A company that surveys broadcast audience for total homes or individuals tuning in or gives percentages of total listening audience for specific stations and specific shows.

ratio Measures based on a true zero point (such as age, as opposed to temperature, which is an internal measure).

raw stock Unexposed film. Called camera stock when it is unexposed film for use in a motion picture camera; called print stock when it is unexposed film for making duplicate copies of still photographs.

reach The number of people or households that a station, commercial or program is heard by in a given time period. Used with frequency to measure a station's audience for evaluation of worth, generally for advertising pricing.

real time Online processing, with data received and processed quickly enough to produce output; interactive.

rear screen projection Projection of positive transparencies onto a translucent screen.

rebate An extra discount on ads earned by using more time or space than the contract specifies.

recap A recapitulation of news.

reduce To decrease the size of anything visual when reproducing it.

register (1) The correct position for a form to print in so that the pages when printed back-to-back will be in their proper places. (2) In color printing, the precise position for superimposition of each color in order for the colors to blend properly.

rejection slip A letter or printed form from a publication's editor accompanying a manuscript returned to its author.

release print In TV, a film print made from a negative and given to stations to use.

relief printing Letterpress. Letters on the block or plate are raised above the general level so that, when an inked roller is passed over the surface, the ink can touch only the raised portions.

remote A videotape recording or live broadcast originating outside the regular studios.

reprint A second or new impression of a printed work, either text or art.

repro *See* camera copy.

respondents Those to whom questions are directed in a survey.

retail rate The local rate (or lower) for advertising.

retouch To improve photographs before reproduction as artwork.

reversal print A copy made on reversal print stock.

reverse To print text or art in white on a dark background, or, in making a cut from a picture, to turn over or "flop" the negative so that everything goes in an opposite direction.

review A critique or commentary on any aspect of human events—politics, society or the arts.

rewrite person A newspaper staff member who rewrites stories and takes phoned-in reports but does not leave the office to cover news.

rim On newspapers, the outer edge of a copy desk where copy readers work under the direction of a "slot" person or copy chief.

ROP Run of paper. Means that an ad may be placed on any page of the publication.

ROS Run of station or run of schedule. Costs less; usually preemptible.

rotary press A press that prints from curved stereotypes or plate attached to a cylinder.

rotogravure Printing by means of a sensitized copper cylinder on which is etched the image to be reproduced.

rough A preliminary visualization of art.

rough cut The first editing of a film, without effects.

roundup A comprehensive story written with information gathered from several sources.

router Routes data on alternative paths if part of a computer network is busy.

routing Cutting out part of a plate or engraving to keep it from printing.

rule A thin strip of type-high metal that prints as a slender line.

run in To join one or more sentences to avoid making an additional paragraph.

running foot Identification information printed in the bottom margin of a magazine.

running head Identification information printed in the top margin of a magazine.

running story or breaking story A fast-breaking story usually written in sections.

saddle stitching Binding pages by stitching with wire through the fold.

SAG Screen Actors Guild.

sample The portion of the total population queried in a survey, intended to be representative of the total population.

sample error The degree to which a sample lacks representativeness; this can be measured and is reduced by having large samples or more homogeneous ones.

sandwich or donut In broadcasting, a commercial with live copy between musical open and close.

sans serif Typeface without serifs, which are the cross lines at the end of the main strokes of many letters.

scaling Measuring and marking illustrations for engraving to ensure that the illustration will appear in the appropriate, designated size and in proper proportion.

scanner Optical scanner.

scanning Movement of an electron beam from left to right and from top to bottom on a screen.

scanning area The picture area scanned by a television camera's pickup tube; more generally, the picture area actually reproduced by the camera and relayed to the studio monitors.

search engine Services such as Yahoo!, Excite and Infoseek that catalog or index Web sites and allow users to search by using key words.

segue An audio transition method whereby the preceding sound goes out and the following sound comes in immediately after.

server *See* host.

service provider Company offering connection to Internet.

set close To thin spaces and omit leads.

set open To open spaces with leads as slugs.

sets in use Rating service term for the percentage of total homes in the coverage area in which at least one radio is on at any given time; the radio equivalent of HUTs (Households Using Television).

set solid To set without extra space between horizontal type lines.

setwise Differentiates the width of a type from its body size.

shared ID When an organization or institution appears on the TV station's channel identification.

share of audience or share The percentage of the total audience tuned into each station at any given time.

shelter books Magazines that focus on housing or related subjects.

short rate A charge back to an advertiser for not fulfilling a contract.

show Program.

side stitching A method of stitching thick booklets by pressing wire staples from the front side of the booklet and clinching them in back, making it impossible to open the pages flat.

SIG Special Interest Group.

sig Signature file such as sender's name, address, phone, fax, etc.

silhouette or outline halftone A halftone with all of the background removed.

silk screen A stencil process using fine cloths painted so that the surface is impenetrable except where color is supposed to come through.

silver print or Van Dyck The proof of negative for an offset plate taken on sensitized paper and used as a final proof before the plates are made.

simulcast Simultaneous transmission over radio and television.

sizing Scaling.

skip frame A process in which only alternate frames are printed, to speed up action on film.

slant Angle. (1) The particular emphasis of a media presentation. (2) To emphasize an aspect of a policy story.

slanting (1) Emphasizing a particular point or points of interest in the news. (2) Disguised editorializing.

slick A publication, usually a magazine, published on coated, smooth paper.

slicks Glossy prints used instead of mattes in sending releases or art to offset publications.

slidefilm Filmstrip. A continuous strip of film with frames in a fixed sequence, but not designed to simulate motion. A recorded soundtrack usually is synchronized with the succession of the film frames.

slides Individual film frames, usually positive but sometimes negative transparencies, projected either in the room where an oral presentation is being given or from a TV control room.

slip sheet Paper placed between sheets of printed paper to prevent smudging.

slot In newspaper rooms, the inside of a copy desk where the copy chief or copy editor sits.

slow motion A scene in which the objects appear to move more slowly than normal. In film, slow motion is achieved through high-speed photography (exposing many frames that differ only minutely from one another) and normal (24 frames per second, for example) playback. In television, slow motion is achieved by multiple scanning of each television frame.

slug Lead thicker than 4 points, used between lines of type.

slug lines The notation placed at the upper left of a story to identify the story during typesetting and makeup of a publication.

slushpile A collection of unsolicited manuscripts received by magazines.

SOF Sound on film.

soft news Feature news or news that does not depend upon timeliness.

software The programs and routines associated with the operation of a computer, as opposed to "hardware."

SOT Sound on videotape.

spin Putting a slant on a story so that it shows the organization or individual in a favorable light even if the situation is much to the contrary. Someone "spinning" or "putting a spin on" a story may be called a "spin doctor." The deception involved in this practice and the deceit associated with the term should be distinguished from the standards of practice endorsed by most public relations people.

splice The spot where two shots are actually joined, or the act of joining two shots. Generally used only when the material (such as film or audiotape) is physically cut and glued (spliced) together again.

split run The regional division of a national magazine before printing to accommodate advertisers desiring to reach a specific regional market and often with regional editorial emphasis.

split screen A divided screen that shows two or more pictures; often used in TV titles and commercials.

sponsor (1) The underwriter of broadcast programming whose messages are presented with the program. Most advertisers buy spot time and are not sponsors. (2) The underwriter of an event or activity, who gets publicity for participation.

spot announcement or spot A broadcast commercial that usually lasts less than one minute.

spread (1) A long story, generally illustrated. (2) An ad group of related photographs. (3) Copy that covers two facing pages in a publication, generally without gutter separation and usually printed from a single plate.

SPSS Social science statistical package used in research.

stakeholder One who has an investment (time, money, etc.) in an organization.

stand-by The signal given in a broadcast studio before the on-air signal is given.

standing head A regularly used title.

standing matter Type kept set from one printing to another, such as staff names on a newspaper.

stat The repro-quality version of line art or other material produced to specified size by a stat machine. Also called photostat.

station break Break to a station for a contracted local spot. May include on-the-hour legal identification required of broadcasters by the FCC.

stereotype A plate cast by pouring molten metal into a matrix or flong. Inexpensive form of duplicating plates generally used by newspapers.

stet A proofreader's designation indicating that the copy should stand as originally written, that the change marked was an error.

stop-motion A slow-motion effect in which one frame jumps to the next, showing the object in a different position.

storyboard (1) Art work that shows the sequence of a TV commercial. (2) In film work, drawings and text showing major visual changes in a proposed show; this grew out of animated film, pioneered by Walt Disney.

straight matter Plain typesetting set in conventional paragraph form, as opposed to some kind of display.

straight news Hard news; a plain recital of news facts written in standard style and form.

stratified sample The population is divided into strata (groups or subpopulations with common traits), and the sample chosen contains the same proportion of desired traits as the population strata from which it is drawn.

stuffer Printed piece intended for insertion into bills and receipts, pay envelopes, packages delivered to customers or any other medium of delivery.

style book A manual setting standards for handling copy and detailing rules for spelling, capitalization, abbreviations, word usage and such.

subhead A small head inserted into the body of a news story to break up long blocks of type.

summary lead The beginning paragraphs in a news story, usually including the H and five W's (who, what, when, where, why and how).

super In film or TV, superimposition of a scene or characters over another scene; also called a take-out or add videotape.

supercard A studio card with white lettering on a dark background, used for superimposing or keying a title over a background scene. For chroma keying, the white letters are on a chroma key blue background.

surprint In printing, superimposing type or lettering on an illustration so the type remains solid, unbroken by a screen.

survey An analysis of a market or of opinions held by a specified group.

suspended interest A news story with the climax at the close.

sync Synchronization—keeping one operation in step with another (1) between sound and picture, or (2) between a scanning beam and a blinking pulse.

synchronization rights Rights granted by a mechanical rights agency to use music licensed by them.

system cue Network identification.

tabloid A newspaper format—usually five columns wide, with each page slightly more than half the size of a standard newspaper page. A tabloid format often involves the use of just a picture and headlines on page one.

tag (1) The final section of a broadcast story, usually stand-up (personally given rather than taped) following a film or VTR. (2) An announcement at the end of a recorded commercial or music at the end of live copy.

tailpiece A small drawing at the end of a story.

take (1) In print, a portion of copy in a running story. (2) in broadcasting, a complete scene. (3) To cut.

talent Any major personality or model for ads or publicity photos. In TV or radio, anyone in front of the camera or on the air.

tally light The red light on a video camera that indicates which camera is on air or being recorded.

TCP/IP Transmission Control Protocol/Internet Protocol rules about transferring data over the Internet.

teaser (1) In print, an ad or statement that piques interest or stimulates curiosity without giving away facts; used to build anticipation. (2) A technique in which the beginning of a film has scenes and sounds related to the theme of the program rather than a title.

telecommunications Long-distance transmission of signals by any means.

teleconference Use of various telecommunication devices (computers, telephones, television and video systems) to permit three or more people at multiple locations to communicate with each other in a "live" and often interactive format.

tele line The equipment room where film and slide projectors are located.

teleprocessing Information handling in which a data processing system uses communication facilities.

teletext A one-way electronic information system; noninteractive.

Teletypesetter (TTS) Trademark applied to a machine that transmits to a linotype and causes news to be set into type automatically.

terminal Any point in a communication system or network where data can enter or leave.

test group People selected and used to measure reactions to or use of a product or idea.

testing Sampling the opinions, attitudes or beliefs of a scientifically selected group on any particular set of questions.

text Written material, generally used in referring to editorial rather than commercial matter; excludes titles, heads, notes, references and such.

TF Till forbid—advertising to run until advertiser terminates or contract expires.

thirty (30) In newspaper code, "that's all." A reporter writing a story places this at the last of the written material to signify the end.

tie-back Previously printed information included in a story to give background or a frame of reference and to refresh the reader's memory.

tie-in (1) Joint or combined activities of two or more organizations on a single promotional project. (2) A promotional activity designed to coincide with an already scheduled event.

tight In broadcast and print media, having little time or space left for additional material.

time base corrector An electronic accessory to a videotape recorder that helps make playbacks or transfers electronically stable; helps maintain picture quality, even in dubbing.

time classifications Broadcast time rated by audience level and priced accordingly, as Class AA, Class A, Class BB, Class B, etc.

timesharing Use of computer hardware by several persons simultaneously.

tint block A solid color area on a printed piece, usually screened.

tip Information offered that could lead to a story.

tipping in Hand insertion or attachment of extra pages in a publication, usually of a different stock than other items.

title slide A graphic giving the name of a TV show.

total audience plan A spot package designed to reach all of a station's audiences.

track The physical location on magnetic tape where the signal is recorded for a specific source—the channel 1, 2, etc., of audio; the video signal; the control signal; etc.

trade publications Periodicals carrying information of interest to a particular trade or industry.

traffic The department in ad agencies that handles production schedules; in broadcasting, traffic handles everything that goes on the air.

trim (1) In newspapers, to shorten copy. (2) In printing, the final process that cuts all pages to the same size.

turnover In advertising, the ratio of *net unduplicated* cumulative audience over several time periods to average audience per time period.

TWX "TWIX," a teletype machine.

typeface A particular type design; may carry the name of the designer or a descriptive name.

type family The name given to two or more type series that are variations of the same basic design.

type page The printed area on a page bordered by margins.

type series The collective name for all sizes of one design of typeface.

typo Typographical error.

UC and LC Upper- and lower-case—capitals and small letters.

UHF Ultra high frequency—TV channels broadcasting at frequencies higher than channel 13.

under and over In broadcasting scripts, using sound dominated by (under) or dominating (over) any other sound.

underrun Printing practice that permits an allowance of 10 percent less than the total printing order as com-

pletion of an order when excessive spoilage in printing or in binding causes a slight shortage. *See* overrun.

upcut In TV or film, to unintentionally overlap a sound picture with another sound.

update To alter a story to include the most recent developments.

UPI United Press International began as an international wire service to which any media could subscribe for news copy and photos, unlike AP, which is a membership cooperative. UPI was bought in 1992 by MBC, a London-based company.

URL Uniform Resource Locator Internet address.

Usenet User Network computer forums or discussion groups.

uplink The transmission of audio, video or digitized computer information to a communications satellite, which relays the information to other receivers.

upper case Capital letters.

Van Dyck *See* silver print.

varitype A typewriter with alternate type fonts.

VDT Visual or video display terminal—an electronic device used in typesetting and word processing, with a television-type screen to display data.

vertical saturation Scheduling commercials heavily one or two days before a major event.

VHF Very high frequency—TV channels broadcasting at channels 2 through 13.

video All television visual projection.

videoconference A teleconference in which full video is transmitted, as well as voice and sometimes even graphics. The video signal can be from one point of origin to many receiving points, or two-way, simultaneously connecting two or more points, each of which can both originate and receive video.

video news release (VNR) A scripted news release that is fully produced and sent to television news directors on a video cassette, usually with some B-roll (background footage) to make editing possible. Often sent by satellite.

videotex An interactive electronic data transmission system; establishes a two-way link from an individual's television set or home computer to a database.

vidicon A special camera tube often used in closed-circuit operations and TV film cameras.

vignette A story or sketch, often a "slice of life" drama.

vignetted halftones A halftone with edges that soften gradually until they completely fade out.

virtual reality A computer-generated environment that can be experienced by wearing special equipment.

Virus Invasive destructive computer software program masked as normal communication.

visual scanner Optical scanner.

VO Voice over—broadcasting or film script designation for a narrator's voice to be used at a certain time in the production.

VTR (1) In TV, videotape recording. Cheaper and more flexible than film, but less permanent. (2) In radio, voice transmitter and receiver—a small device attached to the phone, enabling a reporter to call in a story and preserve broadcast quality.

War file Pronounced "ware" file, a type of digital audio file.

wash drawing A watercolor or diluted India ink brush drawing requiring halftone reproduction.

watermark An identification mark left in the texture of quality paper stock; revealed when the paper is held up to light.

Web site Connected Web pages, usually from one organization.

when room Designation on copy or art that means it is usable at any time.

wide open A publication or news script with ample room for additional material.

widow (1) A short line (one word or two) at the end of a paragraph of type. To be avoided, especially in the first line of a page or column and in captions. (2) In publishing, any less-than-full-measure line ending a paragraph that appears as the top line of a page or column. To be avoided.

wild track Related footage with a sound track not intended to be in sync with the picture.

wipe A transitional television technique in which one scene gradually replaces another.

woodcuts Wooden printing blocks with the impression carved by hand. Now an art form; was the forerunner of zinc engravings,

woodshedding In broadcasting, reading and rehearsing a news script.

word processor A computer software program used to create, edit and manipulate documents. Word processing software is used primarily for text, but also can be used for creating charts and graphs.

working drawings Final drawings, usually black-and-white, prepared for use by an engraver, show how final art will appear.

work print The film print used in first editing. Usually one "light print," not printed for full-quality reproduction.

workstation A group of linked computer equipment used in accomplishing word-processing or design tasks. A workstation often consists of a computer terminal with keyboard and monitor linked to a printer and sometimes to a scanner.

wow Pitch distortion or variation caused by changes in the speed of film or tape; also sound distortions in records.

wrap-up Summary or closing.

wrong font A letter from one font of type mixed with others of a different font.

WWW World Wide Web, collection of computers connected on the Internet.

XCU, ECU In TV or film, an extreme close-up. For a person, this might show eyes and nose only.

yak Narration.

Z-axis The imaginary line that extends in the direction the lens points from the camera to the horizon. Z-axis motion is movement toward or away from the camera. (Not a standardized term in the industry.)

zinc etching A line engraving etched in zinc.

INDEX